FOUNDATIONS

Society, Challenge and Change

Modern Ode to the Modern School

John Erskine

Just after the Board had brought the school up to date
To prepare you for your Life Work
Without teaching you one superfluous thing,
Jim Reilly presented himself to be educated.
He wanted to be a bricklayer.
They taught him to be a perfect bricklayer.
And nothing more.

He knew so much about bricklaying
That the contractor made him a foreman
But he knew nothing about being a foreman.
He spoke to the School Board about it,
And they put in a night course
On how to be a foreman
And nothing more.

He became so excellent a foreman
That the contractor made him a partner.
But he knew nothing about figuring costs
Nor about bookkeeping
Nor about real estate,
And he was too proud to go back to night school.
So he hired a tutor
Who taught him these things
And nothing more.

Prospering at last
And meeting other men as prosperous,
Whenever the conversation started, he'd say to himself
"Just wait till it comes my way—
Then I'll show them!"
But they never mentioned bricklaying
Nor the art of being a foreman
Nor the whole duty of contractors,
Nor even real estate.
So Jim never said anything.

FOUNDATIONS

Society, Challenge and Change

James V. Rudnick, *Editor*

George Brown College of Applied Arts and Technology

Acknowledgements:
The editor would like to thank Dean Ron Waldie, Chair Al Budzin, Co-ordinators Ed Ksenych and Marianne Taylor, and our Editorial Board for their effort, guidance and help during this project.

THOMPSON EDUCATIONAL PUBLISHING, INC.
Toronto

Thompson Educational Publishing, Inc.
14 Ripley Avenue, Suite 105
Toronto, Ontario, Canada M6S 3N9
Tel (416) 766–2763 / Fax (416) 766–0398

Canadian Cataloguing in Publication Data

Main entry under title:

Foundations : society, challenge and change

Includes bibliographical references.
ISBN 1-55077-076-4

1. College readers. I. Rudnick, James.

PE1122.F68 1995 808'.0427 C95-931916-6

Every attempt was made to obtain permision to reproduce the material contained in this book. Corrections or omissions sent to the publisher will be included in future reprints.

Frontispiece: *Modern Ode to the Modern School*, by John Erskine; source unknown.
Cover: Hundertwasser, *78, People (Hommage to "TREES")*
St. Mandé/Seine, 1950; watercolour and charcoal on yellow paper.
Private Collection. Reproduced with permission.

Printed and bound in Canada.
1 2 3 4 99 98 97 96 95

Table of Contents

PART 1
General Education

PART 2
Science and Technology

PART 3
The Social Sciences

PART 4
The Arts and Humanities

APPENDICES

Poems and Visual Art

Poems

Visual Art

PART 1

General Education

'he Thinker, by Auguste Rodin.

\uguste Rodin (1840-1917) was a French sculptor who 'mbued his work with great psychological force. He is egarded as the foremost sculptor of the 19th and early :0th centuries.

'ourtesy of Musée Rodin, Paris, S.1295, bronze

Introduction to General Education

James Rudnick

The teaching of general education to students is increasingly becoming an urgent priority. The "Modern Ode to A Modern School," given as the frontispiece to this book, tells it all. Education today must do more than teach job-specific skills. It must teach students how to think critically with an eye to acquiring knowledge that will help them shape the rest of their lives.

In line with this objective, this text begins to explore the many changes currently affecting each of us, both as individuals and as a wider society. It does so from a multidisciplinary perspective that includes (1) science and technology, (2) the social sciences, and (3) the arts and humanities. This book introduces to the reader some of the key contributions writers have made to understanding these changes. The emphasis throughout is on how these changes affect us as Canadians now and how we can better prepare for the future.

In 1988, the Ontario Council of Regents, the agency that oversees colleges in Ontario, was asked to develop "a vision of the college system in the year 2000." The outcome, known as *Vision 2000*, acknowledges the major changes taking place in Canadian society. It calls for a greater emphasis in the colleges on developing skills and background knowledge with broader applicability to the current and future interests of Ontario's economy and society. This book has been developed to introduce students to the topics and issues outlined in this *Vision 2000* report.

For the authors of *Vision 2000*, "general education" and generic skills are not a substitute for job-specific skills but rather are an increasingly necessary complement to them. Such skills are, as the report noted, also important in promoting good citizenship and helping people cope with the changes taking place today in all aspects of their lives.

Vision 2000: Quality and Opportunity

The Council of Regents

In 1988, the Council of Regents, the body charged with overseeing community colleges in Ontario, was asked to develop "a vision of the college system in the year 2000." Their report, known as *Vision 2000*, acknowledged the major changes taking place in Canadian society. It called for a greater emphasis in the college programs on generic skills and background knowledge with broad applicability to Ontario's economy and society. Edited selections from the *Vision 2000* report are reproduced below.

In October 1988 a comprehensive and far-reaching review of Ontario's system of Colleges of Applied Arts and Technology was set in motion by then Minister of Colleges and Universities, the Honourable Lyn McLeod. The Council of Regents, a policy and planning agency which reports to the Minister, was asked to oversee the project and develop "a vision of the college system in the year 2000."

From the outset, it was vitally important that Vision 2000 be directed by a representative group of people who had a stake in the college system. The Vision 2000 Steering Committee was comprised of educators from colleges, schools and universities, students, employers, and labour and government representatives. The role of these 33 individuals was to guide the overall project.

Founding of the Colleges

When Ontario's colleges were created 25 years ago, it was a time of massive growth and change in the educational system. The baby boom was engulfing the system: new schools and university facilities were being built at an unprecedented rate to accommodate the demand. Not only were there more children coming into the system than ever before, but students were staying in school longer. In addition to the pressures of expansion, school curricula were being overhauled, secondary school programs were being reorganized, and a host of new vocational schools were being built.

It was also the decade in which a human being first walked on the moon; scientific discovery and technological change were starting to accelerate, and a growing gap between the emerging needs of the economy and the skills available in the labour force was seen as a cause for concern. It was to the educational system that leaders turned to ensure that Ontario would have the skilled human resources it would need for the coming decades.

A New Environment

The environment of the 1990s is very different from the one in which the colleges were created, when the economy was dominated by manufacturing and the natural resource sector; the technological base was relatively stable; and production was becoming increasingly automated. At the beginning of the 1960s, population growth rates had reached an historic peak; the population was fairly homogeneous, mainly of European origin, and the traditional household was the nuclear family supported by a male breadwinner. There was a steadily expanding, youthful labour force, and most workers could expect to have one career last a lifetime.

The trends that were just beginning to take shape—and that helped to give rise to the creation of the college system—are in the process of transforming Ontario's economy a quarter of a century later. The demographics of the province are changing significantly, and the social priorities set at that time—the emphasis on equality of opportunity and the responsibility of the colleges to meet the needs of the wider community—have found new impetus in the realities of the 1990s.

Trends such as the aging of the work force, industrial restructuring, technological innovation, and the changing skill content of jobs highlight the need for a dynamic college system which provides high-quality, relevant career education for a broad range of learners.

Ontario's work force is undergoing some fundamental changes because of demographic trends. The growth rate of the population is slowing down.

Coinciding with the lower rate of population growth will be a fairly dramatic increase in the median age of Ontario's population. The median age is projected to rise from about 32 years at the close of the 1980s, to 40 years in 2011.

As the supply of young entrants to the labour force declines, the province is shifting from labour surplus and a relatively young work force, to increasing labour shortages in a number of sectors and a "greying" work force. Critical labour shortages in some industrial fields are already occurring, but at the same time there is unemployment in others, mainly among lower-skilled and older workers. This is occurring at a time when increased competition on a global scale, and the race to keep up with the latest technological innovations are forcing industrialized economies around the world not only to "retool" their factories, plants and offices, but also to retrain their workers. The ability to adapt quickly to new technology and other changes in the marketplace has become a major challenge for employers and employees alike.

Many traditional manufacturing industries are undergoing difficult adjustments in this new environment. Success in many industries is no longer predicated on mass production of a single product, but customized production of products geared to the specific needs of the client. The assembly line is being replaced by multiskilled teams, quality circles and other new-style work environments. Many employers are emphasizing the need for workers who can think critically, communicate well, and work with others in solving problems.

The service sector has become the fastest growing sector of the economy. However, many service jobs continue to be dependent on the goods-producing sector. Many of the high-growth service occupations are low-skill and low-paying, with limited prospects for promotion. On the other hand, the service sector is creating a whole range of new highly-skilled professional-level occupations, in finance, communications and other fields.

Most of the workers in Ontario who will be required to adapt to new technologies, economic restructuring and increased global competition in the year 2000 are already in the labour market. Many of these adult workers will need retraining not just once, but several times in the course of their working lives.

Canadian employers have tended to exhibit significantly lower rates of investment in training than many of this nation's major trading competitors. In the past, employers have been able to import skills from outside Canada to compensate for skills shortage. But the supply-demand disparity in skilled occupations is also being experienced in other industrialized countries; it is not expected, therefore, that immigration will provide the solution. Canada, and Ontario, will have to train—and retrain—their own.

The Economic Council of Canada, in its recent report *Good Jobs Bad Jobs*, makes the case that Canada must provide not only advanced training to produce highly qualified personnel, but also basic skills training for a wide range of underqualified workers, and adjustment training for those whose skills no longer match the demands of the marketplace. The Council warns of a growing segmentation and polarization in terms of earnings, the skill content of jobs, job stability, and the location of employment. Employment problems facing poorly educated and displaced workers appear to be growing, at the same time as the job market for highly skilled, well-paid, stable occupations is expanding.

Economic trends are not the only forces for change in the new environment; Ontario is changing in other ways. We have become an increasingly multicultural society; fewer immigrants now come from Europe, and more from the nations of Asia, Africa and Central and South America. Many new immigrants require language training before they can participate in education or work, and many come from countries which do not have highly developed educational and training opportunities. Those who do have qualifications for professional and technical jobs in Ontario find it difficult to get their credentials validated here. People from other cultures want to be assured that their customs and heritage are respected, and that they will have an equal opportunity to succeed.

The role of women has changed. Women now make up 45 percent of the provincial labour force, and their participation rate continues to increase; however, they continue to earn, on average, only two-thirds of what men earn. Women are also under-represented in many of the occupations that are experiencing critical labour shortage. Many women need support services, particularly child care, to enable them to take advantage of available training opportunities. Other groups, such as persons with disabilities, want better access to education and the labour force so that they, too, can realize their potential.

Demographics may also affect the colleges in future in a more indirect way, through the government's ability to pay for post-secondary eduction. ... The aging population means that a greater proportion of public resources will likely need to be devoted to the health sector.

Together, the economic and social changes in Ontario are putting new pressures on the colleges. While the colleges have filled a much-needed role in career education in the last 25 years, they are being challenged to update their mandate in order to remain relevant to the real needs of the province and its people.

Reorienting the Curriculum

Vision 2000 believes that the provision of general education and generic skills should be significantly increased in programs which receive a college credential.

Insufficient general generic education: In the four principles for the colleges outlined in 1967, colleges were directed to "embrace total education." But from the beginning of the college system, general education (e.g. studies in sociology, world events or the environment) has received less emphasis than vocational skills training in college post-secondary programming, and its position has further declined in the last decade. When funding restraints squeezed college budgets in the late 1970s, program hours were cut back, and the major casualty was general education. General education is supposed to constitute at least 30 percent of post-secondary program content; however, most programs have considerably less.

The rapid pace of change in the workplace, particularly that caused by new technologies, has increased the need for students to acquire generic skills—such as problem-solving and critical thinking, as well as basic literacy, numeracy and computer literacy—so that they can learn new skills or adapt old ones. A worker who does not have the transferable skills to advance to better positions in his or her field may become trapped in a particular job. An over-concentration in many college programs on narrow occupation-specific skills, to the detriment of generic skills and general education, is restricting career opportunities for some college graduates and affecting the ability of business and industry to adapt quickly to the demands of the marketplace.

A greater emphasis in college programs on skills and knowledge that have broad applicability to different current and future uses is needed to serve the interests of Ontario's economy and society. If the diffusion of new technology is dependent on a broadly educated and skilled population, it is important to ensure that as many people as possible have technological literacy and other skills which are transferable to other jobs and occupations. These skills are not a substitute for job-specific skills, but are complementary to them. Moreover, general education and generic skills are important tools for good citizenship and help people cope with change in all aspects of their lives.

General education and generic skills: In the context of the colleges, we define general education to be: "the broad study of subjects and issues which are central to education for life in our culture. Central in, but not restricted to, the arts, sciences, literature and humanities, general eduction encourages students to know and understand themselves, their society and institutions, and their roles and responsibilities as citizens."[1]

We define generic skills to be: "practical life skills essential for both personal and career success. They include language and communications skills, math skills, learning and thinking skills, interpersonal skills, and basic technological literacy. They are not job-specific, but are crucial to mastering changing technologies, changing environments and changing jobs...Facility in some generic skills—reading, listening, writing, learning—is a prerequisite for success in most college level courses."[2]

...There have been concerns raised by both internal and external stakeholders that the college curriculum is overly concentrated on specific skills training, to the detriment, and sometimes to the exclusion, of general education. There is a perception among many people within the colleges, as well as outside, that college career-oriented education must go beyond narrow job-related skills to enable students to realize their personal and career goals.

The debate about how broad a college education should be is not a new one. However, it has been lent more urgency by the rapidly changing economic environment, which demands a labour force which can adapt to new technologies and learn new skills. The need for a refrigeration technologist to understand refrigeration is obvious. However, it is also essential for that technologist to be able to write a clear and concise report, and to communicate and work effectively with customers and co-workers. As new technologies change the process of production and the organization of production and relationships within an enterprise, the ability of the technologist to acquire new skills will be crucial to the future of both the worker and the enterprise.

In the current environment, a worker who lacks appropriate language and communication skills or basic technological literacy is at a distinct disadvantage. In today's fast-changing marketplace, workers require a portable and expandable skills base. Such a base gives them greater security of employment by enabling them to adapt to changing job demands by updating or upgrading skills and to shift between jobs with different skills requirements.

Increasingly, employers are asking that college graduates have ability to learn additional skills, to work with others, to solve problems and to communicate clearly. These skills are becoming more valued because both the speed and nature of economic change make adaptability a requirement. From the perspective of employers, a focus on a generic skill assists them to use both capital and human resources more flexibly in adjusting to the impact of change and competitive pressures. While specific skills training may be firm or job-specific, a focus on generic skills as a foundation of the college curriculum would benefit employers as a whole.

In addition, the communications revolution has expanded the horizons of citizenship so that people can and should feel part of local, national and international debates on issues that affect them, their families and their futures—issues such as poverty, the environment, the Canadian constitution or political change in other parts of the world. To participate actively, they should be aware of the background and context of current events and issues. Helping people to be good citizens, as well as productive workers with marketable skills, should be part of the educational experience at a college.

The need to broaden or enrich college career-oriented education is reinforced at this time by the convergence of opinion among many stakeholders, both within and outside the college system. During the Vision 2000 consultation process, representatives of employers and labour supported a broadening of the curriculum to include more general eduction and generic skills, as did community groups, college faculty and administrators and others:

> Employers, workers, students and teachers have all told Vision 2000 that too many among the current crop of Ontario community college graduates are

A Major Reorientation of the Curriculum

A Mandate for the Future

The Government of Ontario and the Colleges of Applied Arts and Technology should adopt the following mandate for Ontario's colleges:

Preamble

Education has an essential role to play in the development of a world which is peaceful, environmentally sound, equitable and economically viable. Education should help to balance individual and community needs, and foster personal initiative and co-operation within human relationships based on mutual respect.

Education should give people the opportunity to develop the skills and knowledge they need to adapt to and make a constructive contribution to the world in which they live. Education should enhance students' choices and opportunities, and promote the development of individual potential. It should also assist learners in developing their commitment to social responsibility and care for the communities in which they live, and respect for cultural integrity and self-determination of those whose language and traditions may be different from their own.

The Mandate

It is the mandate of the Colleges of Applied Arts and Technology of Ontario:

- To provide high-quality career education that enhances students' ability to acquire information, reason clearly, think critically, communicate effectively, apply their knowledge and participate in society as informed and productive citizens.
- To make a college education as accessible as possible. Accessibility should include the opportunity to succeed, as well as the opportunity to enrol, and it must be provided in a way that achieves educational equity.
- To be responsible, as a system, for quality assurance through system-wide standards and program review.
- To work together and with other educational institutions to offer students opportunities for educational mobility and lifelong learning.
- To create a dynamic, learner-driven system by anticipating and accommodating the diverse needs of students, both full-time and part-time, enrolled in credit and non-credit courses.
- To forge partnerships in and with their communities, including employers, labour, community groups and governments.
- To be participatory institutions in which decision-making involves both internal and external stakeholders
- To be model employers in the manner in which they invest in and manage human resource development, in their commitment to equity and in the creation of a positive, healthy and supportive working environment.

SOURCE: Ontario Council of Regents, *Vision 2000.*

deficient in generic skills and general education, to the detriment of our graduates' career success and the future performance of the Ontario economy.[3]

A growing body of research is also supportive of this direction:

Technological knowledge and capabilities are diffused not through the sale of products or blueprints in international markets, but through national or regional communities which share a certain base of knowledge and the increments to that knowledge...The role of the college system in transmitting the fundamental skills needed by a diverse array of learners will be critical in providing the skills and knowledge base essential for this innovative process.[4]

We are advocating nothing less than major reorientation of the curriculum in the direction of general education and generic skills.

Placing greater emphasis on generic skills and education will not necessarily lead to a lengthening of college programs. Consultations with employers revealed that their willingness and ability to undertake a greater role in providing job-specific training would be enhanced if their employees ,possessed well-developed basic skills. We frequently heard statements such as: "The colleges should give the basic education, and we'll train on the job" and "There is a powerful role for the college in our sector. Don't teach how to operate XYZ machine; teach them the fundamentals in writing, math, and science; and teach them to learn; and prepare them to have to learn and learn again throughout their lifetimes."[5]

While we do not propose that the college diminish the job-specific content of their programs to the extent that might be implied in the preceding statements, it should be possible to revise college curriculum in the directions we have recommended without significantly altering the length of programs. Some judicious reductions in the narrowest specific skills components of existing college programs should be possible without diminishing the overall vocational orientation of college programs. This possibility depends, however, on employers translating their words into action, through taking greater responsibility for job-specific training.

It may also require some reorientation in how students view a college eduction. Many current students are attracted to the college because programs are perceived as providing training which enables them to immediately perform on the job at a high level. The colleges and the secondary schools will need to demonstrate to students the necessity of embarking on a lifelong learning process and the importance of solid foundation skills to this process. Students will need to be convinced, for example, that the acquisitions of these foundations skills will make it easier and faster to acquire specific skills both in an adult educational setting and on the job. Similarly, employers' hiring practices for entry-level jobs will need to be consistent with this thinking and reinforce it.

In short, the success and the costs of educational reform at the college level depend, to a large measure, on complementary actions being undertaken by both secondary schools and employers.

We believe that the explicit and expanded inclusion of generic skills and general education in all programs leading to a college credential is central to the future development of the colleges and their communities. The challenge of equipping learners with the knowledge, skills and abilities needed for Ontario's evolving economy requires that we acknowledge the considerable uncertainty about which specific skills will be needed. We must concentrate on constructing the foundations upon which further skills can be built and from which society will realize the greatest social return.

The focus on general eduction and generic skills will involve a fundamental reorientation of college curricula. To achieve our goals will require that college educators, both faculty, staff and administrators, undertake a major process of renewal of curriculum and delivery methods at each college. The process will need to be guided by the establishment, on a system-wide basis, of clear learning outcomes for each program leading to a college credential. In providing for such outcomes, we envision considerable diversity across the system in the organization and delivery of general education, generic skills and job-specific skills.

Endnotes

1 Michael Park, "Expanding the Core: General Education, Generic Skills, and the Core Curriculum in Ontario Community Colleges," in *Challenges to the Colleges and the College System—Background Papers* (Toronto: Ontario Council of Regents, 1990).

2 Park, op. cit., p. 2.

3 Park, op. cit., p. 5.

4 David Wolfe, "New Technology and Education: A Challenge for the Colleges," in Colleges and the Changing Economy. Background Papers (Toronto: Ontario Council of Regents, 1989), p.16.

5 Audrey Gill, "Role of the Colleges in the Changing Economy: Report on Consultations," in Colleges and the Changing Economy. Background Papers (Toronto: Ontario Council of Regents, 1989), pp. 11,15.

SOURCE: Council of Regents, *Vision 2000: Quality and Opportunity—the Final Report of Vision 2000* (Toronto: Ministry of Colleges and Universities, 1990). The material reproduced was selected and edited for the present work.

The Educational Implications of Our "Technological Society"

James Turk

Microelectronics and the shift from a manufacturing to a service economy are altering the nature and organization of work today. What are the implications of these changes? In a presentation at a conference on liberal education at Ryerson Polytechnical Institute, James Turk challenges conventional views about these changes and their educational implications.

In this talk, I want to do three things. One is to address a prevalent myth about new technologies and their implications for education. The second is to attempt to clarify some terms that are essential for any meaningful discussion of the issues before us. The third is to focus on the educational implications of new technologies for workers—both production workers and salaried workers.

As you may have already surmised, one difference of a *labour* perspective is that we do not assume a session on "Career Implications in Technology" need focus primarily or solely on management. Workers have "careers" too—jobs which they hope to pursue and do well. And post-secondary institutions like Ryerson have had, and should increasingly have, a role to play in the education of these workers for their "careers." More about that later.

Myth about the New "Technology Society"

The context for this conference is the oft-repeated and commonly held notion that the dramatic outpouring of new and sophisticated micro-electronic technologies means that our educational system has to be reshaped. Workers will need more sophisticated job skills, and schools, from the primary to the post-secondary levels, must prepare workers for the new high-tech age by giving greater emphasis to science, by making "computer literacy," a priority, and so forth.

The underlying view is that the employment future lies with those able to perform professional and technically sophisticated work.

I want to call into question much of this conventional wisdom. Let me begin with a myth which does not serve us well in our discussions of education and technology, namely, that the new microelectronic technologies will require a more highly skilled, better trained work force.

Generally, the opposite is the case. The history of the development of the microelectronic technologies, and of their subsequent use, is a history of designing and using machines which deskill work and diminish the role of workers. Insofar as possible, decision making, which formerly was undertaken on the shop or office floor, is removed to the confines of management.

The deskilling is not inherent in new technologies. There is nothing natural or inevitable about deskilling. The new technologies have been consciously designed to deskill work—to allow employers to draw from a larger (and therefore less highly paid) labour pool. Technologies could be designed which enhance and make use of workers' skills, but designers and purchasers of new technologies have little interest in such approaches.[1]

The result is that the design and use of the new

technologies is creating a pear-shaped distribution of skills. On the one hand, jobs are being created for a relatively small number of highly skilled people to design, program, and maintain the equipment. On the other hand, the present skills of the great majority of workers are being diminished, and many of their jobs eliminated.

This pattern applies across the board. Let me give you three examples.

In manufacturing operations, machinists have been one of the more highly skilled trades. Roger Tulin, a skilled machinist who has spent his evenings getting a Ph.D. in social sciences, has written on the changing machinist's work with computer-controlled machine tools:

> For many jobs, the new machines are better and more reliable than conventional methods of machining...computer-numerical-controls could allow skilled machinists who can program, set up, and operate these machines to reach new levels of craftsmanship. The most highly skilled metal workers like to make perfect parts. That's the source of their satisfaction. The new technology could allow them to conceive and execute work that was previously beyond anyone's reach.
>
> However, this hasn't been what shop managers have wanted...their interest is to get the work out with the least amount of labour time possible. So the programming and setting up is usually done by a small group of specialists. "Operators," at lower wages and skill levels, run the production cycles. They are given only the bits of information necessary to keep the cycle running. It's the unused capability, the frustration of the human potential for creative work, that makes the reality of work life so dismal for large numbers of NC and CNC operators.
>
> As machine tools have been made more and more fully automatic, the areas of production which require a full set of conventional skills have been cut back further and further. The "monkey" in the machine shop, who pushes buttons on a task that's broken down to fit so-called monkey intelligence, [this comment is based on a popular ad for CNC equipment which shows a monkey producing "skilled" work] is but a symbol of how management sees the future.[2]

David Noble, in his exceptional work on the history of technology,[3] shows in painstaking detail the history of the development of computer-controlled machine tools and how, at each step in their development and use, the priority was to take skill away from the operator and subject the operator to more direct management control.

One can see the same deskilling in the development and use of office technologies. Evelyn Glenn and Roslyn Feldberg of Boston University have undertaken extensive examinations of the changing character of clerical work. Their conclusions are clear-cut:

> ...narrow, largely manual skills displace complex skills and mental activity...close external control narrows the range of worker discretion...impersonal relationships replace social give and take.[4]

Their study of a number of different organizations adds that "the larger organizations are leading the changes by developing technologies and organizational techniques [for achieving these ends]."[5]

The same pattern of deskilling has also been identified within technical professions. Phillip Kraft, of the State University of New York at Binghamton, has carefully examined the changing nature of programming or software production. His conclusions are remarkably similar to Tulin's, Noble's and Glenn and Feldberg's:

> What is most remarkable about the work programmers do is how quickly it has been transformed. Barely a generation after its inception, programming is no longer the complex work of creative and perhaps even eccentric people. Instead, divided and routinized, it has become mass-production work parcelled out to interchangeable detail workers. Some software specialists still engage in intellectually demanding and rewarding tasks...but they make up a relatively small and diminishing proportion of the total programming work force. The great and growing mass of people called programmers...do work which is less and less distinguishable from that of clerks or, for that matter, assembly line workers.[6]

The point of these comments is to argue that contrary to the widely held (and widely perpetrated) view that the new technologies are increasing the demand for a more highly skilled work force, the opposite is the case.

Evidence for this claim comes not only from scholars studying the workplace, but also from organizations like the U.S. Bureau of Labor Statis-

In Praise of Knowledge

It's Time to Move on from Information

The information age may be at an end. Let's hope so, anyway. Though it has invariably been described as exciting—a word now applied to anything new, whether a corn flake or a challenge—it has in truth been the opposite. It has provided every bore in the world with a limitless supply of the wherewithal to put his victims to sleep. Now, if a harbinger from a Japanese university proves correct, information is giving way to knowledge.

According to two Japanese researchers you will not succeed in business unless you can create new knowledge. That is why, apparently, some companies already have people called "Vice-President, Knowledge." They vice-preside not over the information-technology department but over the hunches, skills and insights of the workforce. This is what is meant by knowledge.

Not perhaps by you. A hunch, after all, may be wrong; if so, it would be better described as information, or maybe misinformation. But at least skills and insights involve something more than just receiving or producing facts. The trouble with the information age is that it seems to place no value upon differentiation.

In this respect, it has been the first retrograde age in history—unless you consider its predecessor the age of Aquarius. Most people, however, prefer to see mankind's development as a slow progression towards something more sophisticated: stone age, iron age, bronze age, age of reason, age of enlightenment, age of analysis, age of—ugh—information. In, with the computer, came the raw, untreated flow of data; out, at least by implication, went the ability to discriminate between useful and useless, good and bad, interesting and dull. With that, the seven ages of mankind suddenly started to look like the seven ages of man: a circular progression towards the stone-age starting-point, a fact-filled oblivion, sans teeth, sans eyes, sans taste, sans everything.

There's nothing wrong with information, of course, so long as you do not worship it. Every library needs a dictionary, a telephone directory, maybe a Wisden; some people can even find a use for the Internet. And the more information around, of course, the greater the need for people to interpret it: *The Economist* can recognise a gift-horse without inspecting its mouth. Still, facts and figures are generally best used as a drunk uses a lamp-post—for support rather than illumination—and the Japanese researchers are right in believing that information alone seldom produces great insights.

Better informed, but none the wiser

Hence another gloomy reflection on the information age: although there are almost as many people alive today as dead, most of the great thinkers, inventors, artists, philosophers and statesmen seem to be under the sod. An optical illusion? Maybe. But perhaps the rate of increase of information, and even of knowledge, has not been matched by the rate of increase of wisdom.

Here surely is a subject clamouring for research: what is the relationship between knowledge and wisdom? If information is to knowledge as instruction is to education, what quality could provide the necessary leap to wisdom? Many questions will have to be asked, many answers weighed, many reports written; a new knowledge-based industry may arise. When the answer is found, it will be a breakthrough, perhaps even an exciting one. Roll on the age of the sage.

SOURCE: *The Economist*, May 27, 1995. Reprinted with permission.

tics which projects job growth over the next decade or so.

Its projections, the most sophisticated in North America, are quite startling for proponents of the high-tech future. Not one technologically sophisticated job appears among their top 15 occupations which are expected to experience the largest job growth.

The category which will contribute the most new jobs through 1995 is janitors—alone accounting for 775,000 new jobs or 3% of all new jobs created in the United States. Following janitors, in order, are cashiers, secretaries, office clerks, sales clerks, nurses, waiters and waitresses, primary school teachers, truck drivers, nursing aides and orderlies.

If you want to go down the list further, the eleventh occupation with the most substantial growth is salespeople, followed by accountants, auto mechanics, supervisors of blue-collar workers, kitchen helpers, guards and doorkeepers, fast food restaurant workers.[7]

In a separate examination of high technology sectors, the Bureau concludes,

> It should be reiterated that even when high tech is very broadly defined...it has provided and is expected to provide a relatively small proportion of employment. Thus, for the foreseeable future the bulk of employment expansion will take place in non-high tech fields.[8]

In short, the persistent deskilling of the majority of existing jobs, and the best forecasts for the nature of future jobs, lead to the same conclusion: a pear, rather than an inverted pyramid, describes the emerging skills distribution in our "technological society." Before, talking about educational implications, I mentioned that I wanted to say a word about definitions. The key term in much of this discussion is "skills."

Many who would dissent from my argument would point to the fact that workers are (and presumably therefore need to be) better educated now than twenty years or forty years ago. Certainly workers today—from the shop floor to the manager's office—on average, have far more schooling than in the past. But that is no evidence that they are, or need be, more skilled. The lengthening of the average period of schooling has relatively little to do with changing occupational requirements for most workers. Rather the lengthening of years in school has resulted from attempts to decrease unemployment levels (beginning in the 1930s), to use the educational system to absorb some of the returning service personnel after World War II, to changing social expectations about the right to more education, and so forth.

In response to the higher level of average grade attained, employers have introduced higher minimum levels of education as requirements for hiring—whether it be a retail clerk at Eaton's, a machine operator at Canadian General Electric or an entry-level management trainee at General Motors.

But there has been no study which has demonstrated that the higher levels were a result of the changing nature of the jobs rather than an increased supply of people who had spent longer in school.[9]

Moreover, one must recognize that traditional designations of "skill" have only an inexact relation to what we would commonly mean by "skill." To put it differently, the definition of "skill" must be understood politically as well as descriptively. For example, things that are required in jobs done primarily by women tend to be defined less as skill than things required in jobs done traditionally by men.[10]

Similarly, there are often necessary "skills" required in the most "unskilled" work—a point employers often discover when they open a new plant in a low-wage area and find that they cannot get the production they expected initially because the inexperienced work force does not have the "skills" required by the "unskilled" work.

I mention this only to highlight for you the fact that the definition of "skill" is more problematic than we conventionally take it to be. When I have argued that' work is being deskilled, I am not referring to job classifications of skill, nor to educational requirements imposed by employers, but to the mastery of craft, that is the knowledge of processes and materials; the ability to conceptualize the product of one's labour and the technical ability to produce it.

As Braverman notes, most discussions of skill use the term as a "a specific dexterity, a limited and repetitious operation, 'speed as skill', etc."[11] He goes on to say that the concept of skill has been degraded to the point that:

> ...today the worker is considered to possess a "skill" if his or her job requires a few days' or weeks' training, several months of training is regarded as unusually demanding, and the job that calls for a learning period of six months or a year—such as computer programming—inspires a paroxysm of awe. (We may compare this with the traditional craft apprenticeship, which rarely lasted less than four years and which was not uncommonly seven years long.)[12]

To this point I have attempted to argue that new technologies in workplaces from a manufacturing plant floor to software production houses to offices are designed and used to deskill the work of the vast majority of workers, and concomitantly, the definition of skill is also being degraded, giving the impression that the real degradation of skill is not as stark as it is.

What has come to be defined as skills training is a distorted and narrow kind of job training of the sort described many years ago by the Gilbreths in the *Primer* on scientific management:

> Training a worker means merely enabling him to carry out the directions of his work schedule. Once he can do this, his training is over, whatever his age.[13]

Even today, with all the mystifying hype about job enrichment and new forms of work organization, Frank Gilbreth's characterization of training is a perfect description of most so-called "skills training."

Educational Implications

The implications of all this are what concern us today.

The most obvious and important implication is that there is little foundation to the view that rising skill levels for the labour force as a whole demand the reshaping of school, college and university curricula to provide more emphasis on mathematics, computer science, and technical training.

While some jobs will require a significant amount of this type of education, the great majority (and a growing percentage) will require little of this knowledge in order to fulfil the requirements of the work. If anything, on average, there will be a diminution of the need for this kind of technical education as essential job prerequisite.

The dangers of a misplaced emphasis on more technical knowledge at all levels of the educational system are several.

First, false expectations are being created. Students will be primed with the myth about the skills their future jobs will require, and then, when they get jobs (if they get jobs), they will discover the cruel joke of their skilled training for what they find to be deskilled jobs.

Second, the rush to emphasize computer literacy and a more technical curriculum can force a de-emphasis of more important educational priorities that today's and tomorrow's students will require, not only for their jobs but for greater fulfilment in their lives.

The deskilling of work means that people will have increasingly to find meaning outside their work. The rapidity of technological change means that people will likely shift jobs (regardless of whether they shift employers) more frequently in their working lives. The greater availability of information and the burgeoning quantity of that information will put greater pressures on people who want to be informed and active participants in their society.

All of these factors mean that the priorities for education from kindergarten through university, including technical and vocational programs, must be to provide people with the capabilities to think critically, and to develop their cognitive, expressive and analytical skills to the fullest. It must, as well, provide people with extensive knowledge of their social, cultural, political and economic institutions, and prepare and encourage them to participate actively in the shaping of decisions that affect their lives.

Far from de-emphasizing a solid general education in the humanities, social and natural sciences, the implications of the emerging "technological society" are that we should be stressing this type of education more than ever.

Certainly there is a necessary place for people specializing in technical matters, but that may be no greater a need in the future than it has been in the past. More likely, there will be a lesser need for such specialized education. Given the power of what can be done with the new technologies, even our scientists will need a sound, general education more than ever. It will be essential for them to have a humanistic perspective from which they pursue their scientific achievements. The quality of our everyday lives, even the future of humankind, is dependent on scientists realizing the broader implications of what they are doing.

Our production and office workers will need narrow job training, which should be provided by the employer. Our skilled craftspeople that survive the deskilling mania of technology designers will continue to need proper apprenticeships (which have increasingly disappeared over the past forty years).

But all will need, as well, a tough, critical, informative general education—beginning at the primary level through to the highest levels—if we are to achieve our fullest potential as individuals and as a society.

Endnotes

[1] See Noble, David. 1984. *Forces of Production: A Social History of Industrial Automation.* New York: Knopf; and Zimbalist, Andrew, ed., 1979. *Case Studies on the Labor Process.* New York: Monthly Review Press.

[2] Tulin, Roger. 1984. *A Machinist's Semi-Automated Life.* San Pedro, California: Singlejack Books, p.14.

[3] Noble, *op. cit.*

[4] Glenn, Evelyn and Roslyn Feldberg. 1977. "Degraded and Deskilled: The Proletarianization of Clerical Work." *Social Problems* 24:42.

[5] Ibid., p.52.

[6] Kraft, Phillip. 1977. *Programmers and Managers: The Routinization of Computer Programming in the United States.* New York: Springer-Verlag, p.97. See also Greenbaum, Joan. 1979. *In the Name of Efficiency: Management Theory and Shopfloor Practices in Data Processing Work.* Philadelphia: Temple University Press.

[7] U.S. Bureau of Labor Statistics. "Occupational Employment Projections through 1995". *Monthly Labor Review* (Nov. 1983): 37–49.

[8] U.S. Bureau of Labor Statistics. "High Technology Today and Tomorrow: A Small Slice of the Employment Pie." *Monthly Labor Review* (Nov. 1983):58.

[9] See Berg, Ivar. 1971. *The Great Training Robbery.* Boston. See also Braverman, Harry. 1974. *Labor and Monopoly Capital.* New York: Monthly Review Press, pp.424–449.

[10] Gaskell, Jane. 1983. "Conceptions of Skill and the Work of Women: Some Historical and Political Issues". *Atlantis* 8(2):11–25.

[11] Braverman, pp.443–444.

[12] Braverman, p.444.

[13] Quoted in Braverman, p.447.

SOURCE: Courtesy of the author.

Questions and Topics for Discussion and Writing

1. How does author James Turk refute the view that "the employment future lies with those able to perform professional and technically sophisticated work"?
2. What is Turk's main point in his discussion of the term "skills" and how the term is defined?
3. According to Turk, what should be the ultimate goal of a solid general education? Does this goal seem reasonable in today's transition from school to work?

Highbrowism is dangerous!

Why Intellectuals Care about the Flintstones

Thomas Hurka

What distinguishes an intellectual? Is it his or her profound interest in "highbrow" things (like poetry, painting and architecture)? This essay takes issue with that idea. The author argues that "real" intellectuals are, or should be, also interested in real things (including the Flintstones). They want to understand the ordinary world around them.

In an SCTV sketch called "Philosophy Today," a group of academics sit around a TV studio waiting for their discussion show to begin. As the cameras roll, the moderator announces the topic for the day: "Were the Flintstones a rip-off of the Honeymooners?" A heated discussion ensues.

The sketch is hilarious, but also deeply insightful. A real intellectual would want to know, would be excited to learn, that the Flintstones *were* a rip-off of the Honeymooners.

What is an intellectual? Some people think intellectuals are distinguished by their interest in certain highbrow subjects. Intellectuals like poetry, painting, and architecture. They talk about international and national (though never local) politics. They think no dinner party complete without some discussion of opera and get annoyed when you interrupt to ask whether they don't think Fred Flintstone was modelled on Ralph Cramden and Barney on Ed Norton.

These aren't intellectuals, just highbrows. Real intellectuals differ not in the subjects they follow, but in the approach they take to any subject. They want to know or understand everything. They care about poetry and architecture, but they also look at the ordinary world around them.

Understanding means knowing generalizations, and real intellectuals look for generalizations on all subjects. They try to spot trends in advertising and popular television. They wonder whether any unifying characteristics distinguish U.S. sports from those popular in other countries. They debate the hypothesis that as you mount through the social classes, the writing on "legible clothing" (clothing with words on it) gets progressively smaller and eventually disappears.

Intellectuals want to unify information. They know the greatest scientific advances occur when what appeared to be distinct phenomena are seen to follow from the same laws as when Newton gave the same explanation of the motions of heavenly bodies and objects on earth. Something similar happens when you see the parallels between Wilma's relationship to Fred and Alice's to Ralph: smarter than, exasperated by, but always lovey-dovey and forgiving at the end of the show.

Intellectuals follow popular culture, but in its social context. They find it curious that in the 1950s, when TV was a luxury of the well-to-do, many popular programs featured working-class characters, whereas in the 1960s, when TV ownership became universal, the subjects were almost exclusively middle-class.

This is reflected in the Flintstones and the Honeymooners. Like Ralph and Ed, Fred and Barney are working men, with ordinary jobs and interests. But where Ralph and Ed live in apartments, Fred and Barney, in a concession to the 1960s, have detached houses in the suburbs.

Even when they discuss the same subjects, highbrows and real intellectuals do so differently. Highbrows think discussing, say, politics intellectually means making lots of references to various Great Dead Political Thinkers. They are demons of quotesmanship. In their writing, "Spinoza said" follows "de Tocqueville remarked" follows "Burke pointed out."

Real intellectuals don't do this. They've read the great philosophers, but they don't need to advertise this fact. And they don't like to bludgeon people with famous names. They know that what made the great thinkers great was not their snappy remarks, but their extended arguments, and that what you need to persuade someone honestly is also an argument—perhaps extended, perhaps complex, but in straightforward language and without needless references.

Once again, it is content versus style. Highbrows think being intellectual means knowing certain facts. For real intellectuals it means thinking logically, precisely, and with an eye to important generalizations.

A persistent hawker of highbrowism is Woody Allen. In his movies a woman is often transformed into an intellectual by a man—in *Annie Hall* by Mr. Allen himself, in *Hannah and Her Sisters* by that awful sculptor. In each case the process is the same: the man recommends some books, the woman reads them and, presto, she's a thinker. At the end she gives full credit for her transformation to her (now ex-) lover.

There's no hint in these movies that reading big books isn't enough. Mr. Allen doesn't consider that you have to challenge the arguments you read, and that if you do, the credit for what you learn goes to you, not to whoever compiled your booklist.

Highbrows want big reforms in education. They want students to stop listening to rock'n'roll and read a series of set Great Books, works approached with reverence as stores of useful quotations and eternal truths. Real intellectuals also want students to read great books, but in the way their authors wanted: as presenting arguments that need to be probed as carefully for weaknesses as for insights, not accepted on faith.

Highbrowism is dangerous, because it erects unnecessary barriers. It discourages would-be intellectuals from addressing ordinary people and creates resentment of the intellectuals' airs. Highbrows want nothing to do with Fred Flintstone and Ralph Cramden, and Fred and Ralph would want nothing to do with them. But real intellectuals care about life in Bedrock and at the bus company, as about anything they can appreciatively understand.

SOURCE: Courtesy of the author.

Questions and Topics for Discussion and Writing

1. Thomas Hurka makes several comparisons to illustrate the difference between intellectuals and "highbrows." If one major distinction had to be made between the two groups, what would it be?
2. Why does Hurka contend that intellectuals are interested in the Flintstones? Why does he use this cartoon as a reference point at all?
3. According to Hurka, what is the intellectual's major aim? Is this goal attainable?

On Being a Critical Thinker

Richard P. Janaro and Thelma C. Altshuler

Why do some people think only during school examinations and then escape to leisure-time activities that require as little thinking as possible? What is "critical thinking" and why does it have such a bad reputation? In this piece, the authors explain how we can make better use of critical faculties.

Toward the end of William Wharton's novel *Dad*, the main character, en route to his father's funeral, gets a glimpse of his own aging and eventual death:

> I'll become a bore to others, a drag in conversation, repeat myself, be slow at comprehension, quick at misunderstanding, have lapses in conceptual sequence. All this will probably be invisible to me. I won't even be aware of my own decline.

What he fears is the loss of a highly treasured human trait, the power of thought. He is clearly a man who has enjoyed the use of his critical faculties, and while they may eventually fail him, his life will have been richer because of their use. He is only one of many who have paid tribute to—and feared the loss of—that unique human skill, the ability to think critically.

Of all the creatures on earth, from the smallest to the largest, only human beings can understand concepts. Other creatures have instincts. They seek food and shelter and cleverly achieve these ends; they have families and nurture their young; they fight, run, and even play. But they don't plan or read or make word jokes or find similarities in apparently unlike objects. They lack the power to contemplate, to speculate, to make valid inferences, and to laugh at foolish inconsistencies. So do computers—those amazingly quick, astonishing storehouses of memories. Computers, however, possess skills that are dependent on the creative imaginations of those who manage their circuits and prepare their software. Human beings are thus the only creatures capable of the joy of thinking.

The man who said he feared the loss of comprehension has at least been able thus far in his life to enjoy thorough use of his brain. What can be said of those who refuse to take advantage of what they have? What would make people reluctant to use that frequently unused human faculty, the mind? Why do some people think only during school examinations and then escape to leisure-time activities that require as little thinking as possible? And why does that special form of thinking called "critical" have such a bad reputation?

We will begin by rejecting one definition of critical thinking. A critic is not necessarily a person who enjoys finding fault, who tears down rather than builds up. Criticism may involve praise of the highest order or the withholding of judgment until more information is available. Criticism is analysis leading to an evaluation. It is the state of mind that should precede choices and actions. Though capable of both spontaneity and intuition, the critical thinker depends less on them than on careful observations and reasoned conclusions.

Criticism, then, is an activity of the mind that carefully defines, describes, and analyzes something—a movie, an event, a presidential decision, a daughter's desire to move into her own apartment. It probably should be, but often is not, the mental activity that people enjoy engaging in more than any other. The following things are opposed to critical thinking: constant complaining; the suspicion that the troubles of the world derive from plots and conspiracies; the habit of claiming to be right at all times; the tendency to form conclusions at once, refusing to be led astray by facts; and the tendency to fall immediately into line with another person's viewpoint.

Critical thinking is also the ongoing process of criticism. It is the disposition of the mind to behave in a certain way, that is, to define, describe, and analyze as accurately, as fairly, and as dispassionately as possible. It is a lifelong commitment.

Critical thinkers quickly become known, become identified as people whose opinions can be trusted. Many times over they have demonstrated a knack for assessing a matter reasonably and making a memorable pronouncement on the subject.

It is not at all difficult to distinguish critical from noncritical thinkers. The latter take things literally and fail to move on quickly to the next step. They have a hard time figuring out why people say what they say. They are not aware of what we might call the shape of experience. The morning after a party, noncritical thinkers cannot put the event into perspective. Critical thinkers, on the other hand, will tell you concisely what happened and what it felt like to be there.

Critical thinking is not an exact science, but it has identifiable characteristics. It has goals. There are certain ways of achieving it. The purpose of this chapter is to systematize these ways as much as possible.

Thinking about Thinking

The first step in becoming a critical thinker is to develop some idea of what is meant by thinking. For centuries, speculations about the mind belonged exclusively to philosophy. It was believed by many that the mind was a spiritual, or at least a nonmaterial, entity, floating somehow within but not connected to the body. Today psychologists believe that all functions of the mind, from dreams to the most complex series of interwoven ideas, are localized in the brain. Take away the brain, and the mind disappears. For all practical purposes, the brain *is* the mind.

Old Brains, New Brains

By making plaster casts of primitive brains on indentations found inside ancient skulls, California anthropologist Ralph Holloway has constructed a theory that the brain has gradually grown larger. Carl Sagan (in *The Dragons of Eden*) describes a three-part division of the brain, the bottom and middle sections being the survivors of millions of years of evolution. These are the "old" brains. The topmost section is most advanced in *Homo sapiens*—humanity in its present form.

The oldest, or *reptilian*, brain once belonged to early inhabitants of planet Earth. These creatures needed a brain to process information delivered by the sense of sight as they foraged about for food and shelter. They also needed to be alert to danger. Hence this brain developed survival techniques, including aggression ("Get them before they get you"); what Robert Ardrey has called the "territorial imperative" ("This area is mine, so keep off!"); and an insistence upon and respect for hierarchy ("You'd better take orders from me, or I'll kill you").

As time went on and mammals began to evolve, a new kind of brain was needed to process information passed on from the sense of hearing, developed out of the necessity for recognizing threatening sounds from a considerable distance. The mammals, travelling at night when the reptiles were sleeping, developed a brain with insights and intuitions of both danger and safety. This brain came to value all those things associated with shelter, including the family instinct, love, charity, and self-sacrifice. As leadership of Earth passed into the keeping of the mammals, brains, not brawn, assumed priority. The reptiles that remained became smaller, and the mammals grew larger. Today whales and especially dolphins exhibit versions of this middle brain. Examples of their intelligence as well as their "tender" qualities have been documented.

The topmost brain in Sagan's theory is, of course, "ours." Courses in the humanities are likely to tell you that by virtue of being *born* human, we have a glorious heritage. The brilliant achievements of our species are proof that to be human is automatically a reason to marvel at oneself. But potentiality is not actuality. Aristotle pointed that out twenty-five hundred years ago, though he stressed that the potential for achievement is always there.

It is clear that we don't always belong to the tradition of human achievement. Consider what humanity is doing to its own environment and to its prospects for survival on this planet. Have we not been told that the present generation is the first to wonder whether it will be the last? Make a list of our present inhumanities and one of our humanities. Which is longer?

As our understanding of the human mind increases, old ideas about the brain's span of usefulness are changing. Traditional notions about aging are being put aside. Loss of the rational faculties and loss of short-term memory (senility), for example, are less and less thought to be inevitable by-products of age. Recent intelligence testing of people as they grow older is revealing that those who continually use their brains can grow *more*, not less, intelligent with age. In his early nineties, Bertrand Russell was still writing, lecturing, and working on complex philosophical puzzles that would have baffled much younger people. George Bernard Shaw lived to be almost a hundred, showing little if any diminution of his mental powers, especially his legendary wit. And George Abbott, to celebrate his own centennial year, opened a play on Broadway. On the other hand, tests indicate that those who spend their lives in nonmental pursuits display brainpower loss at an age when their mentally agile contemporaries are still engaged in productive intellectual labours.

It is important to recognize that the brain needs exercise just as much as do legs and arms. An exercised brain will reward you even more than other parts of the body. Physical well-being is gratifying, but the exhilaration that comes from having completed a taxing bit of mental work—reading a difficult book, writing a complicated paper, solving a tricky puzzle, say—is incomparable.

If some continue to exercise their minds while others do not the future of humanity—assuming we can keep from blowing one another up—could be one in which brain levels can be placed in a large hierarchy. At the top will be those who have powers of analysis and synthesis far beyond anything known today. But how many of these "superbrains" will there be? How many others, with less brainpower, will be placed at the bottom? And more important and more frightening, will the superbrains limit the freedom of those with less developed minds?

Behind Closed Doors

The false but dangerous belief that critical thinking is confined to a small part of the populace is shared by those who have such abilities and by those who don't. Those who think critically may hold this belief in order to retain the skill that sets them apart from others and thus maintain their superiority. If the ability to think is not teachable, then well-paid and prestigious work remains out of reach for the majority, even those willing to work 'hard. If this is the case, critical thinking is something you have to be born with, like an aristocratic title. Education that serves only to develop the intellectual capacity one already has would have value for only a few. With such reasoning, critical thinkers can justify inequitable education systems.

In his satirical anti-utopian novel *Brave New World*, Aldous Huxley created a well-run society in which the brainy people are the ones in power. The Alphas make all the decisions because they have literally been *bred* in test tubes to have the intelligence required for governing the rest. Other groups, conditioned to be pleased with their own special, but lower, qualities, do not expect to improve their ability to think. In the real world, critical thinking is often considered beyond the range of all but a small segment of the people. Corporate bureaucracy is based on the assumption that managing directors and chief executive officers have to make the tough, intricate decisions, or the company will fall into chaos. Power thus remains behind closed doors for the relatively few.

But those with power are not the only ones who claim that critical thought is a special gift. People with poor self-concepts (sometimes the result of parental reinforcement) tend to agree. Sure that they won't be able to do the job, they give up without really trying. Each penalty for poor performance leads them to the certainty that the next failure is preordained. After a time, it is.

The Feeling Level

Those who work outside the closed doors of the critical decision makers often maintain that people who *feel* more than they think are somehow more trustworthy and charitable than their highly paid, less emotional "superiors." The ability to express emotion—even uncontrolled anger—is valued in our thought-suspicious times. "Feeling" people tend to attract our sympathies. They sometimes see themselves as martyrs, perennial victims of injustice at the hands of the callous and calculating. Conversely, those "unable to feel" are often urged to let themselves go and be "human." But there is no reason to equate humanness with feeling, or lack of humanness with critical thinking. The emotional approach to life can be a whole lot easier and a whole lot less effective than trying to analyze what is really happening and coming up with a workable solution to genuine problems.

Thus a lack of perceived compassion for the weakness of others is deplored, while illogical thinking either goes undetected altogether or is dismissed as insignificant. Even when there is little evidence to indicate that nonthinkers are automatically warm and tender, they are often thought to be. Since many people avoid what they believe will be the "pain of thought," they display an easy tolerance for mental lapses in everyone else. The "difficult" subjects in school are always those requiring the closest reading and the most intense concentration; low grades in such subjects tend to be laughed off by many.

Each of us is able to operate on different levels of consciousness. The first we might call "casual." In everyday conversations with friends and family or in just letting the mind ramble on in its usual, undisciplined way, we are hit-or-miss in our thinking. Sometimes some of us carry a thought process in a direct line for a minute or more. Mostly we can't. The level of critical thinking—which is the third level of consciousness and involves sustained, careful manoeuvres of the mind through the shoals of irrelevance—requires time, solitude, and silence. It seldom competes successfully with the second, or feeling, level, which is even less difficult, at least for some, than casual conversation. Frustration, anger, and resentment, or concern, warmth, and passion...all can be summoned front and center without needing our concentration.

The time has come to seek a balance among the three levels of consciousness. We want sometimes to chit-chat with our friends (or ourselves), to let out mind amble along at its own pace and go wherever it will. If we have tenderness or anger to communicate, we want the right to do so. But without the critical level, we run the risk of becoming permanently displaced in a world of never seeing very clearly what we and others are about. We risk not being able to transcend events, observing issues and principles at work.

Bottom-Brain Thoughts

- What shall we have for supper tonight?
- Can we afford to pay the rent?
- I was here first.
- I'll get to the top if it takes me ten years.
- How much does he earn?
- Who does she think she is?
- Who's in charge here?
- Now that I'm the manager, I'll need a larger house.

Middle-Brain Thoughts

- Be home by ten.
- Don't go out with him; he's not for you.
- Married ten years and only one child?
- She's old and helpless; we have to take her in.
- I'll get a job if you promise to stay in college.

Exercising the Critical Faculties

If we believe there is an immediate survival reason for every human skill developed since our species first evolved, we could argue in favor of letting the brain work only when necessary. If we are not trapped in a burning building, lost in a dense forest, adrift in a remote sea, or struggling to remember an obscure date on an important examination, we may safely ease out of the girdle of tight thought and "let our minds go." We may also conclude that if we have no present need of muscle power—for instance, if our car has a flat tire and we need to use the jack—the body may safely be allowed to flop into an easy chair directly after dinner. But not exercising the body could mean not having what it takes to accomplish a physical task when the need arrives. By the same token, when the brain is left to flounder and grow flabby from nonuse, the capacity for sustained logical discourse may just not be there when the need arises.

In this section we look at a few examples of how the critical faculties can be exercised on a daily basis. After all, even great dancers still report to the studio each morning for their barre exercises.

Beyond Chit-Chat

As pointed out in the preceding section, we spend a great deal of time on casual thinking, which is not sustained and nearly always lacks transitions from point to point, and on casual conversation, which is even less organized. Long, rambling conversation seems harmless enough, in the same way that junk food, with its heavy concentration of starch, sugar, and salt, seems safe enough "now and then"—that is, for lunch every day but never for dinner. But chit-chat's cumulative effect on the mind can be every bit as dangerous as the cumulative effect of sweet soft drinks.

Social conversation can be turned into an exercise in critical thought. Avid fans of a sport can spend highly enjoyable time in serious analysis of the coach's strategy. Monday-morning quarterbacks can play their own critical game of "If...then...and that would have provided the opportunity to..." Between games there is talk of player contracts and front-office decisions. When talk is knowledgeable, not merely the recitation of statistics or preferences, it is *critical* talk.

There need be no immediate outcome of critical conversation, of course. Someone remarks, for instance, "I suppose I should root for one of the teams in the playoff." A friend answers, "It makes it more interesting. But I can't find any reason to care about the teams that are left. Neither is from a city I've ever lived in, and there's no one player I care about." Another says, "I usually wait till one team has lost two games in a three-out-of-five series, and then root for the underdog." Yet another pipes in, "Or the team with a lot of older players. It's their last chance to make it." The environmentalist adds, "Or from the standpoint of fuel conservation, teams that are close to each other..." Infuriating to a passionate fan, this type of conversation is critical in that it rises above—or outside of—unexamined "rooting" and makes tentative remarks about the reasons behind a choice. People are making statements and noting their reasons for doing so. At least some kind of thinking is taking place as they talk.

If we always make choices without analyzing them, then we will fail to develop the capacity for making crucial choices when we *really* must. We may "naturally"—for reasons obscure to ourselves—root for *any* underdog, but this basis for choice may not be appropriate or make sense if we think about it.

Solving Problems

The problems of everyday life offer the most obvious chance for most of us to tune the critical faculties. For example, a family member who always needs help of some sort is a problem for almost everyone.

The typical solution, which is to ignore the problem and hope it will go away forever, is not the critical approach. The attitude of "It's easier to help than to have the hassle" may well avoid a painful thought, but not a painful scene further down the line.

The first step in solving a problem is to determine whether there is one at all. Whether to place an aging relative in a nursing home or provide home care yourself may not be a problem if no legitimate choice exists. Should money not be an issue, one obvious question suggests itself: "Do I want to assume the responsibility of caring for my grandmother?" If the answer is no, then the "problem" disappears, unless the original question can be replaced by yet another: "Will I be able to handle the guilt I may feel after I've signed the papers?" However, guilt versus responsibility may be an unbalanced set of alternatives. Is nursing-facility care better suited to your grandmother? Or is she still well enough and alert enough to experience a harmful feeling of rejection? In the first instance, the logic of choosing the nursing home should make guilt unnecessary. In the second, the alternatives seem equally compelling: no, for the good of your relative; yes, for your own good. So you may conclude that you definitely have a problem.

The second step is usually to determine who owns the problem, or, in the case of the nursing-home dilemma, whether you are the sole owner. Are there others in the family who could share the need to choose? Often we make ourselves miserable by supposing that we are not, or ought not to be, sole owners. "Why me?" is a frequent, if rhetorical, question people ask. If there is no answer, then the question is foolish but psychologically damaging. It's necessary to be hard-nosed—that is, brutally realistic—about deciding the question of ownership. To be so saves time and emotional wear and tear.

Recognizing that we seldom receive rewards for good deeds puts us well on the way to not expecting any. The business of living can be much easier without fantasies.

Challenging Assumptions

A good exercise for the critical faculties is to pay close attention to what people say and, just for fun, to freeze the action and examine the statement. If the cost of hurting people's feelings by reporting your "findings" aloud is too high a price, then examining assumptions in the privacy of one's thoughts is fine.

> We allow our ideas to take their own course, and this course is determined by our hopes and fears, our spontaneous desires, their fulfillment or frustration; by our likes and dislikes, our loves and hates and resentments. There is nothing else so interesting to ourselves as ourselves.
>
> *James Harvey Robinson*
>
> The word "criminal" is not only on a much higher level of abstraction than "the man who spent three years in the penitentiary," but it is...a judgment, with the implication "He has committed a crime in the past and will probably commit more crimes in the future." The result is that when John Doe applies for a job and is forced to state that he has spent three years in the penitentiary, prospective employers...may say to him, "You can't expect me to give jobs to criminals?"
>
> *S.I. Hayakawa*
>
> One must become able to transcend the narrow confines of a self-centered existence and believe that one will make a significant contribution to life—if not right now, then at some future time.
>
> *Bruno Bettelhelm*

Suppose, for example, you hear someone say, after reading a front-page story: "They shouldn't let those people out of mental hospitals and turn them loose to hurt innocent people." Immediately you might list a number of assumptions being made:

1. Everyone in a mental hospital deserves to be there.
2. All people admitted to mental hospitals are both incurable and violent.
3. Those in charge of mental hospitals are in no

position to make accurate judgments about the future behavior of any patient released.

4. Confinement to a mental hospital should be permanent.

Having listed the assumptions, you are now in a position to question them.

The noncritical person in a debate is likely to be unable to stay with the subject and will become personal as well as shrill. For instance: "you never come up with any good ideas…just like your brother. I once knew someone who was in a mental hospital…at least I think so. Anyway, all psychiatrists are crooks." Assumptions, such as the latter statement, come to the surface suddenly, then dive below just as rapidly. Personal fears, old prejudices, and unresolved guilt mix with illogical thinking to produce a pandemonium of wild talk that can absolutely stagger you once you set about to really listen.

The highly emotional assumption maker may be too far gone to benefit from your relatively calm analysis of the assumer's argument. But where rational confrontation is possible, you, the critical thinker, advance your own cause and that of the assumer by assisting in the process of recognition. The challenge should, however, be gentle, never officious or self-righteous, for to be such is to throw around a few untested assumptions of your own.

Taking School Examinations

Educators may disagree on principles and strategies, but there is general agreement on the value of critical thinking in school. In order for students to answer critically, they must go beyond the recall level, which consists of factual answers to factual questions. The authorship of *Don Quixote*, the temperature at which water boils, the nationality of Kierkegaard, and the definition of Manifest Destiny are facts worth a few points on objective tests.

The best essay questions are valuable critical exercises, though even straight recall helps tune the brain. If the lecturer has described the court of King Louis XIV and the Palace of Versailles and has then played music of the mid-seventeenth century, the student who can recall what the lecturer said about the history of the time and the way the arts reflect that history is still on the level of recall. An essay question about the relationship between the music and the formal gardens of Versailles forces the student to make a connection on her or his own. Making responsible connections is at the heart of critical thinking.

Or, having given an overview lecture on the neoclassical age with Versailles as a prime example, the instructor may ask the student to provide her or his own overview about an entirely different period. The essay question then might read, "In what way did the arts of the Renaissance indicate a belief in the greatness of humankind?" A wealth of "evidence" could be used by the student—Michelangelo's statue of David, the paintings of Leonardo, the great heroes of Shakespeare, and so on. The essay would require the student to match concrete examples with general principles about the Renaissance as a whole, showing ways in which implicit belief is exemplified in art.

Here are some other critical topics:

1. Explore the possible audience of a local radio station by listening to the vocabulary of the announcers and making inferences about the prospective users of the products advertised. What part of the population seems to be the target? How do you know?
2. Examine the "signals" being transmitted by the people and surroundings in two different parts of the city. Observe carefully the manner of dress, the types of stores, and the lettering on signs that alert visitors would notice. What types of neighborhoods are these areas?
3. Read or see a play that has been called tragedy. Without resorting to quotes from authorities, tell how you think it does or does not match classical principles of tragedy.
4. Describe an incident you have experienced or observed that offers a clear moral choice. Demonstrate your knowledge of two ethical ideas by describing two courses of action and the implications of each.
5. Using all the information you have about a

historical (the French Revolution, for example), tell under what circumstances it might have been avoided.

Note that some of these suggested assignments combine recall information with other kinds of knowledge. The critical thinker knows the basic definition (of tragedy, for example) and is familiar with the plot of the play, but is not willing to be content with mere summary. It is in the matching of plot with definition that the higher order of thinking occurs.

Not included in the exercise on tragedy are the questions "Did you like it?" or "Is it great?" The former question is subjective, often valid, but not basically critical; the latter is evaluative, requiring the ability to describe and compare before the pronouncement that a work of art may be called "great" has any meaning beyond empty words.

For national examinations such as the Scholastic Aptitude Test and the Graduate Record Examination as well as for tests to determine eligibility for law school, critical thinking is apt to be required. [*Editorial note*: The authors are referring here to the standardized testing methods used in the U.S.] Because there is so much variation in the curricula of school systems throughout the country, the test questions must seek evidence of critical thinking rather than the memorization of specific information. A law school candidate may be asked, for example, to match a general principle with a specific situation which involves the ability to recognize the difference between bribery, extortion, and theft. Instead of writing definitions, however, the would-be lawyer must be able to relate the proper charge to the real issue. Doing this requires practice in careful, systematic thinking.

Or one may be asked questions about the meaning of particular lines of words of a poem. In "Loveliest of Trees" by A.E. Housman, for example, there appears the line "Now, of my threescore years and ten, twenty will not come again." The examination asks, "How old is he?" The distracted or impatient test taker translates "three score years and ten" and gives "seventy' as the answer. The more careful test taker answers correctly, "Twenty."

At the end of that same poem are the following lines:

And since to look at things in bloom
Fifty springs are little room,
About the woodlands I will go
To see the cherry hung with snow.

The critical reader, noticing "in bloom," knows at once that the season mentioned is spring. Asked to identify an image in the poem, the critical reader remembers that a poetic image is indirect, figurative, and allusive and answers that "snow" is an image referring to the blossoms rather than to a phenomenon of winter.

How does one develop the critical skills required to score well on essay examinations? The absolutely wrong approach is to use the chit-chat model, whereby you begin writing without the slightest awareness of what will come forth. Instead, you should survey the situation, gain a perspective on the question, formulate precisely in your mind what is being asked, then determine the best available strategy for answering. The skillful essay is clearly introduced and summarized, not long and rambling with no center of gravity.

Looking for Principles

In listening to the statements of others, we sometimes fail to hear principles—or the ones that are *actually* there. A principle is a particular kind of assumption, a moral or ethical judgment that is held to be universally applicable. The confusion of principles is one of our commonest errors.

According to the philosopher Kant, to test the moral validity of a proposed act we should will that it be universally binding. For example, the thief who justifies robbing a grocery store must agree that everyone who has been unfairly treated by society should steal from others. The "others" would, of course, have to include the thief. But a thief who is robbed on the way home from committing a robbery is unlikely to approve the action of the second thief. Therefore the thief's "thinking" prior to the stealing has to be revised: "Robbery is not acceptable, except when I do it."

You are waiting for a bus, and you hear a bystander remark, "Mother's Day came and went, without even a lousy card from my son." As a critical thinker, you entertain yourself by seeking out the principle from which the remark springs. How about starting with "Evidence of love is a greeting card arriving by a certain day." You can push the analysis further: the woman's "even" suggests that a card is minimally acceptable, that an expensive gift would be a stronger sign of love. Turning the assumption into a principle, you have: "Children ought to show their love for their parents by giving them expensive presents by a particular deadline." A moment's reflection should tell us that this is a very dubious universal principle.

Here is a statement reported in a newspaper account of a trial in which a former professional football player was charged with selling drugs: The athlete's attorney quipped, "So this is the thanks he gets for all the pleasure he has given the public!" To turn that remark into a universal principle, try starting out with "People who play football professionally..." or "As long as someone is engaged in an activity that entertains the public, that person may..." Or try this: "In such cases, the public's duty is to..." At the very least the attorney was saying, "Outstanding athletes should be judged by different standards from other people." Having "straightened out" the statement, we are now in a position to analyze it. We may well begin by questioning the phrase "has given the public." Since the man was a highly paid player, "given" seems inappropriate. In light of the hero worship of young fans, we may be tempted to ask why an outstanding athlete should not be held to an even higher standard of behavior than those not in a position to become role models.

Here's another statement, also reported in a newspaper: "It is just as dangerous to allow poisoned literature into the school library as to allow poisoned food into the school cafeteria." The principle seems clear: "We may safely base moral judgments on analogies." But is a valid comparison really being made here? The critical thinker notes differences. The logic of the analogy centers on the equal applicability of "dangerous" in both school areas. Laboratory analysis can tell us what is poison in food and what is not. But what device will detect poison in literature as objectively?

All of us, surely, would like to believe that we operate according to clear and approved principles. Some of us, however, become very confused when we attempt to match a concrete example or detail with an appropriate principle.

Literalists and Figuratists

Because people do not easily fall into categories, it is not fair to insist upon hard-and-fast distinctions. Critical thinkers are not always critical. They are capable of being impulsive, overemotional, and childish. They are inconsistent, too, being hurt on some days by remarks that on other days they would have overlooked or laughed at. Sometimes they become discouraged by the inability to solve a problem, when the brain seems to let them down.

But people who make up their minds to adopt the critical approach to living do acquire certain definite characteristics, and so do those who choose not to. In this section we are concerned with the way in which critical thinkers respond to and talk about experience. Critical thinkers tend to be figurative rather than always literal in their speech and their understanding of things.

On Being Literal

The literal person, or literalist, avoids or does not see general principles but concentrates on specific details. For example, suppose you are making a general complaint about ingratitude. "My brother," you remark, "is so selfish he expects to take, take, take and never give anything in return. After all the times he and his family have come to my house for holiday meals, he never entertains. I've helped him out with money when he needed it, let him use my car, even though he never filled the tank—and now, when I told him I'd appreciate it if he'd take care of our cat for three days while we go to Chicago, he said he wouldn't." There are any number of possible responses your listener could make—a sympathetic nod, a similar story about ungrateful relatives, or even an offer to help with the cat.

The literalist has not really been listening and, in

concentrating on self, remarks, "I've never been to Chicago."

Anyone who has ever listened to the question period following a lecture by a guest speaker will recognize the presence of literalists. No matter how stimulating the subject, the literalist will insist on inquiring of the speaker something totally off the point, like "What do you think of our city?" or "Are you related to...?"

Here is another example of the literalist in action:

> A: I wish life would provide experts. I'd love to have someone whom I could ask important questions: where to live, whether to change jobs, what school is best, what suntan lotion to use.
>
> B: My dermatologist gave me the name of a good suntan lotion. Just a minute. I have the name written down.

A is making a rueful observation that there is no certainty, that in a philosophical sense we are all alone. This is the general principle behind the observation. ***B*** hears only the examples, but not the random nature of them. ***B***, who is not accustomed to hearing or discussing principles, is unaware that ***A*** is uninterested in suntan lotion no matter what his or her actual words may have been.

Consider still another imaginary conversation:

> *Mother:*
> I find the only safe topic with my teenage son is something noncontroversial. I can't talk about his car, expenses, girlfriends, or his plans for school and a career. I know he's interested in baseball, so this morning I mentioned how well the Dodgers are doing. I told him they were six games ahead, and her corrected me. Ten games! It gave him a chance to explain something to me, and it worked. At least we didn't fight this morning.
>
> *Friend A:*
> I know. The only safe topic in our house these days is the new television lineup.
>
> *Friend B:*
> The Dodgers are actually twelve games ahead.

Which friend is the literalist? More important, by what process did either reply come to be what it is? Friend ***A*** listened to what was being said by Mother. Friend ***A*** heard the general principle: Since it is difficult to communicate with the younger generation on our own terms, we must find terms that will work. Knowing the point of the observations, Friend ***A*** replied in kind. Friend ***B***, on the other hand, is probably not in the habit of listening very carefully to begin with.

Literalists see object by object, hear sound by sound, but are unaware of wholes. Their conversation tends to be tedious, except perhaps to other literalists, because they themselves do not speak to significant issues or principles. The literalist back from a trip can give endless details about gas mileage, every morsel of food eaten at each stop, and the cost of items purchased or passed up. Even a pause now and then to sum up—"It wasn't worth it!" or "Travel is a pain, but you have to get away sometimes"—would break the total concentration on pointless detail.

Literalism also stems from self-preoccupation. Literalists are too busy waiting for their turn to speak, too busy thinking of what they might say to hear what others are saying. Even a transition like "I have nothing to contribute to this discussion. May we turn to another?" gives evidence of a critical mind at work and is easier to deal with.

Literalists seldom seek a perspective on world events. They are likely to have some interest in national problems, more in state issues, much more in matters relating to the city, and above all, the neighborhood. Characteristic of literalists, once again, is self-centredness. The closer the problem comes to home, the greater the involvement.

During a conversation, uncritical thinkers will be thinking ahead to what they will say when it is their turn to speak. Perhaps a joke they have just heard the day before will occur to them, which they are anxious to tell to others. They may impose the joke on the group whether the moment is appropriate or not. They are forever changing the subject, not having followed the thread of the conversation to begin with. They are so immersed in their own problems or so anxious to impress others with some good fortune that has befallen them that often their sole concern is to talk as frequently and as long as possible.

The compulsive need to talk and not listen, however, does not always erupt into overt speech. A noncritical person can be shy and introverted, so fearful of being rejected by others that he or she does not dare say much of anything. But reticence does not mean the person is listening. He or she may be carrying on an internal dialogue.

It is surely ironic that unassertive, unassuming people often give the impression of needing to have their egos built up, while the cool and confident critical thinker is often identified as an egotist. This is precisely what the critical thinker is *not.* People who are unsure of themselves, who are defensive, must always personalize whatever happens, whether they do so openly or not. You cannot become a critical thinker until you learn that impulsive, self-centered responses are not the only ones that can be made. A rule of thumb is to delay reacting.

Personalizing what happens and what others say is usually a cover-up for a lack of perception. We may have become so accustomed to leaping without looking or listening that we are easily confused by events. We manipulate them inside our own brains so that they are not confusing: "Oh, I see what that's all about" or "Nobody can fool me on that one." Another ploy is to force someone else to support our manipulations: "Am I right? Wouldn't you have done the same thing? Sure you would have!" Other people, perhaps involved in their own personalizations, may offer positive support just to avoid having to figure out the situation for themselves.

For most of us, the roots of imperception lie buried in our childhood. Think back to dinner table talk. Was it full of silly little details, such as "Who spilled the salt?" or "Finish every mouthful of that meat, or you'll get no ice cream"? Or were real subjects discussed?

Literalism is not always a sign of a nonthinking person. Some very bright people have proved incapable of moving from immediate details in any conversation. One reason may very well be a humourless approach to life, a belief that mind play is childish and that all thought and discussion not directly related to action or the making of money should be avoided. Such people are used to working with the concrete realities of each moment and adjust their responsiveness to experience accordingly. Life is detail after detail. They are often not so much blind to general principles as impatient over wasting time. Sometimes they enjoy discrediting those who are not dedicated to "important" matters but spend their time idly chatting about books or world affairs that obviously have nothing to do with making a living.

Recognizing Contexts

No one goes through life completely isolated. We cannot live on an island, never making contact with others. Therefore, everything we say or do occurs in a context—a framework of circumstances and relationships. The *figuratist* perceives context; the literalist seldom does.

The experience of living is divided into contexts. Home is a fundamental context. There is always some unfinished business or ongoing problem at home. The nature of this context changes constantly, so we must keep tuned in. The literalist easily ignores this context, forgetting the other family members and believing that the peculiar nature of the family circle provides exemption from having to view family matters objectively.

Visiting a new place provides another context. For the figuratist, the first day at college offers many clues about the new environment: messages on bulletin boards; football memorabilia for sale; petitions for either radical or orthodox causes. The figuratist places all these details into a single context to understand the general atmosphere of the new place, perhaps saving herself or himself from the embarrassment of appearing out of place. The literalist only notes the details.

Some contexts happen without warning, and the literalist is caught napping. A nervous twitch, an ironic reply, the exchange of glances between two other people—and a context is set up. Anthropologist Gregory Bateson laments that too many people live in terms of "pieces," but "the pieces of...patterns are not the patterns."

Contexts exist whether recognized or not. Almost any remark contains assumptions that provide a hidden context. For instance, if someone giving a party remarks, "Let's invite Laura for Alberts," there is the assumption that couples are better off at parties than individuals; that Albert can't find his own date; that matchmaking is an honourable enterprise; and even that an "unattached" man or woman would somehow be an intrusion for others at the party.

What is the context of the following remarks?

> "You'll appreciate your college education more if you find a part-time job."
>
> "When you were in India, what did you learn about the country and the people? No, more importantly, what did you learn about yourself?"
>
> "If god had intended women to be men's equals, he would have made them so."
>
> "You come to my house for dinner this time, I went to your house last time."

Literalists make and hear context-ridden statements without knowing they are doing so. Do you think any of the above remarks were made by figuratist? Can you justify your answer?

Linguistic Tip-offs

Figuratists are so called because their language gives them away. It is colorful and imaginative, not literal. Their language declares their independence of the details. Instead of telling you everything that happened, the figuratist sums it all up in a few bold strokes.

> *Don't look back. Something may be gaining on you.* Satchel Paige

> *The law, in its majestic equality, forbids the rich as well as the poor to sleep under bridges.* Anatole France

> *The difficult we do right away. The impossible takes a little longer.* Business sign

Literalists frequently mix their metaphors. The literalist says, "People walk all over me, but I'm putting my foot down!" (Whose foot is down?) The figuratist is likely to reply: "If people walk all over you, make sure you have a good strong mattress." And the literalist may add, "I buy almost everything at Sears."

The secret of figuratism is knowing what is appropriate to think about a given phenomenon. When the state representative reports to a group of his constituents, all teachers, that his bill for a higher educational budget was defeated because "the conservatives literally emasculated me," the figuratist lifts an eyebrow. How well is he handling his job up there in the capital?

> *Parent:*
> You're foolish to go to the dog races so much. Don't you know you win one night and lose it all back the next?
>
> *Offspring:*
> Okay, I'll go every other night.

When it is appropriate—and it is not always appropriate—figuratists operate from general principles rather than from a long string of specific instances. It strikes the figuratist as a waste of time to bore friends with a blow-by-blow description of all the incompetents met during the course of a single day, and the figuratist would rather ignore the matter altogether—on the grounds that everyone is familiar with the existence of incompetence at every turn. The observation "I also did some shopping today and was pleased to see that standards of incompetence are being met in every store" ends the subject.

> *Lady Bracknell:*
> Do you smoke?
>
> *Jack Worthing:*
> Well, yes, I must admit I smoke.
>
> *Lady Bracknell:*
> I am glad to hear it. A man should always have an occupation of some sort.

Literalists relive their days over and over because they never stray very far beyond their own egos. If they do discover a general principle, it is usually that people and events are conspiring against them. They are fearful of being objective, of seeing things as they are, for if they ever do they might not find their way back to their own version of reality.

Figuratists, on the other hand, are free spirits, not easily threatened by situations, not easily cowed by other people. They do not have to talk about themselves all the time, because they are not insecure about their own worth. At the same time, they save themselves from arrogance by the very fact that they do attempt to be objective about all things, including themselves. They make mistakes like everyone else, but do not hide guiltily from them. They may even joke about them. Nobody can be a critical thinker all the time. There are times when only the hard details matter:

Mechanic:
The distributor cap is cracked, the points are worn, and the rotor needs replacing. As a matter of fact, the points should be gapped with a gauge; the dwell should be checked with a tach, and the timing needs resetting. The gap should be set at 35, the rpm at 750, and the timing at 6 degrees before top dead center.

Bewildered:
Why doesn't the car run?

Parents often make the mistake of supposing that children are immature and can thus be dealt with in any way that suggests itself at the moment. Many parents do not bother to prepare their children to act like responsible, critical adults. If the family watches a television show together, is it talked about afterwards? Or does the following happen? "Turn off the set and march right up to bed." If a bedtime story is read, does the parent show an obvious desire to turn out the light and leave the room, or is the story discussed? It is a sad fact of human experience that little of general, impersonal concern is mentioned within the family circle.

Most of us grow up, as Paul Goodman put it, "absurd." Most of us grow up any way we can. There is very little we can do about how we grew up. But we can decide it is high time to start thinking, to start examining our remarks and our thoughts for the amount of personalizing and the lack of general awareness we will find. The very best way to start is in silence and with a determination to hear and notice more.

Situation 1: People are talking about a book you have not read.

Impulsive Noncritical: "I hope they don't ask me to give an opinion."

Delayed Critical: "What is the book basically about?"

Situation 2: You discover your brother in the kitchen bleeding profusely.

Impulsive Noncritical: "I told you to be more careful with a sharp knife!"

Delayed Critical: "We need to get to the emergency room right away."

Situation 3: You read that two small third world countries control much of the Earth's supply of energy.

Impulsive Noncritical: "What's that got to do with me?"

Delayed Critical: "How can we develop new energy sources?"

The Critical Thinker as Critic

In its more formal aspects, criticism is associated with literature and the arts. A professional critic is someone paid to read, view, or listen and then present an informed opinion. Society absolutely needs such people. Critics are to plays and concerts what medical specialists are to designated parts of the body. Professional critics must discern and evaluate with cool detachment.

Once there were two performers—one a literalist, one a figuratist—opening in new plays on the same night. After the performances both entertained friends and fans in their dressing room.

One performer asked, "How was I?"

The other performer asked, "How was it?"

But the general public, too, can increase its enjoyment of the arts by practicing some of the skills of the professional critic. Since no one begins with those skills, we achieve competence gradually. With growing experience and with attentive listening or reading or watching, we begin to discern the various elements of the music or the play; to compare the work with different interpretations of previous performances; and to see what the composer or author is driving at. Each new experience is added to the old. At this stage we require more knowledge and information about the musical or the literary genre, the compositional technique and the sounds of various instruments, and the methods of acting.

Reviews, program notes, and art catalogues for museum exhibits produced by professional critics are often helpful. Professionals have the trained eyes and ears; they are the guides until we are ready to pick our *own* way along unfamiliar trails. Since the artist is frequently ahead of—or at least traveling in a different direction from—the public's taste, we, the critical thinker as critic, should withhold judgment until a work has been thought about for a time. It would be totally unacceptable to make up our minds in advance, pretending to like something because the experts do, or ridiculing it because it is unfamiliar. The opportunity to be a critic does not depend entirely on visits to concert halls or museums. There is always television, which we may approach with an equally dispassionate and an analytical mind. When a news event is considered important enough to be carried simultaneously by major television networks, the critical viewer thinks, "Is this really that important?" And if the news report deals with a government-sponsored program, further questions occur; "What should the state encourage? pay for? or withdraw support from?"

> A well-known entertainer, on in years but still popular, died suddenly and unexpectedly of a heart attack while in Europe. Two of his friends, also famous entertainers, were asked for comments.
>
> One was very personal: "I feel crushed, abandoned. I idolized him. I used him as a model. I would never have become successful had it not been for his encouragement. Life for me will never be the same without him."
>
> The other recognized a larger context: "He changed the entire history of popular songs. He introduced a style of singing that countless have imitated. He was the first performer to use the microphone instead of merely standing behind it. He created a sound that will probably never be forgotten."

After a while, critical thinking becomes an enjoyable part of being a spectator, though there will always be the uncritical friend who insists, "I'd rather not think about what I see. I'd rather enjoy myself." And there's no way to convince that friend it is possible to do both.

Glossary

Context: The environment, the background, the special circumstance that affects understanding.

Critical: an adjective referring to one who makes a habit of standing back and surveying a situation as a whole before teaching a conclusion about it.

Criticism: Analysis leading to evaluation (not used here in the narrower sense of "the act of finding fault with").

Figuratist: One who knows what is appropriate to think and say about a given phenomenon; who engages in "mind play" rather than passively existing; who has acquired the good habit of noticing and listening instead of being preoccupied with self; whose language is full of fancy and good humour; and who, above all, practices the art of critical thinking.

Literalist: One who sees specific instances rather than general principles; who moves from point A to point B in a thought sequence without grasping the essential point of a discussion; who seldom identities contexts, is generally self-centred, and speaks in plodding clichés.

SOURCE: Richard P. Janaro and Thelma C. Altshuler, *The Art of Being Human: Humanities as a Technique for Living*, 3th edition (New York: HarperCollins College Publishers, 1993). Reprinted by permission.

Myths and Facts: How Do We Know?

Robert H. Lauer

How do we distinguish myth from fact? In this piece, Robert Lauer uses examples from life in the United States to look at mistakes that commonly are made when thinking things through. A familiarity with the fallacies of reasoning will help you to formulate your own analyses and to evaluate the arguments of others.

Why do people use drugs? And what can we do about the drug problem? These questions took on an urgency for Americans in the 1980s and early 1990s. The answers given are many and diverse. Here are a few that appeared in a popular column in 1989:

> It's an education problem. We need to guarantee every child as much education as that child can handle, so no one has to grow up in poverty.
>
> It's a religious problem. God is punishing us for deviating from His ways. We must return to the ways taught in the Bible.
>
> The problem is one of our willingness to get tough. We need to crack down on the dealers. They should be put to death, like they do in the People's Republic of China. It doesn't make sense to just put them in prison and continue to house and feed the scum who are destroying us.
>
> The problem is that we are a sick society. Our nation is full of people who abuse their children. Our kids are unhappy because they have parents who are full of anger and greed. You can't expect well-adjusted kids when the parents are so screwed up.
>
> The problem is a political and legal one. We need to decriminalize the use of drugs, and provide free or low-cost drugs to addicts. That would cause the dealers to lose their source of income and would make crime to get money to purchase drugs unnecessary.

To these analyses we could add others... We could say, for example, that drug abuse results from the breakdown of rules that followed the rapid change in all social institutions in our era, from the labels applied to young people who experiment with drugs, or from the definitions of appropriate and inappropriate behavior that prevail in juvenile groups.

There are, in other words, myriad explanations for drug abuse, and for all other social problems as well. The question we raise in this chapter is "How do we know which explanation is correct?" All of the above may sound reasonable, but not all are necessarily true. In fact, many myths surround social problems. How do we distinguish myth from fact?

We will answer the question in two ways. First, we will look at various *intellectual cul-de-sacs*. A cul-de-sac is a street with only one outlet—it is a blind alley. An intellectual cul-de-sac is thinking that does not carry us forward but, rather, leaves us in a "blind alley" because our thinking comes to a dead end. The common intellectual cul-de-sacs in discussions of social problems are various *fallacies of thinking*. We will see how these fallacies have been used to analyze social problems, creating myths that lead to a dead end in our thinking.

We will then look at how sociologists *research* social problems by gathering facts to test various explanations. The facts may lead us to revise our explanations or to abandon a particular explanation. In any case, the study of social problems is not an exercise in speculation. We want explanations that are supported by evidence.

The theoretical perspective we have adopted in this book—social problems as contradictions—is based on research and not merely on reason. Subsequent chapters will show that various kinds of research support the argument that social problems involve multiple-level factors, not single or separate causes operating at only one level of social life.

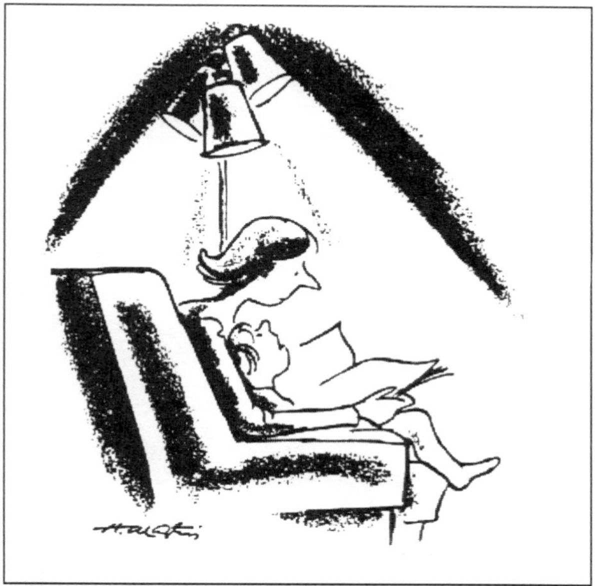

"If the coach and horses and the footmen and the beautiful clothes all turned back into the pumpkin and the mice and the rags, then how come the glass slipper didn't turn back too?"

The Source of Myth: Fallacies of Thinking

In this part of the chapter we will look at nine different fallacies that have been used to analyze social problems. A familiarity with the fallacies will help you to logically formulate your own analyses and to evaluate the analyses and arguments of others.

Fallacy of the Dramatic Instance

The ***fallacy of dramatic instance*** refers to the tendency to *overgeneralize*, to use one, two, or three cases to support an entire argument. This is a common mistake among those who discuss social problems, and it may be difficult to counter because the limited number of cases often are a part of the *individual's personal experience*. For example, in discussing the race problem in the United States, an individual may argue that "Blacks in this country can make it just as much as whites. I know a black businessman who is making a million. In fact, he has a better house and a better car than I have." You might counter this argument by pointing out that the successful businessperson is an exception. The other person might dismiss your point: "If one guy can make it, they all can." The fallacy of the dramatic instance mistakes a few cases for a general situation.

This fallacy is difficult to deal with because the argument is based partly on fact. There are, after all, black millionaires in America. But, does this mean there is no discrimination and that any black person, like any white person, can attain success? Many Americans believe that welfare recipients are "ripping off" the rest of us, that we are subsidizing their unwillingness to work and supporting them at a higher standard of living than we ourselves enjoy. Is that true? Yes, in a few cases. Occasionally, newspapers report instances of individuals making fraudulent use of welfare. But does this mean that most welfare recipients are doing the same? Do people on welfare really live better than people who work for a living?

The point is, in studying social problems, that we must recognize that exceptions always exist. To say that blacks are exploited in America is not to say that *all* blacks are exploited. To say that the poor are victims of a system rather than unwilling workers is not to say that one can't find poor people who are unwilling to work. To say that those on welfare are generally living in oppressive circumstances is not to deny that some welfare recipients are cheating and living fairly well. To use such cases in support of one's argument is to fall into the trap of the fallacy of the dramatic instance, because social problems deal with general situations rather than with individual exceptions.

As this suggests, the fact that someone knows a lazy poor man or a rich black or a cheating welfare recipient may be irrelevant. After all, millions of people are involved in poverty and in the race problem. *Systematic studies* are needed to determine whether the one, two, or three cases we know represent the norm or the exception. The fact that there are black millionaires may be less important than the fact that, in 1988, 13.5 percent of black households had incomes of less than $5,000, compared with 3.2 percent of white households in the same income group. At the other end of the scale, 24.5 percent of white households, compared with 9.5 percent of black households, had an income in excess of $50,000 (U.S. Bureau of the Census 1990:452). Such figures are more pertinent to the race problem than are cases representing exceptions to this general pattern.

Fallacy of Retrospective Determinism

The ***fallacy of retrospective determinism*** is the argument that things could not have worked out any other way than the way they did. It is a *deterministic* position, but the determinism is aimed at the past rather than the future. The fallacy asserts that what happened historically *had* to happen historically, and it had to happen just the way it did. If we accept this fallacy, we would believe that our present social problems are all inevitable. We would say that avoiding racial discrimination or poverty has always been impossible, that there were no alternatives to the wars in which we have been involved, and that the nation's health could not have been any better than it has been. However regrettable any of the problems are or have been, the fallacy of retrospective determinism makes them the unavoidable outcomes of the historical process. This fallacy is unfortunate for a number of reasons. History is more than a tale of *inevitable tragedies*. History is important in enabling us to understand social problems, but we will not benefit from history if we think of it merely as a determined process. We cannot fully understand the tensions between America's minority groups and the white majority unless we know about the decades of exploitation and humiliation preceding the emergence of the modern civil rights movement. Our understanding will remain clouded if we regard those decades as nothing more than an inevitable process. Similarly, we cannot fully understand the tension between the People's Republic of China and the West if we view it only as a battle of economic ideologies. We must realize that the tension is based in the pillage and humiliation that China was subjected to by the West. Again, our understanding will not be enhanced by the study of history if we regard the Western oppression of China in the nineteenth century as inevitable.

If we view the past in terms of determinism, we will have little reason to study it, and we will be deprived of an important source of understanding. Furthermore, the fallacy of retrospective determinism is but a small step from the stoic *acceptance of the inevitable*. That is, if things are the way they had to be, why worry about them? Assuming that the future will also be determined by forces beyond our control, we are left in a position of apathy: There is little point in trying to contest the inevitable. This fallacy is probably less common in discussions about social problems than the fallacy of the dramatic instance, but it does appear in everyday discussions. For example, in responding to the question about the causes of poverty in America, a sixty-four-year-old service station owner said, "To go back through history, it's traditional; there's no special reason, no cause for it. We can't get away from it. It has just always been this way." A similar fatalism cropped up in the response of a young businessman: "I don't actually know the cause of poverty, but it is here to stay and we must learn to live with it. We have to take the good with the bad." Journalists promote this explanation by using phrases like, "It had to happen…" The phrase may be a good lead into a story, but it reinforces the fallacy of retrospective determinism.

An individual might view social problems in deterministic terms for reasons other than intellectual conviction. Determinism can relieve us of responsibility and can legitimate our lack of concern with efforts to effect changes we do not want. Whatever the basis for affirming determinism, the outcome is the same: We may as well accept the problem and learn to live with it, because it is inevitably upon us and inextricably with us.

Whether determinism involves the past, present, future, or all three, thinking about social problems in deterministic terms leads to apathy.

Fallacy of Misplaced Concreteness

There is a tendency to explain some social problems by resorting to ***reification***—making what is abstract into something concrete. "Society," for example, is an abstraction. It is not like a person, an animal, or an object that can be touched. It is an idea, a way of thinking about a particular collectivity of people. Yet we often hear people assert that something is the fault of "society" or that "society" caused a certain problem. This is the ***fallacy of misplaced concreteness***. In what sense can society "make" or "cause" or "do" anything? To say that society caused a problem leaves us helpless to correct the situation because we haven't the faintest notion where to begin. If, for example, society is the cause of juvenile delinquency, how do we tackle the problem? Must we change society? If so, how?

The point is that "society" is an abstraction, a concept that refers to a group of people who interact in particular ways. To *attribute social problems to an abstraction* like "society" does not help us resolve the problems. Sometimes people who attribute the cause of a particular problem to society intend to *deny individual responsibility.* To say that society causes delinquency may be a way of saying that the delinquent child is not responsible for his or her behavior. Still, we can recognize the social causes of problems without either attributing them to an abstraction like society or relieving the individual of responsibility for his or her behavior.

For example, we could talk about the family problems that contribute to delinquency. A family is a concrete phenomenon. Furthermore, we could say that the family itself is a victim of some kind of societal arrangement, such as government regulations that tend to perpetuate poverty and cause stress and disruption in many families. In that case, we could say that families need to be helped by changing the government regulations that keep some of them in poverty and, thereby, facilitate delinquent behavior.

Society, in short, does not cause anything. Rather, problems are caused by that which the concept of society represents—people acting in accord with certain social arrangements and within a particular cultural system.

Fallacy of Personal Attack

A tactic among debaters is to *attack the opponent personally* when one can't support one's position by reason, logic, or facts. This diverts attention from the issue and focuses it on the personality. We will call this the ***fallacy of personal attack*** (philosophers call it *ad hominem*). It can be remarkably effective in avoiding the application of reason or the consideration of facts in a discussion of a social problem. We will extend the meaning when applying this fallacy to the analysis of social problems: we will use it to mean either attacking the opponent in a debate about a problem or *attacking the people who are the victims* of the problem.

Historically, the poor have suffered from this approach to their problem. Matza (1966) detailed how the poor of many nations in many different times have been categorized as "disreputable." Instead of offering sympathy or being concerned for the poor, people tend to label the poor as disreputable and, consequently, deserving of or responsible for their plight. This means, of course, that those of us who are not poor are relieved of any responsibility.

That our nation has the resources to eliminate poverty is generally recognized. We could argue effectively that the problem should be resolved, that no individual in the United States should live in poverty. However, the American poor are commonly castigated. Rather than reasoning about the problem, many Americans dismiss it by attacking the poor as a disreputable group. In research referred to previously (Lauer, 1971), the most common response from 1,400 middle-class people to a question about the cause of poverty was that the poor lack motivation. A young businessman said that poverty exists because of the lazy people, those who "think they deserve things handed to them. They have never worked and probably never will because they expect too much." Similarly, a young woman asserted, "The cause of poverty rests solely on the shoulders of the poverty-stricken people themselves...They have no ambition whatsoever, and it's no one's fault but their own."

A number of problems have been dealt with by attacking the people involved. Ryan (1971) called this "blaming the victim" and said it involves nearly every problem in America.

> The miserable health care of the poor is explained away on the grounds that the victim has poor motivation and lacks health information. The problems of slum housing are traced to the characteristics of tenants who are labeled as "Southern rural migrants" not yet "acculturated" to life in the big city. The "multiproblem" poor, it is claimed, suffer the psychological effects of impoverishment, the "culture of poverty," and the deviant value system of the lower classes; consequently, though unwittingly, they cause their own troubles [Ryan, 1971:5].

The meaning and seriousness of any social problem may be sidestepped by attacking the intelligence or character of the victims of the problem or of those who call attention to the problem. We need only recall a few of the many labels that have been thrown at victims to recognize how common this approach is: deadbeats, draft dodgers, niggers, kikes, bums, traitors, perverts and so forth.

Appeal to Prejudice

In addition to attacking the opponent, a debater may try to support an unreasonable position by using another technique: ***fallacy of appeal to prejudice***. (Philosophers call it argument *ad populum.*) It involves using popular prejudices or passions to convince others of the correctness of one's position. When the topic is social problems, this means using *popular slogans* or *popular myths* to sway people emotionally rather than using reasoning from systematic studies.

For example, a popular slogan that appeared as a car bumper sticker during the early 1970s read "I fight poverty; I work." This appeal to popular prejudice against "freeloaders" used the popular myth that the poor are those who are unwilling to work. This kind of appeal is doubly unfortunate because it assaults the character of the poor unfairly, and it is based upon and helps to perpetuate a myth. As we will see, the poverty problem is not a problem of work. Jobs for the unemployed will not eliminate poverty from America.

Some slogans or phrases last for decades and are revived to oppose efforts to resolve social problems. "Creeping socialism" has been used to describe many government programs designed to aid the underdogs of our society. The term is not used when the programs are designed to help business or industry, or when the affluent benefit from the programs. It has been remarked "What the government does for me is progress; what it does for you is socialism."

In some cases, the slogans use general terms that reflect *traditional values*. Thus, the various advances made in civil rights legislation—voting, public accommodations, open housing—have been resisted in the name of "rights of the individual." Such slogans help to perpetuate the myth that legislation that benefits blacks infringes on the constitutional rights of the white majority.

Myths, in turn, help to perpetuate social problems. In the absence of other evidence, we all tend to rely upon popular notions. Many Americans continue to assume that rape is often the woman's fault because she has sexually provoked the man. These Americans either have seen no evidence to the contrary or have dismissed that evidence as invalid. And, unfortunately, myths tend to become so deeply rooted in our thinking that when we are confronted by new evidence, we may have difficulty accepting it.

Myths are hard to break down. But if we want to understand social problems, we must abandon the poplar ideas and assumptions and resist the popular slogans and prejudices that cloud our thinking, and we must choose instead to make judgments based on evidence.

Circular Reasoning

The ancient Greek physician Galen reportedly praised the healing qualities of a certain clay by pointing out that all who drink the remedy recover quickly—except those whom it does not help. The latter die and are not helped by any medicine. Obviously, according to Galen, the clay fails only in incurable cases. This is an example of the ***fallacy of circular reasoning***: using conclusions to support the assumptions that were necessary to make the conclusions.

Circular reasoning often creeps into analyses of social problems. A person might argue that blacks are inherently inferior and assert that their inferiority is evident in the fact that they can hold only menial jobs and are not able to do intellectual work. In reply, one might point out that blacks are not doing more intellectual work because of discriminatory hiring practices. The person might then reply that blacks could not be hired for such jobs anyway because they are inferior.

Similarly, one may hear the argument that homosexuals are sex perverts. This assumption is supported by the observation that homosexuals commonly have remained secretive about their sexual preference. But, one might counter, the secrecy is due to the general disapproval of homosexuality. No, comes the retort, homosexuality is kept secret because it is a perversion.

Thus, in circular reasoning we bounce *back and forth between assumptions and conclusions.* Circular reasoning leads nowhere in our search for understanding of social problems.

Fallacy of Authority

Virtually everything we know is based on some *authority.* We know comparatively little from personal experience or personal research. The authority we necessarily rely on is someone else's experience or research or belief. We accept notions of everything from the nature of the universe to the structure of the atom, from the state of international relationships to the doctrines of religion—all on the basis of some authority. Most people accept a war as legitimate on the authority of their political leaders. Many accept the validity of capital punishment on the authority of law enforcement officers. Some accept the belief of religious authority that use of contraceptives is morally wrong in spite of the population problem. (They may even deny that there really is a population problem.)

This knowledge that we acquire through authority can be inaccurate, and the beliefs can exacerbate rather than resolve or ameliorate social problems. The ***fallacy of authority*** means an *illegitimate appeal to authority.* Such an appeal obtrudes into thinking about social problems in at least three ways.

First, the *authority may be ambiguous.* Appeal is made to the Bible by both those who support and those who oppose capital punishment and by both those who castigate and those who advocate help for the poor. Supporters of capital punishment point out that the Bible, particularly the Old Testament, decreed death for certain offenses. Opponents counter that the death penalty contradicts New Testament notions of Christian love. Those who castigate the poor call attention to St. Paul's idea that he who does not work should not eat. Those who advocate help for the poor refer us to Christ's words about ministering to the needy and feeding the hungry. Consequently, an appeal to this kind of authority is really an appeal to a particular interpretation of the authority. Because the interpretations are contradictory, we must find other bases for making our judgments.

Second, the *authority may be irrelevant to the problem.* The fact that a man is a first-rate physicist does not mean he can speak with legitimate authority about race relations. We tend to be impressed with people who have made significant accomplishments in some area, but their accomplishments should not overwhelm us if those people speak about a problem outside their area of achievement or expertise. Nor would we be overwhelmed by the wisdom of our forebears. Benjamin Franklin was a remarkable man, and his advice on how to acquire wealth has been heard, in part at least, by millions of Americans throughout history. But whatever the value of that advice for Franklin's contemporaries, it is of little use for for most of America's poor today.

Finally, the *authority may be pursuing a bias* rather than studying a problem. To say that someone is pursuing a bias is not necessarily to disparage that person, because pursuing a bias is part of the job for many people. For example, military officers analyze the problem of war from a military rather than a moral, political, or economic perspective. That is their job. And that is why decisions about armaments, defense, and war should not be left solely to the military. From a military point of view, one way to prevent war is to be prepared to counter any enemy attack. We must be militarily strong, according to this argument, so that other nations will hesitate to initiate an attack upon us.

The result of this line of reasoning is to resist a de-escalation of the arms buildup. In the late 1980s, the Soviet Union initiated efforts to reduce armaments and military spending in both the East and the West. The U.S. government responded positively. Some military voices on both sides, however, warned about the moves and suggested that they were putting the two nations in peril of each other. Social scientists who have studied the problem, on the other hand, point out that the real peril is a continuing arms race, which is more likely to result in, rather than prevent, war.

While some people pursue a bias as an normal part of their work, others pursue it because of *vested interests*. That is, the authority may deliberately or unconsciously allow biases to affect what he or she says because it is personally advantageous to do so. The military leader who inculcates a sense of the treachery of a foreign power and the need for the United States to be preeminent in military strength will obviously benefit from policies that give military needs priority. The corporate executive who talks about federal overregulation would benefit if the government would withdraw from various consumer protection programs. Political leaders like to credit their own policies when crime rates fall and point to uncontrollable circumstances when crime rates rise. Their policies may have no effect on crime rates, but they benefit if they can persuade people that what they have done has lowered the rate or what they will do will lower the rate in the future.

Authority can be illegitimately or arbitrarily assumed and illegitimately or inaccurately used. Both represent the fallacy of authority.

Fallacy of Composition

That the whole is equal to the sum of its parts appears obvious to many people. That what is true of the part is also true of the whole likewise seems to be a reasonable statement. But the former is debatable, and the latter is the ***fallacy of composition*** As economists have illustrated for us, *what is valid for the part is also valid for the whole* is not necessarily true. Consider, for example, the relationship between work and income. If a particular farmer works hard and the weather is not adverse, his income may rise. But if every farmer works hard and the weather is favorable, and a bumper crop results, the total farm income may fall. The latter case is based upon supply and demand, while the former case assumes that a particular farmer outperforms other farmers.

In thinking about social problems, we *cannot assume that what is true for the individual is also true for the group.* An individual may be able to resolve a problem insofar as it affects him or her, but that resolution is not available to all members of the group. For example, a man who is unemployed and living in poverty may find work that enables him to escape poverty by moving, by concentrated effort, or by working for less than someone else. As we will see in our discussion of poverty, that solution is not possible for most of the nation's poor. Something may be true for a particular individual or even a few individuals and yet be inapplicable or counterproductive for the entire group of which the individuals are members (as in the example of farmers).

Non Sequitur

A number of the fallacies already discussed involve non sequitur, but we need to look at this way of thinking separately because of its importance. Literally, non sequitur means "*it does not follow.*" This ***fallacy of non sequitur*** is commonly found when people interpret statistical data.

For example, the data may show that the amount of welfare payments by state governments has increased dramatically over the past few decades. Those are the facts, but what is the meaning? We might conclude that the number of those unwilling to work is increasing, that more and more "freeloaders" are putting their hands into the public treasury. But there are other explanations. The increase may reflect adjustments due to inflation, efforts to get welfare money to eligible recipients who did not receive money because they were unaware of their rights, or it may be the consequence of a sudden rise in unemployment due to governmental efforts to control inflation.

Daniel Bell (1960:chapter 8) showed how statistics on crime can be misleading. In New York one year, reported assaults were up 200 percent, robberies were up 400 percent, and burglaries were up 1,300 percent! Those are the "facts," but what is the meaning? We might conclude that a crime wave occurred that year. Actually, the larger figures represented a new method of crime reporting that was much more effective in determining the total amount of crime. An increase in reported crime rates can mean different things, but it does not necessarily signify an actual increase in the amount of crime.

One other example involves studies of women who work. Some employers have been convinced that women are not desirable as workers because they are less committed to the job than men are. One of the facts that appears to support that notion is the higher turnover rate of women. Women do indeed have a higher rate of leaving jobs than men have. But what is the meaning of that fact? Are women truly less committed to their jobs? Does the employer run the risk of having to find a replacement sooner if a woman rather than a man is hired for a job?

When we look at the situation more closely, we find that the real problem is that women tend to be concentrated in lower level jobs. Also, women who quit a job tend to find another one very quickly. Thus, women may be uncommitted to a particular—low-level—job, but they are strongly committed to work. Furthermore, if we look at jobs with the same status, the turnover rate is no higher for women than men.

In a study of the rates at which women quit, Osterman (1982) found that the rates were lower where employers adhered to federal affirmative-action guidelines. Osterman suggests that the antidiscrimination efforts probably enhanced job opportunities for women, including opportunities for advancement. The better opportunities, in turn, motivated them to remain with their jobs.

In sum, a fact that has been used to discriminate against women turns out to be a result rather than a cause of discrimination. The fact was accurate. The conclusion drawn from it—the unreliability of female workers—was false.

In fact, the correct conclusion may be the very opposite of the one that was drawn. A study of managers found that the women placed greater emphasis on their careers as opposed to family life than did the men (Powell, Posner, and Schmidt, 1984).

These illustrations are not meant to discourage anyone from drawing conclusions. Instead, they are another reminder of the need for thorough study and the need to avoid quick conclusions, even when those conclusions seem logical on the surface. Contrary to popular opinion, *"facts" do not necessarily speak for themselves.* They usually must be *interpreted*, and they must be interpreted in the light of the complexity of social life. Furthermore, numerous logical conclusions usually can be drawn from any particular set of data. The perspective of this book—social problems as contradictions—offers explanations of facts that take into account the complexity of social life.

SOURCE: Robert H. Lauer, *Social Problems and the Quality of Life*, 5th ed.

Drawing Distinctions

Thinking Critically

1. Fact and Opinion

A fact is something that is known on the basis of experience or empirical evidence. It is objectively verifiable to the degree that empirical evidence is verifiable.

Facts should not be accepted uncritically, particularly when they are "facts" about people and society. Examine, for instance, the "fact" that for centuries in the West, the contributions of men to art, literature, science and exploration vastly predominated over those of women. The context, belief system, social roles, distribution of power, health factors of the times and decisions about what is recorded as "important contributions" must be considered in interpreting these "facts". There are limitations to the conclusions which can be drawn from the so-called "facts".

Opinion functions as expression of subjective taste, preference and belief or judgment. Matters of subjective taste do not call for support or justification. We live in a social environment and era which supports the right of people to their own opinions. The right to an opinion is often translated into the equal merit of all opinions. Opinion becomes significant when it functions as a judgment and attempts to persuade. When opinion functions as judgment, it can have serious implications for oneself and others. In this instance, it can be challenged to be supported with evidence.

Opinions can form the basis for an argument. These differ on the basis of their structure more than their purpose. An argument is a collection of claims structured to rationally persuade one of the validity of a conclusion.

2. Premises and Conclusions

A collection of claims or statements (premises) which rationally persuade one to accept a target claim (conclusion) is an argument. Sometime opinions can form the basis for an argument.

A case is a multidimensional argument which advances its own reasons in support of a position as well as systematically and rationally examining and responding to opposing viewpoints.

3. The Person and the Argument

It is important in most instances to separate our response to what is said from who said it. That is, views should be examined on their own merits and not accepted or rejected on the basis of who presented them. Sometimes, the person's reputation is relevant to an acceptance or rejection of her views. For instance, when an idea is advanced by a person who is an expert in the area, greater credibility may be given to the view. Similarly, when a person who has a tarnished record in the area advances an idea, there may be reasonable cause to be especially cautious.

4. Correlation and Causation

Correlation refers to the strength and degree of the association of 2 or more factors. It is not to be confused with proof of a cause/effect relationship. In some cases, correlation may be simply co-incidence; e.g. in the Middle Ages in Europe, it was believed that body lice caused good health. This was based on the observation that only healthy people had lice; sick people didn't have them. Bathing was not a common practice, and the presence of lice was pervasive. Hence, a treatment for illness was to put lice on the sick. (In fact, lice are very sensitive to body temperature and moved to cooler climes when the person developed a fever.)

Causation means that a cause/effect relationship has been established. This requires rigorous investigation.

5. Appropriate/Inappropriate Generalization

Arriving at a conclusion on the basis of insufficient evidence is an inappropriate generalization. Partial or incomplete evidence contributes to hasty conclusions.

SOURCE: Faculty, George Brown College.

PART 2

Science and Technology

Abstract, 1943, by Lawren Harris.

Lawren Harris was the prime leader of Canadian art for many decades. He was a founder and leader of the Canadian Group of Painters, which succeeded the Group of Seven in 1933 (which he also help to found in 1920). (See page 339.)
Courtesy of Hart House Gallery, Toronto.

Introduction to Science and Technology

James Rudnick

Understanding science and technology can often be crucial in our everyday lives, but the ability to predict what will happen tomorrow is beyond most of us. At the root of that problem is the rapidly increasing rate of change in science and technology. While that change is accelerating our world at a faster and faster rate, it is easy to see that many of us are facing a world that becomes ever more arbitrary and unintelligible, mysterious and mercurial every day. And what this rapidly increasing rate of change can mean is that people all over the globe are becoming more and more alienated—the lost and knowledge-abandoned inhabitants of planet Earth.

And while all of us can see these marked changes occuring around us, many of us are not equipped to understand or react to this process. What was new a mere two years ago is now obsolete and has been replaced by generation after generation of technological advancement. This rapid development in everything from kitchen blenders to biotechnology, from snack foods to chaos theory has made it difficult for even the most "up to date" of us to keep up! Our grandparents struggled for decades to understand electricity—while we duel with black holes in a 20 second sound bite on the nightly news. Change has made time spiral inwards in an ever-tightening helix, and to understand is not only difficult, but once that knowledge is attained, it must be updated continually. Hence the oft-heard idiom that "knowledge is power."

And at the root of that search for knowledge is the scientific method, a tried and true process of coming up with an hypothesis or prediction and then testing it. The hypothesis may range from the mundane, like the conductivity of copper wire, to the remarkable, like the theoretical work of Hawking featured in this section on black holes. But no matter, the rules are the same: predict and then subject the prediction to rigorous testing. Replication, reliability and validity form the methodological trio necessary for successful advancements in the areas of science and technology and the resulting quest for knowledge. And it is the adherence to the scientific method that has resulted in the accelerating curve of change we now see all around us.

Understanding the scientific method is important. But it is equally important to keep in mind that the ways in which we think and do things in our world must go hand in hand with the process of questioning technological progress, and should form a necessary part of the civilization around us. Should society use all the technology now available? And how should we balance their use with the ethical issues posed by these technologies?

This Science and Technology unit attempts to answer these and other questions posed by some of the world's best known scientists and writers,—like Hawking, Asimov, Suzuki, Sagan and Marie Curie—on various scientific and technological issues. It is hoped that the reader will come away with a better understanding of these issues and their importance to each and every one of us.

Go to the movies...

The Eureka Phenomenon

Isaac Asimov

Science is rigorous and exacting work. But there would be no body of scientific knowledge at all without the creative process that conceived the scientific propositions to begin with. In this article prolific science writer Isaac Asimov discusses the creative process in science. He also describes some famous examples of this creative process at work.

In the old days, when I was writing a great deal of fiction, there would come, once in a while, moments when I was stymied. Suddenly, I would find I had written myself into a hole and could see no way out. To take care of that, I developed a technique which invariably worked.

It was simply this—I went to the movies. Not just any movie. I had to pick a movie which was loaded with action but which made no demands on the intellect. As I watched, I did my best to avoid any conscious thinking concerning my problem, and when I came out of the movie I knew exactly what I would have to do to put the story back on the track.

It never failed.

In fact, when I was working on my doctoral dissertation, too many years ago, I suddenly came across a flaw in my logic that I had not noticed before and that knocked out everything I had done. In utter panic, I made my way to a Bob Hope movie—and came out with the necessary changes in point of view.

It is my belief, you see, that thinking is a double phenomenon like breathing.

You can control breathing by deliberate voluntary action: you can breathe deeply and quickly, or you can hold your breath altogether, regardless of the body's needs at the time. This, however, doesn't work well for very long. Your chest muscles grow tired, your body clamours for more oxygen, or less, and you relax. The automatic involuntary control of breathing takes over, adjusts it to the body's needs and unless you have some respiratory disorder, you can forget about the whole thing.

Well, you can think by deliberate voluntary action, too, and I don't think it is much more efficient on the whole than voluntary breath control is. You can deliberately force your mind through channels of deductions and associations in search of a solution to some problem and before long you have dug mental furrows for yourself and find yourself circling round and round the same limited pathways. If those pathways yield no solution, no amount of further conscious thought will help.

On the other hand, if you let go, then the thinking process comes under automatic involuntary control and is more apt to take new pathways and make erratic associations you would not think of consciously. The solution will then come while you *think* you are *not* thinking.

The trouble is, though, that conscious thought involves no muscular action and so there is no sensation of physical weariness that would force you to quit. What's more, the panic of necessity tends to force you to go on uselessly, with each added bit of useless effort adding to the panic in a vicious cycle.

It is my feeling that it helps to relax, deliberately, by subjecting your mind to material complicated enough to occupy the voluntary faculty of thought, but superficial enough not to engage the deeper involuntary one. In my case, it is an action movie; in your case, it might be something else.

I suspect it is the involuntary faculty of thought that gives rise to what we call "a flash of intuition," something that I imagine must be merely the result of unnoticed thinking.

Perhaps the most famous flash of intuition in the history of science took place in the city of Syracuse in third-century B.C. Sicily. Bear with me and I will tell you the story.

About 250 B.C., the city of Syracuse was experiencing a kind of Golden Age. It was under the protection of the rising power of Rome, but it retained a king of its own and considerable self-government; it was prosperous; and it had a flourishing intellectual life.

The king was Hieron II, and he had commissioned a new golden crown from a goldsmith, to whom he had given an ingot of gold as raw material. Hieron, being a practical man, had carefully weighed the ingot and then weighed the crown he received back. The two weights were precisely equal. Good deal!

But then he sat and thought for a while. Suppose the goldsmith had subtracted a little bit of the gold, not too much, and had substituted an equal weight of the considerably less valuable copper. The resulting alloy would still have the appearance of pure gold, but the goldsmith would be plus a quantity of gold over and above his fee. He would be buying gold with copper, so to speak, and Hieron would be neatly cheated.

Hieron didn't like the thought of being cheated any more than you or I would, but he didn't know how to find out for sure if he had been. He could scarcely punish the goldsmith on mere suspicion. What to do?

Fortunately, Hieron had an advantage few rulers in the history of the world could boast. He had a relative of considerable talent. The relative was named Archimedes and he probably had the greatest intellect the world was to see prior to the birth of Newton.

Archimedes was called in and was posed the problem. He had to determine whether the crown Hieron showed him was pure gold, or was gold to which a small but significant quantity of copper had been added.

If we were to reconstruct Archimedes' reasoning, it might go as follows. Gold was the densest known substance (at that time). Its density in modern terms is 19.3 grams per cubic centimetre. This means that a given weight of gold takes up less volume than the same weight of anything else! In fact, a given weight of pure gold takes up less volume than the same weight of *any* kind of impure gold.

The density of copper is 8.92 grams per cubic centimetre, just about half that of gold. If we consider 100 grams of pure gold, for instance, it is easy to calculate it to have a volume of 5.18 cubic centimetres. But suppose that 100 grams of what looked like pure gold was really only 90 grams of gold and 10 grams of copper. The 90 grams of gold would have a volume of 4.66 cubic centimetres, while the 10 grams of copper would have a volume of 1.12 cubic centimetres; for a total value of 5.78 cubic centimetres.

The difference between 5.18 cubic centimetres and 5.78 cubic centimetres is quite a noticeable one, and would instantly tell if the crown were of pure gold, or if it contained 10 percent copper (with the missing 10 percent of gold tucked neatly in the goldsmith's strongbox).

All one had to do, then, was measure the volume of the crown and compare it with the volume of the same weight of pure gold.

The mathematics of the time made it easy to measure the volume of many simple shapes: a cube, a sphere, a cone, a cylinder, any flattened object of simple regular shape and known thickness, and so on.

We can imagine Archimedes saying, "All that is necessary, sire, is to pound that crown flat, shape it into a square of uniform thickness, and then I can have the answer for you in a moment."

Whereupon Hieron must certainly have snatched the crown away and said, "No such thing. I can do that much without you; I've studied the principles of mathematics, too. This crown is a highly satisfactory work of art and I won't

Famous Scientist / Writer

ISAAC ASIMOV (1920-92)

Isaac Asimov was born in Petrovichi, Russia in 1920. During his lifetime he wrote over 400 publications. Asimov grew up in Brooklyn, New York. He entered Columbia University at the age of 15 and his youth was marked by the development of a stong interest in science fiction. At 18, he sold his first story to a science fiction magazine and eventually became one of the world's best-known science fiction writers.

After serving in World War II, Asimov earned a Ph.D. at Columbia in 1948 in enzyme chemistry. He then taught biochemistry at the Boston University School of Medicine, subsequently becoming a full-time writer in 1958. His first science-fiction novel, *Pebble in the Sky*, appeared in 1950. Asimov's writings included not only works of science fiction, but also mystery stories, humour and history, as well as books on the Bible and Shakespeare.

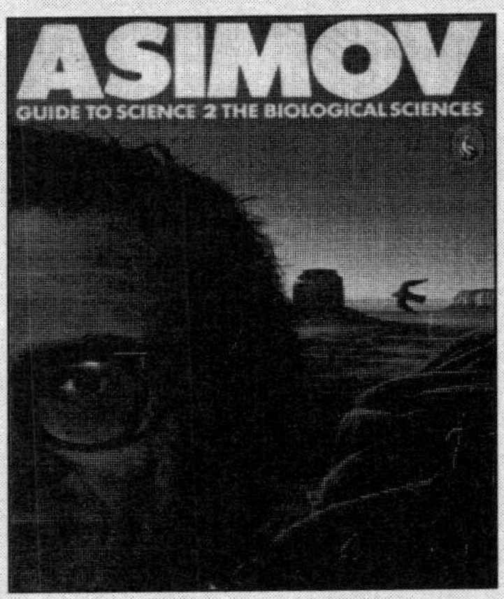

Asimov's best-known science-fiction works are *I, Robot* (1950); *The Foundation Trilogy* (1951-53), and the trilogy's sequel, *Foundation's Edge* (1982); *The Naked Sun* (1957) and *The Gods Themselves* (1972). His major science books are the *Biographical Encyclopedia of Science and Technology* (1964; revised 1982) and *Asimov's New Guide to Science* (1984), a revised edition of his renowned *Intelligent Man's Guide to Science* (1960). Later works include *Foundation and Earth* (1986); *Prelude to Foundation* (1988); and *Forward the Foundation* (1992). Asimov's 800-page autobiography, *In Joy Still Felt*, appeared in 1980.

have it damaged. Just calculate its volume without in any way altering it."

But Greek mathematics had no way of determining the volume of anything with a shape as irregular as the crown, since integral calculus had not yet been invented (and wouldn't be for two thousand years, almost). Archimedes would have had to say, "There is no known way, sire, to carry through a non-destructive determination of volume."

"Then think of one," said Hieron testily.

And Archimedes must have set about thinking of one, and gotten nowhere. Nobody knows how long he thought, or how hard, or what hypotheses he considered and discarded, or any of the details.

What we do know is that, worn out with thinking, Archimedes decided to visit the public baths and relax. I think we are quite safe in saying that Archimedes had no intention of taking his problem to the baths with him. It would be ridiculous to imagine he would, for the public baths of a Greek metropolis weren't intended for that sort of thing.

The Greek baths were a place for relaxation. Half the social aristocracy of the town would be there and there was a great deal more to do than wash. One steamed one's self, got a massage, exercised, and engaged in general socializing. We can be sure that Archimedes intended to forget the stupid crown for a while.

One can envisage him engaging in light talk, discussing the latest news from Alexandria and

Carthage, the latest scandals in town, the latest funny jokes at the expense of the country-squire Romans—and then he lowered himself into a nice hot bath which some bumbling attendant had filled too full.

The water in the bath slopped over as Archimedes got in. Did Archimedes notice that at once, or did he sigh, sink back, and paddle his feet awhile before noting the water-slop? I guess the latter. But, whether soon or late, he noticed, and that one fact, added to all the chains of reasoning his brain had been working on during the period of relaxation when it was unhampered by the comparative stupidities (even in Archimedes) of voluntary thought, gave Archimedes his answer in one blinding flash of insight.

Jumping out of the bath, he proceeded to run home at top speed through the streets of Syracuse. He did *not* bother to put on his clothes. The thought of Archimedes running naked through Syracuse has titillated dozens of generations of youngsters who have heard this story, but I must explain that the ancient Greeks were quite lighthearted in their attitude toward nudity. They thought no more of seeing a naked man on the streets of Syracuse, than we would on the Broadway stage.

And as he ran, Archimedes shouted over and over, "I've got it! I've got it! " Of course, knowing no English, he was compelled to shout it in Greek, so it came out, "Eureka! Eureka! "

Archimedes' solution was so simple that anyone could understand it—once Archimedes explained it.

If an object that is not affected by water in any way, is immersed in water, it is bound to displace an amount of water equal to its own volume, since two objects cannot occupy the same space at the same time.

Suppose, then, you had a vessel large enough to hold the crown and suppose it had a small overflow spout set into the middle of its side. And suppose further that the vessel was filled with water exactly to the spout, so that if the water level were raised a bit higher, however slightly, some would overflow.

Next, suppose that you carefully lower the crown into the water. The water level would rise by an amount equal to the volume of the crown, and that volume of water would pour out the overflow and be caught in a small vessel. Next, a lump of gold, known to be pure and exactly equal in weight to the crown, is also immersed in the water and again the level rises and the overflow is caught in a second vessel.

If the crown were pure gold, the overflow would be exactly the same in each case, and the volume of water caught in the two small vessels would be equal. If, however, the crown were of alloy, it would produce a larger overflow than the pure gold would and this would be easily noticeable.

What's more, the crown would in no way be harmed, defaced, or even as much as scratched. More important, Archimedes had discovered the "principle of buoyancy."

And was the crown pure gold? I've heard that it turned out to be alloy and that the goldsmith was executed, but I wouldn't swear to it.

How often does this "Eureka phenomenon" happen? How often is there this flash of deep insight during a moment of relaxation, this triumphant cry of "I've got it! I've got it!" which must surely be a moment of the purest ecstasy this sorry world can afford?

I wish there were some way we could tell. I suspect that in the history of science it happens *often*; I suspect that very few significant discoveries are made by the pure technique of voluntary thought; I suspect that voluntary thought may possibly prepare the ground (if even that), but that the final touch, the real inspiration, comes when thinking is under involuntary control.

But the world is in a conspiracy to hide the fact. Scientists are wedded to reason, to the meticulous working out of consequences from assumptions to the careful organization of experiments designed to check those consequences. If a certain line of experiments ends nowhere, it is omitted from the final report. If an inspired guess turns out to be correct, it is *not* reported as an inspired guess. Instead, a solid line of voluntary thought is invented after the fact to lead up to the thought, and that is what is inserted in the final report.

The result is that anyone reading scientific papers would swear that *nothing* took place but voluntary thought maintaining a steady clumping stride from origin to destination, and that just can't be true.

It's such a shame. Not only does it deprive science of much of its glamour (how much of the dramatic story in Watson's *Double Helix* do you suppose got into the final reports announcing the great discovery of the structure of DNA?[1]), but it hands over the important process of "insight," "inspiration," "revelation" to the mystic.

The scientist actually becomes ashamed of having what we might call a revelation, as though to have one is to betray reason—when actually what we call revelation in a man who has devoted his life to reasoned thought, is after all merely reasoned thought that is not under voluntary control.

Only once in a while in modern times do we ever get a glimpse into the workings of involuntary reasoning, and when we do, it is always fascinating. Consider, for instance, the case of Friedrich August Kekule von Stradonitz.

In Kekule's time, a century and a quarter ago, a subject of great interest to chemists was the structure of organic molecules (those associated with living tissue). Inorganic molecules were generally simple in the sense that they were made up of few atoms. Water molecules, for instance, are made up of two atoms of hydrogen and one of oxygen (H_2O). Molecules of ordinary salt are made up of one atom of sodium and one of chlorine (NaCl), and so on.

Organic molecules, on the other hand, often contained a large number of atoms. Ethyl alcohol molecules have two carbon atoms, six hydrogen atoms, and an oxygen atom (C_2H_6O); the molecule of ordinary cane sugar is $C_{12}H_{22}O_{11}$, and other molecules are even more complex.

Then, too, it is sufficient, in the case of inorganic molecules generally, merely to know the kinds and numbers of atoms in the molecule; in organic molecules, more is necessary. Thus, dimethyl ether has the formula C_2H_6O, just as ethyl alcohol does, and yet the two are quite different in properties. Apparently, the atoms are arranged differently within the molecules—but how to determine the arrangements?

In 1852, an English chemist, Edward Frankland, had noticed that the atoms of a particular element tended to combine with a fixed number of other atoms. This combining number was called "valence." Kekule in 1858 reduced this notion to a system. The carbon atom, he decided (on the basis of plenty of chemical evidence) had a valence of four; the hydrogen atom, a valence of one; and the oxygen atom, a valence of two (and so on).

Why not represent the atoms as their symbols plus a number of attached dashes, that number being equal to the valence? Such atoms could then be put together as though they were so many Tinker Toy units and "structural formulas" could be built up.

It was possible to reason out that the structural formula of ethyl alcohol was

```
    H   H
    |   |
H — C — C — O — H
    |   |
    H   H
```

while that of dimethyl ether was

```
    H       H
    |       |
H — C — O — C — H
    |       |
    H       H
```

In each case, there were two carbon atoms, each with four dashes attached; six hydrogen atoms, each with one dash attached; and an oxygen atom with two ashes attached. The molecules were built up of the same components, but in different arrangements.

Kekule's theory worked beautifully. It has been immensely deepened and elaborated since his day, but you can still find structures very much

[1] I'll tell you, in case you're curious. None! [Asimov's note.]

like Kekule's Tinker Toy formulas in any modern chemical textbook. They represent oversimplifications of the true situation, but they remain extremely useful in practice even so.

The Kekule structures were applied to many organic molecules in the years after 1858 and the similarities and contrasts in the structures neatly matched similarities and contrasts in properties. The key to the rationalization of organic chemistry had, it seemed, been found.

Yet there was one disturbing fact. The well-known chemical benzene wouldn't fit. It was known to have a molecule made up of equal numbers of carbon and hydrogen atoms. Its molecular weight was known to be 78 and a single carbon-hydrogen combination had a weight of 13. Therefore, the benzene molecule had to contain six carbon-hydrogen combinations and its formula had to be C_6H_6.

But that meant trouble. By the Kekule formulas, the hydrocarbons (molecules made up of carbon and hydrogen atoms only) could easily be envisioned as chains of carbon atoms with hydrogen atoms attached. If all the valences of the carbon atoms were filled with hydrogen atoms, as in "hexane," whose molecule looks like this—

```
    H H H H H H
    | | | | | |
  H-C-C-C-C-C-C-H
    | | | | | |
    H H H H H H
```

the compound is said to be saturated. Such saturated hydrocarbons were found to have very little tendency to react with other substances.

If some of the valences were not filled, unused bonds were added to those connecting the carbon atoms. Double bonds were formed as in "hexene"—

```
    H H H H H H
    | | | | | |
  H-C-C-C=C-C-C-H
    | |     | |
    H H     H H
```

Hexene is unsaturated, for that double bond has a tendency to open up and add other atoms. Hexene is chemically active.

When six carbons are present in a molecule, it takes fourteen hydrogen atoms to occupy all the valence bonds and make it inert—as in hexane. In hexene, on the other hand, there are only twelve hydrogens. If there were still fewer hydrogen atoms, there would be more than one double bond; there might even be triple bonds, and the compound would be still more active than hexene.

Yet benzene, which is C_6H_6 and has eight fewer hydrogen atoms than hexane, is *less* active than hexene, which has only two fewer hydrogen atoms than hexane. In fact, benzene is even less active than hexane itself. The six hydrogen atoms in the benzene molecule seem to satisfy the six carbon atoms to a greater extent than do the fourteen hydrogen atoms in hexane.

For heaven's sake, why?

This might seem unimportant. The Kekule formulas were so beautifully suitable in the case of so many compounds that one might simply dismiss benzene as an exception to the general rule.

Science, however, is not English grammar. You can't just categorize something as an exception. If the exception doesn't fit into the general system, then the general system must be wrong.

Or, take the more positive approach. An exception can often be made to fit into a general system, provided the general system is broadened. Such broadening generally represents a great advance and for this reason, exceptions ought to be paid great attention.

For some seven years, Kekule faced the problem of benzene and tried to puzzle out how a chain of six carbon atoms could be completely satisfied with as few as six hydrogen atoms in benzene and yet be left unsatisfied with twelve hydrogen atoms in hexane.

Nothing came to him!

And then one day in 1865 (he tells the story himself) he was in Ghent, Belgium, and in order to get to some destination, he boarded a public bus. He was tired and, undoubtedly, the droning

Isaac Newton in 1726.

Isaac Newton, the discoverer of the fundamental laws of physics and the inventor of calculus, has long been considered one of the greatest scientists that ever lived. Legend has it that his "eureka" moment occurred when he was hit by a fallling apple, thereby "discovering" the law of gravity!

beat of the horses' hooves on the cobblestones lulled him. He fell into a comatose half-sleep.

In that sleep, he seemed to see a vision of atoms attaching themselves to each other in chains that moved about. (Why not? It was the sort of thing that constantly occupied his waking thoughts.) But then one chain twisted in such a way that head and tail joined, forming a ring—and Kekule woke with a start.

To himself, he must surely have shouted "Eureka," for indeed he had it. The six carbon atoms of benzene formed a ring and not a chain, so that the structural formula looked like this:

To be sure, there were still three double bonds, so you might think the molecule had to be very active—but now there was a difference. Atoms in a ring might be expected to have different properties from those in a chain and double bonds in one case might not have the properties of those in the other. At least, chemists could work on that assumption and see if it involved them in contradictions.

It didn't. The assumption worked excellently well. It turned out that organic molecules could be divided into two groups: aromatic and aliphatic. The former had the benzene ring (or certain other similar rings) as part of the structure and the latter did not. Allowing for different properties within each group, the Kekule structures worked very well.

For nearly seventy years, Kekule's vision held good in the hard field of actual chemical techniques, guiding the chemist through the jungle of reactions that led to the synthesis of more and more molecules. Then, in 1932, Linus Pauling applied quantum mechanics to chemical structure with sufficient subtlety to explain just why the benzene ring was so special and what had proven correct in practice proved correct in theory as well.

* * *

Other cases? Certainly.

In 1764, the Scottish engineer James Watt was working as an instrument maker for the University of Glasgow. The university gave him a model of a Newcomen steam engine, which didn't work well, and asked him to fix it. Watt fixed it without trouble, but even when it worked perfectly, it didn't work well. It was far too inefficient and consumed incredible quantities of fuel. Was there a way to improve that?

Thought didn't help, but a peaceful, relaxed walk on a Sunday afternoon did. Watt returned with the key notion in mind of using two separate chambers, one for steam only and one for cold water only, so that the same chamber did not have to be constantly cooled and reheated to the infinite waste of fuel.

The Irish mathematician William Rowan Hamilton worked up a theory of "quaternions" in 1843 but couldn't complete that theory until he grasped the fact that there were conditions under which $p \times q$ was *not* equal to $q \times p$. The necessary thought came to him in a flash one time when he was walking to town with his wife.

The German physiologist Otto Loewi was working on the mechanism of nerve action, in particular, on the chemicals produced by nerve endings. He awoke at 3 A.M. one night in 1921 with a perfectly clear notion of the type of experiment he would have to run to settle a key point that was puzzling him. He wrote it down and went back to sleep. When he woke in the morning, he found he couldn't remember what his inspiration had been. He remembered he had written it down, but he couldn't read his writing.

The next night, he woke again at 3 A.M. with the clear thought once more in mind. This time, he didn't fool around. He got up, dressed himself, went straight to the laboratory and began work. By 5 A.M. he had proved his point and the consequences of his findings became important enough in later years so that in 1936 he received a share in the Nobel prize in medicine and physiology.

How very often this sort of thing must happen, and what a shame that scientists are so devoted to their belief in conscious thought that they so consistently obscure the actual methods by which they obtain their results.

"Look, an apple is about to land on him—he's got a great future ahead of him in physics!"

Questions and Topics for Discussion and Writing

1. Why does Asimov put so much emphasis on the "Eureka Phenomenon" and Archimedes' sudden discovery?
2. Why is it important that the scientist *not* be concentrating on the problem to be solved to make the breakthrough insight possible?
3. What comparisons does Asimov make between grammar and science? How does this affect the work of writers and scientists in different ways.

Technology—Onward and Upward

There's No Way to Go But Ahead

Isaac Asimov

Some would argue that modern advances in scientific knowledge threaten our very existence. In this article, scientist and popular science writer Isaac Asimov is adamant, on the contrary, that scientific and technological advances are the only possible solutions to world's problems.

We are all now aware that some new scientific or technological advance, though useful, may have unpleasant side effects. More and more, the tendency is to exert caution before committing the world to something that may not be reversible.

The trouble is, it's not always easy to tell what the side effects will be. In 1846, Ascanio Sobrero produced the first nitroglycerine. Heated, a drop of it exploded shatteringly. The Italian chemist realized in horror its possible application to warfare and stopped his research at once. It didn't help, of course. Others followed up, and it and other high explosives were indeed being used in warfare by the close of the 19th century.

Did that make high explosives entirely bad? In 1867, Alfred Nobel learned how to mix nitroglycerine with diatomaceous earth to produce a safer-to-handle mixture he called "dynamite." With dynamite, earth could be moved at a rate far beyond that of pick and shovel and without brutalizing men by hard labour. It was dynamite that helped forge the way for railroads, that helped build dams, subways, foundations, bridges, and a thousand other grand-scale constructions of the industrial age.

A double-edged sword of good and evil has hung over human technology from the beginning. The invention of knives and spears increased man's food supply—and improved the art of murder. The discovery of nuclear energy now places all the earth under threat of destruction—yet it also offers the possibility of fusion power as an ultimate solution to man's energy problems.

Or think back to the first successful vaccination in 1796 and the germ theory of disease in the 1860s. Do we view medical advance as dangerous to humanity, or refuse to take advantage of vaccines and antitoxins, of anesthesia and asepsis, of chemical specifics and antibiotics? And yet the side effects of the last century's medical discoveries have done more to assure civilization's destruction than anything nuclear physicists have done. For the population explosion today is caused not by any rise in average birth rate but by the precipitous drop—thanks to medicine—in the death rate. Does that mean science should have avoided improving man's lot through medicine and kept mankind a short-lived race? Or does it mean we should use science to correct the possibly deleterious side effect, devise methods that would make it simpler to reduce the birth rate and keep it matching the falling death rate? The latter, obviously!

Science and technology are getting a bad press these days. Increasingly scornful of the materialism of our culture, young people speak about returning to a simpler, pre-industrial, pre-scientific day. They fail to realize that the "good old days" were really the horrible bad old days of ignorance, disease, slavery and death. They fancy themselves in Athens, talking to Socrates, listening to the latest play by Sophocles—never as a slave brutalized in the Athenian silver mines. They imagine themselves as medieval knights on armoured chargers—never as starving peasants.

Yet, right down to modern times, the wealth and prosperity of a relative few have been built on the animal-like labour and wretched existence of many—peasants, serfs and slaves. What's more, nothing could be done about it. Slavery and peonage were taken for granted. Not until science became prominent did slavery come to be recognized as a dreadful wrong, to be abolished. It was the scientist, supposedly cold and concerned with things rather than ideals, who brought this about. His investigations made possible the harnessing of the energy of the inanimate world. With steam, electricity and radio beams to do our work for us, there was less need for the comparatively weak and fumbling human muscle—and slavery began to vanish.

It is also a fact that, before modern technology, the full flower of art and human intellect was reserved for the few. It was the technical advances of printing that scattered books widely, made universal literacy practical. It was the movies, radio, the record player and television that brought many of the marvels of mankind (along with much of the refuse) to even the poorest.

Yes, science has helped create problems, too—serious ones. And we must labour to solve them—in the only way history tells us problems have been solved: by science. If we were to turn away now, if a noble young generation abandoned the materialism of an industry, what would happen? Without the machinery of that industry, we would inevitably drift back to slavery.

In these days of urban decay and energy crisis, there is a constant longing to return to the land and flee back to a simpler way of life. But it can't be done. We have a tiger by the tail and we can't go home again. We never could.

When mankind learned how to make use of fire some 50,000 years ago, it meant protection against predators, and more and better food. It also meant that man could venture out of the tropics into colder climates. Do you suppose this didn't bring problems? When the fire went out in the cave on a winter night and could not be relighted, there was the danger of freezing. Or the smoke would ruin one's lungs.

Why not give up fire, then, go back to the tropics and the simpler, carefree ways? Ah, one could not. Extending his range, man had increased his numbers. Returnees would find the tropics full, and there would be a catastrophic struggle for the smaller supply of food. So, having once learned to use fire, people either endured its discomforts—or did away with them by further technological advance. They learned better ways of making fire, heating dwelling places, handling smoke.

No fundamental technological advance has ever been given up willingly by any society. There has been no way to do it.

About 8000 B.C., mankind invented agriculture. Again it made possible an increase in numbers. People had never eaten so well, but it meant they had to give up the free, nomadic life and remain bound to the soil. It meant hard labour. It meant banding together to fight off surrounding tribes who, still food gathering, might help themselves to your crops. It also meant the risk of crop failures.

Where irrigation was introduced to make harvest more dependable, it meant the formation of a large political unit, the social tyranny of a king, an aristocracy, a priesthood. And, even if the land grew prosperous and populous, any infectious disease that got started ran through the crowded population like wildfire.

Why not, then go back to the wilder, freer ways of hunting and food gathering? Wouldn't that mean less work and worry, less war, less pestilence?

But you can't! Abandon agriculture and, out of every 10,000 people, only 100 survive. No, the problems to which agriculture gave rise could be solved only by moving forward with additional advances in technology—the use of oxen in place of men, horses in place of oxen, crop rotation, fertilizer, etc.

So it is now with our industrial age, which has once again increased man's numbers and his range—and brought new problems. If there is a shortage of gasoline, can't we in a pinch abandon our automobiles and go back to horse-and-wagon? Give up our oil furnaces for the fireplace? Give up electric lights and use candles?

No, we can't. There are no longer enough horses to move us about, or enough wood to warm us, or enough candles to light our way.

Besides, if we try it for long, we will quickly find that the simple life just won't do.

In 1800, when the earth was still supported almost entirely by nonindustrial methods, the population of the planet was 900 million. Now it is pushing four billion. Where does the food come from to support the extra three billion? It comes from the industrialization of the farm: from the use of high-energy machinery to plow and seed and weed and reap. It comes from fertilizers and insecticides produced by sophisticated high-energy chemical factories.

We can't abandon industrialization, if only because our food supply depends on it. You can talk about "natural" food all you want, but if everyone decided to grow food without chemical fertilizers or insecticides or machinery, it would mean that only one quarter of the world population could be fed.

Can we abandon some of our industrial technology and hold onto the rest? That would be very difficult, since it all hangs together.

We can save, conserve, cut out waste, but what we have we must keep. The only solution, as always in the history of mankind, is to solve problems by still further advances in technology.

SOURCE: From *Reader's Digest,* November 1975. Reprinted with permission of *Readers Digest* and King Features Syndicate.

DNA—Cracking the Code

Human Genome Project

It was not until 1909 that the term "gene" was used to describe the fundamental units of heredity which transmitted characteristics from one being to another. By the 1920s it was known that it was the chromosomes which carried the genes and the information of heredity. However, a major breakthrough occurred in chemistry in 1953. While working in Cambridge, James Watson and Francis Crick discovered the DNA molecule (deoxyribonucleic acid) which finally disclosed the fundamental mechanism of heredity.

Watson's and Crick's model explained how the DNA carried the genetic information. The DNA molecule consists of a "double helix" which looks like two ladders twisted together. The DNA molecule in turn consists of smaller molecules called nucleotides which consist of four base elements or compounds: A (adenine), T (thymine), C (cytosine), and G (guanine). A gene is a section or substring of the DNA molecule; it consists of a combination of nucleotides which determine a certain trait or characteristic. The genes which carry the basic genetic information are located in the 23 pairs of chromosomes.

Many scientists working on the Human Genome Project are confident that given time, money and new developments in technology, they will be able to map the 100,000 genes which make up our genome, that is, all the genes located in the 23 pairs of chromosomes. By uncovering the secrets of heredity and understanding the genetic code, they hope to gather enough knowledge to detect "faulty" or "defective" genes which produce crippling diseases such as Huntington's disease, cystic fibrosis, Down's Syndrome, muscular dystrophy, and cancer. They hope that the genome map will give them enough genetic information to detect genetic abnormalities and to find cures and treatments for the over 50,000 diseases which are currently known to be caused by defective or faulty genes.

Questions and Topics for Discussion and Writing

1. Isaac Asimov's "There's No Way to Go But Ahead" presents a widely differing view about the relationship of technology and the world than the ones espoused by E.F. Schumacher and David Suzuki later in this book. How is Asimov's view different?

2. Asimov's piece was written in 1975. What has happened since then to weaken his argument?

3. Why does Asimov say it is impossible to go anywhere but "ahead" or "up?" What is his response to those who praise the "good old days" and criticize technological advances.

We All Use the Scientific Method

Thomas Henry Huxley

Thomas Huxley is known best as the dynamic popularizer and advocate of the theory of evolution in the nineteenth century. They called him "Darwin's Bulldog". What is the scientific method and how does it relate to the real world? This lecture, given by Huxley to "workingmen" to help advance the cause of technical education, tries to explain the method by reference to everyday life situations.

The method of scientific investigation is nothing but the expression of the necessary mode of working of the human mind. It is simply the mode at which all phenomena are reasoned about, rendered precise and exact. There is no more difference, but there is just the same kind of difference, between the mental operations of a man of science and those of an ordinary person, as there is between the operations and methods of a baker or of a butcher weighing out his goods in common scales, and the operations of a chemist in performing a difficult and complex analysis by means of his balance and finely-graduated weights. It is not that the action of the scales in the one case, and the balance in the other, differ in the principles of their construction or manner of working; but the beam of one is set on an infinitely finer axis than the other, and of course turns by the addition of a much smaller weight.

You will understand this better, perhaps, if I give you some familiar example. You have all heard it repeated, I dare say, that men of science work by means of induction and deduction, and that by the help of these operations, they, in a sort of sense, wring from Nature certain other things, which are called natural laws, and causes, and that out of these, by some cunning skill of their own, they build up hypotheses and theories. And it is imagined by many, that the operations of the common mind can be by no means compared with these processes, and that they have to be acquired by a sort of special apprenticeship to the craft. To hear all these large words, you would think that the mind of a man of science must be constituted differently from that of his fellow men; but if you will not be frightened by terms, you will discover that you are quite wrong, and that all these terrible apparatus are being used by yourselves every day and every hour of your lives.

There is a well-known incident in one of Moliere's plays, where the author makes the hero express unbounded delight on being told that he had been talking prose during the whole of his life. In the same way, I trust that you will take comfort, and be delighted with yourselves, on the discovery that you have been acting on the principles of inductive and deductive philosophy during the same period. Probably there is not one here who has not in the course of the day had occasion to set in motion a complex train of reasoning, of the very same kind, though differing of course in degree, as that which a scientific man goes through in tracing the causes of natural phenomena.

A very trivial circumstance will serve to exemplify this. Suppose you go into a fruiterer's shop, wanting an apple,—you take up one, and, on biting it, you find it is sour; you look at it, and see that it is hard and green. You take up another one, and that too is hard, green, and sour. The shopman offers you a third; but, before biting it, you examine it, and find that it is hard and green, and you immediately say that you will not have it, as it must be sour, like those that you have already tried.

Nothing can be more simple than that, you

think; but if you will take the trouble to analyse and trace out into its logical elements what has been done by the mind, you will be greatly surprised. In the first place, you have performed the operation of induction. You found that, in two experiences, hardness and greenness in apples went together with sourness. It was so in the first case, and it was confirmed by the second. True, it is a very small basis, but still it is enough to make an induction from; you generalise the facts, and you expect to find sourness in apples where you get hardness and greenness. You found upon that a general law, that all hard and green apples are sour; and that, so far as it goes, is a perfect induction. Well, having got your natural law in this way, when you are offered another apple which you find is hard and green, you say, "All hard and green apples are sour; this apple is hard and green, therefore this apple is sour." That train of reasoning is what logicians call a syllogism, and has all its various parts and terms—its major premise, its minor premise, and its conclusion. And, by the help of further reasoning, which, if drawn out, would have to be exhibited in two or three other syllogisms, you arrive at your final determination, "I will not have that apple." So that, you see, you have, in the first place, established a law by induction, and upon that you have founded a deduction, and reasoned out the special conclusion of the particular case. Well now, suppose, having got your law, that at some time afterwards, you are discussing the qualities of apples with a friend: you will say to him, "It is a very curious thing—but I find that all hard and green apples are sour!" Your friend says to you, "But how do you know that?" You at once reply, "Oh, because I have tried them over and over again, and have always found them to be so." Well, if we were talking science instead of common sense, we should call that an experimental verification. And, if still opposed, you go further, and say, "I have heard from the people in Somersetshire and Devonshire, where a large number of apples are grown, that they have observed the same thing. It is also found to be the case in Normandy, and in North America. In short, I find it to be the universal experience of mankind wherever attention has been directed to the subject." Whereupon, your friend, unless he is a very unreasonable man, agrees with you, and is convinced that you are quite right in the conclusion you have drawn. He believes, although perhaps he does not know he believes it, that the more extensive verifications are—that the more frequently experiments have been made, and results of the same kind arrived at—that the more varied the conditions under which the same results are attained, the more certain is the ultimate conclusion, and he disputes the question no further. He sees that the experiment has been tried under all sorts of conditions, as to time, place, and people, with the same result; and he says with you, therefore, that the law you have laid down must be a good one, and we must believe it.

In science we do the same thing—the philosopher exercises precisely the same faculties, though in a much more delicate manner. In scientific inquiry it becomes a matter of duty to expose a supposed law to every possible kind of verification, and to take care, moreover, that this is done intentionally, and not left to a mere accident, as in the case of the apples. And in science, as in common life, our confidence in a law is in exact proportion to the absence of variation in the result of our experimental verifications. For instance, if you let go your grasp of an article you may have in your hand, it will immediately fall to the ground. That is a very common verification of one of the best established laws of nature—that of gravitation. The method by which men of science establish the existence of that law is exactly the same as that by which we have established the trivial proposition about the sourness of hard and green apples. But we believe it in such an extensive, thorough, and unhesitating manner because the universal experience of mankind verifies it, and we can verify it ourselves at any time; and that is the strongest possible foundation on which any natural law can rest.

So much, then, by way of proof that the method of establishing laws in science is exactly the same as that pursued in common life. Let us now turn to another matter (though really it is but another phase of the same question), and that is, the method by which, from the relations of certain phenomena, we prove that some stand in the position of causes towards the others.

I want to put the case clearly before you, and I will therefore show you what I mean by another familiar example. I will suppose that one of you, on coming down in the morning to the parlour of your house, finds that a tea-pot and some spoons which had been left in the room on the previous evening are gone—the window is open, and you observe the mark of a dirty hand on the window-frame, and perhaps, in addition to that, you notice the impress of a hob-nailed shoe on the gravel outside. All these phenomena have struck your attention instantly, and before two seconds have passed you say, "Oh, somebody has broken open the window, entered the room, and run off with the spoons and the tea-pot!" That speech is out of your mouth in a moment. And you will probably add, "I know there has; I am quite sure of it!" You mean to say exactly what you know; but in reality you are giving expression to what is, in all essential particulars, an hypothesis. You do not *know* it at all; it is nothing but an hypothesis rapidly framed in your own mind. And it is an hypothesis founded on a long train of inductions and deductions.

What are those inductions and deductions, and how have you got at this hypothesis? You have observed, in the first place, that the window is open; but by a train of reasoning involving many inductions and deductions, you have probably arrived long before at the general law—and a very good one it is—that windows do not open of themselves; and you therefore conclude that something has opened the window. A second general law that you have arrived at in the same way is, that tea-pots and spoons do not go out of a window spontaneously, and you are satisfied that, as they are not now where you left them, they have been removed. In the third place, you look at the marks on the window-sill, and the shoe-marks outside, and you say that in all previous experience the former kind of mark has never been produced by anything else but the hand of a human being; and the same experience shows that no other animal but man at present wears shoes with hob-nails in them such as would produce the marks in the gravel. I do not know, even if we could discover any of those "missing links" that are talked about, that they would help us to any other conclusion! At any rate the law which states our present experience is strong enough for my present purpose. You next reach the conclusion, that as these kinds of marks have not been left by any other animals than men, or are liable to be formed in any other way than by a man's hand and shoe, the marks in question have been formed by a man in that way. You have, further, a general law, founded on observation and experience, and that, too, is, I am sorry to say, a very universal and unimpeachable one—that some men are thieves; and you assume at once from all these premises—and that is what constitutes your hypothesis—that the man who made the marks outside and on the window-sill, opened the window, got into the room, and stole your tea-pot and spoons. You have now arrived at a *vera causa*—you have assumed a cause which, it is plain, is competent to produce all the phenomena you have observed. You can explain all these phenomena only by the hypothesis of a thief. But that is a hypothetical conclusion, of the justice of which you have no absolute proof at all; it is only rendered highly probable by a series of inductive and deductive reasonings.

I suppose your first action, assuming that you are a man of ordinary common sense, and that you have established this hypothesis to your own satisfaction, will very likely be to go off for the police, and set them on the track of the burglar, with the view to the recovery of your property. But just as you are starting with this object, some person comes in, and on learning what you are about, says, "My good friend, you are going on a great deal too fast. How do you know that the man who really made the marks took the spoons? It might have been a monkey that took them, and the man may have merely looked in afterwards." You would probably reply, "Well, that is all very well, but you see it is contrary to all experience of the way tea-pots and spoons are abstracted; so that, at any rate, your hypothesis is less probable than mine." While you are talking the thing over in this way, another friend arrives, one of that good kind of people that I was talking of a little while ago. And he might say, "Oh, my dear sir, you are certainly going on a great deal too fast. You are most presumptuous. You admit that all

Thomas Henry Huxley

We All Use A Scientific Method ... of Sorts

When Thomas Henry Huxley claimed that "we all use the scientific method," he was simply stating that people, in their day-to-day lives, base their actions on many of the same principles that scientists use in conducting experiments.

By recalling events that have happened in the past, making theories about how similar events are likely to happen in the future, and testing these assumptions time and time again, we are able to base our actions on what seems to us to be certain and infallible suppositions. For example, a person who inserts a specific key into the ignition of the same car every morning can expect, barring mechanical failure, that the car will start. We use past experiences to predict future ones and unless unusual circumstances arise, which we can almost always identify, we are proven correct.

Scientists use their expectations about the physical world to develop laws about the way things work. If a bowling ball were to leave the hand of a bowler and float up to the ceiling, we would immediately begin to question whether the laws of gravity had somehow stopped working (or we would check the ball for helium!).

The first great modern proponent of the scientific method, which hinges upon a regular set of laws that governs the world around us, was Sir Isaac Newton (1642-1727). Newton rigorously applied it to his experiments on gravity. But what Newton also demonstrated was that people must be willing to question previously-held views about scientific "truths" in order for scientific progress to be made.

Some people actually question the assumptions that lie at the very core of the scientific method. Challenging the premise that certain natural laws are unchanging is known as "skepticism." Philosophical skeptics ask questions like "what if future events somehow *do not* resemble past events? Is there really any guarantee that when we wake up tomorrow, the grass will be green and the sky will be blue? Why couldn't the turning of the ignition key produce Beethoven's 4th Symphony, and not the usual sound of a car starting?" This mode of thought found perhaps its fiercest expression in the writings of philosopher David Hume (1711-1776), whose *Enquiry Concerning Human Understanding* (1748) is a classical formulation of philosophical skepticism.

Many people, when confronted with this type of logic, find themselves unable to say for sure exactly *why* it is that the world keeps on working in the same manner, day after day—it just *does*, and this regularity forms the basis for our actions. After all, it would be an extremely staunch skeptic indeed that would jump in front of a moving train whilst maintaining that there is no guarantee that future events will be like past ones.

these occurrences took place when you were fast asleep, at a time when you could not possibly have known anything about what was taking place. How do you know that the laws of Nature are not suspended during the night? It may be that there has been some kind of supernatural interference in this case." In point of fact, he declares that your hypothesis is one of which you cannot at all demonstrate the truth, and that you are by no means sure that the laws of Nature are the same when you are asleep as when you are awake.

Well, now, you cannot at the moment answer that kind of reasoning. You feel that your worthy friend has you somewhat at a disadvantage. You will feel perfectly convinced in your own mind, however, that you are quite right, and you say to him, "My good friend, I can only be guided by the natural probabilities of the case, and if you will be kind enough to stand aside and permit me to pass, I will go and fetch the police." Well, we will suppose that your journey is successful, and that by good luck you meet with a policeman; that eventually the burglar is found with your property on his person, and the marks correspond to his hand and to his boots. Probably any jury would consider those facts a very good experimental verification of your hypothesis, touching the cause of the abnormal phenomena observed in your parlour, and would act accordingly.

Now, in this suppositious case, I have taken phenomena of a very common kind, in order that you might see what are the different steps in an ordinary process of reasoning, if you will only take the trouble to analyse it carefully. All the operations I have described, you will see, are involved in the mind of any man of sense in leading him to a conclusion as to the course he should take in order to make good a robbery and punish the offender. I say that you are led, in that case, to your conclusion by exactly the same train of reasoning as that which a man of science pursues when he is endeavouring to discover the origin and laws of the most occult phenomena. The process is, and always must be, the same; and precisely the same mode of reasoning was employed by Newton and Laplace in their endeavours to discover and define the causes of the movements of the heavenly bodies, as you, with your own common sense, would employ to detect a burglar. The only difference is, that the nature of the inquiry being more abstruse, every step has to be most carefully watched, so that there may not be a single crack or flaw in your hypothesis. A flaw or crack in many of the hypotheses of daily life may be of little or no moment as affecting the general correctness of the conclusions at which we may arrive; but, in a scientific inquiry, a fallacy, great or small, is always of importance, and is sure to be in the long run constantly productive of mischievous, if not fatal results.

Do not allow yourselves to be misled by the common notion that an hypothesis is untrustworthy simply because it is an hypothesis. It is often urged, in respect to some scientific conclusion, that, after all, it is only an hypothesis. But what more have we to guide us in nine-tenths of the most important affairs of daily life than hypotheses, and often very ill-based ones? So that in science, where the evidence of an hypothesis is subjected to the most rigid examination, we may rightly pursue the same course. You may have hypotheses and hypotheses. A man may say, if he likes, that the moon is made of green cheese: that is an hypothesis. But another man, who has devoted a great deal of time and attention to the subject, and availed himself of the most powerful telescopes and the results of the observations of others, declares that in his opinion it is probably composed of materials very similar to those of which our own earth is made up: and that is also only an hypothesis. But I need not tell you that there is an enormous difference in the value of the two hypotheses. That one which is based on sound scientific knowledge is sure to have a corresponding value; and that which is a mere hasty random guess is likely to have but little value. Every great step in our progress in discovering causes has been made in exactly the same way as that which I have detailed to you. A person observing the occurrence of certain facts and phenomena asks, naturally enough, what process, what kind of operation known to occur in Nature applied to the particular case, will unravel and explain the mystery? Hence you have the scientific hypothesis; and its value will be proportionate to the care and completeness with which its basis had been tested and verified. It is in these matters as in the commonest affairs of practical life: the guess of the fool will be folly, while the guess of the wise man will contain wisdom. In all cases, you see that the value of the result depends on the patience and faithfulness with which the investigator applies to his hypothesis every possible kind of verification.

Questions and Topics for Discussion and Writing

1. According to Huxley, how do we establish good scientific "laws?" How has the passage of time dealt with what people have laid down as the "unchanging" laws of nature?

2. What are some examples from the history of science in which something that has been "proven", using all of the steps required by the scientific method, has later been found to be untrue? Does this invalidate the method used by scientists?

Can We Know the Universe?

Carl Sagan

Why *can't* we travel faster than the speed of light? In this article, astronomer, popular science writer, and TV host, Carl Sagan discusses science and scientific knowledge in general. He also considers the limits of human knowledge.

> Nothing is rich but the inexhaustible wealth of nature. She shows us only surfaces, but she is a million fathoms deep.
>
> *Ralph Waldo Emerson*

Science is a way of thinking much more than it is a body of knowledge. Its goal is to find out how the world works, to seek what regularities there may be, to penetrate to the connections of things—from subnuclear particles, which may be the constituents of all matter, to living organisms, the human social community, and thence to the cosmos as a whole. Our intuition is by no means an infallible guide. Our perceptions may be distorted by training and prejudice or merely because of the limitations of our sense organs, which, of course, perceive directly but a small fraction of the phenomena of the world. Even so straightforward a question as whether in the absence of friction a pound of lead falls faster than a gram of fluff was answered incorrectly by Aristotle and almost everyone else before the time of Galileo. Science is based on experiment, on a willingness to challenge old dogma, on an openness to see the universe as it really is. Accordingly, science sometimes requires courage—at the very least the courage to question the conventional wisdom.

Beyond this the main trick of science is to *really* think of something; the shape of clouds and their occasional sharp bottom edges at the same altitude everywhere in the sky; the formation of a dewdrop on a leaf; the origin of a name or a word—Shakespeare, say, or "philanthropic"; the reason for human social customs—the incest taboo, for example; how it is that a lens in sunlight can make paper burn; how a "walking stick" got to look so much like a twig; why the Moon seems to follow us as we walk; what prevents us from digging a hole down to the center of the Earth; what the definition is of "down" on a spherical Earth; how it is possible for the body to convert yesterday's lunch into today's muscle and sinew; or how far is up—does the universe go on forever, or if it does not, is there any meaning to the question of what lies on the other side? Some of these questions are pretty easy. Others, especially the last, are mysteries to which no one even today knows the answer. They are natural questions to ask. Every culture has posed such questions in one way or another. Almost always the proposed answers are in the nature of "Just So Stories," attempted explanations divorced from experiment, or even from careful comparative observations.

But the scientific cast of mind examines the world critically as if many alternative worlds might exist, as if other things might be here which are not. Then we are forced to ask why what we see is present and not something else. Why are the Sun and the Moon and the planets spheres? Why not pyramids, or cubes, or dodecahedra? Why not irregular, jumbly shapes? Why so symmetrical, worlds? If you spend any time spinning hypotheses, checking to see whether they make sense, whether they conform to what else we know, thinking of tests you can pose to substantiate or deflate your hypotheses, you will find yourself doing science. And as you come to practice this habit of thought more and more you will get better and better at it. To penetrate into the heart of the thing—even a little thing, a blade of grass, as Walt Whitman said—is to experience a kind of exhilaration that, it may be, only human beings of all the beings on this planet can feel. We are an intelligent species and the use of our intelligence quite properly gives us pleasure. In this respect the brain is like a muscle. When we think well, we feel good. Understanding is a kind of ecstasy.

But to what extent can we really know the universe around us? Sometimes this question is posed by people who hope the answer will be in the negative, who are fearful of a universe in which everything might one day be known. And sometimes we hear pronouncements from scientists who confidently state that everything worth knowing will soon be known—or even is already known—and who paint pictures of a Dionysian or Polynesian age in which the zest for intellectual discovery has withered, to be replaced by a kind of subdued languor, the lotus eaters drinking fermented coconut milk or some other mild hallucinogen. In addition to maligning both the Polynesians, who were intrepid explorers (and whose brief respite in paradise is now sadly ending), as well as the inducements to intellectual discovery provided by some hallucinogens, this contention turns out to be trivially mistaken.

Let us approach a much more modest question: not whether we can know the universe or the Milky Way Galaxy or a star or a world. Can we know, ultimately and in detail, a grain of salt? Consider one microgram of table salt, a speck just barely large enough for someone with keen eyesight to make out without a microscope. In that grain of salt there are about 10^{16} sodium and chlorine atoms. This is a 1 followed by 16 zeros, 10 million billion atoms. If we wish to know a grain of salt, we must know at least the three-dimensional positions of each of these atoms. (In fact, there is much more to be known—for example, the nature of the forces between the atoms—but we are making only a modest calculation.) Now, is this number more or less than the number of things which the brain can know?

How much *can* the brain know? There are perhaps 10^{11} neurons in the brain, the circuit elements and switches that are responsible in their electrical and chemical activity for the functioning of our minds. A typical brain neuron has perhaps a thousand little wires, called dendrites, which connect it with its fellows. If, as seems likely, every bit of information in the brain corresponds to one of these connections, the total number of things knowable by the brain is no more than 10^{14}, one hundred trillion. But this number is only one percent of the number of atoms in our speck of salt.

So in this sense the universe is intractable, astonishingly immune to any human attempt at full knowledge, We cannot on this level understand a grain of salt, much less the universe.

But let us look a little more deeply at our microgram of salt. Salt happens to be a crystal in which, except for defects in the structure of the crystal lattice, the position of every sodium and chlorine atom is predetermined. If we could shrink ourselves into this crystalline world, we would see rank upon rank of atoms in an ordered array, a regularly alternating structure—sodium, chlorine, sodium, chlorine, specifying the sheet of atoms we are standing on and all the sheets above us and below us. An absolutely pure crystal of salt could have the position of every atom specified by something like 10 bits of information.[1] This would not strain the information-carrying capacity of the brain.

If the universe had natural laws that governed its behavior to the same degree of regularity that determines a crystal of salt, then, of course, the universe would be knowable. Even if there were many such laws, each of considerable complexity, human beings might have the capability to understand them all. Even if such knowledge exceeded the information-carrying capacity of the brain, we might store the additional information outside our

[1] Chlorine is a deadly poison gas employed on European battlefields in World War I. Sodium is a corrosive metal which burns upon contact with water. Together they make a placid and unpoisonous material, table salt. Why each of these substances has the properties it does is a subject called chemistry, which requires more than 10 bits of information to understand.

Famous Scientist / Writer

CARL SAGAN (1934-)

Carl Edward Sagan (1934-) is an American astrophysicist based at Cornell University in Ithaca, N.Y. Sagan was born in Brooklyn and received his Doctorate in Astronomy and Astrophysics from the University of Chicago in 1960.

Sagan's research has focussed on a number of scientific areas, and he is a leading figure in the field of exobiology, the search for extraterrestrial life.

Because of his expertise in this area and in astrophysics, Sagan has participated in several space-exploration initiatives. He has been the Director of the Laboratory for Planetary Studies at Cornell since 1968.

Sagan is the author of a vast number of specialized scientific

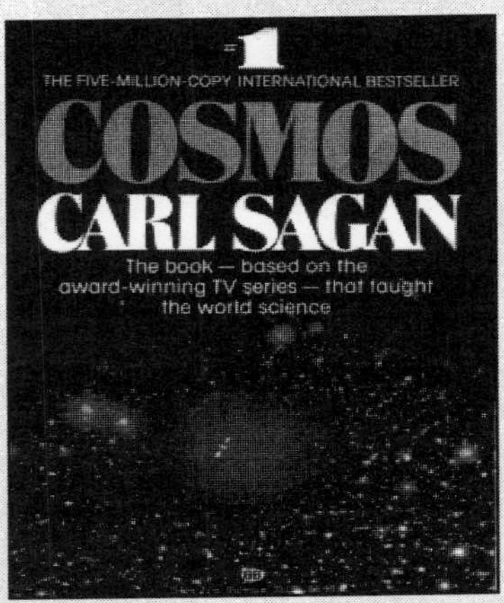

articles, but is more widely known world-wide for his television show, *Cosmos*, and his popular books, *The Dragons of Eden* (1977), *Broca's Brain* (1979), *Comet* (1985) and *Contact* (1985).

In 1990, Sagan convened the Global Forum of Spiritual and Parliamentary Leaders in Moscow. There he presented a document entitled "Preserving and Cherishing the Earth" which was written by Sagan himself and 32 world-renowned scientists.

This statement was signed by 370 spiritual leaders from 83 countries. It represents the most profound appeal ever compiled by global scientific and religious leaders for responsible management of the planet's resources and technology in the face of the worsening environmental crisis.

bodies—in books, for example, or in computer memories—and still, in some sense, know the universe.

Human beings are, understandably, highly motivated to find regularities, natural laws. The search for rules, the only possible way to understand such a vast and complex universe, is called science. The universe forces those who live in it to understand it. Those creatures who find everyday experience a muddled jumble of events with no predictability, no regularity, are in grave peril. The universe belongs to those who, at least to some degree, have figured it out.

It is an astonishing fact that there *are* laws of nature, rules that summarize conveniently—not just qualitatively but quantitatively—how the world works. We might imagine a universe in which there are no such laws, in which the 10^{80} elementary particles that make up a universe like our own behave with utter and uncompromising abandon. To understand such a universe we would need a brain at least as massive as the universe. It seems unlikely that such a universe could have life and intelligence, because beings and brains require some degree of internal stability and order. But even if in a much more random universe there were such beings with an intelligence much greater than our own, there could not be much knowledge, passion or joy.

Fortunately for us, we live in a universe that has at least important parts that are knowable. Our common-sense experience and our evolutionary history have prepared us to understand something of the workaday world. When we go into other realms, however, common sense and ordinary intuition turn out to be highly unreliable guides. It is stunning that as we go close to the speed of light our mass increases indefinitely, we shrink toward zero thickness in the direction of motion, and time for us comes as near to stopping as we would like. Many people think that this is silly, and every week or two I get a letter from someone who complains to me about it. But it is a virtually certain consequence not just of experiment but also of Albert Einstein's brilliant analysis of space and time called the Special Theory of Relativity. It does not matter that these effects seem unreasonable to us. We are not in the habit of traveling close to the speed of light. The testimony of our common sense is suspect at high velocities.

Or consider an isolated molecule composed of two atoms shaped something like a dumbbell—a molecule of salt, it might be. Such a molecule rotates about an axis through the line connecting the two atoms. But in the world of quantum mechanics, the realm of the very small, not all orientations of our dumbbell molecule are possible. It might be that the molecule could be oriented in a horizontal position, say, or in a vertical position, but not at many angles in between. Some rotational positions are forbidden. Forbidden by what? By the laws of nature. The universe is built in such a way as to limit, or quantize, rotation. We do not experience this directly in everyday life; we would find it startling as well as awkward in sitting-up exercises, to find arms outstretched from the sides or pointed up to the skies permitted but many intermediate positions forbidden. We do not live in the world of the small, on the scale of 10^{-13} centimetres, in the realm where there are twelve zeros between the decimal place and the one. Our common-sense intuitions do not count. What does count is experiment—in this case observations from the far infrared spectra of molecules. They show molecular rotation to be quantized.

The idea that the world places restrictions on what humans might do is frustrating. Why *shouldn't* we be able to have intermediate rotational positions? Why *can't* we travel faster than the speed of light? But so far as we can tell, this is the way the universe is constructed. Such prohibitions not only press us toward a little humility; they also make the world more knowable. Every restriction corresponds to a law of nature, a regularization of the universe. The more restrictions there are on what matter and energy can do, the more knowledge human beings can attain. Whether in some sense the universe is ultimately knowable depends not only on how many natural laws there are that encompass widely divergent phenomena, but also on whether we have the openness and the intellectual capacity to understand such laws. Our formulations of the regularities of nature are surely dependent on how the brain is built, but also, and to a significant degree, on how the universe is built.

For myself, I like a universe that includes much that is unknown and, at the same time, much that is knowable. A universe in which everything is known would be static and dull, as boring as the heaven of some weak-minded theologians. A universe that is unknowable is no fit place for a thinking being. The ideal universe for us is one very much like the universe we inhabit. And I would guess that this is not really much of a coincidence.

SOURCE: From Carl Sagan, *Broca's Brain* (New York: Random House, 1979).

Questions and Topics for Discussion and Writing

1. How does Sagan draw the distinction between science and non-science?
2. How does Sagan treat the verb "to know" when he asks "can we know the universe?"
3. Why does Sagan suppose that humans are driven to find natural, regular laws governing our universe? Could the same thing be said of people 1,000 years ago, or has technological developments altered this drive?

The Cosmic Connection

Carl Sagan

This selection consists of three short essays by Carl Sagan. In the first, Sagan notes, in discussions with first-graders, the enormous untapped reservoir of interest and excitement to things astronomical. In the second, he describes how one correspondent assure him that the planets are definitely inhabited. In the third, Sagan discusses time travel and the possibility that black holes may be conduits to advanced technological civilizations.

On Teaching the First Grade

A friend in the first grade asked me to come to talk to his class which, he assured me, knew nothing about astronomy but was eager to learn. With the approval of his teacher, I arrived at his school in Mill Valley, California, armed with twenty or thirty color slides of astronomical objects—the Earth from space, the Moon, the planets, exploding stars, gaseous nebulae, galaxy, and the like—which I thought would amaze and intrigue and, perhaps to a certain extent, even educate. But before I began the slide show for these bright-eyed and cherubic little faces, I wanted to explain that there is a big difference between stating what science has discovered and describing how scientists found it all out. It is pretty easy to summarize the conclusions. It is hard to relate all the mistakes, false leads, ignored clues, dedication, hard work, and painful abandonment of earlier views that go into the initial discovery of something interesting.

I began by saying, "Now you have all *heard* that the Earth is round. Everybody *believes* that the Earth is round. But *why* do we believe the Earth is round? Can any of you think of any evidence that the Earth is round?"

For most of the history of mankind, it was reverently held that the Earth is flat—as is entirely obvious to anyone who has stood in a Nebraska cornfield around planting time. The concept of a flat Earth is still built into our language in such phrases as "the four corners of the Earth." I thought I would stump my little first-graders and then explain with what difficulty the sphericity of Earth had come into general human consciousness. But I had underestimated the first grade of Mill Valley.

"Well," asked a moppet in the sort of one-piece coverall worn by railroad engineers, "what about this business of a ship that's sailing away from you, and the last thing you see is the master, or whatever it's called, that holds up the sail? Doesn't that mean that the ocean has to be curved?"

"What about when there's an *ellipse* of the moon. That's when the Sun is behind us and the shadow of the Earth is on the Moon, right? Well, I saw an *ellipse*. That shadow was round, it wasn't straight. So the Earth has to be round."

"There's better proof, much better proof," offered another. "What about that old guy who sailed around the world—Majello? You can't sail *around* the world if it isn't round, right? And people today sail around the world and fly around the world all the time. How can you fly around the world if it isn't round?"

"Hey, listen, you kids, don't you know there's *pictures* of the Earth?" added a fourth. "Astronauts have been in space, they took pictures of the Earth; you can look at the pictures, the pictures are all round. You don't have to use all these funny reasons. You can *see* that the Earth is round."

And then, as the *coup de grâce*, one pinafored little girl, recently taken on an outing to the San Francisco Museum of Science, casually inquired. "What about the Foucault pendulum experiment?"

It was a very sobered lecturer who went on to describe the findings of modern astronomy. These children were not the offspring of professional astronomers or college teachers or physicians or the like. They were apparently ordinary first-grade children. I very much hope—if they can survive twelve to twenty years of regimenting "education"—that they will hurry and grow up and start running things.

Astronomy is not taught in the public schools, at least in America. With a few notable exceptions, a student can pass from first to twelfth grade without ever encountering any of the findings or reasoning processes that tell us where we are in the universe, how we got here, and where we are likely to be going; without any confrontation with the cosmic perspective.

The ancient Greeks considered astronomy one of the half dozen or so subjects required for the education of free men. I find, in discussions with first-graders and hippie communards, congressmen and cab drivers, that there is an enormous untapped reservoir of interest and excitement to things astronomical. Most newspapers in America have a daily syndicated astrology column. How many have a daily syndicated astronomy column, or even a science column?

Astrology pretends to describe an influence that pervades people's lives. But it is a sham. Science really influences people's lives, and in only a slightly less direct sense. The enormous popularity of science fiction and of such movies as *2001: A Space Odyssey* is indicative of this unexploited scientific enthusiasm. To a very major extent, science and technology govern, mold, and control our lives—for good and for ill. We should make a better effort to learn something about them.

"The Ancient and Legendary Gods of Old"

The sorts of scientific problems that I am involved in—the environments of other planets, the origin of life, the possibility of life on other worlds—engage the popular interest. This is no accident. I think all human beings are excited about these fundamental problems, and I am lucky enough to be alive at a time when it is possible to perform scientific investigation of some of these problems.

One result of popular interest is that I receive a great deal of mail, all kinds of mail, some of it very pleasant, such as from the people who wrote poems and sonnets about the plaque on *Pioneer 10*; some of it from schoolchildren who wish me to write their weekly assignments for them; some from strangers who want to borrow money; some from individuals who wish me to check out their detailed plans for ray guns, time warp, spaceships, or perpetual motion machines; and some from advocates of various arcane disciplines such as astrology, ESP, UFO-contact stories, the speculative fiction of von Danniken, witchcraft, palmistry, phrenology, tea-leaf reading, Tarot cards, the I-Ching, transcendental meditation, and the psychedelic drug experience. Occasionally, also, there are sadder stories, such as from a woman who was talked to from her shower head by inhabitants of the planet Venus, or from a man who tried to file suit against the Atomic Energy Commission for tracking his every movement with "atomic rays." A number of people write that they can pick up extraterrestrial intelligent radio signals through the fillings in their teeth, or just by concentrating in the right way.

But over the years there is one letter that stands out in my mind as the most poignant and charming of its type. There came in the post an eighty-five-page handwritten letter, written in green ballpoint ink, from a gentleman in a mental hospital in Ottawa. He had read a report in a local newspaper that I had thought it possible that life exists on other planets; he wished to reassure me that I was entirely correct in this supposition, as he knew from his own personal knowledge.

To assist me in understanding the source of his knowledge, he thought I would like to learn a little of his personal history—which explains a good bit of the eighty-five pages. As a young man in Ottawa, near the outbreak of World War II, my correspondent chanced to come upon a recruiting poster for the American armed services, the one showing a goateed old codger pointing his index finger at your belly button and saying, "Uncle Sam Wants You." He was so struck by the kindly visage of gentle Uncle Sam that he determined to make his acquaintance immediately. My informant boarded a bus to California, apparently the most plausible habitation for Uncle Sam. Alighting at the depot, he inquired where Uncle Sam could be found. After some confusion about surnames, my informant was greeted by unpleasant stares. After several days of earnest inquiry, no one in California could explain to him the whereabouts of Uncle Sam.

He returned to Ottawa in a deep depression, having failed in his quest. But almost immediately, his life's work came to him in a flash. It was to find "the ancient and legendary gods of old," a phrase that reappears many times throughout the letter. He had the interesting and perceptive idea that gods survive only so long as they have worshippers. What happens then to the gods who are no longer believed in, the gods, for example, of ancient Greece and Rome? Well, he concluded, they are reduced to the status of ordinary human beings, no longer with the perquisites and powers of the godhead. They must now work for a living—like everyone else. He perceived that they might be somewhat secretive about their diminished circumstances, but would at times complain about having to do menial labor when once they supped at Olympus. Such retired deities, he reasoned, would be thrown into insane asylums. Therefore, the most reasonable method of locating these defrocked gods was to incarcerate himself in the local mental institution—which he promptly did.

While we may disagree with some of the steps in his reasoning, we probably all agree that the gentleman did the right thing.

My informant decided that to search for all the ancient and legendary gods of old would be too tiring a task. Instead, he set his sights on only a few: Jupiter, Mercury, and the goddess on the obverse face of the old British penny—not everyone's first choice of the most interesting gods, but surely a representative trio. To his (and my) astonishment, he found—incarcerated in the very asylum in which he had committed himself—Jupiter, Mercury, and the goddess on the obverse face of the old English penny. These gods readily admitted their identities and regaled him with stories of the days of yore when nectar and ambrosia flowed freely.

And then my correspondent succeeded beyond his hopes. One day, over a bowl of Bing cherries, he encountered "God Almighty," or at least a facsimile thereof. At least the Personage who offered him the Bing cherries modestly acknowledged being God Almighty. God Almighty luckily had a small spaceship on the grounds of the asylum and offered to take my informant on a short tool around the Solar System—which was no sooner said than done.

"And this, Dr. Sagan, is how I can assure you that the planets are inhabited."

The letter then concluded something as follows: "But all this business about life elsewhere is so much speculation and not worth the really serious interest of a scientist such as yourself. Why don't you address yourself to a really important problem, such as the construction of a trans-Canadian railroad at high northern latitudes?" There followed a detailed sketch of the proposed railway route and a standard expression of the sincerity of his good wishes.

Other than stating my serious intent to work on a trans-Canadian railroad at high northern latitudes, I have never been able to think of an appropriate response to this letter.

A Passage to Elsewhen

One of the most pervasive and entrancing ideas of science fiction is time travel. In *The Time Machine*, the classic story by H.G. Wells, and in most subsequent renditions, there is a small machine, constructed usually by a solitary scientist in a remote laboratory. One dials the year of interest, steps into the machine, presses a button, and *presto*, here's the past or the future. Among the common devices in time-travel stories are the logical paradoxes that accompany meeting yourself several years ago; killing a lineal antecedent; interfering directly with a major historical event of the past few thousand years; or accidentally stepping on a Precambrian butterfly—you are always changing the entire subsequent history of life.

Such logical paradoxes do not occur in stories about travel to the future. Except for the element of nostalgia—the wish we all have to relive or reclaim some elements of the past—a trip forward in time is surely at least as exciting as one backward in time. We know rather much about the past and almost nothing about the future. Travel forward in time has a greater degree of intellectual excitement than the reverse.

There is no question that time travel into the future is possible: We do it all the time merely by aging at the usual rate. But there are other, more interesting possibilities. Everyone has heard about, and now even a fair number of people understand, Einstein's special theory of relativity. It was Einstein's genius to have subjected our usual views of space, time, and simultaneity to a penetrating logical analysis, which could have been performed two centuries earlier. But special relativity required for its discovery a mind divested of the conventional prejudices and the blind adherence to prevailing beliefs—a rare mind in any time.

Some of the consequences of special relativity are counterintuitive, in the sense that they do not correspond to what everybody knows by observing his surroundings. For example, the special theory says that a measuring rod shrinks in the direction in which it is moving. When jogging you are thinner in the direction you are jogging—and not because of any weight loss. The moment you come to a halt you immediately resume your usual paunch-to-backbone dimension. Similarly, we are more massive when running than when standing still. These statements appear silly only because the magnitude of the effect is too small to be measured at jog velocities. But were we able to jog at some close approximation to the speed of light (186,000 miles per second), these effects would become manifest. In fact, expensive synchrotons—machines to accelerate charged particles close to the speed of light—take account of such effects, and work only because special relativity happens to bc correct. The reason these consequences of special relativity seem counterintuitive is that we are not in the habit of traveling close to the speed of light. It is not that there is anything wrong with common sense; common sense is fine in its place.

There is a third consequence of special relativity, a bizarre effect important only close to the speed of light: The phenomenon called time dilation. Were we to travel close to the speed of light, time, as measured by our wristwatch or by our heartbeat, would pass more slowly than a comparable stationary clock. Again, this is not an experience of our everyday life, but it is an experience of nuclear particles, which have clocks built into them (their decay times) when they travel close to the speed of light. Time dilation is a measured and authenticated reality of the universe in which we live.

Time dilation implies the possibility of time travel into the future. A space vehicle that could travel arbitrarily close to the speed of light arranges for time, as measured on the space vehicle, to move as slowly as desired. For example, our Galaxy is some sixty thousand light-years in diameter. At the velocity of light, it would take sixty thousand years to cross from one end of the Galaxy to the other. But this time is measured by a stationary observer. A space vehicle able to move close to the speed of light could traverse the Galaxy from one end to the other in less than a human lifetime. With the appropriate vehicle we could circumnavigate the Galaxy and return al-

Courtesy of NASA.

"I cannot believe that God plays dice with the cosmos."—Albert Einstein.

A view of Earth from Apollo 11.

most two hundred thousand years later, as measured on Earth. Naturally, our friends and relatives would have changed some in the interval—as would our society and probably even our planet.

According to special relativity, it is even possible to circumnavigate the entire universe within a human lifetime, returning to our planet many billions of years in our future. According to special relativity, there is no prospect of traveling *at* the speed of light, merely very close to it. And there is no possibility in this way of traveling backward in time; we can merely make time slow down, we cannot make it stop or reverse.

The engineering problems involved in the design of space vehicles capable of such velocities are immense. *Pioneer 10*, the fastest man-made object ever to leave the Solar System, is traveling about ten thousand times slower than the speed of light. Time travel into the future is thus not an immediate prospect, but it is a prospect conceivable for all advanced technology on planets of other stars.

There is one further possibility that should be mentioned; it is a much more speculative prospect. At the end of their lifetimes, stars more than about 2.5 times as massive as our Sun undergo a collapse so powerful that no known forces can stop it. The stars develop a pucker in the fabric of space—a "black hole"—into which they disappear. The physics of black holes does not involve Einstein's special theory of relativity; it involves his much more difficult general theory of relativity. The physics of black holes—particularly, rotating black holes—is rather poorly understood at the present time. There is, however, one conjecture that has been made, which cannot be disproved and which is worthy of note: Black holes may be apertures to elsewhen. Were we to plunge down a black hole, we would re-emerge, it is conjectured, in a different part of the universe and in another epoch in time. We do not know whether it is possible to get to this other place in the universe faster down a black hole than by the more usual route. We do not know whether it is possible to travel into the past by plunging down a black hole. The paradoxes that this latter possibility imply could be used to argue against it, but we really do not know.

For all we do know, black holes are the transportation conduits of advanced technological civilizations—conceivably, conduits in time as well as in space. A large number of stars are more than 2.5 times as massive as the Sun; as far as we can tell, they must all become black holes during their relatively rapid evolution.

Black holes may be entrances to Wonderlands. But are there Alices or white rabbits?

Questions and Topics for Discussion and Writing

1. Why would a high-level astronomer like Carl Sagan think it valuable to recount his experiences with a first-grade class?
2. What implication does the letter-writer's contention that "gods survive only so long as they have worshippers" have for science?
3. What relationship does Sagan see between order in the universe and our ability to know and understand it?

Our Picture of the Universe

Stephen Hawking

Despite being afflicted with the debilitating ALS, or "Lou Gherig's Disease," physicist Stephen Hawking is often mentioned in the same breath as such figures as Aristotle, Copernicus, Galileo, Newton and Einstein. In this selection taken from his world famous book, *A Brief History of Time* (also turned into a popular film of the same name) Hawking describes highlights in the history of his science and its goal of nothing less than a complete description of the universe we live in, a single theory that describes the whole universe.

A well-known scientist (some say it was Bertrand Russell) once gave a public lecture on astronomy. He described how the earth orbits around the sun and how the sun, in turn, orbits around the center of a vast collection of stars called our galaxy. At the end of the lecture, a little old lady at the back of the room got up and said: "What you have told us is rubbish. The world is really a flat plate supported on the back of a giant tortoise." The scientist gave a superior smile before replying, "What is the tortoise standing on?" "You're very clever young man, very clever," said the old lady. "But it's turtles all the way down!"

Most people would find the picture of our universe as an infinite tower of tortoises rather ridiculous, but why do we think we know better? What do we know about the universe, and how do we know it? Where did the universe come from, and where is it going? Did the universe have a beginning, and if so, what happened *before* then? What is the nature of time? Will it ever come to an end? Recent breakthroughs in physics, made possible in part by fantastic new technologies, suggest answers to some of these longstanding questions. Someday these answers may seem as obvious to us as the earth orbiting the sun—or perhaps as ridiculous as a tower of tortoises. Only time (whatever that may be) will tell.

As long ago as 340 B.C. the Greek philosopher Aristotle, in his book *On the Heavens*, was able to put forward two good arguments for believing that the earth was a round sphere rather than a flat plate. First, he realized that eclipses of the moon were caused by the earth coming between the sun and the moon. The earth's shadow on the moon was always round, which would be true only if the earth was spherical. If the earth had been a flat disk, the shadow would have been elongated and elliptical, unless the eclipse always occurred at a time when the sun was directly under the center of the disk. Second, the Greeks knew from their travels that the North Star appeared lower in the sky when viewed in the south than it did in more northerly regions. (Since the North Star lies over the North Pole, it appears to be directly above an observer at the North Pole, but to someone looking from the equator, it appears to lie just at the horizon.) From the difference in the apparent position of the North Star in Egypt and Greece, Aristotle even quoted an estimate that the distance around the earth was 400,000 stadia. It is not known exactly what length a stadium was, but it may have been about 200 yards, which would make Aristotle's estimate about twice the currently accepted figure. The Greeks even had a third argument that the earth must be round, for why else does one first see the sails of a ship coming over the horizon, and only later see the hull?

Aristotle thought that the earth was stationary

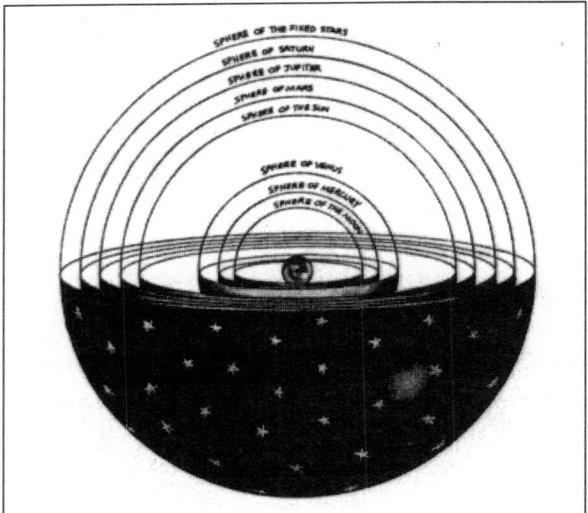

Figure 1.1: Ptolemy's cosmological model (second century AD): The Earth stood at the centre and was surrounded by eight spheres that carried the moon, the sun, the stars, and the five planets known at that time (Mercury, Venus, Mars, Jupiter and Saturn). The Polish priest Copernicus developed a simpler model in 1514 in which the sun was stationary at the centre. Kepler and Galileo later started to publicly support and elaborate the Copernican view.

and that the sun, the moon, the planets, and the stars moved in circular orbits about the earth. He believed this because he felt, for mystical reasons, that the earth was the center of the universe, and that circular motion was the most perfect. This idea was elaborated by Ptolemy in the second century A.D. into a complete cosmological model. The earth stood at the center, surrounded by eight spheres that carried the moon, the sun, the stars, and the five planets known at the time, Mercury, Venus, Mars, Jupiter, and Saturn (Fig. 1.1). The planets themselves moved on smaller circles attached to their respective spheres in order to account for their rather complicated observed paths in the sky. The outermost sphere carried the so-called fixed stars, which always stay in the same positions relative to each other but which rotate together across the sky. What lay beyond the last sphere was never made very clear, but it certainly was not part of mankind's observable universe.

Ptolemy's model provided a reasonably accurate system for predicting the positions of heavenly bodies in the sky. But in order to predict these positions correctly, Ptolemy had to make an assumption that the moon followed a path that sometimes brought it twice as close to the earth as at other times. And that meant that the moon ought sometimes to appear twice as big as at other times! Ptolemy recognized this flaw, but nevertheless his model was generally, although not universally, accepted. It was adopted by the Christian church as the picture of the universe that was in accordance with Scripture, for it had the great advantage that it left lots of room outside the sphere of fixed stars for heaven and hell.

A simpler model, however, was proposed in 1514 by a Polish priest, Nicholas Copernicus. (At first, perhaps for fear of being branded a heretic by his church, Copernicus circulated his model anonymously.) His idea was that the sun was stationary at the center and that the earth and the planets moved in circular orbits around the sun. Nearly a century passed before this idea was taken seriously. Then two astronomers—the German, Johannes Kepler, and the Italian, Galileo Galilei—started publicly to support the Copernican theory, despite the fact that the orbits it predicted did not quite match the ones observed. The death blow to the Aristotelian/Ptolemaic theory came in 1609. In that year, Galileo started observing the night sky with a telescope, which had just been invented. When he looked at the planet Jupiter, Galileo found that it was accompanied by several small satellites or moons that orbited around it. This implied that everything did *not* have to orbit directly around the earth, as Aristotle and Ptolemy had thought. (It was, of course, still possible to believe that the earth was stationary at the center of the universe and that the moons of Jupiter moved on extremely complicated paths around the earth, giving the *appearance* that they orbited Jupiter. However, Copernicus' theory was much simpler.) At the same time, Johannes Kepler had modified Copernicus' theory, suggesting that the planets moved not in circles but in ellipses (an ellipse is an elongated circle). The predictions now finally matched the observations.

As far as Kepler was concerned, elliptical orbits were merely an ad hoc hypothesis, and a rather repugnant one at that, because ellipses were clearly less perfect than circles. Having discovered almost by accident that elliptical orbits fit the observations well, he could not reconcile them with his idea that the planets were made to orbit the sun by magnetic forces. An explanation was provided only much later, in 1687, when Sir Isaac Newton published his *Philosophiae Naturalis Principia Mathematica*, probably the most important single work ever published in the physical sciences. In it Newton not only put forward a theory of how bodies move in space and time, but he also developed the complicated mathematics needed to analyze those motions. In addition, Newton postulated a law of universal gravitation according to which each body in the universe was attracted toward every other body by a force that was stronger the more massive the bodies and the closer they were to each other. It was this same force that caused objects to fall to the ground. (The story that Newton was inspired by an apple hitting his head is almost certainly apocryphal. All Newton himself ever said was that the idea of gravity came to him as he sat "in a contemplative mood" and "was occasioned by the fall of an apple.") Newton went on to show that, according to his law, gravity causes the moon to move in an elliptical orbit around the earth and causes the earth and the planets to follow elliptical paths around the sun.

The Copernican model got rid of Ptolemy's celestial spheres, and with them, the idea that the universe had a natural boundary. Since "fixed stars" did not appear to change their positions apart from a rotation across the sky caused by the earth spinning on its axis, it became natural to suppose that the fixed stars were objects like our sun but very much farther away.

Newton realized that, according to his theory of gravity, the stars should attract each other, so it seemed they could not remain essentially motionless. Would they not all fall together at some point? In a letter in 1691 to Richard Bentley, another leading thinker of his day, Newton argued that this would indeed happen if there were only a finite number of stars distributed over a finite region of space. But he reasoned that if, on the other hand, there were an infinite number of stars, distributed more or less uniformly over infinite space, this would not happen, because there would not be any central point for them to fall to.

This argument is an instance of the pitfalls that you can encounter in talking about infinity. In an infinite universe, every point can be regarded as the center, because every point has an infinite number of stars on each side of it. The correct approach, it was realized only much later, is to consider the finite situation, in which the stars all fall in on each other, and then to ask how things change if one adds more stars roughly uniformly distributed outside this region. According to Newton's law, the extra stars would make no difference at all to the original ones on average, so the Stars would fall in just as fast. We can add as many stars as we like, but they will still always collapse in on themselves. We now know it is impossible to have an infinite static model of the universe in which gravity is always attractive.

It is an interesting reflection on the general climate of thought before the twentieth century that no one had suggested that the universe was expanding or contracting. It was generally accepted that either the universe had existed forever in an unchanging state, or that it had been created at a finite time in the past more or less as we observe it today. In part this may have been due to people's tendency to believe in eternal truths, as well as the comfort they found in the thought that even though they may grow old and die, the universe is eternal and unchanging.

Even those who realized that Newton's theory of gravity showed that the universe could not be static did not think to suggest that it might be expanding. Instead, they attempted to modify the theory by making the gravitational force repulsive at very large distances. This did not significantly affect their predictions of the motions of the planets, but it allowed an infinite distribution of stars to remain in equilibrium—with the attractive forces between nearby stars. However, we now believe such an equilibrium would be unstable: if the stars in some region got only slightly nearer each other, the attractive forces between them would become stronger and dominate over the repulsive forces so that the stars would continue to fall toward each other. On the other hand, if the stars got a bit farther away from each other, the repulsive forces would dominate and drive them farther apart.

Another objection to an infinite static universe is normally ascribed to the German philosopher Heinrich Olbers, who wrote about this theory in 1823. In fact, various contemporaries of Newton had raised the problem, and the Olbers article was not even the first to contain plausible arguments against it. It was, however, the first to be widely noted. The difficulty is that in an infinite static universe nearly every line of sight would end on the surface of a star. Thus one would expect that the whole sky would be as bright as the sun, even at night. Olbers' counterargument was that the light from distant stars would be dimmed by absorption by intervening matter. However, if that happened the intervening matter would eventually heat up until it glowed as brightly as the stars. The only way of avoiding the conclusion that the whole of the night sky should be as bright as the surface of the sun would be to assume that the stars had not been shining forever but had turned on at some finite time in the past. In that case the absorbing matter might not have heated up yet or the light from distant stars might not yet have reached us. And that brings us to the question of what could have caused the stars to have turned on in the first place.

The beginning of the universe had, of course, been discussed long before this. According to a number of early cosmologies and the Jewish/Christian/Muslim tradition, the universe started at a finite, and not very distant, time in the past. One argument for such a beginning was the feeling that it was necessary to have "First Cause" to explain the existence of the universe. (Within the universe, you always explained one event as being caused by some earlier event, but the existence of the universe itself could be explained in this way only if it had some beginning.) Another argument was put forward by St. Augustine in his book *The City of God*. He pointed out that civilization is progressing and we remember who performed this deed or developed that technique. Thus man, and so also perhaps the universe, could not have been around all that long. St. Augustine accepted a date of about 5000 B.C. for the Creation of the universe according to the book of Genesis. (It is interesting that this is not so far from the end of the last Ice Age, about 10,000 B.C., which is when archaeologists tell us that civilization really began.)

Aristotle, and most of the other Greek philosophers, on the other hand, did not like the idea of a creation because it smacked too much of divine intervention. They believed, therefore, that the human race and the world around it had existed, and would exist, forever. The ancients had already considered the argument about progress described above, and answered it by saying that there had been periodic floods or other disasters that repeatedly set the human race right back to the beginning of civilization.

The questions of whether the universe had a beginning in time and whether it is limited in space were later extensively examined by the philosopher Immanuel Kant in his monumental (and very obscure) work, *Critique of Pure Reason*, published in 1781. He called these questions antinomies (that is, contradictions) of pure reason because he felt that there were equally compelling arguments for believing the thesis, that the universe had a beginning, and the antithesis, that it had existed forever. His argument for the thesis was that if the universe did not have a beginning, there would be an infinite period of time before any event, which he considered absurd. The argument for the antithesis was that if the universe had a beginning, there would be an infinite period of time before it, so why should the universe begin at any one particular time? In fact, his cases for both the thesis and the antithesis are really the same argument. They are both based on his unspoken assumption that time continues back forever, whether or not the universe had existed forever. As we shall see, the concept of time has no meaning before the beginning of the universe.

This was first pointed out by St. Augustine. When asked: What did God do before he created the universe? Augustine didn't reply: He was preparing Hell for people who asked such questions. Instead, he said that time was a property of the universe that God created, and that time did not exist before the beginning of the universe.

When most people believed in an essentially static and unchanging universe, the question of whether or not it had a beginning was really one of metaphysics or theology. One could account for what was observed equally well on the theory that the universe had existed forever or on the theory that it was set in motion at some finite time in such a manner as to look as though it had existed forever. But in 1929, Edwin Hubble made the landmark observation that wherever you look, distant galaxies are moving rapidly away from us. In other words, the universe is expanding. This means that at earlier times objects would have been closer together. In fact, it seemed that there was a time, about ten or twenty thousand million years ago, when they were all at exactly the same place and when, therefore, the density of the universe was infinite. This discovery finally brought the question of the beginning of the universe into the realm of science.

Hubble's observations suggested that there was a time, called the big bang, when the universe was infinitesimally small and infinitely dense. Under such conditions all the laws of science, and therefore all ability to predict the future, would break down. If there were events earlier than this time, then they could not affect what happens at the present time. Their existence can be ignored because it would have no observational consequences. One may say that time had a beginning at the big bang, in the sense that earlier times simply would not be defined. It should be emphasized that this beginning in time is very different from those that had been considered previously. In an unchanging universe a beginning in time is something that has to be imposed by some being outside the universe; there is no physical necessity for a beginning. One can imagine that God created the universe at literally any time in the past. On the other hand, if the universe is expanding, there may be physical reasons why there had to be a beginning. One could still imagine that God created the universe at the instant of the big bang, or even afterwards in just such a way as to make it look as though there had been a big bang, but it would be meaningless to suppose that it was created *before* the big bang. An expanding universe does not preclude a creator, but it does place limits on when he might have carried out his job!

In order to talk about the nature of the universe and to discuss questions such as whether it has a beginning or an end, you have to be clear about what a scientific theory is. I shall take the simple-minded view that a theory is just a model of the universe, or a restricted part of it, and a set of rules that relate quantities in the model to observations that we make. It exists only in our minds and does not have any other reality (whatever that might mean). A theory is a good theory if it satisfies two requirements: It must accurately describe a large class of observations on the basis of a model that contains only a few arbitrary elements, and it must make definite predictions about the results of future observations. For example, Aristotle's theory that everything was made out of four elements, earth, air, fire, and water, was simple enough to qualify, but it did not make any definite predictions. On the other hand, Newton's theory of gravity was based on an even simpler model, in which bodies attracted each other with a force that was proportional to a quantity called their mass and inversely proportional to the square of the distance between them. Yet it predicts the motions of the sun, the moon, and the planets to a high degree of accuracy.

Any physical theory is always provisional, in the sense that it is only a hypothesis: you can never prove it. No matter how many times the results of experiments agree with some theory, you can never be sure that the next time the result will not contradict the theory. On the other hand, you can disprove a theory by finding even a single observation that disagrees with the predictions of the theory. As philosopher of science Karl Popper has emphasized, a good theory is characterized by the fact that it makes a number of predictions that could in principle be disproved or falsified by

Famous Scientist

STEPHEN HAWKING (1942-)

Stephen William Hawking was born in London, England in 1942. He received his doctorate at Cambridge University, and was appointed Lucasian Professor of Mathematics there in 1979, a position held many years before by Isaac Newton. In 1974, Hawking was made a Fellow of the Royal Society of London.

Because of his revolutionary work in physics, especially concerning black holes and the creation of the universe, Hawking is usually mentioned in the same breath as such figures as Aristotle, Copernicus, Galileo, Newton and Einstein. Those with an eye for coincidences will note, as Hawking has, that he was born exactly 300 years after the death of Galileo. Hawking wrote *The Large Scale Structure of Spacetime* with George Ellis in 1973, a book he calls "highly technical, and quite unreadable." His 1988 attempt to put his theories about the " big bang" theory of the creation of the universe, general relativity and black holes, *A Brief History of Time*, proved much more accessible to the general public and sold over one million copies. *A Brief History of Time* was also turned into a popular film of the same name. As well as outlining Hawking's ideas about physics, the film provides autobiographical detail about his life. Hawking has become one of the major scientific innovators of all time despite being afflicted with ALS, or "Lou Gherig's Disease." Although this disease has affected his life in many ways, Hawking has written that "I was...fortunate in that I chose theoretical physics, for that is all in the mind."

observation. Each time new experiments are observed to agree with the predictions the theory survives, and our confidence in it is increased; but if ever a new observation is found to disagree, we have to abandon or modify the theory. At least that is what is supposed to happen, but you can always question the competence of the person who carried out the observation.

In practice, what often happens is that a new theory is devised that is really an extension of the previous theory. For example, very accurate observations of the planet Mercury revealed a small difference between its motion and the predictions of Newton's theory of gravity. Einstein's general theory of relativity predicted a slightly different motion from Newton's theory. The fact that Einstein's predictions matched what was seen, while Newton's did not, was one of the crucial confirmations of the new theory. However, we still use Newton's theory for all practical purposes because the difference between its predictions and those of general relativity is very small in the situations that we normally deal with. (Newton's theory also has the great advantage that it is much simpler to work with than Einstein's!)

The eventual goal of science is to provide a single theory that describes the whole universe. However, the approach most scientists actually follow is to separate the problem into two parts. First, there are the laws that tell us how the universe changes with time. (If we know what the universe is like at any one time, these physical laws tell us how it will look at any later time.) Second, there is the question of the initial state of the universe. Some people feel that science should be concerned with only the first part; they regard the question of the initial situation as a matter for metaphysics or religion. They would say that God, being omnipotent, could have started the universe off any way he wanted. That may be so, but in that case he also could have made it develop in a completely arbitrary way. Yet it appears that he chose to make it evolve in a very regular way according to certain laws. It therefore seems equally reasonable to suppose that there are also laws governing the initial state.

It turns out to be very difficult to devise a theory to describe the universe all in one go. Instead, we break the problem up into bits and invent a number of partial theories. Each of these partial theories describes and predicts a certain limited class of observations, neglecting the effects of other quantities, or representing them by simple sets of numbers. It may be that this approach is completely wrong. If everything in the universe depends on everything else in a fundamental way, it might be impossible to get close to a full solution by investigating parts of the problem in isolation. Nevertheless, it is certainly the way that we have made progress in the past. The classic example again is the Newtonian theory of gravity, which tells us that the gravitational force between two bodies depends only on one number associated with each body its mass, but is otherwise independent of what the bodies are made of. Thus one does not need to have a theory of the structure and constitution of the sun and the planets in order to calculate their orbits.

Today scientists describe the universe in terms of two basic partial theories—the general theory of relativity and quantum mechanics. They are the great intellectual achievements of the first half of this century. The general theory of relativity describes the force of gravity and the large-scale structure of the universe, that is, the structure on scales from only a few miles to as large as a million million million million (1 with twenty-four zeros after it) miles, the size of the observable universe. Quantum mechanics, on the other hand, deals with phenomena on extremely small scales, such as a millionth of a millionth of an inch. Unfortunately, however, these two theories are known to be inconsistent with each other—they cannot both be correct. One of the major endeavors in physics today, and the major theme of this book, is the search for a new theory that will incorporate them both—a quantum theory of gravity. We do not yet have such a theory, and we may still be a long way from having one, but we do already know many of the properties that it must have. And we shall see, in later chapters, that we already know a fair amount about the predictions a quantum theory of gravity must make.

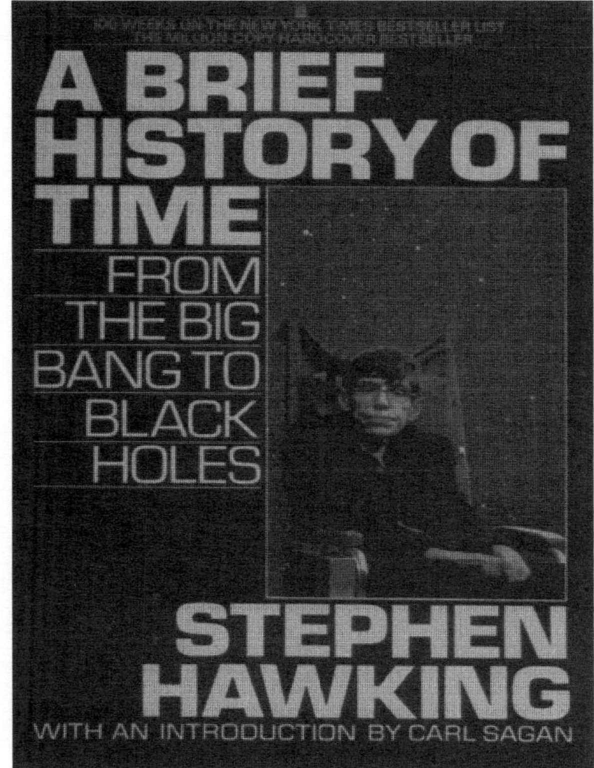

Cover of Stephen Hawking's world-famous book, *A Brief History of Time*, published in1988.

Now, if you believe that the universe is not arbitrary, but is governed by definite laws, you ultimately have to combine the partial theories into a complete unified theory that will describe everything in the universe. But there is a fundamental paradox in the search for such a complete unified theory. The ideas about scientific theories outlined above assume we are rational beings who are free to observe the universe as we want and to draw logical deductions from what we see. In such a scheme it is reasonable to suppose that we might progress ever closer toward the laws that govern our universe. Yet if there really is a complete unified theory, it would also presumably determine our actions. And so the theory itself would determine the outcome of our search for it! And why should it determine that we come to the right conclusions from the evidence? Might it not equally well determine that we draw the wrong conclusion? Or no conclusion at all?

The only answer that I can give to this problem is based on Darwin's principle of natural selection. The idea is that in any population of self-reproducing organisms, there will be variations in the genetic material and upbringing that different individuals have. These differences will mean that some individuals are better able than others to draw the right conclusions about the world around them and to act accordingly. These individuals will be more likely to survive and reproduce and so their pattern of behavior and thought will come to dominate. It has certainly been true in the past that what we call intelligence and scientific discovery has conveyed a survival advantage. It is not so clear that this is still the case: our scientific discoveries may well destroy us all, and even if they don't, a complete unified theory may not make much difference to our chances of survival. However, provided the universe has evolved in a regular way, we might expect that the reasoning abilities that natural selection has given us would be valid also in our search for a complete unified theory, and so would not lead us to the wrong conclusions.

Because the partial theories that we already have are sufficient to make accurate predictions in all but the most extreme situations, the search for the ultimate theory of the universe seems difficult to justify on practical grounds. (It is worth noting, though, that similar arguments could have been used against both relativity and quantum mechanics, and these theories have given us both nuclear energy and the microelectronics revolution!) The discovery of a complete unified theory, therefore, may not aid the survival of our species. It may not even affect our life-style. But ever since the dawn of civilization, people have not been content to see events as unconnected and inexplicable. They have craved an understanding of the underlying order in the world. Today we still yearn to know why we are here and where we came from. Humanity's deepest desire for knowledge is justification enough for our continuing quest. And our goal is nothing less than a complete description of the universe we live in.

SOURCE: From *A Brief History of Time: From the Big Bang to Black Holes* by Stephen Hawking (New York: Bantam Books, 1990).

Questions and Topics for Discussion and Writing

1. What key connection does Hawking make between theory and technology in his discussion of the early astronomers? How has this connection been strengthened over time?
2. What is Hawking's definition of a theory? What are the advantages for a theoretical physicist such as Hawking of approaching theories in this way?
3. How does Hawking make the connection between theoretical physics and Darwinian evolution? Is this connection convincing?
4. What does Hawking define as the ultimate goal of humankind? Is it likely that this will ever be achieved?

Playing Russian Roulette with the World Environment

David Suzuki

David Suzuki is a Canadian geneticist, columnist, and popular host of television and radio programs on science. In this article, he deplores the degradation of our environment. He sees part of the explanation for this deterioration in our blind adherence to "sacred truths" with no basis in reality.

In the mid-fifties, while I was returning from college in the United States for the summer, I glanced down at the Niagara River as my train passed over. Below, I could see fishermen on the banks flailing away at the water and yanking silver objects from the river as fast as they could cast. The were catching silver bass on a massive annual spawning run.

Those spring runs petered out years ago.

Old fishermen on the east and west coasts of Canada describe an abundance and size of salmon, cod and lobsters when they were starting out that younger fishermen have never seen. It wasn't long ago that we drank from the Great Lakes with confidence in the water's purity, and relished fresh fruits and vegetables without concern about chemical contamination. Only a few decades ago, the quality of our water, soil and air was radically different and there were an abundance and variety of life that now are found only in the most remote parts of the country. The planet has changed almost beyond recognition within the life-time of Canada's elder citizens. Their recollections are not simply old folks' romantic musings on the good old days; they are a living record of the cataclysmic degradation that has taken place around us. In the past, men took canaries into coal mines as biological indicators of the quality of the air; today, our elders are the ones who know that canaries are falling all around us.

Our species boasts the highest ratio of "brain to brawn" of all life forms, and that mental power has gifted us with a conscious strategy for survival. We have invented a notion called the "future," which provided us with options and enabled us to deliberately select a future toward which we aimed. Yet today, with all the amplified brainpower of computers, communications networks, scientists and engineers, we seem unable to use the strategy that got our forebearers to where we took over. What has gone wrong?

I believe that we continue to cling to certain "sacred truths" that blind us to many problems and often cause the ones that we do recognize. Let me list some of those sacred truths.

We equate "progress" with *growth*—growth in the economy, income, consumer goods, material comfort. A need for steady economic growth is repeated like a catechism by every politician, economist and businessperson, and has led us to link *profit* with the goal of society. But human beings today are the most ubiquitous and numerous large mammal in the world, and it is our unrelenting commitment to growth that now has us consuming 40 percent of the net primary production of energy on the planet. We are only one species among perhaps 30 million. When our population doubles again within 50 years, will we then demand 80 percent? Nothing on this planet continues indefinitely to grow steadily.

The current increases in consumption and material wealth are a historical aberration, a blip that will come to a stop within our children's lifetime. The only question is whether we will deliberately bring our demands and consumption under control or allow pestilence, famine or war to do the job.

We have come to believe in the ability of science to provide us with the knowledge to understand and manage our natural resources. Yet the unique power of science is that its practitioners focus on an isolated part of nature, and thus increase knowledge in fragmented bits and pieces. Modern physicists have learned that it is not possible to put these fragments of knowledge together into a complete picture, because in real life, unlike a jigsaw puzzle, the pieces interact synergistically. Thus, properties emerge from the complex that cannot be anticipated from the known properties of the component parts.

As a result, there are fundamental reasons why it is not possible to comprehend the behavior of entire ecosystems or even complex components within them. In addition, the degree of our ignorance remains vast. We know very little, for example, about chinook salmon during their four-year stay in the ocean, yet we maintain the illusion that we are managing them scientifically.

We believe we can manage the effects of new technologies by doing proper cost/benefit analysis to maximize the benefits while minimizing costs. History informs us that every technology, however beneficial, has costs. And invariably the benefits of new technologies are immediate and obvious. That's why we (including me) love technology; it does such wonderful things for us. But the costs of these technologies are almost always hidden, and cannot be anticipated.

If all technologies exact a price that cannot be foreseen, can we continue to mortgage the future by opting for the immediate benefits of new inventions while postponing the solution to their accompanying costs? Today scientists speak of building machines that can think, tampering with the heredity of babies, manipulating the human mind and releasing genetically engineered organisms into the environment—yet we cannot predict their long-term consequences.

We believe we can minimize environmental damage from our activity by carrying out environmental assessments. Thus, for example, oil exploration in the high Arctic or off Georges Bank or building a fixed link to Prince Edward Island, depend on the success of an environmental assessment review process (**EARP**). Of course, there should be such assessments, but in view of how little we know of the constituents of ecosystems and their interactions, fluctuations over time and the tiny window our tests provide, the **EARP** is far too limited in scope, duration and scale to provide information that is statistically meaningful.

We cannot assume that once an **EARP** indicates no hazard, development should have an unconditional green light. Approval should always be provisional, with a continued accumulation of information on which reassessments of that approval are constantly made.

We believe that in a democracy, we elect people to political office to represent and lead us into the future. Yet most politicians come from two professions, business and law, the two areas whose practitioners have the poorest comprehension of issues scientific and technological.

Today, the most important factor shaping our lives and society is science when applied by industry, medicine and the military. Yet, jurisdictional concerns such as Meech Lake and economic priorities of free trade preoccupy our leaders and subsume the priorities of the planet's ecosystem.

"Conventional wisdom" assumes the truth of the above assumptions. Unless we expose them to the light of critical examination, we will continue to ravage the ecosystem for short-term benefits. We desperately need a new paradigm, a new vision of the human place in nature.

We live in a time when satellites have sent back images of this planet that graphically demonstrate its oneness. I think ecologist Jack Valentyne, who poses as Johnny Biosphere to instruct children about the environment, is on the right track. He reminds us that we all have built into our cells and tissues, atoms and molecules that were once in the bodies of all other people on the planet and of people who lived one or two thousand years ago. Not only that, but we are made of atoms respired by trees and insects and mammals and birds. That's because all life forms share the atmosphere around the world.

Famous Canadian Scientist / Writer

DAVID SUZUKI (1936 -)

Born in British Columbia in 1936, David Takayoshi Suzuki has become one of the world's leading environmental advocates. Shortly after graduating, he accepted a post at the University of British Columbia and has been there ever since.

David Suzuki's early life was far from pleasant however. When he was five, his family was sent to an internment camp in B.C. because of World War II suspicions that Japanese-Canadians posed "security risks." This experience had a profound impact on the young Suzuki.

Although Suzuki's early work was in developmental genetics, he began to become increasingly interested in the ethical issues that surround science. Perhaps it was his early work on the ability of genes to mutate, or to be mutated by humans, that caused him to question the responsibility that people have to the natural world.

Whatever the cause of his interest, Suzuki has, through newspaper columns, books such as *Time to Change* (1994), radio programs like *Quirks and Quarks* and his hugely successful television show, *The Nature of Things*, been able to transmit his ideas to millions of people world wide. As Suzuki has said, in reference to what he views as a world-wide crisis, "We have become drunk with the power of our technology, and we have bought the illusion that we have control."

Johnny Biosphere tells of an Indian who, on a hot day hundreds of years ago, swam in Lake Superior. Sodium ions from the sweat of his body are still contained in each drink of water that we take from Lake Ontario. And when one realizes that everything we eat for nutrition was itself once living, we realize that we remain inextricably linked to the rest of life on this planet. Seen in this perspective of sharing and connectedness, we have to behave in a radically different way when we dispose of our wastes or apply new technologies that affect other parts of the ecosystem.

Throughout human history, the boast of our species has been that we love our children and hope that they will have a richer, fuller life than we did. Yet now, for the first time, we know with absolute certainty that our children's lives will be immeasurably poorer in bio-diversity and filled with massive problems that we have foisted on them in our shortsighted pursuit of immediate profit and power.

Can we continue to mortgage our children's future so thoughtlessly? Not if we mean it when we say we love them.

David Suzuki, "Playing Russian Roulette with World Environment" *The Globe and Mail* (April 23, 1988) D1-D2. Reprinted with the permission of the author.

Questions and Topics for Discussion and Writing

1. Suzuki disparages of the mindset that equates "progress" with "growth." Assuming that a biologist like Suzuki is not opposed to certain types of progress, how is he suggesting we continue?
2. What does Suzuki have in mind when he refers to the "hidden costs" of new technologies?
3. Why does Suzuki oppose EARP tests in the form they currently take?

Science and Technology

David Suzuki

Many scientists believe that their work will solve global hunger, pollution, or overpopulation. Author David Suzuki argues, on the contrary, that there are social, economic, religious, and political roots to these concerns. In the essays that follow, Scientists argues that scientists and the rest of us have to realize that science and technology cannot solve all our problems.

One of the major underlying causes of the global ecocrisis is the dominant attitude within society today. It is based on a profound faith in the power of science and technology to give us insight and understanding that enable us to control and manipulate our environment.

Technology has revolutionized human evolution since the earliest records of our species. While providing practical dividends in the past, technology—whether pottery, painting, bow and arrow, or metalwork—did not require scientific explanation. But today, it is science that drives technological innovation, from telecommunications to biotechnology and nuclear power. And now, our insights and inventions have given our species unprecedented power to change our surroundings with unpredictable consequences. For this reason, it is essential to understand the nature of the scientific enterprise, what it reveals, and where its limits lie.

As a brand-new assistant professor in the early 1960s, I taught a course in genetics, my field of specialty, with all of the enthusiasm of an ambitious hotshot on the ladder to tenure, recognition, and bigger grants. After one of my first students had been in my lab a while, he remarked that he had assumed that geneticists knew almost everything. "Now that I've been doing experiments for a year," he went on, "I realize we know almost nothing."

He was absolutely right, of course. In spite of the vaunted "success" of modern science, it has a terrible weakness, one that is inherent in its methodology. Scientists focus on a part of the world that they then isolate, control, and measure. They gain an understanding of and power over that fragment of nature without knowing how it meshes with other components of a system. The insights we acquire are a fractured mosaic of bits and pieces instead of an integrated whole. Thus, we may invent powerful techniques to manipulate genetic material, for example, without knowing what it will do to the whole animal.

Those who have been practising science for a while know that experiments are far more likely to yield a puzzle than a satisfying answer. So while the spectacular pictures from satellites passing by our neighbouring planets may have eliminated a few theories, they generated far more questions. There is something reassuring in knowing that nature is a lot more complex than we can imagine.

But the practice of science has changed radically during the past decades. After Sputnik was launched in 1957, the United States responded by pouring money into universities and students to catch up. It was a golden period for scientists as good research in just about any area was supported. When I graduated in 1961 as an expert on the behaviour of chromosomes in fruit flies, my peers and I could choose from several job offers and grants. We were engaged in a quest for knowledge purely for the sake of knowing, and we took it for granted that good research would eventually lead to ideas that could be applied.

In the ensuing years, science has become extremely competitive because of the high stakes that come with success. Thirty years ago, a productive scientist in my field might publish one major paper a year. Now several articles are expected annually while a publication record of a dozen or more is not unusual. But today's articles are often repetitive or report small incremental additions of knowledge, thereby fragmenting knowledge even further.

Since scientific ideas and techniques have created spectacular new high-tech industries, governments perceive research as vital fuel for the economic engine. Consequently, research funding agencies now look for work that promises to pay off in some practical way, and when applying for grants, scientists have to play a game by claiming or implying that the research being proposed will lead to some beneficial discovery. If you look at the titles of Canadian research grant proposals, you would think that all of the world's problems could be solved by scientists right here.

Of course, that's not true at all. Even if we funded people adequately (which Canada does not), few if any of those solutions will be achieved as projected. The game of grant-seeking perpetrates a mistaken notion of how science is done. Scientists do not proceed linearly to a specific goal, going from experiment 1 to 2 to 3 to a cure for cancer, for example. If research worked that way, doing science would be routine and far less interesting. The fact is, most scientists start from an initial curiosity about some aspect of nature. They design experiments to satisfy that interest, then lurch down unexpected side streets, blunder into blind alleys and, perhaps, through luck and perceptiveness, connect unrelated ideas to produce something useful.

But many young scientists actually believe that science advances in a straight line and that the claims made in grant proposals can be achieved. And the media tend to reinforce the notions with breathless reports of new discoveries and liberal use of the word *breakthrough*. People are relying

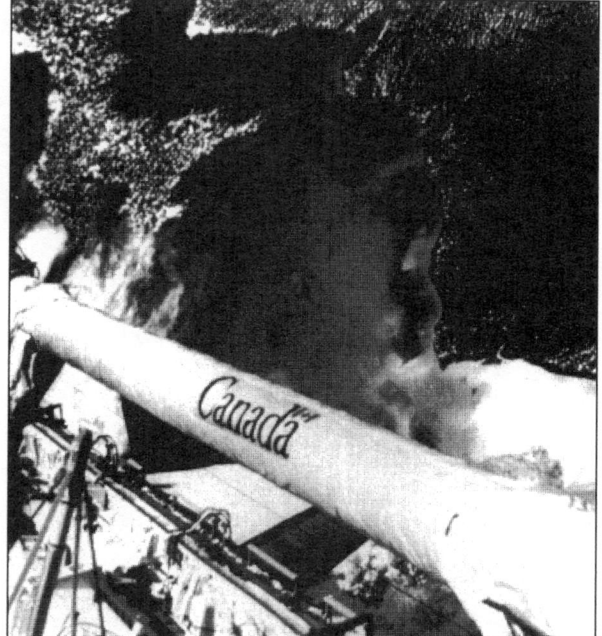

Courtesy of NASA.

The Canadarm—Canada's contribution to the US space shuttle program.

on this unwarranted optimism when they believe the "experts" will take care of a problem.

But the consequences of the major hazards facing us today—atmospheric change, pollution, deforestation, overpopulation, species extinction, et cetera—cannot be scientifically predicted, let alone resolved, because we have only a fragmentary understanding of nature. When scientists say "more information is needed" before a course of action can be planned for an issue like global warming, they give a mistaken impression that such knowledge can be quickly acquired and that, until it is, the problem isn't real, so we can carry on with business as usual.

Scientists who claim their work will solve global hunger, pollution, or overpopulation do not understand the social, economic, religious, and political roots of the problems that preclude scientific solution. There is a vital role for science today in detecting and warning of changes and unpredictable hazards, but scientists have to get rid of the pernicious myth about the potential of their work to solve all our problems.

Science, Technology, and the Environment

by David Suzuki

DON'T WORRY. *They'll* find an answer" is a common response to a news report on some impending disaster. "They," of course, are scientists and engineers, and the widespread faith in them is easy to understand. We are surrounded by a technological cornucopia that attests to their success while the media regularly announce. "breakthroughs" that promise to make life better. The achievements of science and technology are remarkable. My father's cure from cancer and the effective treatment of my father-in-law's heart disease fill me with gratitude for the advances in medical science. I couldn't do what I do without a telephone, fax, or laptop computer. And there will be more miracles from science in the future. But history amply shows that every technology, however powerful and beneficent also has costs, side effects that cannot be anticipated because our knowledge of the world is so limited and fragmentary.

Nevertheless, there is a widespread belief that scientists and engineers can solve all problems, including environmental ones. Consider the threat of global warming that results from the buildup of greenhouse gases like carbon dioxide. The United States has vigorously opposed setting targets for carbon dioxide reduction and expects instead that new technological solutions will allow continued increases in greenhouse gases *and* protection of the biosphere. Thus, a workshop sponsored by the prestigious U.S. National Academy of Sciences recommended starting a two-year search for major ways to manipulate the atmosphere. One idea being actively studied was advanced by California scientist John Martin. He suggests that spreading massive amounts of iron across the Antarctic Ocean will fertilize the iron-deficient waters and stimulate huge algal blooms, which will then remove carbon dioxide from the atmosphere. To support his scheme, Martin showed that added iron stimulated a tenfold increase in algal growth in bottles of Antarctic water.

Scientists learn by separating a phenomenon from everything else so that they can focus on it alone. They thus gain insights into the properties of isolated *fragments* of nature, but what they learn is of little value in predicting the consequences of applying the information gained. Iron added to a bottle may stimulate algae growth, but it is absurd to expect such a simple cause-effect consequence from spreading iron over the Antarctic Ocean!

Many schemes for atmospheric modification are in the same class as Martin's in scale and hubris. Californian Dwain Spencer proposes towing huge grids along the ocean to "farm" seaweed. Two and a half million square kilometres of ocean surface, he calculates, could grow enough plants to remove a billion tonnes of carbon dioxide a year. Then the plants can be harvested and allowed to ferment. The methane produced could be used as fuel, while the $C0_2$ would be trapped. On the basis of a Japanese report that $C0_2$ near deep-sea vents liquefies and behaves like a solid, Spencer suggests waste carbon dioxide could be liquefied and dumped onto the ocean floor.

It has been proposed that as global temperature increases, the oceans could be covered with white polystyrene balls, or all house rooftops painted white to reflect solar energy back into space. Another idea is to launch a series of satellites that will spread an immense sheet of thin film in outer space and cast a shadow over part of the Earth to cool it down. An area equivalent to "only" two percent of the Earth's surface, it is estimated, would compensate for an increase of twice as much carbon dioxide.

Columbia University geochemist Wallace Broecker points out that volcanic eruptions release sulphur dioxide, which reflects sunlight. Broecker calculates that warming due to a doubling in $C0_2$ levels could be cancelled out by spreading 35 million tonnes of sulphur dioxide from a fleet of several hundred jumbo jets working around the clock. Unfortunately, sulphur dioxide causes acid rain, but his logic would suggest that another fleet of planes could spray a neutralizing agent into the air, and we could let technology run amok.

The ecological consequences of the proposed

technological "solutions" to atmospheric change cannot be predicted. But we can say with full confidence there will be enormous, unexpected results that could be as destructive as the condition being treated. However, if the solution is uncertain, the *cause* of atmospheric change is obvious—it is *us*, our numbers, our technology, our lifestyles. And the safest, easiest "answer" is equally clear: we have to reduce output of the offending molecules. We don't need more science, only political will.

Belief in technological know-how was implicit in Robert Bourassa's grand scheme to harness every major watershed in Québec's north, thereby converting James Bay into a freshwater lake. The same belief allows the forest industry to state that large-scale clear-cut logging, slash burning, monoculture planting, fertilizing, and chemical spraying preserve "forests forever." Techno-optimism enables "experts" to claim they can predict and manage the consequences of massive dams, oil developments, and pulp mills.

While technological innovation has created unprecedented levels of health, consumer goods, physical comfort and affluence for a privileged minority on the planet, life has not improved for most of humankind. Indeed, global degradation through atmosphere change, toxic pollution, overpopulation, agricultural land loss, deforestation, and species extinction now threatens all life and is often caused and exacerbated by our use of more science and technology. Yet we remain oblivious to the costs and negative consequences of new technologies.

I was once a guest on Peter Gzowski's *90 Minutes Live*, along with writer Kurt Vonnegut, Jr., and ex-Harvard psychologist Timothy Leary. Leary expounded the benefits of SMIILE—Space Migration, Intelligence Increase and Life Extension. He was deadly serious, but Vonnegut and I dismissed his ideas as the result of too much LSD. But in a delightful book with the zany title *Great Mambo Chicken and the Transhuman Experiment*, Ed Regis makes it clear that Leary was simply following some of the leading scientists of our time. The book is an entertaining but serious chronicle of the history and personalities behind mind-popping notions. Cryonics is the freezing of the dead for resuscitation by advanced societies of the future. The L5 Society envisions the construction of immense colonies in outer space to absorb Earth's excess population. Nanotechnology is the creation of machines the size of molecules. Immortality is promised by duplicating all of human memory in a computer and beaming millions of backup copies across the universe. Star lifting refers to taking the sun apart and "harvesting" its energy more efficiently. Cosmic engineering is done by moving entire galaxies with vast solar sails. And as Regis documents, respectable, often preeminent, scientists promulgate and legitimate these ideas.

The resulting techno-optimism is fed by what Regis calls "fin-de-siècle hubristic mania," an irrepressible urge to break past the physical limits restraining humankind and a belief in the power of the human intellect to do so. Columbia University physicist Gerald Feinberg sums it up in a catechism that "everything possible will eventually be accomplished."

Fear of death and an ache for immortality also impel the technological drive. Whether it's cryonics, computer duplication of human memory, or engineering a more "efficient" universe, the goal is to exist forever. And if death is unacceptable, so, too, are the inadequacies of the human condition. Thus, Regis quotes Carnegie-Mellon computer whiz Hans Moravec on biological needs like food and sex: "I resent the fact that I have these very insistent drives which take an enormous amount of effort to satisfy and are never completely appeased." Regis cites aeronautical engineer Bob Truax, asking, "What right-minded engineer would try to build any machine out of lime and jelly! Bone and protoplasm are extremely poor structural materials."

To technocrats, nature itself can be improved. Austrian physicist Cesar Marchetti believes that "a trillion people can live beautifully on the Earth for an unlimited time and without exhausting any primary resource and without overloading the environment." It just requires remaking the planet so that our "coupling with the Earth will be practically nil." Princeton physicist Gerard O'Neill prefers space colonies because they would be "far more comfortable, productive, and attractive than is most of Earth." His colleague Freeman Dyson regards galaxies "in a wild state" as "wastefully shining all over the Galaxy." He suggests they be brought under human control and put to use. This is the very attitude underlying many megaprojects on Earth.

Regis shows that our techno-faith is rooted in hubris, fear of death, and an alienation from our biological roots so profound that we actually loathe our bodies and hold nature in contempt. It is a tragically perverse and misguided basis for applying the enormous power of science and technology.

Biosphere II—A Stunt

by David Suzuki

The complex and elegant balance of land, sky, oceans, and living things that keeps the planet habitable lies far beyond our scientific understanding at this moment. Nevertheless, as global destruction continues, the search for technological fixes continues.

Perhaps nothing better illustrates this self-deceptive faith than a project attempting to duplicate the entire biosphere.

At a conference in Kyoto in 1990, the Japanese multimillionaire who paid for the meeting held up a flask half filled with water containing a water plant and a live goldfish. The neck of the flask was completely sealed. "I have had this for over a month," he said, "and it has changed my life." He went on to tell us how astonished he was at the ability of sunlight alone to keep plant photosynthesis and fish respiration going. It is an impressive lesson. Still, the closed system will become unbalanced, the water will turn foul, and the fish and plant will die. But for weeks, even months, such a flask gives the comforting *illusion* of being in equilibrium.

In February 1992, with much fanfare, four men and four women were sealed in an immense steel-and-glass structure just north of Tucson, Arizona, at the edge of the Sonora Desert. The complex, called Biosphere II, houses an expensive and ambitious attempt to mimic the complex community of organisms on the planet (Biosphere I is the entire planet). Biosphere II is a huge greenhouse covering 1.2 hectares in which the diverse ecosystems of the planet are simulated in seven different *biomes*, representations of biogeographical settings, including deserts, tropical rainforests, and a 25-foot-deep "ocean."

Until 1994, the inhabitants of this structure will live off the "land," on the productive output of more than 3,800 species of plants and animals that have been assembled there. The "bionauts" are supposed to depend only on the air, water, and food recycled and generated within the structures. These high-tech hunter-gatherers live in apartments and are linked to the outside world through computers, while the entire system is supposed to be completely physically sealed off from Biosphere I.

Biosphere II was originally developed to determine whether selfsustaining and self-regenerating units could be created in outer space for interplanetary travel or permanent stations on the moon or Mars. But now that the global environment is in crisis, the project is being promoted as an attempt to learn about the way Earth's ecosystems work. Already over $30 million has been invested in a project that could end up costing well over $100 million.

Its scientific pretensions are absurd. Like the sealed bottle with plant and fish, Biosphere II has sufficient complexity to maintain an illusion of equilibrium and balance in a closed system. But it would take decades to be sure such a habitat is stable, and it would be astonishing if it were. Biosphere II is like the popular mechanical dinosaurs currently touring museums—impressive at first sight, but actually grotesque simplifications of the real thing.

We know so little about the components and interactions of stable ecosystems that we *cannot* duplicate them. Besides, Biosphere II maintains its "environment" only with computers that regulate temperature, humidity, tides, and seasonal change, while an entire basement of machinery is needed to cool and filter the air, store water, and recycle animal waste. Biosphere II is nothing but a very elaborate zoo or herbarium in which every component is selected and managed by people, not nature.

For over three billion years, life on earth survived and changed with only sunlight as an external energy source. Today, in the span of less than a century, much of this is now endangered. Of course, even if the environment is so changed that humanity can no longer survive, life of some sort will persist. But it will be a radically different mix of organisms, and many of the products of billions of years of evolution will have been snuffed out. Biosphere II diverts attention from our real need to study authentic ecosystems that could provide serious insights into the basis of stability on Biosphere I.

By embarking on a stunt with a lot of media hype, the proponents of Biosphere II divert money and attention away from a more urgent challenge—saving the planet's diversity of lifeforms by protecting their habitats. Harvard biologist E.O. Wilson once told me that more money is spent in New York City bars in two weeks than total world expenditures to study tropical rainforests over a year. The effort and money invested in Biosphere II is of little scientific value and merely adds to the widespread public impression that we are in control and can create our own livable environment. That is what is killing the planet.

Pandora's Box

by David Suzuki

The planet today is undergoing a massive ecological transformation as a result of the application of science and technology. We therefore have to consider the long-term ecological effects of everything we do today, especially when using new technologies. But from local controversies over urban aerial spraying and industrial pollution all the way to megaprojects like nuclear power plants and hydroelectric dams, long-term deleterious costs simply cannot be avoided. The reason is that with *any* new development the potential benefits

such as jobs, profit, consumer products, or material comfort are immediate, obvious, and attractive. But it is impossible to anticipate their long-term social and ecological impacts. We are too ignorant about the physical and biological makeup of the planet to make even the crudest predictions. As well each action we take has complex synergistic interactions with its surroundings. And the ultimate in unpredictability is human motives and behaviour.

Every technology, however beneficial, has negative costs, but because we lack predictive powers, those who raise questions about possible dangers end up sounding like party poopers whose arguments are weak or contrived. The clear and tangible benefits of new ideas are compelling compared to vague negative concerns and so technological development becomes almost inevitable.

If inevitable but unpredictable hazards accompany any new technology, how are we to learn to

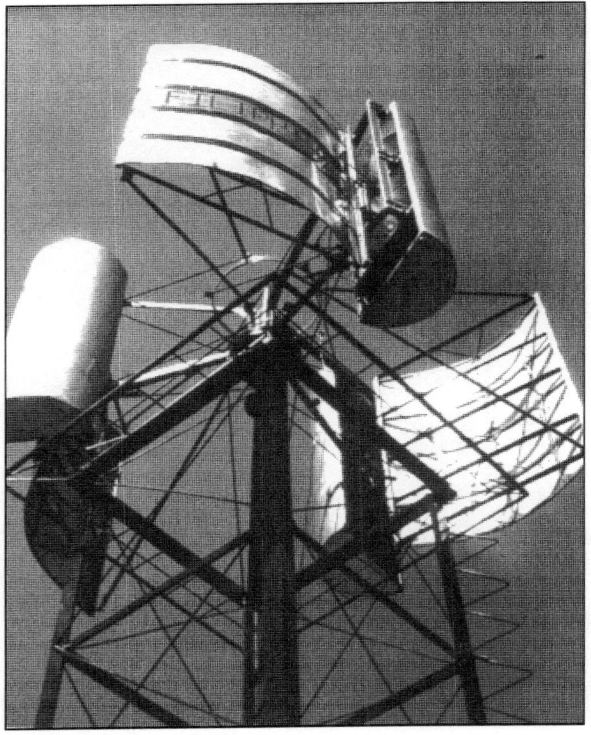

deal with innovations to minimize their deleterious effects? It's a losing cause if we continue to weigh immediate and obvious benefits against only what we know to be the obvious consequences, because again and again we encounter entirely new phenomena after the fact. The only help we have to guide us in navigating those novel waters of the future is the past.

History provides the only real data against which today's proposed projects can be evaluated. Unfortunately, we pay too little attention to the lessons of the past. For example, as a genetics student, I was never taught that ill-considered attempts to manage human heredity were spurred on and legitimated by the exaggerated claims of geneticists early in the century. Nor was I told that Hitler's program of race purification was built on these claims. Instead, I was taught science's history as a series of triumphant intellectual "breakthroughs" that have advanced Western civilization to its present heights.

The history of science and its application as it is usually taught is a fabrication in which the negative consequences of new ideas have been omitted or so minimally portrayed as to seem insignificant. Scientists are depicted as larger-than-life heroes driven by a search for truth in the service of humankind. Of course, a few of them are, but as a group, scientists exhibit the entire range of human foibles from idealism to greed, zeal, and bigotry. And when their powerful ideas and inventions are co-opted for political or economic purposes, all the noble intentions get shoved aside.

I arrived in England in 1992 just as a six-part series called *Pandora's Box* was broadcast on the BBC. It looked at the history of new technological developments from the time they were conceived to the present. Programs were devoted to documenting the track record of economics as a science, the story of DDT, the history of nuclear power, the use of mathematics in systems analysis, the Volta River power project in Ghana, and the way society in the Soviet Union was managed scientifically. The programs were based primarily on historical film footage and interviews with survivors of the events documented in the reports. Each story was a devastating chronicle of high expectations and promise of new scientific and technological ideas and their ultimate subversion and perversion by political or economic imperatives.

Pandora's Box is not an anti-scientific diatribe but a serious look at the way our lives and surroundings have been changed by technology and science. The programs demand that we examine more deeply such glibly promoted notions as sustainable development or genetic engineering. Let's consider one of them, the story of hydroelectric development in Africa that is particularly poignant and relevant to Canadians.

In 1951, a British colony then known as Gold Coast became the first African nation whose citizens voted for independence. A charismatic leader, Kwame Nkrumah, was swept into power as head of what would become Ghana. The country seemed to be a model for the rest of Africa—rich in natural resources, with its own universities, doctors, and lawyers, and led by a man with vision. Nkrumah wanted to transform Ghana into a modern industrial state within a generation and believed his goal could be achieved through hydro power.

Since the 1920s, British engineers had proposed to harness the Volta River. As a student in the United States, Nkrumah had been inspired by the post-Depression dam projects of President Roosevelt. Cheap electricity, Nkrumah reasoned, would light up Ghanaian homes and attract foreign industrial investment. Britain encouraged this vision with promises of technical and financial help for the project in return for cheap aluminum.

However, uncontrollable events deflected these plans in 1956 when Britain invaded Egypt to protect its interests in the Suez Canal. This costly venture forced Britain to back out of the Volta River project. Nkrumah turned to the United States for financing and was encouraged by President Eisenhower to contact Edgar Kaiser, who needed power for his aluminum company. Kaiser's promise to build a plant in Ghana allowed Nkrumah to secure the largest loan ever given by the World Bank to that time to build the Volta River dam.

Ghana had its own rich bauxite deposits, and with an educated citizenry had the potential to create its own indigenous aluminum industry that would take everything from mining the ore to processing it and manufacturing finished products. Fearful that Ghanaian politicians might be tempted to nationalize the industry and keep the profits in the country, Kaiser forced Nkrumah to agree to import and process American bauxite. And once the World Bank loan was assured, Kaiser demanded electricity at the lowest rate paid by its global competitors. In essence, Ghana would be subsidizing an American company to process American bauxite to provide aluminum ingots to American manufacturers. By then, too much was riding on the project for Nkrumah to pull out.

By the time the dam was completed early in 1966, Ghana was deeply in debt, its foreign reserves depleted. Ghana was also caught up as a pawn in the Cold War, and two months later, a coup that some claim was engineered by the CIA overthrew Nkrumah. He fled to Guinea where he died in 1972. By the end of the 1970s, Ghana had endured seven coups. The World Bank loan was repaid and the aluminum company profited, but the country failed to realize its bright promise. Instead, Ghana and Nkrumah seemed to fulfill all the negative expectations of the industrialized world, even though their fate was largely the result of exploitation by the rich countries.

The BBC program barely hints at the considerable environmental and social consequences of the Volta River project. But as Canadians debate the ecological and economic costs of large dams, the tragic story of Ghana resonates familiarly. As we chart our way into the future, we cannot afford to ignore the painful lessons already provided by the history of others.

James Bay Project

by David Suzuki

In our concern with serving the immediate needs of our own species, politicians make decisions based on economic, social, or political imperatives that have vast repercussions for other species, whole ecosystems and, eventually, other human beings.

Some of the planet's priceless and irreplaceable ecosystems in exotic places like Sarawak, the Amazon, and Zaire are now being invaded by human activity. But if poverty and ignorance in poor countries blind people to the consequences of their actions, what is our excuse?

At this moment, Hydro-Québec is pressing on to fulfill Premier Robert Bourassa's grand vision of harnessing for hydroelectric power all of the major rivers draining into James and southern Hudson bays from Québec. The James Bay Project (JBP) is the largest development ever undertaken in the history of North America and is a technological experiment with ecological repercussions that extend far beyond the confines of Québec. The land area affected is as large as France, while the enormous inland sea formed by James and Hudson bays will be seriously affected.

Every spring in these waters, ice formed with salt water melts in the bays and the freshwater runoff into estuaries stimulates a bloom of ice algae, the basis of a food chain extending to cod, seals, and whales. Each year, hundreds of beluga whales of the eastern herd return to the estuaries. In the fall, millions of migratory birds—ducks, geese, shorebirds—stop at biological oases on the bay edges to fatten up for flights as far as the tip of South America!

Phase I of the JBP, begun in 1971, has already flooded 10,000 square kilometres. Phase II will inundate 5,000 more. Having been exempted from environmental impact assessments on Phase I, Hydro-Québec wants to carry on with the second phase before even assessing the ecological effects already caused by the first!

In the Arctic, *timing* is everything. Plants and animals in the north have evolved an impeccable synchrony with seasonal productivity in specific regions. Through narrow temporal and geographic windows, life has flourished, but unlike human beings, wild organisms can't change their growth cycle, feeding, nesting areas, or time of arrival. They are locked into a genetic destiny that has been honed over aeons of time. Phase II will completely reverse the seasonal water cycles in fertile estuaries—spring meltwater will be held back in reservoirs and released in winter to serve peak energy demands. What will the beluga do?

The JBP would never be allowed in the urban areas of the south but went ahead because Bourassa considers northern Québec a wasteland. Yet Cree and Inuit maps are crisscrossed with family hunting and fishing territories, seasonal routes, and campsites—the entire area is fully occupied and developed. The JBP is not only flooding Native land, it is poisoning the water. In the Lagrande River reservoirs of Phase I, mercury in soil and sediment has been converted by bacteria into methyl mercury, then ingested and concentrated up the food chain to reach toxic levels in fish. Hydro-Québec's proposed solution for the Cree? Stop eating the fish. Native people may physically survive the shopping malls, junk food, and television brought by the JBP, but their way of life can't. The body of knowledge acquired by aboriginal people over thousands of years allowed them to live rich lives in balance with the animals and plants that have sustained them. But now that irreplaceable traditional knowledge is being erased in a single generation.

Québecois in unprecedented numbers are asking, "What is the value of the JBP for Québec?" With programs of conservation and alternate energy, the province has no need for more energy for decades. Critics in Québec say the JBP Phase I has already saddled Québec with a debt of $20 billion, while all the planned building to come could add at least $60 billion more. Hydro-Québec says it has lucrative contracts to export electricity to the United States but has not made the details public. And cheap energy is being used to attract aluminum smelting plants that yield relatively few jobs while polluting air and water with highly toxic effluents that put both wildlife and workers at risk. Québec is competing with Brazil to be the world's top aluminum producer. Like a desperate Third World country, the Québec government is willing to destroy unique ecological treasures, ignore indigenous people, increase pollution, and add to massive debt for an illusion of political action and economic responsibility.

In Québec, groups representing one of every six Québecois are demanding a moratorium on the JBP. They range from churches to labour unions, hunters, fishers, environmentalists, and the Parti Québecois.

The JBP II can and must be stopped. Outside Québec, we must make sure that Manitoba and Ontario do not go ahead with plans to dam and divert their rivers into James and Hudson bays and demand federal imposition of jurisdictional rights to protect the environment.

The fate of many ecosystems in Canada now seems to hinge on the application of an environmental assessment (EA) of proposed developments like dams. It's ironic that so much rests on an EA. Scientists are still trying to describe the elementary units of matter and how they interact, while our knowledge about how gene activity is controlled or cells function is primitive. When it comes to communities of organisms in complex ecosystems, most of the component species are not yet identified, so we have very little insight into their interaction and interdependence.

Given the state of our ignorance, the notion that in only a few months enough information can be collected to assess the consequences of massive projects like dams, aluminum plants, or pulp mills is absurd. The so-called "data" assembled in an EA are so limited in scale, scope, and duration as to be virtually worthless scientifically. At the very least, an EA should be initiated from a profound sense of humility at the inadequacy of our knowledge. At best, the EA can highlight questions, reveal areas of ignorance, and warn of potentially sensitive effects. Anyone who claims to know enough to predict with confidence the consequences of new developments simply doesn't understand the limited nature of scientific knowledge.

In our form of government, only *people* vote; owls, trees, or rivers don't. A minister designated to protect the environment must therefore act according to the demands of a human electorate. So a watershed, old-growth forest, ocean bottom, or newly discovered oil deposit can be assessed only in terms of potential human utility. If trees could vote, we would have radically different priorities. Since they can't, society must incorporate an ecological perspective in our value system.

None of the three federal environment ministers appointed since the 1988 election (Lucien Bouchard, Robert de Cotret, Jean Charest) has exhibited any understanding of the value of ecological diversity, nor have they developed a vision of current events in the perspective of past and future generations. In their feeble attempts to force legally required EAs on the provinces, the ministers have dickered, threatened, and perhaps made secret deals, yet all the while, development continued! What use is debate over the future of an old-growth forest, for example, if the contentious trees are being cut down as the argument is going on? Yet that's what de Cotret did in allowing the Rafferty and Alameda dams. De Cotret claimed an EA on the Oldman Dam could be carried out *after* its completion. That's like doing an EA on the future of a forest after it's been clear-cut.

Phase II of the James Bay Project represents a critical test of federal commitment to the environment. There are compelling reasons—economic, environmental, cultural, and social—to question the sanity of this immense undertaking. The Inuit and Cree who live in the area are militantly opposed to the dam and argue that no amount of money will make up for the complete devastation of their traditional way of life. Economists say the project is a fiscal swamp that will be paid for by future generations, while environmentalists predict an ecological disaster.

People are what they *do*, not what they *say*. The provincial premiers, for all their rhetoric of environmental concern, are preoccupied with maximizing economic returns regardless of environmental consequences. Inadequate as the EA is, it is the only way at present to raise substantive ecological questions. The federal government must demand a full EA on the entire James Bay Project *before* any more work is done on Phase II.

Even as the Québec Cree were battling with Hydro-Québec and the Québec government in the fall of 1991, their relatives, the Cree of northern Ontario, were granted a reprieve by Ontario Hydro on their plans to build more dams on the Moose River system. But each province regards its plans as its own business.

We assess the impact of human activity on a piecemeal basis that seems to suggest whatever we're looking at, whether a dam, new coal plant, or another logging road, can be examined by itself in isolation from anything in its neighbourhood. But as we learned when British Columbia's Bennett Dam was built, 1,200 kilometres away, in Alberta, the world's largest freshwater delta was severely impacted. Everything on the planet is interlinked in a single, finite global biosphere. From this perspective, it's clear the human borders we construct for political, social, or economic reasons do not conform to the geological, climatic, and ecological factors that govern the distribution of animals and plants.

We should be looking at the *cumulative* effect of all of the dams and development affecting the James-Hudson Bay eco-complex. There should be mechanisms and structures like the International Joint Commission on the Great Lakes to carry out such transprovincial assessments. On too many issues—clear-cut logging of a B.C. old-growth forest, oil exploration in the Arctic, fishing policy in the face of declining stocks—we act as if each is a local matter to be resolved as an isolated problem. In failing to assess the total ecological context within which the issue falls, we nickle-and-dime the biosphere to pieces.

This failing is just as evident at the transnational level. We believe, for example, that the vastness of Canada somehow buffers us against the air pollution of Los Angeles or Mexico City and that it is really their problem, not ours. Yet air is part of a single entity that is contributed to and partaken of by all living things on earth. Bad air in Mexico City or Los Angeles may be more concentrated around their environs, but life everywhere will eventually be exposed to it. The solution to pollution is not dilution. In a finite sphere, there is no way to escape the buildup of whatever we put into the atmosphere.

For the same reason, the fate of huge areas such as the boreal forests of the Prairie provinces, British Columbia's coastal rainforests, and James and Hudson bays is of vital interest to people in the United States and Europe, indeed, everyone on earth. And for the same reason, Canadians are concerned about the future of the rainforests in tropical areas of the planet. We need to transcend borders and to take into account the cumulative impacts of what has already been done around the world. These are the issues that our EAs should address.

Reproductive Biology

by David Suzuki

Most North Americans live in a human-created urban environment. In such surroundings it is easy to consider ourselves as separate from the natural world. But we are constantly reminded of our biological nature on the occasions of birth and death and when faced with disease, aging, and accidents. Women remind us of our biological rhythms each month at menstruation and throughout the process of fertilization, pregnancy, childbirth, and parenting.

Lactation is a definitive characteristic of mammals and has evolved exquisitely to provide infants with antibodies, nutrition, and physical contact. Yet we have attempted to replace that "animal" process with infant formula or cow's milk. We now know that the replacement of mother's milk exacts costs, in the case of cow's milk, by inducing juvenile diabetes and allergies. As well there are studies that suggest children fed cow's milk as babies score significantly lower in IQ tests. It all leads one to ask why there was ever a need to replace mother's milk in the first place. For a growing infant, there is no food more nutritious—always at the right temperature, clean, and made without effort or waste packaging.

In our world today, it seems when there is money to be made, we forget to ask questions like: Do we need it? Is it good for the baby or the mother? What could the medical, social, and environmental costs be? In the case of poor countries, these questions are especially important. But conventional economics doesn't seem to reckon these "externalities" in its costs.

There is an even more powerful and insidious factor than economics at play in the replacement of mother's milk by cow's milk and that is the symbolic conquest of nature by human intellect and technology. Twentieth-century civilization can be characterized by its determination to stamp the imprint of human prowess on the planet. So we try to "manage" the natural world by forcing it to conform to human economic priorities, bureaucratic portfolios, and political boundaries. This attempt to control and dominate is at the core of our global ecocrisis.

That impulse to intervene and manipulate extends to ourselves. We have done it with war, religious proselytizing, and commercials and ads to sell products. And, of course, it has led us to the improvement of human health, nutrition, sanitation, and disease control. But we seem to have lost any sense of boundaries to our reach. At a panel discussion about aging and death, a young man in the audience got up to ask, "When will you geneticists cure the disease of aging?" Senescence and death are natural (and necessary) processes but once converted into a "disease" become a legitimate target for scientists to "cure."

Many people will argue vehemently that human beings are not animals. Every technological "triumph" over human nature in the form of a new drug, cosmetic surgery, infant formula, or oral contraceptive extends our separation from the natural world. It is no wonder then that less and less food is purchased "in the raw" as we attempt to banish all biological traces of blood, feathers, fur, scales, or blemishes. In fact, within the elaborate packaging that often contains it, processed food could be the ultimate distancing from nature—extracts of molecules that no longer bear even traces of their cellular origin.

Like a baby nursing at a mother's breast, birth is an undeniable affirmation of our rootedness in nature. During pregnancy and delivery, all the evolutionary programming in a woman's body takes over. But increasingly, we insert our need to control.

Very early preemies have long been objects for medical intervention and management, and now embryos and fetuses are. Fetal surgery is already being practised in utero and no doubt will increase as diagnostic and surgical techniques are refined and broadened. And now that an egg can be removed from a woman, fertilized in vitro, and allowed to divide several times before insertion into a uterus, new manipulations are possible. At the eight-cell stage, one cell can be removed, its sex determined and its DNA analyzed. Then foreign DNA can be injected into the embryo, which in turn can be inserted into the mother. Thus, embryos can be monitored by quality control and modified if necessary. In the process, the scientist/doctor has become an essential part of the reproductive process, thereby taking us farther from our biological roots and installing greater human control over our own destiny.

What drives us down this path is the belief that we are gifted with the power and the mandate to conquer nature. The more we live in a human-created environment and the more we are separated from our biological roots, the easier it is to see the imposition of the human will as natural. And over and over, we will discover unexpected results, as we are now learning with the totally unnecessary widespread replacement of mother's milk. In order to restore a balance with the natural world, we need a shift in attitude that reinserts us into the natural realm.

SOURCE: From *Time to Change* by David Suzuki, Toronto: Stoddart Publishing Co. Limited, 1994. Reprinted with the permission of the author.

Questions and Topics for Discussion and Writing

1. What does Suzuki mean when he says "we don't need more science, only political will?" How does this statement mesh with the claim advanced by another scientist at the end of the article that "everything possible will eventually be accomplished?"
2. According to Suzuki, why is Biosphere II actually more harmful than helpful to Biosphere I?
3. Suzuki invokes the metaphor of "Pandora's Box" to emphasize his views on African development. What are the origins of this metaphor, and why is it an appropriate one in this case?
4. Despite the increasing number of groups cited by Suzuki that oppose the James Bay Project, it continued. How was this possible?
5. Suzuki disparages medical intervention into the DNA structures of unborn babies. But how does one refute the argument often put forward by those who support the production of "designer genes" that if science allows people to produce the kind of child they want, and they are able to pay for this service, there is no reason not to avail themselves of this technology?

Darwinism Defined

Stephen Jay Gould

Stephen Jay Gould is a professor of biology, geology, and the history of science at Harvard University and a popular writer on natural evolution. In this selection Gould takes to task those commentators who confuse the fact of evolution with theories that explain it. In doing so, he sheds light on not only Darwin's theory of natural selection but the nature of science itself.

Charles Darwin, who was, perhaps, the most incisive thinker among the great minds of history, clearly divided his life's work into two claims of different character: establishing the fact of evolution, and proposing a theory (natural selection) for the mechanism of evolutionary change. He also expressed, and with equal clarity, his judgment about their different status: confidence in the facts of transmutation and genealogical connection among all organisms, and appropriate caution about his unproved theory of natural selection. He stated in the *Descent of Man*: "I had two distinct objects in view; firstly, to show that species had not been separately created, and secondly, that natural selection had been the chief agent of change...If I have erred in...having exaggerated its [natural selection's] power...I have at least, as I hope, done good service in aiding to overthrow the dogma of separate creations."

Darwin wrote those words more than a century ago. Evolutionary biologists have honored his fundamental distinction between fact and theory ever since. Facts are the world's data; theories are explanations proposed to interpret and coordinate facts. The fact of evolution is as well established as anything in science (as secure as the revolution of the earth about the sun), though absolute certainty has no place in our lexicon. Theories, or statements about the causes of documented evolutionary change, are now in a period of intense debate—a good mark of science in its healthiest state. Facts don't disappear while scientists debate theories. As I wrote in an early issue of this magazine (*Discover*, May 1981), "Einstein's theory of gravitation replaced Newton's, but apples did not suspend themselves in mid-air pending the outcome."

Since facts and theories are so different, it isn't surprising that these two components of science have had separate histories ever since Darwin. Between 1859 (the year of publication for the *Origin of Species*) and 1882 (the year of Darwin's death), nearly all thinking people came to accept the fact of evolution. Darwin lies beside Newton in Westminster Abbey for this great contribution. His theory of natural selection has experienced a much different, and checkered, history. It attracted some notable followers during his lifetime (Wallace in England, Weismann in Germany), but never enjoyed majority support. It became an orthodoxy among English-speaking evolutionists (but never, to this day, in France or Germany) during the 1930s, and received little cogent criticism until the 1970s. The past fifteen years have witnessed a revival of intense and, this time, highly fruitful debate as scientists discover and consider the implications of phenomena that expand the potential causes of evolution well beyond the unitary focus of strict Darwinism (the struggle for reproductive success among organisms within populations). Darwinian selection will not be overthrown; it will remain a central focus of more inclusive evolutionary theories. But new findings and interpretations at all levels, from molecular change in genes to patterns of overall diversity in geological time, have greatly expanded the scope of important causes—from random, selectively neutral change at the genetic level, to punctuated equilibria and catastrophic mass extinction in geological time.

In this period of vigorous pluralism and intense debate among evolutionary biologists, I am greatly saddened to note that some distinguished commentators among non-scientists, in particular Irving Kristol in a *New York Times* Op Ed piece[1] of Sept. 30, 1986 ("Room for Darwin and the Bible"), so egregiously misunderstand the character of our discipline and continue to confuse this central distinction between secure fact and healthy debate about theory.

I don't speak of the militant fundamentalists who label themselves with the oxymoron "scientific creationists," and try to sneak their Genesis literalism into high school classrooms under the guise of scientific dissent. I'm used to their rhetoric, their dishonest mis- and half-quotations, their constant repetition of "useful" arguments that even they must recognize as nonsense (disproved human footprints on dinosaur trackways in Texas, visible misinterpretation of thermodynamics to argue that life's complexity couldn't increase without a divine boost). Our struggle with these ideologues is political, not intellectual. I speak instead of our allies among people committed to reason and honourable argument.

Kristol, who is no fundamentalist, accuses evolutionary biologists of bringing their troubles with creationists upon themselves by too zealous an insistence upon the truths of Darwin's world. He writes: "...the debate has become a dogmatic crusade on both sides, and our educators, school administrators, and textbook publishers find themselves trapped in the middle." He places the primary blame upon a supposedly anti-religious stance in biological textbooks: "There is no doubt that most of our textbooks are still written as participants in the 'warfare' between science and religion that is our heritage from the 19th century. And there is also little doubt that it is this pseudoscientific dogmatism that has provoked the current religious reaction."

Kristol needs a history lesson if he thinks that current creationism is a product of scientific intransigence. Creationism, as a political movement against evolution, has been a continually powerful force since the days of the Scopes trial. Rather than using evolution to crusade against religion in their texts, scientists have been lucky to get anything at all about evolution into books for high school students ever since Scopes's trial in 1925. My own high school biology text, used in the liberal constituency of New York City in 1956, didn't even mention the word evolution. The laws that were used against Scopes and cowed textbook publishers into submission weren't overturned by the Supreme Court until 1968 (*Epperson v. Arkansas*).

But what about Kristol's major charge—anti-religious prejudice and one-dimensional dogmatism about evolution in modern textbooks? Now we come to the heart of what makes me so sad about Kristol's charges and others in a similar vein. I don't deny that some texts have simplified, even distorted, in failing to cover the spectrum of modern debates; this, I fear, is a limitation of the genre itself (and the reason why I, though more of a writer than most scientists, have never chosen to compose a text). But what evidence can Kristol or anyone else provide to demonstrate that evolutionists have been worse than scientists from other fields in glossing over legitimate debate within their textbooks?

Consider the evidence. Two textbooks of evolution now dominate the field. One has as its senior author Theodosius Dobzhansky, the greatest evolutionist of our century, and a lifelong Russian Orthodox; nothing anti-religious could slip past his watchful eye. The second, by Douglas Futuyma, is a fine book by a kind and generous man who could never be dogmatic about anything except intolerance. (His book gives a fair hearing to my own heterodoxies, while dissenting from them.)

[1] An invited editorial article published on the page opposite to the newspaper's own editorials—hence an "Op Ed" piece. *[The Editor.]*

"Survival of the Fittest"

Charles Darwin

Charles Darwin (1809–1882) was the author of *The Origin of Species* and the major exponent of the theory of evolution.

Darwin's voyages to the Galapagos islands and examination of the fossil record convinced him that species had evolved over millions of years through a mechanism which he called natural selection.

Darwin saw that there were a number of variations within each species; he deduced, therefore, that there was a struggle for existence within each species. Those members of a species which could best adapt to changing conditions in

the environment would survive and reproduce. Darwin called this process of natural selection and adaptation the "survival of the fittest"—those beings who were best suited or "fitted" to the environment would survive and leave offspring.

The principles of evolution were, therefore, the mechanism of natural selection, adaptation, and struggle for existence or survival. The memorable line from the poet Tennyson, "Nature red in tooth and claw," symbolized the idea of evolution through natural selection.

Darwin's theory of natural selection is to this day the main unifying basis of biology.

When we come to popular writing about evolution, I suppose that my own essays are as well read as any. I don't think that Kristol could include me among Darwinian dogmatists, for most of my essays focus upon my disagreements with the strict version of natural selection. I also doubt that Kristol would judge me anti-religious, since I have campaigned long and hard against the same silly dichotomy of science versus religion that he so rightly ridicules. I have written laudatory essays about several scientists (Burnet, Duvier, Buckland, and Gosse, among others) branded as theological dogmatists during the nineteenth-century reaction; and, while I'm not a conventional believer, I don't consider myself irreligious.

Kristol's major error lies in his persistent confusion of fact with theory. He accuses us—without giving a single concrete example, by the way—of dogmatism about *theory* and sustains his charge by citing our confidence in the *fact* of transmutation. "It is reasonable to suppose that if evolution were taught more cautiously, as a conglomerate idea consisting of conflicting hypotheses rather than as an unchallengeable certainty, it would be far less controversial."

Well, Mr. Kristol, evolution (as theory) is indeed "a conglomerate idea consisting of conflicting hypotheses," and I and my colleagues teach it as such. But evolution is also a fact of nature, and so do we teach it as well, just as our geological colleagues describe the structure of silicate minerals, and astronomers the elliptical orbits of planets.

Rather than castigate Mr. Kristol any further, I want to discuss the larger issue that underlies both this incident and the popular perception of evolution in general. If you will accept my premise that evolution is as well established as any scientific fact (I shall give the reasons in a moment), then why are we uniquely called upon to justify our chosen profession; and why are we alone subjected to such unwarranted infamy? To this central question of this essay, I suggest the following answer. We haven't received our due for two reasons: (1) a general misunderstanding of the different methods used by all historical sciences (including evolution), for our modes of inference don't match stereotypes of "*the* scientific method"; and (2) a continuing but unjustified fear about the implication both of evolution itself and of Darwin's theory for its mechanism. With these two issues resolved, we can understand both the richness of science (in its pluralistic methods of inquiry) and the absence of any conflict, through lack of common content, between proper science and true religion.

Our confidence in the fact of evolution rests upon copious data that fall, roughly, into three great classes. First, we have the direct evidence of small-scale changes in controlled laboratory experiments of the past hundred years (on bacteria, on almost every measurable property of the fruit fly *Drosophila*), or observed in nature (color changes in moth wings, development of metal tolerance in plants growing near industrial waste heaps), or produced during a few thousand years of human breeding and agriculture. Creationists can scarcely ignore this evidence, so they respond by arguing that God permits limited modification within created types, but that you can never change a cat into a dog (who ever said that you could, or that nature did?).

Second, we have direct evidence for large-scale changes, based upon sequences in the fossil record. The nature of this evidence is often misunderstood by non-professionals who view evolution as a simple ladder of progress, and therefore expect a linear array of "missing links." But evolution is a copiously branching bush, not a ladder. Since our fossil record is so imperfect, we can't hope to find evidence for every tiny twiglet. (Sometimes, in rapidly evolving lineages of abundant organisms restricted to a small area and entombed in sediments with an excellent fossil record, we do discover an entire little bush—but such examples are as rare as they are precious.) In the usual case, we may recover the remains of side branch number 5 from the bush's early history, then bough number 40 a bit later, then the full series of branches 156–161 in a well preserved sequence of younger rocks, and finally surviving twigs 250 and 287.

In other words, we usually find sequences of structural intermediates, not linear arrays of ancestors and descendants. Such sequences provide superb examples of temporally ordered evolutionary trends. Consider the evidence for human evolution in Africa. What more could you ask from a record of rare creatures living in terrestrial environments that provide poor opportunity for fossilization? We have a temporal sequence displaying clear trends in a suite of features, including threefold increase of brain size and corresponding decrease of jaws and teeth. (We are missing direct evidence for an earlier transition to upright posture, but wide-ranging and unstudied sediments of the right age have been found in East Africa, and we have an excellent chance to fill in this part of our story.) What alternative can we suggest to evolution? Would God—for some inscrutable reason, or merely to test our faith—create five species, one after the other (*Australopithecus afarensis, A. Africanus, Homo habilis, H. erectus, and H. sapiens*), to mimic a continuous trend of evolutionary change?

Or, consider another example with evidence of structurally intermediate stages—the transition from reptiles to mammals. The lower jaw of mammals contains but a single bone, the dentary. Reptiles build their lower jaws of several bones. In perhaps the most fascinating of those quirky changes in function that mark pathways of evolution, the two bones articulating the upper and lower jaws of reptiles migrate to the middle ear and become the malleus and incus (hammer and anvil) of mammals.

Creationists, ignorant of hard evidence in the fossil record, scoff at this tale. How could jaw bones become ear bones, they ask. What happened in between? An animal can't work with a jaw half disarticulated during the stressful time of transition.

The fossil record provides a direct answer. In an excellent series of temporally ordered structural intermediates, the reptilian dentary gets larger and larger, pushing back as the other bones of a reptile's lower jaw decrease in size. We've even found a transitional form with an elegant solution to the problem of remaking jaw bones into ear bones. This creature has a double articulation—one between the two bones that become the mammalian hammer and anvil (the old reptilian joint), and a second between the squamosal and dentary bones (the modern mammalian condition). With this built-in redundancy, the emerging mammals could abandon one connection by moving two bones into the ear, while retaining the second linkage, which becomes the sole articulation of modern mammals.

Third, and most persuasive in its ubiquity, we have the signs of history preserved within every organism, every ecosystem, and every pattern of biogeographic distribution, by those pervasive quirks, oddities, and imperfections that record pathways of historical descent. These evidences are indirect, since we are viewing modern results, not the processes that caused them, but what else can we make of the pervasive pattern? Why does our body, from the bones of our back to the musculature of our belly, display the vestiges of an arrangement better suited for quadrupedal life if we aren't the descendants of four-footed creatures? Why do the plants and animals of the Galapagos so closely resemble, but differ slightly from the creatures of Ecuador, the nearest bit of land 600 miles to the east, especially when cool oceanic currents and volcanic substrate make the Galapagos such a different environment from Ecuador (thus removing the potential argument that God makes the best creatures for each place, and small differences only reflect a minimal disparity of environments)? The similarities can only mean that Ecudorian creatures colonized the Galapagos and then diverged by a natural process of evolution.

This method of searching for oddities as vestiges of the past isn't peculiar to evolution, but a common procedure of all historical science. How, for example, do we know that words have histories, and haven't been decreed by some all-knowing committee in Mr. Orwell's bureau of Newspeak? Doesn't the bucolic etymology of so many words testify to a different life style among our ancestors? In this article, I try to "broadcast" some ideas (a mode of sowing seed) in order to counter the most "egregious" of creationist sophistries (the animal *ex grege*, or outside the flock), for which, given the *quid pro quo* of business, this fine magazine pays me an "emolument" (the fee that millers once received to grind corn).

I don't want to sound like a shrill dogmatist shouting "rally round the flag boys," but biologists have reached a consensus, based on these kinds of data, about the fact of evolution. When honest critics like Irving Kristol misinterpret this agreement, they're either confusing our fruitful consonance about mechanisms of change, or they've misinterpreted part of our admittedly arcane technical literature.

Once such misinterpretation has gained sufficient notoriety in the last year that we crave resolution both for its own sake and as an illustration of the frustrating confusion that can arise when scientists aren't clear and when commentators, as a result of hidden agendas, don't listen. Tom Bethell argued in *Harper's* (February 1985) that a group of young taxonomists called pattern cladists have begun to doubt the existence of evolution itself.

This would be truly astounding news, since cladistics is a powerful method dedicated to reforming classification by using only the branching order of lineages on evolutionary trees ("propinquity of descent" in Darwin's lovely phrase), rather than vague notions of overall similarity in form or function. (For example, in the cladistic system, a lungfish is more closely related to a horse than to a salmon because the common ancestor of lungfish and horse is more recent in time than the link point of the lungfish-horse lineage with the branch leading to modern bony fishes (including salmon).

Cladists use only the order of branching to construct their schemes of relationships; it bothers them not a whit that lungfish and salmon look and work so much alike. Cladism, in other words, is the purest of all genealogical systems for classification, since it works only with closeness of common ancestry in time. How preciously ironic then, that this most rigidly evolutionary of all taxonomic systems should become the subject of such extraordinary misunderstanding—as devised by Bethell, and perpetuated by Kristol when he writes: "...many younger biologists (the so-called 'cladists') are persuaded that the differences among species—including those that seem to be closely related—are such as to make the very concept of evolution questionable."

This error arose for the following reason. A small splinter group of cladists (not all of them, as Kristol claims)—"transformed" or "pattern" cladists by their own designation—have adopted what is to me an ill-conceived definition of scientific procedure. They've decided, by misreading Karl Popper's philosophy, that patterns of branching can be established unambiguously as a fact of nature, but that processes causing events of branching, since they can't be observed directly, can't be known with certainty. Therefore, they say, we must talk only of pattern and rigidly exclude all discussion of process (hence "pattern cladistics").

This is where Bethell got everything arse-backwards and began the whole confusion. A philosophical choice to abjure all talk about process isn't the same thing as declaring that no reason for patterns of branching exists. Pattern cladists don't doubt that evolution is the cause behind branching; rather, they've decided that our science shouldn't be discussing causes at all.

Now I happen to think that this philosophy is misguided; in unguarded moments I would even deem it absurd. Science, after all, is fundamentally about process; learning why and how things happen is the soul of our discipline. You can't abandon the search for cause in favor of a dry documentation of pattern. You must take risks of uncertainty in order to probe the deeper questions, rather than stopping with sterile security. You see, now I've blown our cover. We scientists do have our passionate debates—and I've just poured forth an example. But as I wrote earlier, this is a debate about the proper approach to causes, not an argument about whether causes exist, or even whether the cause of branching is evolution or something else. No cladist denies that branching patterns arise by evolution.

This incident also raises the troubling issue of how myths become beliefs through adulterated

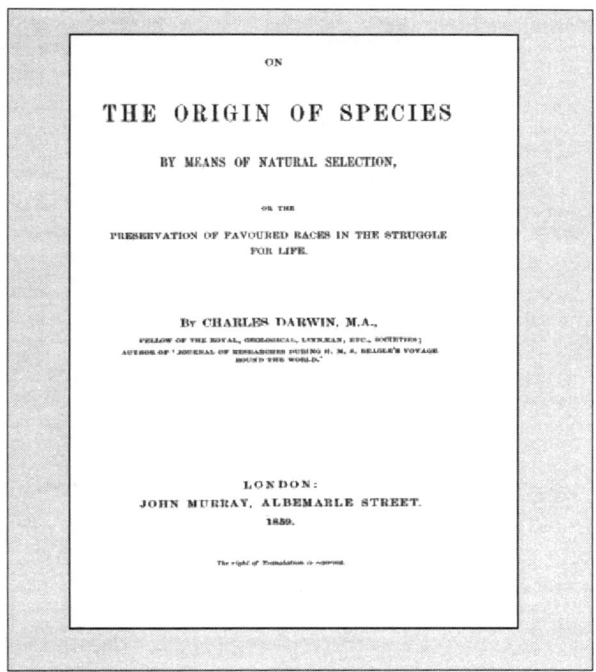

ON

THE ORIGIN OF SPECIES

BY MEANS OF NATURAL SELECTION,

OR THE

PRESERVATION OF FAVOURED RACES IN THE STRUGGLE FOR LIFE.

BY CHARLES DARWIN, M.A.,

FELLOW OF THE ROYAL, GEOLOGICAL, LINNÆAN, ETC., SOCIETIES;
AUTHOR OF 'JOURNAL OF RESEARCHES DURING H. M. S. BEAGLE'S VOYAGE ROUND THE WORLD.'

LONDON:
JOHN MURRAY, ALBEMARLE STREET.
1859.

The right of Translation is reserved.

The title page from Charles Darwin's *On the Origin of Species,* first published in 1859.

"The *Origin* is one of the most important books ever published, and a knowledge of it should be a part of the intellectual equipment of every educated person... The book will endure in future ages so long as a knowldege of science persists among mankind."—*Nature* magazine.

repetition without proper documentation. Bethell began by misunderstanding pattern cladistics, but at least he reports the movement as a small splinter, and tries to reproduce their arguments. then Kristol picks up the ball and recasts it as a single sentence of supposed fact—and all cladists have now become doubters of evolution by proclamation. Thus a movement, by fiat, is turned into its opposite—as the purest of all methods for establishing genealogical connections becomes a weapon for denying the mechanism that all biologists accept as the cause of branching on life's tree: evolution itself. Our genealogy hasn't been threatened, but my geniality has almost succumbed.

Short Excerpt from "On the Origin of Species" by Charles Darwin

Illustrations of the Action of Natural Selection

"In order to make it clear how, as I believe, natural selection acts, I must beg permission to give one or two imaginary illustrations. Let us take the case of a wolf, which preys on various animals, securing some by craft, some by strength, and some by fleetness; and let us suppose that the fleetest prey, a deer for instance, had from any change in the country increased in numbers, or that other prey had decreased in numbers, during that season of the year when the wolf is hardest pressed for food. I can under such circumstances see no reason to doubt that the swiftest and slimmest wolves would have the best chance of surviving, and so be preserved or selected—provided always that they retained strength to master their prey at this or at some other period of the year, when they might be compelled to prey on other animals. I can see no more reason to doubt this, than that man can improve the fleetness of his greyhounds by careful and methodical selection, or by that unconscious selection which results from each man trying to keep the best dogs without any thought of modifying the breed.

"Even without any change in the proportional numbers of the animals on which our wolf preyed, a cub might be born with an innate tendency to pursue certain kinds of prey. Nor can this be thought very improbable; for we often observe great differences in the natural tendencies of our domestic animals; one cat, for instance, taking to catch rats, another mice; one cat, according to Mr. St. John, bringing home winged game, another hares or rabbits, and another hunting on marshy ground and almost nightly catching woodcocks or snipes. The tendency to catch rats rather than mice is known to be inherited. Now, if any slight innate change of habit or of structure benefited an individual wolf, it would have the best chance of surviving and of leaving offspring. Some of its young would probably inherit the same habits or structure, and by the repetition of this process, a new variety might be formed which would either supplant or coexist with the parent-form of wolf. Or, again, the wolves inhabiting a mountainous district, and those frequenting the lowlands, would naturally be forced to hunt different prey; and from the continued preservation of the individuals best fitted for the two sites, two varieties might slowly be formed...."

Charles Darwin, *On the Origin of Species*, London: John Murray, 1859.

When I ask myself why the evidence for evolution, so clear to all historical scientists, fails to impress intelligent nonscientists, I must believe that more than simple misinformation lies at the root of our difficulty with a man like Irving Kristol. I believe that the main problem centers upon a restrictive stereotype of scientific method accepted by most non-practitioners as the essential definition of all scientific work.

We learn in high school about *the* scientific method—a cut-and-dried procedure of simplification to essential components, experiment in the controlled situation of a laboratory, prediction and replication. But the sciences of history—not just evolution but a suite of fundamental disciplines ranging from geology, to cosmology, to linguistics—can't operate by this stereotype. We are charged with explaining events of extraordinary complexity that occur but once in all their details. We try to understand the past, but don't pretend to predict the future. We can't see past processes directly, but learn to infer their operation from preserved results.

Science is a pluralistic enterprise with a rich panoply of methods appropriate for different kinds of problems. Past events of long duration don't lie outside the realm of science because we cannot make them happen in a month within our laboratory. Direct vision isn't the only, or even the usual, method of inference in science. We don't see electrons, or quarks, or chemical bonds, any more than we see small dinosaurs evolve into birds, or India crash into Asia to raise the Himalayas.

William Whewell, the great English philosopher of science during the early nineteenth century, argued that historical science can reach conclusions as well confirmed as any derived from experiment and replication in laboratories, by a method he called "consilience" (literally "jumping together") of inductions. Since we can't see the past directly or manipulate its events, we must use the different tactic of meeting history's richness head on. We must gather its wondrously varied results and search for a coordinating cause that can make sense of disparate data otherwise isolated and uncoordinated. We must see if a set of results so diverse that no one had ever considered their potential coordination might jump together as the varied products of a single process. Thus plate tectonics can explain magnetic stripes on the sea floor, the rise and later erosion of the Appalachians, the earthquakes of Lisbon and San Francisco, the eruption of Mount St. Helens, the presence of large flightless ground birds only on continents once united as Gondwanaland, and the discovery of fossil coal in Antarctica.

Darwin, who understood the different rigor of historical science so well, complained bitterly about those critics who denied scientific status to evolution because they couldn't see it directly or reproduce its historical results in a laboratory. He wrote to Hooker in 1861: "Change of species cannot be directly proved...The doctrine must sink or swim according as it groups and explains phenomena. It is really curious how few judge it in this way, which is clearly the right way." And later, in 1868: "This hypothesis may be tested...by trying whether it explains several large and independent classes of facts; such as the geological succession of organic beings, their distribution in past and present times, and their mutual affinities and homologies."

If a misunderstanding of the different methods of historical inquiry has impeded the recognition of evolution as a product of science at its best, then a residual fear for our own estate has continued to foster resentment of the fact that our physical bodies have ancient roots in ape-like primates, waddling reptiles, jawless fishes, worm-like invertebrates, and other creatures deemed even lower or more ignoble. Our ancient hopes for human transcendence have yet to make their peace with Darwin's world.

But what challenge can the facts of nature pose to our own decisions about the moral value of our lives? We are what we are, but we interpret the meaning of our heritage as we choose. Science can no more answer the questions of how we ought to live than religion can decree the age of the earth. Honourable and discerning scientists (most of us, I trust) have always understood that the limits to what science can answer also describe the power of its methods in their proper domain. Darwin himself exclaimed that science couldn't touch the problem of evil and similar moral conundrums: "A dog might as well speculate on the mind of Newton. Let each man hope and believe what he can."

There is no warfare between science and religion, never was except as a historical vestige of shifting taxonomic boundaries among disciplines. Theologians haven't been troubled by the fact of evolution, unless they try to extend their own domain beyond its proper border (hubris and territorial expansionism aren't the sins of scientists alone, despite Mr. Kristol's fears). The Reverend Henry Ward Beecher, our greatest orator during Darwin's century, evoked the most quintessential of American metaphors in dismissing the entire subject of conflict between science and religion with a single epithet: "Design by wholesale is grander than design by retail"—or, general laws rather than creation of each item by fiat will satisfy our notion of divinity.

Similarly, most scientists show no hostility to religion. Why should we, since our subject doesn't intersect the concerns of theology? I strongly dispute Kristol's claim that "the current teaching of evolution in our public schools does indeed have an ideological bias against religious belief." Unless at least half my colleagues are inconsistent

A caricature of Charles Darwin that appeared in "Vanity Fair," sketched by British cartoonist Leslie Ward (1851-1922) under the heading "Natural Selection." A caricature is a drawing or sketch of a person in which particular or unusual characteristics are emphasized for comic effect.

dunces, there can be—on the most raw and direct empirical grounds—no conflict between science and religion. I know hundreds of scientists who share a conviction about the fact of evolution, and teach it in much the same way. Among these people I note an entire spectrum of religious attitudes—from devout daily prayer and worship to resolute atheism. Either there's no correlation between religious belief and confidence in evolution—or else half these people are fools.

The common goal of science and religion is our shared struggle for wisdom in all its various guises. I know no better illustration of this great unity than a final story about Charles Darwin. This scourge of fundamentalism had a conventional church burial—in Westminster Abbey no less. J. Frederick Bridge, Abbey organist and Oxford don, composed a funeral anthem especially for the occasion. It may not rank high in the history of music, but it is, as my chorus director opined, a "sweet piece." (I've made what may be the only extant recording of this work, marred only by the voice of yours truly within the bass section.) Bridge selected for this text the finest biblical description of the common aim that will forever motivate both the directors of his building and the inhabitants of the temple of science—wisdom. "Her ways are ways of pleasantness and all her paths are peace" (Proverbs 3: 17).

I am only sorry that Dr. Bridge didn't set the very next metaphor about wisdom (Proverbs 3: 18), for it describes, with the proper topology of evolution itself, the greatest dream of those who followed the God of Abraham, Isaac, and Jacob: "She is a tree of life to them that lay hold upon her."

SOURCE: From *Discover* (January, 1987), 64–70. Reprinted with the permission of the author.

Questions and Topics for Discussion and Writing

1. What does Gould mean when he refers to the "fundamental distinction between fact and theory?"
2. How does Gould illustrate what he calls "the troubling issue of how myths become beliefs through adulterated repetition without proper documentation?"
3. What connections do Darwin and Gould make between morality and science? Do scientists have a duty to be "moral?"

The Discovery of Radium

Marie Curie

The following short article is from an address by one of the world's greatest experimental physicists. Marie Curie gave this presentation to an audience at Vassar College in New York State acknowledging a gift by American women to her of a gram of radium for use in her research. Radium was (and is) extremely expensive and difficult to produce. In this article she describes the general course of her work on radiation.

I could tell you many things about radium and radioactivity and it would take a long time. But as we cannot do that, I shall give you only a short account of my early work about radium. Radium is no more a baby; it is more than twenty years old, but the conditions of the discovery were somewhat peculiar, and so it is always of interest to remember them and to explain them.

We must go back to the year 1897. Professor Curie and I worked at that time in the laboratory of the School of Physics and Chemistry where Professor Curie held his lectures. I was engaged in some work on uranium rays which had been discovered two years before by Professor Becquerel. I shall tell you how these uranium rays may be detected. If you take a photographic plate and wrap it in black paper and then on this plate, protected from ordinary light, put some uranium salt and leave it a day, and the next day the plate is developed, you notice on the plate a black spot at the place where the uranium salt was. This spot has been made by special rays which are given out by the uranium and are able to make an impression on the plate in the same way as ordinary light. You can also test those rays in another way, by placing them on an electroscope. You know what an electroscope is. If you charge it, you can keep it charged several hours and more, unless uranium salts are placed near to it. But if this is the case the electroscope loses its charge and the gold or aluminum leaf falls gradually in a progressive way. The speed with which the leaf moves may be used as a measure of the intensity of the rays; the greater the speed, the greater the intensity.

I spent some time in studying the way of making good measurements of the uranium rays, and then I wanted to know if there were other elements, giving out rays of the same kind. So I took up a work about all known elements and their compounds and found that uranium compounds are active and also all thorium compounds, but other elements were not found active, nor were their compounds. As for the uranium and thorium compounds, I found that they were active in proportion to their uranium or thorium content. The more uranium or thorium, the greater the activity, the activity being an atomic property of the elements, uranium and thorium.

Then I took up measurements of minerals and I found that several of those which contain uranium or thorium or both were active. But then the activity was not what I would expect; it was greater than for uranium or thorium compounds, like the oxides which are almost entirely composed of these elements. Then I thought that there should be in the minerals some unknown element having a much greater radioactivity than uranium or thorium. And I wanted to find and to separate that element, and I settled to that work with Professor Curie. We thought it would be done in several weeks or months, but it was not so. It took many years of hard work to finish that task. There was

Famous Scientist at Work

Marie Curie (1867-1934)

Marie Curie (1867-1934) and her husband Pierre Curie (1859-1906) were French physicists and Nobel laureates. Together, they discovered the chemical elements radium and polonium.

The Curies' study of radioactive elements contributed to the understanding of atoms on which modern nuclear physics is based.

Originally named Marja Sklodowska, Marie Curie was born in Warsaw on November 7, 1867. Her father taught high school physics. In 1891 she went to Paris (where she changed her name to Marie) and enrolled in the Sorbonne.

Two years later she passed the examination for her degree in physics, ranking in first place. She met Pierre Curie in 1894, and they married in 1895.

Marie Curie was interested in the recent discoveries of radiation. When she found that the radiations from pitchblende, an ore containing uranium, were more intense than those from uranium itself, she realized that unknown elements, even more radioactive than uranium, must be present. Marie Curie was the first to use the term "radioactive" to describe elements that give off radiations as their nuclei break down.

Marie Curie was the first female recipient of a Nobel Prize. Marie Curie's final illness was diagnosed as pernicious anemia, caused by overexposure to radiation. She died in Haute Savoie on July 4, 1934.

not *one* element; there were several of them. But the most important is radium, which could be separated in a pure state.

All the tests for the separation were done by the method of electrical measurements with some kind of electroscope. We just had to make chemical separations and to examine all products obtained, with respect to their activity. The product which retained the radioactivity was considered as that one which had kept the new element; and, and as the radioactivity was more strong in some products, we knew that we had succeeded in concentrating the new element. The radioactivity was used in the same way as a spectroscopical test.

The difficulty was that there is not much radium in a mineral; this we did not know at the beginning. But we now know that there is not even one part of radium in a million parts of good ore. And, too, to get a small quantity of pure radium salt, one is obliged to work up a huge quantity of ore. And that was very hard in a laboratory.

We had not even a good laboratory at that time. We worked in a hangar where there were no improvements, no good chemical arrangements. We had no help, no money. And because of that, the work could not go on as it would have done under better conditions. I did myself the numerous crystallizations which were wanted to get the radium salt separated from the barium salt, with which it is obtained, out of the ore. And in 1902 I finally succeeded in getting pure radium chloride and determining the atomic weight of the new element, radium, which is 226, while that of barium is only 137.

Later I could also separate the metal radium, but that was a very difficult work; and, as it is not necessary for the use of radium to have it in this state, it is not generally prepared that way.

Now, the special interest of radium is in the intensity of its rays, which is several million times greater than the uranium rays. And the effects of the rays make the radium so important. If we take a practical point of view, then the most important property of the rays is the production of physiological effects on the cells of the human organism. These effects may be used for the cure of several diseases. Good results have been obtained in many cases. What is considered particularly important is the treatment of cancer. The medical utilization of radium makes it necessary to get that element in sufficient quantities. And so a factory of radium was started, to begin with, in France, and later in America, where a big quantity of ore named carnotite is available. America does not produce many grams of radium every year but the price is still very high because the quantity of radium contained in the ore is so small. The radium is more than a hundred thousand times dearer than gold.

But we must not forget that when radium was discovered no one knew that it would prove useful in hospitals. The work was one of pure science. And this is a proof that scientific work must not be considered from the point of view of the direct usefulness of it. It must be done for itself, for the beauty of science, and then there is always the chance that a scientific discovery may become, like the radium, a benefit for humanity.

But science is not rich; it does not dispose of important means; it does not generally meet recognition before the material usefulness of it has been proved. The factories produce many grams of radium every year, but the laboratories have very small quantities. It is the same for my laboratory, and I am very grateful to the American women who wish me to have more of radium, and give me the opportunity of doing more work with it.

The scientific history of radium is beautiful. The properties of the rays have been studied very closely. We know that particles are expelled from radium with a very great velocity, near to that of light. We know that the atoms of radium are destroyed by expulsion of these particles, some of which are atoms of helium. And in that way it has been proved that the radioactive elements are constantly disintegrating, and that they produce, at the end, ordinary elements, principally helium and lead. That is, as you see, a theory of transformation of atoms, which are not stable, as was believed before, but may undergo spontaneous changes.

Radium is not alone in having these properties. Many having other radioelements are known already: the polonium, the mesothorium, the radiothorium, the actinium. We know also radioactive gases, named emanations. There is a great variety of substances and effects in radioactivity. There is always a vast field left to experimentation and I hope that we may have some beautiful progress in the following years. It is my earnest desire that some of you should carry on this scientific work, and keep for your ambition the determination to make a permanent contribution to science.

SOURCE: From a lecture given by Marie Curie at Vassar College in the 1920s.

Questions and Topics for Discussion and Writing

1. Why do you think that Marie Curie was so interested in radioactivity that she would devote so many years of strenuous work, and ultimately her life, to isolating and measuring radium?

2. Describe the "beauty of science" that Curie refers to. What do you think are some of the "beautiful" aspects of her research work, as she might have seen them?

Technology with a Human Face

E. F. Schumacher

Radical economist E.F. Schumacher takes issue with the view that more technology is the only answer to world problems. This is a short excerpt from his world-famous book, *Small is Beautiful (1973).*

As Gandhi said, the poor of the world cannot be helped by mass production, only by production by the masses. The system of mass production, based on sophisticated, highly capital-intensive, high energy-input dependent, and human labour-saving technology, presupposes that you are already rich, for a great deal of capital investment is needed to establish one single workplace. The system of production by the masses mobilises the priceless resources which are possessed by all human beings, their clever brains and skilful hands, and supports them with first-class tools. The technology of mass production is inherently violent, ecologically damaging, self-defeating in terms of non-renewable resources, and stultifying for the human person. The technology of production by the masses, making use of the best of modern knowledge and experience is conducive to decentralization, compatible with the laws of ecology, gentle in its use of scarce resources, and designed to serve the human person instead of making him the servant of machines. I have named it intermediate technology to signify that it is vastly superior to the primitive technology of bygone ages but at the same time much simpler, cheaper, and freer than the super-technology of the rich. One can also call it self-help technology, or democratic or people's technology—a technology to which everybody can gain admittance and which is not reserved to those already rich and powerful. Although we are in possession of all requisite knowledge, it still requires a systematic, creative effort to bring this technology into active existence and make it generally visible and available. It is my experience that it is rather more difficult to recapture directness and simplicity than to advance in the direction of ever more sophistication and complexity. Any third-rate engineer or researcher can increase complexity; but it takes a certain flair of real insight to make things simple again. And this insight does not come easily to people who have allowed themselves to become alienated from real, productive work and from the self-balancing system of nature, which never fails to recognize measure and limitation. Any activity which fails to recognise a self-limiting principle is of the devil. In our work with the developing countries we are at least forced to recognise the limitations of poverty, and this work can therefore be a wholesome school for all of us in which, while genuinely trying to help others, we may also gain knowledge and experience of how to help ourselves.

I think we can already see the conflict of attitudes which will decide our future. On the one side, I see the people who think they can cope with our threefold crisis by the methods current, only more so; I call them the people of the forward stampede. On the other side, there are people in search of a new life-style, who seek to return to certain basic truths about man and his world; I call the home-comers. Let us admit that the people of the forward stampede, like the devil, have all the best tunes or at least the most popular and familiar tunes. You cannot stand still, they say; standing still means going down; you must go forward; there is nothing wrong with modern technology except that it is as yet incomplete; let us complete it. Dr. Sicco Mansholt, one of the most prominent chiefs of the European Economic Community, may be quoted as a typical representative of this group. "More, further, quicker, richer," he says, "are the watchwords of present-day society." And he thinks we must help people to adapt, "for there is no alternative." This is the authentic voice of the forward stampede, which talks in much the same tone as Dostoyevsky's Grand Inquisitor: "Why have you come to hinder us?" They point to the population explosion and to the possibilities of world hunger. Surely, we must take our flight forward and not be fainthearted. If people start protesting and revolting, we shall have to have more police and have them better equipped. If there is trouble with the environment, we shall need more stringent laws against pollution, and faster economic growth to pay for antipollution measures. If there are problems about natural resources, we shall turn to synthetics; if there are problems about fossil fuels, we shall move from slow reactors to fast breeders and from fission to fusion. There are no insoluble problems. The slogans of the people of the forward stampede burst into the newspaper headlines every day with the message, "a breakthrough a day keeps the crisis at bay."

And what about the other side? This is made up of people who are deeply convinced that technological development has taken a wrong turn and needs to be redirected. The term "home-comer" has, of course, a religious connotation. For it takes a good deal of courage to say "no" to the fashions and fascinations of the age and to question the presuppositions of a civilization which appears destined to conquer the whole world; the requisite strength can be derived only from deep convictions. If it were derived from nothing more than fear of the future, it would be likely to disappear at the decisive moment. The genuine "home-comer" does not have the best tunes, but he has the most exalted text, nothing less than the Gospels. For him, there could not be a more concise statement of his situation, of our situation, than the parable of the prodigal son. Strange to say, the Sermon on the Mount gives pretty precise instructions on how to construct an outlook that could lead to an Economics of Survival.

- How blessed are those who know that they are poor; the Kingdom of Heaven is theirs.
- How blessed are the sorrowful; they shall find consolation.
- How blessed are those of a gentle spirit; they shall have the earth for their possession.
- How blessed are those who hunger and thirst to see right prevail; they shall be satisfied.
- How blessed are the peacemakers; God shall call them his sons.

It may seem daring to connect these beatitudes with matters of technology and economics. But may it not be that we are in trouble precisely because we have failed for so long to make this connection? It is not difficult to discern what these beatitudes may mean for us today:

- We are poor, not demigods.
- We have plenty to be sorrowful about, and are not emerging into a golden age.
- We need a gentle approach, a non-violent spirit, and small is beautiful.
- We must concern ourselves with justice and see right prevail.
- And all this, only this, can enable us to become peacemakers.

The home-comers base themselves upon a different picture of man from that which motivated the people of the forward stampede. It would be very superficial to say that the latter believe in "growth" while the former do not. In a sense, everybody believes in growth, and rightly so, because growth is an essential feature of life. The whole point, however, is to give to the idea of growth a qualitative determination; for there are always many things that ought to be growing and many things that ought to be diminishing.

Equally, it would be very superficial to say that the home-comers do not believe in progress, which also can be said to be an essential feature of all life. The whole point is to determine what constitutes progress. And the home-comers believe that the direction which modern technology has taken and is continuing to pursue—towards ever-greater size, ever-higher speeds, and ever-in-

Is Small Beautiful?

E.F. Schumacher

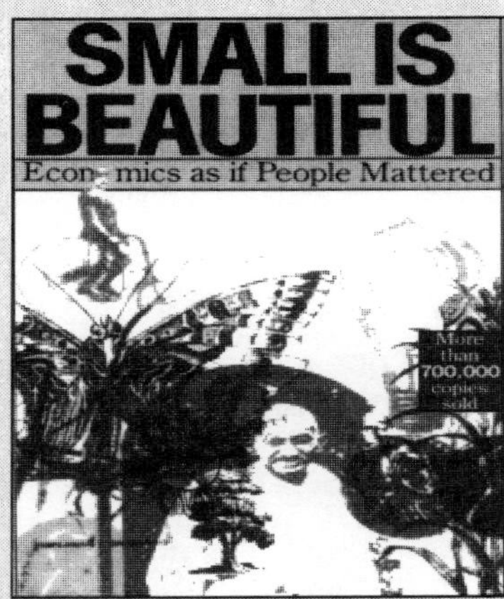

When E.F. Schumacher wrote *Small is Beautiful* in 1973, he probably had only a vague idea of the impact that technology was going to have on the lives of the ordinary person a scant twenty years later.

Today, advances in computer technology, coupled with our much-publicized shift into an "information society," have made almost everybody familiar with things such as credit cards and direct-debit systems, instant-cash banking and bill payments, faxes, modems, desktop publishing and the Internet.

While these advances have certainly made the world "small," to use Schumacher's phrase, in the sense that we can now send intricate digital information to people around the globe and complete complicated financial transactions just by punching a few buttons, it has also created an extremely "big," and often unwieldy, mass of available information. One need only log onto the Internet for a few minutes to see just how much material there is "out there" in "cyberspace."

In 1990, an American writer by the name of Bill McKibben conducted an interesting experiment: He watched one complete day's programming on all of the 93 cable television stations in the city of Fairfax, Virginia. McKibben's television "day" actually lasted over 2,000 hours, as he and his friends compiled videotapes of 24 continuous hours on each of the 93 stations, which McKibben then proceeded to watch in eight-hour shifts for several months.

To balance this information overload, he also spent 24 continuous hours on a mountaintop near his home, watching nature, swimming and thinking. These experiences were detailed in McKibben's 1992 book, *The Age of Missing Information.*

McKibben's experiences taught him one essential lesson: He was unable to glean, from over 2,000 hours of TV watching, even one piece of what he calls "fundamental information" about the world around us—information that was easy to gather in one day on top of a mountain, and came without wires, plugs or cable bills.

creased violence, in defiance of all laws of natural harmony—is the opposite of progress. Hence the call for taking stock and finding a new orientation. The stocktaking indicated that we are destroying our very basis of existence, and the orientation is based on remembering what human life is really about.

In one way or another everybody will have to take sides in this great conflict. To "leave it to the experts" means to side with the people of the forward stampede. It is widely accepted that politics is too important a matter to be left to experts. Today, the main content of politics is economics, and the main content of economics is technology. If politics cannot be left to the experts, neither can economics and technology.

The case for hope rests on the fact that ordinary people are often able to take a wider view, and a more "humanistic" view, than is normally being taken by experts. The power of ordinary people, who today tend to feel utterly powerless, does not lie in starting new lines of action, but in placing their sympathy and support with minority groups which have already started. I shall give two examples relevant to the subject here under discussion. One relates to agriculture, still the greatest single activity of man on earth, and the other relates to industrial technology.

Modern agriculture relies on applying to soil, plants, and animals ever-increasing quantities of chemical products, the long-term effect of which on soil fertility and health is subject to very grave doubts. People who raise such doubts are generally confronted with the assertion that the choice lies between "poison or hunger." There are highly successful farmers in many countries who obtain excellent yields without resort to such chemicals and without raising any doubts about long-term soil fertility and health. For the last twenty-five years, a private, voluntary organization, the Soil Association, has been engaged in exploring the vital relationships between soil, plant, animal, and man; has undertaken and assisted relevant research; and has attempted to keep the public informed about developments in these fields. Neither the successful farmers nor the Soil Association have been able to attract official support or recognition. They have generally been dismissed as "the muck and mystery people," because they are obviously outside the mainstream of modern technological progress. Their methods bear the mark of non-violence and humility towards the infinitely subtle system of natural harmony, and this stands in opposition to the life-style of the modern world. But if we now realise that the modern life-style is putting us into mortal danger, we may find it in our hearts to support and even join these pioneers rather than to ignore or ridicule them.

On the industrial side, there is the Intermediate Technology Development Group. It is engaged in the systematic study of how to help people to help themselves. While its work is primarily concerned with giving technical assistance to the Third World, the results of its research are attracting increasing attention also from those who are concerned about the future of the rich societies. For they show that an intermediate technology, a technology with a human face, is in fact possible; that it is viable; and that it reintegrated the human being, with his skilful hands and creative brain, into the productive process. It serves production by the masses instead of mass production. Like the Soil Association, it is a private, voluntary organization depending on public support.

I have no doubt that it is possible to give a new direction to technological development, a direction that shall lead it back to the real needs of man, and that also means: to the actual size of man. Man is small, and, therefore, small is beautiful. To go for giantism is to go for self-destruction. And what is the cost of a reorientation? We might remind ourselves that to calculate the cost of survival is perverse. No doubt, a price has to be paid for anything worth while: to redirect technology so that it serves man instead of destroying him requires primarily an effort of the imagination and an abandonment of fear.

SOURCE: From E. F. Schumacher, *Small is Beautiful* (New York: Harper & Row, 1973).

Questions and Topics for Discussion and Writing

1. More than 20 years have passed since Schumacher wrote this piece. What did he mean when he referred to "the conflict of attitudes that will decide our future?" How has this conflict manifested itself since Schumacher made his prediction?

2. Which contemporary figures would fit into Schumacher's category of "home-comers?" He also speaks of the "forward stampede." Which representatives of the latter group come to mind?

3. Despite his claims that "small is beautiful," Schumacher states that he is still not completely opposed to progress. How is Schumacher's belief in progress different from the one held by the "stampeders" he opposes?

Science and Culture for the 21st Century

Digby J. McLaren

Dr. Digby J. McLaren is past President of the Royal Society of Canada, Ottawa. This presentation was given to a conference on Ethics and Technology in Guelph, Ontario, in 1989. In this presentation McLaren discusses ethical issues in an age of pervasive technology.

In this presentation which I had occasion to present at the UNESCO Symposium of the same title in September 1989, I would like to consider five themes, and to generalize from them in the context of ethics and technologies. They include: (1) Science and the New World View; (2) Predicting the Elements, the Evolution and the Cultural Dimensions of Change; (3) Reconciling the Diversity of Interests with Social Freedoms, Human Rights and Human Values; (4) Determining Remedial Activities; and finally, Ethics and the Responsibilities of Scientists.

Science and the New World View

I choose to take the term "new world view" literally and look at this planet as we perceive it today and as it has developed through time.

Our ideas about the Earth have changed since James Hutton first gave us a model two hundred years ago. He recognized the existence of an earth system and correctly outlined a pattern of on-going change through small increments over an enormous time period. He thus paved the way for Darwin's still broader biological conceptions on the same basis. Hutton's model, however, was not evolutionary, and he really did make the oft-quoted remark, "We find no vestige of a beginning—no prospect of an end." It is ironical, today, when we are at last approaching an approximation to a new model of the Earth that we are faced with the very real prospect of an end to the current era of human dominance. We now see the Earth as a small planet in space that is inherently changeable. Its liquid core and mantle are heated by radioactive elements that still remain from its origins some four and a half billion years ago. This heat induced on-going crustal and mantle movement is described under the term of plate tectonics. Within this system there are many subsystems of change acting at different rates, some rhythmic others episodic. As a consequence, it is beyond our capacity to predict future changes accurately. Some are manifest in earthquake and volcanic activity on land and at the ocean ridges. They are linked to change in the relative position of the plates leading, in turn, to changes in climate and ocean circulation, and in the ambient life forms at or near the surface of the planet. All are on-going and currently unpredictable.

The planet, with its life forms, is part of the solar system and is thus influenced by the sun, and by variations in earth tilt and orbit round the sun. These induce further changes in atmospheric and ocean circulation, and therefore climate. Finally, the planet has been constantly bombarded by material in the form of meteorites and comets; some large enough to cause further massive changes in the Earth system and its biomass. We are far from being able to tie all these variables together into a coherent model.

Life has played an important role in shaping the

physical and chemical nature of the planetary surface and atmosphere. Life developed in balance with the changing environment as a result of an evolutionary process driven by those changes. In the very recent past, the emergence of the human race has begun to cause change in the environmental flux more rapidly than, and in a different manner from, the established system. With essentially free energy supplied by fossil fuels, our race has become, during the last two centuries, a dominant force for change on Earth by any measure we may apply.

We are now able to chart past and current environmental changes, and techniques recently developed enable us to view the land, oceans and atmosphere from space, and measure secular changes in climate, cloud and ice cover, soil moisture, and marine and land bio-productivity. Ice cores have furnished an accurate record as far back as one hundred and sixty thousand years of global temperature, levels of atmospheric carbon dioxide and variations year by year in wind-borne sediments, including volcanic events. Other techniques allow us to penetrate more deeply into the past.

Direct measurement may now be made of the accelerating effects of quarrying by humans of soils, forests and ground water, encouraged by an economic system not yet adjusted to evaluating the sustainability of a resource, commonly assumed to be renewable, by overuse to such a degree that recovery will not occur on a human time-scale, if at all.

The scientist may point out and measure many of the changes that are taking place in our immediate environment and in a time scale of our own lives. But it will take very much more than science to change our current system, and persuade us to learn to live in balance with earth's ecosystem.

Predicting the Elements, the Evolution and the Cultural Dimensions of Change

In the present world, we must take certain facts into account that are not open to dispute in assessing the cultural dimension. The physical reality is that the ecology of the planet is out of equilibrium and change is out of control. This must surely be dictated by human behaviour. The facts are:

Population Growth. The world reached its first billion in population about the middle of the last century. In this century, it has increased to 5 billion, and, barring catastrophe, will double within the next thirty-five to forty years.

Energy Use. The use of fossil fuels in this century has increased twelve-fold, and the rate of increase is accelerating. This accounts for about seventy-nine percent of the world's total energy usage, but more than three-quarters of these fuels are used by less than a quarter of the world's population. The increase of carbon dioxide in the atmosphere, generated largely by fossil fuel use, has reached danger levels and cannot continue for very much longer. This also is largely the waste from the minority—the so-called developed world.

Biodiversity Reduction. We are in the midst of a major extinction event comparable to some of the largest in the geological past. By eliminating wildlife habitat we condemn animals and plants to individual extinction. We now use and therefore interfere with forty percent of all the net primary productivity of the Earth. It is this activity above all others that is inevitably changing the ecological balance of the total biosphere—an activity largely unplanned and without regard for the consequences.

Global Military Expenditures. These now total about one trillion dollars a year. In the light of problems facing the world today, these figures represent an enormous, almost unimaginable, waste of resources and human ingenuity.

Contemplating these facts, we observe that the global economy, this century, has grown twenty-nine fold, and is expected to grow another five times during the next doubling of the population. The largest growth in human population takes place in the tropics, but North Americans, for example, use two hundred times as much energy per capita as a citizen of Bangladesh or Bolivia, and produce the equivalent amount of pollution and CO_2.

There is one major observation that may be made concerning the changes we are inducing on

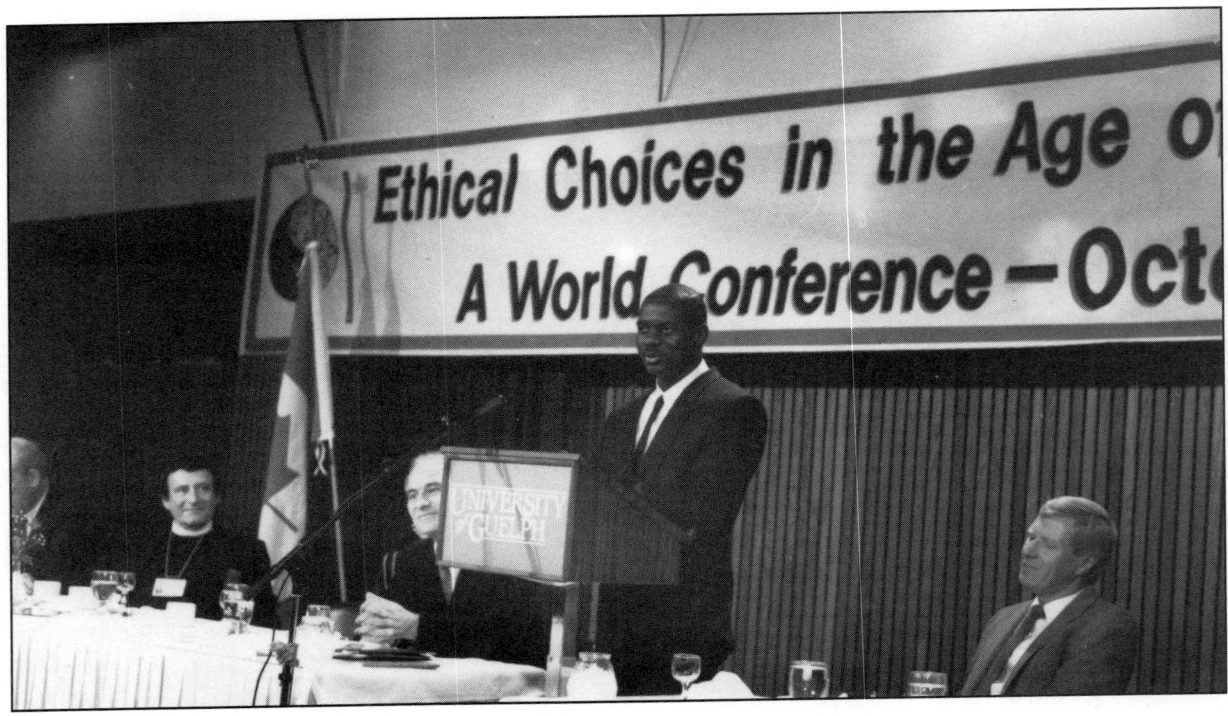

Ethical Choices in the Age of Pervasive Technology.

This article by Digby J. McLaren (as well as the two following selections) were presented at a 1989 conference on ethics and technology at the University of Guelph, Ontario. The above photograph shows athlete Ben Johnson, at that time embroiled in a steroid-use scandal, describing the pressures on him as a competitive sprinter to disregard ethical principles in order to win at all costs.

Earth: almost all the disrupting phenomena, from CFCs in the stratosphere, acid rain, greenhouse gases in the atmosphere, quarrying of soils and soil erosion, quarrying of ground water, overconsumption of energy and resultant further damage to the atmosphere, are reversible. We may not choose to do so, but they could be stopped, repaired and/or recovered if we took measures today. We are technically fully capable to undertake this task. It is simply a question of political and economic will, of rethinking our cultural values and taking the ecological warning signals seriously. The destruction of the forests and other wildlife habitats, however, is irreversible. The current accelerating extinction rate, if it continues for a hundred years more, will equal the massive extinction of seventy to eighty percent of all species on Earth that took place sixty-five million years ago at the end of the Cretaceous—the well-known end of the dinosaurs. It takes millions of years to recover from such extinction events and the ecology is never the same. This is perhaps the greatest single danger facing this planet, and humankind.

Reconciling the Diversity of Interests with Social Freedoms, Human Rights and Human Values

Certain things are very difficult for us to grasp today, and are becoming more difficult:

(a) The worth of a human being is inevitably associated with things that we value most ourselves and that we recognize in others. We send food to the starving, but if we truly valued those who receive our help, then we would try to prevent the situation that they are faced with from happening. In fact, by our current actions we are contributing to the onset of much greater starvation than the world has ever known.

(b) It is necessary to understand what is meant when we use the word "we." In all discussions on the future, "we" is always present, even though it may be unvoiced. When we claim that humankind is emerging or advancing or mastering their environment, does this mean all humankind? In fact, proportionally, most of our claims for the "we," as it is tacitly assumed, are false. Those living in the privileged corner of the world cannot encompass the fact of five billion people on Earth and the fact of ninety million babies born each year and all that this demands of us. How may "they" become "we?"

(c) Our system of thought has grown out of our background, our history. But we have nothing to learn from history today. Indeed, we must forget it if we are to come to terms with the exponential growth currently, but temporarily, dominating humankind in resource use, waste production, soil erosion, water depletion, and so on.

Some of us alive today will live to see the end of growth. How will this come about? By planning, education and control, by famine and disaster, or by war on an unimaginable scale? Growth, surely, cannot continue, so that culturally we must come to terms with the idea that we live on a finite planet, and that most of us (the "we") are living lives of ultimate degradation, and that it appears very likely that this will get worse while growth continues. We (local) must recognize our legitimate diversity of interests and reconcile them with ideas of social freedoms, human rights, or human values. In each case, we must ask for whom?

Determining Remedial Activities

Science may be entering, or is already in a period of history for which we have been preparing since the Greeks who suggested about 2600 years ago that perhaps nature is intelligible. We find we are now faced with a task which is more difficult than anything we have ever contemplated: to decide how we may continue to live on this small planet. The human being is an animal that has moved out of ecological balance with its environment. Man is a wasteful killer and a despoiler of other life on the planet. This normal and apparently acceptable behaviour is licensed by a belief in God-given resources and encouraged by an economic system that emphasizes short-term profit as a benefit, and has not learned to put a real cost on the resources we consume. If we depart from an ecological balance to the extent that we destroy most of the remaining life on Earth, then, surely, we are dooming ourselves to a similar fate. In other words, we must live in balance with the world in which we find ourselves.

There must be a price put on such commodities as soils, as well as groundwater, surface waters, atmosphere and biosphere—or the sum total of all kinds of life on Earth. Such a price must include the cost of protection, replacement and substitution. Current economic thinking appears to be caught in a system which assumes limitless resources and ignores the production of waste products. This system worked when resources did appear to be limitless and when waste was easily disposed of and self-cleansing. Neither of these variables exist any longer.

The economic subsystem takes in resources and excretes wastes, and is thus irrevocably and closely linked to the ecosystem. Both input and output are finite and the main variable is the one-way flow of matter-energy. Such a way of looking at things raises the question of how big the economic system should be in relation to the physical dimensions of the global system. This also necessarily questions the concept of growth economics and the impossibility of generalizing current Western standards of living to the world as a whole. An important factor must be included: human welfare and equity.

If we begin to think this way, we shall be confronted by some extremely hard decisions, which may not be taken. But we shall also be confronted by a massive questioning of the current beliefs, axioms and myths, which lie behind much of today's economic and social thought, and we may look to the emergence of new understandings of what constitutes our enlightened self-interest.

Ethics and the Responsibilities of Scientists

These remarks may be considered presumptuous on the part of a scientist, but we are all in this together. I believe, therefore, that it is perfectly proper to appeal for an inductive approach in looking at our present condition on Earth, to draw empirical conclusions, including constructing some worst-case scenarios, and to attempt to put probabilities on them. I began these remarks with the Earth System, and I find that the human species has taken over. I suggest that we do not know enough to decide how to run this planet. We are forcing our will upon it, using the depleting resources and increasing waste discharge, while at the same time claiming that we must aim for sustainability. May we attain this globally, or have we passed the limits within which it may be achieved?

Perhaps a way might be found to judge our actions by a new principle: the health of the planet. Perhaps the economy could be seen as being within the environment, and not the environment within the economy. Perhaps we should ask the question of any action that we take: "Does it increase or decrease survivability?" The problems in relation to this way of looking at things would be scientific and social, and in their solution, we would strive to discover reality.

The term "quality of life" might take on a new meaning. We could try to limit our own needs in keeping with a consciousness of global resources and needs in the broadest terms. We could live in balance with all life, and crop and harvest according to preference and needs, provided that this does not reduce the capacity of future generations to also do so. In agriculture, food could be produced through appropriate land use in balance with the capacity of the environment to supply, rather than imposing our will on it by force for short-term benefit. Such an approach does not require a high degree of altruism, although it does require some degree of sacrifice. It is inevitable that what we now consider justifiable freedoms may be seriously constrained.

In a similar way, we may look on sovereignty in a different light. We may assume common cause with all people on Earth against a common enemy—action that threatens balance within our environment, or reduces our legacy to future generations. Somehow, a way must be found to permit us to look, for one brief moment, at the world without the filters of belief, axiom, model or political theory. During this moment, we could observe the planet and draw conclusions from our observation as to the health of our planet and the probability that life may be self-sustaining indefinitely into the future in terms of human lifetimes. We must examine the presuppositions that lie behind all our beliefs, and realize that sustainability is the ultimate criterion by which we judge our actions in our use of Earth resources and our discharge of wastes within the confines of our planet.

SOURCE: *Critical Choices: Ethics, Science and Technology,* edited by Henry Wiseman, Jokelee Vanderkop and Jorge Nef. (Toronto: Thompson Educational Publishing, Inc.,1991).

Questions and Topics for Discussion and Writing

1. The work of biologists like Stephen Jay Gould and David Suzuki, astronomers like Carl Sagan and physicists like Stephen Hawking have been highly publicized for their originality and for their revolutionary insights. Why, then, does McLaren state that "we are far from being able to tie all these variables together into a coherent model?"

2. What does McLaren mean by "biodiversity reduction?" Why is this dangerous for the biosphere?

3. McLaren's most provocative statement is that humans are "wasteful killers" and "despoilers of life on this planet" because we have somehow come to believe that we have inherited certain rights in relation to other species of life. Is McLaren's claim justified, or simply a rhetorical device intended to provoke (remembering that this piece was initially delivered as a speech)?

Ethics in the Use of Technology

James M. Stewart

Modern industry is perhaps the main vehicle through which we advance our quest for more and better technology. In this selection, James M. Stewart, Senior Vice-President of Du Pont Canada Ltd., focuses on the ethical issues underlying recent advances in technology for industrialists. He concludes that it is the responsibility of the leaders of industry to ensure that the ethical ramifications of decision-making are kept in the forefront.

I certainly feel like Daniel in the lion's den at this conference—one of the very few industrialists in a sea of distinguished thinkers from academia and the public sector! Yet, industry is one of the main vehicles through which society derives the benefits and sustains the costs and penalties of technology. So industry must play a vital role in ethical decisions on technology. It is also necessary to reflect on the way we, as a society, go about making technological choices and why this process must be improved. Some practical examples from our experience at Du Pont might be useful in helping others comprehend the kind of approach we think should be taken in weighing the advantages and disadvantages of new technologies. Finally, I will offer a few specific suggestions about how industry can make a more meaningful contribution to technological decisions.

I will start with a few of my beliefs:

(1) Technology is neither ethical nor unethical. The ethical dimension comes in the decision-making process on how technology will be used. An ethical decision-making process is one which is fair and open, and gives all those with a stake in the outcome a chance to be heard. Decisions will be ethical only if they are made after balanced and thoughtful consideration of all the implications, by and for all constituencies, and within a short and long-term global context.

(2) By and large, the use of technology by industry has been ethical: a higher standard of living, longer life spans, dramatic reduction in disease, better and more plentiful food, more universal education. These are the important benefits that society wants, and in helping to develop them, industry has acted in an ethical manner.

(3) As a last premise, the survival of industry depends on meeting public expectations. As Peter Drucker has pointed out, "The [business] enterprise exists on sufferance and exists only as long as society and the economy believes it does a job—a necessary, useful and productive one."

Technology can continue to be a positive force for good. Yet today, we face enormous and critical decisions on its use. We are just beginning to understand that in an interdependent world, technological decisions can have far-reaching, sometimes global implications. In this respect, we must ask ourselves whether these decisions will be made in a balanced, thoughtful and ethical way? Will all important constituencies be heard from and their points of view considered? To attain this balance, we are going to have to radically change our decision-making processes.

Although I will be using some environmental examples to outline the decision-making process that takes place at Du Pont, we face similar ethical issues in technology in many other areas. My company, and for that matter myself, are involved not only in technological decisions relating to the environment, but also to the use of energy, worker and community safety and occupational health, employment and job creation, urban development, health care, and Third World development. In few of these areas do we see a really balanced and thoughtful decision-making process. Instead, we can observe a decision-making process characterized by the following traits:

(1) Single issue lobbyists with strong, partisan, emotional biases tend to get the most media coverage. They have a legitimate role to play but they tell only one side of the story.

(2) The public is woefully unprepared and largely uneducated regarding technology. Yet technology is the dominant force affecting our lives. Naturally, fear, often unreasoning fear, dominates the thinking.

(3) Industry, suspect because of its vested interest, and in some cases because of its record, is reluctant to get openly involved. Its essential input is often disregarded.

(4) Most of our politicians do not have the background or knowledge to understand fully the complexities of modern technology or the implications of its use.

In this context, it is no wonder that we stumble ahead uncertainly, unable to really come to grips with major technological decisions.

Industry Responsibility

What can industry do to improve this situation? First of all, we must recognize our responsibility to speak up publicly. It is industry that in many ways has the best information, knowhow, and resources to contribute to decisions involving technology. But we have been too reticent, too secretive, not willing enough to take the public into our confidence, reluctant to share the information needed for balanced decision-making. Maybe that is because it has seemed easier to try to reach decision-makers through quiet lobbying behind closed doors.

The low-key approach is not working. Politicians are more sensitive than ever to the media and the polls. To make an impact, industry will have to inform and win over public opinion. We will have to speak in terms to which the public can relate—about the concrete benefits and hazards to them in what we do. We must also be prepared for emotional and unreasoned attack, as well as valid and reasoned criticism.

Industry must inform the public that there are important but controversial issues that need to be considered not to mention some difficult balancing of interests. For example, we may all endorse the call of the Brundtland Commission for sustainable development, but translating that principle into decisions and actions is a very challenging task. In the developing world, the balance will be even harder to find since technology is crucial to improving living standards, health and nutrition.

Canadian industry is operating in a fiercely competitive world—an increasingly interdependent world. The health, even the survival, of Canadian industry depends on the aggressive development and application of technology. In many areas, we are already behind competitor nations. If we do not introduce new processes and new products, for sure others will, and Canadians would then solely import the results of successful application of technology elsewhere. All Canadians would be the worse for that through unemployment, lower standards of living, lessened ability to make public investments whether it be as assistance for the disadvantaged in our society or support for the arts. In the developing world, the balance will be even harder to find since technology is crucial to improving living standards, health and nutrition. If groundless fears and ill-conceived arguments deprive Canadian industry of the tools it needs to compete, the price will be high, and ultimately, it will be paid by all of us. Industry must bring forward these considerations so that the tradeoffs can be made in an ethical decision-making process.

At this point, I would like to highlight some specific cases that illustrate ethical decisions on the use of technology at a practical level. At Du Pont, we are producers of plastic packaging materials, so I will address the issue of plastics in food packaging and garbage disposal. Both are, needless to say, controversial subjects. My purpose is to highlight the kinds of questions that we in this company believe must be asked and answered as part of an ethical decision-making process.

(1) The Solid Waste Crisis: Some Practical Examples

Our biggest enemy is the tendency to reach for simple, popular solutions based on superficial analysis. Unfortunately, these issues are anything but simple. It takes rigorous thinking to arrive at an ethical decision that truly considers all implications—long- and short-term—by and for all constituencies.

The municipal garbage issue is a case in point. Public opinion has somehow become convinced that plastics are the problem. If only they could be eliminated, recycled or made degradable, the problem would be solved. In the United States and elsewhere, plastics are being singled out for restrictive legislation. But this snap judgment overlooks a whole range of relevant factors. A key point is that plastics make up only about 7 percent by weight of municipal garbage, although, true enough, more than that on a volume basis.

Advances in plastic packaging, from bread bags to microwave dishes, have not only reduced the costs of distribution and greatly increased consumer convenience. They have also played a major role in the dramatic reductions in food spoilage and disease transmission. It cannot be denied that there have been some frivolous uses of plastics in packaging. These, however, will not survive. On the other hand, the movement to restrict plastic packaging threatens to deprive the public of useful, and in some cases, essential products. It will not help the environment much either, given the relatively moderate contribution of plastics to the solid waste stream. On the contrary, it could be counterproductive if plastics are replaced by containers that are less environmentally compatible.

We need to put the role of plastics in municipal waste disposal into context. The major components of municipal garbage are one-third compost waste (leaves, lawn and kitchen waste, etc.), and one-third paper products. Why are our politicians not working more strongly on recycling the large compost portion? Is it ethical to concentrate on the visible and emotionally charged plastics issue?

Maybe we could learn something from European countries that seem to be handling the solid waste problem more effectively. In the most progressive jurisdictions, cardboard and paper, glass and metal, and some plastics, are separated and recycled; and compost materials are removed for separate recycling. What remains is burned in high-tech incinerators. Even Sweden, which once banned incineration because of environmental concerns, has now found waste incineration environmentally safe and uses energy-from-waste incinerators to dispose of a large part of unrecycled waste. After all, most plastics are made from oil and their reuse for energy saves oil and coal. Few people seem to realize that every kilogram of polyethylene used to recover energy avoids the use of two kilograms of coal.

What about recycling? All thermoplastics, and they are the ones in everyday use, can be recycled. It is just a question of cost. But that is a big question. An infrastructure is needed to collect plastics in sufficient quantity to warrant building a reprocessing plant. Different plastics have different properties so sorting is a big and costly problem. The net result is that the cost of recycled plastic can be much more than virgin plastic. Du Pont strongly supports recycling where it makes sense. But in some cases, we have to ask if it is the best way to spend our waste management dollars, particularly if the energy value of plastics can be recovered in efficient incinerators.

While the environment is not the only criterion for deciding which packaging to use, it is obviously very important. But assessing the environmental impact of a packaging system is a more complicated task than many people realize.

I believe we must compare plastics with other forms of packaging in terms of the total environmental impact *over the entire life cycle* of the technology. That means considering the effects of raw material production, transportation, use, disposal—in other words—the full span from cradle to grave. Only if we do this objectively and thoroughly can ethical decisions be made. In this assessment plastic packages should survive only if it is the best packaging system, on an ethical decision-making basis.

(2) Plastic Packaging

Milk pouch packaging is a more specific example of an environmental impact assessment in food packaging. Half of Canadian milk is sold in plastic pouches. This system was developed and commercialized in North America by Du Pont and we lead the world in this technology. The main alternatives are the paper carton or the plastic jug. Many consumers, and some consumer groups, favour the use of paper products because they are based on a resource that is at least potentially renewable. Some people propose a return to the glass bottle, believing it to be a more natural, usable container. Which is friendlier to the environment?

The plastic pouch generates less than one quarter of the packaging waste by weight than does the carton. Also, the process of manufacturing the pouch generates 60 percent less air pollution than does the production of paper packaging for the same quantity of milk. In a landfill site, the pouch takes up less than 10 percent of the space of the milk carton because it is completely compressed. Furthermore, it can be recycled while the carton cannot. Whether recycling makes economic sense is a debatable point but Du Pont is working on an experiment to find this out.

What about the returnable glass bottle? It appears that a British Colombia dairy is promoting glass as the environmentally friendly solution. But once the total system is examined, glass is quickly rejected. Why? The high energy in its manufacture; the transportation cost for a heavy container; the chemicals, energy and water required for cleaning; the spoilage and health risks. A study done by the University of Minnesota a decade ago compared the environmental impact of glass bottles, paper cartons, returnable polyethylene bottles and polyethylene pouches. The study assumed that the glass and returnable polyethylene bottles would last for 25 trips. The pouch won hands down in all categories. An environmentally friendly winner? An ethical decision?

It should be mentioned that pouch packaging of food products is in use today largely in the rich countries. Should we be promoting it for use in the developing world? Is that not just another example of exporting our wasteful and environmentally damaging technology? Again, a total impact assessment should help us to make an ethical decision.

In Puerto Rico, school milk is rapidly being switched from paper cartons to individual "mini-sip" polyethylene pouches. Why? Cafeteria garbage is reduced 40 percent and schools pay for garbage disposal on the amount generated. There is a major saving in the refrigerator volume required, thus also, less energy. Kids like it and it costs less. To us it seems an ethical decision.

In India we are working on pouch packaging of edible oil. Edible oil is a huge volume commodity there. It is handled in bulk—in tanks and drums, and consumers take their individual needs home in their own containers. Seems like a perfect environmental packaging system—everything reusable, perhaps indefinitely. But is it? Are we ethical in promoting a switch to polyethylene pouch packaging? The immediate reaction of the environmental critic is predictable. But consider this. In the present system, leakage and spoilage are high—conservatively estimated to be at least 10 percent or even double that amount.

Consumers face serious hazards through spoilage and contamination. The mass sickness and paralysis from the adulteration of cooking oil by industrial lubricating oil in Calcutta in 1988 was widely reported. But this was just one of a long list of such incidents. There is also the serious problem of consumers receiving both poor quality and suspect quantity.

The plastic pouch is less than half the cost of competing rigid plastic or paper-based containers. Considering all aspects of the present system, the advantages of the plastic pouch system in cost, safety and health and environment, are apparent. It is no wonder the Indian government is enthusiastic about the potential of plastic pouch packaging.

Such mundane examples may seem out of place with more elevated, philosophical concepts on ethics. The examples themselves may even sound self-serving. This was not the purpose. As mentioned beforehand, plastic packaging will survive or fail on its merits. It is just an example with which I am familiar. It is also one where things are not necessarily what they might seem to be on the surface; where total environment impact assessments are necessary so that the right answer—the ethical decision ensues. Without airing the total picture, public pressure might push the decision in the wrong direction.

What Industry Should Do

What can industry do to contribute more to ethical decision-making on the use of technology? There are a number of aspects to be considered in building a set of ethical guidelines:

(1) It goes without saying that industry should view technological decisions holistically, and strive to see that they are ethical.

(2) Business has an obligation to share its knowledge and expertise to increase understanding of the issues and the advantages and disadvantages of proposed solutions.

(3) Corporations should work harder and more openly to break down the barriers of fear and mistrust between themselves and the community at large—including, of course, environmental groups.

(4) Business should participate more fully in open public debates on technology. Our only plea is that we be treated as responsible citizens with honest and valid points of view.

(5) Industry should work harder to promote improved education on the benefits and perils of science and technology. It should provide tomorrow's leaders and voters with enough technological awareness that they can make balanced decisions. Du Pont is assisting in several projects in this area.

Industry has stewardship of capital and human resources as well as environmental resources. It is our responsibility to see that, in the process of making decisions, society considers the full dimensions of the issues at stake and the valid perspectives of industry on these issues.

As I have tried to show with the plastic packaging examples, ethical decisions on technology are often more complex than meets the eye. To make informed, sustainable choices, we need thorough research, rigorous thinking, and an understanding of the total life cycle of the product or technology under assessment. Industry has the analytical tools and the technical knowledge to make a vital contribution to the debate. Ethical decision-making is very much about weighing and balancing. It is the obligation of industry, as far as possible, to see that all relevant factors are placed on the scale.

SOURCE: *Critical Choices: Ethics, Science and Technology,* edited by Henry Wiseman, Jokelee Vanderkop and Jorge Nef. (Toronto: Thompson Educational Publishing, Inc.,1991). Reprinted with permission.

Questions and Topics for Discussion and Writing

1. As Senior Vice President of a large chemical company, how can James M. Stewart's views on the relationship between technology and society be expected to differ from those of scientists like David Suzuki? Do his opinions as stated in this article match these expectations?

2. It would seem paradoxical that an industrialist like Stewart places the onus of waste-disposal problems on politicians, and not on corporations. Why does he do this, and why is this shifting of responsibility not as surprising at it might first seem?

3. What does Stewart mean when he says that "industry should view technological decisions holistically?" How would a corporation's accountant view such a mandate in terms of profits and losses?

Scientific Research and Social Values

Geraldine Kenney-Wallace

This presentation was given to a conference on Ethics and Technology in Guelph, Ontario, in 1989. Dr. Geraldine Kenney-Wallace, President of McMaster University, Hamilton and formerly Chair of the Science Council of Canada, examines the ethical choices we face in an age of pervasive technology.

I am both challenged and honoured by being on this platform today to talk about ethics and technology, and to try and share with you a direction in which I believe we must go—with science, with technology, and unquestionably with wise ethical choices. I am going to elaborate these arguments in some detail, but first, let me deliver a prologue on the conference.

When Henry Wiseman came to see me this time two years ago, I had been Chair of the Science Council for barely two months. A mutual colleague had put us in touch, and a few phone calls later, we sat in Ottawa and had an animated discussion on ethics and on the possibilities of this as yet unshaped conference. The Science Council of Canada became a co-sponsor in an act of faith as much as an intellectual and business decision because we believed in the general thesis of the argument. Ethics *is* everybody's business, and yet too little attention is given to this theme.

That is in a sense what this conference is about: making value judgments in a highly complex and rapidly changing technological society. Sometimes not all the facts are in, not all the plans are in shape. But you must move ahead, make decisions and get on with life. How to do that wisely is intimately tied up with choices, with technology, and in particular, with cooperation and collaboration among traditionally different groups of academe, business, labour and government.

Thus, I want to congratulate the organizers of this conference, all the other sponsors and the delegates. All of you have had the insight to participate in what promises to be a stimulating few days, whose impact on you, as individuals or institutions, may very well shape the way you personally enter the twenty-first century.

I am neither a professional philosopher nor professional historian, but I am fascinated by one reoccurring theme which reflects on our disciplinary culture. We will probably all agree that "it is self-evident," and "history has shown" are loose statements just as dangerous as "science has proven!" We all work on what we believe is the nature of evidence, but the way we assemble our evidence varies between philosophy, history, and the physical or life sciences. We translate our ideas beyond the facts and data and in doing so enfold beliefs and values. As a physical scientist, I am constrained in my interpretations by the (so-far) constraints of the universe or the laws of physics. There is no ideology attached to the speed of light. There are, however, values in interpreting history. We must share an understanding of our disciplinary cultures in order to move ahead in the wider debates on ethical choices.

My theme today is very simple: "*The Global Village is Restless.*" We are electronically tuned to each other like a giant nervous control system. But the reasons for the restlessness are a little confused. Thus I would like to present my remarks today in the context of these global events and from the *perspective of discovery.*

As a scientist, I am intrigued by the act of discovery. The essence of being alive scientifically is to ask questions and shape solutions. This process is a voyage of intellectual discovery in which uncertainties and judgment play a major role. Discovery is intrinsically a human activity of choice and one in which we revel. We rejoice, in an often surprisingly generous way, the first time we discover a range of events that have a fresh personal meaning. Let me give you some examples:

- Discovery that a child can link words haltingly into a full sentence;
- Discovery that a disease may have hope for a cure or be eradicated, such as the case for polio in the 1950s and 1960s;
- Discovery that against all competitive odds, the race was run and won;
- Discovery that a new author can transport the imagination and light up our minds;
- Discovery that a space probe can transport us to images of another universe, at least electronically;
- Discovery that the tax bills are less than projected;
- Discovery of personal tranquillity;
- Discovery that human warmth can eventually heal the pain.

From such a perspective of discovery, let me state the three central points I wish to make and elaborate in the context of ethics and technology.

(1) Discovery through Nature: The science and technologies of tomorrow to which we must respond, positively and wisely, are here because the scientific principles are already well established. What neither I nor you know is the breakthroughs that may occur, indeed, will occur, over the next decade or two. Science and Technology must progress wisely in order to maintain harmony in times of almost bewildering change. In biotechnology, for example, every breakthrough will cause further restlessness unless ethical consideration keeps pace.

(2) Discovery through Human Society (both individually and collectively): The issues of ethics can be grouped into a set of four umbrella issues which refer to the needs of society. These are material needs, social needs, the needs of the interface of human and machine, and finally, the needs inside of each one of us. The latter need is to express and to fulfil our human potential which is the single and possibly loneliest voyage of discovery each one of us takes. It is critically important we do not confuse one need for another. Nor must we let the failure of society to grapple with one need delay the progress on others by default.

(3) Discovery for the Future: Can we identify the grand questions that have achieved marked prominence today as a consequence of globalization of news, markets, medicine, ideas translated into dozens of languages, books, trade and technology, scientific research and educational goals, and environmental challenges? Our restlessness is heightened because of the decentralization of decision-making in all sectors and because of knowledge-driven economics that open markets in the face of crumbling ideologies. It is indeed a time demanding courage, conscience and confidence. We must identify and understand the questions of the future. Perhaps the most important question is about ourselves. Is our human software up to this? Yes, I believe it is, but as humans we have also shown remarkable resistance to change. Complacency is not an option—that is a point on which we might all agree. Evolution or revolution? That is always the question, and the point upon which there will be debate.

I believe the answer is that we need a blend of both evolution and revolution. In those issues where an evolutionary or environmental change is appropriate to move individuals or society ahead, a radical change will have disastrous consequences; and in those issues where "more the same" is a pathway to obsolescence, intellectually or economically, then clearly revolutionary concepts are needed to shift the paradigm. Revolution can be peaceful, as the extraordinary events unfolding in October 1989 in Hungary showed us, in contrast to the tragic events of 1956. It is political and public will that determine the difference.

In other words, change must be accompanied with a clearly articulated set of clauses which I will call sunrise and sunset. These must be discussed when considering our voyages of discovery whether they be in research terms, societal terms or in individual terms. To give a concrete example: keeping an older technology facility fully operational in a hospital, although it has been overtaken by far newer techniques capable of similar or better results for the patients and doctors, seems to be a waste of hard-earned tax-payers' money. The important skilled human resources could be applied elsewhere. When the newer technology is less invasive and more effective in diagnostic terms, surely the decision in "cost-benefit" terms should be clear? But if maintaining the older technology means limiting patient access to the newer facility because constrained hospital operating budgets result in cutting down the hours of access, then this becomes an ethical issue as well. Do not blame the technology. Ask who is accountable in setting hospital priorities. Where are the barriers to common sense decisions? Unfortunately, this is too common a problem in the health care sector.

Evolution or revolution? Sunset or sunrise? Keep these in mind when, in the conference workshops, you look carefully at the ethical choices and the wise actions that you would recommend in the context of rapidly changing and pervasive technologies. To be wise you need to be informed before choices are made. Therefore, let me now move back into my modes of discovery.

(1) Discovery through the Natural Sciences

First of all I would like to analyze the title of the Conference, "Ethical Choices in an Age of Pervasive Technology." As a scientist, I thought: every age is an age of pervasive science and technology, every age is an information age. It is what you *perceive* as science and technology that changes.

Consider a rather different timescale than that of rotation of the earth and sun. Consider a timescale from a state of magic to a state of art, from a state of science, a state of technology, a state of convenience, a state of antique, a state of *objet d'art.* Let me illustrate this timescale and show how perceptions of technology change.

In 3000 B.C., Babylonians had a superb sense of mathematical symmetry and pattern recognition that is the envy of modern robots. Look at the jewellery, the copper and bronze tools and armlets, or at the trumpets they blew. We do not call this advanced materials, metallurgy, acoustics, differential equations and symmetry theory. We call this archaeology now, and exhibit just such artifacts in museums as art, and as beautiful, eloquent expressions of the age.

In Renaissance times, Michelangelo painted the Sistine Chapel magnificently. He must have worked in an empirical way. He and the members of his atelier were smart and experimented extensively. It was natural for them to discover. Michelangelo knew, as an artisan, that what we now call inorganic transition metal pigments lasted longer and could withstand the bleaching of the sun. He used them literally to brilliant effect on the ceiling in contrast to many other painters of the time, and since, who used organic pigments which indeed bleach and fade rapidly. Secondly, he also knew as an artist much about the science of optics, perspective and illusion. Close to the ceiling, the larger than life figures are immensely distorted, but on the chapel floor, looking up, the three-dimensional images stand out clearly and naturally.

We see here a brilliant blend of art and science at a time when creativity flourished and the arts and sciences were sponsored by major institutions such as the Church, the State, the Court, the Medicis, and a range of other private sponsors or patrons. Some citizens were prepared to pay or could afford to pay; many more over the centuries have enjoyed the results.

They are now restoring the ceilings covered with 500 years of smoke from flickering candles and bustling human activity that brought the dust and grime of daily life into the Chapel and eventually on the surfaces of the walls. The ceiling restoration is astonishingly beautiful, bold in colour and alive with imagery. The chapel is closed to the public now and will be for some years. A Japanese company has the rights on the filming and release of pictures of the new cleaned ceiling, to be revealed in a few years time. It has invested in the rediscovery of this art. While some may grumble about access during the 1980s and 1990s, no one else was prepared to foot a bill of such

"The Global Village is Restless."

Science and Social Values

One of the key issues in Geraldine Kenney-Wallace's piece is the concept of "access." This issue emphasizes a self-evident and powerful truth about discovery, namely that technological innovations are only useful to the people that can actually use them.

We have witnessed this phenomenon in full force over the last two decades. Computers were formerly available only to a very select number of people who used them for specific tasks. In 1995 about 80% of Canadians have access to computers, and an increasing number are become active on the Internet. This new technology will bring with it a whole new set of questions related to the issue of access: Can information be copyrighted on the "Information Highway?" How can publication bans, which affect television and radio media, be enforced? Do national laws and borders need to be respected in cyberspace?

New technologies always bring with them entirely new ethical issues, and there are usually several figures who set themselves up as "experts" or even "gurus" who explain not only how to use the new apparatus, but what its larger meaning to society will be.

One of the paradoxes of the Information Age is that the advent of computer technology is, according to its champions, supposed to render books and magazines obsolete as the electronic forms of these publications take over. But it appears as though the opposite has been true—with each new computer tool comes articles, manuals and books about it and detailing how to use it. One needs only to go to the nearest bookstore to observe the proliferation of books about the Internet.

And this represents yet another paradox, because all of the instructional and directional material one needs to use the Internet effectively is in fact contained within the Internet itself. But unless one cracks open one of the many "how-to" manuals available at the bookstore, it is very difficult for the average person to find much of the useful information contained within!

magnitude. There is a moral here, analogous to the familiar free lunch story, in both the hospital and chapel anecdotes. There is no access without cost and that can be an ethical issue, if access *is* the goal. But then, citizens must be prepared to pay the cost, financial or otherwise, if it is unethical to impede access to the science and its technological applications which are of a public good nature.

You might be surprised to realize that it is only over the past two decades we have learned why inorganic transition metal compounds are so colourful and stable. The answers lie in quantum mechanics, spectroscopy, and the excitation of electrons. Indeed, some of these pigments are dropped into crystal lattices and polished to make rods for lasers. This rather unexpected blend of science and art today underlies a 10 billion dollar global industry built upon lasers and optoelectronics. In many areas, lasers have become commonplace. Medical applications abound, from ophthalmology or treatments of eyes in outpatient clinics to laser photoradiation therapy treatment of skin cancer. Lasers, communications, satellites and fibre-optic networks: these are the components of the global communications network through which we live, do business, receive information and are challenged today. These dramatic changes are all sources of our restlessness as well as our wonder.

In a society based upon socialized medicine, there are few access problems in principle. In practice, we have to have policies that answer the question wisely, "access to what?" The ethical issues arise from privacy and access to information. Who has access to medical information as a consequence of the diagnosis and treatment? There are ethical issues arising from invasive surgery, when the choice is, perhaps, no surgery at all. There are issues on priorities of funding, on fiscal allocation and on human resource allocation, in days of competing technologies in hospitals and clinics. These all happen after the discovery-through-nature phase and should be discussed and widely debated. These issues should not be used as a vehicle to prevent science and discovery from moving on. Today, without a car, or public transportation, you would be surprisingly inconvenienced. This may change in the future. The rapid diffusion of information technologies may soon see us back in the equivalent of electronic cottage industries as work, decisions, manufacturing and services become increasingly decentralized and globalized. You may not identify with radar, which emerged from World War II, but you would not like to give up a microwave oven. It is now a matter of convenience.

Do our perceptions of risk change along this state of magic to a state of modern convenience time-scale? Undoubtedly yes! But science is and always has been part of our culture. Technology is, and always has been pervasive. It is our perspective of what Science and Technology are, how pervasive technology is, and our personal knowledge base that are changing all the time. More and more people are exposed to a greater store of knowledge over which they are not necessarily in control, or empowered to control. Thus our notions of risk change and evolve in this context of discovery and uncertainty. Today, the global village is electronically wired and pervasiveness is constantly impressed upon us. Sharing other peoples' risk by proxy, through remote control of television drama or environmental devastation around the world, is in itself a source of restlessness to many in the global village.

(2) Discovery through Society: Issues of Needs

Let me now move to some modern examples of the science and technology affecting our lives but which have come about through our societal needs. First, let us look at material needs, and through a few examples to identify the demands on technology and science-based innovation.

Canada is a country which historically has relied on trading its natural comparative advantage in raw materials and wealth of natural resources. In days of intense global trade challenges, the market issues of competitiveness focus on the need to put value-added into that resource base. The resource sector is in a period of trade deficits, and there are plentiful alternative suppliers to the world markets. The nation's economy is at stake.

Through biotechnology, in particular through advances in genetics over the past two decades, transgenetic experiments are now taking place which have an impact on fish, trees, plants, insects. There is, furthermore, a new movement towards sustainable agriculture in Canada. The degree of transgenetic research and its implications are not fully known. This is a modern cellular version of grafting orchard trees to produce fruit through hybrids. But in watching the most fundamental research move ahead, and in acknowledging the needs of society for a stronger resource base, there are still voices of disquiet. Now scientists are working at the DNA, RNA, and cellular level, across previously distinct species. They are beginning to touch matters very close to the human being, to life in all forms. The ethical choices will lie in how we apply the results. The closer the results come to us, the more complex those ethical choices seem to be...or are they? Let me give you an example of what I mean by "close to us." Consider the already proven and partially available genetic screening. A person's disposition to genetic-based disease can be mapped out, a little like finger printing. This is a wonderful breakthrough towards early diagnosis and the prevention of certain genetic-based diseases, if treatments are known.

However, a few moments reflection raises very important questions. Who does the screening, and who pays? Who gets the information, and who acts? Who is liable if refusing to act? These are profound issues of privacy, control, and health care economics which could lead to the setting of targets and priorities in a health care system. Should we prevent genetic research for screening? No. In any event, it is too late. Articles on genetics appear in business journals and fashion magazines. But we must debate the ethical issues clearly, and soon, before we get too emotionally involved because it is "close to us."

Thus a marvellous leap forward in genetic medicine, giving hope for some individual lives, must be thought out carefully from a perspective of individual rights, freedoms and responsibilities. Society, too, has a collective responsibility to build on our knowledge, to utilize science and technology for the greater public good. Health is a key public good responsibility in modern industrialized societies. In the developing world, health is an economic factor which encompasses a broad range of issues from food security to disease prevention. From agriculture, to vaccines, to safe water supplies, biotechnology, biosciences and genetic research have revolutionized the way we can meet the legitimate demands and needs of society. The ethics of meeting those needs still requires debate and thoughtful action on the standards, regulatory practices, codes of behaviour, and priorities in research to allay fears that a Brave New World is too "close to us."

I believe we, in 1989, are really dealing with the most revolutionary and evolutionary of human activities: the management of transition and change in real-time in our global village. Information technologies sharpen the focus on the decentralization of decision-making, on the dramatic geo-political shifts in our village, on the swell of democracy, and on the fluidity and rapidity of response in fiscal markets.

To accomplish this, we are realizing that we must go beyond the village borders, beyond the bounds of conventional wisdom, beyond the bounds of isolated academic disciplines, or yesterday's science and older technology, beyond the long established divisions of private and public sectors. We are compelled to acknowledge that the pervasive nature of technology has challenged us, and our village peace is disturbed because our values and ethics need to be assessed or reaffirmed. And the greatest unease can often be found at the human-machine interface because it is there that our personal sense of control, of being empowered to freely make decisions, is most often questioned or vulnerable to challenge.

Finally, let me say a few words about our inner individual needs. What do you personally want to do or to be or to give to society? What are the personal ethics that drive your human engine? Science and technology have opened up incredible vistas for each one of us and forced us to deal with a remarkably wide set of choices for personal action. Knowing and not knowing is a debate that carries on in our conscious and subconscious mind, leading us along a personal voyage of discovery from uncertainty to confidence and back again. Developing our human potential is the loneliest, and yet the most extraordinary experience each one of us survives. We make choices all the time, sometimes by default.

(3) Discovery for the Future

Little free time is spent on things that are free today, and little free time is spent freely. Life seems rushed. I have tried to imagine the future world and pose questions that undoubtedly will absorb whatever free time we may choose to spend in trying to answer them. In the new realm of work, the conventional old lines of demarcation and responsibility will at first sight seem blurred. The old rules and old management styles do not always work. I hope we are clear in our goals, in what evidence we see, because if we are, we will ask the right questions. Ethics are not an add-on to this future. Ethical issues are central to decision-making and codes of behaviour which are set by, and also govern the norms of society. From the electronic board room to the computerized factory floor, ethical behaviour is everyone's business.

In the future, we will still sense that the bounds of time and space are collapsing. Stock markets now communicate around the globe in nanoseconds (10^{-9}s) and the space probe Voyager II launched a dozen years ago, has left our universe as this remarkably robotic vehicle travelled 4.6 billion miles, passed Neptune on its way, and now continues to another universe. Ice sheets, 500 km in length and 50 km wide are found in space and the frontiers of our galaxy continue to tantalize our minds.

The new work realm is digital but culturally we seem analogue in response. In the research world, whether in space or on earth, we are trying to understand what happens to the materials at the atomic level. The atoms and molecules can influence or scramble the encoding and decoding of information from electronic or optical sources. Versatility is the hallmark of our future capability. We must be both digital and analogue, both precise and uncertain, but always know our direction.

Whether deforestation, excessive grazing, or depletion of resources as demand escalates beyond delivery, both industrialized and developing countries share the global commons and the mutual responsibility for environmental integrity. What is ownership? Ownership of the broadcasting frequency spectrum, of space, of deep ocean floors, of the environment, must all be considered as much as ownership of firms or intellectual property. These are very interesting and important questions which have ethical dimensions in an age of pervasive technology. Once again, courage and conscience must meet imaginatively in our decision-making on ownership, public and private good issues.

Finally, imagine in our future world, the very real scenario that the store of human knowledge (such as the U.S. Library of Congress, the Canadian National Archives, the Bodleian, the great yet still hidden libraries of other cultures) comprising facts and interpretations, history and future trends are all stored holographically in a device the size of a sugar cube. Who has access to the sugar cube? How do you as individuals have access to the sugar cube? What do we do with the overwhelming volume of knowledge? Technology may be pervasive, but how pervasive is our understanding of all the facts, of the management of human change and our own personal voyages of discovery?

Science and technology are agents of change. Like love and betrayal, whether of ideas, or a country, a person or a personal future, science and technology carry a duality. They have already made us reflect upon, and be motivated by rapid changes in our village which have propelled us into a global realm of unprecedented opportunity. As developed and developing countries come to grips with opposite sides of a complex and environmentally common global coin, let us all commit to individual and societal leadership in placing ethical issues as high on our new agenda as education and the global environment. Science is a pervasive way of thinking about our culture, and so is ethics. Tension can be creative, not destructive. Atoms and molecules, at the microscopic level, move with uncertainty according to the laws of physics manifested in quantum mechanics. Learning to live wisely with change and uncertainty and to embrace the sense of discovery in nature and science is perhaps after all part of our natural order in this universe. We are part of this symbiotic sugar cube in the galaxy. The future challenges are ours to accept, and ours to decide.

SOURCE: *Critical Choices: Ethics, Science and Technology,* edited by Henry Wiseman, Jokelee Vanderkop and Jorge Nef. (Toronto: Thompson Educational Publishing, Inc.,1991). Reprinted with permission.

Questions and Topics for Discussion and Writing

1. What does the author mean when she asserts that "the global village is restless?" Why does she think that what she calls "the perspective of discovery" is the correct perspective through which this restlessness should be viewed?

2. Why does Kenney-Wallace claim that "every age is an information age?" She provides some historical examples to back up her claim; what other instances from history can be used to illustrate this point?

3. What is the duality that science and technology carry, according to Kenney-Wallace, and why does she conclude that this duality impels us to act ethically when making decisions about their impact on society?

A Consumer's Guide

Pseudoscience and Science

James S. Trefil

James S. Trefil (1938-) is professor of physics at the University of Virginia. In this selection on "pseudoscience" Trefil illustrates how information, when presented in a way that seems "scientific," can fool people. He is convinced that the world could use a do-it-yourself guide to the Alice-in-Wonderland realm of unorthodox scientific claims.

I have mixed feelings about the current boom in things parascientific—movies like *Star Wars* and *Close Encounters of the Third Kind*, TV shows about weekly UFO landings, and books about spaceships that descended to earth in prehistoric times. As a physicist, I realize that today's flights of fancy may well be tomorrow's scientific orthodoxy. But it worries me that a public ill equipped to distinguish between razzle-dazzle and sound speculation is swallowing whole many pseudoscientific notions that strike me as silly at best and as a species of intellectual junk food at worst.

My concern here is not, incidentally, altogether cool and disinterested; I still brood about the time several years ago when my son, then ten, was watching a TV "documentary" about ancient civilizations that had been visited by extraterrestrials. When I ventured something mildly skeptical about the show, my son turned on me and cried, "But didn't you *see!* They *proved* it!"

Repeated experiences like this with my children, my students, and my contemporaries have left me convinced that the world could use a kind of do-it-yourself guide to getting one's bearings in the Alice-in-Wonderland realm of unorthodox scientific claims. Before launching into this guide, however, I'd like to make some general remarks about off-beat claims and mention some concrete examples.

As I said above, it's important to realize that unorthodox views are not alien to conventional science. When you come down to it, every accepted scientific principle started out in life as an unorthodox thought in the mind of one man. It follows, then, that in every living science there is a frontier area where new basic principles are being sought and where innovative ideas can gain a hearing. In my own field of physics there are several frontier areas, the most wide-open one being the study of elementary particles (the subatomic objects that in some way contain the key to the ultimate structure of matter). So newness in itself is not now and never has been a basis for the rejection of an idea by the scientific community.

One can visualize the situation in science in terms of concentric circles: At the *center* is that body of time-tested, universally accepted ideas that are set forth in school and college texts. The first circle out from the center is the *frontier*, which interacts constantly with the center, feeding it new ideas that the center, after lengthy testing, adopts and assimilates.

If we move beyond the frontier region of a science, however, we come to a hazy outer circle area that I like to call the *fringe*. The fringe is characterized by a scarcity of hard data and by a general fuzziness of ideas that make the average scientist very uncomfortable. It is a zone in which neither accepted scientific writ nor reasonable extrapolations of scientific knowledge seem to apply. For these reasons, it is an area that scientists generally prefer to avoid. Yet the fringe has its uses, for it feeds ideas to the frontier, much as the frontier feeds ideas to the center. Fifty years ago, the notion that we should attempt to communicate with extraterrestrial intelligences would most emphatically have been a fringe concept. Yet today this idea has moved into the more respectable frontier circle. (Incidentally, this move illustrates an important point about the ideas contained within both the fringe and the frontier. The soundest, most useful of them keep gravitating inward, ring by ring, toward the orthodox center.)

Now there is only one thing that will make the average scientist more uneasy than talking about what lies beyond his particular frontier and that is having someone express doubts about the validity of ideas that he considers to be established at the center of his discipline and therefore no longer open to question. For example, in the time of Isaac Newton the law of gravity was a frontier subject, but now it is regarded as a principle that has been validated by centuries of experiment and use. This law has passed from the frontier of science and is firmly ensconced within the vital center. Anyone who suggests that the law ought to be abandoned or modified is not going to get a sympathetic hearing unless he presents a very convincing argument.

The progression of scientific ideas from frontier circle to "center" acceptance isn't always smooth. The germ theory of disease and the theory of continental drift are examples of ideas that were considered too "fringy" when they were first introduced. Only long, often acrimonious campaigns won them official recognition.

There have of course been thousands of fringe ideas that never made it to the frontier and thousands of frontier ideas that never gained centrist respectability. The basic problems, then, that anyone, scientist or layman, faces when confronted with a new theory are how to decide where it belongs on the concentric-circle scale and how to determine its chances of eventual acceptance.

In making such judgments, scientists have to keep two criteria in mind: A new idea may be rejected because it is too far beyond the frontier—for instance, too fringy and unprovable; or it may be rejected because it is too far behind the frontier—for instance, a clumsy, complicated way of accomplishing ends already being accomplished by simple, efficient, economical centrist theories. Thus, an overly elaborate, hard-to-prove, Rube Goldberg-like notion could be rejected because it might be at once too fringy and too inefficient in comparison with well-established centrist theories.

With this framework in mind, let's look at some current offbeat theories and the problems they pose for the citizen who is wondering whether to accept or reject their striking claims.

Velikovsky and *Worlds in Collision*

In 1950 Immanuel Velikovsky, a Russian-born psychoanalyst, published a book called *Worlds in Collision* that touched off a minor tempest among astronomers and served as a model for an entire generation of pseudoscientific writing. The premise of his work was that the recent history of our solar system has been marked by a series of catastrophic events and that these events are faithfully recorded in ancient writings. Thus, according to Velikovsky the planet we now know as Venus was ejected from Jupiter about 5,000 years ago (an event recorded in Greek mythology). Thereafter, Venus wandered about the solar system as a comet, experiencing several close encounters with our earth before settling into its present orbit. One of these encounters coincided with the parting of the Red Sea for the Israelites and another, with the stopping of the rotation of the earth for the benefit of the ancient Hebrew leader Joshua. Both of these events and other "catastrophes" too numerous to mention are recorded in the Old Testament.

To substantiate these claims, Velikovsky cited examples from other legends about massive floods and about days when the sun stood still in the sky. He also used the ancient writings to predict the properties of the planets. For example, since the manna that fell on the Israelites during their wanderings in the desert was supposed to have been material from the Venusian comet, he predicted that hydrocarbons (or many carbohydrates—the distinction between the two isn't clear in the book) would be found in the Venusian atmosphere. He also predicted that Venus would be found to be "candescent."

When these claims were made, very little was known about planetary science, so they could be classified as fringe ideas. At the same time, they required that known physical laws (such as the conservation of energy) had to have been violated at some time in the past or the events Velikovsky described would have been impossible. Thus, the scientific community rejected his thesis because his ideas were both too far ahead of and too far behind the frontier. (Velikovsky's followers also claim that a group of professors tried to suppress publication of the book. If this is true, I can only say that professors have less clout now than in the early fifties.)

Velikovsky's claims are set forth in a book that runs to 389 pages in the paperback edition. Faced with this avalanche of fact and hypothesis, what is the reader supposed to do? Well, in Velikovsky's case we're lucky because his book caused so much furore that a number of refutations have been written. The most recent of these refutations is the published proceedings of a symposium held in 1973 by the American Association for the Advancement of Science (AAAS) (Donald Goldsmith, ed., "Scientists Confront Velikovsky," Cornell University Press, 1977). A quick look at the *Reader's Guide to Periodical Literature* or at the card catalog of a public library will turn up other books and articles *contra* Velikovsky. The counterarguments fall into three categories: questions of fact, questions of logical consistency, and questions of alternative explanations.

Let's take the category of factual questions. As we noted above, Velikovsky claimed flatly that hydrocarbon-based manna from Venus fell upon the Israelites during their desert wanderings. Yet National Aeronautics and Space Administration space probes have turned up no evidence of hydrocarbons in the atmosphere of Venus—although once a scientist was misquoted as saying that an early probe did find such evidence—and the temperature of the planet is about what you'd expect on the basis of the greenhouse effect. (Certainly it's not hot enough to make the surface candescent.) Such evidence helps to clear the air, but it's hardly the kind of knowledge that most of us would have at our fingertips. In keeping with my goal of providing a do-it-yourself system for analyzing theories then, I'll have to turn to the other two categories, logical consistency and alternative explanations.

About logical consistency: If you look over Velikovsky's argument, it becomes apparent that the central point is his idea that ancient writings are supposed to be taken as literal, eyewitness accounts of celestial events. Fair enough. But when I read the Bible's account of the Israelites' wanderings, I find that the manna fell from heaven daily *except for the Sabbath*. Now I can imagine a comet whose tail contains edible material, and I can even conceive of this edible material falling only on one small area of the earth for an extended period, but I cannot for the life of me imagine a comet that keeps the Sabbath. That doesn't seem to me "logically consistent." This sort of example can be multiplied ad infinitum by anyone who looks seriously into the thousands of statements in *Worlds in Collision*.

In the same way—and here we come to the category of alternative explanations—we can ask if it's really necessary to suspend the laws of nature in order to explain the accounts of natural disasters in ancient writings. Isn't there some less complicated way of interpreting these phenomena? Surely disaster is one experience that has been shared, at one time or another, by the entire human race. And of course, the idea that ancient writers never took liberties with facts in order to achieve literary effect is a notion that doesn't stand scrutiny very well. If it did, we'd be faced with trying to explain why ancient writers were so different from their modern counterparts...

ETI and UFO Phenomena

If I had been writing this article 10 years ago, the field of extraterrestrial intelligence (ETI) and unidentified flying objects (UFOs) would have been relegated to the farthest reaches of the fringe. The whole thing reeked of little green men and bug-eyed monsters, and the Condon report had pretty well established that the great majority

Serious Scientific Chicanery

The "Science" of Intelligence Testing

James Trefil's article on "pseudoscience" illustrates the ways in which information, when presented in a way that seems sufficiently "scientific" can fool many people into believing things that are untrue, or only half-true.

Most of Trefil's examples are farily innocent — even if people watching a television show on the Great Pyramids or the Bermuda Triangle *do* believe what is convincingly presented by an authoritative-sounding narrator, backed by forceful music and reams of impressive facts and figures, the end result is that they will stop and think about what they have learned only rarely, and in a not-so-serious way at that. As Trefil suggests, this kind of mis-information is spread around at cocktail parties and offhand conversations around the office photocopier. It rarely goes further than that.

But what happens when the implications of false science are far more serious? Unfortunately, history is filled with scientists who have used their research for purposes that are less than admirable.

There is an unfortunate and long-standing tradition of researchers advancing theories about human intelligence and its connection to people's racial background. This research is objectionable for a number of reasons, not the least of which is that it ignores the effects of environment on intelligence-test results.

One of the worst perpetrators of the this form of scientific fraud was the noted English psychologist, Sir Cyril Burt, who at the time of his death in 1971 had become the first psychologist to be knighted. Burt had been honoured for his services to the British educational system, since he had "proven" that almost 80 percent of intelligence is inherited.

Burt's published research had great implication for educational systems worldwide, since it raised the implication that if intelligence was a fixed and inherited characteristic, there was little sense in attempting to work with children whose capacity for improvement was limited. Burt's theories were seized upon eagerly by many in the United States, who used his work to bolster their claim that government funding for lower-class and minority educational programs should be eliminated.

Fortunately, Burt's research was found to be almost completely fabricated. The amazing thing was that he had managed to fool the world-wide scientific community for nearly thirty years, with his imposing, authoritative manner, and his constant reference to a busy team of "co-workers" that never existed!

As James Trefil suggests, certain tricks can be used to dupe the lay public into believing pseudo-scientific information. But the career of Cyril Burt, who managed to deceive top-level psychologists for three decades, illustrates that scientific chicanery can exist at the highest levels.

of UFO sightings could be assigned a perfectly natural (although sometimes complex) explanation. There seemed to be nothing more to say on the subject.

In the past few years, however, a number of developments have occurred to alter this picture. Astronomers have started to give serious thought to the idea that radio telescopes might be able to "listen in" on signals from other planetary systems. In fact, the search for evidence of ETI has already begun with existing telescopes, and proposals are in the wind to build new ones just for this purpose. In a sense, the interest in ETI constitutes a success story in which a formerly unacceptable idea has moved into the realm of serious scientific consideration.

Although the UFO phenomenon hasn't achieved this sort of status, in recent years a few reputable scientists have been willing to look into UFO sightings to see if there might be something there beyond optical illusion. The results to date are not impressive, but the fact that some scientists are willing to take the time to examine the question is itself significant. I know it may sound terribly elitist to say so, but one of the best indicators of the soundness of a new idea is the willingness of scientists to devote their time to developing it.

Most scientists aren't wealthy, so about the only things they can invest in their career are the time and effort that go into research. Like an investor looking through stock offerings, each scientist has to make a judgment as to where his energies should go to produce the maximum return. Thus, when a scientist passes up "sure thing" conventional research to devote his time to something like listening with a radio telescope for extraterrestrial signals, he's doing the equivalent of putting his money where his mouth is.

Of course, the presence of reputable scientists in a field doesn't guarantee that the ideas being investigated will turn out to be right. On the other hand, there are a lot of conventional research projects that don't prove out either. So although the ETI-UFO subject still has a very fringy flavour to it, the past few years have seen some parts of it move tentatively into the legitimate frontier area of conventional science.

Pyramid Power

This whole pyramid-power business is so far out that I wasn't going to deal with it at all. I changed my mind when I saw the following ad in the catalog of a respected scientific-supplies company:

> **CAN THE GREAT PYRAMID UNLOCK THE MYSTERIES OF ENERGY & AGING?** .... *Did the ancient Egyptians build Cheops's Pyramid in such a way that the laws of nature are contradicted? Some people have been using exact scale models of the pyramids and are claiming all kinds of things...meat doesn't rot, razor blades stay sharp, things don't rust, and other strange phenomena. All these claims are based on energy resonating in an exact scale model of Cheops's Pyramid oriented to magnetic North.*

From this ad, it's clear we're dealing with something firmly established behind the frontier. Oh well, back to Volume 18 of the *Britannica* for the pyramid dimensions. Assemble, as I did, a cardboard pyramid. Put a piece of hamburger inside and line the pyramid up with a compass. Wait a few days. Whew!

Do-It-Yourself Checklist

On the basis of the foregoing examples, I think we can now try to list general techniques that anyone can use when confronted with the next plausibly presented arguments for God-only-knows-what new idea. Here are some useful questions to ask:

Are the facts really what the author says they are?

Further (and more to the point), has someone already been sufficiently irritated by the author's claims to answer this question for you? Some of the "facts" presented in any argument just might be wrong, but it's not always convenient to check them out yourself. It's always easier if someone else does the work. For example, trying to run down all the half truths, rumours, and inaccuracies about the Bermuda Triangle would be a prodigious task. Fortunately, you don't have to do it because it's been done and the results published by Lawrence Kusche in The Bermuda Triangle Mystery—Solved (Harper & Row, 1975). In a similar vein, the proceedings of the AAAS symposium mentioned previously give a pretty good overall critique of Velikovsky, so you don't have to go searching around for scattered articles.

Therefore the first thing to do is to check your local library listings on the subject you want to look into.

Is the author trying to overload your circuits?

Although Erich von Daniken is the best (or worst) example of this technique of bludgeoning the reader into quiescence, all such authors that I have read use it. The only defense against the ploy is to pick out a few statements made about a field you know something of and look into them thoroughly. The chances are that if the author hasn't gotten those right, he hasn't done too good a job on the material you don't check.

Given the author's facts, is there a simpler explanation of them?

If I had to pick the single failing that characterizes pseudoscientific theories, I would choose their tendency *to propose complex solutions to simple problems.* We have already seen in the case of Velikovsky that the existence of old manuscripts describing cataclysmic events can easily be explained in terms of shared human experiences and of the known tendency of writers to exaggerate. What are we to do then when given the choice between revising almost the whole body of physics and astronomy and accepting as literal truth "facts" that may be only-too-human exaggerations? It seems to me that the most sensible path is to take the explanation that does the least amount of damage to other ideas.

I can't resist mentioning another example of how this criterion works. In the ancient-astronaut documentary mentioned earlier, there was an episode in which a subterranean vault with painted walls was shown. The announcer made a big point of claiming that there was no evidence of soot (such as a torch would have left) anywhere in the vault. The program's conclusion was that the ancient Egyptians must have had access to electric lights and hence had been visited by extraterrestrials.

Now, even assuming that it is correct that this chamber was put together without any soot being left behind by the workmen, does it necessarily follow that the Egyptians were visited by astronauts? Putting it another way, if you were an Egyptian engineer, could you think of a way to get a chamber built without leaving deposits of soot? A few minutes' reflection turns up (1) washing the soot off after the work is finished, (2) sinking a shaft to the chamber to let smoke out and light in, (3) doing it all with mirrors.

The interested citizen should always take a little time to play devil's advocate on such questions because the penchant for ignoring the very existence of a simpler explanation of the facts—an explanation that doesn't require a wildly complicated set of theories—is the besetting weakness of almost all pseudoscience.

Does the whole thing boil down to being unable to prove a negative?

It is impossible to prove that there are no unicorns. All we can prove is that we've found none so far. If the end result of a long argument (the "bottom line," if you prefer) is nothing more than the statement that a particular theory can't be disproved, you are probably safe putting it in the same class as unicorns.

Are established scientists putting time in on the phenomenon?

In the case of UFOs and ETIs, discussed above, one element in our considerations was the fact that a number of reputable scientists have been willing to bet their valuable time that the idea has something to it. While this doesn't guarantee that an idea is right, it does mean that someone has looked into it thoroughly and has come up with the conclusion that it's worth looking into a little more.

Having said this, let me hasten to add a caveat. There is no proposition on God's green earth so silly that it can't find at least one Ph.D. to support it. If you're going to use this criterion in judging a theory, find out who the scientists are. A quick check in *American Men and Women of Science* or in *Who's Who* will give you some idea of the credentials of the person involved. If you want a standard of comparison, look up Peter Sturrock, of Stanford University—he's one of the people with sound credentials who are investigating UFO sightings these days.

Finally, you have to realize that this "credentials" criterion is only one of several you should use in making a judgment. If the theory sounds fishy to you, if you feel that the conclusions are unreasonable, and if the arguments of the scientists don't convince you, then so be it. In the final analysis, you have to make up your own mind anyway.

Can you test the theory yourself?

If you have a mechanical turn of mind, you can occasionally check out a claim yourself, as I did with the pyramid-power test.

Ask such simple questions as those on the checklist when you're reading the next book that reveals the secret of the ages; they will help you decide whether you're looking at a genuine scientific breakthrough or at just another addition to the fringe. There are two areas in which such questioning will be of little help, however, and we might as well get them straight right now. If outright fraud is involved—as it is reputed to have been in the famous "demonstration" by Uri Geller at the Stanford Research Institute—going through this sort of questioning will do you little good. There is no way that fraud can be detected secondhand by the layman, and there is probably no one more ill equipped than the average scientist to deal with outright duplicity. Also, the test questions really don't apply to writings that are specifically nonrational, such as the mystical and drug-oriented books that were so common a few years ago. Such books aren't playing the same game as those by the pseudoscientists and therefore can't be judged by the same rules.

No discussion of pseudoscience would be complete without some comment on its social implications. I am well aware that many of my colleagues regard modern pseudoscience as the forerunner of an antirational swing in our society and denounce it in terms that are worthy of that doom-crying German philosopher Oswald Spengler. I feel that this is something of an overreaction. Pseudoscience has been around at least as long as (and perhaps even longer than) conventional science. Perhaps it serves some deep need of human beings to believe that there is still some mystery—something unknown—left in life. Maybe the unknown thrives because people like to see the pompous scientific establishment discomfited ("Okay, Mr. Know-it-all, explain *this* one"). Or maybe it's just that P.T. Barnum was right about a sucker being born every minute. None of these interpretations constitutes a threat to conventional science.

After all, Luigi Galvani's "animal electricity" cures in the nineteenth century didn't impair the development of the science of electricity. Mme. Blavatsky's theosophy certainly had little effect on American science. And despite the apocalyptic terms with which it was greeted, it would be hard to show that Velikovsky's *Worlds in Collision* has had much of an effect on modern astronomy. At its worst, pseudoscience is a minor inconvenience of the cocktail party variety; and at its best, it is good entertainment. I certainly make no apology for the fact that I enjoyed reading Velikovsky and von Daniken, even though I think they are wrong.

SOURCE: Reprinted from *The Saturday Review*, 29 April 1978.

Questions and Topics for Discussion and Writing

1. What is the main issue illustrated by Trefil's anecdote about his ten-year-old son? Why is the author still brooding over this incident? How does this story compare with Sagan's experience as a guest in a first-grade classroom? (See the earlier article by Sagan.)

2. Is Trefil's construction of the concentric-circle model (centre, frontier and fringe) a useful one in assisting his reader in envisioning the separate realms of scientific theory? Why or why not? It is possible to construct a better model?

3. What is the relationship of the Scientific Method to Trefil's contentions about being unable to prove a negative?

Is There a Lesson Here for the Internet?

Déjà Vu—All over Again!

Todd Lappin

In the beginning, when the frontier was wide open, 12 year-old Maynard Mack wanted to see what the fuss was all about.

He'd heard about the hip new technology. He'd been told about the miracles the future would bring. And he'd picked up a few copies of the latest specialty magazines. But the prefab boxes he saw advertised in those pages were hard to come by and far too expensive for a country kid from Ohio. "They may have been available for sale somewhere, but I certainly never saw them," Maynard says.

So he assembled his equipment on a wing and a prayer. Yet even as he was entranced by the new medium, Maynard—like thousands of other amateurs—didn't know what would become of his efforts.

The high-powered corporate executives didn't know either, but they were sure they wanted a piece of the action. The pundits didn't know, despite their predictions that the new technology would bring the blessings of Knowledge, Culture, and Democracy into every home across the land. And the politicians in Washington didn't know, though they recognized that the frontier was developing so quickly that hordes of voters would soon be breathing down their necks.

They all knew they were onto something.

"Let us not forget that the value of this great system does not lie primarily in its extent or even in its efficiency. Its worth depends on the use that is made of it … For the first time in human history we have available to us the ability to communicate simultaneously with millions of our fellowmen, to furnish entertainment, instruction, widening vision of national problems and national events. An obligation rests on us to see that it is devoted to real service and to develop the material that is transmitted into that which is really worthwhile."

Mitch Kapor? Newt Gingrich? Al Gore? Alvin Toffler?

Nope. Herbert Hoover, speaking in 1924 as the Secretary of Commerce. And the "great system?" Not the Internet. Nor the Infobahn. It was radio. Plain ol' broadcast radio.

In 1922, the "radio craze" was taking the country by storm. Journalists wrote ecstatic articles describing the newest developments in wireless technology. Politicians hailed radio as the latest product of American entrepreneurial genius. The term "broadcasting"—previously used by farmers to describe the "act or process of scattering seeds" was rapidly becoming a household word, complete with all its contemporary mass media connotations. Radio stations were popping up like dandelions across the land. Meanwhile, back in Ohio, young Maynard Mack kept track of these advances by poring over the pages of the nearest big-city newspaper, Cleveland's *The Plain Dealer*.

Maynard didn't want to miss out on the fun. So he gathered together a mad scientist's assortment of hardware—a few scraps of plywood, a couple yards of wire, two or three control knobs, a cylindrical oatmeal carton, and a surplus vacuum tube he got from the chemistry department of the local college—and went to work building himself a radio receiver based on a set of plans he'd seen in a magazine.

That's what you did if you were an inquisitive kid growing up in the early 1920s, says Maynard, now a retired Yale University literature professor. You went cruising along the frontier of high-tech electronic communications. In other words, you built a crude, homemade radio receiver, strapped on a clunky set of headphones, and tried to listen to the signals being exchanged through the ether. Maynard remembers that sometimes he'd hear nothing but static for hours on end. Sometimes he'd struggle to decipher a few stray dots and dashes of Morse code conversation hammered out by other amateur radio enthusiasts on their jury-rigged transmitters. And when he really struck gold, he'd manage to catch one of the night-time music or news programs emanating from KDKA in Pittsburgh, Pennsylvania, one of the nation's first radiobroadcast stations. "Back then, you had to make your own entertainment," Maynard muses.

If Maynard Mack had been born 60 years later—in 1970 instead of 1910—he still might have kept busy manufacturing his own entertainment. But in 1982, he would have been staying up late to construct a Frankenclone PC up in his bedroom. And nowadays, he'd probably be puttering around with motherboards and high-speed modems instead of all those goofy radio parts. Maybe he'd spend hours surfing the Web, skimming Usenet groups, or loitering in America Online chat rooms. That's what you do if you're an inquisitive kid growing up in the 1990s. You cruise along the frontier of high-tech electronic communications. You get wired, you go online, and you explore the world of activity unfolding in cyberspace. But when Maynard Mack was growing up, the goal was to get wireless.

Get wired! Get wireless! They may sound contradictory, but historically, they mean the same thing. It's about riding the wave. Actualizing tomorrow. Plugging in. Checking it out. Getting the scoop on the Next Big Something.

Today's Next Big Something is so wrapped in hype it's tough to see what's really going on. And as the hype solidifies into conventional wisdom, almost anyone can recite the narrative. It goes like this: The online revolution is happening now. The revolution will facilitate interaction through the digital exchange of information. By exchanging information, we grow closer as a community. By exchanging information, we become free. Blah, blah, blah.

But what if conventional wisdom is wrong? What if the crystalball narrative doesn't turn out as planned? What if, a decade or so from now, we wake up to find that the digisphere has been overrun by swarms of inane mass marketeers—people who believe that "interacting" is something you do with a set-top box that provides only an endless stream of movies-on-demand, bargains overflowing from virtual shopping malls, and spiffy videogames?

It has happened before.

This isn't the first time a new medium has come along, promising to radically transform the way we relate to one another. It isn't even the first time a fellowship of amateur trailblazers has led the charge across the new media hinterland. Radio started out the same way. It was a truly interactive medium. It was user-dominated and user-controlled. But gradually, as the airwaves became popular, that precious interactivity was lost. We need to understand how that happened.

We've come a long way since the early 1920s—so far that it's difficult to imagine a time when the radios now on our bed tables and in the dashboards of our cars were worshipped as objects of cultic fascination and mystery. Radio long ago lost its shimmering, high-tech gloss. Since the early 1920s, a science fiction writer's dreamscape of new communications technologies have come along to nudge radio from the spotlight. In the 1950s, we got black-and-white televisions. In the 1960s, color television. In the 1970s, cable. Then came infatuation with VCRs. Satellite dishes. Cellular telephones. And now we've got PCs with online hookups.

The glitter may be gone, but broadcast radio is alive and well. After all, radios are a fixture in 98 percent of American homes and in almost as many automobiles. Radio broadcasting remains a staple of our mass-media diet. We listen to it while getting dressed in the morning. During the daily commute. At work. Or while doing chores around the house. And as we continue to tune in, we also transform radio's most adept practitioners into national celebrities. Rush, Garrison, and Howard, to name a few. But 75 years ago, there was no such thing as a radio celebrity. Radio sets were an expensive novelty. In 1922, for example, when less than 0.2 percent of American households owned a radio receiver, the average radio set cost a whopping 50 bucks. (At the time, US$50 was about 2 percent of an average American family's annual household income—which means that a radio would have set you back about as much as a well-equipped home computer today.) Few anticipated that listening to the radio was an activity that would someday appeal to broad segments of the population. Seventy-five years ago, radio broadcasting resembled the PC industry during the days of Jobs and Wozniak—it was an infant technology struggling to establish a niche for itself in the food chain of modern mass communications.

Yet even during those early days, enough people were listening for the medium to catch on. Radio listeners fell into two categories. First, there were the professionals. These were people who worked for companies that sought to turn a profit from wireless technology—business giants like General Electric Corp., Westinghouse Electric and Manufacturing Corp., the American Telephone and Telegraph Company, and the newly formed Radio Corporation of America (RCA). The men at the helm of these corporations thought radio had only limited consumer appeal. As if mesmerized by the old media paradigm of the telephone, they convinced themselves that the future of wireless radio lay in the direction of targeted, point-to-point communications. Specifically, they concluded that radio was naturally suited for use in environments where wired telephone networks were either too expensive or too impractical to operate. Thus the professionals went to market offering wellheeled clients premium services such as ship-to-shore maritime communication and intercontinental messaging services.

Then there were the amateurs, who didn't care much about radio's profit-making potential. They got involved with wireless because they were fascinated by the new technology. The amateurs were hackers, basically hobbyists, tinkerers, and technofetishists who huddled in their garages, attics, basements, and woodsheds to experience the wondrous possibilities of the latest communications miracle. Unlike the professionals, the amateurs didn't view radio exclusively as a tool for point-to-point communications. They also used it to communicate with anyone who happened to be listening.

The airwaves were wide open, more or less. The professionals had ignored the mass-market potential of wireless technology, leaving plenty of room for amateur enthusiasts to stake their claims along the bandwidth spectrum. Licensing requirements issued by the Department of Commerce were reasonably easy to meet for anyone who wanted to set up a transmitter. (Proficiency in Morse code was the most daunting requirement.) And once you got on the bandwagon, there was a whole community of likeminded early enthusiasts who were eager to welcome you aboard. It wasn't fancy, but then again, neither was Arpanet back in the days when Vint Cerf was calling the shots.

In his 1928 history, *The Electric Word: The Rise of Radio*, author Paul Schubert describes what it was like to be one of those primordial broadcasters in 1917, the period just prior to America's entry into World War I. "Before the war," Schubert writes, "there had been some five thousand licensed radio amateurs scattered throughout the nation, most of them youngsters. Limitations on power and wavelength had made the achievement of great distances generally impossible by them, but through their organization, The American Radio Relay League, they had been able to exchange communications from coast to coast. And they had filled one most important place in radio activities—they served as a cooperating audience to the serious experimenters who were striving to perfect the more subtle utilizations of the art."

Just after World War I, the radio ranks swelled even further, as thousands of Army-trained radio operators were demobilized. At the time, transmitting equipment was confusing, temperamental, and hard to come by, but figuring out how to get it all together and make it work was part of the sport (as anyone who's ever spent a few hours wrestling with initialization strings for a SLIP connection understands). And in the end, it was worth the effort. After all, there was nothing like the intoxicating rush that came from connecting with strangers in ways that had never been possible before.

"I think I can sympathize with and understand the passion of the wireless amateur who goes fishing in the electrical ocean, hoping to draw a congenial spirit out of the unknown depths," a contributor wrote in a 1924 edition of *Radio Broadcast* magazine. "This type of amateur sits in his laboratory and sends out a little message, baited with 10 watts, say, and then listens with a beating heart for a response from the void. Usually his cry is in vain. He draws a blank. But sometimes he hears, mixed up with his heart throbs, a reply from another 'brass pounder' calling him by his sign letters. What a thrill!"

Tuning in was something that was done actively—not passively.

For the thousands of amateurs who owned radio transmitters, the ether crackled to life as a two-way communications medium, whenever they strapped on headphones to begin tapping out Morse code or speaking into the microphone. Meanwhile, there were thousands more, like Maynard Mack, who chose the easier path—setting up a receiving outfit without the transmitter. But they too were encouraged to get in on all the interactive programming by sending amateur broadcasters "Applause Cards"—postcards confirming receipt of their transmissions. "Although not a hundred miles from N.Y. I must write to tell you how I heard your signals last night," a Connecticut listener scribbled after hearing a 1920 broadcast by station 2XB in Manhattan. "I happened to catch a part of the 10:45 period. At 11:15 when I found you were on a longer wavelength than I expected, I heard every word beautifully. Monday night we are having a little company to listen to you and if you can acknowledge by a word or two to me, I will be more than delighted."

For a while, the amateurs had a pretty good thing going. It was all very nice and ever-so civil. While blazing a path through the airwaves and attracting a growing following among members of the general public, the amateurs built an iconoclastic virtual community within the static-plagued nether world of the broadcast ether. In the early 1920s, it was a community spearheaded by thousands of precocious young Americans who could easily "talk inductance, capacity, impedance, resistance, and the other technical terms with a pretty thorough grasp on their meaning and a good appreciation of their application in radio work," according to *Electrical World* magazine. It was a wireless community that operated according to its own set of rules, protocols, customs, and taboos. Creative experimentation with radio programming was encouraged. Monopolizing bandwidth was considered bad form. And blatant commercialism was completely uncool.

Radio Broadcast magazine was a mouthpiece for the amateurs and the burgeoning broadcast audience. It was also a focal point for the articulation of their values and their interests. *Radio Broadcast* sought to chronicle the ways in which the advent of a new communications medium promised to permanently alter the face of culture and society.

Thumbing through back issues of *Radio Broadcast* is an eye-opening experience: it is startling to discover how much like us our radio precursors were. They spoke with similar enthusiasm and asked many of the same questions. They believed in their new technology, and they believed that it should be harnessed to help make the future better than the past.

"Will Radio Make the People the Government?" demanded a headline in a 1924 issue of *Radio Broadcast*. Political columnist Mark Sullivan was reluctant to answer the question definitively, but he had little doubt that the confluence of radio and politics was destined to profoundly impact on American democracy. "The fundamental merit of the radio in Congress will be that it will enable the public to get its information direct," Sullivan prophesied in proto-Gingrichian tones. "At present, aside from those speeches from men who, because of one distinction or another, have all their speeches printed in full—aside from these, the public is now dependent on the vicarious censorship of the newspaper reporter. It is the reporter who ignores some speeches, makes mere allusions to some, and transmits extracts from others. In all this exercise of judgment and taste, there are the aberrations that inevitably accompany any individual judgment." But radio would change all that. "The person who wants to listen to Congress will be able to do so, and there will be many who will want to listen."

Others speculated that radio would put politics on a more rational footing and bring civility back into the campaign process. "There is no doubt whatever that radio broadcasting will tend to improve the caliber of speeches delivered at the average political meeting," a *Radio Broadcast* editor wrote in his monthly column. "Personality will count for nothing as far as the radio audience is concerned. Ill-built sentences expressing weak ideas cannot succeed without the aid of forensic gesticulation. The flowery nonsense and wild rhetorical excursions of the soap box spellbinder are probably a thing of the past if a microphone is being used. The radio listener, curled comfortably in his favorite chair is likely to criticize the vituperations of the vote pleader quite severely. Woe be unto the candidate who depends for public favor upon wild rantings and tearings of hair."

Politics would not be alone in feeling the impact of radio's growing reach. Religion, too, was destined for dramatic transformation. On January 2, 1921, the Reverend Edwin J. Van Etten of the Calvary Episcopal Church on Shady Avenue in Pittsburgh became the first minister in the United States to broadcast a church service by wireless radio. (The pilot broadcast went without a hitch, with the help of two wireless engineers—one Jewish and one Catholic—who spent the duration of the service camouflaged in choir robes.) Response to the experiment was strong, and in subsequent months, donations from the Calvary Church's "Unseen Congregation" flowed in steadily. But as more and more churches took to the airwaves, Van Etten developed a strangely Darwinistic view of the trend he had unleashed.

"Broadcasting of church services will prove something of a disintegrating force on the church organizations," he warned in a 1923 issue of *Radio Broadcast*. "Only the fittest preachers will survive, and struggling churches will, more or less, go to the wall."

Apparently, such fears were shared by Van Etten's superiors. A few months later, Episcopal Bishop Stearly wrote a letter to *Radio Broadcast* asking, "Why go to your parish church when you can sit at ease in your parlour and hear the heavenly music of a capable choir and be charmed by the fervid eloquence of a magnetic preacher? There seems to have entered into our crowded and throbbing life another ally of those forces which make difficult the assembling of the faithful for praise and prayer...Now it becomes necessary for the clergy to make the church more attractive than the world's entertainments, to discover to men the possibilities within it for strength and refreshment, and the gifts of grace in its bestowings, more precious than earthly things."

The future of radio was so bright even the sacred aura of the Almighty looked faded by comparison.

Nevertheless, the editors of *Radio Broadcast* had their own demons to contend with. All of a sudden, radio broadcasting had become wildly popular. Everyone was taking to the airwaves—broadcasters and listeners alike. In early 1921, only five stations had received the new "broadcast class" licenses that were being issued by the Department of Commerce for transmissions of "market or weather reports, and music, concerts, lectures, etc." By early 1923, that number had shot up to 576.

Meanwhile, as radio receivers got easier to use and broadcast programming more interesting, hundreds of thousands of Americans started tuning in for the first time. Hardware practically flew off dealers' shelves as sales of radio receivers jumped sixfold, from $60 million in 1922 to $358 million in 1924.

As more and more listeners began hearing an ever-growing variety of radio broadcasts, programming tastes became increasingly sophisticated. Newcomers didn't want to hear radio geeks chatting among themselves in Morse code. Like newbies on America Online, they wanted their information to arrive in neatly wrapped packages. They wanted to hear professional-quality programs broadcast with professional-quality transmitting equipment. They wanted to be entertained and informed. That meant live music. And speeches. Sporting events. News and weather reports. And they wanted it all to come in crystal clear, with little static or interference.

The sudden popularity put the squeeze on broadcasters, because meeting the expectations of this growing audience was an expensive proposition. Not only did it cost anywhere from $3,000 to $50,000 and up to build and equip a broadcast station, but there were plenty of operating costs to account for even after the station was up and running—staff salaries, equipment maintenance, compensation for musicians and performers. All these costs were borne by broadcast station owners, while broadcast listeners paid nothing at all for the programming they received and enjoyed. And nobody had yet figured out an acceptable way to recover all that station investment, as the idea of "direct advertising" remained beyond the pale of public tolerance. It was a problem many impoverished Web site administrators should appreciate.

Radio broadcasting was an expensive proposition, yet few station owners were prepared to bear these costs indefinitely. The 576 radio broadcast stations operating in 1923 were run by an eclectic assortment of business people, starry-eyed idealists, public-service organizations. and hardcore wireless addicts. Few regarded radio broadcasting as a profit-making venture unto itself—most broadcast stations were created to serve as high-tech promotional gimmicks that would draw attention to the station owners' primary line of business. Thus in Philadelphia, Gimbel's Brothers department store operated station WIF. Retailer L. Bamberger & Co. founded WOR in New York. WAAF in Chicago was run by the Union Stock Yards & Transit Co. In New Lebanon, Ohio, the Nushawg Poultry Farm owned station WPG. And in Los Angeles, the City Dye Works and Laundry Co. started station KUS.

The broadcast landscape of the early 1920s might have seemed pretty familiar to us if somebody had tacked a suffix of -.com, -.edu, -.gov, or -.org onto the call letters of each radio station. In 1923, for example, 39 percent of radio broadcast stations were owned by companies that manufactured or sold radio hardware and equipment. An assortment of retail stores and commercial businesses owned another 14 percent. Thirteen percent was owned by educational institutions such as schools and universities. Twelve percent was owned by newspapers or publishing houses. Churches and YMCAs owned 2 percent. Municipalities and publicly regulated utilities each owned 1 percent. And the rest were operated by a motley collection of "others," whose ranks included everyone from ranchers and Boy Scouts to eccentric millionaires and backyard amateurs.

Unfortunately, nobody had yet figured out a way to make money from radio broadcasting. And until that happened, the "wireless craze" could be dismissed as just another pop-culture fad. Industry experts argued that wireless wouldn't end up in every American home until broadcast quality was improved on a nationwide basis, but such obvious conclusions didn't help much when it came time to figure out a way to finance all this mass media

Internet Glossary

Welcome to Cyberspace

Information Highway—A popular term for the network or networks capable of transporting voice, interactive television, full-motion video, sound, graphics and data: a single system connecting telephones, television cable and computers.

Cyberspace—Known as the online world, this term is used to describe the intertwining of more than 15,000 computer networks around the world whereby people can communicate through the use of computers and the internet system.

Internet— A network of computers that connects more than 30 million people, used for communicating by electronic mail (email), the transfer of files, and the searching of vast databases of information.

World Wide Web—The WWW is an enormous system of interlinked computer systems that provides the user with information that includes text, sound, and images.

infrastructure development. Thus a single question appears over and over on the pages of *Radio Broadcast* magazine throughout the first half of the 1920s: Who will pay for radio broadcasting?

There were plenty of ideas floating around. In 1921, *Radio Broadcast* proposed that since the airwaves were a public treasure, it was only natural that each radio station should seek out a "public spirited citizen"—preferably one with very deep pockets—to act as a patron. "We have gymnasiums, athletic fields, libraries, museums, etc. endowed and for what purpose? Evidently for the amusement and education of the public. But it may be that in the early future the cheapest and most efficient way of dispensing amusement and education may be by radiophone," the magazine suggested.

Two years later, the editors of *Radio Broadcast* thought they had their sugar daddy. An assortment of Wall Street financiers—gentlemen "who could not possibly be suspected of any idea of profit-taking, and who have been intimately connected with other musical ventures"—announced that they planned to form a non profit group called the Radio Music Fund Committee to "solicit funds from the listening public, calling for contributions of a dollar up, from all those who are entertained." The funds received would then be "directly applied to the securing of artists of the highest caliber."

A similar plan was tested at WHB, a station owned by the Sweeny Auto School in Kansas City. After issuing a statement pleading that "it is only fair for those sharing the pleasure to pay a portion of the expense," WHB's station head managed to pry $3,100 from his "invisible audience." Such results were encouraging, but encouragement and $3,100 wouldn't cover all the bills. "Of course that amount won't go far towards keeping a broadcast station running," *Radio Broadcast* admitted, "but the audience is indeed showing an appreciative spirit." There were other suggestions. Broadcast programming could be delivered as a public utility to American homes through wired networks, much like electricity or telephone service. Shortwave transmitters could be pressed into action, since the greater range of shortwave broadcasts would eliminate the need to operate so many local stations. David Sarnoff, vice president and general manager of RCA, volunteered that leading equipment manufacturers would be happy to aid the cause by tacking a broadcast surcharge onto the cost of radio hardware. And in New York, an experiment in municipal financing was launched in 1924 with the founding of radio station WNYC.

Finally, in 1925, *Radio Broadcast* announced that after having reviewed roughly a thousand entries, a winner had been chosen in the magazine's first-ever, "Who Is to Pay for Broadcasting and How?" essay contest. The $500 first prize was awarded to H.D. Kellogg Jr. of Haverford, Pennsylvania, for his suggestion that the federal government collect a sales tax of $2 per amplifier tube and $0.50 per radio crystal sold. The amassed tax revenues would then be distributed to broadcast stations nationwide by a new bureaucracy, the Federal Bureau of Broadcasting. The plan seemed comprehensive, but was coolly received by many analysts. Professor J.H. Morecroft, a former president of the Institute of Radio Engineers, wrote, "I do not see how a fund collected from the taxing measure can be equitably distributed. I dislike the idea of Government getting into the game because of its well-known and frequently proved inefficiency and blighting effect in attempting to carry out technical expertise. Let us keep broadcasting as far as possible out of Government hands." Sound familiar?

Herbert Hoover shared this free market bias, and his critique of the *Radio Broadcast* plan made that perfectly clear. In 1922, the English had launched a centralized system of hardware taxation on behalf of a new radio trust called the British Broadcasting Company, or BBC. Hoover wasn't about to let the same thing happen in the United States. "I do not believe that your prize-winning plan is feasible under conditions as they exist in this country, however well it may work elsewhere," he huffed.

There may have been as many different proposals about how to pay for broadcasting as there were frequencies on the radio dial, but everyone seemed to agree on two things: federal management wasn't an option, and selling air time to advertisers was absolutely out of the question.

"I believe that the quickest way to kill broadcasting would be to use it for direct advertising," Secretary Hoover argued in 1924. "The reader of the newspaper has an option whether he will read an ad or not, but if a speech by the President is to be used as the meat in a sandwich of two patent medicine advertisements, then there will be no radio left."

Hoover uttered these words during his opening address at the Third Annual Radio Conference—a meeting of radio executives and government technocrats held in Washington, DC, to chart the future of the broadcast industry. Two years earlier, during the 1922 conference, Hoover had been heard making similarly negative comments about the evils of "other advertising."

"It is inconceivable that we should allow so great an opportunity for service to be drowned in advertising chatter," he had said.

After Herbert Hoover sketched out his ideal of commercial-free broadcasting at the first Washington radio conference, *Radio Broadcast* reported that several bigwigs from American Telephone and Telegraph had "agreed with this point of view." But back in Manhattan, a group of AT&T colleagues were busy working on a project that would soon lead to the near total commercialization of the broadcast airwaves. It was to be the "killer app" of the radio broadcast industry—an innovation that would, in a single stroke, solve the "who is going to pay" riddle and create a mechanism for financing the production of audience-attracting radio shows. It was a new programming format that would suburbanize the wireless frontier. But nobody realized that at the time. Not Herbert Hoover. Not the editors of *Radio Broadcast.* Not the amateurs. Not even the guys at AT&T. Nobody knew that big change was afoot.

It was all taking place out in the open—right under everybody's nose. Two weeks before the start of the 1922 radio conference, AT&T issued a press release announcing that the nation's premier telecommunications company planned to inaugurate a brand-new wireless service. It was going to be called "toll broadcasting."

"The American Telephone and Telegraph Company will provide no program of its own, but provide the channels through which anyone with whom it makes a contract can send out their own programs," the press release explained. "Just as the company leases its long-distance wire facilities for the use of newspapers, banks and other concerns, so it will lease its radio telephone facilities and will not provide the matter which is sent out from this station."

It sure sounded innocent enough. AT&T simply planned to build a giant pay phone. Toll broadcasting would work like a radio phone booth in which anyone with something to say or a song to sing could walk in, stand before the microphone, and get the word out to thousands of fellow citizens. One-to-one communication would give way to one-to-many, but the basic pay-phone idea would remain the same. You plunk down your money, and you speak your piece. Pay as you play. The phone company would merely rent you some hardware—in the form of radio station WEAF. And instead of needing pocket change, you'd have to bring along some pretty big bills to use this new phone booth. Rates started at $40 for a 15-minute period in the afternoon, or $50 in the evening.

It took a few months for the idea to catch on, but toll broadcasting was a hit. At 5:15 in the afternoon on August 28, 1922, WEAF sent out its first commercial message. The groundbreaking broadcast came in the form of an infomercial by the Queensboro Corporation, a New York development company that sought to educate the listening audience about American novelist Nathaniel Hawthorne—and perhaps unload a few units in the company's new "Hawthorne Court" apartment complex over in Jackson Heights, Queens, at the same time.

"I wish to thank those within the sound of my voice for the broadcasting opportunity afforded to me to urge this vast radio audience to seek the recreation and the daily comfort of a home far removed from the congested part of the city, right at the boundaries of God's great outdoors, and within a few minutes by subway from the business section of Manhattan," began Mr. Blackwell

A New Age of Information Technology?

The Internet and the World Wide Web

We are told we are entering a new era of **information technology**. Nowhere is this revolution better seen than in the recent rapid development of the **Internet**.

Below we briefly describe what this thing is, show what you can expect to see on it, explain how you can cruise the **information superhighway**, and finally speculate where this technology might be leading us. It is fairly easy to gain access to this technology, so you should consider exploring it.

E-mail and Newsgroups

The Internet is a network of computers around the world. Originally designed for research and military purposes, the "net" has become widely popular.

Recently, the biggest area of expansion is simply **e-mail**—messages sent from individuals to other individuals across the country or around the world at telephone-connection speeds. The network is already in place, so there is no additional cost to send these messages. More and more individuals (estimated at around 30 million) are now on the Internet using e-mail. All that is needed is an e-mail account name (such as thompson@epas.utoronto.ca) and you can send and receive e-mail to anyone else on the Internet, providing you know their address. If you have a friend in Australia, then you could have virtually instantaneous connection with him or her.

As an extension of this idea, you can "join" **newsgroups**. These are electronic forums where you can discuss with others around the world on any topic area that might interest you. By joining (usually simply by sending an e-mail message), you can receive from and send mail to any other subscriber in that newsgroup. There are thousands upon thousands of these newsgroups.

The World Wide Web

Recently, there has been an expansion in the graphic side of the internet, known as the **World Wide Web**. Here you are looking at full-colour photographs, the possibility of sound and even motion pictures. It is definitely the way of the future.

Increasingly, countless associations (Windsurfing clubs and the like) and commercial businesses (a great many enterprises, large and small) are setting up their own **WWW sites** where they show their products and take orders. There are also major internet/WWW directories (*www.akebono.com*, for example in California) which can be starting off points to the sites around the world. In addition, you can also search for information at major "search sites". These **search engines** will find key words by scrounging around sites registered with them.

What will I see?

The adjacent photographs are taken from the World Wide Web itself (though they are printed here in only black and white). They are typical of what you might find once you **log on**.

The idea is to call in, using your modem, to a WWW site (which has a special address). This brings you to the site owner's **home page**.

The home page will likely contain highlighted words (like the bold words in this article) that can be clicked with your mouse. If you click on a word, you will then be shunted off to another page. This new page might be on the same site or in another part of the world.

The new page will contain more **hyperlinks**, as they are called, which again will move you on to another page, possibly in still another part of the world. This all happens very quickly, depending on the speed of your connection to the internet.

Already the number of such hyperlinks is practically endless, so you can spend a lot of time cruising around in **cyperspace**.

How do I get Connected?

You will need a telephone link to an internet "service provider," a computer (MacIntosh or an IBM486 compatible with Windows software) with a fast modem, and the appropriate software.

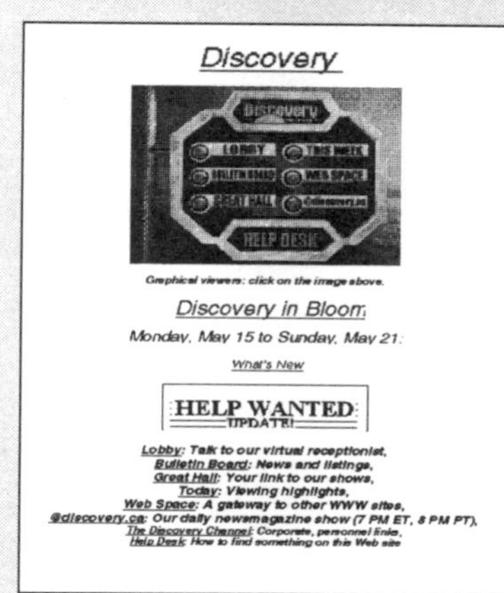

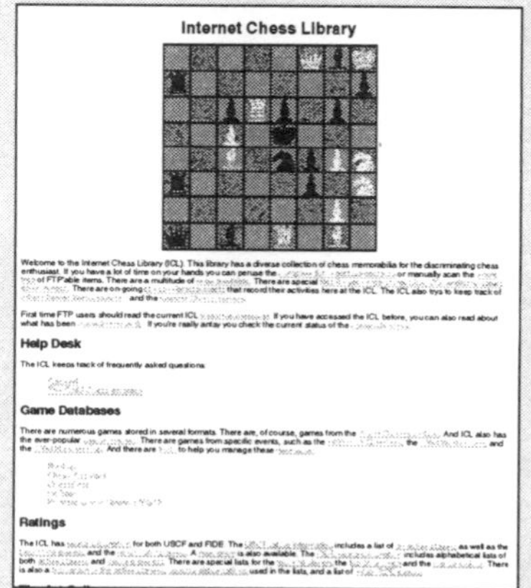

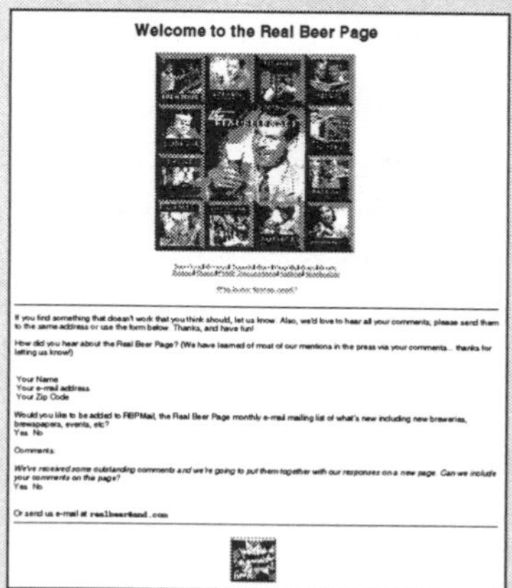

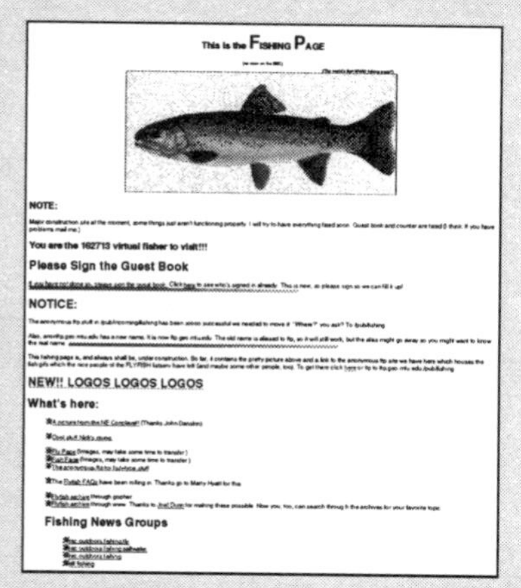

The computer, modem, and connection cost money, but after you are connected there is nothing to buy: **the software for browsing the web is all out there on the Internet itself and it is free** (Netscape or Mosaic are the common ones).

What Can I Do with It?

By and large people on the net are just browsing around. But increasingly the net is being used to disseminate information and to help to locate it. It is probably a just a matter of time before we become dependant on it for our information. For example, most major league sports scores are "posted" on the net as is information on upcoming games. The news is available. And you can read about and, of course, purchase all sorts of things.

Pictures, video and audio

The World Wide Web can also transmit back to your computer audio sounds (for example, samples of radio broadcasts), still pictures (you can take a "virtual" visit to the Louvre Museum in Paris, for example) and motion picture (clips from recent movies or rock concerts). You can also track down your favourite interest or hobby.

Where Is It All Going?

Where this will lead, it is not altogether clear. What is clear is that we are on the edge of a big technological change—we have entered an information age.

By their nature, technological revolutions on this scale are "progressive"(indeed, they themselves define our idea of progress!). Whether or not they are used to improve the lot of humans is another matter. Progress in this important sense depends, as always, on how these technologies are used by humans.

from the Queensboro Corporation. "This sort of residential environment strongly influenced Hawthorne, America's greatest writer of fiction. He analyzed with charming keenness the social spirit of those who had thus happily selected their homes, and he painted the people inhabiting those homes with good-natured relish." (Apparently, Hawthorne Court survives to this day as an urban oasis. According to Harold Thompson, president of the Hawthorne Court Council, life at the complex "just keeps getting better." "This is a wonderful place to live!" he gushed during a phone interview.)

Similar programs by Tidewater Oil and the American Express Company followed a month later. Straight-ahead advertising was still considered a no-no, but sponsorship seemed to be OK. Other companies began signing up as sponsors for professional entertainment. The "Happiness Boys" was a name given to Billy Jones and Ernie Hare, two vaudeville comedians whose weekly show was sponsored by the Happiness Candy Company. (Jones and Hare would also be heard under the guises of the "Best Foods Boys" and the "Taystee Loafers.") Clicquot Ginger Ale brought us music by the "Clicquot Club Eskimos." "The Eveready Hour" was a slick variety show that received production help from the N.W. Ayer advertising agency.

It may have been commercial, but it was also reasonably subtle, and audiences ate it up. And as they did, the money began rolling in. AT&T realized that it could offer toll broadcasters access to an even larger listening audience (not to mention some impressive production economies of scale) by linking a few radio stations together with phone wires. AT&T called this innovation "chain broadcasting," and it was first tried successfully in the summer of 1923, when programming that originated from WEAF in New York was simultaneously broadcast by WJAR in Providence, Rhode Island, and WMAF in South Dartmouth, Massachusetts. It was the first broadcast network.

RCA, Westinghouse, and General Electric figured out that there was big money to be made in network broadcasting, and in September 1926, they teamed up to start a network of their own. They called their new company the National Broadcasting Corporation.

NBC then made AT&T an offer for WEAF. AT&T was beginning to get cold feet in the uncharted waters of programming distribution, so the phone company decided to unload the golden goose. NBC's offer to pay $1 million for WEAF was accepted. WEAF was renamed WNBC and became the flagship station of the new network. NBC prospered and in 1927 spawned a competitor—the Columbia Broadcasting System. And by 1930, when radio had become a fixture in almost 46 percent of American homes, the commercial networks dominated the broadcast airwaves and little remained of the amateurs or the wireless community they had so proudly created.

So where does that leave us?

It leaves us at the beginning.

According to Odyssey Ventures Inc. of San Francisco, only 7 percent of American households currently have access to any online media. We still don't know who's going to pay for a nationwide system of high-bandwidth pipes—never mind the question of how this new media will evolve as those household penetration numbers climb ... ever higher...into double digits. Right now, we are present at the creation of yet another great system whose worth will depend on the use we make of it.

Radio was an interactive medium during its early days. It was cherished by people much like ourselves. But later it changed. The interactivity was lost. Radio junkies had fewer opportunities to create broadcast programming. Passivity became the norm.

Maybe things will be different this time. Online media enables us to be both consumers and suppliers of electronic media content. Today, we have a second chance to "develop the material that is transmitted into that which is really worthwhile," as Hoover put it in 1924. Perhaps radio wasn't the right technology. But the Web and the Net may well be. Our job is to make sure that glorious potential doesn't get stuffed into yet another tired, old media box.

SOURCE: *Wired*, May 1995.

PART 3

The Social Sciences

Early Sunday Morning, 1930, by Edward Hopper.

Edward Hopper (1882-1967) was an American painter whose works are landmarks of American realism. His paintings embody a style based on simple, large geometric forms, flat masses of color, and the use of architectural elements in his scenes for their strong verticals, horizontals, and diagonals.

Introduction to the Social Sciences

James Rudnick

This unit is focused on the individual and his or her relation to the wider social world. That is, it examines not only the nature of society (i.e. its social institutions, politics and economy), but the more introspective dimensions of human conduct as well. The first few articles examine, a little provocatively, whether or not our individual actions are simply "programmed" (similar to the proverbial rats in a psychologist's cage) by forces beyond our immediate control.

Social scientists frequently remind us that our behaviour, even at its seemingly most individualistic, is more than a programmed response, and that the ever-changing patterns of human relationships are really much more complex than a superficial investigation might suggest. Most of the writers whose works are reprinted in this section speak to this very point—namely, that the human personality and society at large are very complex and not easy to understand. The task of the social and psychological sciences, with all their theories and research findings, is to help us understand these issues better. Only by understanding them can we possibly shape the world in which we live to everyone's advantage.

As an example of a social scientist at work, the Miligram field experiment in the New York subway included herein illustrates the importance of "social norms," the accepted beliefs and practices not normally recognized by us at all. Such norms are clearly an important part of the larger social institutions that bind us all all. Miligram's subway experiment is a fascinating example of one social scientist in a particular setting attempting to uncover some of the reasons underlying human interaction.

This unit also covers a great deal of wider ground from the perspective of the social sciences. For example, several selections examine the way women traditionally have been, and still are, often regarded as second-class citizens, and how this is beginning to change partly as a result of the organized women's movement. Other articles examine the questions of racial discrimination against visible minorities and the significance of multiculturalism in Canadian society today. Still other articles examine our politics (e.g. the Charter of Rights) and changes in our economy ("MacDonaldization") and working life ("Life in a Fast Food Factory").

The purpose of this unit as a whole is to provide a general introduction to the social sciences, touching on as many important issues as possible in the short number of pages available. It is not possible to cover every point, but each piece seeks to help inform us a little more about our individual lives and the wider society in which we live. It is hoped that these selections will provide much food for thought and lively discussion.

Bridge and the Principle of Variable-Ratio Reinforcement

Marilyn White

Operant conditioning theory leads us to expect that people will avoid unrewarding experiences. In this article Marilyn White suggests, perhaps on the contrary, that aficionados of games like bridge, like herself, even though they often lose, keep coming back for more. What might explain the underlying psychology of the dedicated bridge player and other such sport and game "fanatics"?

The January *Canadian Masterpoint* arrived just about the time I was lecturing on Behaviouristic theory to my Nursing classes, and I was struck by what a brilliant idea it would be to use John Gowdy's question, "Why do we do it?" (i.e. play competitive bridge) as a discussion topic, to see if my students had grasped and could apply (I'm such a dreamer) the principles we had been working with.

My students were not familiar with the game of bridge, so I explained briefly what competitive bridge was about (winning) and referred to the article that appeared a couple of years ago (I think in the *Toronto Star*), which pointed out that the level of individual stress in a room full of tournament bridge players was roughly equivalent to, and possibly higher than, that of a neurosurgeon about to cut into a difficult case; and I read John's poignant questions aloud:

"Why do we suffer through the losses and the pain, and the sometimes unpleasant opponents or partners?"

How that moved me! What memories were roused! (Bottom boards, hurt feelings, insults received, drained self-esteem...) Voice faltering with emotion, I summarized briefly John's experiences at a "very important tournament" where a mixed crowd of Americans and Canadians twice broke into "O Canada" when he and his team entered a bar, once when they had won, and once when they had lost.

My groundwork complete, I stood back and waited for eager replies to my reiterated question, "So, why do they do it?"

My students appeared to have reached a level of boredom unusual even for them, but I persisted: "Come on. This is so easy. Pretend it's an exam question: *Apply the principle of classical conditioning to explain why this person continues to play competitive bridge*."

At last a hand went up. "Maybe because the playing of bridge has become associated with feelings of warmth and belonging?"

"Yes!" I cried delightedly. "And what would have been the original unconditioned stimulus?"

"The anthem sung by the crowd?"

"Wonderful!" (More people were getting interested now.) "And what was the unconditioned response?"

"The good feelings?"

"YES! And...who can finish it?"

"How about this, Miss? Bridge, originally a neutral stimulus, became associated by repeated pairings with strong positive emotions, and thus became in itself the conditioned stimulus, which had the power to elicit the positive feelings, which have now become *conditioned responses*!" The student finished on a note of triumph, which indeed we all shared; but I was hungry for more.

"Excellent." I responded briskly. "And let's remind ourselves that a classically conditioned response is a powerful, automatic, and permanent piece of learning...Now, are we saying that, for this gentleman, bridge will always be a preferred pastime?"

Long pause. "No," the blonde girl in the corner finally ventured. "If he never ever at any time again had another positive experience, then the original learning would weaken and extinguish over time, and bridge would again become either a neutral or perhaps even a negative pastime, and he could give it up."

"That's right. That would be the principle of *extinction*. Good. But what would happen if, after a long string of negative experiences and bad losses, he should win even one game again?"

"Then the whole original learning would be back, due to the principle of *spontaneous recovery!*"

Ah. It was moments like this that made life worthwhile..."Okay, that's really good, and I want everyone to take a moment right now to think about something in your life that you do because of classical conditioning...Good. Now, let's ask ourselves why lesser mortals, who have never had the powerful aphrodisiac of public applause associated with the game of bridge, continue to play in spite of multitudinous horrible experiences. Why do gamblers gamble, even after their wives threaten to leave them? What, in fact, is Thorndike's *Law of Effect?*"

That was an easy one. Hands shot up.

"That's the law which states that behaviours followed by positive outcomes are strengthened, whereas behaviours followed by negative outcomes are weakened."

"Exactly. And, as we know, B.F. Skinner expanded on Thorndike's ideas in the theory of *operant conditioning*, which holds that reinforcement of a behaviour (a positive consequence) increases the probability that the behaviour will be repeated, and punishment (a negative consequence) decreases that probability."

I took a deep breath. "Now, what I want somebody to do is explain why a person, such as a bridge player, would continue an activity that is expensive, time-consuming, frustrating, and often painful, in the face of repeated losses and bad games, we're talking about your average, everyday-type player."

Another long silence.

"But, Miss," (I love that term of address) "wouldn't operant conditioning theory predict that a behaviour that is punished that badly tend to decrease? Wouldn't the person just, like, quit playing?"

"One would certainly think so," I responded. "But simple observation at any bridge club would prove that not to be the case. These places are full of players whose behaviour is repeatedly "punished," to use the correct jargon, yet—they show up again, week after week."

I saw that this was going nowhere "Let me jog your memory," I said, smiling (can't anyone ever remember anything?). "In real life do you get reinforced every time you perform a behaviour? For example, do you get praised every time you make your bed? Brush your teeth? Eat your veggies? Does a golfer win every tournament? Does a chess player win every match? Of course not! That's not the way the world works...What happens is that we get partial (or intermittent) reinforcement—and schedules of intermittent reinforcement are simply rules that determine when a response will be reinforced."

"Does that ring any bells?" I asked. Silence.

"Okay, come on now. Remember when I said intermittent schedules are very important in maintaining a learned behaviour? And that there was one particular type of schedule that was incredibly powerful in maintaining a behaviour? Who can recall the schedules?"

"Oh, Miss, I remember, you told us about that guy playing the slot machine that was rigged to pay off after every 20th play. But the player wouldn't know when the payoff will be—it might pay off twice in a row, and then again 58 plays later averaging out to every 20 plays."

"That's right. And what do you call that?"

"That's a variable-ratio schedule—and you said it was different from the other kind, the fixed-ratio (where you know that the machine would pay off exactly after every 20 plays) because it was much more powerful in maintaining behaviour!"

I would probably have to marry this kid. What a genius.

"Perfect, you've got it...The thing is, when you have learned to expect a reinforcement (*contingency theory*—but hey, what's in a name) and you do not know when that reinforcement is coming, then you'll keep on trying practically forever. The big win could be just around the corner. It could be next time. It could be now."

I looked benignly at my class. Had they learned anything? "I want you all to write a short essay for next week. Describe a behaviour, belief, value, or attitude that you have learned through operant conditioning, and discuss the reinforcement schedule by which you think it is being maintained... we have to stop for now. It's my bridge night, and I'm feeling lucky!"

SOURCE: From *Canadian Masterpoint,* April 1995. Reprinted by permission of the author.

Personal Bests

Operant Conditioning and the Big Fix

Marilyn White's article about bridge and the effects of the principle of "variable-ratio reinforcement" on the game's aficionados must certainly raise a number of questions in the mind of anyone who pursues his or her hobby seriously.

White's bridge players, at least insofar as they operate within her psychological paradigm, appear to be driven by their desire for rewards, however small. The unpredictability of these rewards keeps people coming back; it is almost as though the suspense of not knowing just *when* one's rewards will occur makes participants endure all kinds of hardships and setbacks while waiting for their big payoff.

But isn't this what really occurs for most of us? We would all like to be world-renowned figures in our chosen sport or hobby, whether it is ice hockey or ice sculpture. For most people, this just is not a reasonable goal, so we tend to focus more on "personal bests."

Swimmers and runners try to cover 100 meters faster than they ever have before, regardless of their finishing position. Bowlers shoot not for a perfect score, but just for a higher total than they have ever tallied. Golfers are often heard to say that what was turning out to be an unsuccessful day was "saved" by that one perfect shot. On an even more abstract level, people who practice Tai Chi or Yoga are usually unconcerned with scores or finishing times, seeking instead to improve on their own level of mastery in these disciplines.

As life for most of us becomes stressful and complicated—through the pressures of work, personal finances, etc.—maintaining what Marilyn White terms "schedules of intermittent re-inforcement" through whatever hobbies we choose often seems like the best way of maintaining sanity!

Questions and Topics for Discussion and Writing

1. According to this article, what is the most important reason that the average club-level player continues to play bridge? Can this argument be extended to players of a higher calibre, ones who win tournaments and receive recognition and fame?
2. One of White's students makes an analogy with slot-machine gambling, which could be used to explain the behaviour of a compulsive gambler. Does the principle of variable-ratio reinforcement apply to people with other types addictions—i.e. dependence on drugs or alcohol—or is a completely different paradigm at work in these instances?
3. Are there any flaws or weaknesses in the principle of variable reinforcement? Why is it deemed a "principle" and not a "theory"? Does the principle explain why certain people appear to engage in pastimes for fun, without any regard to the "pay-offs" that dominate the variable reinforcement argument?

The Town B.F. Skinner Boxed

Steve Fishman

In the dusty reaches of the Mexican desert, a handful of utopians are trying to prove that what worked for the psychologists' pigeons can work for humans, too.

Lately Ivan, who is two years old, has been emitting some undesirable verbal behaviour.

Where Ivan lives, the Code of Children's behaviour is quite explicit about what is desirable: Orderliness and cleanliness; for example, singing, laughing, dancing. And speaking positively. "great!" "I like it." "I'm happy"—these are the kinds of statements Ivan should be making. But Ivan has been negative. Linda, the leader of the committee on children's behaviour, reports that he has been saying things like "The sky is not blue," or "You can't run," or "No, that is not yours, that is everyone's"—which could be considered desirable "sharing behaviour," if it weren't for all the other negatives.

It's Thursday night and the committee is holding its weekly meeting in the children's house, where the community's four youngest children live. In these get-togethers, the adults discuss everything about the kids, from how they ought to behave to what medical care they should receive to how long their hair should be. The eleven adults listening to Linda's recitation of Ivan's negatives—two biological parents and nine "behavioural" parents—sit in the dining room clumped around the long, low children's table.

Linda explains that for the past week, the grownups who care for the youngest children have been wearing counters around their necks—little silvery devices like those that ticket takers use to click off the number of people entering a theatre. Every time Ivan, who has brown bangs, brown eyes, and a voice that penetrates like a foghorn, has emitted a negative verbal behaviour, click. "I don't like the beans." Click. "It's too cold outside." Click.

Linda holds up a piece of peach-coloured graph paper with pencilled peaks: Ivan has averaged 18 negative verbal behaviours per day. She poses the crucial question: "Should we intervene now to correct Ivan's behaviour?"

Welcome to Los Horcones, a tiny enclave in the barely hospitable stretches of Mexico's Sonora Desert, 175 miles south of the U.S. border. Here 26 adults and children are attempting to live according to the teachings of the late Harvard behaviourist Burrhus Frederic (B.F.) Skinner—one of the most widely recognized and most often maligned of psychologists.

In the cultural lab they call home, this outpost community of Mexicans has been at it for 17 years, experimenting with Skinner's ideas, working away on themselves and their children. So that no visitor will miss the point, there is this welcome sign at the edge of their land, written in both Spanish and English: "We apply the science of behaviour to the design of a new society."

The idea, first Skinner's and now theirs, is as ambitious as it sounds: By the methodical application of the science of behaviourism, the little band at Los Horcones believes it can transform selfish human beings into cooperative, sharing ones.

Until his death this past August, B.F. Skinner argued that his psychology was both potent and practical. His fundamental discoveries, made 55 years ago, rest on this idea: If any particular behaviour is reinforced, it will continue. If not, it will cease.

For pigeons, Skinner found, reinforcement came in the form of dry, hard food pellets. What a hungry pigeon wouldn't do for the promise of a pellet! Climb stairs, peck a key 10,000 times, even guide a missile—which Skinner demonstrated to U.S. Army officials in World War II.

Give Skinner some lab time—he was one of psychology's first great experimenters—and he'd figure out which reinforcers, administered how often and for how long, would not only make people share but make them *like* to share. "We can *make* men adequate for group living," boasted the protagonist in Skinner's classic 1948 utopian novel, *Walden Two.*

Over the past two decades, Skinner's behaviourism and his ideas about what motivates people have largely been supplanted in the world of academic psychology. The trend now is toward cognitive psychology, which concentrates on the unconscious causes of human behaviour, processes that cognitive psychologists say cannot or should not be subject to systems of reward and punishment.

But in this desert proving ground, behaviourism is as alive as the tarantulas that take up guard on the drainpipes, as hardy as the boa constrictors that swallow live rabbits whole. In the children's house and the other whitewashed bungalows of the community of Los Horcones, behaviourism still has a shot.

"It's true," says Juan Robinson, the community's coordinator of adult behaviour. "A person can be made to enjoy what he did not at first enjoy."

Take Ivan.

Ivan's biological parents, Luciano Coronado Paredes, 26, and Maria Guadalupe Cosio de Coronado, 26, better known as Lucho and Lupita, sit in the tiny children's chairs with the other adults. They met elsewhere, but heard about Los Horcones and were married here. They vowed to put the community first. "If you ever decide to leave, just go, don't even tell me," said Lupita. Both Ivan and his brother Sebastian, aged four, were born at Los Horcones, and live together in the children's house.

Lucho and Lupita are tired after a long day's work, and remain quite even when the subject is their younger son. Lucho, in fact, peruses a book on rabbits while Linda's discussion goes on. "Did you know," he asks a neighbor, "that rabbits eat their food twice?" No one is really worried about Ivan. It is just behaviour, after all. Ivan used to cry when he wanted something, instead of a asking for it. That took but a few weeks to correct.

An approach is suggested for Ivan's negative emissions—straightforward Skinnerian science. When Ivan says something positive, he'll be reinforced with attention—hugs and kisses, pats on the head, and M&Ms. His negative comments will be ignored (but still counted with the clickers). Punishment isn't shunned out of principle; it is just, as Skinner saw it, that the consequences can turn out to be troublesome.

Linda (the children all call her La Linda) asks if everyone agrees. In the community's open family, all decisions must be made unanimously. One by one, the adults, all of whom are considered parents, nod. "Adults are difficult to change," says a parent. "Pigeons and children are easy."

B.F. Skinner experimented on pigeons and also on rats. In his crucial experiments of the 1930s, he demonstrated that by offering a simple food pellet as a "reinforcer"—a term first used by the famed Russian physiologist Ivan Pavlov—he could condition laboratory rats to press a bar when a light came on, to hold it down for as long as 30 seconds, and to keep pressing harder.

To Skinner, humans were bigger and more complex but not fundamentally different from lab animals. For the right reinforcers, he claimed, they would do almost anything.

Critics denounced Skinner's science, when it came to humans, as simplistic, manipulative, and reductionist—as well as down right unflattering. They argued that people, unlike pigeons, have rich inner lives and complex, hidden motivations. What, for goodness' sake, of a person's free will? cried the critics. Skinner harrumphed. Free will, he said, was illusory. He preferred to talk about the predictability of people.

Famous Psychologist

B.F. Skinner

This article and the following by John Staddon touch on the work of psychologist B.F. Skinner (1904–1990), one of the most controversial psychologists of all time.

Following up on the ideas advanced by the Russian psychologist Ivan Pavlov, Skinner's writings on *behaviourism* outlined his contention that human activity can be predicted and controlled by reinforcing certain types of behaviours while discouraging others. He is also well known for his application of psychology to education, where he supported the theory of "programmed instruction," which transfers learning principles derived through experimentation into the classroom. In his 1948 book *Walden Two*, Skinner outlined his ideas for an ideal society which would be constructed through careful planning and application of the principles of programmed instruction.

Born Burrhus Frederic Skinner in Susquehanna, PA in 1904, he obtained his Ph.D. degree at Harvard in 1931, and after stints at other universities began teaching there in 1948. Besides *Walden Two*, Skinner's books include *The Behavior of Organisms* (1938), *Science and Behavior* (1953), *Verbal Behavior* (1957), *Beyond Freedom and Dignity* (1971) and *About Behavioursim* (1974). In each of these works, Skinner ex-

pounded on his principle of "operant conditioning" which rests upon the simple-sounding premise that the actions of an organism can be re-inforced or discouraged through a system or "schedule" of rewards. The implications of this principle are multiple, and Skinner drew several important conclusions from his research about human behaviour and its ability to be controlled by outside stimuli.

For example, when a child refuses to eat certain food, the punishment she might get from parents by throwing a tantrum actually re-inforces this behaviour instead of discouraging it, since the child's attempt to get her parents' attention has succeeded. According to Skinner, punishing a child in order to persuade her to eat her broccoli actually encourages future refusals. The answer would be to eliminate the negative re-inforcement and to support some other desired behaviour.

Another implication of Skinner's research is illustrated by the article by Marilyn White in this section, which shows how the unpredictability of rewards for certain actions acts as a powerful stimulus for people continuing to perform these actions.

Opponents of Skinner's views, like John Staddon, contend that his theories about how human behaviour is determined suffer from one fundamental weakness, namely that people are not seen to have any free will in deciding how they will act—their actions are all determined by their environment. In fact, the free will vs. determinism debate is one of the key questions in philosophy as well as psychology, and has been argued over for centuries.

Skinner's response to his critics was that our behaviour really is completely controlled by our environment—through our genetic makeups as determined by our ancestors, our upbringing, our social and economic conditions, etc. Skinner believed that through research like his, people obtain the means of knowing just which factors collaborate to determine our lives, thereby allowing us to regulate and alter them.

But as Staddon's piece illustrates, not everybody agrees.

The late psychologist wasn't, however, a cold, impersonal manipulator. Rather, he seems to have been as cheery and optimistic as a handyman who says, Hey, I can fix that. After his wife complained that the first years of child-rearing were hell, he devised the "baby tender," a glass-enclosed, temperature-controlled crib that eliminated the need to change the baby's clothes so often. His own daughter tried it out and became the notorious baby in the "Skinner box." After noticing how dull his other daughter's grammar school was, Skinner built a "teaching machine," decades ahead of today's interactive learning systems.

In the same problem-solving spirit, the late behaviourist sat down in 1947 and in seven weeks wrote the book outlining his plan to ease society's woes through behaviourism. In Skinner's utopia, 1,000 citizens work four hours a day for no money, share their children, develop their artistic talents. As literature, *Walden Two* is a bore, freighted with long arguments between the proselytizing Frazier and his skeptical foil, a character named Castle. But the ideas have had a long life.

The book became a staple of college psychology classes as behaviourism flourished in the 1950s and 1960s. Two million copies are in print today. To a disposed mind, it can read like a do-it-yourself kit.

In the late 1960s, Juan Robinson, a handsome young middle-class Mexican (descended from a Scottish grandfather), was a university psychology student in Mexico City. Robinson read *Walden Two* and quickly became a convert.

In 1972, on the dusty edge of the Mexican town of Hermosillo, he and his wife, Mireya Bustamente Norberto, then 21, decided to give behaviourism a practical try. They founded a school for retarded children, many of them so unmanageable that their parents were prepared to ship them to an institution. Subjected to behavioural techniques, the 20 students fell into line.

Consider the case of Luis, an autistic teen who threw as many as three tantrums a day. Did Luis sit quietly? Very nice, the behaviourists said, and handed him a coin. Shake hands? One more coin. Merchant Luis began bartering half hours of appropriate behaviour—he even did chores!—for coins redeemable for meals, and his tantrums virtually ceased. "We can modify antisocial behaviour," Juan concluded, "in three months."

At the end of the school day, Juan and Mireya hosted gatherings. Linda (La Linda), just 19, a volunteer at the school, attended; so did her husband, Ramon Armendariz, 21. Juan, old man of the group at 24, would break out his copy of *Walden Two* and read aloud. Juan's voice is high and breathy, like the sound produced by blowing air into a Coke bottle. Night after night, his audience listened to that eerie hoot go on about how, with the aid of Skinner's science, a new society could be formed.

Among the small following, the idea started to take. They would start a community called Los Horcones—or "the pillars"—of a new society, nothing less. It would be a living experiment, a "cultural lab." They would be the researchers, they and their children the pigeons. Together they'd take Skinner's behaviourism another step down the road.

They drafted a Code of Adult behaviour—41 pages in a green plastic binder, written in a style about as lively as a traffic ticket's—and in it they spelled out the details of the communitarian lifestyle. All adults would be parents to all children. Residents would be discouraged from saying "mine" and encouraged to say "ours"—as in "This is our daughter," even if one was not a blood relation. If an adult was working and a child asked a question, the adult would drop everything and explain what was going on. In addition, the older children would serve as teachers for the younger ones. Casual sex would not be considered a good example for "our" children.

In general, residents were to keep the community in mind at all times. They had to stop getting satisfaction from receiving more—whether pie or praise—and start getting excited about giving more. "Have approving thoughts about others" was a key dictum. The worst adjective that could be applied to someone at Los Horcones was "individualistic."

In all, six young urban friends gave up the career track in society—"the outside"—and moved to the countryside to build houses and to farm.

They knew nothing about these endeavour, and Ramon recalls that for a few moments in 1973, the idea of building a new society with these ragtag city kids seemed like a very silly idea. It was dawn and the brand new behaviourists found themselves circling a fawn and white Guernsey cow, trying to figure out how to milk it.

In 1980, the citizens of Los Horcones departed that first desolate site for the current patch of desert: an even more remote 250 acres of brush, cactus, and mesquite, 40 miles from Hermosillo. The new land might as well have been a stretch of concrete. They dug a small reservoir and carved out irrigation ditches to compensate for the parching lack of rain, and they hauled in trees. With a mania for systems, they not only planted but numbered every one of them. "Orderliness," Mireya says with a chortle, "is reinforcing."

Today Los Horcones is an oasis. "Everywhere you look, there we have done something," says Lucho. Vegetables grow in flawless stripes on seven acres. Orchards produce grapefruits as big as melons and lemons the size of baseballs. There are pigs, rabbits, chickens, 13 cows, electric milking machines, and a cheese factory. The community is, in fact, 75 percent food self-sufficient, buying only such staples as rice and flour. They have a Caterpillar tractor, trucks, and a school bus converted into a touring vehicle—sleeps nine—for occasional group forays to the outside world.

There's a basketball court and a plaza where they hold pig roasts and dances for guests from Hermosillo. They've dug a swimming hole, called Walden Pond, and built wood and metal shops. There's a dormitory for the dozen or so mentally impaired children they care for, which earns them cash to buy supplies. Luis is still there, helping to milk the cows for coins. The huge main house has a living room, communal dining room and an office featuring a couple of computers. A lab contains cages of cooing pigeons used in behavioural experiments.

This has taken considerable work, far more than the four hours a day Skinner projected in his book. "I did like to play sports, but for me, it's not so important now," says Lucho, who, as all the adults do, works six and a half days a week. What's important to him now? "Building a building, fixing a toilet," he says simply. The only space an adult can call his or her own at Los Horcones is one of the 25 assigned white stucco residences, each no more than a bedroom. Meagre quarters for a private life, but the idea, after all, was to build a place where people shared not only space but belongings and emotions. The bedrooms are starkly utilitarian, with perhaps a table, an overhead fan—and no closets.

That's because the clothes at Los Horcones belong to everybody and are stored on one building: rows or jeans, neatly pressed and arranged by size, rows shirts on hangers. First come, first served; too bad what goes best with your eyes. "I have four or five shirts I like," says Ramon. "I don't care who uses them. How could you build a community on sharing and be worried about who uses shirts?"

At first, it's fair to say, newcomers couldn't believe they had to do this clothes-swap thing. Even those dedicated to the design of a new society found it strange to see someone else in the clothes they were wearing yesterday. And yet, in the long run, sharing clothes has turned out to be one of the easier things to adjust to. Some of the less tangible behaviours have been tougher to master. The main hurdle for the individual and for the new society is this: How can someone who's been reared to believe that if you don't look out for yourself, no one else will, suddenly believe that other people's happiness is your happiness, too?

"It's like being born again," says Juan.

But how to be reborn?

Fortunately, a day at Los Horcones is chock-full of strategies. Every activity can, it seems, be a form of reinforcement. Not only do the residents pick beans side by side, and take turns cooking together, they hold meetings to air any thoughts about how everyone behaved during the picking and cooking.

If you don't show up where you are supposed to, or if your tone of voice is too authoritarian, someone will take note of it. Alcohol, and even coffee, are allowed only in moderation because they aren't good for you. The place is like a big self-improvement camp, with lots of monitors. Lucho wrote in his notebook how many times his coworker was late for his shift at the cheese factory. That way, he said, there would be no argument when they were both sitting down with the behaviour coordinator, trying to improve the situation.

If the extended family's kindhearted badgering can't haul a newcomer into line, there are, of course, other weapons for promoting utopia in the desert. That's where Skinner's science comes in. "That's right," says Juan, "we have the technology to change behaviour."

In theory, no behaviour is beyond the technology's reach. One woman—who prefers to remain anonymous, so we'll call her Susan—was interested in improving her relationship with her husband, so she deigned a self-management program. She translated relationship-with-husband into graphable entities—positive verbal contacts, or PVCs, and negative verbal contacts, NVCs. She collected the data on a notepad she hid in her pocket, and after nine days she checked her chart: on average, 3.5 PVCs and 1.8 NVCs per day. Secretly, she also tallied her husband's communications. His score: 2.5 PVCs and 1.5 NVCs.

For Susan, or anyone, to learn a new behaviour, it's essential to figure out what reinforces that behaviour. Busi, 15 years old, taught Sebastian, just four, how to read in an astonishingly quick 15 hours. As he sounded out words, syllable by syllable, she patted his head and pushed a few of his reinforcers, Fruit Loops, into his mouth. But pats and sweets don't work for everybody. There is also the "participative reinforcer." To reward someone for cooking a nice meal, you not only applaud—though they like applause here—you offer to help afterwards with the dishes.

The most reliable reinforcer, though, is what the behaviourists at Los Horcones call "natural" one, in which the person practising a new behaviour is reinforced by the consequences of that behaviour. When Linda, for instance, discovered that she didn't run to other people's babies when they cried, she made herself run. The babies smiled in her arms, which, she explained, reinforced her response, naturally.

Susan, too, chose a natural reinforcer: her husband's response. She set a goal for herself: She would emit seven PVCs a day, and drop her NVCs to zero. Her husband had no idea about this particular behaviour management program—it's hard to always know who's managing whose behaviour at Los Horcones—but Susan noted that his PVCs increased to almost eight a day and his NVCs fell to zero. Both their PVCs up, Susan felt a lot better about their relationship.

PVCs? NVCs? They make lovely points on a graph, but are they love? It's not a distinction that behaviourists are troubled by. They're interested in observable behaviour, not hidden recesses of the psyche. "How can you see what is inside except by the outside product?" explains Linda. "Anyone can imagine that if you, as a wife, have more pleasing interactions with your husband, you feel like he loves you more."

Despite the behaviourist lingo and the laboratory overtones, there is a bit of common sense to all this. A baby's smile can make someone feel good. And many people know that lending a hand, the essence of "participative reinforcement," or making tender comments, as Susan did to increase her PVCs, brings returns in good will. The difference is that at Los Horcones, these insights are applied in a deliberated system.

What's more, in a community that's also a behaviourism laboratory, reinforcers are the object of methodical study. Every morning, Linda experiments with the little ones. One current topic: can children learn to consider future consequences? Linda doles out the investigative tool: M&Ms. "You can eat it now," she tells the two- through seven-year-olds, "but if you wait until I say 'eat,' you get another." On a wall are the graphs she has charted; the lines reveal that the children will wait up to four minutes.

Los Horcones may, in fact, be one of the most self-studied communities in history. The results of the group's self-scrutiny, 20 papers, have been published in academic journals over the past 15 years—each signed communally, of course: "Los Horcones." The articles have examined the steps the community has taken its system of government by consensus more democratic, or revealed some of the reinforcers they've discovered to be most effective in motivating people to clean their rooms (candy and praise for a 14-year-old) or help harvest the crops (participation rather than sweets).

Still, when it comes to human overhaul, there are sticky areas. Even the technology, apparently, cannot always correct a history of individualistic living. Jealousy, for instance. That most individualistic of emotions, which says this is mine and not yours, seems to be stubborn as hell.

At Los Horcones possessiveness is discouraged. You aren't supposed to waltz into the dining room where the kids slide from one adult's lap to another's and check that your child or your husband has enough of Lupita's special rabbit-garlic stew on his or her plate. Spouses rarely sit together, often don't acknowledge each other, and a visitor doesn't at first know who the pairs are. One couple who became too much of a couple, walking hand in hand and generally behaving like honeymooners, was booted out. The community may be sexually monogamous, but it is emotionally polygamous. "You're married to everyone," Lupita explains.

"Yes, I had jealousy," says Ramon. "I went to Juan, the behaviour manager. Here, your problem is everybody's. We had long meetings about it. It helped, though I think behaviours that you have when you are an adult you can't entirely get rid of."

Clearly, the brightest hopes for the redesigned society are the people without an individualistic past, those who have benefited from the technology starting at the earliest stages of their lives: the children. If anyone is to carry out the caring and cooperative ideal, it ought to be those who have grown up here. "I never wanted kids before this," says Ramon, who is the father of four. "I didn't think I had anything to offer them, not until Los Horcones."

The children receive an enormous amount of attention from lots of adults. They're bright and outgoing, and from all appearances, feel capable and loved and useful. Skinner himself, who met the youngsters on several visits they paid to the United States, approved. "They've done wonderful things with their children," he said.

The first wave of the community's children are teenagers now. They have spent weekends with friends from the outside, and have had their friends visit them at Los Horcones. They know their upbringing has been different, but they dismiss the issue with a big shrug.

Ask them, for instance: If you had a problem, would you go to your mother?

"Sometimes when I have a problem I go to La Linda because she is the coordinator of child behaviour," says Esteban, 12, son of Juan and Mireya.

Or you could ask: Who won the game of Monopoly?

"I think we all did," one child says. "We were all rich."

Or, Wouldn't you like a little pocket money?

Another shrug, confused, like when you try to explain something to a cat. "I have the money I need," says a teenager named Javier. "Whenever I go to town, they give me some money to buy a soda or something."

Or, Wouldn't you like to live somewhere else?

"I can't stand to stay away more than a couple of days," says Busi, her hands filled with fruit from the orchard.

None of the kids can; but none have had to. That may all change. The teenagers may soon be sent to Tucson, Arizona, to a branch of the community to be opened there, so they can enrol at the University of Arizona—not for a diploma, just to attend classes and learn. The prospect of this exodus makes some nervous, and not just the kids.

Who known how many of the five teenagers will return? Or will these behaviourally brought up young people make their lives elsewhere?

"I accept both possibilities," says Juan.

Walden Two was a community of a thousand people; Los Horcones hovers at 25 to 30, and can seem at times on the verge of depopulating. They would like to boost the population to 100 or 200; that would be much more reinforcing. Then at midday, children could greet workers with fresh lemonade and maybe a band would be playing.

"Then, even the people we lost would return," says Ramon. As it is now, members, even those who share the ideals, fall away, beyond the reach of the technology. Over the past 17 year, 60 people have come and gone—from South America, the United States, even as far away as Europe. Perhaps some were simply lonely, or seeking food and shelter, or curious because they'd heard about the community or seen an ad. (Yes, Los Horcones advertised in the local newspaper.) They stayed a few months or a couple of years, and drifted away. Leaving is the worst anticommunitarian behaviour, and yet, it would seem, the toughest to change.

Last spring, just as the counter revealed that four in five of tiny, horn-voiced Ivan's commentaries were positive, Lupita and Lucho packed up their sons and left for Lupita's family home in Hermosillo. Lucho said he had wearied of trying, against his nature, to put the community first, whether by working more or organizing better. Lupita was torn, but followed her husband.

Lucho had succeeded through behavioural self-management in giving more approval to the kids, but he had never found a program that would make him think less often of his family and himself. "I just didn't want to change for what the community was offering me," he says. "It was simply that."

It was an awful failure of the technology—that was the shared analysis of the members who remained, though the discussions weren't so analytical. There were tears. The departure was like divorce, an angry divorce.

With the exception of one founder who stayed 12 years before leaving, Lupita and Lucho had been there longer than any of the dozens who had passed through. But years spent at the community were evidently no guarantee of continued commitment.

Outside Los Horcones, Lucho said, things seemed easier. "Here it's not the same as starting a new society and defining everything. Here, the rules of the game are easy. I feel energized to do something. I think this energy I got at Los Horcones, and I am thankful for that." He got other things, too, like knowledge of how to make cheese, which is the business he and Lupita have chosen to go into for themselves—competing, of all things, for Los Horcones's customers.

"If there had been those, I would have felt much better," Lucho said after he left.

Maybe Lucho would have liked some other reinforcers: additional time for himself, more trips outside the community, perhaps a few more economic incentives?

And now, into this 17-year-old utopia, new "experimental" reinforcers soon may be creeping: credits for work, and paid vacations. That's what Los Horcones is considering. "People won't try to live communitarianly if they are not earning something more individualistic," says Juan pragmatically.

Individual rewards for living together? It sounds against the grain. Could behaviourism have pecked up against its limits?

"With investigation, you rise above the limits," says Juan, faithful as Skinner's *Walden Two* hero, Frazier. "We must investigate in more detail the variables that control these problems."

As the late great experimenter himself might have said: Back to the lab.

SOURCE: Steve Fishman, "The Town B.F. Skinner Boxed", from *In Health*, January/February 1991:50–57.

Questions and Topics for Discussion and Writing

1. Why does the author begin and end this article with anecdotes about little "Ivan" and his parents? Does he succeed in making his point?
2. Fishman leaves unanswered his question about whether the act of plotting points on a behavioural graph are the same as parental love. From the evidence presented in this article, does it appear that these two ways of shaping a child's behaviour can be compatible?
3. This piece does not contain complex tables and is not filled with a great deal of hard and complicated data, but the author has managed to construct a compelling argument. What techniques has he used to make this piece so effective?

On Responsibility and Punishment

John Staddon

Consider the following propositions. First, because human behaviour is ultimately determined by outside factors, human beings cannot be held responsible for their actions. Second, punishment doesn't work anyway. These propositions are legacies of modern psychology. And, the author argues, they are nonsense.

The litany of social dysfunction is now familiar. The rates of violent crime are 40 percent higher than they were a decade ago; Americans kill and maim one another at per capita rates five to ten times as high as those of other industrialized nations. The rate of illegitimacy continues to climb. Tens of thousands of children have no fathers and no family members or close acquaintances who hold regular jobs; this pattern is now repeating into the second and third generations. Illiteracy is a big problem, and schools have so lost authority that the accepted response to armed pupils is to install metal detectors. Senator Daniel Patrick Moynihan, in a celebrated article, recently pointed out that we cope with social disintegration by redefining deviance so that crimes become "normal" behaviour.

How did we arrive at this condition? There's no short answer, but I have increasingly come to believe that my own profession—psychology—bears a large part of the blame. The story began many years ago, when psychology defined itself as a science. Thus self-anointed, the discipline gained great prestige. People accepted with little demur prescription that would earlier have been condemned on moral grounds. Don't spank your child. Don't attempt to deter sexual exploration by young people—deterrence is probably bad and will certainly fail. Punishment is ineffective and should be replaced by positive reinforcement. Self-esteem is good, social stigma bad. It is not clear that this advice was all wrong. What is clear, and what I will show in this article, is that it was not based on *science.*

Some questions about behaviour can be answered—either now or in the future—through the methods of science. How does visual perception work? What are the effects of different reward schedules? How accurate is memory for words and faces? What lighting conditions are best for different kinds of tasks? Which people are likely to succeed in which professions? Other questions, including apparently simple ones such as the value of some teaching techniques and the legitimacy of corporal punishment, cannot be answered by science, because they have consequences that go beyond the individual or far into the future. Corporal punishment and teaching methods affect not just the child but, eventually, the nature of society. Society cannot be the subject of experiments, and even if it could, the effects of social changes usually take decades or even centuries to play out. Hence we often cannot expect to get hard scientific answers to social questions.

Obviously, we need to separate those questions that belong in the domain of science from those that do not—to separate questions that can be answered definitively from those that cannot. Unfortunately, psychology as a profession tends to assume that all questions about human action fall within its domain and that all can eventually be answered with the authority of science—and this imperialism has gone largely unquestioned.

Psychologists and behavioural psychiatrists seem

a diverse crew. At one end of the spectrum we have touchy-feelies who say things like "Any of us who were raised in the traditional patriarchal system have trouble relating because we've been 'mystified' to some degree by an upbringing that compels obedience and rules by fear. A raising that can be survived only by denial of the authentic self" (John Bradshaw). At the other we have the behaviourists, who say things like "In the scientific view...a person's behaviour is determined by a genetic endowment traceable to the evolutionary history of the species and by the environmental circumstances to which as an individual he has been exposed" (B.F. Skinner).

Bradshaw and Skinner seem to agree on little. It may come as a surprise, therefore, to learn that psychological pundits from Bradshaw to Skinner agree on several important things. Almost all focus entirely on the individual. All reject what Bradshaw calls "fear," Skinner called "aversive contingency," and the rest of us call punishment. Nearly all psychologists believe that behaviour is completely determined by heredity and environment. A substantial majority agree with Skinner that determinism rules out the concept of personal responsibility. This opposition between determinism and responsibility is now widely accepted, not just by behaviourists but by every category of mental-health professional, by journalists, by much of the public and by many in the legal profession.

Behaviourism is the most self-consciously "scientific" of the many strands that make up psychology. Although somewhat overshadowed recently by cognitive psychology and other movements, behaviourism has had overwhelming influence during most of the short history of psychology. Consequently, when behaviourists have produced hard evidence in favor of beliefs already shared by other psychologists, the combined effect has always been decisive. I will describe just such a confluence in this article.

About moral positions, argument is possible. But about scientific facts there can be no argument. Skinner, and the behaviourist movement of which he was the head, delegitimized both individual responsibility and punishment. Responsibility was dismissed by philosophical argument. Punishment was ruled out not by moral opposition but by supposedly scientific laboratory results. Less science-oriented psychologists and psychiatrists have agreed that punishment is bad, but the reasons for their consensus are more complex, and have to do with the social function of psychotherapy. Nevertheless, for the majority of psychologists and psychiatrists. The facts established by the behaviourists have always constituted an unanswerable argument—especially if these have supported pre-existing beliefs. This "scientific" consensus has had a devastating effect on the moral basis of American society.

I will argue, first, that there is no opposition between behavioural determinism and the notion of individual responsibility, and second, that the scientific basis for blanket opposition to punishment as a legitimate social instrument—in the family, the school, the workplace, and the judicial system—is nonexistent. My focus is Skinnerian behaviourism because it is the area of psychology that has been most concerned with large social issues. But the key ideas have been carried forward by a much larger number of psychologists and psychiatrists who have never thought of themselves as behaviourists.

B.F. Skinner's 1971 best seller *Beyond Freedom and Dignity* contains his most concerted, and successful, attack on traditional methods of social control. Most psychotherapists, behaviourist and nonbehaviourist alike, have come to agree with the substance of Skinner's message: that punishment is bad and that the idea of individual responsibility is a myth. Skinner's argument is simply wrong. It will be a task for future sociologists to understand why such a bad argument received such ready assent.

Skinner contrasted the "prescientific" view that "a person's behaviour is at least to some extent his own achievement" with the "scientific" view that behaviour is completely determined by heredity and environment. The conventional view, he wrote, is that a person is free:

> He is autonomous in the sense that his behaviour is uncaused. He can therefore be held responsible for what he does and justly punished if he offends. That view, together with its associated practices, must be

> re-examined when a scientific analysis reveals unsuspected controlling relations between behaviour and environment.

What's wrong with this apparently judicious line of reasoning?

Freedom

Is man free? Well, as the professor used to say, it depends on what you mean by "freedom." The bottom line is that you're free *if you feel free.* Skinner's definition is simpler: to him, freedom was simply the absence of punishment ("aversive contingencies"). But we are all "punished" by gravity if we seek to disobey its rules. The punishment can sometimes be quite severe, as beginning cyclists and skaters can attest. Yet we don't feel unfree when we learn to skate or cycle. Punishment doesn't always abolish freedom—and freedom is not just the absence of punishment.

Skinner had another definition of freedom: absence of causation ("autonomous man"). This is an odd notion indeed. How can one ever prove the *absence* of causation? In science conjecture like this is called a null hypothesis, and everyone accepts that such a thing is impossible to prove. We might prove the obverse, however, that people are unfree when their behaviour is determined—that is to say when it can be predicted. For example, suppose a rich and generous aunt offers her young niece a choice between a small sum of money and a large sum. In the absence of any contrary factors, the niece will doubtless pick the larger over the smaller. (Classical economics rests on the assumption that this will always be the choice made.) Can we predict the niece's behaviour? Certainly. Is her behaviour determined? Yes, by all the usual criteria. Is she unfree? She certainly doesn't feel unfree. People generally feel free when they follow their preferences. No matter how predictable those preferences may be. Behaviour can be predicted in other contexts as well. Mathematicians predictably follow the laws of arithmetic, architects the laws of geometry, and baseball players the laws of physics. The behaviour of all is determined; yet all feel free. Ergo, predictability—determinism—doesn't equal the absence of freedom, as Skinner proposes.

So even if we could predict all human behaviour with absolute precision, this wonderful new science would have no bearing at all on the idea of freedom.

Punishment

There is another strand in Skinner's assault on traditional practices—his attack on punishment. He rejected punishment not because it's morally wrong but because it doesn't work. (W.H. Auden had no such doubts about punishment when he remarked, "Give me a no-nonsense, down-to-earth behaviourist, a few drugs, and simple electrical appliances, and in six months I will have him reciting the Athanasian Creed in public.") Since everyone knows that some punishments sometimes work, you may be curious to hear how Skinner defended his position. His argument boils down to three points: punishment is ineffective because when you stop punishing, the punished behaviour returns; punishment provokes "counterattack"; positive reinforcement is better. Let's look at each of these.

Punishment is ineffective. Well, no, it isn't. Common sense aside, laboratory studies with pigeons and rats (the basis for Skinner 's argument) show that punishment (usually a brief electric shock) works very well to suppress behaviour, as long as it is of the right magnitude and follows promptly on the behaviour that is to be suppressed. If a rat gets a moderate shock when he presses a bar, he stops pressing it more or less at once. If the shock is too great, the rat stops doing anything; if the shock is too weak. he may still press the bar once in a while; if it's just right, he quits pressing but otherwise behaves normally. Does the punished behaviour return when the punishment is withdrawn? That depends on the training procedure. An avoidance procedure called shock postponement, in which the rat gets no shock so long as he presses the bar once in a while, produces behaviour that can persist indefinitely when the shock schedule is withdrawn. That is to say, the rat continues periodically to press the bar.

Punishment provokes counterattack. Sure: if a food-producing lever also produces shock, the rat will try to get the food without getting the shock. A famous picture in introductory-psychology texts is called "Breakfast in Bed." It shows a rat that learned in a shock-food experiment to press the lever while lying on his back, insulated by his fur from the metal floor grid. Skinner was right that rats, and people, try to beat a punishment schedule.

Positive reinforcement is more effective. Not true. The effects of positive reinforcement also dissipate when the reinforcement is withdrawn, and there is no positive-reinforcement procedure that produces behaviour as persistent as that produced by a shock-postponement schedule. Positive reinforcement also provokes counterattack. Every student who cheats, every gambler who rigs the odds, every robber and thief, shows the counterattack provoked by positive-reinforcement schedules.

There are other arguments on both sides, but the net conclusion must be that the scientific evidence is pretty much neutral in deciding between reward and punishment. Each has its advantages and disadvantages: punishment is better for suppressing behaviour, positive reinforcement better for generating behaviour; punishment tends to produce more-persistent behaviour than rewards; and so on. If we wish to favor reward over punishment, we must make a moral, not a scientific, case.

Justice and Determinism

All this might be academic but for its impact on legal thinking. The opposition between determinism and responsibility, and the doubts cast on punishment, do seem to raise issues of justice. If the devil—or, at least, "my environment"—made me do it, surely I should be spared the rigors of just punishment (of dubious effectiveness in any case, according to psychologists). In the era of Lorena Bobbitt, Reginald Denny's attackers, and the Menendez brothers, this argument evidently strikes a receptive chord in the hearts of American juries. Too bad, because the argument is false. I've already argued that behaviour can be both determined (in the sense of predictable) and free. I'll argue now that the legal concept of personal responsibility is founded on this kind of predictability. Personal responsibility demands that behaviour be predictable—not the opposite, as Skinner contended.

What is the purpose of judicial punishment? Legal scholars normally identify two purposes, retribution and deterrence. Retribution is a moral concept, which need not concern us here. But deterrence is a practical matter. Arguments about deterrence are clouded by ideology and the impossibility of deciding the issue by the methods of science. Nevertheless, there is a straightforward approach to deterrence that would much simplify a jury's task. The idea is that the purpose of legal punishment is to minimize the total amount of suffering in society—the suffering caused by crime as well as the suffering caused by punishment. The concept is simple: If thievery is punished by amputation, the level of thievery will be low but the level of suffering of thieves will be very high—higher, perhaps, than warranted by the reduction in theft. On the other hand, if murderers go free, the level of murder will be high and the ease of the killers will not balance the suffering of the rest. We may argue about how to measure suffering and how to assess the effect of a given level of legal punishment for a given crime, but the principle, which I call the social view of punishment, seems reasonable enough. It is consistent with the fundamental principle that government exists for the welfare of society as a whole, not for the good of any particular individual. Once they understand the argument, most people seem to agree that the social view of punishment is acceptable, although not, perhaps, the whole story. What people do not seem to realize is that this perfectly reasonable view is not opposed to determinism; it requires determinism.

From an objective point of view—the only legitimate point of view for science—"holding a man responsible" for his actions means nothing more than making him subject to punishment if he breaks the law. The social view of punishment assumes that people are sensitive to reward and punishment—that behaviour is predictably subject to causal influences. If criminal behaviour is predictably deterred by punishment, the justly punished criminal is less likely to disobey the law again, and serves as an example to other potential lawbreakers. This is the only objective justification for punishment. But if behaviour were unpredictable and unaffected by "reinforcement contingencies"—if it were uncaused, in Skinner's caricature of freedom—there would be absolutely no point to punishment or any other form of behavioural control, because it would have no predictable effect. In short, legal responsibility requires behavioural determinism.

It is interesting to reflect that the objective case for *personal* responsibility rests entirely on the beneficial *collective* effects of just punishment (on minimizing the sum total of human suffering). It does not rest on philosophical notions of individual autonomy, or personal intent, or anything else at the level of the individual—other than normal susceptibility to reward and punishment. The idea that the law is somehow concerned with the mental state of the accused, rather than with the consequences of judicial action, has taken root because Skinner, like most other psychologists, focused almost exclusively on the individual.

If a person's "behaviour is at least to some extent his own achievement." Skinner wrote, then he can be praised for success and blamed for failure. Since personal responsibility is a myth (he concluded), praise and blame are irrelevant. But if personal responsibility is defined as I have defined it, praise and blame need not—should not—be abandoned. In the social view, the use of praise and blame has nothing to do with the ontology of personal responsibility, the epistemology of intention, or whatnot. It has everything to do with reward and punishment (in other contexts Skinner admitted as much, at least with respect to praise). We praise good behaviour because we wish to see more of it: we censure the criminal because we wish to see less crime. Praise and blame are perhaps, the strongest incentives available to society. By giving them up, Skinner gave up our best tools for social order.

It is extraordinary that Skinner seems to have missed the connection between determinism and the sanctions imposed by the legal system. He spent his life studying how the behaviour of animals is determined by the conditions of reward and punishment. He and his students discovered dozens of subtle and previously unsuspected regularities in the actions of reward and punishment. Yet he failed to see that the system of rewards and punishments imposed by society works in much the same way as his reinforcement schedules.

Remarkably, law and science seem to agree on the social view of punishment. Only when punishment is likely to be completely, ineffective as a deterrent does the law limit its use. If the criminal is insane, or if injury was the unintended result of actions whose harmful outcome was unforeseeable, no guilt is attached to the perpetrator and no punishment is meted out—presumably because punishment can play no role in preventing a recurrence of the crime or the injury. There is surprising congruence between the legal concept of responsibility and the function of punishment as a deterrent. "Guilt" is established not so much by the act as by the potential of punishment to deter the act.

The "Victim" Defense: What Should the Jury Do?

These arguments greatly simplify a jury's task. Jurors have no need to puzzle through philosophical questions about intent or knowledge of right and wrong. Nor do they need to ask whether criminal behaviour was determined by the defendant's history. (The scientific answer will almost always be yes, because almost all behaviour is determined.) History is not the point. The point is, Did the defendant know that his actions would have an illegal outcome? And if he had known in advance of the act that sure punishment would follow, would he still have acted as he did? *If the criminal would have been deterred by the prospect of punishment*, the social view says, then he should be punished. Did the Menendez brothers know that their actions would result in the death of their parents? Presumably yes. If they had known that those acts would result in severe punishment (life in prison or death), would they have acted nevertheless? Probably not. Verdict: *Guilty.* On the other hand, if the jury had reason to believe that the defendants' history was so horrific that they would have murdered even in the face of certain punishment, then some other verdict (which might still involve removing these damaged men from society) would be appropriate.

The Proper Role or Psychology

The social view of punishment is as far as psychology can go toward prescribing social policy. Given a certain set of values, psychology may help us decide what system of rewards and punishments will be helpful in promoting them. But the social view of reward and punishment does not by itself prescribe social policy. Our value system, our morality, plays a legitimate role in measuring suffering, in evaluating known outcomes, and in judging the rightness or wrongness of particular rewards and punishments. We're less moved by the plight of the disappointed thief who breaks open an empty safe than by the suffering of a mugging victim, for example. Psychology can tell us a little (only a little, since we don't do such experiments on human beings) about the effects on individuals of corporal punishment versus the effects of a jail term; it cannot tell us whether corporal punishment is cruel or not. Social science can tell us that more people will be killed by guns if guns are freely available than if they are not; it cannot tell us whether the freedom to bear arms is an inalienable right. Psychology can tell us something, about the extent of homosexuality in different cultures; it cannot tell us whether homosexuality is good, bad, or a matter of indifference. Psychology can also tell us that social opprobrium—Hester Prynne's *A*, blame, or the big red D some have proposed for drunk drivers—is often an effective deterrent. It cannot tell us whether such punishment is right or not. Scientific psychology, like all science, is amoral: it tells us what is or what might be—not what should be. Psychologists who offer more, promoters of the "authentic self" or punishment-free societies, are peddling not science but faith.

SOURCE: John Staddon, "On Responsibility and Punishment," *Atlantic Monthly*, February 1995. Reprinted with the permission of the author.

Questions and Topics for Discussion and Writing

1. For several decades, B.F. Skinner argued that punishment was ineffective in achieving desired behaviour. John Staddon says that it is. How do both psychologists support their arguments about punishment? Which is the more convincing?
2. What stance does Staddon take on the free will vs. determinism question? What does he say about the concept of "predictability" as it relates to this debate?
3. What role does Staddon advocate for the behavioural psychologist in the criminal justice system? Why does he feel that the issues he is writing about have such wide applicability to the law.

The Problem that Has No Name

Betty Friedan

Betty Friedan (1921-) has been the senior spokesperson for women's rights in the USA over the past quarter of a century. Her book *The Feminine Mystique* (1963), from which this selection was taken, was responsible for starting a nationwide feminist movement. She was a founder and the first president (1966–70) of the National Organization for Women (NOW).

The problem lay buried, unspoken, for many years in the minds of American women. It was a strange stirring, a sense of dissatisfaction, a yearning that women suffered in the middle of the twentieth century in the United States. Each suburban wife struggled with it alone. As she made the beds, shopped for groceries, matched slipcover material, ate peanut butter sandwiches with her children, chauffeured Cub Scouts and Brownies, lay beside her husband at night—she was afraid to ask even of herself the silent question—"Is this all?"

For over fifteen years there was no word of this yearning in the millions of words written about women, for women, in all the columns, books and articles by experts telling women their role was to seek fulfilment as wives and mothers. Over and over women heard in voices of tradition and of Freudian sophistication that they could desire no greater destiny than to glory in their own femininity. Experts told them how to catch a man and keep him, how to breastfeed children and handle their toilet training, how to cope with sibling rivalry and adolescent rebellion; how to buy a dishwasher, bake bread, cook gourmet snails, and build a swimming pool with their own hands; how to dress, look, and act more feminine and make marriage more exciting; how to keep their husbands from dying young and their sons from growing into delinquents. They were taught to pity the neurotic, unfeminine, unhappy women who wanted to be poets or physicists or presidents. They learned that truly feminine women do not want careers, higher education, political rights—the independence and the opportunities that the old-fashioned feminists fought for. Some women, in their forties and fifties, still remembered painfully giving up those dreams, but most of the younger women no longer even thought about them. A thousand expert voices applauded their femininity, their adjustment, their new maturity. All they had to do was devote their lives from earliest girlhood to finding a husband and bearing children.

By the end of the nineteen-fifties, the average marriage age of women in America dropped to 20, and was still dropping, into the teens. Fourteen million girls were engaged by 17. The proportion of women attending college in comparison with men dropped from 47 percent in 1920 to 35 percent in 1958. A century earlier, women had fought for higher education; now girls went to college to get a husband. By the mid-fifties, 60 percent dropped out of college to marry, or because they were afraid too much education would be a marriage bar. Colleges built dormitories for "married students," but the students were almost always the husbands. A new degree was instituted for the wives—"Ph.T." (Putting Husband Through).

Then American girls began getting married in high school. And the women's magazines, deploring the unhappy statistics about these young marriages, urged that courses on marriage, and marriage counsellors, be installed in the high schools. Girls started going steady at twelve and thirteen, in junior high. Manufacturers put out brassieres with false bosoms of foam rubber for little girls of ten. And an advertisement for a child's dress, sizes 3–6x, in the *New York Times* in the fall of 1960, said: "She Too Can Join the Man-Trap Set...."

In a New York hospital, a woman had a nervous breakdown when she found she could not breast-feed her baby. In other hospitals, women dying of cancer refused a drug which research had proved might save their lives: its side effects were said to be unfeminine. "If I have only one life, let me live it as a blonde," a larger-than-life-sized picture of a pretty, vacuous woman proclaimed from newspaper, magazine, and drugstore ads. And across America, three out of every ten women dyed their hair blonde. They ate a chalk called Metrecal, instead of food, to shrink to the size of the thin young models. Department-store buyers reported that American women, since 1939, had become three and four sizes smaller. "Women are out to fit the clothes, instead of vice-versa," one buyer said.

Interior decorators were designing kitchens with mosaic murals and original paintings, for kitchens were once again the center of women's lives. Home sewing became a million-dollar industry. Many women no longer left their homes, except to shop, chauffeur their children, or attend a social engagement with their husbands. Girls were growing up in America without ever having jobs outside the home. In the late fifties, a sociological phenomenon was suddenly remarked: a third of American women now worked, but most were no longer young and very few were pursuing careers. They were married women who held part-time jobs, selling or secretarial, to put their husbands through school, their sons through college, or to help pay the mortgage. Or they were widows supporting families. Fewer and fewer women were entering professional work. The shortages in the nursing, social work, and teaching professions caused crises in almost every American city. Concerned over the Soviet Union's lead in the space race, scientists noted that America's greatest source of unused brain power was women. But girls would not study physics: it was "unfeminine." A girl refused a science fellowship at Johns Hopkins to take a job in a real-estate office. All she wanted, she said, what every American girl wanted—to get married, have four children and live in a nice house in a nice suburb.

The suburban housewife—she was the dream image of the young American women and the envy, it was said, of women all over the world. The American housewife—freed by science and labour-saving appliances from the drudgery, the dangers of child-birth and the illnesses of her grandmother. She was healthy, beautiful, educated, concerned only about her husband, her children, her home. She had found true feminine fulfilment. As a housewife and a mother, she was respected as a full and equal partner to man in his world. She was free to choose automobiles, clothes, appliances, supermarkets; she had everything that women ever dreamed of.

In the fifteen years after World War II, this mystique of feminine fulfilment became the cherished and self-perpetuating core of contemporary American culture. Millions of women lived their lives in the image of those pretty pictures of the American suburban housewife, kissing their husbands goodbye in front of the picture window, depositing their stationwagonsfull of children at school, and smiling as they ran the new electric waxer over the spotless kitchen floor. They baked their own bread, sewed their own and their children's clothes, kept their new washing machines and dryers running all day. They changed the sheets on the beds twice a week instead of once, took the rug-hooking class in adult education, and pitied their poor frustrated mothers, who had dreamed of having a career. Their only dream was to be perfect wives and mothers; their highest ambition to have five children and a beautiful house, their only fight to get and keep their husbands. They had no thought for the unfeminine problems of the world outside the home; they wanted the men to make the major decisions. They gloried in their role as women, and wrote proudly on the census blank: "Occupation: housewife."

For over fifteen years, the words written for women, and the words women used when they talked to each other, while their husbands sat on the other side of the room and talked shop or politics or septic tanks, were about problems with their children, or how to keep their husbands happy, or improve their children's school, or cook chicken or make slipcovers. Nobody argued whether women were inferior or superior to men; they were simply different. Words like "emancipation" and "career" sounded strange and embarrassing; no one had used them for years. When a Frenchwoman named Simone de Beauvoir wrote a book called *The Second Sex*, an American critic commented that she obviously "didn't know what life was all about," and besides, she was talking about French women. The "woman problem" in America no longer existed.

If a woman had a problem in the 1950s and 1960s, she knew that something must be wrong with her marriage, or with herself. Other women were satisfied with their lives, she thought. What kind of a woman was she if she did not feel this mysterious fulfilment waxing the kitchen floor? She was so ashamed to admit her dissatisfaction that she never knew how many other women shared it. If she tried to tell her husband, he didn't understand what she was talking about. She did not really understand it herself. For over fifteen years women in America found it harder to talk about this problem than about sex. Even the psychoanalysts had no name for it. When a woman went to psychiatrist for help, as many women did, she would say, "I'm so ashamed," or "I must be hopelessly neurotic." "I don't know what's wrong with women today," a suburban psychiatrist said uneasily. "I only know something is wrong because most of my patients happen to be women. And their problem isn't sexual." Most women with this problem did not go to see a psychoanalyst, however. "There's nothing wrong really," they kept telling themselves. "There isn't any problem."

But on an April morning in 1959, I heard a mother of four, having coffee with four other mothers in a suburban development fifteen miles from New York, say in a tone of quiet desperation, "the problem." And the others knew, without words, that she was not talking about a problem with her husband, or her children, or her home. Suddenly they realized they all shared the same problem, the problem that has no name. They began, hesitantly, to talk about it. Later, after they had picked up their children at nursery school and taken them home to nap, two of the women cried, in sheer relief, just to know thy were not alone.

Gradually I came to realize that the problem that has no name was shared by countless women in America. As a magazine writer I often interviewed women about problems with their children, or their marriages, or their houses, or their communities. But after a while I began to recognize the telltale signs of this other problem. I saw the same signs in suburban ranch houses and split-levels on Long Island and in New Jersey and Westchester County; in colonial houses in a small Massachusetts town; on patios in the Midwest. Sometimes I sensed the problem, not as a reporter, but as a suburban housewife, for during this time I was also bringing up my own three children in Rockland County, New York. I heard echoes of the problem in college dormitories and semi-private maternity wards, at PTA meetings and luncheons of the League of Women Voters, at suburban cocktail parties, in station wagons waiting for trains, and in snatches of conversation overheard at Schrafft's. The groping words I heard from other women, on quiet afternoons when children were at school or on quiet evenings when husbands worked late, I think I understood first as a woman long before I understood their larger social and psychological implications.

Source: Betty Friedan. *The Feminine Mystique*, New York: W.W. Norton, 1963. Reprinted by permission of W.W. Norton & Company, Inc.

Questions and Topics for Discussion and Writing

1. What is the underlying "problem" that Friedan is referring to? Does it now have a name?
2. Has the situation in which women find themselves in our society changed since Friedan wrote her book in the early 1960s? In what way?
3. One of the biggest changes in our society since the 1950s has been the extent to which women have become part of the employed labour force. What has been the effect of this change on the status of women in our society? To what extent do you think this has placed a "double burden" on women.

Men as Success Objects and Women as Sex Objects

Simon Davis

Some people believe that we've come a long way toward gender equality. But this excerpt describing research into personal advertisements casts doubt on the validity of this optimistic belief. In it, Simon Davis shows that women and men still play traditional roles when looking for a mate. The study looks at differential mate selection by men and women as reflected in newspaper companion ads.

Personal advertisements were taken from the *Vancouver Sun*, which is the major daily newspaper serving Vancouver, British Columbia. The *Sun* is generally perceived as a conservative, respectable journal—hence it was assumed that people advertising in it represented the "mainstream." It should be noted that people placing the ads must do so in person. For the sake of this study, gay ads were not included. A typical ad would run about 50 words, and included a brief description of the person placing it and a list of the attributes desired in the other party. Only the parts pertaining to the attributes desired in the partner were included for analysis. Attributes that pertained to hobbies or recreations were not included for the purpose of this study.

The ads were sampled as follows: Only Saturday ads were used, since in the *Sun* the convention was for Saturday to be the main day for personal ads, with 40–60 ads per edition—compared to only 2–4 ads per edition on weekdays. Within any one edition *all* the ads were included for analysis. Six editions were randomly sampled, covering the period of September 30, 1988, to September 30, 1989. The attempt to sample through the calendar year was made in an effort to avoid any unspecified seasonal effect. The size of the sample (six editions) was large enough to meet goodness-of-fit requirements for statistical tests.

The attributes listed in the ads were coded as follows:

- *Attractive*: specified that a partner should be, for example, "pretty" or "handsome."
- *Physique*: similar to 1; however, this focused not on the face but rather on whether the partner was "fit and trim," "muscular," or had "a good figure." If it was not clear if body or face was being emphasized, this fell into variable (1) by default.
- *Sex*: specified that the partner should have, for instance, "high sex drive," or should be "sensuous" or "erotic," or if there was a clear message that this was an arrangement for sexual purposes ("lunchtime liaisons—discretion required").
- *Picture*: specified that the partner should include a photo in his/her reply.
- *Profession*: specified that the partner should be a professional.
- *Employed*: specified that the partner should be employed, e.g. "must hold steady job" or "must have steady income."
- *Financial*: specified that the partner should be, for instance, "financially secure" or "financially independent."
- *Education*: specified that the partner should be, for instance, "well educated" or "well read," or should be a "college grad."
- *Intelligence:* specified that the partner should be "intelligent," "intellectual," or "bright."

- *Honest*: specified, for instance, that the partner should be "honest" or have "integrity."
- *Humour*: specified "sense of humour" or "cheerfulness."
- *Commitment*: specified that the relationship was to be "long term" or "lead to marriage," or some other indication of stability and longevity.
- *Emotion*: specified that the partner should be "warm," "romantic," "emotionally supportive," "emotionally expressive," "sensitive," "loving," "responsive," or similar terms indicating an opposition to being cold and aloof.

In addition to the 13 attribute variables, two other pieces of information were collected: The length of the ad (in lines) and the age of the person placing the ad. Only if age was exactly specified was it included; if age was vague (e.g. "late 40s,") this was not counted.

Variables were measured in the following way: any ad requesting one of the 13 attributes was scored once for that attribute. If not explicitly mentioned, it was not scored. The scoring was thus "all or nothing," e.g. no matter how many times a person in a particular ad stressed that looks were important it was only counted as a single score in the "attractive" column; thus, each single score represented one person. Conceivably, an individual ad could mention all, some, or none of the variables. Comparisons were then made between the sexes on the basis of the variables, using percentages and chi-squares [a statistical test of whether two things are related]. Chi-square values were derived by cross-tabulating gender (male/female) with attribute (asked for/not asked for).... Finally, several of the individual variables were collapsed to get an overall sense of the relative importance of (a) physical factors, (b) employment factors, and (c) intellectual factors.

Results

A total of 329 personal ads were contained in the six newspaper editions studied. One ad was discarded in that it specified a gay relationship, leaving a total sample of 328. Of this number, 215 of the ads were placed by men (65.5%) and 113 by women (34.5%).

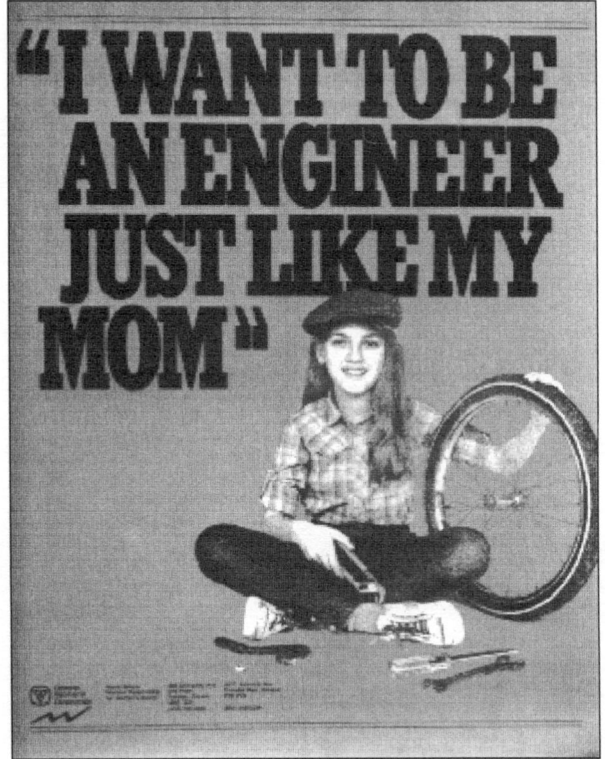

Ontario WOmen's Directorate.

The mean [average] age of people placing ads was 40.4. One hundred and twenty-seven cases (38.7%) counted as missing data in that the age was not specified or was vague. The mean age for the two sexes was similar: 39.4 for women (with 50.4% of cases missing) and 40.7 for men (with 32.6% of cases missing)...

For 10 of the 13 variables a statistically significant difference was detected. The three largest differences were found for attractiveness, professional and financial status. To summarize: in the case of attractiveness, physique, sex, and picture (physical attributes) the men were more likely than the women to seek theses. In the case of professional status, employment status, financial status, intelligence, commitment, and emotion (nonphysical attributes) the women were more likely to seek these. The women were also more likely to specify education, honesty and humour, however not at a statistically significant level.

Methodological Issues

Mate Selection

In *Men as Sucess Objects and Women as Sex Objects*, Simon Davis studies classified personal advertisements from the Vancouver *Sun*. His objective was to find out what qualities people are looking for in members of the opposite sex (he did not analyze same-sex personals). This technique is fascinating because personal ads are really just very plain, up-front lists of desireable traits people wish to have published for a wide audience to read and respond to.

As reflected in the title of his article, Davis found that, generally, men are looking for qualities based on physical attractiveness, whereas women are looking for qualities that have more to do with "success" and personality.

A study like this might be argued to have only limited applicability to real life. After all, Davis looked at the classified ads in only one city, in the far western part of Canada. Maybe people in the Prairies or the Maritimes have completely different preferences? Can the data collected from Vancouver be used to make generalizations about Canada, or even more broadly, about the nebulous entity we often call "society," which usually means something like "North America and pehaps the rest of the Western world?"

As long as a survey like this is not being used to support the premise that what is true of the data collected in Vancouver is completely and unerringly true in every part of the world, the answers to the above question is "yes." Honest social scientists like Davis take presuppositions or hypotheses about a certain aspect of society and test them on certain specific cases. When they have collected their research data, they interpret it, being careful not to lay down their findings as iron-clad rules or laws about the way people behave.

Men as Success Objects ... provides us with an excellent example of how such a survey can move from hypothesis to research to conclusion, while maintaining objectivity and conciseness in its presentation.

The data were explored further by collapsing several of the categories: the first 4 variables were collapsed into a "physical" category, Variables 5–7 were collapsed into an "employment" category and Variables 8 and 9 were collapsed into an "intellectual" category. The assumption was that the collapsed categories were sufficiently similar (within the three new categories) to make the new larger categories conceptually meaningful; conversely, it was felt the remaining variables (10–13) could not be meaningfully collapsed any further...

The men were more likely than the women to specify some physical attribute. The women were considerably more likely to specify that the companion be employed, or have a profession, or be in good financial shape. And the women were more likely to emphasize the intellectual abilities of their mate.

One can, incidentally, also note...an overall indication of attribute importance by collapsing across sexes; i.e. it is apparent that physical characteristics are the most desired regardless of sex.

Sex Differences

This study found that the attitudes of the subjects, in terms of desired companion attributes, were consistent with traditional sex role stereotypes. The men were more likely to emphasize stereotypically desirable feminine traits (appearance) and deemphasize the nonfeminine traits (financial, employment, and intellectual status). One inconsistency was that emotional expressiveness is a feminine trait but was emphasized relatively less by the men. Women, on the other hand, were more likely to emphasize masculine traits such as financial, employment, and intellectual status, and valued commitment in a relationship more highly. One inconsistency detected for the women concerned the fact that although emotional expressiveness is not a masculine trait, the women in this sample asked for it, relatively more than the men, anyway. Regarding this last point, it may be relevant to refer to Basow's (1986, p.210) conclusion that "women prefer relatively androgynous men, but men, especially traditional ones, prefer relatively sex-typed women."

These findings are similar to results from earlier studies, e.g. Deaux and Hanna (1984), and indicate that at this point in time and in this setting sex role stereotyping is still in operation.

One secondary finding that was of some interest to the author was that considerably more men than women placed personal ads—almost a 2:1 ratio. One can only speculate as to why this was so; however, there are probably at least two (related) contributing factors. One is that social convention dictates that women should be less outgoing in the initiation of relationships: Green and Sandos (1983) found that women who initiated dates were viewed less positively than their male counterparts. Another factor is that whoever places the ad is in a "power position" in that they can check out the other person's letter and photo, and then make a choice, all in anonymity; one could speculate that this need to be in control might be more an issue for the men.

Methodological Issues

Content analysis of newspaper ads has its strengths and weaknesses. By virtue of being an unobtrusive study of variables with face validity, it was felt some reliable measure of gender-related attitudes was being achieved. That the mean age of the men and women placing the ads was similar was taken as support for the assumption that the two sexes in this sample were demographically similar. Further, sex differences in desired companion attributes could not be attributed to differential verbal ability in that it was found that length of ad was similar for both sexes.

On the other hand, there were some limitations. It could be argued that people placing personal ads are not representative of the public in general. For instance, with respect to this study, it was found that the subjects were a somewhat older group—mean age of 40—than might be found in other courting situations. This raises the possibility of age being a confounding variable. Older singles may emphasize certain aspects of a relationship, regardless of sex. On the other hand, there is the possibility that age differentially affects women in the mate selection process, particularly when children are desired. The strategy of controlling for age in the analysis was felt problematic in that the numbers for analysis were fairly small, especially given the missing data, and further, that one cannot assume the missing cases were not systematically different (i.e. older) from those present.

References

Basow, S. (1986). Gender Stereotypes: Traditions and Alternatives. Brooks/Cole Pub.

Deaux, K. and Hanna, R. (1984) "Courtship in the personals column," *Sex Roles* 11: 363-375.

SOURCE: Simon Davis. "Men as Success Objects and Women as Sex Objects: A Study of Personal Advertisements," *Sex Roles*, 23, 1–2, July (1990) 43–50. Reprinted by permission.

Questions and Topics for Discussion and Writing

1. Why do you think it is that personal advertisements have become a popular way of finding mates? Why was it not so popular in the past?
2. Have a look at the personal ads yourself in a local newspaper. How does Davis' argument hold up?
3. What limitations can one put on Davis' findings from a methodological perspective? Can they be generalized? What inherent limits are there in the survey? How could one improve on the validity and generalizability of the results?

Sex Inequality in Cultural Symbolism and Interpersonal Relations

Jean Stockard and Miriam M. Johnson

Male dominance is hard to see unless one has become sensitized to it. The difficulty arises because male dominance is imbedded in our everyday language and in our ways of thought. This selection focuses on male dominance in two areas: (1) language/culture, and (2) face-to-face interaction. Male dominance weaves its way through our language, religion, social roles, and interpersonal power. It is changed when it is challenged by men and women. Although this article was written in 1980, and therefore is somewhat dated in specifics, many of the points the authors make are still valid today.

Male dominance refers to the beliefs, values, and cultural meanings that give higher value and prestige to masculinity than to femininity, which value males over females, men over women. Many anthropologists consider all known societies to be male dominant to some degree.

Male dominance does not mean that individual males in a society consciously conspire to keep women subordinate. Neither does it mean that women are helpless victims who have no way to prevail against men. Indeed, male dominance is hard to see unless one has become sensitized to it. The difficulty arises because male dominance is imbedded in our language and ways of thought. These built-in presuppositions limit the potential of all people and have personal costs for both males and females. In this chapter, we show how male dominance operates at the level of culture and in our everyday interactions.

Cultural Symbolism and Male Dominance

A cultural level of analysis or way of viewing human action focuses on the shared meanings individuals use in their interactions. Male dominance is passed from one generation to another partly through these shared symbol systems, including language and religions, as well as the mass media. These symbol systems picture and define our world for us and constrain us to interpret the world in masculine terms.

It is important to remember that ultimately culture is a human product: we humans construct our social world. However, no one individual ever constructs an entire culture singlehandedly. Most of our culture was originally made by other people, and some of it is quite old. This is the reason why we often see cultural meanings as if they were facts of nature, like the weather, objective necessities that exert an irresistible control over us rather than the products of human activity. Thus, humans are both creators and victims of culture. But because culture is a human product, created and re-created in human interaction, it can be changed and controlled by human will.

Language

Language, the means of our thought and of our communication with others, embodies male dominance. What is male in a language is generally basic; what is female is usually subsidiary and/or deprecated. Some languages, such as Japanese, are used differently by male and female speakers. Although the basic form and syntax of the language do not change, males and females use different prefixes and suffixes, and at times the two "languages" sound quite different. When this happens, however, the language that the males use is always seen as the language of the society; the female version is called "women's language." Other languages such as those in the Romance and Germanic families use gender-differentiated pronouns for both the singular and plural forms, but again the male form is basic. In French, while *elles* refers to a group of females and *ils* to men, only *ils* may be used to describe a group of mixed sex. In English, this same practice appears in the use of the generic *he*. To refer in a general sense to a single person, one must use the masculine singular pronouns *he, him,* or *his*. The result can be absurd: "No person may require another person to perform, participate in, or undergo an abortion against his will" (Key, 1975:89). In other instances, the term *man* is used to refer to all human beings. We have many phrases with this meaning, including "good will to men," "Man in the street," and even "all men are created equal."

English often describes females in terms of males. Thus, we may speak of an usherette, a poetess, an actress, even a tigress and a lioness. With occupations, we usually attach appendages, such as lady doctor or woman lawyer, to signify that the occupant is not a male. Only with family-related terms such as widower or with traditionally female occupations, such as male nurse or male prostitute, do we signify that the occupant is a male (Adams and Ware, 1979:491). Even the terms of address Mrs. and Miss indicate a woman's marital status. There are no comparable terms in the language to indicate whether a man is married. Even the recent attempt in English to use the undifferentiated Ms. for women may be in danger of being subverted. Although the originators of the term hoped it would be used to refer to all adult women, it now appears that Ms. is informally coming to refer only to single women or even to women who had been divorced! Thus, out of an undifferentiated category, yet a third differentiation has been made—a formerly married woman.

Finally, language usage deprecates and devalues women. In some instances, this may take the form of trivializing what women are and do, as in phrases such as "wine, women, and song" or using the term *girl* for women of all ages. One of our mature students described how she developed new sensitivity when a college choir director regularly called for women's voices with the phrase, "Now, girls" while eliciting male vocalization with "Now, men." To call a full-grown adult male "boy" is an insult, but until recently it was no insult at all to call a full-grown adult female "girl." Actually, the words *woman* and *female* themselves have several deprecatory meanings. For example, the 1956 edition of Webster's dictionary gives, in addition to neutral meanings, the following meanings for *woman*: "One who is effeminate, cowardly, emotional, or weak, used of a man, as, he seemed to me a very woman." Another meaning given was "to cause to act like a woman, to subdue to weakness like a woman." In 1967, the Random House dictionary eschews the foregoing list but notes that the word *female*, which used to be used interchangeably with *woman*, has now developed a contemptuous implication, as in "a strong-minded female." The 1916 collegiate edition of Webster's dictionary was even more straightforward. It defined male as "denoting an intensity or superiority of the characteristic qualities of anything—contrasted with female"!

Perhaps the ultimate form of this deprecation involves sexual overtones to words connected with women. One study found close to 1,000 English words and phrases that describe women in sexually derogatory ways, and many fewer such phrases describing men. While there are over 500 synonyms for prostitute, there are only about 65 for the masculine term of whoremonger (Schulz, 1975). Even terms that were once sexually neutral (such as hussy, which comes from an old English term for housewife; broad, which meant a young woman; and spinster, which once meant someone who ran a spinning wheel) have over the years developed negative meanings with sexual overtones (Schulz, 1975).

These language patterns reflect our male-dominated culture. They may also, however, reinforce and reproduce this culture because language reflects the ways in which we see the world....

Religion

The major functionaries of religious systems are also male. For instance, although there have been a few strong women prophets, the major prophets and figures of Western religions, including Moses, Jesus, and Mohammed, were male. Females are included in Biblical stories, but their role is generally minor. They may be maternal and devoted helpmates as Mary Magdalene and Ruth were, or they may be evil or stupid, as were Lot's wife, Jezebel, and most especially, Eve.

Religions have different official roles for males and females, and males always have the closest ceremonial ties to the deities. In the Catholic church, men are priests and women are nuns. While nuns teach, nurse, and may hold very responsible administrative positions in hospitals and schools, they cannot celebrate Mass. Only priests may perform the ceremony that links the faithful directly with God. In some Protestant groups, only elders and deacons—who are men—may make the congregational decisions. Among conservative and orthodox Jews, only men may be rabbis. Jewish women serve important functions in the home, but in the orthodox and conservative synagogues they are seated apart from the men and are not involved in the official prayers and ceremonies.

Finally, religious rituals reflect and reinforce systems of male dominance. This occurs partly because the major religious functionaries are male. Thus, in Christianity, men ordain other men; in most denominations only men serve communion; and men generally perform wedding ceremonies. Sometimes the ceremonies themselves embody the principles of male dominance. For instance, the traditional Jewish male regularly repeats a prayer in which he thanks God that he was not born a woman. The initiation rites of males through which young men learn the sacred rules of a society may serve to bond men together and to separate them from and elevate them over women. Even female initiation rites serve to promote male dominance by legitimizing and helping women rationalize men's control over their lives (Weitz, 1977:185–87).

Because religion defines the ultimate meaning of the universe for a people, the impact may be deep and often emotional rather than intellectual. When male dominance is embodied within religion, it enters the arena that a society considers sacred. This may make it even less open to question and more resistant to change than other social areas.

The Mass Media

The way men and women are depicted in the media—in television shows, magazines, popular songs, and even school textbooks—reflects the assumptions of a male-dominant society.

Women tend to be both underrepresented and misrepresented in television programming, from children's shows and cartoons to prime-time comedies and dramas, game shows, crime shows, and commercials. With the exception of soap operas, where men are only about 50 percent of the characters, men are vastly overrepresented as characters. A study in 1975 found that 69 percent of the characters in all prime-time shows (74 percent of the characters in dramas and 60 percent in comedies) are men (McNeil, 1975). On children's programs, there are over twice as many males as females (Sternglanz and Serbin, 1974, cited by Schuetz and Sprafkin, 1978:72). A study of spot messages during children's shows, including commercials and public service announcements, revealed that over 60 percent of the characters, both human and cartoon, were male (Schuetz and Sprafkin, 1978:73). The situation on public television is even more dismal. An analysis of programs other than music and dramas found that only 15 percent of the participants were women (Cantor, 1978). This situation had not changed appreciably by the 1977–78 season (U.S. Commission on Civil Rights, 1979).

The roles men and women play also differ. Studies of commercials find that males are much more likely to do the selling, either in a factual or an "aggressive sales-pitchy" manner. Females tend to be seductive or soft-spoken in commercials (Chafetz, 1978). Analyses of role interactions of characters in prime-time shows also reveal sex differences that reflect male dominance. One study analyzed activities intended to influence or control the behaviour of others in prime-time situation comedies and crime dramas in 1975. Both social class (measured by occupational status) and race influence dominance attempts, with higher-status people and whites more likely to dominate others. However, ignoring the impact of occupational status, men dominated women in 23 percent of the interactions involving both men and women in situation comedies and 47 percent of these interactions in crime shows. The reverse situation, with women dominating men, occurred in 13 percent of the interactions in comedies and in only 6 percent of the crime show interactions. Even though having a female star helped decrease the number of times men were dominant, the incidence of men dominating women on these shows was still much higher than the reverse (Lemon, 1978)...

An analysis of the top ten popular songs in each year from 1955 through 1974, songs that were so popular that they were played many times each day on radios and phonographs (especially by teenagers), found that while they made many references to women's beauty and sex appeal in the songs, they rarely mentioned males' physical attractiveness. The author concludes that the songs convey the message to boys that they "*should* dominate every relationship and that a girl's refusal to participate as the subordinate partner is evidence of the boy's personal failure." Girls would get the message that beauty, sex appeal, passivity, submissiveness, and dependence are appealing to boys and that by manipulating a boy's sexual impulses, a girl may control him (Talkington, 1976:149).

Finally, a number of studies have examined children's reading, mathematics, science, and social studies textbooks and found similar results there. Females are less often included as characters and, when they are included, are much less likely to be the main character. The behaviours that characterize the children and adults of each sex group in the stories also differ. Men are often portrayed outdoors, in business, and at school; women are much more often portrayed in the home (Saario et al., 1973).

In short, these images of males and females in the mass media as well as in school curricular materials attest to the male-dominant culture. That females are less often portrayed than males has been called a "symbolic annihilation," the removal of women from our cultural imagery (Tuchman, 1978). Women are more limited in the roles they hold and may be shown in devalued characterizations and in interactions controlled by men. While these portrayals reflect the male-dominated culture, by their very existence they—like religion and language—may also reinforce and support the existence of male dominance on the cultural level.

Interpersonal Relations and Male Dominance

Not only does male dominance pervade our language, religion, and media; it also influences the everyday interactions of males and females. Sex segregation and the devaluation of women appear in everyday life. This involves *social roles*, individuals' actions in social groups based on the expectations of others in that group. When people are expected to play certain roles simply because they are males or females, these roles are called *sex roles* or *gender roles*. These sex roles are both different and differentially evaluated.

Sex Role Differentiation in Everyday Life

Extensive role segregation appears in day-to-day interactions at home, at work, and in organizations. For instance, in the United States, men more often change the oil in the car and mow the lawn, and women more often dust and clean closets. At work, women much more often use a typewriter or copy machine; men more often use a dictaphone. While both upper-class men and women belong to exclusive clubs, the men may belong to the city clubs or the university clubs, and the women belong to the Junior League or have auxiliary membership in their husbands' groups. Middle- and working-class organizations are also sex-segregated. Only men may usually belong to the Elks Club, the Moose, the Eagles, the American Legion, and the Junior Chamber of Commerce. While women may belong to auxiliary groups such as the American Legion Auxiliary or the Jaycee-ettes and participate in social and service functions, they are generally barred from participating in the ceremonial activities of the groups. (These groups have also been segregated by race and religion. Nonwhites and non-Protestants have sometimes formed their own lodges, which are also sex-segregated.)

The intensity of people's feelings about this role segregation is most apparent in organizations threatened by change. For a number of years the Episcopal church had a strong controversy over the ordination of women into the priesthood. Before women were officially ordained, dissident priests who allowed women to give communion were threatened with excommunication. After women joined the priesthood, dissent continued. Some clergy and some parishes even left the established church for other church bodies or their own fellowship. Similarly, the United States Jaycees once expelled several chapters when they admitted women. Supporters of integrating the group took the case to court, and the Jaycees have spent much time and money fighting the possibility of integration.

The Devaluation of Women in Everyday Life

Not only women's activities, but also their very being are devalued in everyday interactions. This is well illustrated by the way men avoid anything feminine. For instance, if nursery school boys display behaviour usually associated with girls, they tend to redefine the activity as masculine. Heuser (1977) tells about a boy who one day wore white tights and a woman's wig. He vehemently rejected other children's derision of his "girlish" behaviour by explaining that his tights were "boy's tights" and his wig covered his balding head! Heuser did not find the parallel behaviour of girls avoiding masculine activities. It is far worse for a boy to be called a sissy than for a girl to be called a tomboy. Grown men continue this pattern. The unisex fashion pattern primarily involves women adopting masculine clothes such as pants and T-shirts. Men may wear brighter clothes and jumpsuits and even carry purses, but they never wear skirts or dresses, and the purses they carry are always, as the fashion coordinators say, distinctively masculine.

Even the attribution of womanly traits may be considered an insult. In an informal basketball game we observed, when a boy would miss a basket the other boys would call him "woman!" On another occasion, we heard a younger boy turn to an older boy in the midst of an argument and say, "Shaddup, boy!" in the most deprecating tone he could muster. The older boy, however, immediately gained the upper hand by saying to his younger brother, "You shaddup, girl!" There is no comparable phenomenon among women, for young girls do not insult each other by calling each other "man."

By adulthood most men temper the open comments they make about women as they become more intimately involved with them. Yet signs of men's devaluation still appear, especially in all-male settings. In his classic study, *The American Soldier*, Samuel Stouffer describes how training for combat becomes entwined with the soldiers' definitions of themselves as men (Stouffer et al., 1976:180):

> The fear of failure in the role [of combat soldier], as by showing cowardice in battle, could bring not only fear of social censure, but also more central and strongly established fears related to sex-typing. To fail to measure up as a soldier in courage and endurance was to risk the charge of not being a man. ("Whatsa matter, bud—got lace on your drawers!")

Even in modern times men are urged on to war by threats to their masculinity. Wayne Eisenhart (1975) describes an "endless litany" from the drill sergeant in the Vietnam War along the lines of "Can't hack it, little girls?"

Men's sexual jokes may also reveal antagonistic attitudes toward women. Jokes about dumb blondes or traveling salesmen and the farmer's daughter are typical ways to convey devaluation of females. The woman in these jokes "is represented as naive or simply stupid, easily outmanoeuvred by the male, who gets what he wants with cost" (Fry, 1972:139).

The Reproduction of Male Dominance in Everyday Interactions

In the final analysis cultural patterns of sex segregation and devaluation continue to exist because individuals perpetuate them. Sex segregation is usually much more strongly supported by men than by women, and it is men who express jokes and comments that devalue women. Men communicate their expectations of role segregation and devaluation to each other and thus reinforce these views. Obviously some men do not care as deeply as others about maintaining sex segregation. However, because they must actively

Sex Stereotyping

I Want to Be an Engineer

In their article on "Sex Inequality in Cultural Symbolism and Interpersonal Relations," authors Stockard and Johnson argue that male dominance is so firmly entrenched in our society that it often occurs unnoticed by most people.

One of the ways through which these differing attitudes are manifested is language. As the authors indicate, language is one important medium that has been adversely affected by male dominance.

Keeping in mind, however, that this article was written in 1980, it is possible to see ways in which gender bias is being eliminated from society. For example, it is not uncommon today to hear of "letter-carriers," "firefighters" and "police officers" instead of "mailmen," "firemen" and "policemen." People are starting to use more flexible third-person pronouns when speaking and writing about someone whose gender is not specified, such as "If a person doesn't pay *his or her* rent, *he or she* can be threatened with eviction." People who disagree with these kinds of linguistic changes argue that they make language unneccessarily cluttered, but as authors Johnson and Stockard imply, this is one medium through which we can—and should—try to reverse the trend of excessive gender domination.

Another way in which the authors claim male dominance is perpetuated in our society is through advertising. One of the most pervasive techniques used in this regard is to reduce women to one-dimensional characters who are consumed with enthusiasm for a particualr product or service. For example, a recent radio spot for a nation-wide chain of department stores features two effusive young women displaying what seems to be far too much anticipation about an upcoming national sale. Admittedly, a certain degree of "suspension of disbelief" is expected by the advertiser—they don't really think that anyone in their right mind is going to be as excited as the two women about the sale.

In addition, commercials will sometimes feature unrealistic male caricatures doing exactly the same thing. But the strong implication still resides in the media, in all its forms, that women don't have anything better to do than get excited about discount sales, spend time looking attractive for beer-drinking males on beaches or in bars, or looking for new ways to get their clothes as white and bright as possible.

This implication is becoming increasingly paradoxical, since women have taken a firm place in the workforce and are no longer confined to what had been known as "women's" roles in society.

work against long-established traditions and the often deeply held views of others, their attempts to end sex segregation and devaluation usually meet a good deal of opposition. Women also may reinforce sex segregation, the devaluation of women, and male dominance through their responses to these expectations.

Male power in everyday life. In male-dominant societies, men have, as a group, greater power than women. Their verbal communications of women show that they know that this power differential exists. Males and females in our society tend to speak in different ways. Women tend to be more polite and less assertive than men are. Women also soften their requests more often with phrases like "Would you mind?" while men tend to be more direct and demanding (Lakoff, 1975). Men tend to interrupt women when they are speaking more than women interrupt men (Zimmerman and West, 1975). Contrary to the stereotype of talkative women, when men and women are in the same group, the men actually dominate the conversation and talk more than the women do (Henley, 1977).

Men's greater power also shows in non-verbal interactions. Men take up more space than women do, even when the size of their bodies is taken into account. When both men and women are seated, for instance, men take up more space relative to their bodies than women do. Men also touch women without permission more than women touch men (Henley, 1977). In all of these interactions, women's actions are those found to characterize lower-status persons generally. This suggests that women recognize that men have greater power than they do and demonstrate this recognition in their interpersonal relations....

Studies of women in male-dominated arenas suggest that women who emphasize some aspect of a feminine role meet with the fewest interpersonal problems on the job. For example, John Y. Brown, a millionaire from his investments in Kentucky Fried Chicken, once bought the Kentucky Colonels basketball team. His wife, Ellie, became chair of the board and placed her friends from the Junior League on the other seats on the board. Basketball team administrators up to that time had always been men. Yet, these women eliminated criticism of their entrance into the field by emphasizing their femininity in their statements, their dress, and their manners. As one member of the board put it, "We're all wives and mothers first" (Rich, 1974:56). Similarly, interviews with women professionals suggest that women who "act professional, but not especially formal or aggressive, who try to be gracious as women and not be one of the boys, face the fewest problems in male dominated work situations" (Epstein, 1970:979). Being feminine may take the form of playing the mother who is sympathetic and helpful to others, the sex object or seductress who plays on her sexuality, or the "pet" or kid sister who encourages the men in their work or acts as a mascot (Kanter, 1975; Tavris and Offir, 1977:211)...

Summary

Male dominance pervades both cultural symbols and day-to-day interactions. Males are depicted in different roles than women and are given more value and authority than women in languages, in religions, and in the mass media. In day-to-day interactions, men show their devaluation of women and the roles of the sexes are often sharply differentiated. While the actions of women often reinforce differentiation and devaluation, contemporary feminists have challenged these patterns of male dominance.

SOURCE: Taken from Jean Stockard and Miriam Johnson, *Sex Roles: Sex Inequality and Sex Role Development*. Englewood Cliffs, N.J.: Prentice-Hall, Inc., 1980, pp. 3–20. Reprinted by permission of Prentice-Hall.

Questions and Topics for Discussion and Writing

1. Give examples of how our language, in relation to gender issues, has improved over the past few decades. What are examples of areas where our language continues to regard women as second-class citizens and therefore needs improvement?

3. Analyze some of the TV advertisements during typically male dominated sports. Do they reflect sex equality or are women still cast as sex objects? What about normal TV advertising?

By Any Means Necessary

Malcolm X

This piece is the transcript of a speech given by Malcolm X at the Harvard Law School Forum on December 16, 1964. In it, Malcolm X articulates his views on the civil rights struggle in the United States. His aggressive and at times confrontational views stand in contrast to those of more moderate black leaders of the day, such as Martin Luther King, Jr. The moderator of this forum, Alan Dershowitz, has gone on to become one of the highest-profile attorneys in the United States.

Alan Dershowitz, Moderator:

"Our speaker this evening was born Malcolm Little about forty years ago in Omaha, Nebraska. Not much is known about his early life except that in 1948 he joined the Black Muslim Movement and adopted the last name of X, which he maintains today. Although still a Muslim, he has recently broken with the Black Muslim Movement, where he served as Chief Minister. He is now Chairman of an organization known as The Organization of Afro-American Unity—the description of which I shall leave to him. Now he prefers to be known as Brother Malcolm when he is speaking in a religious capacity, but as Malcolm X when he is speaking in a political capacity. The New York Times reported not very long ago that Malcolm X was the second most sought-after speaker on college and university campuses. The first was Barry Goldwater.

"Mr. Malcolm X."

I first want to thank the Harvard Law School Forum for the invitation to speak here this evening, more especially to speak on a very timely topic—The African Revolution and Its Impact on the American Negro. I probably won't use the word "American Negro," but substitute "Afro-American." And when I say Afro-American, I mean it in the same context in which you usually use the word Negro. Our people today are increasingly shying away from use of that word. They find that when you're identified as Negro, it tends to make you "catch a whole lot of hell" that people who don't use it don't catch.

In the present debate over the Congo, you are probably aware that a new tone and a new tempo, almost a new temper, are being reflected among African statesmen toward the United States. And I think we should be interested in and concerned with what impact this will have upon Afro-Americans and how it will affect America's international race relations. We know that it will have an effect at the international level. It's already having such an effect. But I am primarily concerned with what effect it will have on the internal race relations of this country—that is to say, between the Afro-American and the white American.

When you let yourself be influenced by images created by others, you'll find that oftentimes the one who creates those images can use them to mislead you and misuse you. A good example: A couple of weeks ago I was on a plane with a couple of Americans, a male and a female sitting to my right. We were in the same row and had a nice conversation for about thirty-five to forty minutes. Finally the lady looked at my briefcase and said, "I would like to ask you a personal question," and I knew what was coming. She said,

"What kind of last name could you have that begins with X?" I said, "Malcolm." Ten minutes went by, and she turned to me and said, "You're not Malcolm X?" You see, we had a nice conversation going, just three human beings, but she was soon looking at the image created by the press. She said so: "I just wouldn't believe that you were that man," she said.

I had a similar experience last week at Oxford. The Oxford Union had arranged a debate. Before the debate I had dinner with four students. A girl student looked kind of cross-eyed, goggle-eyed and otherwise, and finally just told me she wanted to ask me a question. (I found out she was a conservative, by the way, whatever that is.) She said, "I just can't get over your not being as I had expected." I told her it was a case of the press carefully creating images.

Again I had a similar experience last night. At the United Nations a friend from Africa came in with a white woman who is involved with a philanthropic foundation over there. He and I were engaged in conversation for several minutes, and she was in and out of the conversation. Finally I heard her whisper to someone off to the side. She didn't think I was listening. She said—she actually said this—"He doesn't look so wild, you know." Now this is a full-grown, so-called "mature" woman. It shows the extent to which the press can create images. People looking for one thing actually miss the boat because they're looking for the wrong thing. They are looking for someone with horns, someone who is a rabble-rouser, an irrational, antisocial extremist. They expect to hear me say [that Negroes] should kill all the white people—as if you could kill all the white people! In fact, if I had believed what they said about the people in Britain, I never would have gone to Oxford. I would have let it slide. When I got there I didn't go by what I had read about them. I found out they were quite human and likable. Some weren't what I had expected.

Now I have taken time to discuss images because one of the sciences used and misused today is this science of [image making]. The power structure uses it at the local level, at the national level, at the international level. And oftentimes when you and I feel we've come to a conclusion on our own, the conclusion is something that someone has invented for us through the images he has created.

I'm a Muslim. Now if something is wrong with being Muslim, we can argue, we can "get with it." I'm a Muslim, which means that I believe in the religion of Islam. I believe in Allah, the same God that many of you would probably believe in if you knew more about Him. I believe in all of the prophets: Abraham, Moses, Jesus, Muhammad. Most of you are Jewish, and you believe in Moses; you might not pick Jesus. If you're Christians, you believe in Moses and Jesus. Well, I'm Muslim, and I believe in Moses, Jesus, and Muhammad. I believe in all of them. So I think I'm "way up on you."

In Islam we practice prayer, charity, fasting. These should be practiced in all religions. The Muslim religion also requires one to make the pilgrimage to the Holy City of Mecca. I was fortunate enough to make it in April, and I went back again in September. Insofar as being a Muslim is concerned, I have done what one is supposed to do to be a Muslim.

Despite being a Muslim, I can't overlook the fact that I'm an Afro-American in a country which practices racism against black people. There is no religion under the sun that would make me forget the suffering that Negro people have undergone in this country. Negroes have suffered for no reason other than that their skins happen to be black. So whether I'm Muslim, Christian, Buddhist, Hindu, atheist or agnostic, I would still be in the front lines with Negro people fighting against the racism, segregation, and discrimination practiced in this country at all levels in the North, South, East, and West.

I believe in the brotherhood of all men, but I don't believe in wasting brotherhood on anyone who doesn't want to practice it with me. Brotherhood is a two-way street. I don't think brotherhood should be practiced with a man just because his skin is white. Brotherhood should hinge upon the deeds and attitudes of a man. I couldn't practice brotherhood, for example, with some of those Eastlands or crackers in the South who are responsible for the condition of our people.

I don't think anyone would deny either that if

The Views of Malcolm X

Malcolm X

Malcolm X

Malcolm X was born Malcolm Little in Omaha, Nebraska. He was assassinated in 1965. His life has recently been portrayed in the film *Malcolm X.*

While in prison, Malcolm X joined the Nation of Islam. He took on the surname "X" to signify that, like most descendants of the slaves forcibly brought to the United States from Africa, he had lost his ancestral name. He joined the Nation of Islam in prison and became a devoted follower of the Islamic religion. The Nation of Islam maintained that the solution for black people in the United States was complete separation for blacks.

Malcolm X's views underwent a radical change in 1964. During a series of religious trips to Mecca and the newly independent African states, he encountered good people of all races. His views began to change accordingly. He came to the conclusion that he had yet to discover true Islam. He came to regard not all whites as racists, and saw the struggle of black people as part of a wider freedom struggle. He established his own religious group and a political organization, the Organization for Afro-American Unity.

Along with Martin Luther King, Malcolm X symbolized the civil rights movement in the United States during the 1960s.

Before Going to Mecca

"No *sane* black man really wants integration! No *sane* white man really wants integration. No sane black man really believes that the white man ever will give the black man anything more than token integration. No! The Honorable Elijah Muhammad teaches that for the black man in America the only solution is complete *separation* from the white man!"
The Autobiography of Malcolm X, p.248.

"And this is one thing that whites—whether you call yourselves liberals or conservatives or racists or whatever else you might choose to be—one thing that you have to realize is, where the black community is concerned, although the large majority you come in contact with may impress you as being moderate and patient and loving and long-suffering and all that kind of stuff, the minority who you consider to be Muslims or nationalists happen to be made of the type of ingredient that can easily spark the black community. This should be understood. Because to me a powder keg is nothing without a fuse."
Malcolm X Speaks, p.48.

After Going to Mecca

"Never have I witnessed such sincere hospitality and the overwhelming spirit of true brotherhood as is practiced by people of all colors and races here in this Ancient Holy Land, the home of Abraham, Muhammad, and all the other prophets of the Holy Scriptures. For the past week, I have been utterly speechless and spellbound by the graciousness I see displayed all around me by people of *all colors.*"
The Autobiography of Malcolm X, p.344.

"My pilgrimage broadened my scope. It blessed me with a new insight. In two weeks in the Holy Land, I saw what I never had seen in thirty-nine years here in America. I saw all *races*, all *colors*,—blue-eyed blonds to black-skinned Africans—in *true* brotherhood! In unity! Living as one! Worshipping as one! No segregationists—no liberals; they would not have known how to interpret the meaning of those words.

"In the past, yes, I have made sweeping indictments of *all* white people. I never will be guilty of that again—as I know now that some white people *are* truly sincere, that some truly are capable of being brotherly toward a black man. The true Islam has shown me that a blanket indictment of all white people is as wrong as when whites make blanket indictments against blacks.

"Yes, I have been convinced that *some* American whites do want to help cure the rampant racism which is on the path to *destroying* this country!"
The Autobiography of Malcolm X, p.366.

you send chickens out of *your* barnyard in the morning, at nightfall those chickens will come home to roost in your barnyard. Chickens that you send out always come back home. It is a law of nature. I was an old farm boy myself, and I got in trouble saying this once [about President Kennedy's assassination], but it didn't stop me from being a farm boy. Other people's chickens don't come to roost on your doorstep, and yours don't go to roost on theirs. The chickens that this country is responsible for sending out, whether the country likes it or not (and if you're mature, you look at it "like it is"), someday, and someday soon, have got to come back home to roost.

Victims of racism are created in the image of racists. When the victims struggle vigorously to protect themselves from violence of others, they are made to appear in the image of criminals; as the criminal image is projected onto the victim. The recent situation in the Congo is one of the best examples of this. The headlines were used to mislead the public, [to create] wrong images. In the Congo, planes were bombing Congolese villages, yet Americans read that (How do they say it?) American-trained anti-Castro Cuban pilots were bombing rebel strongholds. These pilots were actually dropping bombs on villages with women and children. But because the tags "American-trained" and "anti-Castro Cubans" were applied, the bombing was legal. Anyone against Castro is all right. The press gave them a "holier than thou" image. And you let them get away with it because of the labels. The victim is made the criminal. It is really mass murder—murder of women, children, and babies. And mass murder is disguised as a humanitarian project. They fool nobody but the people of America. They don't fool the people of the world, who see beyond the images—their man in the Congo is Tshombe, the murderer of the rightful Prime Minister of the Congo. No matter what kind of language you use, he's purely and simply a murderer. The real Prime Minister of the Congo was Patrice Lumumba. The American government—your and my government—took this murderer and hired him to run the Congo. He became their hired killer. And to show what a hired killer he is, his first act was to go to South Africa and to hire more killers, paying them with American dollars. But he is glorified because he is given the image of the only one who could bring stability to the Congo. Whether he can bring stability or not, he's still a murderer. The headlines spoke of white hostages, not simply hostages, but white hostages, and of white nuns and priests, not simply nuns and priests, but white nuns and priests. Why? To gain the sympathy of the white public of America. The press had to shake up your mind in order to get your sympathy and support for criminal actions. They tricked you. Americans consider forty white lives more valuable than four thousand black lives. Thousands of Congolese were losing their lives. Mercenaries were paid with American dollars. The American press made the murderers look like saints and the victims like criminals. They made criminals look like victims and indeed the devil look like an angel and angels like the devil.

A friend of mine from Africa, who is in a good position to know, said he believed the United States government is being advised by her worst enemy in the Congo, because an American citizen could not suggest such insane action-especially identifying with Tshombe, who is the worst African on earth. You cannot find an African on earth who is more hated than Tshombe. It's a justifiable hatred they have toward him. He has won no victory himself. His Congolese troops have never won a victory for him. Every victory has been won by white mercenaries, who are hired to kill for him. The African soldiers in the Congo are fighting for the Stanleyville government. Here Tshombe is a curse. He's an insult to anyone who means to do right, black or white. When Tshombe visited Cairo, he caused trouble. When, he visited Rome last week, he caused trouble, and the same happened in Germany. Wherever Tshombe goes, trouble erupts. And if Tshombe comes to America, you'll see the worst rioting, bloodshed, and violence this country has ever seen. Nobody wants this kind of man in his country.

What effect does all this have on Afro-Americans? What effect will it have on race relations in this country? In the U.N. at this moment, Africans are using more uncompromising language and are heaping hot fire upon America as the racist and neo-colonial power par excellence. African statesmen have never used this language before. These statesmen are beginning to connect the criminal, racist acts practiced in the Congo with similar acts in Mississippi and Alabama. The Africans are pointing out that the white American government—not all white people—has shown just as much disregard for lives wrapped in black skin in the Congo as it shows for lives wrapped in black skin in Mississippi and in Alabama. When Africans, therefore, as well as we begin to think of Negro problems as interrelated, what will be the effect of such thinking on programs for improved race relations in this country? Many people will tell you that the black man in this country doesn't identify with Africa. Before 1959, many Negroes didn't. But before 1959, the image of Africa was created by an enemy of Africa, because Africans weren't in a position to create and project their own images. The image was created by the imperial powers of Europe.

Europeans created and popularized the image of Africa as a jungle, a wild place where people were cannibals, naked and savage in a countryside overrun with dangerous animals. Such an image of the Africans was so hateful to Afro-Americans that they refused to identify with Africa. We did not realize that in hating Africa and the Africans we were hating ourselves. You cannot hate the roots of a tree and not hate the tree itself. Negroes certainly cannot at the same time hate Africa and love themselves. We Negroes hated the American features: the African nose, the shape of our lips, the color of our skin, the texture of our hair. We could only end up hating ourselves. Our skin became a trap, a prison; we felt inferior, inadequate, helpless. It was not an image created by Africans or by Afro-Americans. but by an enemy.

Since 1959 the image has changed. The African states have emerged and achieved independence. Black people in this country are crying out for their independence and show a desire to make a fighting stand for it. The attitude of the Afro-American cannot be disconnected from the attitude of the African. The pulse beat, the voice, the very life-drive that is reflected in the African is reflected today here among the Afro-Americans. The only way you can really understand the black man in America and the changes in his heart and mind is to fully understand the heart and mind of the black man on the African continent; because it is the same heart and the same mind, although separated by four hundred years and by the Atlantic Ocean. There are those who wouldn't like us to have the same heart and the same mind for fear that that heart and mind might get together. Because when our people in this country received a new image of Africa, they automatically united through the new image of themselves. Fear left them completely. There was fear, however, among the racist elements and the State Department. Their fear was of our sympathy for Africa and for its hopes and aspirations and of this sympathy developing into a form of alliance. It is only natural to expect us today to turn and look in the direction of our homeland and of our motherland and to wonder whether we can make any contact with her.

Courtesy of the Bettman Archives.

Malcolm X.

I grew up in Lansing, Michigan, a typical American city. In those days, a black man could have a job shining shoes or waiting tables. The best job was waiting tables at the country club, as is still the case in most cities. In those days, if a fellow worked at the State House shining shoes, he was considered a big shot in the town. Only when Hitler went on the rampage in 1939, and this country suffered a manpower shortage, did the black man get a shot at better jobs. He was permitted a step forward only when Uncle Sam had his back to the wall and needed him. In 1939, '40, and '41, a black man couldn't even join the Army or Navy, and when they began drafting, they weren't drafting black soldiers but only white. I think it was well agreed upon and understood: If you let the black man get in the Army, get hold of a gun, and learn to shoot it, you wouldn't have to tell him what the target was. It was not until the Negro leaders (and in this sense I use the word Negro purposely) began to cry out and complain—"If white boys are gonna die on the battlefields, our black boys must die on the battlefields too!"—that they started drafting us. If it hadn't been for that type of leadership, we never would have been drafted. The Negro leaders just wanted to show that we were good enough to die too, although we hadn't been good enough to join the Army or Navy prior to that time.

During the time that Hitler and Tojo were on the rampage, the black man was needed in the plants, and for the first time in the history of America, we were given an opportunity on a large scale to get skills in areas that were closed previously to us. When we got these skills, we were put in a position to get more money. We made more money. We moved to a better neighborhood. When we moved to a better neighborhood, we were able to go to a better school and to get a better education, and this put us into a position to know what we hadn't been receiving up to that time. Then we began to cry a little louder than we had ever cried before. But this advancement never was out of Uncle Sam's goodwill. We never made one step forward until world pressure put Uncle Sam on the spot. And it was when he was on the spot that he allowed us to take a couple of steps forward. It has never been out of any internal sense of morality or legality or humanism that we were allowed to advance. *You have been as cold as an icicle whenever it came to the rights of the black man in this country.* (Excuse me for raising my voice, but I think it's time. As long as my voice is the only thing I raise, I don't think you should become upset!)

Because we began to cry a little louder, a new strategy was used to handle us. The strategy evolved with the Supreme Court desegregation decision, which was written in such tricky language that every crook in the country could sidestep it. The Supreme Court desegregation decision was handed down over ten years ago. It has been implemented less than ten percent in those ten years. It was a token advancement. even as we've been the recipients of "tokenism" in education, housing, employment, everything. But nowhere in the country during the past ten years has the black man been treated as a human being in the same context as other human beings. He's always being patronized in a very paternalistic way, but never has he been given an opportunity to function as a human being. Actually, in one sense, it's our own fault, but I'll get to that later on. We have never gotten the real thing. (Heck, I'll get to it right now.) The reason we never received the real thing is that we have not displayed any tendency to do the same for ourselves which other human beings do: to protect our humanity and project our humanity.

I'll clarify what I mean. Not a single white person in America would sit idly by and let someone do to him what we black men have been letting others do to us. The white person would not remain passive, peaceful, and nonviolent. The day the black man in this country shows others that we are just as human as they in reaction to injustice, that we are willing to die just as quickly to protect our lives and property as whites have shown, only then will our people be recognized as human beings. It is inhuman, absolutely subhuman, for a man to let a dog bite him and not fight back. Let someone club him and let him not fight back, or let someone put water hoses on his women, his mother and daughter and babies and let him not fight back...then he's subhuman. The day he becomes a human being he will react as other human beings have reacted, and nobody [in humanity] will hold it against him.

In 1959, we saw the emergence of the Negro revolt and the collapse of European colonialism on the African continent. Our struggle, our initiative, and our militancy were in tune with the struggle and initiative and militancy of our brothers in Africa. When the colonial powers saw they couldn't remain in Africa, they behaved as somebody playing basketball. He gets the basketball and must pass it to a teammate in the clear. The colonial powers were boxed in on the African continent. They didn't intend to give up the ball. They just passed it to the one that was in the clear, and the one that was in the clear was the United States. The ball was passed to her, and she picked it up and has been running like mad ever since. Her presence on the African continent has replaced the imperialism and the colonialism of Europeans. But it's still imperialism and colonialism. Americans fooled many of the Africans into thinking that they weren't an imperialist power or colonial power until their intentions were revealed, until they hired Tshombe and put him back to kill in the Congo. Nothing America could have done would have ever awakened the Africans to her true intentions as did her dealings with this murderer named Tshombe.

America knew that Africa was waking in '59. Africa was developing a higher degree of intelligence than she reflected in the past. America, for her part, knew she had to use a more intelligent approach. She used the friendly approach: the Peace Corps, Crossroads. Such philanthropic acts disguised American imperialism and colonialism with dollar-ism. America was not honest with what she was doing. I don't mean that those in the Peace Corps weren't honest. But the Corps was being used more for political purposes than for moral purposes. I met many white Peace Corps workers while on the African continent. Many of them were properly motivated and were making a great contribution. But the Peace Corps will never work over there until the idea has been applied over here.

Of course the Civil Rights Bill was designed supposedly to solve our problem. As soon as it was passed, however, three civil rights workers were murdered. Nothing has been done about it, and I think nothing will be done about it until the people themselves do something about it. I, for one, think the best way to stop the Ku Klux Klan is to talk to the Ku Klux Klan in the only language it understands, for you can't talk French to someone who speaks German and communicate. Find out what language a person speaks, speak their language and you'll get your point across. Racists know only one language, and it is doing the black man in this country an injustice to expect him to talk the language of peace to people who don't know peaceful language. In order to get any kind of point across our people must speak whatever language the racist speaks. The government can't protect us. The government has not protected us. It is time for us to do whatever is necessary by any means necessary to protect ourselves. If the government doesn't want us running around here wild like that, then I say let the government get up off its...whatever it's on and take care of it itself. After the passage of the Civil Rights Bill, they killed the Negro educator Pitt in Georgia. The killers were brought to court and then set free. This is the pattern in this country, and I think that white people (I use the word white people because it's cut short: it gets right to the point) are doing us an injustice. If you expect us to be nonviolent, you yourselves aren't. If someone came knocking on your door with a rifle, you'd walk out of the door with your rifle. Now the black man in this country is getting ready to do the same thing.

I say in conclusion that the Negro problem has ceased to be a Negro problem. It has ceased to be an American problem and has now become a world problem, a problem for all humanity. Negroes waste their time confining their struggle to civil rights. In that context the problem remains only within the jurisdiction of the United States. No allies can help Negroes without violating United States protocol. But today the black man in America has seen his mistake and is correcting it by lifting his struggle from the level of civil rights to the level of human rights. No longer does the United States government sit in an ivory tower where it can point at South Africa, point at the Portuguese, British, French, and other European colonial powers. No longer can the United States hold twenty million black people in second-class citizenship and think that the world will keep a silent mouth. No matter what the independent African states are doing in the United Nations, it is only a flicker, a glimpse, a ripple of what this country is in for in the future, unless a halt is brought to the illegal injustices which our people continue to suffer every day.

The Organization of Afro-American Unity (to which I belong) is a peaceful organization based on brotherhood. Oh yes, it is peaceful. But I believe you can't have peace until you're ready to protect it. As you will die protecting yours, I will die protecting mine. The OAAU is trying to get our problem before the United Nations. This is one of its immediate projects on the domestic front. We will work with all existing civil rights organizations. Since there has been talk of minimizing demonstrations and of becoming involved in political action, we want to see if civil rights organizations mean it. The OAAU will become involved in every move to secure maximum opportunity for black people to register peacefully as voters. We believe that along with voter registration, Afro-Americans need voter education. Our people should receive education in the science of politics so that the crooked politician cannot exploit us. We must put ourselves in a position to become active politically. We believe that the OAAU should provide defense units in every area of this country where workers are registering or are seeking voting rights, in every area where young students go out on the battlefront (which it actually is). Such self-defense units should have brothers who will not go out and initiate aggression, but brothers who are qualified, equipped to retaliate when anyone imposes brutally on us, whether it be in Mississippi, Massachusetts, California, or New York City. The OAAU doesn't believe it should permit civil rights workers to be murdered. When a government can't protect civil rights workers, we believe we should do it. Even in the Christian Bible it says that he who kills with the sword shall be killed by the sword, and I'm not against it. I'm for peace, yet I believe that any man facing death should be able to go to any length to assure that whoever is trying to kill him doesn't have a chance. The OAAU supports the plan of every civil rights group for political action, as long as it doesn't involve compromise. We don't believe Afro-Americans should be victims any longer. We believe we should let the world know, the Ku Klux Klan know, that bloodshed is a two-way street, that dying is a two-way street, that killing is a two-way street. Now I say all this in as peaceful a language as I know.

There was another man back in history whom I read about once, an old friend of mine whose name was Hamlet, who confronted, in a sense, the same thing our people are confronting here in America. Hamlet was debating whether "To be or not to be"—that was the question. He was trying to decide whether it was "nobler in the mind to suffer (peacefully) the slings and arrows of outrageous fortune," or whether it was nobler "to take up arms" and oppose them. I think his little soliloquy answers itself. As long as you sit around suffering the slings and arrows and are afraid to use some slings and arrows yourself, you'll continue to suffer. The OAAU has come to the conclusion that it is time to take up whatever means necessary to bring these sufferings to a halt.

SOURCE: From *The Speeches of Malcolm X*, Edited with an introductory essay by Archie Epps (London: Peter Owen, 1969).

Questions and Topics for Discussion and Writing

1. What point is Malcolm X trying to make through his remarks on image-making? Is he convincing? Can people be blamed for accepting images created by the media?

2. What parallels does Malcolm X make between revolutionary events in Africa and inter-racial relations in his own country? What is significant about the United States government's actions in both of these areas?

3. Malcolm X's speech to the Harvard Law School Forum deals with several issues that were relevant to the U.S. of the 1960s. Do any of his ideas have anything to do with Canada in the 1990s?

The Milgram Experiment on Social Norms

Stanley Milgram

Stanley Milgram was born in 1933 in New York City. Milgram spent from 1960 to 1963 at Yale University conducting the obedience experiments for which he became internationally famous. The full series of experiments was first published in his 1974 book *Obedience to Authority*, which was nominated for a National Book Award. These edited excerpts describe his subway experiments.

The general question that motivated this research was: How are social norms maintained? Our focus was on the type of...norms which regulate everyday activity and which are neither made explicit nor codified. Scheff (1960) refers to this class of norms as "residual rules," residual in the sense that they are the restraints on behaviour that persist after the formal social norms have been sorted out of the analysis. Scheff isolates these rules on the basis of two criteria: (1) people must be in substantial agreement about them; and (2) they are not noticed until a violation occurs. These rules have been likened to the rules of grammar in that one can follow them without an explicit knowledge of their content and yet notice a violation immediately.

The fact that these residual rules are usually unexpressed creates a serious obstacle to their study: We are virtually inarticulate about them. When compared with formal laws, for example, which have been explicitly codified, residual rules have been left unarticulated by the culture.

An important distinction between these residual rules and laws can be drawn in terms of enforcement. The mechanism for the maintenance of laws is obvious. The entire law enforcement establishment is charged with the responsibility of keeping behaviour within the law. Society is quite explicit about the consequences of breaking the law and about who should administer punishment. But who is charged with maintaining residual rules? What consequences should the residual rule breaker expect?...

The residual rule selected for study was a rule of social behaviour on the New York City subway system. The requirements of appropriate social behaviour on the subway are, on the face of it, simple. People get on the subway for a very clear and specific reason: to get from one place to another in a brief period of time. The amount of interaction among the riders required for this purpose is minimal and the rules governing this interaction are widely adhered to. One rule of subway behaviour is that seats are filled on a first-come, first-served basis. Another implicit rule is one that discourages passengers from talking to one another. Even though riders are often squeezed into very close proximity, they are rarely observed to converse. The experimenters in this study violated these rules by asking people for their seats. This procedure allowed for discrete, measurable responses: people could either give up their seats or refuse to do so....

Common sense suggests that it is impossible to obtain a seat on the subway simply by asking for it. Harold Takooshian obtained data on this last point. He asked 16 people to predict what percentage of requests would result in the offer of a seat. Answers ranged from 1% to 55%; the median

Excerpt

Stanley Milgram

"As a social psychologist, I look at the world not to master it in any practical sense, but to understand it and to communicate that understanding to others. Social psychologists are part of the very social matrix they have chosen to analyze, and thus they can use their own experience as a source of insight. The difficulty is to do this in a way that does not drain life of its spontaneity and pleasure.

"A wish to understand social behaviour is not, of course, unique to psychologists; it is part of normal human curiosity. But for social psychologists, this need is more central, more compelling, and thus they go a step further and make it their life's work...

"The implicit model for the experimental work is that of the person influenced by social forces while often believing in his or own independence of them. It is thus a social psychology of the reactive individual, the recipient of forces and pressure emanating from outside oneself. This represents, of course, only one side of the coin of social life, for we as individuals also initiate action out of internal needs and actively construct the social world we inhabit...

"Every experiment is a situation in which the end is unknown; it is tentative, indeterminate, something that may fail. An experiment may produce only a restatement of the obvious or yield unexpected insights. The indeterminacy of its outcome is part of its excitement.

"Although experiments may be objective, they are rarely entirely neutral. There is a certain viewpoint that is implicit in the experiments that were carried out. Thus, in my studies of conformity and obedience, the moral value always rests with the person who rejects the group or authority....

"The most interesting experiments in social psychology are produced by the interplay of naivete and skepticism. The experimenter must be sufficiently naive to question what everyone thinks is a certainty. Yet he must be skeptical at every point—in his interpretation of data, and in the too hasty assimilation of a discovery to a preexisting framework of thought...."

prediction was that 14% of those who were asked would give up their seats.

Before we describe the experimental procedure, it is worth pointing out some things that the procedure was *not*. The procedure was not an attempt to obtain seats by demanding that riders give them up. Experimenters were instructed to be sure to phrase their questions as requests, not as demands. The procedure was not designed to question the subjects' right to their seats. The subjects' right to their seats was affirmed in the request; you do not request things from people which they do not rightfully possess. The procedure does *not* involve some momentous or unreasonable request. Nothing of any great or lasting value was requested from the subjects. It is, in fact, the observation that this request is so reasonable and yet so rare that suggests the operation of some strong inhibitory social force.

Procedure

The experimenters were six male and four female graduate students. One woman was black; the other experimenters were white. Experimenters worked in pairs; as one performed the manipulation, the other recorded the data and observations.

The passengers on several mid-town routes of the New York City subway system formed the subject pool for the experiment. Experimenters were free to select their own subjects under the following constraints: Each experimenter asked one passenger from each of the following categories: man under 40 (by experimenter's approximation), woman under 40, man over 40, woman over 40. One member of each category was approached by each experimenter in each of the three conditions described in the following. Experimenters approached members of their own race only.

1. In the first condition (no justification), the experimenter approached a seated subject and said, "Excuse me. May I have your seat?" The observer recorded the age and sex of the subject, whether or not the subject gave up the seat, and other reactions of the subjects and

Methodological Concerns in the Social Sciences

An Interview with Stanley Milgram

The following interview with Stanley Milgram, conducted by Carol Tavris for *Psychology Today*, touches on a broad range of substantive and methodological concerns pertaining to the social sciences.

CAROL TAVRIS: Much of your work is directed toward the experience of living in cities, isolating the intangibles that make Oslo different from Paris, Topeka different from Denver, and New York different from anything. How do you go about defining those intangibles?

STANLEY MILGRAM: First, you keep your eyes open; you generalize on the basis of numerous specific incidents; you try to determine whether particular incidents lead up to a definable pattern; you attempt to find an underlying coherence beneath the myriad surface phenomena in a particular city. You generalize from your own experience and formulate a hypothesis.

Then you become systematic about it. You ask people what specific incidents seem to them to characterize a particular urban setting, and you see whether any patterns or dimensions emerge. When you ask Americans to cite specific incidents they think typical of London, for example, they often center on the civility of the Londoner. Typical comments about New York focus on its pace of activity, and diversity. The psychologist differs from the

novelist or travel writer in that he tries to measure whether these features—pace, friendliness, diversity—actually correspond to what is out there, and differ from one urban setting to the next....

TAVRIS: What features of urban life have interested you most recently?

MILGRAM: For years I've taken a commuter train to work. I noticed that there were people at my station whom I had seen for many years but never spoken to, people I came to think of as *familiar strangers....*

TAVRIS: How do our dealings with familiar strangers differ from with total those strangers?

MILGRAM: The familiar-stranger phenomenon is not the absence of a relationship but a special kind of frozen relationship. For example, if you wanted to make a trivial request or get the time of day, you are more likely to ask a total stranger, rather than a person you had seen for many years but had never spoken to. Each of you is aware that a history of noncommunication exists between you, and you both have accepted this as the normal state.

But the relationship between familiar strangers has a latent quality to it that becomes overt on specific occasions. I heard of a case in which a woman fainted in front of her apartment building. Her neighbor, who had seen her for 17 years and never spoken to her, immediately went into action. She felt a special responsibility; she called the ambulance, even went to the hospital with her. The likelihood of speaking to a familiar stranger also increases as you are removed from the scene of routine meeting. If I were out strolling in Paris and ran into one of my commuter strangers from Riverdale, we would undoubtedly greet each other for the first time.

And the fact that familiar strangers often talk to each other in times of crisis or emergency raises an interesting question: is there any way to promote solidarity without having to rely on emergencies and crises?

TAVRIS: To study the familiar stranger, your students directly confronted commuters for information. Is this typical of your experimental style?

MILGRAM: Methods of inquiry must always be adapted to the problem at hand, and not all of life's phenomena can be assembled in a laboratory. You must often go out to meet the problem, and it doesn't require a license to ask someone a question. My experimental style aims to make visible the social pressures that operate on us unnoticed.

And an experiment has a tangible quality to it; you see people really behaving in front of you, which stimulates insight. It is a matter of bringing issues down to a level where you can see them clearly, rendering processes visible. Social life is highly complex. We are all fragile creatures entwined in a cobweb of social constraints. Experiments often serve as a beam that helps clarify the murky aspects of experience. And I do believe that a Pandora's box lies just beneath the surface of everyday life, so it is often worthwhile to challenge what you most take for granted. You are often surprised at what you find.

TAVRIS: For example?

MILGRAM: We've recently looked at the subway experience which is so characteristic of New York life. If you consider that at rush hour total strangers are pressed against each other in a noisy hot car, surrounded by poking elbows, it is astonishing how little aggression this produces. It is a remarkably regulated situation, and we tried to probe the norms that keep it manageable. The best way to start was to be simple-minded and not too sophisticated, since sophistication assumes too much about the structure you wish to illuminate.

TAVRIS: What did you do?

MILGRAM: I suggested to the class that we each go up to someone on the subway and simply ask for his seat. The immediate reaction of the class was exactly the same as yours—laughter. But anxious laughter is often a sign that you are on to something important. Many members of the class felt that no one in New York would give up his seat simply because a stranger asked him to. My students did a second thing that uncovered their prejudices. They said that the person would have to justify his request by asserting illness, nausea, dizziness; they assumed that the request itself would not gain the seat. A third clue: I asked for volunteers from a class of graduate students, but they recoiled *en masse.* That's very revealing. After all, they merely had to make a trivial request. Why was it so frightening a project? In other words, the very formulation of the research question began to generate emotional clues to its answer. Finally, one brave soul, Ira Goodman, took on the heroic assignment, accompanied by a student observer. Goodman was asked to make the request courteously, and without initial justification, to 20 passengers.

TAVRIS: What happened?

MILGRAM: Within a week, rumors started to circulate at the Graduate Center. "They're getting up! They're getting up!" The news provoked astonishment, delight, wonder. Students made pilgrimages to Goodman as if he had uncovered a profound secret of survival in the New York subway, and at the next session of the seminar, he announced that about half of those he had asked had gotten up. He didn't even have to give a reason.

But one discrepancy struck me in Goodman's report. He had only approached 14 people instead of the hoped-for 20. Since he was normally quite conscientious, I asked why. He said: "I just couldn't go on. It was one of the most difficult things I ever did in my life." Was there something idiosyncratic about Goodman, or was he telling us something profoundly revealing about social behaviour generally? There was only one way to find out. Each of us would repeat the experiment, and neither I nor my colleague, Professor Irwin Katz, would be exempted.

Frankly, despite Goodman's initial experience, I assumed it would be easy. I approached a seated passenger and was about to utter the magical phrase. But the words seemed lodged in my trachea and would simply not emerge. I stood there frozen, then retreated, the mission unfulfilled. My student observer urged me to try again, but I was overwhelmed by paralyzing inhibition. I argued to myself: "What kind of craven coward are you? You told your class to do it. How can you go back to them without carrying out your own assignment?" Finally, after several unsuccessful tries, I went up to a passenger and choked out the request, "Excuse me, sir, may I have your seat?" A moment of stark anomic panic overcame me. But the man got right up and gave me the seat. A second blow was yet to come. Taking the man's seat, I was overwhelmed by the need to behave in a way that would justify my request. My head sank between my knees, and I could feel my face blanching. I was not role-playing. I actually felt as if I were going to perish. Then the third discovery: as soon as I got off the train, at the next station, all of the tension disappeared.

TAVRIS: What underlying social principles does such an experiment reveal?

MILGRAM: First, it points up the enormous inhibitory anxiety that ordinarily prevents us from breaching social norms. Asking a person for his seat is a trivial matter, yet it was extremely difficult to make the request. Second, it highlights the powerful need to justify one's request by appearing sick or exhausted. I must stress that this is not acting, but a compelled playing out of the logic of social relations. Finally, the fact that all of these intense feelings were synthesized in, and were limited to the particular situation, shows the power of immediate circumstances on feelings and behaviour. I was relieved and back to normal the instant I was off the train.

TAVRIS: Your reaction sounds typical of the subjects in the obedience experiment. Many of them felt obliged to follow the experimenter's orders to shock an innocent victim, even though they felt great anxiety.

MILGRAM: Yes. The subway experience gave me a better understanding of why some subjects obeyed. I experienced the anxiety they felt as they considered repudiating the experimenter. That anxiety forms a powerful barrier that must be surmounted, whether one's action is consequential—disobeying an authority—or trivial—asking for a seat on the subway.

Do you know there are people who choose to die in a burning building rather than run outside with their pants off? Embarrassment and the fear of violating apparently trivial norms often lock us into intolerable predicaments. And these are not minor regulatory forces in social life, but basic ones.

TAVRIS: Can you recommend a similar experiment for those of us in cities without subways?

MILGRAM: If you think it is easy to violate social constraints, get onto a bus and sing out loud. Full-throated song now, no humming. Many people will say it is easy to carry out this act, but not one in a hundred will be able to do it.

The point is not to *think* about singing, but to try to *do* it. Only in action can you fully realize the forces operative in social behaviour. That is why I am an experimentalist....

TAVRIS: Your obedience work and city work both consider the network of social rules that constrain us. In the galaxy of factors that make up a city's atmosphere, for example, which do you think are the most important?

MILGRAM: Clearly I the degree of moral and social involvement people have with each other, and the way this is limited by the objective circumstances of city life. There are so many people and events to cope with that you must simply disregard many possible inputs, just to get on. If you live on a country road you can say hello to each of the occasional persons who passes by; but obviously you can't do this on Fifth Avenue.

As a measure of social involvement for instance, we are now studying the response to a lost child in big city and small town. A child of nine asks people to help him call his home. The graduate students report a strong difference between city and town dwellers; in the city, more people refused to extend help to the nine-year-old. I like the problem because there is no more meaningful measure of the quality of a culture than the manner in which it treats its children.

TAVRIS: But is it inevitable that big cities breed impersonal treatment of others? You don't find drunks or beggars on the streets in Chinese cities, but if you did it would be everyone's responsibility to help. The moral norms are to aid the other guy, so no one person must play lone Samaritan.

MILGRAM: I would be reluctant to compare a city such as Peking, in which the atmosphere is permeated with political doctrines and imperatives, to Western cities. Beyond that, it is true that not all large cities are alike. But the most general movement is toward an adaptation common to all cities. Paris today seems more like New York than it did 20 years ago, and 50 years from now they will be even more alike, as adaptive needs come to dominate local color. There will be some cultural differences, but these ill fade, and I regard this as most unfortunate....

TAVRIS: Let's back up a moment if we may. How did you get into the field of psychology?

MILGRAM: My boyhood interests were scientific. I edited the high-school science magazine, and my first article in 1949 was on the effects of radiation on the incidence of leukemia in the Hiroshima and Nagasaki survivors. I was always doing experiments; it was as natural as breathing, and I tried to understand how everything worked.

I fell away from science in college to pursue courses in political philosophy, music and art. But I finally came to the realization that although I was interested in the questions raised by Plato, Thomas Hobbes and John Locke, I was unwilling to accept their mode of arriving at answers. I was interested in human questions that could be answered by objective methods. In the '50s the Ford Foundation had a program to move people into the behavioural sciences. It seemed like a perfect opportunity, and I shifted into social psychology at the Department of Social Relations at Harvard. Men of uncommon wisdom ran things at the time, and created a climate in which ideas and excellence found ready support and encouragement....

Harvard was full of lively souls like Henry Murray; some are still there. Roger Brown was a brilliant assistant professor 20 years ago and remains an inspiring scholar; Jerome Bruner was a vital and dynamic force, though he's now settled at Oxford.

TAVRIS: What would you say are the ingredients that make for a creative social psychologist?

MILGRAM: It is complicated. On the one hand, he needs to be detached and objective. On the other hand, he will never discover anything if he lacks feeling for the pulse and emotionality of social life. You know, social life is a nexus of emotional attachments that constrain, guide and support the individual. To understand why people behave as they do you have to be aware of the feelings aroused in everyday social situations.

TAVRIS: And beyond that?

MILGRAM: Out of your perception of such feelings, insights may arise. They may take the form of explicit principles of social behaviour. But, more often, they express themselves in symbolic form, and the experiment is the symbol. I mean, just as a playwright's understanding of the human situation reveals itself in his own mind in dramaturgical form, so for the creative investigator, intuition translates directly into an experimental format that permits him both to express his intuition and critically examine it....

SOURCE: Tavris, Carol. "The Frozen World of the Familiar Stranger" in *Psychology Today* magazine, vol 8 (June 1974). Reprinted with permission from *Psychology Today Magazine*, other passengers. Information about the time of day, subway line, and nearest station was also recorded.

As Table 1 shows, 56% of the subjects got up and offered their seats to the experimenters. An additional 12.3% of the subjects slid over to make room for the experimenter. (Experimenters had been instructed to ask for seats only if all of the seats in a car were taken, but it sometimes occurred that, although there did not appear to be any seats, room could be generated if the passengers squeezed together.) If these two responses are combined, we see that 68.3% of the subjects obtained seats by asking for them.

2. A second condition tested the hypothesis that subjects gave up their seats because they assumed the experimenters had some important reason for requesting it. In order to rule out this assumption, experimenters were instructed to say "Excuse me. May I have your seat? I can't read my book standing up." The experimenter stood holding a paperback mystery. It was expected that by supplying this trivial reason, experimenters would receive fewer seats. The expectation was confirmed; experimenters received significantly fewer seats (41.9% of the requests, $z = 2.3$, $p < .05$) ....

3. A third condition was included because we believed that subjects might have been so startled by the request that they didn't have time to formulate an adequate reply. It seemed that they might have surrendered their seats because it was easier to do so than to figure out how to refuse in the brief time allowed. This condition was, therefore, designed to allow more time to formulate a reply.

   To do this, it was necessary to alert the passenger that a seat might be requested. An experimenter and confederate entered the subway car from different doors and converged in front of the subject. They then engaged in the following conversation, while giving the impression that they were strangers:

TABLE 1: SUBWAY EXPERIMENTS: RESPONSES IN EACH EXPERIMENTAL CONDITION[a]

No Justification Condition n = 41	
Subjects who gave up their seats	56.0%
Subjects who slid over to make room for E	12.3%
Subjects who did not give up their seats	31.7%
Trivial Justification Condition n = 43	
Subjects who gave up their seats	37.2%
Subjects who slid over to make room for E	4.7%[b]
Subjects who did not give up their seats	58.1%
Overheard Condition n = 41	
Subjects who gave up their seats	26.8%
Subjects who slid over to make room for E	9.8%[c]
Subjects who did not give up their seats	63.4%
Written Condition n = 20	
Subjects who gave up their seats	50.0%
Subjects who slid over to make room for E	0.0%[d]
Subjects who did not give up their seats	50.0%

[a]Overall Chi square for four conditions collapsing subjects who gave up their seats with those who slid over = 9.44, $df = 3$, $p < .05$.

[b]Z test between No Justification and Trivial Justification conditions (collapsing as above): Z = 2.3, $p < .05$.

[c]Z test between No Justification and Overheard conditions (collapsing as above): Z = 2.7, $p < .05$.

[d]Z test between No Justification condition and Written condition (collapsing as above): not significant.

E to confederate, "Excuse me. Do you think it would be alright if I asked someone for a seat?" The confederate replied "What?" *E* repeated, "Do you think it would be alright if I asked someone for a seat?" The confederate replied, noncommittally, "I don't know."

This conversation was enacted in a sufficiently loud voice so that the passengers seated in front of the pair would definitely overhear it. The seated passengers would be alerted to the possibility that one of them might be approached with a request to surrender his or her seat. It gave the seated passengers time to formulate a response to the request, eliminating the startle component of the earlier conditions.

Thus, after acting out the foregoing exchange, the experimenter paused for approximately 10 seconds, then turned to the nearest seated passenger, and requested his or her seat. In this condition, experimenters received seats only 36.5% of the time, compared to 68.3% in Condition 1. The additional time between the overhearing of the conversation and the direct request was used to advantage. Subjects were better prepared to turn down the request.

4. Finally, we wished to separate the content of the request from the oral manner in which it was delivered. An orally delivered question directed to a person seems to demand an immediate oral response. We wondered whether a written message would reduce the demand for an immediate and obliging response. Accordingly, in this condition, the experimenter stood in front of the subject and wrote the following message on a sheet of notebook paper: "Excuse me. May I have your seat? I'd like very much to sit down. Thank you." The experimenter then passed the message to the subject, saying, "Excuse me." We expected fewer seats than in the basic variant, as the request on paper seemed less direct and somewhat more distant, especially since the subject was not forced to engage the experimenter in eye contact as he formulated a reply. Our expectation was wrong. Experimenters received seats 50.0% of the time, a nonsignificant decrease from the initial condition. (Each experimenter carried out this procedure twice rather than four times; the overall n equalled 20.) The reason for this result is not clear. This method seemed to add a touch of the bizarre to the procedure, perhaps adding to the subject's eagerness to end the whole interaction by simply giving up his seat.

Observers also recorded other aspects of the subjects' reactions. Subjects often had a vacant and bewildered facial expression. Of the subjects who gave up their seats in the initial condition, 70% did so without asking, "Why?" Other subjects responded by simply saying, "No." Some subjects didn't seem to be distressed at all. Subjects who attributed sickness to the experimenter were often very concerned and comforting.

Information was also gathered about the reactions of other passengers who witnessed the incident. On a few occasions, other passengers openly chided a subject who had given up a seat. A more common reaction was for one rider to turn to another and say something such as, "Did you see that? He asked for a seat!" Such a comment points to the abnormal nature of the event and invites criticism of it. Witnesses to the exchange often turned and stared at the experimenter as he or she left the car...

An important aspect of the maintenance of social norms is revealed in the emotional reaction of the experimenters. Most students reported extreme difficulty in carrying out the assignment. Students reported that when standing in front of a subject, they felt anxious, tense, and embarrassed. Frequently, they were unable to vocalize the request for a seat and had to withdraw. They sometimes feared that they were the center of attention of the car and were often unable to look directly at the subject. Once having made the request and received a seat, they sometimes felt a need to enact behaviour that would make the request appear justified (e.g. mimicking illness; some even felt faint)...

Why does the act of making this simple request cause such an acute emotional response?

One might approach this question by focusing on the content of the request; after all, the experimenters did ask for a seat from someone when they had no clear right to do so. But this focus on the seat seems misguided. The intensity of the emotion the experimenters experienced is incommensurate with the small cost involved in the subjects' giving up their seats. The significance of the request lies not in the seat (that is not the heart of the matter), but in the redefinition of the immediate relationship between experimenters and subjects that the request involves. Since it is this disruption of relationships that constitutes the essence of the violation, it can better be understood as a breach of a structure of social interaction than as merely a violation of rules of equity in interaction.

One analysis of the structure of social interaction that may help us to understand the sources of this effect has been provided by Goffman (1959). His description of the breakdown of interaction that results when an actor discredits his role fits well the description our experimenters gave of their experiences:

> At such moments the individual whose presentation has been discredited may feel ashamed while the others present may feel hostile, and all the participants may come to feel ill at ease, nonplussed, out of countenance, embarrassed, experiencing the kind of anomy that is generated when the minute social system of face-to-face interaction breaks down (p.12).

One might argue with some cogency that the experimenters were playing a social role, that of a subway rider, and that they discredited it by asking for the seat. But this use of "role" and "discrediting" seems strained and forced. Our results indicate, rather, that this "anomy" is a more general phenomenon resulting directly from doing something that "just isn't done" in a particular setting, whether it is related to the performance of any important social role or not....

To be sure the concept of "those things that just aren't done" is itself a complex one, containing both a statistical proposition (such actions *do not* occur) and a normative proposition (such actions *ought not* to occur). Moreover, there remains the problem of specifying the precise content of those things that "just aren't done," a discussion we shall not develop here.

The results of our experience in doing something that "just isn't done" suggest that knowledge of the objective social order controls behaviour not only cognitively (people may simply never have thought of asking for a seat), but emotionally: actions outside of understood routine paths appropriate to the social setting, at least in this case, give rise to an intense, immediate, inhibitory emotion. This emotion restricts individual action to the routine patterns that constitute the stable background of everyday life.

References

Chomsky, N. (1959). Review of *Verbal Behavior, Language,* Jan.-Mar., 35, 26–58.

Goffman, E. (1959). *The Presentation of Self in Everyday Life,* Anchor Doubleday, New York.

Goffman, E. (1971). *Relations in Public,* Harper, New York.

Scheff, T. (1960). *Being Mentally Ill: A Sociological Theory,* Aldine, Chicago.

Takooshian, H. (1972). Report on a Class Field Experiment, Unpublished manuscript.

SOURCE: Baum, A., J.E. Singer, and S. Valins (eds). *Advances in Environmental Psychology* 1, *The Urban Environment.* Hillsdale, New Jersey: Lawrence Erlbaum Associates. 1978. Reprinted by permission of Lawrence Erlbaum Associates, Inc.

Questions and Topics for Discussion and Writing

1. Why did Stanley Milgram pick the New York City subway system as the testing-ground for his theories about social behaviour? What is unique about this "laboratory"?
2. What was Milgram able to observe in his experiments that was more revealing than the observations he made on his subjects. Did these observations prove or disprove his expectations about the "rules of social behaviour"?
3. Milgram claims that he became a social scientist in order to "understand" the social world. How does an experiment like this one help the social psychologist understand the larger world around us?

From The New York Times Magazine

Just a Damn Minute

James Gleick

Writer James Gleick argues in this article that life is simply becoming too fast-paced. He maintains that time-saving advance in technology have other, more serious side effects that should be considered seriously before the new technology is embraced.

You are short of time. Technologists know this and are trying to help—in their fashion.

First, your symptoms:

- A 60-second television commercial (these dinosaurs do turn up on some obscure cable channels) feels like a full-length feature film. You can't believe how it goes on and on.
- Before you reheat leftovers in the microwave, you plan an activity to fill the 90 seconds that might otherwise be spent watching your food through the little window.
- You keep your wristwatch within a minute of the correct time. Dialling 976-TIME (big business since the telephone companies spun it off) is not good enough any more. Now you have software that connects with the United States Naval Observatory to recalibrate your computer's clock.
- You've started to notice that some recorded music has longer intervals between tracks than others. (Even if you haven't noticed, someone must have—my new Sony Discman lets you do something about it. The instructions crow: "You can enjoy playing with less blank space between the tracks.")

Everyone knows that in the era of channel flipping and fast food, a minute is an eternity. But those gaps between songs are no more than a second or two. The problem is, even a second is long—not an instant anymore. It stretches out before us as a container, with events and voids to be filled with millinano or picothings. A second is long enough for impatience to begin welling up.

The evolution of technology has long been about saving time, but on grosser scales than now. The cotton gin, the automobile and the vacuum cleaner let people work, move and clean faster—savings to be measured in hours and minutes. But now we're thinking in fractional seconds. A millisecond here, a millisecond there—does it really add up?

The consumer-product laboratories think so. They are slicing time ever more finely for us, catering to our sense of urgency, hurrying us along. Toasters are toasting faster. It might take two or three minutes for a liquid based under-the-tongue thermometer to rise to your temperature; new thermometers are electronic and, naturally, faster.

The household-products groups at companies like Black & Decker, developers of the Dustbuster (don't have to spend time walking to the closet; don't have spend time plugging it in), find time-saving opportunities all through the standard household day. There are still seconds wasted in ironing (heat-up time) and coffee making (brewing, steeping), which the Black & Decker people have plucked with their new Handy Xpress iron and Brew'n Go Coffeemaker (for the "hurry-up market"). They cite a Gallup survey showing that a majority of Americans, and especially baby boomers, says they "do not have time to do everything that needs to be done." The answer may be self-evident; the question, surely, is revealing.

The technologies can be simple (quicker-heating coils in toasters and irons) or clever. Portable CD players use memory chips to store a few seconds of music and process it before feeding it back—recovering from skips and, as a side benefit, squeezing the blank intervals between programmed songs. Some new telephone-answering machines have quick-playback buttons, for when your callers drone on and on with their shaggy-dog messages. Because the technology is digital, the pitch doesn't rise a la the Chipmunks; the sound just goes...faster. How did they know I was so busy I couldn't stand to listen to my friends speak with normal languor? The current generation of answering machines seems to favor a 25 percent speedup. No doubt we'll soon learn to expect—and understand—even more rapid-fire speech.

Who can say just where we began the slide down this long, strange slope? One place may have been the New York World's Fair in 1964 and 1965. Many thousands of people waited in line at the AT&T pavilion to try out Touch Tone dialling. They got to dial numbers the old, rotary way and then the new, push-button way, for purposes of comparison. An electric readout showed just how many tenths of a second they could bank. However much it was, we now know it wasn't enough. In the post Touch-Tone generation, you probably have speed-dial buttons on your telephone; if you're willing to invest a half hour in learning to program them, you can earn that investment back four seconds at a time. And in some places—especially in restless cities like New York, where the car behind you commences honking just milliseconds after the light turns green—telephone directory assistance now offers callers the option of automatically dialling the number they just retrieved, for a price. A case study in what time is worth: in the New York metropolitan area, it appears that 21 percent of us are willing to pay 35 cents to save about four seconds.

So, what are we doing with all these seconds?

Money can be acquired, saved and spent on demand. We sometimes act as though we could treat time the same way. "But we only seem to shift time from one activity to another of equal distraction," says Greg Blonder, director of human-centered engineering research at AT&T. If a time-optimized device enables you to do more work faster, that may be a boon. Then again, if you happen to be a telemarketer, the benefit may not reach those of us on the receiving end of the extra calls you squeeze in.

By tradition, impatience is a vice. Haste makes waste. Even if our technological world seems inspired by the modernist Benjamin (Time Is Money) Franklin, we can all think of a few remaining human activities that cannot profitably be rushed.

"There are two cardinal sins," Kafka said, "from which all the others spring: impatience and laziness." There's the paradox—maybe it's laziness, not industriousness, when we succumb to our time-saving machines. Just how much time do we save—net—when we dash to the gym so that we can spend 30 minutes on the Stairmaster increasing our heart rate and listening to our digitally optimized Discman? Technology can't help us walk the fine line between time wasted and time spent ruminating or daydreaming—not acting, not doing. For most of us, coffee breaks have gone the way of enforced Sabbaths, and neither transcendental meditation nor the sensory-deprivation tank seems likely to replace them.

It may help to think of time as a continuous flow, rather than a series of segmented packages. Or to find aggressive ways of squandering the time we save. Or at least to recognize that devices can't really acquire more time for us, because time is not a thing we have; it is a thing we are in. We can drift or we can swim, but it will carry us along either way.

SOURCE: *The New York Times Magazine*, May 14, 1995.

Questions and Topics for Discussion and Writing

1. Since author James Gleick admits that the progress of time-saving technology has not been harmful to society, what is his major objection to the new ways of saving time he ridicules?
2. What does Gleick mean when he talks about a "long, strange slope?" Why does he say that finding "aggressive ways of squandering the time we save" might be a good way of halting our slide down this slope?

Canadian Charter of Rights and Freedoms

With the proclamation of the Canadian Charter of Rights and Freedoms in 1982, a great many legal disputes have focused on the interpretations of the rights and freedoms defined under the Charter. Below is the full text of the Canadian Charter of Rights and Freedoms, which comprises Part I of the *Constitution Act, 1982.*

Whereas Canada is founded upon principles that recognize the supremacy of God and the rule of law:

Guarantee of Rights and Freedoms

Rights and freedoms in Canada

1. *The Canadian Charter of Rights and Freedoms* guarantees the rights and freedoms set out in it subject only to such reasonable limits prescribed by law as can be demonstrably justified in a free and democratic society.

Fundamental Freedoms

Fundamental freedoms

2. Everyone has the following fundamental freedoms:

(a) freedom of conscience and religion;

(b) freedom of thought, belief, opinion and expression, including freedom of the press and other media of communication;

(c) freedom of peaceful assembly; and

(d) freedom of association.

Democratic Rights

Democratic rights of citizens

3. Every citizen of Canada has the right to vote in an election of members of the House of Commons or of a legislative assembly and to be qualified for membership therein.

Maximum duration of legislative bodies

4. (1) No House of Commons and no legislative assembly shall continue for longer than five years from the date fixed for the return of the writs at a general election of its members.

Continuation in special circumstances

(2) In time of real or apprehended war, invasion or insurrection, a House of Commons may be continued by Parliament and a legislative assembly may be continued by the legislature beyond five years if such continuation is not opposed by the votes of more than one-third of the members of the House of Commons or the legislative assembly, as the case may be.

Annual sitting of legislative bodies

5. There shall be a sitting of Parliament and of each legislature at least once every twelve months.

Mobility Rights

Mobility of citizens

6. (1) Every citizen of Canada has the right to enter, remain in and leave Canada.

Rights to move and gain livelihood

(2) Every citizen of Canada and every person who has the status of a permanent resident of Canada has the right

(a) to move and to take up residence in any province; and

(b) to pursue the gaining of a livelihood in any province.

Limitation

(3) The rights specified in subsection (2) are subject to

(a) any laws or practices of general application in force in a province other than those that discriminate among persons primarily on the basis of province of present or previous residence; and

(b) any laws providing for reasonable residency requirements as a qualification for the receipt of publicly provided social services.

Affirmative action programs

(4) Subsections (2) and (3) do not preclude any law, program or activity that has as its object the amelioration in a province of conditions of individuals in that province who are socially or economically disadvantaged if the rate of employment in that province is below the rate of employment in Canada.

Legal Rights

Life, liberty and security of person

7. Everyone has the right to life, liberty and security of the person and the right not to be deprived thereof except in accordance with the principles of fundamental justice.

Search or seizure

8. Everyone has the right to be secure against unreasonable search or seizure.

Detention or imprisonment

9. Everyone has the right not to be arbitrarily detained or imprisoned.

10. Everyone has the right on arrest or detention

(a) to be informed promptly of the reasons therefor;

(b) to retain and instruct counsel without delay and to be informed of that right; and

(c) to have the validity of the detention determined by way of *habeas corpus* and to be released if the detention is not lawful.

11. Any person charged with an offence has the right

(a) to be informed without unreasonable delay of the specific offence;

(b) to be tried within a reasonable time;

(c) not to be compelled to be a witness in proceedings against that person in respect of the offence;

(d) to be presumed innocent until proven guilty

The Constitution Act, 1982

The Charter of Rights and Freedoms

The Canadian Charter of Rights and Freedoms is actually Part I, Sections 1–34 of the Constitution Act of 1982.

Historically, most Canadians had been content to have their personal rights and freedoms ensured by the British legal tradition. Even after Confederation in 1867, little concern was expressed that Canadians' individual rights were not being adequately protected.

In 1960, however, the government of John Diefenbaker passed the Canadian Bill of Rights. With the proclamation of Constitution Act in 1982, the Charter of Rights and Freedoms combined with the 1960 Bill to strengthen the legal protection of the rights of all Canadians.

The Charter of Rights and Freedoms has met with both praise and criticism since its adoption in 1982. On the positive side, observers note that it contains two key statements that seem particularly relevant to the times.

The first provides for the equality of men and women (Clause 15[1]). The second (Clause 15[2]) is an affirmative action provision, which allows for the advancement of groups that have traditionally been placed at a disadvantage because of race, ethnic background, gender, sexual orientation or physical disability. Since its passage, a great many legal disputes have been focused around interpretations of the rights and freedoms defined under the Charter.

Critics of the Charter, known as "Charter Skeptics" argue that while it has advanced the cause of disadvantaged groups in Canadian society, it has not gone far enough. Furthermore, they contend that the Charter has placed too much important decision-making power in the hands of judges who often misuse it, causing the Charter to look good "on paper" while failing in reality.

ELIZABETH THE SECOND

By the Grace of God of the United Kingdom, Canada and Her other Realms and Territories Queen, Head of the Commonwealth, Defender of the Faith.

To all to whom these presents shall come or whom the same may in anyway concern,

GREETING:

A PROCLAMATION

Attorney General of Canada

WHEREAS in the past certain amendments to the Constitution of Canada have been made by the Parliament of the United Kingdom at the request and with the consent of Canada;

AND WHEREAS it is in accord with the status of Canada as an independent state that Canadians be able to amend their Constitution in Canada in all respects;

AND WHEREAS it is desirable to provide in the Constitution of Canada for the recognition of certain fundamental rights and freedoms and to make other amendments to the Constitution;

AND WHEREAS the Parliament of the United Kingdom has therefore, at the request and with the consent of Canada, enacted the Canada Act, which provides for the patriation and amendment of the Constitution of Canada;

AND WHEREAS section 58 of the Constitution Act, 1982, set out in Schedule B to the Canada Act, provides that the Constitution Act, 1982 shall, subject to section 59 thereof, come into force on a day to be fixed by proclamation issued under the Great Seal of Canada:

NOW KNOW You that We, by and with the advice of Our Privy Council for Canada, do by this Our Proclamation, declare that the Constitution Act, 1982 shall, subject to section 59 thereof, come into force on the Seventeenth day of April, in the Year of Our Lord One Thousand Nine Hundred and Eighty-two.

OF ALL WHICH Our Loving Subjects and all others whom these Presents may concern are hereby required to take notice and to govern themselves accordingly.

IN TESTIMONY WHEREOF We have caused these Our Letters to be made Patent and the Great Seal of Canada to be hereunto affixed.

At Our City of Ottawa, this Seventeenth day of April in the Year of Our Lord One Thousand Nine Hundred and Eighty-two and in the Thirty-first Year of Our Reign.

By Her Majesty's Command

Registrar General of Canada

Prime Minister of Canada

GOD SAVE THE QUEEN

ELIZABETH DEUX

PAR LA GRÂCE DE DIEU REINE DU ROYAUME-UNI, DU CANADA ET DE SES AUTRES ROYAUMES ET TERRITOIR CHEF DU COMMONWEALTH, DÉFENSEUR DE LA FOI,

À TOUS CEUX QUE LES PRÉSENTES PEUVENT DE QUEL MANIÈRE CONCERNER,

SALUT:

PROCLAMATION

Le procureur général du Canada

CONSIDÉRANT:

qu'à la demande et avec le consentement du Canada, le Parlement du Royaume-Uni a déjà modifié à plusieurs reprises la Constitution du Canada;

qu'en vertu de leur appartenance à un État souverain, les Canadiens se doivent de déte tout pouvoir de modifier leur Constitution au Canada;

qu'il est souhaitable d'inscrire dans la Constitution du Canada la reconnaissance d certain nombre de libertés et de droits fondamentaux et d'y apporter d'autres modific

que le Parlement du Royaume-Uni, à la demande et avec le consentement du Canad adopté en conséquence la Loi sur le Canada, qui prévoit le rapatriement de la Const canadienne et sa modification;

que l'article 58, figurant à l'annexe B de la Loi sur le Canada, stipule que, sous ré de l'article 59, la Loi constitutionnelle de 1982 entrera en vigueur à une date fixée p proclamation sous le grand sceau du Canada,

NOUS PROCLAMONS, sur l'avis de Notre Conseil privé pour le Canada, que la Loi constitutionnelle de 1982 entrera en vigueur, sous réserve de l'article 59, le dix-sep jour du mois d'avril en l'an de grâce mil neuf cent quatre-vingt-deux.

NOUS DEMANDONS À Nos loyaux sujets et à toute autre personne concernée de pr acte de la présente proclamation.

EN FOI DE QUOI, Nous avons rendu les présentes lettres patentes et y avons fait apposer l grand sceau du Canada.

Fait en Notre ville d'Ottawa, ce dix-septième jour du mois d'avril en l'an de grâce neuf cent quatre-vingt-deux, le trente et unième de Notre règne.

Par ordre de Sa Majesté

Le registraire général du Canada

Le premier ministre du Canada

DIEU PROTÈGE LA REINE

The Canadian Charter of Rights and Freedoms, 1982.

The Charter was signed by Queen Elizabeth II, Jean Chrétien (presently the Prime Minister of Canada who was Minister of Justice in 1982), André Quellet (then Registrar General) and Pierre Trudeau (then the Prime Minister).

according to law in a fair and public hearing by an independent and impartial tribunal;

(e) not to be denied reasonable bail without just cause;

(f) except in the case of an offence under military law tried before a military tribunal, to the benefit of trial by jury where the maximum punishment for the offence is imprisonment for five years or a more severe punishment;

(g) not to be found guilty on account of any act or omission unless, at the time of the act or omission, it constituted an offence under Canadian or international law or was criminal according to the general principles of law recognized by the community of nations;

(h) if finally acquitted of the offence, not to be tried for it again and, if finally found guilty and punished for the offence, not to be tried or punished for it again; and

(i) if found guilty of the offence and if the punishment for the offence has been varied between the time of commission and the time of sentencing, to the benefit of the lesser punishment.

Treatment or punishment

12. Everyone has the right not to be subjected to any cruel and unusual treatment or punishment.

Self-crimination

13. A witness who testifies in any proceedings has the right not to have any incriminating evidence so given used to incriminate that witness in any other proceedings, except in a prosecution for perjury or for the giving of contradictory evidence.

Interpreter

14. A party or witness in any proceedings who does not understand or speak the language in which the proceedings are conducted or who is deaf has the right to the assistance of an interpreter.

Equality Rights

Equality before and under law and equal protection and benefit of law

15. (1) Every individual is equal before and under the law and has the right to the equal protection and equal benefit of the law without discrimination and, in particular, without discrimination based on race, national or ethnic origin, colour, religion, sex, age or mental or physical disability.

Affirmative action programs

(2) Subsection (1) does not preclude any law, program or activity that has as its object the amelioration of conditions of disadvantaged individuals or groups including those that are disadvantaged because of race, national or ethnic origin, colour, religion, sex, age or mental or physical disability.

Official Languages of Canada

Official languages of Canada

16. (1) English and French are the official languages of Canada and have equality of status and equal rights and privileges as to their use in all institutions of the Parliament and government of Canada.

Official Languages of New Brunswick

(2) English and French are the official languages of New Brunswick and have equality of status and equal rights and privileges as to their use in all institutions of the legislature and government of New Brunswick.

Advancement of status and use

(3) Nothing in this Charter limits the authority of Parliament or a legislature to advance the equality of status or use of English and French.

Proceedings of Parliament

17. (1) Everyone has the right to use English or French in any debates and other proceedings of Parliament.

Proceedings of New Brunswick legislature

(2) Everyone has the right to use English or French in any debates and other proceedings of the legislature of New Brunswick.

Parliamentary statutes and records

18. (1) The statutes, records and journals of Parliament shall be printed and published in English and French and both language versions are equally authoritative.

New Brunswick statutes and records

(2) The statutes, records and journals of the legislature of New Brunswick shall be printed and published in English and French and both language versions are equally authoritative.

Proceedings in courts established by Parliament

19. (1) Either English or French may be used by any person in, or in any pleading in or process issuing from, any court established by Parliament.

Proceedings in New Brunswick courts

(2) Either English or French may be used by any person in, or in any pleading in or process issuing from, any court of New Brunswick.

Communications by public with federal institutions

20. (1) Any member of the public in Canada has the right to communicate with, and to receive available services from, any head or central office of an institution of the Parliament or government of Canada in English or French, and has the same right with respect to any other office of any such institution where

(a) there is a significant demand for communications with and services from that office in such language; or

(b) due to the nature of the office, it is reasonable that communications with and services from that office be available in both English and French.

Communications by public with New Brunswick institutions

(2) Any member of the public in New Brunswick has the right to communicate with, and to receive available services from, any office of an institution of the legislature or government of New Brunswick in English or French.

Continuation of existing constitutional provisions

21. Nothing in sections 16 to 20 abrogates or derogates from any right, privilege or obligation with respect to the English and French languages, or either of them, that exists or is continued by virtue of any other provision of the Constitution of Canada.

Rights and privileges preserved

22. Nothing in sections 16 to 20 abrogates or derogates from any legal or customary right or privilege

The Supreme Court of Canada, Ottawa.

The most important legal decisions under the Charter of Rights and Freedoms are made here by Supreme Court judges.

acquired or enjoyed either before or after the coming into force of this Charter with respect to any language that is not English or French.

Minority Language Educational Rights

Language of instruction

23. (1) Citizens of Canada

(a) whose first language learned and still understood is that of the English or French linguistic minority population of the province in which they reside, or

(b) who have received their primary school instruction in Canada in English or French and reside in a province where the language in which they received that instruction is the language of the English or French linguistic minority population of the province,

have the right to have their children receive primary and secondary school instruction in that language in that province.

Continuity of language instruction

(2) Citizens of Canada of whom any child has received or is receiving primary or secondary school instruction in English or French in Canada, have the right to have all their children receive primary and secondary school instruction in the same language.

Application where numbers warrant

(3) The right of citizens of Canada under subsections (1) and (2) to have their children receive primary and secondary school instruction in the language of the English or French linguistic minority population of a province

(a) applies wherever in the province the number of children of citizens who have such a right is sufficient to warrant the provision to them out of public funds of minority language instruction; and

(b) includes, where the number of those children so warrants, the right to have them receive that instruction in minority language educational facilities provided out of public funds.

Enforcement

Enforcement of guaranteed rights and freedoms

24. (1) Anyone whose rights or freedoms, as guaranteed by this Charter, have been infringed or denied may apply to a court of competent jurisdiction to obtain such remedy as the court considers appropriate and just in the circumstances.

Exclusion of evidence bringing administration of justice into disrepute

(2) Where, in proceedings under subsection (1), a court concludes that evidence was obtained in a manner that infringed or denied any rights or freedoms guaranteed by this Charter, the evidence shall be excluded if it is established that, having regard to all the circumstances, the admission of it in the proceedings would bring the administration of justice into disrepute.

General

Aboriginal rights and freedoms not affected by Charter

25. The guarantee in this Charter of certain rights and freedoms shall not be construed so as to abrogate or derogate from any aboriginal, treaty or other rights or freedoms that pertain to the aboriginal peoples of Canada including

(a) any rights or freedoms that have been recognized by the Royal Proclamation of October 7, 1763; and

(b) any rights or freedoms that now exist by way of land claims agreements or may be so acquired.

Other rights and freedoms not affected by Charter

26. The guarantee in this Charter of certain rights and freedoms shall not be construed as denying the existence of any other rights or freedoms that exist in Canada.

Multicultural heritage

27. This Charter shall be interpreted in a manner consistent with the preservation and enhancement of the multicultural heritage of Canadians.

Rights guaranteed equally to both sexes

28. Notwithstanding anything in this Charter, the rights and freedoms referred to in it are guaranteed equally to male and female persons.

Rights respecting certain schools preserved

29. Nothing in this Charter abrogates or derogates from any rights or privileges guaranteed by or under the Constitution of Canada in respect of denominational, separate or dissentient schools.

Application to territories and territorial authorities

30. A reference in this Charter to a province or to the legislative assembly or legislature of a province shall be deemed to include a reference to the Yukon Territory and the Northwest Territories, or to the appropriate legislative authority thereof, as the case may be.

Legislative powers not extended

31. Nothing in this Charter extends the legislative powers of any body or authority.

Application of Charter

Application of Charter

32. (1) This Charter applies

(a) to the Parliament and government of Canada in respect of all matters within the authority of Parliament including all matters relating to the Yukon Territory and Northwest Territories; and

(b) to the legislature and government of each province in respect of all matters within the authority of the legislature of each province.

Exception

(2) Notwithstanding subsection (1), section 15 shall not have effect until three years after this section comes into force.

Exception where express declaration

33. (1) Parliament or the legislature of a province may expressly declare in an Act of Parliament or of the legislature, as the case may be, that the Act or a provision thereof shall operate notwithstanding a provision included in section 2 or sections 7 to 15 of this Charter.

The House of Commons, Ottawa.

Operation of exception

(2) An Act or a provision of an Act in respect of which a declaration made under this section is in effect shall have such operation as it would have but for the provision of this Charter referred to in the declaration.

Five-year limitation

(3) A declaration made under subsection (1) shall cease to have effect five years after it comes into force or on such earlier date as may be specified in the declaration.

Re-enactment

(4) Parliament or the legislature of a province may re-enact a declaration made under subsection (1).

Five-year limitation

(5) Subsection (3) applies in respect of a re-enactment made under subsection (4).

Citation

Citation

34. This Part may be cited as the Canadian Charter of Rights and Freedoms.

On Immigration, Multiculturalism and Employment Equity

Carl James

In this excerpt from his 1995 book *Seeing Ourselves*, sociologist Carl James, with the help of a number of his students, examines the ways in which contemporary Canadian society is affected by immigration and multiculturalism. Notably, the young people he surveyed express a wide range of views, reflective of the society as a whole.

Three of the most significant issues that produced some of the most heated discussions and debates in classes were immigration, multiculturalism and employment equity. The significance of these issues to the participants at this particular stage of their lives not only had to do with their hopes of eventually realizing their career goals after graduation, but their understanding of how difficult the job market had become. For most of the students, particularly young white males, immigration, multiculturalism and employment equity were seen as impediments to their achievements. Immigrants were perceived as "a drain on our social services," who "were taking jobs away from Canadians," "causing an increase in crimes" (particularly Blacks and Asians), and were "coming into our country bringing their culture and changing our culture" (particularly Sikhs).

Connections were often made between the increase in immigration and "what is wrong with multiculturalism." The latter was seen as facilitating changes in the "Canadian way of life." Employment equity was also perceived, like multiculturalism as making it difficult for "Canadians" to eventually achieve the jobs to which they aspire. Participants spoke about these factors causing "unneeded tension and frustrations among 'Canadians' (read white and British), 'immigrants,' the target groups and the government."

The following essays illustrate how participants, particularly young, white males and females related these three issues. The discussion that follows attempts to put into context and clarify the ideas and some of the misinformation and myths that underlie several of the prevailing attitudes and positions that are so often displayed in the general society. It is worth repeating that the ideas that are written here do not only reflect those of these participants, but are also ideas which represent many of the perspectives which can be found in our society generally and in major socializing institutions such as the media, schools, governments and others.

Immigrants and Immigration

Todd: *"It is expected that many traditional habits and practices have to be simmered down..."*

People coming to Canada should be informed or enlightened as to what to expect when they arrive here. It is for this reason the transition period is so difficult for so many people. I respect peoples' culture, traditions and beliefs and I expect people to respect mine. In many Middle Eastern cultures, westerners are often subjected to harsh reprimands if they dress in what we call western clothing, especially women. Many westerners often complain of the treatment they are given if they dress "disrespectfully" i.e. in the western clothing, especially women. Many times they are not allowed to commute or live in certain areas of the society, because it is felt they would corrupt the natives with their culture. Yet these very people come here to Canada and expect us Canadians to accept them in their traditional garments, and to work side by side with them. That is not fair. Canada is a sovereign nation with an identity.

I wonder what a foreigner would say when they arrive in Canada to find people with various modes of dress, some with turbans as police officers, some with daggers attending schools, while others wear kimonos (Japanese dress), saris, and a wide variety of dress. They would obviously be confused. I don't believe that Canadians should wear a national uniform or dress, but I disagree with immigrants coming to Canada and insisting on being employed with their traditional dress. The world must be able to recognize Canadians for who they are; Canadians should have an identity. This I believe is one of the many reasons that white people are viewed as Canadians and most non-whites are seen as immigrants. I am not saying that we (non-whites) should try to conform to the ideals and mouldings of the white, but the integration process is a blending-in process, where it is expected that many traditional habits and practices have to be simmered down, because for the immigrant Canada is a new country, a different culture, and a new way of life.

Nancy: *"I think that heritage is something that should be shared with others and not kept to yourself..."*

The issue that I wish to discuss deals with the immigrants that come to Canada and settle with their own ethnic group. I realize that when someone comes to a new country they feel safe in a community that is similar to the one they left behind, but I feel that this only brings people of different cultures further apart rather than closer together. I am not saying that it is wrong for people to be actively involved in their cultural community, I feel that it is important to keep up with your heritage and pass it down to future generations, but I think that heritage is something that should be shared with others and not kept to yourself.

I am an active participant in a Ukrainian dance group and have been for eight years, within this time I have seen how these people interact with other non-Ukrainians. It seems as though they want nothing to do with people that are not of their ethnic background. They all belong to Ukrainian churches, schools, sports teams, camps, country clubs, they have relatives in Ukrainian rest homes and on their vacation they drive up to their Ukrainian community cottages.

When I first joined this group it seemed as though the co-ordinators wanted me to forget my Scottish and Irish background and to just concentrate on being a Ukrainian. There came a time when I was almost embarrassed to admit that I also had another heritage.

When people of the same ethnicity cling together they become so involved in their own culture that they are not willing to open their eyes and experience what other cultures have to offer. This becomes impossible for them to do when they have spent so much time in their own community that they cannot communicate with anyone outside of it. For example, I knew someone who had been in this country for sixty years and could hardly speak a word of English, therefore how was he suppose to communicate with anyone outside his ethnic community, he had trapped himself in it.

I don't feel that to be a Canadian you have to change your name or behaviour but I do feel that a true Canadian is one that can admit that they are. I myself almost found that I was considering myself to be Ukrainian and I hardly ever called myself Canadian which my family has been for three generations.

Bill: *"I resented that a Canadian didn't come first...."*

I used to resent immigrants and refugees. I always looked at them as taking away from the Canadian social service system that I thought was unfair. This negative attitude was formed when I was out of work and looked into upgrading my education through the unemployment office. The waiting list was so long, and what infuriated me was the list of names waiting to enrol were names that I couldn't pronounce. All these people were ahead of me and I resented that a Canadian didn't come first. It has taken a bit of attitude adjusting to come to terms that—this is what Canada is all about. These people belong to Canada, just as I do.

Dave: *"I would like to see these people protesting only Canadian issues..."*

I cannot understand why immigrants coming to Canada, making the choice to leave their place of birth and adopting Canada as their new home, would protest in the streets of Canada about issues back in their country. Canada is filled with problems and the country needs people who would come here to contribute to the welfare, progress and development of the country. I would like to see these people protesting about Canadian issues such as the lack of jobs, the GST, no more taxes and other social issues that affect them and relate to Canada because here is where they are living.

Jane: *"Should protection from abuse be grounds for immigration?..."*

On the issue of immigrants (women) being allowed to stay in Canada because of persecution and harassment in their home country, I believe most of them should be allowed to stay. I say most of them because Canada cannot be seen as a dumping ground or a place where people can concoct a story and easily get in. Also Canada must respect the culture of laws of another sovereign country and we cannot be viewed as a judgmental country that decides what is right or wrong for other peoples or how they should live their lives. But I do believe once someone has embraced our shores and expressed a desire to remain here in Canada because of justified fears and a dissatisfaction with the oppressive, sexist and discriminatory policies of their government, then I believe they should be allowed to stay.

One of the issues I find irritating is immigrants coming to Canada, an English/French speaking country, and apparently making little or no effort to speak English or even to get involved in E.S.L. classes (English as a second language) and continuing to wear traditional clothes, and also wanting to be employed wearing their traditional clothes.

Claire: *"From immigrant to Canadian: How easy is the transition?..."*

Race and ethnicity are terms one rarely uses or prefers as a topic of discussion among friends, acquaintances or fellow workers. They seem to be taboo in Canadian society. And yet when people see each other, their first thought is "this person is yellow or brown or mulatto or black or white." It is known that visual images have a far greater impact than those produced by any of the other senses and hence the impact of skin colour or general features cannot be underestimated. As an individual, and being a first generation immigrant, I have been rather fortunate in not having had the nasty experience of a "culture shock" after having moved to Canada. My knowledge of English and previous experiences in dealing with people from different countries around the world during work and travel made my adaptation and integration into Canadian society easier than it might have been otherwise. Besides, having grown up in a large cosmopolitan city, awash in western influence, was also a major contributing factor in my familiarity with western culture.

Before arriving in Toronto I had never really given much thought to the importance of race, ethnicity and culture. In fact, I rarely thought about my own culture, probably because I lived it daily. However, after being here for a few days I realized that knowing the language and wearing Canadian-style clothing was not enough to make the transition to being a Canadian. Also, initially I wasn't sure if I wanted to be one. When asked who I was, my immediate reply was "Indian." I began to wonder if I was the target of discrimination and was going to be judged on the basis of my skin colour. I did my best to acquire the "Canadian" accent so as not to sound like a foreigner and even became rather good at blowing my own trumpet during job interviews (which is very much against my nature) but I could do nothing to change the way I looked. It was also very frustrating to know that my long years of education in India meant almost nothing here. I began to perceive discrimination in every rejection. Yet, I did manage to get a job and thought I'd won a great victory. One hurdle had been overcome and I felt nothing could stop me from becoming a successful Canadian. And yet, when at work, white-Canadian fellow workers would ask me "How come you speak such good English?" I could not take it as a compliment. In fact, I always felt insulted and angered that they thought only whites could master the English language. Unfortunately, I felt I was in no position to counter their perceptions except by making an exception of myself.

After being in Toronto for three years, watching people on the transit system, in malls and other public places, experiencing first hand what it's like to be a first-generation immigrant and becoming partly "Canadianized" I ask myself: "Is Canada a racist country?" The answer, of course, is "Yes." Not only do I see and hear and read about racist and discriminatory acts being perpetuated in this country, but also experience it first-hand—among neighbours, fellow workers, in the malls, on the transit system, etc. However, this does not drive me away from the country because, in spite of this, I have been able to achieve a certain amount of success and I'm sure I'll do even better in the future.

Anthony: *"Growing up as a child of immigrants..."*

I was born here in Canada. I am white, and have no trace of any accent. The language that is spoken in my home is English, and my family does not practice any religious customs other than status quo Christianity. Yet I think I can still empathize with the way in which many new, non-Anglo Canadians must certainly feel during this latest craze of immigrant-bashing.

My Mother emigrated from Poland at a young age, my Father, while being born here, is Italian and was socialized in Toronto's large Italian community, thus preserving many cultural traits. My name is obviously Italian and my physical features make it seem quite easy for everyone I meet to assume that I am Italian, a fact that brought me much grief growing up.

I was very aware of the stigma that was carried with the word "immigrant" while growing up in Toronto. Although it simply means a person who was born beyond the borders of one country and moved to another one, it carried other connotations as well. I didn't want to be called an immigrant, I perceived it as an insult. Although I was somewhat aware that the stereotypes of immigrants who were racial minorities were much more harmful and negative, the stereotypes of Eastern and Southern Europeans were still very much there. While playing down my Italian background as much as possible, I flat out denied being Polish.

There was no one single incident that brought these feelings on, I was never singled out in front of a large group to have my ethnicity ridiculed, I was not taught to hate myself the way Natives or Africans were, I have never known first hand the dehumanizing racism that people of colour must go through everyday. Most Italian and Polish people I have known have been very proud of their heritage. Yet, as a youngster I did not feel this way.

I can not in honesty remember the first specific incidents that I can justify my feelings with. But as far back as I can remember I thought that the word "immigrant" meant stupid, unclean, strange, outsider. I also remember the first day of school nearly every year when the teacher called my name and asked if I was Italian. The word instantly conjured up images of the greasy, over-sexed uneducated "wop" that seemed so prevalent on T.V. I was young, and wanted to be like everyone else, not an unwanted immigrant. I often answered "no" to the teacher's question. However, I was even more embarrassed to be Polish. After hearing years of Polish jokes, I actually began wondering if Polish people were really inherently unintelligent.

I can remember when my grandmother dealt with the neighbourhood people; they were also immigrants. She was friendly and warm, she felt quite comfortable in her dealings with them. They appeared to me as neighbourhood people that were just like us, nothing to be intimidated by. When she had dealings with authority figures—they were exclusively Anglo, native-born Canadians—she became immediately apprehensive, telling me to always watch what I say around these people, to make sure to never insult them. Many of these people were polite, but I remember the ones who were rude and insulting towards her. She was just another dumb immigrant who couldn't speak English. Besides being intimidated by authority figures, these situations reinforced the idea that immigrants were second class citizens and native-born Anglos were the ideal Canadians who were to be revered and respected.

There were many days I went hungry as I could not bear to be seen eating the ethnic foods my mother made me for lunch. I often avoided having friends over for fear that they might hear my mother speaking Polish. These were the marks of the lowly immigrant that I desperately wanted no part of. I wanted the blond hair, blue eyes, and a cool, "Canadian" name like Brett Smith or Jay Johnson which were the marks of the Canadian.

To me, being other than Anglo meant being an immigrant. It meant being a janitor or cleaning woman. It meant dressing in strange attire and speaking peculiar languages. It brought images of my grandmother being scolded and humiliated by a cop, as if she were a child, it brought images of the leering immigrant who both steals jobs and drains the welfare system.

Through high school I never dated girls who weren't Anglo. I joined in with my exclusively "Canadian" friends in ridiculing the "wops" and "Ginos" and other immigrant kids at school. After twenty years of this, I systematically self-destroyed a very important part of who I am, a part I can never get back.

Maria: *"Having been born in a different country...I feel that being a member of the white race enables me to blend into the Canadian society much easier..."*

Having been born in a different country has enabled me to develop a greater awareness of my own ethnicity. When I first came to Canada, I realized that I was different from the people around me. Mainly because the language I spoke was Polish, not English. At that time I felt inferior because of the language barrier, but as my English improved, I was readily accepted by those around me. Since I spoke English, I was seen as a Canadian and no longer as an immigrant. Then and only then, I was able to say that I was Polish. At the present time I feel very strongly about my ethnic background. Even though I now live in Canada, I still want my children to speak the Polish language and practise the Polish traditions and customs.

I feel that being a member of the white race enables me to blend into the Canadian society much easier. My major barrier was being unable to communicate with the language of the dominant culture. But once that barrier was removed, combined with the fact that I was white, I was no longer considered as an outsider.

Multiculturalism

Ed: *"Is multiculturalism destroying Canadian identity?..."*

I was never a fan of the Multicultural Act and if anything I find myself even more opposed to it now. Although many people would like to say that this makes me a racist, I believe that I am not. A racist is someone who hates or discriminates against a person or people because of a difference (or perceived difference) in colour or religion. While I have never been like that, it sure makes my blood boil to hear that Sikhs can wear their turbans in police forces, or that schools are required to remove all references to Christmas from the classroom. Just because I do not like to see these events happen, doesn't mean that I dislike the person for succeeding in his or her quest. I am developing a strong discriminatory attitude towards the government.

On the topic of a Canadian identity, I can remember a government official (I cannot remember who) stating that one of Canada's greatest problems is that we haven't been able to create a feeling of being truly Canadian. This same politician stated that many of the problems that we are experiencing with Quebec could be amended if we could just inspire a feeling of Canadian-ness within the people. That statement blew my mind. This same politician supports the very Act which is, with the government's blessing and money, destroying what remaining Canadian identity there was. Not only does Canada open its arms and borders to accept immigrants from all over the world, something that doesn't bother me, it also willingly changes CANADIAN traditions and customs to accommodate them. In essence, what the Canadian government is doing is saying, "Hi, welcome, culture, don't worry about learning one of the two official languages of the country. In fact, if there are any traditions that have been around in Canada for a long time that you do not like, let us know, we will either exclude you from them or change them all just for you."

What this Multicultural Act has really done is given everyone a chance to change Canada and make it more like the countries they left in the first place. If you want to inspire a feeling of Canadian pride, leave Canada's laws and customs as they were and encourage people to assimilate, and contribute to the country in a positive way. As John F. Kennedy so eloquently put it, "Ask not what your country can do for you, but what you can do for your country!" Although this was an American President, I believe this country needs to do some real flag waving to wake it up.

Ron: *"Religious Symbols: Do they contravene Canadian laws and policies?..."*

The idea that Sikhs are being allowed to wear their turbans on a police force makes me very, very mad. I know that in Canada everyone has the freedom of religion and there is nothing wrong with that. However, the Charter of Rights and Freedoms is like rules and regulations. The police force has rules and regulations and under those there is a uniform rule that states that every police officer must wear a hat. I don't think that it is right that a Sikh may change that rule. It is not fair to the rest of the police force. In fact, I think that it is an insult to this country. If I went to their country there would be no way in hell that I or any other white man would be able to change any of their rules. I do not have any prejudices against the Sikhs or any other nationality or skin colour but people from other countries are treating Canada like garbage and they are taking advantage of Canada and its people. I think that in order to change this problem Canada has to take away some of its privileges. One of these would be changing the Charter of Rights and Freedoms.

Simon: *"Freedom of Religion: Essence of the multicultural policy..."*

Although the past few decades have seen numerous changes in Canada's constitution regarding racist attitudes, statutes and laws founded on bigotry, the recent confrontation between the minority Sikhs and the majority white Canadians over the issue of the Sikhs wearing their ceremonial daggers in my opinion proves that the system of social stratification and inequality among minority groups is far from being eradicated.

Being labelled as a minority within the Canadian culture tends to lead to certain stigmas and attacks that are being built up around the colour of people's skin, as well as what rites or rituals take place within the sub-culture of minority groupings. Recently Sikhs have become the target for attacks such as these regarding this traditional dagger, which a great many Sikhs see as an essential part of their heritage.

When Sikhs come to Canada and become citizens of this country, they, as well as all other minority groups, are granted full freedom of religion, language and all heritage rights. I believe that by depriving the Sikhs of their right to wear the kirpan, the very essence of the multicultural policy within Canada is being ignored. The Sikhs view their dagger as something to be honoured and deeply treasured, just as Christians view their cross—not as weapons.

I think it is sad that the prevalent attitude among so many Canadians is the thought that "we let them in to this country so they should do as we tell them to. You don't see us going to their country and making all these demands." I believe that this type of statement reflects as a whole, the way in which the Canadian population has been reared, with close-minded and bigoted attitudes which have been handed down from generation to generation.

Many more changes need to be made before Sikhs or any other minority group can appreciate the freedom that they deserve. Although Canada is proclaimed to be a multicultural country we really are not, and until multiculturalism is fully enforced and regulated, minority rights will continue to be undermined and stepped on. Changes need to be made now.

Avinder: *"All I would like is the same respect back..."*

I am seen to others as a minority. Some people tend to see me differently because I am of a different race. But what they do not know is that I am not so different from them. I speak the same language, eat the same food, and do the same activities. Just because I am a different race they think that I do different things. I try to fit in with other groups and appreciably try to learn what others can teach me. All I would like is the same respect back. Religion is important to me and also very important to my parents. But that does not mean that everywhere I go I take my religion with me, because this is not so. Since I was brought to this country, I try to do what others do, and I practise my religion in my own home. I believe that my family and I carry out our responsibilities as Canadians ought to. Everyone should have their religion in them somewhere, but practice it on your own time.

James: *"Misconceptions about the French..."*

During the last week, Quebec's sovereignty issue has been competing with the Gulf War for news headlines. The issue sparked after the failure of the Meech Lake Accord. The collapse of the Accord created an even stronger feeling of patriotism in Quebec. This event sealed the fate of Canada's future. French Canadians are often thought to be extremists, separatists and selfish. I believe that English Canadians don't know enough about the history of French Canada to be able to be make a fair and unbiased assessment of the situation. During the next few paragraphs, I will express my opinion and try to clarify the situation as a "Québécois."

I don't believe anyone can get a full understanding of the situation unless they've lived it. I was born in Montreal and I went to a French school until I came to college in Ontario. I believe that this enabled me to see through many of the lies that the media was reporting. The greatest concern for the French is the preservation of their language. They live in a continent dominated by English. They feel this influence through the music that they listen to, television, the media and of course the political system. Many tactics taken by the Quebec government to ensure the safety of the language are questionable. The greatest example is Bill 101; this affected the province on many levels: economic, educational, social, etc. ... I believe that it violates human rights especially in the domain of freedom of speech. But is it justified? I believe it is, if the rest of Canada is almost solely English (road signs, store signs), why not! Although there is one aspect that I haven't made up my mind on: Immigrants or Canadians whose parents never went to an English school are obliged to go to a French school, although I believe going to a French school is the first step towards becoming a "true Canadian" (most immigrants already know a bit of English)!

If you had taken a good history course, you will know that Canada did not start with equality among the English and the French. I remember learning that the English had tried to assimilate the French by forcing them to go to English schools and by not allowing them to have any Catholic establishments. Eventually, they got some of their rights back, not because of the fairness of the English, but because of their strong will and their patriotism towards each other. That is one thing that will never change, their devoted patriotism towards the Quebec flag and

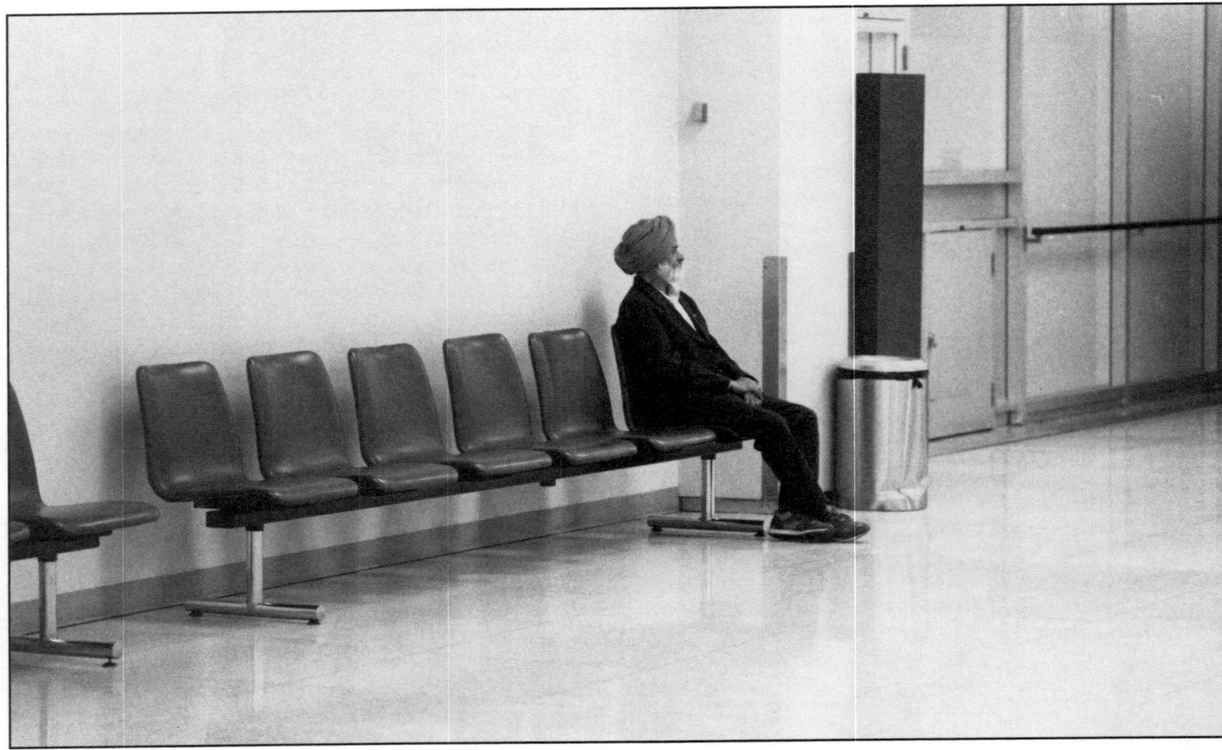

Photo by Dick Hemingway.

their language. Proof of that is in Quebec's music, theatre and especially on Saint Jean Baptist day (National holiday). For the first time this summer I participated in it and I was blown away by the amount of people in the streets with flags and chanting "Vive le Québec." That day I was proud to be a "Québécois!"

The thing that annoys me the most is when other Canadians complain that when they went to Quebec nobody spoke to them in English. What do you expect? The French know just as much English as the rest of Canada knows French. If a French person were to travel in the rest of Canada, they wouldn't expect everyone to speak French to them. Let's not have double standards!

I believe it's time Canada realizes that Quebec is a completely different culture. The way things are going, Quebec will separate and it will prove to be a great loss to all Canadians. It's time we open our eyes and accept Quebec for what it is and not for what we want it to be! Without "La Belle Province," there will be no Canada. It's about time all Canadians discard their differences and try to live together as one!

Troy: *"Police and the Black community..."*

We argued and argued over the matter of the Black community and the police. My argument, and I think I can speak for at least one quarter of the class, was that Black people tend to be more involved in crime. From statistics or police documents I can draw this conclusion. But one cannot make this type of conclusion because statistics mean nothing. All that they are saying is that so many crimes are being committed by these types of people. There are bad apples on every tree. I believe that all people are good, and just because there are some bad ones does not mean that the entire race should be discriminated against. I also hold the belief that a criminal has no colour. A criminal is a wrongdoer, and all criminals shall be dealt with by the law.

Employment Equity

Randy: *"Employment equity: Discrimination against White males?..."*

Almost every time someone begins to talk about employment opportunities, you can bet the topic of employment equity will come up. This seems to be on a lot of people's minds, especially those who are interested in police or fire fighting employment.

It doesn't really matter how these agencies wish to carry out their hiring procedures, because in the end they are all under close supervision. By who? By the N.D.P. government, that's who. Bob Rae, the party leader, has implemented an employment equity legislation. The rules were sent down to the agencies and it was explained that they were to hire a certain percentage of women and minorities within a given time. This is good because it forces police and fire agencies to open the doors to these prescribed groups that have been discriminated against in the past. On the other hand it's also kind of bad.

Being a member of the "white male" group, I have now come up against an annoying obstacle. Because of this new employment equity legislation the police forces are trying to increase their enrolment numbers of women, minority and disabled groups in order to meet Mr. Rae's requirements.

I think the phrase "employment equity" should be changed to "employment inequity." According to Webster's New World dictionary equity means "fairness and impartiality." From the same dictionary I found the word equal to mean "of the same value, having the same rights, to be equal to." Perhaps Mr. Rae has a different dictionary in which his translations come from.

The majority of the population should realize that women, minorities and the disabled have been discriminated against and in many cases still are. They may not admit it, but they know it's true. If this is the case...why turn everything upside down by trying to make amends with these prescribed groups over such a short time? Why turn the white male into the minority, because this is what's happening, the white male is being discriminated against for something that happened beyond his/her control; it's a form of reverse discrimination. The police forces actually tell us (the white applicants), that our chances are slim of getting hired until the employment equity numbers balance out. This is where I start to get my back up. Equality should mean that everyone gets the same chance of being hired. If the top 10 applicants are black, they are hired, if they are white males, they are hired and the same if they are female. Forget about balancing the numbers, give the job to the person who best deserves it. That's equal!

Employment equity has played a minor role in my personal life. A couple of years back when this legislation came into effect I was applying to the Toronto Police with a East Indian friend of mine. I received a higher mark than him on the physical testing, and we were close on the written. After these tests the Toronto Police put out a hiring freeze and I was asked to re-apply at a later date. Two weeks after this, my friend received a phone call from Toronto Police asking him to come in for an interview. Toronto pushed him through the hiring process in less than two months and had him signed up to go to police college the following month. On average, the normal hiring procedure takes roughly six to twelve months, start to finish. The main difference between our two applications was that mine said "white male" and his said "visible minority," I'm sure there was more but this stuck out and bothered me. From that point I know I had to make myself a more attractive applicant to recruiters because the competition had just became tougher.

I'm a firm believer in the saying "two wrongs don't make a right," but this is what's happening now with employment equity. I truly wish I had a solution to offer that may rectify the situation and make it fair for everyone.

Will employment equity benefit society as a whole?, I don't think so. If anything it has created greater tension between the white applicants and the prescribed groups. It has brought our society into a state of disrepute. Eventually when employment equity has succeeded society as a whole may be better off, but then again I'm not sure. Even the minorities when asked say they want to be hired because they were the best, not because they were the minority. But on the other hand, if some recruiter told me I was wanted because I was white, and they were short of whites I wouldn't think twice about the so called "equity."

Competition is very tough in the job market these days and spreads further than the police and fire fighting professions. It's very common for someone to make an excuse, or to blame someone else for their own problems. For example, the fisherman always has ten reasons why the "big one" got away. Well, for some, not being hired on a police or fire department brings about a similar set of excuses, such as "I didn't get hired because some minority took my spot," and various other reasons. Being in a Police Education class I hear too many of these excuses every day, and it's usually before people even go to write their exam. In my opinion these people are probably not qualified and their preparing themselves for defeat, in turn using the minorities as their scapegoats. In the long run all employment equity is doing is making the competition that much more stiff. Therefore, if you want the opportunity, you have to go and get it because it's not going to come to you, and that's the bottom line.

Roger: *"Employment equity: Reverse racism?..."*

I come from an Irish-English family (75%–25% mix), and was raised in a white middle-class household. My family has never been overly rich, nor have we ever starved. I was born in Toronto, but raised in the suburbs, so in essence I have lived a rather sheltered life.

Even though I grew up in a good, financially stable home, I don't consider this fact to be an advantage created by my race or ethnicity. Through school and social clubs, I've had many friends from different races and ethnic backgrounds who were in a home of equal to greater financial stability. Like many others, my parents are both fairly uneducated, by today's standards, yet through hard work and determination have managed to make a success of themselves.

All through talking with other people, I've been trying to think of an instance where my race, or my ethnicity has been of an advantage to me, and I haven't been able to think of one. Sure, there is the fact that I came from a stable home, but this has nothing to do with my race, it has to do with loving parents who have shown a genuine concern with what I do. Maybe the fact that I am fairly well educated can be considered an advantage, but my race didn't put me through school. My parents' guidance, my own drive to better myself and a desire to reach a certain goal, are what completed my education. Maybe always having money in my pocket can be considered an advantage, but even this fact is not a result of my race; the fact that I have always had a part-time job and worked hard to earn the money is.

So even after listening to other people's stories and points of view, I have found no situation were my being white is an advantage. I have always been a believer in the human spirit, I believe that what a person is, not what a person looks like, determines his or her future.

Just as I have not been able to think of a past experience or incident were my race or ethnicity has been an advantage, I am not able to think of an incident were my race or ethnicity has been a disadvantage. That is up until recently.

As my graduation quickly approaches, I am becoming more and more frustrated by the tough uphill battle which I will have to undertake. As is obvious, my future goal is to become a police officer, a profession which has been drastically affected by special interest groups, pathetic government policies and government appointed "overseers" such as the infamous Susan Eng. Through the media and schools, we are constantly bombarded with messages and slogans denouncing racism and discrimination. We are told that these types of acts will no longer be tolerated by society, and will be slushed through Government policies and public awareness. In our tireless search for racism and discrimination, two very interesting and disturbing phenomena have appeared: Everything has become a "racial issue," and "reverse discrimination."

This government's "Employment Equity Program" and "Multicultural Act" have in essence turned my race and my ethnicity into a disadvantage. The fact that I am a high school and college graduate no longer carries any significant merit when applying to a police force or any other Government agency. The prime qualification has become skin colour.

Although many "experts" and government officials will deny the existence of reverse discrimination and hiring quotas, professionals within the affected fields will give you a completely different story. The agencies' personnel tell horror stories about the government-imposed "hiring of minorities at all cost" tactics. Stories like these do little to add optimism to my view of a future career.

Many people talk about instances were they have been denied jobs in the past because of their race; well, in the near future I too will be able to relate to these people very easily. The only difference is I will be affected by a Government-endorsed policy.

The next question is, how does this make me feel? Quite simply put, nauseated. Now the fact that I am qualified, and possess more than sufficient skills to perform my job, has little to no bearing. I may now be forced to sit back and watch less qualified and less educated persons pass me in line because they are members of a race which the government has targeted.

The Employment Equity program is a topic of which I have very mixed emotions. The concept behind the program is good; it prevents employers from denying people positions within companies or agencies according to their colour or religion. The problem is in how the government has implemented the program. In government agencies, and in the public service sector, this program has made it extremely difficult to almost impossible for a white person (especially a white male) to find employment. In the business world, competition is not restricted to just business transactions, the whole application process is also a competition. If a person is more qualified because of English skills, education and experience he/she should get the job. This is not necessarily true now with the implementation of this Employment Equity.

My example of how this government has gone overboard with this program is the same as my cousin Brent's. During the summer, I had to go to the OHIP building to straighten up a problem I had with my health card. As soon as I entered the office, I was taken aback, not only was I the only white in the office, I was the only one capable of speaking English at an understandable level. After approximately 10 minutes of trying to understand what the OHIP employee was saying to me, the supervisor finally showed up (just returning from her lunch break). I was relieved to find out that not only was the lady capable of speaking English, but was also very understandable (and yes she also was of a visible minority group). My point here is, if these jobs are posted publicly, there would have to be applicants who possess good English skills. Did these people just not show up during the interviews for these jobs? In these economic times, I find that very hard to believe. Also if the purpose of the Employment Equity is to show an equal representation of the community which it belongs, someone obviously made a mistake.

Eugene: *"Employment Equity is a course of events which is inevitable..."*

The things that I feel have affected me the most while in this class were the topics of reverse discrimination, and of whites of this generation "paying" for the mistakes and ignorance of our forefathers. This in particular because I have Chinese background and I also have white background. Is it necessary then, to split me in half so that my white half may be condemned, and my Chinese half may receive retribution? And finally, the ignorant and extremely racist attitudes that were displayed by certain classmates really appalled, shocked, dismayed, and insulted me. Having people like this in my class really made the issue of racism hit close to home.

The topic of reverse discrimination basically made me realize that even though I am willing to make this effort to understand, it does not mean that those I encounter will feel similarly. And I cannot allow these people to make me lose sight of what I feel is right, nor let them weaken my determination.

The topic of whites of this generation paying for the mistakes of their forefathers also affects me greatly. I realize that this is a course of events which must inevitably come about but it is hard to see past the fact that I am losing out. I guess where one stands on this topic depends on whether they feel their life is more important than the future or vice versa.

Radcliffe: *"Employment Equity—A necessary hiring practice..."*

I intend to discuss that employment equity is a necessary hiring practice that needs to stay in effect until an acceptable balance in employment is achieved.

When I first learned of employment equity I felt that it was reverse discrimination. I thought that minorities were getting an unfair advantage over those who had more experience in their field. Now I understand that equity means giving people a fair chance at getting hired. Equity means that other factors are taken into consideration when hiring. A man who has worked just as hard as a man who has been hindered by prejudice and unfair hiring practices should be credited for what he has endured to enter the job market.

As children we learn through example. When minorities are growing up in our society they are socialized with cultural bias and unequal representation in their curriculum. If at a young age they are taught that positions of power are open to all people and yet no minority has occupied such powerful positions, they will not perceive themselves "Good" enough for the job. For common sense would dictate that if there were a equitable hiring practice in effect there would be people of all races occupying such power positions. For example a young black female has never seen a black woman police officer. So she does not take the necessary steps in order to reach that position. With the employment equity in place the disadvantaged youth is given merit for enduring a culturally biased educational system. Now when a young black girl sees someone like her in such a power position she will take the necessary steps to become a police officer and she can get the job regardless of whether or not employment equity exists. When equal representation of cultures is met within the police force, or any other profession for that matter, employment equity should be discontinued. As the demographics of the surrounding area fluctuate employment equity should be able to go with those changes.

Discussion

A poll conducted in 1989 found that 49 percent of the people polled agreed that immigrants take away jobs from Canadians. The same study also found that Canadians were concerned that newcomers, particularly racial minorities, do not make enough effort to integrate into the society (Angus Reid, 1989). These ideas remain and are reflected in the above essays. More generally, it is felt that the changes in the economy, the double-digit unemployment rate, the need to preserve "our" cultural identity, and the rising tensions among the various ethnic and racial groups are enough reasons for "the Canadian government to stop immigration altogether or drastically reduce the numbers coming in." Unfortunately, this position fails to take into consideration Canada's needs and the significant role of immigrants in the economic wellbeing of Canada.

Before proceeding, it is important to clarify the difference between an immigrant and a refugee, a confusion that was often reflected in the comments made by participants. An immigrant is a person who takes up permanent resident in Canada, while a refugee, or Convention refugee, according to the United Nations definition and adopted by all member countries like Canada, is:

> *Any person who, by reason of a well-founded fear of persecution for reason of race, religion, nationality, membership in a particular social group or political opinion, (a) is outside the country of his (her) nationality and is unable or, by reason of such fear, is unwilling to avail himself (herself) of the protection of that country, or, (b) not having a country of nationality, is outside the country of his (her) former habitual residence and is unable, or by reason of such fear, is unwilling to return to the country.*[1]

It is estimated that we would experience a decline in population if we were to significantly reduce the number of immigrants and refugees entering Canada. This is so, since according to Statistics Canada, we have a birth rate of 1.8 and an aging population; there are more Canadians dying than are born; and well over 10,000 people emigrate from Canada (most going to the United States) each year. This is the situation that makes the Canadian government, despite many Canadians' opposition to immigration, continue to allow some 250,000 immigrants into the country each year. This supports the claim made by many demographers and statisticians that we need this number of immigrants entering Canada each year if we are to have a viable economy and social stability.[2] The aging of our population is of particular importance here. It is estimated that by 2036 one in every four Canadians will be 65 years or older (Gauthier, 1994). So as the post-war baby boom generation gets older and drops out of the labour force, there will be an increased need for immigrants to fill the labour force's needs, which in turn will provide a steady tax base to fund the high quality health and social service needs of that generation.

In order to sustain population levels and meet labour force demands, Canada's immigration policies have traditionally sought to attract the youngest, healthiest, best-educated and most resourceful people. Since the introduction of the immigration point system[3] in 1967, all immigrants except close

[1] It should be noted that people just do not enter Canada and claim refugee status, Canada must first recognize the country of which claimants are citizens as refugee-producing countries, of course with reference to the United Nations definition. Other factors that are taken into account to qualify as a refugee are: age, level of education, job skills, knowledge of English or French and security and health considerations.

[2] In fact, according to the Law Union of Ontario (1981), Canada's population would begin to decline to by the year 2000 with an annual immigrant rate of 100,000.

[3] In addition to the refugee class of immigrants, there are also, as set out by the Immigration Act of 1976, family and independent classes. The family class refers to those immigrants who may be sponsored by relatives (e.g. parents, siblings, children), or nominated by husband, wife or fiancee who are Canadian residents or citizens, 18 years or older. The sponsors must agree to provide maintenance for up to 10 years. Independent immigrants include assisted relatives (not in the above category), entrepreneurs, investors and retirees. Those entering through this class must qualify by scoring a minimum of 70 points out of a possible 100 based on age, level of education, job skills, occupational demand, knowledge of English or French, "personal suitability" (i.e.

family relatives of Canadian citizens and permanent residents, have been assessed according to age, education, training and experience, demand for their occupation in Canada, presence of pre-arranged employment and/or knowledge of one or more of Canada's official languages. Over three quarters (77 percent) of all immigrants admitted to Canada during the 1980s were under the age of 40; over half (57 percent) were under 30 (Logan, 1991:11). Adjusted for age, the 1986 census shows that 28.2 percent of immigrants compared to 22.3 percent of native-born Canadians had some university education (Jansen and Richmond, 1990: 6). More current data indicate that this percentage has increased in recent years. Although educational attainment data includes pre-school and school age children, a full 33 percent of newcomers had some postsecondary education; among refugees, 28 percent had some postsecondary education (Employment and Immigration, 1989b: 22).

People are particularly sensitive to factors which might operate as barriers or hurdles to the realization of their aspirations and goals when they are at the point of entering the job market. It is understandable therefore that the class participants would think, given the degree to which this view is supported in the media, that immigrants are taking jobs to which Canadians citizens are entitled. Economists argue that by creating demands for goods and services, immigrants create jobs for Canadians. According to one government study, immigrants and refugees admitted to Canada between 1983 and 1985, created 9,000 jobs over and above those they filled, and that single immigrant entrepreneurs were expected to create or maintain an average of six jobs (Employment and Immigration, 1992a). Another study estimated that immigrant investigators created an estimated 10,000 jobs between January 1986 and December 1991 (Employment and Immigration, 1992b). While immigrants are to be found in significant numbers, and are in some cases over-represented, in some industries and businesses compared to native-born workers, this is certainly not the cases in the labour force as a whole. As has already been mentioned, because the majority of immigrants are selected on the basis of education, skills, experience, "national and regional population goals and labour market needs" (Employment and Immigration, 1978:25), they tend to fill labour market gaps. So immigrants fill jobs which there are no Canadians to fill or jobs which Canadians do not want. The notion that immigrants are a drain on our social services is not supported by research data either. For instance, according to the Economic Council of Canada, between 1981 and 1986, 12.5 percent of the newcomers to Canada received some government social assistance cheques compared to 13.8 percent of Canadian-born adults; and only 3.5 percent of foreign-born received welfare in 1987 compared with 5.5 percent of those born in Canada (Jensen and Richmond, 1990). This indicates, as has so often been said, that newcomers tend to make less use of the social service system than native-born Canadians. In cases of social and financial needs they tend to turn for assistance from their sponsoring relative or community rather than to government. immigrants tend to aspire to be self sufficient and this can only be achieved through their own work efforts; they are inexperienced with such government assistance programs, particularly immigrants from "developing nations"; they would feel that accepting such assistance would be an admission of failure, something that is contrary to the reason for which they immigrated in the first place; and the immigration policies require that they are economically self-sufficiency and/or they are the responsibility of their sponsor for at least 10 years or until they become citizens.

Similarly, the myth that there is a correlation between an increase in crime and an increase in immigration is an example of media-fed xenophobia in Canada. This is fuelled by stereotypes based on race, ethnicity and the countries of origin of members of minority groups. The immigration act

capacity to adapt to Canada), and security and health considerations. Entrepreneurs must intend to operate a business and employ one or more Canadians. Investors must have a net worth of $500,000 and must invest a minimum of $150,000 in a project that create jobs and is economically beneficial.

spells out that persons convicted of criminal offenses or believed to have committed a crime, and persons who would constitute a danger to national security are inadmissible. A study by Samuel (1989) showed that the criminality rate of immigrants from source areas like Africa, Asia and the Caribbean was less than one third of that of immigrants from the United States and Europe. Generally, the criminal behaviours of any population must be examined in relations to that group's access to opportunities. For immigrants, in particular, we need to examine how, as the host society, our accommodation practices provide immigrants access to the necessary employment and education opportunities. Before leaving this point, there is one question I think we should think about: When does a person cease to be regarded as an immigrant? What are the criteria that makes one a Canadian?

The above essays indicate that a distinction is not made between immigrants and racial and ethnic minorities. In fact, these minorities, especially racial minorities, are often constructed as immigrants. They are perceived as having "come to our country" settling within "their own ethnic groups" and protesting "in the streets of Canada about issues back in their country." Some suggest that Canada's multicultural policy is responsible for what is seen as immigrants (or racial and ethnic minority group members) "taking advantage of our liberalism" to the extent that they try to change "our identity," "our laws," and "our culture." But an honest examination of our demography will indicate that "ethnic" neighbourhoods abound throughout the country, and have for many, many generations. Neighbourhoods populated by people of similar background, whether by language, social class, ethnicity, race, nationality or sexual orientation, provide members of that community with an available support system. Associations, organization and businesses located in these neighbourhoods strengthen individual and group identity, nurture community spirit and foster economic self-sufficiency and productivity. As one minority member of metropolitan Toronto comments: "You have to understand that back home, we don't have social insurance or anything of that kind...Everyone's social insurance policy is [their] relatives and friends. If you grow older, or you are somewhat poor, you always rely on the people you know and your relatives. We always depend on each other" (Watson, 1991:A11).

Insofar as immigrants must adjust to a new environment, and they are likely to experience barriers to full participation in the society, particularly as racial and ethnic minorities, then it is inevitable that they would seek alternative ways of participating. It is within these communities that they find the space and the voice to experience the life they would wish. Further, we maintain that in a democratic society, everyone has the right to live where and with whom they choose, as well as participate in the way they wish. Hence, where they live and the ways in which they participate are individual choices rather than prescribed options or privileges.

In one of the above essays, the writer points out that immigrants should not "protest in the streets of Canada about issues in their country," they should protest "about Canadian issues." An interesting question that this raises is: Do not *all* Canadians have the freedom to exercise their rights as citizens—the right to express their political positions about—and hence influence—local, national and international issues? Similar objections about how people choose to participate and explain their opinions are not often articulated when members of the dominant group protest about international issues. In such cases, they are not perceived to be protesting out of self-interest but from a position of concern and empathy. This same behaviour, when exhibited by racial and ethnic minorities, is invariably interpreted as the actions of "others"—"outsiders" and "immigrants."

Earlier, we observed that all societies are multicultural and that racial, ethnic, religious, linguistic and regional groups have different subcultures. In Canada, with the exception of Aboriginals, all of our ethnic groups are immigrants, some more recent than others. Tensions and conflicts are often found within culturally diverse societies. They are sometimes a result of differences in political perspectives, lack of recognition of respective differences, lack of access to political and economic resources, and the society's inability to manage and accommodate these differences. Canada is not unique with the difficulties we experience between the various subcultural groups. The French-English issue is an example of historic tensions that exist in culturally diverse societies such as ours. Similar tensions and conflict can be observed in other nations. How we address these issues and tensions reflect how we come to understand and accept our cultural diversity, as well as how we accommodate our minority population.

One aspect of our cultural diversity with which many Canadians seem to struggle is that of "religious freedom"—individuals' right to engage in their particular religious practices. As some of the essays indicate, religious practices, for example those of Sikhs (the ones that are often cited) are perceived to contravene our laws, and to change "our Canadian identity." Particular references are made to "Sikhs being allowed to wear turbans on the police force, or the RCMP." Participants insist that religious practices such as those of Sikhs are contrary to our laws even when informed that the Constitution of Canada and the Multiculturalism Act support these practices. Specifically, the Constitution

> *provides that every individual is equal before and under the law and has the right to equal protection and benefit of the law without discrimination and that everyone has the freedom of conscience, religion, thought, belief, opinion, expression, peaceful assembly and association …*

And the Multiculturalism Act states in part:

> *And whereas Canada is a party to the International Convention on the Elimination of All Forms of Racial Discrimination, which Convention recognizes that all human beings are equal before the law and are entitled to equal protection of the law against any discrimination and against any incitement to discrimination, and to the International Covenant on Civil and Political Rights, which Covenant provides that persons belonging to ethnic, religious or linguistic minorities shall not be denied the right to enjoy their own culture, to profess and practise their own religion or to use their own language …*

Very often criticisms are made by dominant group Canadians whose religious practices and symbols are very well preserved by the laws and institutions of our society. Generally, Canadians do not know that the Sikh religion has been in Canada for generations, that the first Sikh temple or *gurdwara* was opened in Vancouver, British Columbia in 1908 (Burnet and Palmer, 1989). On the basis of longevity alone, this should be seen as an established Canadian religion.

The principle of equity and social justice underlie any practices that is established to ensure the rights and privileges of Canadians. The fact that the multiculturalism policy exists is because in a democratic society, measures must be taken to ensure that the rights and freedom of all members of society are protected; that there is full and equitable participation of all members of the society; and that barriers to participation do not exist. Similarly, the employment equity[1] policy seeks to remove barriers in accessing employment opportunities. Employment equity policies, as Fish argues in his essay: "Reverse Racism or How the Pot Got To Call The Kettle Black," are "not intended to disenfranchise white males. Rather the policy was driven by other considerations, and it was only as a by-product of those considerations—not as a goal—that white males have been rejected" (Fish, 1993:136). These considerations include such things as minority representation and an acknowledgement that barriers to employment opportunities have existed historically and systemically, and continue to exist for racial and ethnic minorities. In making this point in class, I often get the response: "Two wrongs don't make a right; if it is unfair to discriminate against Blacks, it is just as unfair to discriminate against Whites."

[1] The term employment equity is seen as uniquely Canadian. It was coined by the 1984 Royal Commission on Equity in Employment (Judge Rosalie Abella). It is used to "describe programs designed to improve the situation of individuals who, because of they are or can be identified as being in a particular group, find themselves adversely affected by certainly systems or practices in the workplace" (Moreau, 1994:147). The four groups that have been identified as disadvantaged because of their labour force participation, unemployment rates, levels of income, and persistent occupational segregation are: women, Aboriginal people, "visible" minorities, and people with disabilities (Moreau, 1994:147).

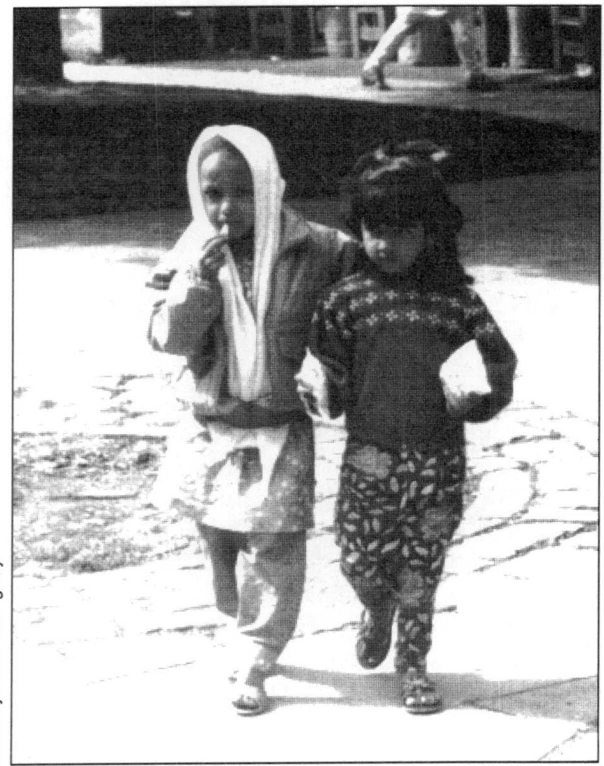
Photo by Dick Hemingway.

Awareness and a willingness to look at more than skin colour is crucial to the elimination of prejudice.

This position is posited on the notion that everyone is or should be the *same,* and ignores the historical fact that groups have been excluded historically or treated inequitably. It is a dismissal of individual and group differences, and a disregard for the existing power imbalance that provides advantages to some members of society and forces disadvantages upon others. Fairness is a notion that must be evaluated in relation to the histories of respective groups to which individuals belong. Equity programs are "attempts to undo the effects of arbitrary and racist policies and practices that have historically been barriers to access and opportunities" (James, 1995) for some.

The claim that employment equity is "reverse racism" or "reverse discrimination" has merit only if racism or discrimination are constructed in terms of individuals' attitudes and ignorance, rather than a product of historical and structural factors. But we know, as discussed earlier, that racism is not based merely on individuals' ignorance or negative attitudes, but more importantly on structural inequality. It is more than individuals' attitudes and acts of discrimination. It is a cultural and historical fact that structures the norms and values of this society, consequently finding expressions in the laws, policies and practices of institutions. As I argued elsewhere:

> Essentially, the phase "reverse racism" seems oxymoronic. It negates the inherent inequalities in resources and power among groups posited by racial categorization in our society. It is a phrase that has important carriage for young white males, for it gives political weight to their feelings of powerlessness and loss of privilege. The term allows them to wear the banner of oppression as victims of a system over which, like racial minorities, they have no control...It fails to construct power in structural and historical terms which would account for the cultural capital that they possess because of their membership in their particular racial group. Inherent in their conceptualization of racism is their neglect to acknowledge their own power and privilege, and to recognize that their own power is rooted in the historical and cultural conditions upon which this society has been built. Not to recognize the structural roots of racism and their white privilege is a way of denying their own racism, the benefit they derive from its existence, and their responsibility for participating in changing it (James, 1994).

We cannot minimize the importance of the fact that some who articulate this sense of victimization are students. As young people, they attend postsecondary institutions, with the hope that they will "have the edge" on other job applicants, eventually realizing their occupational goals. They are particularly sensitive to the job market and the employment opportunities that await them. Whatever is perceived as a barrier would contribute frustration and anger. Their anger and frustration stem also from what they see as meritocracy being compromised. As an article in *BusinessWeek* magazine points out, "At the heart of the issue for many white males is the question of merit—that in the rush for a more diverse workplace, they will lose out to less qualified workers" (January, 1994:52). This might in part explain why, in their bid to maintain some sense of self-confident and optimism, some individuals see employment equity as premised on a quota system in which "less qualified minorities are being hired."

But studies reveal that racial and ethnic minorities experience significant barriers to employment opportunities. For instance, in a survey of employers in Toronto, Billingsley and Muzynski (1985) found that most employers relied on informal employee and friendship networks to recruit and fill job positions. Moreover, a survey of 672 corporate recruiters, hiring mangers and agency recruiters conducted by Canadian Recruiters Guild in 1989 showed that 87 percent of corporate and 100 percent of agency recruiters surveyed received direct discriminatory requests. Nearly three-quarters of corporate and 94 percent of agency recruiters complied with these requests. The survey also showed that out of 6,720 available positions, only four target group members were placed by the recruiting agencies (Currents, April 1989:19–20). In their 1985 study "Who Gets the Work: A Test of Racial Discrimination in Employment" in Toronto, Henry and Ginzberg concluded that:

> ...there is a very substantial racial discrimination affecting the ability of members of racial minorities to find employment even when they are well qualified and eager to find work...Once an applicant is employed, discrimination can still affect opportunities for advancement, job retention, and level of earnings, to say nothing of the question of the quality of work and the relationship with co-workers (1990:20).

And in a study of Black youth employment experiences, James (1993) quotes respondents as saying that racism and discrimination were "challenges" with which they had to contend, both in terms of obtaining a job and while they were on the job. They suggested that "who you know" is even more important than education, "particularly in competition against a white person for a job." As one respondent stated, "while education can help, I have seen that who you know gets you further" (p.10).

Information that challenges the myth of meritocracy is difficult for anyone to accept, particularly middle-class, postsecondary students, when they have been socialized to believe that the principles of democracy and correspondingly, meritocracy, work well to provide all Canadians the same opportunities and chances to succeed once they have gained the ability, education, training and skill, and the opportunity to apply themselves. Such people subscribe to the notion that it is individuals' efforts and ability, and not systemic factors that determine achievement. It is inconceivable therefore, that governments and other institutions should support what these students perceive as "unfairness"—a situation in which race or gender or ability is seen as operating to advantage some (i.e. Aboriginals, women, racial minorities, and people with disabilities). When governments and institutions by these practice admit to inequalities, they appear to deny the young men's traditional beliefs in meritocracy.This raises doubts in their minds, shakes their confidence in the system, and has them asking questions such as "why me, why now?" Or, "why do I have to pay for things that I am not responsible for creating?" Nonetheless, it remains that at some point, remedies like these must be developed to address the situations of those citizens who are, and have been in the past, disadvantaged by structural inequalities. If not now, when?

Summary

The essays on immigration, multiculturalism and employment equity tend to suggest that participants see these phenomena as impediments to economic growth and positive social relations in Canada. Immigration is perceived as largely unnecessary particularly at this time of high unemployment and social tensions due to crime and ethnic differences. But as Darren rightly mentions in his answer to the question: "Are immigrants a strain on our society?"

> One of the benefits from having immigrants come into the country is economic. The immigrants will obtain jobs and receive wages in return, they then will spend the money on necessities, such as food, shelter, and clothing. When more products like these have to be supplied, the companies that produce them have to accommodate the demands of the new immigrants. When this happens new jobs are cre-

> ated. This is also beneficial to economic growth, and will eventually benefit all the country. This is the aspect that a number of Canadians do not take into consideration when they oppose new arrivals to the country.
>
> Without immigrants, we would not be able to increase in population. The reason for this is that the number of children born is very low and will not compensate for the number of deaths and emigration that occur each year. The influx of new immigrants into the country will help to compensate and eventually even out and expand the population. This will enable Canada to become economically stable and prosperous.

And as Fleras and Elliot (1992) state: "the immigrants of today are likely to underwrite the costs of the delivery of social services in the future. For this reason alone, we are as dependent on immigrants as they are on us" (p.46).

Many people see a link between immigration and multiculturalism—two unnecessary evils. It is believed that the large numbers of immigrants, their assertiveness and expectations that their ethnic and religious values and practices be recognized, contribute to disharmony and a loss of "Canadian identity." But as one participant argues, this perception of multiculturalism, immigration and immigrants is due to the fact that "we are resistant to change and anything foreign. What we don't understand, we destroy. The cold hard fact is that we need immigrants more than they need us." The subcultures expressed by minority group members is related to the social situation or context in which they find themselves. "It is identification with select objective markers of that cultural lifestyle—not the degree of intensity of involvement or the number of distinguishing cultural traits—that is crucial" (Fleras and Elliott, 1992:51). Furthermore, remind us, the ethnic culture is not necessarily based on the original immigrant culture but on a "reconstructed" ethnicity in which tradition is "invented" on the basis of ongoing adaptations to the environment and to the social situation in Canada (Fleras and Elliot, 1992:51).

On the issue of employment equity many of the white class participants see it as "reverse racism," "reverse discrimination," and/or an unfair policy in which "less qualified racial minorities" are being hired. One participant argues that because of employment equity "white males are not being hired and this causes some sort of negative feelings towards the designated groups. I believe this created more tension and frustration among each other." However, with reference to the career to which he aspires, he admits that as "a corrective measure," employment equity "would definitely help" since having coworkers from "all racial minority backgrounds can and will benefit a multicultural society."

It can be said that myths, misinformation and half-truths characterize much of the discussion about immigration, immigrants, multiculturalism and employment equity. These myths are largely based on the lack of acknowledgement of the inherent economic and social inequities within our society, a fear of social change, and an anticipated loss of political, economic, and social power and privilege. They are also coloured by prejudices, stereotypes, and racism aimed toward the groups who are characterized as their benefactors. If we are to build a democratic and equitable society in Canada, then we must be prepared for social change and we all must play a part in initiating and fighting for that change.

SOURCE: Carl James, *Seeing Ourselves: Exploring Race, Ethnicity and Culture* (Toronto: Thompson Educational Publishing, Inc., 1995). Reprinted with permission.

Questions and Topics for Discussion and Writing

1. Discuss the historical significance of immigration and immigrants to the economic, social, political and technological development of Canada. How will immigration play a role in the future development of Canada?
2. What is meant by the term "hyphenated Canadian"? What role does the population in general play in maintaining the "hyphen" in some Canadians' lives?
3. Is there such a thing as "reverse racism"? Do multiculturalism and employment equity contribute to reverse racism and discrimination in Canada?

McDonaldization

George Ritzer

In his piece on the "McDonaldization" of society, sociologist George Ritzer describes how the organizational methods of fast-food chain restaurants have moved into society as a whole, and have become standard practice for people in all aspects of business and society.

The place to begin is with some of my early background. My thinking about McDonaldization was shaped by the fact that I grew up before the fast-food restaurant was developed and was raised in a city, New York, which was in many ways during those years the antithesis of a society dominated by the fast-food restaurant and its principles and mentality.

I was born in 1940; Ray Kroc did not found the first McDonald's franchise until 1955. Furthermore, the early Mcdonald's fast-food restaurants were primarily medium-sized town and suburban phenomena; they did not make their way into the big cities until much later....

I was an adult before I ever saw a McDonald's, and that gives me a perspective different from that of the vast majority of students reading this...who were born into a society already dominated by McDonald's and its clones not only in the fast-food business but in other businesses as well (for example, AAMCO Transmissions and H&R Block). Unlike most of you, I am able to remember a world without McDonald's. By virtue of my age, I lived through the revolution wrought by the fast-food restaurant and saw the changes it brought about in society. This gives me a longer-term perspective with which to look at the phenomenon of McDonaldization....

From the late 1950s on I was certainly conscious of McDonald's and its clones and their expansion throughout society. While I was observing what was occurring, I don't remember feeling alarmed by it. Then, in 1975, I lived in Europe for the first time. While I lived in the Netherlands, I was able to travel around most of Western Europe and a bit of Eastern Europe as well. I particularly remember an extended visit to Vienna and the feeling that it reminded me of what New York had been like when I was growing up in the 1940s. While one could find a fast-food restaurant here and there in Europe in 1975, by and large that continent had not yet undergone the process of McDonaldization. The contrast between Europe and the rampant McDonaldization taking place in the United States made me acutely aware of what was happening back home....

In 1992 I spent some time in Moscow and was struck again by the spread and significance of McDonaldization. There, in the heart of an otherwise depressing and decaying city, stood the new McDonald's. It had been the world's largest and busiest until 1992, when an even larger and busier McDonald's was opened in the center of Beijing. Despite its being supplanted in this exalted position by the newer outlet in China, this restaurant still attracted droves of Moscovites. Many things drew them to it, not the least of which was that it was the symbol of the rationalization of America and its coveted market economy....

These personal experiences are part of the background for my concerns with and about McDonaldization, but there is also an academic backdrop. After I started teaching sociology at the university level in 1968, I devoted more and more attention to reading and teaching sociological theory. One of the theorists who appealed to me most was Max Weber, especially his theory of rationalization.... Weber was interested in the ra-

Rationalization for What?

Max Weber

In his piece on the "McDonaldization" of society, sociologist George Ritzer describes how "the principles of the fast-food restaurant are coming to dominate more and more sectors of American society as well as the rest of the world."

As a serious researcher Ritzer, who teaches at the University of Maryland, is doing more than simply drawing a few parallels between the way a fast-food chain produces hamburgers and the way our fast-paced society operates. Ritzer is following in the footsteps of social scientists before him who have attempted to look at the ways in which society changed as it became more bureaucratized and more "rational."

According to Ritzer, the major inspiration for his thoughts on McDonaldization and rationalization was Max Weber, one of the leading figures of nine-

teenth-century philosophy, sociology and political science.

Weber was born in Thuringia (Germany) in 1864, and died in Munich in 1920. Weber studied at the Universities of Heidelberg, Berlin and Gottingen, earning his doctorate in 1891. He began his career as a professor in 1894, but a serious nervous disorder forced him to suspend his teaching and research in 1897 for four years. He resumed his teaching at Heidelberg in 1902. Weber concentrated on three broad areas in his writing: the social sciences and sociology, history, and religion.

Weber's most famous works include *The Protestant Ethic and the Spirit of Capitalism* (1905), *Economy and Society* and his *General Economic History* (published posthumously, in 1924).

It was in the first of these books that Weber developed his now-famous idea of the "Protestant Work Ethic," which held that certain tenets of Protestant Christianity made it extremely adaptable to capitalist economic systems. This theory was strengthened by the fact that the Industrial Revolution had combined with Protestantism in the nineteenth century in both the U.S.A. and England to produce flourishing economies on a large scale.

tionalization process in the West. More generally, he was interested in why the West had rationalized while the rest of the world had failed to do so. Weber was ambivalent about the rationalization process taking place in the West. While he recognized the many advantages flowing from rationalization, he was very much aware of the negative aspects and consequences. Most generally, he was afraid of the possibility of what he called the "iron cage of rationality." His fear was that when all aspects of modern society were rationalized to a high degree, there would be no way for us to escape and no place to which we could flee.

While Weber analyzed many aspects of rationalization in the West, his model case was the bureaucracy. To Weber, the bureaucracy was the epitome of rationalization. The bureaucracy represented a kind of iron cage, and those who worked in a bureaucracy were locked into it. Furthermore, as more and more sectors of society were bureaucratized, the cage would grow larger, enclosing more and more people. Weber was writing in turn-of-the century Germany, where the modern bureaucracy was a relatively new and expanding phenomenon. However, in today's society, while still an important example of rationalization and still posing the dangers suggested by Weber, the bureaucracy no longer seemed to me to be the model of rationalization. From my vantage point, the fast-food restaurant had replaced it as the model....

Mcdonaldization is *"the process by which the principles of the fast-food restaurant are coming to dominate more and more sectors of American society as well as the rest of the world"* (Ritzer, 1993:1)....

The Spreading Tentacles of McDonaldization

The most obvious and perhaps least important extension of McDonaldization is the fact that fast-food restaurants have grown and expanded. The McDonald's chain, which began operation in 1955, opened its twelve thousandth branch in 1991; the leading 100 restaurant chains operate over 110,000 outlets in the United States lone (Ramirez, 1990)....

Another area of expansion consists of the locales in which one finds fast-food chains. As was mentioned above McDonald's began in suburbs and medium-sized towns. In more recent years it has moved into the big cities, even the most desirable (at least from a business point of view) areas, such as Times Square. Fast-food restaurants have also migrated into even smaller towns that people thought could not support them (L. Shapiro, 1990). They have expanded in other ways as well. Instead of being content to surround college campuses, fast-food restaurants are increasingly found *on* campus. We are even beginning to see more involvement by the chains in the food served at high schools and grade schools (Farhi, 1990).... Fast-food outlets are turning up increasingly *in* hospitals in spite of innumerable attacks on the nutritional value of the food. The latest, but undoubtedly not the last, incursion of the fast-food chains is into the nation's baseball parks and other sports venues.

Still another element of the expansion of fast-food restaurants involves the degree to which a wide array of other kinds of businesses are coming to be operated in accordance with the principles...pioneered by fast-food chains. For example, the vice chairman of one of those businesses, Toys 'R Us, said: "We want to be thought of as a sort of McDonald's of toys" (Egan, 1990:29). Other chains with a similar model and similar ambitions include Jiffy-Lube, AAMCO Transmissions, Midas Muffler, Hair Plus, H&R Block, Pearle Vision Centers, Kampgrounds of America (KOA), Kinder Care (dubbed "Kentucky Fried Children"), Nutri/System, and Jenny Craig.

The influence of McDonald's is also felt in the number of social phenomena that have come to be prefaced by "Mc." Examples include McDentists, McDoctors, McChild Care Centers, McStables (for the nationwide racehorse training operation of Wayne Lucas), and McPaper (Prichard, 1987) (for *USA Today*, whose short news articles are sometimes called "News McNuggets"). When *USA Today* began a television program modeled after the newspaper, it was immediately dubbed "News McRather" (Zoglin, 1988)....

The derivatives of McDonald's are in turn having their own influence. For example, the success of *USA Today* ("McPaper") has led to changes (for example, shorter stories, color weather maps) in many newspapers across the nation. As one *USA Today* editor put it: "The same newspaper editors who call us McPaper have been stealing our McNuggets" (Pritchard, 1987:32–33)....

The objective of the remainder of this...is to get at the full reach of the influence of McDonaldization throughout society. I will do this by breaking McDonaldization down into its key elements and then demonstrating how each element is being manifested in more and more sectors of society.

Efficiency

The first element of Mcdonaldization is *efficiency*, or the choice of the optimum means to an end. Many aspects of the fast-food restaurant illustrate efficiency (drive-though windows, for example), especially from the viewpoint of the restaurant, but none illustrates it better than the degree to which the customer is turned into an unpaid laborer. For example, customers are expected to stand in line and order their own food rather than having a waiter do it and to "bus" their own paper, plastic, and Styrofoam rather than having it done by a busperson.

Fast-food restaurants have also pioneered the movement toward handing the consumer little more than the basics of a meal. The consumer is expected to take the naked burger to the "fixin' bar" and there turn it into the desired sandwich by adding such things as lettuce, tomatoes, and onions. We all therefore are expected to log a few minutes a week as sandwich makers....In these and other ways, the fast-food restaurant has grown more efficient, often by imposing inefficiencies on the consumer....

Of course, the fast-food restaurant did not create the idea of imposing work on the consumer, getting the consumer to be in effect an unpaid employee, but it institutionalized and expedited this development. There are many other examples of this process of imposing work on the consumer. Old-time grocery stores where the grocer retrieved the needed items have been replaced by supermarkets where the shopper may put in several hours a week "working" as a grocery clerk seeking out wanted items during lengthy treks down seemingly interminable aisles. Having obtained the groceries, the shopper then unloads the food at the checkout counter and in some cases even bags the groceries. This is all efficient from the point of view of the supermarket, but it is clearly inefficient from the perspective of the shopper.

Virtually gone are gas station attendants who filled gas tanks, checked oil, and cleaned windows. At self-service stations we all now put in a few minutes a week as unpaid attendants pumping gas, checking oil, and cleaning windows. Furthermore, instead of having a readily available attendant to pay for our gasoline, we must trek into the station to pay....

Efficiency has been extended to the booming diet industry, which encompasses diet drugs, diet books, exercise videotapes, diet meals, diet drinks, weight-loss clinics and "fat farms" (Kleinfeld, 1986). Diet books promising all sorts of efficient shortcuts to weight loss are often at the top of the best-seller lists. Losing weight is normally difficult and time-consuming; this explains the lure of diet books that promise to make weight loss easier and quicker, that is, more efficient....

A fairly recent development is the growth of diet centers such as Nutri/System...Dieters at Nutri/System are provided (at substantial cost) with prepackaged freeze-dried food. All the dieter needs to do is add water when it is time for the next meal. Freeze-dried foods are efficient not only for the dieter but also for Nutri/System because they can be efficiently packaged, transported, and stored. Furthermore, the dieter's periodic visits to a Nutri/System center are efficiently organized....Counselors learn their techniques at Nutri/System University, where after a week of training (no inefficient years of matriculation here) they earn certification and an NSU diploma.

Calculability

The second dimension of McDonaldization is *calculability*. McDonaldization involves an emphasis on things that can be calculated, counted, quantified. Quantification refers to a tendency to emphasize quantity rather than quality. This leads to a sense that quality is equal to certain, usually (but not always) large quantities of things.

As in many other aspects of its operation, the emphasis on quantity at McDonald's (for example, the Big Mac) is mirrored by other fast-food restaurants. The most notable is Burger King, which stresses the quantity of the meat its hamburger called the "Whopper" and of the fish in its sandwich called the "Whaler." At Wendy's we are offered a variety of "Biggies." Similarly, 7-Eleven offers its customers a hot dog called the "Big Bite," a large soft drink called the "Big Gulp," and the even larger "Super Big Gulp." This emphasis on quantity in McDonaldized society is not restricted to fast-food restaurants. For example, United Airlines boasts that it serves more cities than does any other airline.

What is particularly interesting about this emphasis on quantity is the seeming absence of interest in communicating anything about quality. Thus, United Airlines does not tell us anything about the quality (for example, passenger comfort) of its numerous flights. The result is a growing concern about the decline or even absence of quality not only in the fast-food business but in society as a whole (Tuchman, 1980). If fast-food restaurants were interested in emphasizing quality, they might give their products names such as the

"Delicious Mac," the "Mac with Prime Beef," and the "All-Beef Frankfurter," but the fact is that typical McDonald's customers know they are *not* getting that highest-quality food.

One observer has argued that we do not go to McDonald's for a delicious, pleasurable meal but to "refuel" as rapidly as possible (Bergere, 1983:126). McDonald's is a place to which we go when we need to fill our stomachs with calories and carbohydrates so that we are able to move on to the next rationally organized activity. It is far more efficient to think of eating as refuelling rather than as a dining experience.

As with efficiency, calculability has been extended from fast-food restaurants to many other settings, including dieting. Given its nature, the diet industry is obsessed with things that can be quantified. Weight, weight loss or gain, and time periods are measured precisely. Food intake is carefully measured and monitored. Diet foods detail the number of ounces of food, the number of calories, and many other things....

Organizations such as Weight Watchers and Nutri/System are obsessed with calculability....

Predictability

Rationalization involves an increasing effort to ensure *predictability* from one time or place to another. In a rational society people want to know what to expect in all settings and at all times. They neither want nor expect surprises. They want to know that when they order a Big Mac today, it is going to be identical to the one they ate yesterday and the one they will eat tomorrow.

The movie industry is increasingly characterized by predictability. One manifestation of this is the growing reliance on sequels to successful movies rather than the production of completely new movies based on new concepts, ideas, characters. The Hitchcock classic, *Psycho*, for example, was followed by several sequels (of course, not made by Hitchcock), as have less artistically successful horror films such as *Halloween* and *Nightmare on Elm Street*. Outside the horror movies genre, a range of other movies have been succeeded by one or more sequels, including *Star Wars, The Godfather, Back to the Future,* and *Terminator*.

The routine use of sequels is a relatively new phenomenon in Hollywood. Its development parallels and is part of the McDonaldization of society. The attraction of sequels lies in their predictability. From the point of view of the studios, the same characters, actors, and basic plot lines can be used over and over. Furthermore, there seems to be a greater likelihood that sequels will be successful at the box office than is the case with completely original movies; profit levels are more predictable. Form the viewers' perspective, there is great comfort in knowing that they will once again encounter favourite characters played by familiar actors who find themselves in accustomed settings. Thus, in a series of *Vacation* movies Chevy Chase plays the same character. The only thing that varies is the vacation setting in which he practices his familiar antics. Moviegoers seem to be more willing to shell out money for a safe and familiar movie than for a movie that is completely new to them. Like a McDonald's meal, sequels are typically not of as high quality as the originals, but at least the consumers know what they are getting. In fact, it is almost always the case that the first sequel is not as good as the original movie and that each succeeding sequel is worse than its predecessor....

Much of the attraction of the shopping mall is traceable to its predictability. For example, the unpredictability of weather is eliminated: "One kid who works here told me why he likes the mall... It's because no matter what the weather is outside, it's always the same in here. He likes that. He doesn't want to know it's raining—it would depress him" (Kowinski, 1985:27). This quotation points to another predictable aspect of shopping malls: They are always upbeat and rosy. Malls, like fast-food restaurants, are also virtually the same from one place or time to another: One finds the same chains represented in malls throughout the country. Finally, those who spend their days wandering through malls are relatively free from the unpredictabilities of crime that beset them when they wander through the city streets....

I close this discussion of predictability in a McDonaldized society with the example of modern suburban housing. Many of Steven Spielberg's movies take place in these rationalized and highly predictable suburbs. Spielberg's strategy is to lure the viewer into this highly predictable world and then have a highly unpredictable event occur. For example, in *E.T.—The Extra-Terrestrial*, the extra-terrestrial wanders into a suburban development of tract houses and is discovered by a child who lives in one of those houses and who up to that point has lived a highly predictable suburban existence. The unpredictable ET eventually disrupts not only the lives of the child and his family but also that of the entire community. Similarly, *Poltergeist* takes place in a suburban household, and the evil spirits ultimately disrupt its predictable tranquillity. (The spirits first manifest themselves through that key element of a McDonaldized society: the television set.) The great success of Spielberg's movies may be traceable to our longing for some unpredictability, even if it is frightening and menacing, in our increasingly predictable lives.

Control through the Substitution of Nonhuman for Human Technology

I now combine the discussion of two elements of McDonaldization: *increased control* and *the replacement of human by nonhuman technology.* The reason for the combination is that these two elements are closely linked. Specifically, replacement of human by nonhuman technology is often oriented toward greater control. The great sources of uncertainty and unpredictability in a rationalizing system are people—either the people who work within those systems or the people who are served by them. McDonald's seeks to exert increasing control over both its employees and its customers. It is most likely to do this by steadily replacing people with nonhuman technologies. After all, technologies such as robots and computers are far easier to control than are humans (except, perhaps, for fictional computers like HAL in *2001: A Space Odyssey*). In addition to the elimination of some people and their replacement by technologies, those who continue to labor within McDonald's are better controlled by the new technologies. These nonhuman technologies also exert increasing control over the people served by the system.

As in the production and consumption of food in the fast-food restaurants, the production of some of the raw materials required by such restaurants—bread, fish, meat, and eggs—has come to be characterized by increasing control through the substitution of nonhuman for human technology. For example, in the case of the raising of animals for food, relatively small, humanized family-run farms are being rapidly replaced by "factory farms" where people and animals are controlled by nonhuman technologies (Singer, 1975)...

The replacement of human by nonhuman technology and the consequent increase in control are found not only in food production and the fast-food restaurant but also in home cooking. Technologies such as the microwave oven or the conventional oven with a temperature probe "decide" when food is done rather than leaving that judgment to the cook. Ovens, coffee makers, and other appliances now turn themselves on and off. The instructions on all kinds of packaged foods dictate precisely how the food is to be prepared and cooked. Premixed products such as Mrs. Dash combine an array of seasonings, eliminating the need for the cook to come up with creative combinations of seasonings. Even the now old-fashioned cookbook was designed to take creativity away from the cook who was inclined to flavour to taste and put it in the hands of the rigid guidelines laid down by the cookbook....

A very similar development has taken place in supermarkets. In the past, prices were marked on food products and the supermarket checker had to read the price and enter it into the cash register. As with all human activities, there was a chance for human error. To counter this problem, many supermarkets have installed optical scanners. Instead of the human checker reading the price, the mechanical scanner "reads" the code, and the price for a given code number has been entered into the computer that is the heart of the modern cash register. This nonhuman technology has eliminated some of the human uncertainty from the job of supermarket checker. It has also reduced the number and level of sophistication of tasks performed by the checker. The checker no longer needs to read the amount and enter it in the cash register. Less skilled tasks such as scanning the food and bagging it are all that is left. In other words, the supermarket checker has undergone "deskilling," a decline in the amount of skill required on the job.

The next step in this development is to have the customer do the scanning, eliminating the need for a checkout person. In fact, a nearby Safeway has instituted such a system. To make things easier, Safeway is providing its customers with a brochure entitled "Checkout for Yourself Just How Easy It Is" (of course, one might ask, "Easy for whom?"). Here are three "easy" steps as described in the brochure:

1. Pass the item's bar code over the scanner. Wait for beep. Place item on conveyor belt.
2. When you are finished scanning all items, touch END ORDER button on screen.
3. Pick up receipt at the end of the lane. Proceed to the pay station.

Such military-like orders exert great control over the customer and allow for elimination of the checkout person. Self-checkout is also part of the process, discussed above, of passing more work on to the customer. Indeed, after they are done scanning, customers must then bag their own groceries. The developer of one of these systems predicted that "within five years, self-service grocery technology could be as pervasive as the automatic cash machines used by bank customers" (E. Shapiro, 1990:D1). One customer, obviously a strong believer in McDonaldization, said of the system: "It's quick, easy and efficient...You get in and out in a hurry" (E. Shapiro, 1990:D8). The next "advance" will be a technology that permits the insertion of the customer's credit or debit card in the scanning system, avoiding the need to move on to a human cashier and pay for the food.

Supermarket scanners allow other kinds of control over customers. Before the scanner, customers could examine their purchases and see how much each one cost; they could also check to make sure that they were not being overcharged at the cash register. With the advent of the scanner, prices no longer appear on goods, only bar codes. This change has given the supermarket greater control over customers: It is almost impossible now for the consumer to keep tabs on the checkers. When the scanners were instituted at my local market, the management announced that it was issuing markers to customers who were interested in writing the price on each item. This is consistent with the trend toward getting consumers to do work historically done by others, in this case by grocery clerks who worked deep into the night to mark each item. In any case, the supermarkets did not keep the markers very long since few hurried shoppers had the desire to put in several additional minutes a day as grocery clerks....

Irrationality of Rationality

Great gains in increasing rationalization have resulted from increases in efficiency, predictability, calculability, and control through the substitution of nonhuman for human technology. The economic columnist Robert Samuelson (1989) confesses that he "openly worship[s] McDonald's" and thinks of it as "the greatest restaurant chain in history." [However, Samuelson does recognize that there are those who "can't stand the food and regard McDonald's as the embodiment of all that is vulgar in American mass culture" (1989: A25).] Let me enumerate some of the advantages of the fast-food restaurant and, more generally, of other elements of a McDonaldized society.

The fast-food restaurant has expanded the alternatives available to consumers: More people now have ready access to Italian, Mexican, Chinese, and Cajun foods; the salad bar enables people to make salads exactly the way they want them; and microwave ovens and microwavable foods allow us to have dinner in minutes or even seconds. For those with a wide range of shopping needs, supermarkets and shopping malls are very efficient sites and home shopping networks allow us to shop more efficiently without leaving home. Today's high-tech for-profit hospitals are likely to provide higher-quality medical care than did their predecessors, and we can get almost instantaneous medical attention at the local drive-in McDoctors. Computerized phone systems allow people to do things, such as getting a bank balance in the middle of the night, that were impossible before, and automated bank teller machines allow people to obtain money any time of the day or night. Package tours permit large numbers of people to

Photo by Dick Hemingway.

visit countries they would otherwise be unable to see; diet centres such as Nutri/System allow people to lose weight in a carefully regulated and controlled system; the twenty-four-second clock in professional basketball has enabled outstanding athletes such as Michael Jordan to more fully demonstrate their extraordinary talents; RVs let the modern camper avoid excessive heat, rain, and insects; and suburban tract houses have permitted large numbers of people to afford single-family homes.

Rational systems also allow us to avoid the problems created by nonrational systems in other societies. Here is a description of a recent visit to a pizzeria in Havana, Cuba:

> The pizza's not much to rave about—they scrimp on tomato sauce, and the dough is mushy...
>
> It was about 7:30 p.m., and as usual the place was standing-room-only, with people two deep jostling for a stool to come open and a waiting line spilling out onto the sidewalk...
>
> The menu is similarly Spartan...To drink, there is tap water. That's it—no toppings, no soda, no beer, no coffee, no salt, no pepper. And no special orders...
>
> A very few people are eating. Most are waiting...Fingers are drumming, flies are buzzing, the clock is ticking. The waiter wears a watch around his belt loop, but he hardly needs it; time is evidently not his chief concern. After a while, tempers begin to fray...
>
> But right now, it's 8:45 p.m. at the pizzeria, I've been waiting an hour and a quarter for two small pies...(Hockstader, 1991:A12).

Few would prefer such irrational systems to the rationalized elements of our society.

However, while there are many advantages to a McDonaldized society, there are also great costs which can be dealt with largely under the heading of *the irrationality of rationality.* In other words, it is my thesis, following Weber, that rational systems inevitably spawn a series of irrationalities that limit, ultimately compromise, and perhaps even defeat their rationality.

We can conceive of the irrationality of rationality in several ways. At the most general level, it is simply an overarching label for the negative aspects and effects of McDonaldization. More specifically, it can be seen as the opposite of rationality and its several dimensions. That is, McDonaldization can be viewed as leading to inefficiency, unpredictability, incalculability, and loss of control. Most specifically, irrationality means that rational systems are *unreasonable systems*. By that I mean that they deny the basic humanity, the human reason, of the people who work within or are served by them. In order words, rational systems are dehumanizing systems. Thus, while in other contexts rationality and reason are often used interchangeably, here they are employed to refer to antithetical phenomena.

The most obvious manifestations of the inefficiency of the fast-food restaurant are long lines of people that are often found at the counters and the long lines of cars that snake by the drive-through windows. What is purported to be an efficient way of obtaining a meal turns out to be quite inefficient....The fast-food restaurant is far from the only aspect of our McDonaldized society that operates inefficiently. Here is the way columnist Richard Cohen describes the inefficiencies of automated teller machines (ATMs) and in the process...the tendency in a rational society to utilize the consumer as an unpaid worker:

> Oh Lord, with each advance of the computer age, I was told I would benefit. But with each "benefit," I wind up doing more work. This is the ATM rule of life...I was told—nay promised—that I could avoid lines at the bank and make deposits, or withdrawals any time of the day. Now, there are lines at the ATMs, the bank seems to take a percentage of whatever I withdraw or deposit, and of course, I'm doing what tellers (remember them?) used to do. Probably, with the new phone, I'll have to climb telephone poles in the suburbs during ice storms (Cohen, 1990:5).

At least three different irrationalities are underscored in this quotation: Rational systems are not less expensive, they force us to do a range of unpaid work, and most important from the point of view of this discussion, they are often inefficient. The fact is that a rationalized system is often not the most efficient means to an end. It may be more efficient to deal with a human teller, either in the bank or at drive-through window, than to wait on line at an ATM machine, perhaps on a cold, snowy night. For many people it would be far more efficient to prepare a meal at home than to load the family in the car, drive to McDonald's, fill up on food, and then drive home again. This may not be true of some meals cooked at home form scratch, but it is certainly true of TV dinners, microwave meals, and full-course meals brought in from the supermarket. Yet many people persist in the belief, fuelled by endless propaganda from fast-food chains, that it is more efficient to eat there than to eat at home.

The main reason why I think of McDonaldization as irrational and ultimately unreasonable is that it tends to be a dehumanizing system that may become antihuman or even destructive of human beings. There are a number of ways in which the health and perhaps the lives of people have been threatened by progressive rationalization (Spencer, 1983). One example is the high caloric, fat, cholesterol, salt, and sugar content of the food served in fast-food restaurants.... It can be argued that with their appeal to children, fast-food restaurants are creating not only lifelong devotees of fast food but also people who will grow addicted to diets high in salt, sugar, and fat.

The fast-food industry has run afoul not only of nutritionists but also of environmentalists. It produces an enormous amount of trash, some of which is nonbiodegradable. Many people have been critical of the eyesores created by litter from innumerable fast-food meals strewn across the countryside. Almost two decades ago, before much of its enormous expansion, it was estimated that it took 315 square miles of forest to provide the paper needed for a year by McDonald's (Boas and Chain, 1976). That figure must be far greater today even though some paper containers have been replaced by Styrofoam and other products. Even greater criticism has been levelled at the widespread use by the fast-food industry of virtually indestructible plastics. Styrofoam debris piles up in landfills, creating mountains of waste that will remain there for years, if not forever.

McDonaldized institutions have a negative effect not only on our health and the environment but also on some of our most cherished institutions, most notably the family. For example, a key technology in the destruction of the family meal has been the microwave oven and the vast array of microwavable foods it has helped generate (Visser, 1989)... In fact, the microwave in a McDonaldizing society is seen as an advance over the fast-food restaurant. Said one consumer researcher: "It has made even fast-food restaurants not seem fast because at home you don't have to wait in line" (Wall Street Journal, 1989:B1). Consumers are demanding meals that take no more than ten minutes to microwave, whereas in the late 1970s people were willing to spend about a half hour cooking dinner and in the early 1970s were willing to spend an hour. This emphasis on speed has of course brought with it poorer taste and lower quality, but people do not seem to mind this loss: "We're just not as critical of food as we used to be" (Wall Street Journal, 1989:B1)....

Thus, we see that contrary to McDonald's propaganda and the widespread belief in it, fast-food restaurants and other McDonaldized institutions are not truly reasonable systems. They spawn all sorts of problems for the health of their customers and the well-being of the environment, tend to be dehumanizing and therefore unreasonable in various ways, and often lead to the opposite of what they are supposed to create (for example, they lead to inefficiency rather than increased efficiency). All this is not to deny the many advantages of McDonald's that were mentioned above, but it points to the fact that counterbalancing and perhaps even overwhelming problems are associated with a fast-food society. These problems, these irrationalities, need to be understood by a population which has been exposed to little more than an unrelenting set of superlatives created by McDonaldized institutions to describe themselves.

Perhaps the ultimate irrationality of McDonaldization is the possibility that we could come to lose control over the system while it could come to control us. Already, many aspects of the lives of most people are controlled by these rational systems, although it at least appears that these systems are ultimately controlled by people. However, these rational systems can spin beyond the control of even the people who occupy the highest positions within them. This is one of the senses in which we can, following Weber, talk of an "iron cage of McDonaldization." It can become a system that comes to control all of us.

There is another fear here, and that is that these interlocking rational systems can fall into the hands of a small number of leaders who will then be able to exercise control over all of society. Thus, there are authoritarian and totalitarian possibilities associated with the process of McDonaldization. We may come to be increasingly controlled by the rational systems themselves or by a few leaders who master those systems....

Ritzer, George, *Sociological Beginnings: On the Origins of Key Ideas in Sociology* (New York: McGraw-Hill, Inc. 1994), pp. 131–157. Reprinted with permission.

Questions and Topics for Discussion and Writing

1. What does Ritzer say about the pervasiveness of "McDonaldization" that would help to explain the chain's appeal, despite the rather unhealthy food being offered to customers?

2. As Ritzer points out, McDonald's restaurants in countries outside of North America tend to be located in prominent areas. How does this fit in with the larger scheme of McDonaldization?

3. Ritzer cites examples of the ways society has "McDonaldized," from self-serve salad bars to coffee-makers. Is he suggesting that every aspect of our fast-paced society is in some way a copy of the McDonald's model, or that some larger force is at work?

Work in a Fast-Food Factory

Ester Reiter

Picture yourself working in a "Post-industrial information age economy." Chances are you're seeing a futuristic-looking office filled with computers, fax machines, and other high-tech equipment rather than a high-tech restaurant, wearing a uniform and giving people their burgers, shakes and fries. In this excerpt, Ester Reiter describes the work that goes on in a Burger King.

Fast-food workers, like factory workers, use expensive pieces of machinery to perform simple repetitive tasks under close supervision in an assembly line environment. Like factory workers, they have little scope for individual innovation and find their workplace set by the machines they tend. Any deviation from the routine prescribed by head office is forbidden since it would likely reduce efficiency.

But fast-food workers face an added burden: as service workers who meet the public, they become part of the package being sold. They are on display, so they must submit to having their personal appearance, speech and demeanour monitored, moulded and, as much as possible, standardized. An irregular personality, it seems, is every bit as unacceptable to the system as an underdone french fry or burnt burger.

This paper focuses on the technology and the labour process in the fast-food industry. Using Marx's description of the transitions from craft to manufacture to large-scale industry, it considers the changes in the restaurant industry brought about by the development of fast-food chains. The description of life in a fast-food factory is based on my experience working in a Burger King outlet in 1980/1.

Founded in 1954 by James McLamore and David Edgerton, Burger King became a wholly-owned subsidiary of Pillsbury in 1967. The company grew from 257 restaurants at the time of the merger to 3,022 by May 1981. About 130,000 people are employed in Burger Kings all over the world. By November 1982, there were 87 Burger King stores in Canada, 40 of them company owned.[1]

Transforming the Operations of a Kitchen

Until approximately 25 years ago, all restaurant work involved an extensive division of labour: a complex hierarchy within the kitchen required workers with levels of skill and training. For a restaurant to be successful, all workers had to co-ordinate their efforts. A supervisor's function was not only to ensure that the work was done, but to see that the various parts of the operation were synchronized.

This production arrangement resembles what Marx called "manufacture." The skill of the worker remains central to the production process. The commodity created (the meal served to the customer) is the social product of many workers' efforts. Human beings, using tools to assist them in their work, remain the organs of the productive mechanism.

In the fast-food industry, the machines, or the instruments of labour, assume a central place. Instead of assisting workers, the machines are dominant. Marx described this as transition from "manufacture" to "large-scale industry."[2] Since the motion of the factory proceeds from the machinery and not from the worker, working personnel can continually be replaced. Frequent change in workers will not disrupt the labour process—a shift in organisation applauded by Harvard Business Review contributor, Theodore Levitt.[3] According to Levitt, this new model is intended to

Class Conflict

Karl Marx

Ester Reiter, the author of this selection, bases her analysis in part on the writings of Karl Marx. Like Max Weber, who was profiled in the previous article, Karl Marx was an influential social thinker. Marx's writings and his political followers are still highly influential today.

Karl Marx (1818-1883) was born into a middle-class family in Trier, a town in the Rhineland region of Germany— a fact that is perhaps surprising to those who, due to the nature of Marx's economic and political theories, might have imagined him to have grown up in a working-class household. Marx first attended the University of Bonn and later the University of Berlin, where he came under the influence of the so-called "Young Hegelians," a group of students and professors dedicated to furthering the work of the renowned German philosopher Georg Wilhelm Friedrich Hegel.

Marx moved to Belgium in 1845, then returned to Germany in 1848. He was expelled from Germany in 1849, and after spending a short time in France, departed for England where he would live for the rest of his life under fairly dire financial circumstances.

Regarded by many as the most influential social critic and revolutionary of all time, Marx's best known work, aside from the *Communist Manifesto* (co-written with Frederick Engels), was *Das Kapital* (*Capital*).

The entire body of Marx's writings is vast. Many terms and phrases that are commonplace today in politics and economics are attributable to Marx, such as "surplus value," "labour power," the "lumpenproletariat" and the "alienation of the working class."

Marx's basic political/economic theory held that the capitalist ruling class was doomed to failure, and its weakening would encourage the workers to take over not only the means of industrial production but the political realm as well. It was the exploitation, Marx claimed, of the labour of those who did not own the means of production by those who did that constituted the core of capitalism. Marx saw conflict between workers and capitalists as a necessary and inevitable stage in the economic history of the industrialized world.

replace the "humanistic concept of service" with the kind of technocratic thinking that in other fields has replaced "the high cost and erratic elegance of the artisan with the low-cost munificence of the manufacturer."

The labour process admired by Levitt has been adopted by many of the large fast-food companies including Burger King.

Managing a Store

The brain centre of all Burger King outlets lies in Burger King headquarters in Miami, Florida. There the Burger King bible, the *Manual of Operating Data*, is prepared. The procedures laid down in the manual must be followed to the letter by all Burger King stores. To ensure procedures are followed, each outlet is investigated and graded twice yearly by a team from regional headquarters.

In order to maximize volume and minimize labour costs, there is tremendous emphasis on what Burger King management calls speed of service. Demand is at its peak during the lunch hour, which accounts for about 20 percent of sales for the day; the more people served during the hour of twelve to one, the higher the sales volume in the store.

Ideally, service time should never exceed three minutes.[4] Labour costs are also kept down by minimizing the use of full-time workers and by hiring minimum-wage part-time workers. Workers fill out an availability sheet when they are hired, indicating the hours they can work. Particularly when students are involved, management pressures them to make themselves as available as possible, though no guarantees are provide for how many hours a week of work they will be given, or on which days they will be asked to work.

Scheduling is done each week for the coming week and workers are expected to check the schedule each week to see when they are supposed to show up. *The Manual of Operating Data* recommends as many short shifts as possible be assigned, so that few breaks will be required.

Food and paper costs make up about 40 percent of the cost of sales in Burger King outlets. These costs are essentially fixed, owing to company requirements that all Burger King outlets buy their stock from approved distributors. In effect, individual stores have control over food costs in only two areas—"waste" of food and meals provided to employees. Both together make up less than four percent of the cost of sales.

Store operations are designed from head office in Miami. By late 1981, it was possible to provide store managers not only with a staffing chart for hourly sales—indicating how many people should be on the floor given the predicted volume of business for that hour—but also where they should be positioned, based on the type of kitchen design. Thus, what discretion managers formerly had in assigning and utilizing workers has been eliminated.

Having determined precisely what workers are supposed to be doing and how quickly they should be doing it, the only remaining issue is getting them to perform to specifications. "Burger King University," located at headquarters in Miami was set up to achieve this goal. Burger King trains its staff to do things "not well, but right," the Burger King way.[5] Tight control over Burger King restaurants throughout the world rests on standardizing operations—doing things the "right" way—so that outcomes are predictable.

Working at Burger King

I did fieldwork at a Burger King outlet in suburban Toronto in 1980/1. The Burger King at which I worked was opened in 1979, and by 1981 was the highest volume store in Canada with annual sales of over one million dollars.

Workers use the back entrance at Burger King when reporting for work. Once inside, they go to a small room (about seven by twelve feet), which is almost completely occupied by an oblong table where crew members have their meals. Built-in benches stretch along both sides of the wall, with hooks above for coats. Homemade signs, put up by management, decorate the walls.

The crew room is usually a lively place. An AM/FM radio is tuned to a rock station while the teenage workers coming off or on shift talk about school and weekend activities or flirt with each other. Children and weddings are favourite topics of conversation for the older workers. Each worker must punch a time card at the start of a shift. A positioning chart, posted near the time clock, lists the crew members who are to work each meal, and indicates where in the kitchen they are to be stationed.

There are no pots and pans in the Burger King kitchen. As almost all foods enter the store ready for the final cooking process, pots and pans are not necessary. The major kitchen equipment consists of the broiler/toaster, the fry vats, the milkshake and coke machines, and the microwave ovens. In the near future, new drink machines will be installed in all Burger King outlets that will automatically portion the drinks. At Burger King, hamburgers are cooked as they pass through the broiler on a conveyor belt at a rate of 835 patties per hour. Furnished with a pair of tongs, the worker picks up the burgers as they drop off the belt, puts each on a toasted bun, and places the hamburgers and buns in a steamer.

The more interesting part of the procedure lies in applying condiments and microwaving the hamburgers. The popularity of this task among employees rests on the fact that it is unmechanized and allows some discretion to the worker. However, management is aware of this area of worker freedom and makes efforts to eliminate it by outlining exactly how this job is to be performed.

Despite such directives, the "Burger and Whopper Board" positions continue to hold their attraction for the workers, for this station requires two people to work side by side, and thus allows the opportunity for conversation. During busy times, as well, employees at this station also derive some work satisfaction from their ability to "keep up." At peak times, the challenge is to not leave the cashiers waiting for their orders.

As with the production of hamburgers, the cooking of french fries involves virtually no worker discretion. The worker, following directions laid out in the *Manual of Operating Data*, empties the frozen, pre-cut, bagged fries into fry baskets about two hours before they will be needed. When cooked fries are needed, the worker takes a fry basket from the rack and places it on a raised arm above the hot oil, and presses the "on" button. The arm holding the fry basket descends into the oil, and emerges two minutes and twenty seconds later; a buzzer goes off and the worker dumps the fries into the fry station tray where they are kept warm by an overhead light. To ensure the proper portions are placed into bags, a specially designed tool is used to scoop the fries up from the warming table.

Even at this station, though, management is concerned about limiting worker discretion. Despite the use of a specially designed scoop to control the portions each customer is given, a sign placed in the crew room for a few weeks admonished crew about being too generous with fry portions.

At the cash register, the "counter hostess" takes the order and rings it up on the computerized register. The "documentor" contains 88 colour coded items, ensuring that all variations of an order are automatically priced. As a menu item is punched in at the counter, it will appear on printers in the appropriate location in the kitchen. In this manner, the worker at sandwiches, for example, can look up at the printer and check what kind of sandwich is required. When the customer hands over the money, the cashier ring in "amount tendered" and the correct amount of change to be returned to the customer is rung up. Thus, cashiers need only remember to smile and ask customers to come again.

The computerized cash register not only simplifies ordering and payment, but is used to monitor sales and thus assist in staffing. If sales are running lower than expected, some workers will be asked to leave early. Output at each station is also monitored through the cash register. Finally, the computer at all company stores is linked through a modem to the head office in Miami. Top management has access to information on the performance of each store on a daily basis, and this information is routed back to the Canadian division headquarters in Mississauga.

Skill levels required in a Burger King have been reduced to a common denominator. The goal is to reduce all skills to a common, easily learned level and to provide for cross-training. At the completion of the ten-hour training program, each worker is able to work at a few stations. Skills for any of the stations can be learned in a matter of hours; the simplest jobs, such as filling cups with drinks, or placing the hamburgers and buns on the conveyor belt, can be learned in minutes. As a result, although labour turnover cuts into the pace of making hamburgers, adequate functioning of the restaurant is never threatened by people leaving. However, if workers are to be as replaceable as possible, they must be taught not only to perform their jobs in the same way, but also to resemble each other in attitudes, disposition, and appearance. Thus, workers are also drilled on personal hygiene, dress (shoes should be brown leather or vinyl, not suede), coiffure (hair tied up for girls and not too long for boys), and personality. Rule 17 of the handout to new employees underlines the importance of smiling: "Smile at all times, your smile is the key to our success."

While management seeks to make workers into interchangeable tools, workers themselves are expected to make a strong commitment to the store. If they wish to keep jobs at Burger King, they must abide by the labour schedule. Workers, especially teenagers, are expected to adjust their activities to the requirements of Burger King.

The Workers

One of the results of the transformation of the labour process from one of "manufacture" to that of "large-scale industry" is the emerging market importance of the young worker. While artisans require long training to achieve their skills, a machine-tender's primary characteristics are swiftness and endurance. Thus, young workers become ideal commodities: they are cheap, energetic, and plentiful. As well, they can be used as a marketing tool for the industry: the mass produced, smiling teenager, serving up the symbols of the good life in North America—hamburgers, cokes and fries.

Making up about 75 percent of the Burger King work force, the youngsters who worked after school, on weekends, and on holidays were called "part-timers." The teenager workers (about half of them boys, half girls) seemed to vary considerably in background. Some were college-bound youngsters who discussed their latest physics exam while piling on the pickles. Others were marking time until they reached age 16 and could leave school.

The daytime workers—the remaining 25 percent of the work force—were primarily married women of mixed economic backgrounds. Consistent with a recent study of part-time workers in Canada, most of these women contributed their wages to the family budget.[6] Although they were all working primarily because their families needed the money, a few expressed their relief at getting out of the house, even to come to Burger King. One woman said: "At least when I come here, I'm appreciated. If I do a good job, a manager will say something to me. Here, I feel like a person. I'm sociable and I like being amongst people. At home, I'm always cleaning up after everybody and nobody ever notices!"[7]

Common to both the teenagers and the housewives was the view that working at Burger King was peripheral to their major commitments and responsibilities; the part-time nature of the work contributed to this attitude. Workers saw the alterative available to them as putting up with the demands of Burger King or leaving; in fact, leaving seemed to be the dominant form of protest. During my period in the store, on average, eleven people out of ninety-four hourly employees quit at each two-week pay period. While a few workers had stayed at Burger King for a few years, many did not last through the first two weeks. The need for workers is constant.

Burger King's ability to cope with high staff turnover means virtually no concessions are offered to workers to entice them to remain at Burger King. In fact, more attention is paid to the maintenance of the machinery than to "maintaining" the workers; time is regularly scheduled for cleaning and servicing the equipment, but workers may not leave the kitchen to take a drink or use the bathroom during the lunch and dinner rushes.

The dominant form—in the circumstances, the only easily accessible form—of opposition to the Burger King labour process is, then, the act of quitting. Management attempts to head off any other form of protest by insisting on an appropriate "attitude' on the part of the workers. Crew members must constantly demonstrate their satisfaction with working at Burger King by smiling at all times. However, as one worker remarked, "Why should I smile? There's nothing funny around here. I do my job and that should be good enough for them." It was not, however, and this worker soon quit. Another woman who had worked in the store for over a year also left. A crew member informed me that she had been fired for having a "poor attitude."

Management control and lack of worker opposition is further explained by the fact that other jobs open to teenagers are no better, and in some cases are worse, than the jobs at Burger King. The workers all agreed that any job that paid the full rather than the student minimum wage would be preferable to a job at Burger King; but they also recognized that their real alternatives would often be worse. Work at a donut shop, for example, also paid student minimum wage, under conditions of greater social isolation; baby sitting was paid poorly; and the hours for a paper route were terrible. Work at Burger King was a first job for many of the teenagers, and they enjoyed their first experience of earning their own money. And at Burger King, these young men and women were in the position of meeting the public, even if the forms of contact were limited by a vocabulary developed in Burger King headquarters: "Hello.

Welcome to Burger King. May I take your order?" Interaction with customers had some intrinsic interest.

In sum, workers at Burger King are confronted with a labour process that puts management in complete control. Furnished with state-of-the-art restaurant technology, Burger King outlets employ vast numbers of teenagers and married women—a population with few skills and little commitment to working at Burger King. In fact, this lack of commitment is understood through reference to a labour process that offers little room for work satisfaction. Most jobs can be learned in a very short time (a matter of minutes for some) and workers are required to learn every job, a fact that underlines the interchangeable nature of the jobs and the workers who do them. The work is most interesting when the store is busy. Paradoxically, work intensity, Burger King's main form of assault on labour costs, remains the only aspect of the job that can provide any challenge for the worker. Workers would remark with pride how they "didn't fall behind at all," despite a busy lunch or dinner hour.

It would be reassuring to dismiss the fast-food industry as an anomaly in the workplace; teenagers will eventually finish school and become "real workers," while housewives with families are actually domestic workers, also not to be compared with adult males in more skilled jobs. Unfortunately, there are indications that the teenagers and women who work in this type of job represent an increasingly typical kind of worker, in the one area of the economy that continues to grow—the service sector. The fast-food industry represents a model for other industries in which the introduction of technology will permit the employment of low-skilled, cheap, and plentiful workers. In this sense, it is easy to be pessimistic and agree with Andre Gorz's depressing formulation of the idea of work:

> The terms "work" and "job" have become interchangeable: work is no longer something that one does but something that one has. Workers no longer "produce" society through the mediation of the relations of production; instead, the machinery of social production as a whole produces "work" and imposes it in a random way upon random, interchangeable individuals.[8]

The Burger King system represents a major triumph for capital. However the reduction of the worker to a simple component of capital requires more than introduction of a technology; workers' autonomous culture must be eliminated as well, including the relationships among workers, their skills, and their loyalties to one another. The smiling, willing, homogeneous worker must be produced and placed on the Burger King assembly line.

While working at Burger King, I saw the extent to which Burger King has succeeded in reducing its work force to a set of interchangeable pieces. However, I also, saw how insistently the liveliness and decency of the workers emerged in the informal interaction that occurred. Open resistance is made virtually impossible by the difficulty of identifying who is responsible for' the rules that govern the workplace: the workers know that managers follow orders from higher up. The very high turnover of employees indicates workers understand that their interests and Burger King's are not the same. As young people and women realize that their jobs in the fast-food industry are not waystations en route to more fulfilling work, they will perhaps blow the whistle on the Burger King "team." The mould for the creation of the homogeneous worker assembling the standardized meal for the homogeneous consumer is not quite perfected.

SOURCE: Reiter, Ester (1986). "Life in a Fast-Food Factory," pp. 309–326 in Craig Heron and Robert Storey (eds.), *On the Job: Confronting the Labour Process in Canada*. Kingston and Montréal: McGill-Queen's University Press. Reprinted with permission.

Endnotes

1. Promotional material from Burger King Canada head office in Mississauga, Ontario.
2. Karl Marx, *Capital*, vol.1 ([1867]; New York 1977), ch. xv.
3. Theodore Levitt, "Production Line Approach to Service," *Harvard Business Review* 50, no.1, (Sept.-Oct. 1972): 51–2.
4. A "Shape Up" campaign instituted at the beginning of 1982 attempted to set a new goal of a 2 1/2-minute service time.
5. Personal communication, Burger King "professor," 4 January 1982.
6. Labour Canada, *Commission of Inquiry into Part-Time Work* (Ottawa 1983) [Wallace commission].
7. Personal communication, Burger King worker, 8 August 1981.
8. Andre Gorz, *Farewell to the Working Class* (Boston 1982), 7l.

Body Ritual Among the Nacirema

Horace Miner

In this article Miner takes a satirical look at the "Nacirema," a people whose culture is riddled with magic, and whose everyday lives are based in superstition and the supernatural. Miner subtly sensitizes the reader to his or her own ethnocentricity, and presses the reader to recognize that the primitive and the magical are less a matter of specific practices than the assumptions that we draw upon to interpret those practices.

The anthropologist has become so familiar with the diversity of ways in which different peoples behave in similar situations that he is not apt to be surprised by even the most exotic customs. In fact, if all of the logically possible combinations of behaviour have not been found somewhere in the world, he is apt to suspect that they must be present in some yet undescribed tribe. This point has, in fact, been expressed with respect to clan organization by [George] Murdock. In this light, the magical beliefs and practices of the Nacirema present such unusual aspects that it seems desirable to describe them as an example of the extremes to which human behaviour can go.

Professor [Ralph] Linton first brought the ritual of the Nacirema to the attention of anthropologists twenty years ago, but the culture of this people is still very poorly understood. They are a North American group living in the territory between the Canadian Cree, the Yaqui and Tarahumare of Mexico, and the Carib and Arawak of the Antilles. Little is known of their origin, although tradition states that they came from the east. According to Nacirema mythology, their nation was originated by a culture hero, Notgnihsaw, who is otherwise known for two great feats of strength—the throwing of a piece of wampum across the river Pa-To-Mac and the chopping down of a cherry tree in which the spirit of Truth reside.

Nacirema culture is characterized by a highly developed market economy which has evolved in a rich natural habitat. While much of the people's time is devoted to economic pursuits, a large part of the fruits of these labours and a considerable portion of the day are spent in ritual activity. The focus of this activity is the human body, the appearance and health of which loom as a dominant concern in the ethos of the people. While such a concern is certainly not unusual, its ceremonial aspects and associated philosophy are unique.

The fundamental belief underlying the whole system appears to be that the human body is ugly and that its natural tendency is to debility and disease. Incarcerated in such a body, man's only hope is to avert these characteristics through the use of the powerful influences of ritual and ceremony. Every household has one or more shrines devoted to this purpose. The more powerful individuals in the society have several shrines in their houses and, in fact, the opulence of the house is often referred to in terms of the number of such ritual centres it possesses. Most houses are of wattle and daub construction, but the shrine rooms of the more wealthy are walled with stone. Poorer families imitate the rich by applying pottery plaques to their shrine walls.

While each family has at least one such shrine, the rituals associated with it are not family ceremonies but are private and secret. The rites are normally only discussed with children, and then only during the period when they are being initiated into these mysteries. I was able, however, to establish sufficient rapport with the natives to examine these shrines and to have the rituals described to me.

The focal point of the shrine is a box or chest which is built into the wall. In this chest are kept the many charms and magical potions without which no native believes he could live. These preparations are secured from a variety of specialized practitioners. The most powerful of these are the medicine men, whose assistance must be rewarded with substantial gifts. However, the medicine men do not provide the curative potions for their clients, but decide what the ingredients should be and then write them down in an ancient and secret language. This writing is understood only by the medicine men and by the herbalists who, for another gift, provide the required charm.

The charm is not disposed of after it has served its purpose, but is placed in the charm-box of the household shrine. As these magical materials are specific for certain ills, and the real or imagined maladies of the people are many, the charm-box is usually full to overflowing. The magical packets are so numerous that people forget what their purposes were and fear to use them again. While the natives are very vague on this point, we can only assume that the idea in retaining all the old magical materials is that their presence in the charm-box, before which the body rituals are conducted, will in some way protect the worshipper.

Beneath the charm-box is a small font. Each day every member of the family, in succession, enters the shrine room, bows his head before the charm-box, mingle different sorts of holy water in the font, and proceeds with a brief rite of ablution. The holy waters are secured from the Water Temple of the community, where the priests conduct elaborate ceremonies to make the liquid ritually pure.

In the hierarchy of magical practitioners, and below the medicine men in prestige, are specialists whose designation is best translated "holy-mouth-men." The Nacirema have an almost pathological horror of and fascination with the mouth, the condition of which is believed to have a supernatural influence on all social relationships. Were it not for the rituals of the mouth, they believe that their teeth would fall out, their gums bleed, their jaws shrink, their friends desert them, and their lovers reject them. They also believe that a strong relationship exists between oral and moral characteristics. For example, there is a ritual ablution of the mouth for children which is supposed to improve their moral fibre.

The daily body ritual performed by everyone includes a mouth-rite. Despite the fact that these people are so punctilious about care of the mouth, this rite involves a practice which strikes the uninitiated stranger as revolting. It was reported to me that the ritual consists of inserting a small bundle of hog hairs into the mouth, along with certain magical powders, and them moving the bundle in a highly formalized series of gestures.

In addition to the private mouth-rite, the people seek out a holy-mouth-man once or twice a year. These practitioners have an impressive set of paraphernalia, consisting of a variety of augers, awls, probes, and prods. The use of these objects in the exorcism of the evils of the mouth involves almost unbelievable ritual torture of the client. The holy-mouth-man opens the client's mouth and, using the above mentioned tools, enlarges any holes which decay may have created in the teeth. Magical materials are put into these holes. If there are no naturally occurring holes in the teeth, large sections of one or more teeth are gouged out so that the supernatural substance can be applied. In the client's view, the purpose of these ministrations is to arrest decay and to draw new friends. The extremely sacred and traditional character of the rite is evident in the fact that the natives return to the holy-mouth-men year after year, despite the fact that their teeth continue to decay.

It is to be hoped that, when a thorough study of the Nacirema is made, there will be careful inquiry into the personality structure of these people. One has but to watch the gleam in the eye of a holy-mouth-man, as he jabs an awl into an exposed nerve, to suspect that a certain amount of sadism is involved. If this can be established, a very interesting pattern emerges, for most of the population shows definite masochistic tendencies. It was to these that professor Linton referred in discussing a distinctive part of the daily body ritual which is performed only by men. This part of the rite involves scraping and lacerating the surface of the face with a sharp instrument. Special women's rites are performed only four times during each lunar month, but what they lack in frequency is made up in barbarity. As part of this ceremony, women bake their heads in small ovens for about an hour. The theoretically interesting point is that what seems to be a preponderantly masochistic people have developed sadistic specialties.

The medicine men have imposing temple, or *latipso*, in every community of any size. The more elaborate ceremonies required to treat very sick patients can only be performed at this temple. These ceremonies involve not only the thaumaturge but a permanent group of vestal maidens who move sedately about the temple chambers in distinctive costume and headdress.

The *latipso* ceremonies are so harsh that it is phenomenal that a fair proportion of the really sick natives who enter the temple ever recover. Small children whose indoctrination is still incomplete have been known to resist attempts to take them to the temple because "that is where you go to die." Despite this fact, sick adults are not only willing but eager to undergo the protracted ritual purification, if they can afford to do so. No matter how ill the supplicant or how grave the emergency, the guardians of many temples will not admit a client if he cannot give a rich gift the custodian. Even after one has gained admission and survived the ceremonies, the guardians will not permit the neophyte to leave until he makes another gift.

The supplicant entering the temple is first stripped of all his or her clothes. In every-day life the Nacirema avoids exposure of his body and its natural functions. Bathing and excretory acts are performed only in the secrecy of the household shrine, where they are ritualized as part of the body-rites. Psychological shock results form the fact that the body secrecy is suddenly lost upon entry into the *latipso*. A man, whose own wife has never seen him in an excretory act, suddenly finds himself naked and assisted by a vestal maiden while he performs his natural functions into a sacred vessel. This sort of ceremonial treatment is necessitated by the fact that the excreta are used by a diviner to ascertain the course and nature of the client's sickness. Female clients, on the other

Anthropology Today

In his piece on *The Body Ritual of the Nacirema*, Horace Miner takes a satirical look at our society and anthropology, the science that studies the development, customs and origins of the human race.

Anthropology is broadly divided into two main groups. *Cultural anthropology* looks at people's society, beliefs, rituals and practices, while *physical anthropology* examines anatomical and physiological development. So an article like Miner's would be an example of cultural anthropology at work, while an archaeological expedition that uncovers information about the shape of the human skull in the Stone Age would contribute to the field of physical anthropology.

Cultural anthropologists often engage in field research travelling to live among distant and so-called "primitive" people in order to study their culture. They try to compare these societies to cultures elsewhere in order to learn something about how societies originate and how they develop.

One of anthropology's fascinations is that it uses methods derived from psychology, physiology, mythology, history and sociology and combines them to study cultures. Sigmund Freud (1856–1939), although noted as the "father of psychoanalysis" for his studies of the unconscious mind, also devoted considerable effort to anthropological questions. He believed, for example, that in early human cultures, the murder of older males (fathers) was replaced by the sacrificial eating of symbolic animals; this led to the development of the so-called "Oedipal" complex in modern-day males. Anthropologists and psychologists alike took (and still take) exception to many of Freud's theories, but his combination of the two disciplines illustrates the way anthropological research is informed by other disciplines.

Polish anthropologist Bronislaw Malinowski (1884–1942) is cited by Horace Miner as a pioneer of intensive, thorough field research.

hand, find their naked bodies are subjected to the scrutiny, manipulation and prodding of the medicine men.

Few supplicants in the temple are well enough to do anything but lie on their hard beds. The daily ceremonies, like the rites of the holy-mouth-men, involve discomfort and torture. With ritual precision, the vestals awaken their miserable charges each dawn and roll them about on their beds of pain while performing ablutions, in the formal movements of which the maidens are highly trained. At other times they insert magic wands in the supplicant's mouth or force him to eat substances which are supposed to be healing. From time to time the medicine men come to their clients and jab magically treated needles into their flesh. The fact that these temple ceremonies may not cure, and may even kill the neophyte, in no way decreases the people's faith in the medicine men.

There remains one other kind of practitioner, known as a "listener." This witch-doctor has the power to exorcise devils that lodge in the heads of people who have been bewitched. The Nacirema believe that parents bewitch their own children. Mothers are particularly suspected of putting a curse on children while teaching them the secret body rituals. The counter-magic of the witch-doctor is unusual in its lack of ritual. The patient simply tells the "listener" all his troubles and fears, beginning with the earliest difficulties he can remember. The memory displayed by the Nacirema in these exorcism sessions is truly remarkable. It is not uncommon for the patient to bemoan the rejection he felt upon being weaned as a babe, and a few individuals even see their troubles as going back to the traumatic effects of their own birth.

In conclusion, mention must be made of certain practices which have their base in native aesthetics but which depend upon the pervasive aversion to the natural body and its functions. There are ritual fasts to make fat people thin and ceremonial feasts to make thin people fat. Still other rites are used to make women's breasts larger if they are small, and smaller if they are large. General dissatisfaction with breast shape is symbolized in the fact that the ideal form is virtually outside the range of human variation. A few women afflicted with almost inhuman hypermammary development are so idolized that they make a handsome living simply going form village to village and permitting the natives to stare at them for a fee.

Reference has already been made to the fact that excretory functions are ritualized, routinized, and relegated to secrecy. Natural reproductive functions are similarly distorted. Intercourse is a taboo as a topic and scheduled as an act. Efforts are made to avoid pregnancy by the use of magical materials or by limiting intercourse to certain phases of the moon. Conception is actually very infrequent. When pregnant, women dress so as to hide their condition. Parturition takes place in secret, without friends or relatives to assist, and the majority of women do not nurse their infants.

Our review of the ritual life of the Nacirema has certainly shown them to be a magic-ridden people. It is hard to understand how they have managed to exist so long under the burdens which they have imposed upon themselves. But even such exotic customs as these take on real meaning when they are viewed with the insight provided by [Bronislaw] Malinowski when he wrote:

> Looking from far and above, from our high places of safety in the developed civilization, it is easy to see all the crudity and irrelevance of magic. But without its power and guidance early man could not have mastered his practical difficulties as he has done, nor could man have advanced to the higher stages of civilization.

SOURCE: Harold Miner, "Body Ritual Among the Nacirema." *American Anthropologist* 58(3), 1956. Reprinted with permission of *American Anthropologist* and Agnes Miner.

Questions and Topics for Discussion and Writing

1. What is the first clue author Horace Miner provides that indicates that the "Nacirema" are actually the subject of a satirical article? What is the main danger of using satire as a means of social criticism?

2. What techniques does Miner use to make this piece seem like a legitimate scholarly article? Is he successful in deceiving the reader to a certain extent?

PART 4

The Arts and Humanities

The Luncheon of the Boating Party, 1881, by Pierre Auguste Renoir (oil on canvas; 129.5 x 172.7 cm.).
Renoir (1841-1919) was a French impressionist painter who is recognized by critics as one of the greatest and most independent painters of his period.

Courtesy of The Phillips Collection, Washington, D.C.

Introduction to the Arts and Humanities

James Rudnick

The study of art is not a science. That is, to enjoy art you must come up with a subjective personal criticism of a given work based on your own interpretation of what you read, see or hear. The formal rules of scientific experimentation do not apply. More often than not, art summons emotions. It can disturb us, enlighten us and even threaten us as we seek to understand the intended message of the artist. But since we all initially percieve works of art as individuals, what one person sees in a painting might or might not be seen by others. The mere fact that you can or can't see things the same way others do is of no matter in the arts—it's the viewer who matters most, for art is subjective by its very nature. Hence, what one sees as a call to arms another might condemn as utter nonsense. Because of the vast potential of art to inspire people in so many different ways, we can say that "art is as art does."

The perception of art and one's reflection upon it often opens up a door to fundamental truths. There is a sense of disclosure made by the artist, no matter what form his or her work takes, that speaks to us all. If one accepts the premise that there are two poles of life—the individual and his or her polar opposite, society—then the following might also be true.

As an individual begins to relate to himself or herself through art, there occurs a deepening personal enrichment that goes beyond the bounds of simple perception. This in turn often leads to a personal quest for meaning as an introspective, reflective and individual act.

On the larger social scale, art helps us to understand the universality of human nature, to discover the building blocks of the civilization within which we all live. Although a popular painting might not mirror everybody's own experiences *exactly*, its appeal rests upon the fact that the artist or writer has, through the chosen medium, managed to capture certain emotions or truths with which a broad range of people can readily identify. Take, for example Joanna Wos's piece in this section, *The One Sitting There*. The actual circumstances of the story do not matter as much as the sense of identification that almost everyone has with the themes of love and loss the story embodies.

This section on the Arts and Humanities focuses on a broad foundation of both the expressive and reflective arts for the reader to ponder. From the monochromatic reproductions of fine art and sculpture, to literature, poetry, essays and more, a broad range of artistic forms and points of view is represented. What we have included are works from well-known scholars, sculptors, philosophers, professors, painters, poets, critics, curators and novelists. Art can open inner doors of discovery and wonder unlike anything else. It is hoped that this section will begin to do so for the curious reader.

Portrait of the Arts

Morton Ritts

What is the place of art in our daily lives? How does an artistic work differ from a scientific work or routine everyday work in general? In this short but insightful essay, author Morton Ritts explores the relevance of art and concludes that the artist has a special place in our world: he or she helps to redraw and enlarge the boundaries of our emotional and intellectual experience.

In this unit we examine the role of the arts. Sometimes it's harder to say what art is than what it isn't. Art, for example, isn't science. As we saw in an earlier unit, science is factual and propositional. It tries to provide knowledge that is objective and clear, with verifiable observations based on a rigorous method of enquiry.

Art, on the other hand, tends to be ambiguous and problematic. It is both factual and fictional. Indeed, on one level, narrative arts like literature and film proclaim themselves to be not "true" at all, to be "made-up." How can something that's made up be true? And yet, we know from our own experience that when we read certain novels or see certain films we're struck by just how "true to life" they are.

There is a profound paradox here. Characters in novels and films who are invented, who are fictions, often reveal more about human nature than real people. Fiction, in other words, has the capacity to provide us with greater insight to truth than truth. But fiction is just another kind of truth. All art is.

Of course, psychology and biology also provide us with truth. But their focus is always general, while art portrays the particular. For example, as a psychological theory, Sigmund Freud's "oedipal complex" is universal and abstract. But in his novel *Sons and Lovers*, D.H. Lawrence gives this theory specific, concrete form by creating a rich and complex character whose intense, troubled relationship with his mother dominates his life.

For another example compare the description of anxiety and fear in a psychology textbook with how these same emotions are depicted in a novel or film. The textbook account is analytical, factual. This is fine, but such an account doesn't convey to us what anxiety and fear "feel" like. A well-written novel or well-made film does, however, by locating these emotions in actions that compel our interest. This difference between fact and fiction is the difference between science and the arts. Science and the social sciences "tell" whereas the arts "show."

We've said that the arts "show" by giving us knowledge of the particular. As the *Sons and Lovers* example suggests, we come to know an important universal relationship (mothers and sons) in the depiction of a specific relationship.

The arts "show" by way of creativity, discipline, expressiveness. They give form to our experience. Sometimes the result is indirect, as in expressionist painting. Sometimes it's brutally direct, as in *The Killing Fields*, a powerful film about the genocide that occurred in Cambodia in the 1970s. Different as they are, both examples represent some important aspect of truth.

Art and society

One thing we can say for certain is that artists work in a social context. On the walls of the vast cathedral-like caves at Lascaux in southwestern France, our paleolithic ancestors painted picture-stories of their communal hunts. These extraordinary images bind us to our own prehistoric beginnings some 20,000 years ago. At the same time, they're a good example of one of the underlying impulses behind art—the impulse to leave our mark, to say we were here...

Is there a difference between work and art? Yes and no. No doubt, what a good painter or a writer produces is always the result of hard work. But if all art is work, the opposite—that all work is art—is not true. This is because most of us work to please someone else, while most artists work primarily to please themselves. In this sense, the more a job allows you to please yourself the closer you are to being an artist.

Most of us don't have this luxury. If we work in a factory, in an office or retail store, or in a school, our individual needs count for less than those of the company or our clients. Certainly we can find fulfilment in our work, but never at the expense of the group. While enlightened employers try to create the conditions for a balance between our individual interests and those of the company, this isn't often possible.

So in this way art is different from work. Unlike work, art, in western culture at least, stresses the primacy of the individual. In this tradition, even performing artists, like musicians, actors and dancers have a healthy regard for their own uniqueness. They may be part of a team, but some will always insist on shining more brightly than others—on being "stars."

Throughout history, societies have often objected to the idea of artists as individuals, arguing that their first loyalty is not to themselves but to the state. This was the case in the former Soviet Union, and is still the case in China. Even in democracies like Canada and the U.S., books, magazines, paintings, photographs and films are censored because they are deemed in some way a threat to society for reasons of obscenity, libel or blasphemy.

The Greek philosopher Plato would have heartily endorsed such censorship. For him, art was at best a distraction, at worst a danger. He believed it was difficult enough to know reality. Art only made it harder—instead of showing things as they were, it offered distorted representations of those things. Drama, poetry, painting gave us a kind of secret second-hand version of life, he argued. They served no constructive purpose.

According to Plato, only the study of science, philosophy or history enlightened us because these disciplines appealed to the mind, to our rational selves. Drama, poetry, music, the visual arts appealed to our senses, our irrational and emotional selves. In doing so, they not only distorted reality, they threatened the security and well-being of the state because they tended to mislead, confuse and excite people.

The need to imagine

Just as art differs from philosophy, science and history, writers, actors, dancers and other artists differ from philosophers, scientists and historians. Like them, artists attempt to impose their own sense of order on the random flow of life around them. But as we've already seen, their method is different—artists work with their senses, with feeling and intuition, with metaphor and imagination.

In his play, *A Midsummer Night's Dream*, William Shakespeare compared artists (poets) to lovers and lunatics. What connects them, he suggests, is precisely this power of the imagination:

And, as imagination bodies forth,
The form of things unknown, the poet's pen
Turns them to shapes, and gives to airy nothing
A local habitation and a name.

The artist, then, is someone whose imagination makes the unknown known, the invisible visible and the unconscious conscious—which is very close to the therapeutic process of Freudian psychoanalysis. Art itself is a way of exploring the mysteries of the human condition, not in the linear fashion of scientific enquiry but in the associative, circular manner of therapy. "We shed our sicknesses in books," D.H. Lawrence wrote. Art, he meant, heals.

That's perhaps one reason why people feel the need to write, paint, play an instrument or sing. Another reason, we've suggested, is the desire to leave some sign, some evidence of our existence. As children we seek even the most trivial kind of immortality, nothing more sometimes than carving

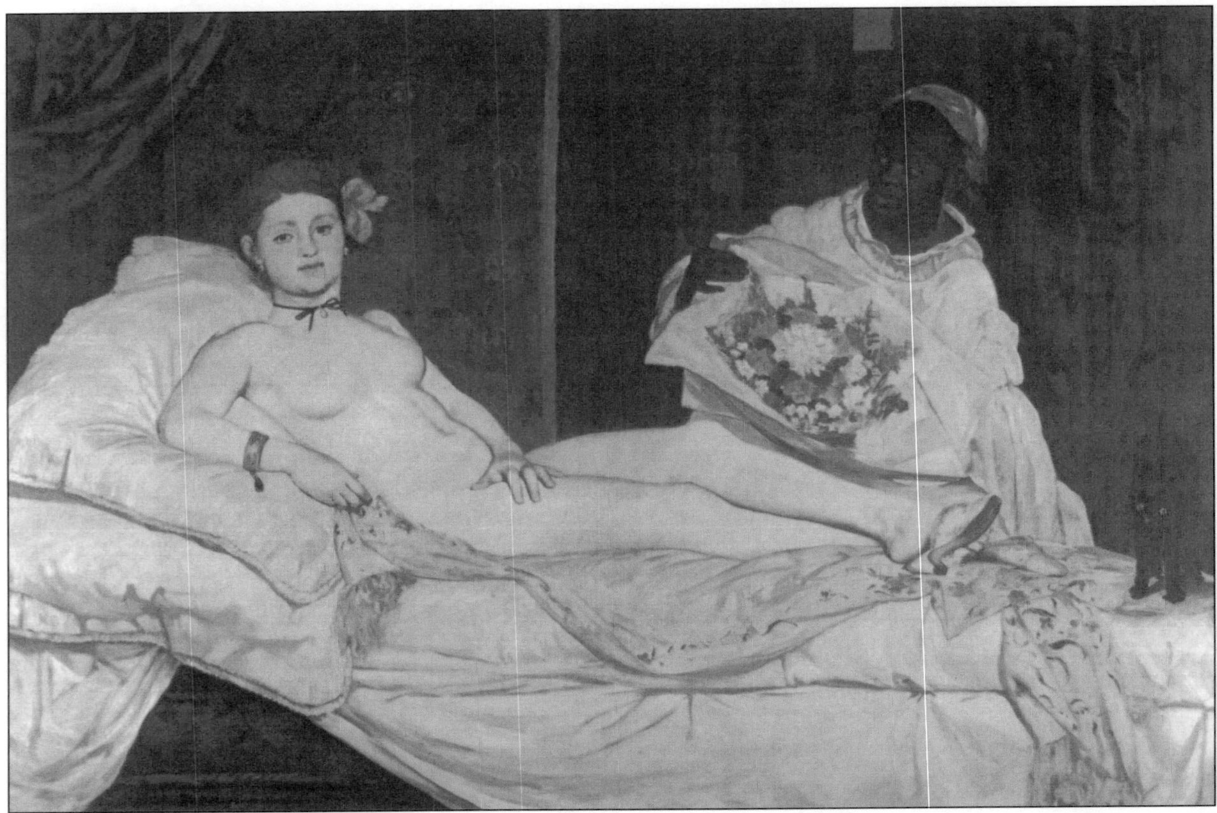

Olympia, 1863, by Edouard Manet.

Manet (1832-1883) was a French painter whose work inspired the impressionist style although he himself refused to so label his own work.

Courtesy of Musée d'Orsay, Paris.

our initials into the trunk of a tree or printing our name in the fresh concrete of a sidewalk.

The humanistic psychologist Abraham Maslow offers still another way of looking at the desire to create. We may recall that in his hierarchy of needs, Maslow speculates that physical survival is basic. Someone who lacks the requirements for physiological well being, including food and shelter, isn't much interested in writing novels or painting landscapes.

But once these basic needs are satisfied, we often ask ourselves, "What more is there to life?" What's more, Maslow says, are the higher level needs for love, esteem and, above all, self-actualization. More than most people, artists are obsessed by the need to self-actualize, to be the best they can at whatever they are. A tale about two modern painters, Amadeo Modigliani and Chaim Soutine, illustrates this point.

Modigliani and Soutine were friends who shared a studio in a small garret in Paris at the turn of the century. They were almost stereotypes of the starving artist, deprived of material comforts but endowed with rich and productive imaginations.

One day, the story goes, they bought a chicken at the local butcher shop, as the subject for a "still life." They hung it from the rafters in their studio and set up their easels. In the midst of their preparation, however, it occurred to them that they hadn't had a decent meal in weeks. They'd spent their last francs on a chicken, but incredibly—foolishly, it seemed at that moment—they were intending to paint it, not eat it.

Maslow might explain their dilemma this way: If the two friends cooked the chicken, they'd satisfy their basic survival needs but not their need for art. On the other hand, if they painted the chicken, they'd satisfy their need for self-actualization, but might starve to death in the process. What to do? In fact, they arrived at one of those inspired compromises that are the mark of true genius—they painted very quickly (while the chicken was still fresh).

The story is a good example of the struggle between the demands of life and those of art. Someone once asked the great artist Picasso whether, if his house caught fire, he'd rescue his cat first or his paintings. He answered his cat. Picasso's point was that artists draw their inspiration from life. Without life there can be no art.

Art redraws the boundaries of our lives

As much as artists deal with the world of imagination and subjective perception, their messages of pain or celebration correspond in some way to life outside them, to the common experiences of humanity. When we see a film or hear a song that absorbs us, we feel this connection too. The artist redraws and enlarges the boundaries of our emotional and intellectual landscape.

At their best, the books and films and music that mean most to us tell us stories in provocative new ways. Since the beginning, the human species has always felt compelled to tell stories. There are the hunting pictures in the caves at Lascaux. There was remarkable poetry, music and painting in the Nazi concentration camps. Plato was right to suggest that art is dangerous, but perhaps that's exactly what art should be—something that pricks the bubble of illusion, that exposes pain and injustice, that challenges us to think about old things in new ways.

Art is often most dangerous when it creates an experience for us that defies what is considered politically and morally "correct." That's why one of the first acts of dictatorial regimes is to imprison a country's writers. Or why police shut down exhibitions of "offensive" paintings and photographs. Or why some governments issue death threats against artists who have allegedly committed crimes against the state.

Yet those who want to create art, and not propaganda, will always affirm their right to see with their own eyes, to speak in their own voice. Their messages may indeed be subversive. But we soon forget books or paintings or music or films or plays that merely entertain us. We remember instead those that have astonished or disturbed, moved or changed us. They're part of who we are.

SOURCE: Morton Ritts, "Portrait of the Arts" in *Humanities: Self Society and Culture*, edited by W.R. Hanna and C. Cockerton (Toronto: Thompson Educational Publishing, Inc., 1993). Reprinted by permission.

Questions and Topics for Discussion and Writing

1. What does the author mean when he says "the more a job allows you to please yourself the closer you are to being an artist"?
2. The author argues that the tools the artist uses are different from those used by philosophers, scientists and historians. What are the main tools of the artist?
3. In this article, the author refers to the work of psychologist Abraham Maslow. What were the different levels of human needs Maslow distinguished and where does art fit in Maslow's hierarchy of needs?

The Dimensions of a Complete Life

Martin Luther King, Jr.

Martin Luther King, Jr. (1929-1968) was one of the leaders of the American civil rights movement. He was a proponent of the philosophy of non-violent resistance, leading and organizing such protests during this turbulent period in U.S. history. In this piece, King outlines his views on how spirituality should be combined with humility and social awareness to comprise a complete life.

Many, many centuries ago, out on a lonely, obscure island called Patmos, a man by the name of John caught a vision of the new Jerusalem descending out of heaven from God. One of the greatest glories of this new city of God that John saw was its completeness. It was not partial and one-sided, but it was complete in all three of its dimensions. And so, in describing the city in the twenty-first chapter of the book of Revelation, John says this: "The length and the breadth and the height of it are equal." In other words, this new city of God, this city of ideal humanity, is not an unbalanced entity but it is complete on all sides.

Now John is saying something quite significant here. For so many of us the book of Revelation is a very difficult book, puzzling to decode. We look upon it as something of a great enigma wrapped in mystery. And certainly if we accept the book of Revelation as a record of actual historical occurrences it is a difficult book, shrouded with impenetrable mysteries. But if we will look beneath the peculiar jargon of its author and the prevailing apocalyptic symbolism, we will find in this book many eternal truths which continue to challenge us. One such truth is that of this text. What John is really saying is this: that life as it should be and life at its best is the life that is complete on all sides.

There are three dimensions of any complete life to which we can fitly give the words of this text: length, breadth, and height. The length of life as we shall think of it here is not its duration or its longevity, but it is the push of a life forward to achieve its personal ends and ambitions. It is the inward concern for one's own welfare. The breadth of life is the outward concern for the welfare of others. The height of life is the upward reach for God.

These are the three dimensions of life, and without the three being correlated, working harmoniously together, life is incomplete. Life is something of a great triangle. At one angle stands the individual person, at the other angle stand other persons, and at the top stands the Supreme, Infinite Person, God. These three must meet in every individual life if that life is to be complete.

Now let us notice first the length of life. I have said that this is the dimension of life in which the individual is concerned with developing his inner powers. It is that dimension of life in which the individual pursues personal ends and ambitions. This is perhaps the selfish dimension of life, and there is such a thing as moral and rational self-interest. If one is not concerned about himself he cannot be totally concerned about other selves.

Some years ago a learned rabbi, the late Joshua Liebman, wrote a book entitled *Peace of Mind*. He has a chapter in the book entitled "Love Thyself Properly." In this chapter he says in substance that it is impossible to love other selves adequately unless you love your own self properly. Many people have been plunged into the abyss of emotional fatalism because they did not love themselves properly. So every individual has a responsibility to be concerned about himself enough to discover what he is made for. After he discovers his calling he should set out to do it with all of the strength and power in his being. He should do it as if God Almighty called him at this particular moment in history to do it. He should seek to do his job so well that the living, the dead, or the unborn could not do it better. No matter how small one thinks his life's work is in terms of the norms of the world and the so-called big jobs, he must realize that it has cosmic significance if he is serving humanity and doing the will of God.

To carry this to one extreme, if it falls your lot to be a streetsweeper, sweep streets as Raphael painted pictures, sweep streets as Michelangelo carved marble, sweep streets as Beethoven composed music, sweep streets as Shakespeare wrote poetry. Sweep streets so well that all the hosts of heaven and earth will have to pause and say, "Here lived a great street-sweeper who swept his job well." In the words of Douglas Mallock:

> If you can't be a highway, just be a trail;
> If you can't be the sun, be a star,
> For it isn't by size that you win or you fail—
> Be the best of whatever you are.

When you do this, you have mastered the first dimension of life—the length of life.

But don't stop here; it is dangerous to stop here. There are some people who never get beyond this first dimension. They are brilliant people; often they do an excellent job in developing their inner powers; but they live as if nobody else lived in the world but themselves. There is nothing more tragic than to find an individual bogged down in the length of life, devoid of the breadth.

The breadth of life is that dimension of life in which we are concerned about others. An individual has not started living until he can rise above the narrow confines of his individualistic concerns to the broader concerns of all humanity.

You remember one day a man came to Jesus and he raised some significant questions. Finally he got around to the question, "Who is my neighbor?" This could easily have been a very abstract question left in mid-air. But Jesus immediately pulled that question out of mid-air and placed it on a dangerous curve between Jerusalem and Jericho. He talked about a certain man who fell among thieves. Three men passed; two of them on the other side. And finally another man came and helped the injured man on the ground. He is known to us as the good Samaritan. Jesus says in substance that this is a great man. He was great because he could project the "I" into the "thou."

So often we say that the priest and the Levite were in a big hurry to get to some ecclesiastical meeting and so they did not have time. They were concerned about that. I would rather think of it another way. I can well imagine that they were quite afraid. You see, the Jericho road is a dangerous road, and the same thing that happened to the man who was robbed and beaten could have happened to them. So I imagine the first question that the priest and the Levite asked was this: "If I stop to help this man, what will happen to me?" Then the good Samaritan came by, and by the very nature of his concern reversed the question: "If I do not stop to help this man, what will happen to him?" And so this man was great because he had the mental equipment for a dangerous altruism. He was great because he could surround the length of his life with the breadth of life. He was great not only because he had ascended to certain heights of economic security, but because he could condescend to the depths of human need.

All this has a great deal of bearing in our situation in the world today. So often racial groups are concerned about the length of life, their economic privileged position, their social status. So often nations of the world are concerned about the length of life, perpetuating their nationalistic concerns, and their economic ends. May it not be that the problem in the world today is that individuals as well as nations have been overly concerned with the length of life, devoid of the breadth? But there is still something to remind us that we are interdependent, that we are all involved in a single process, that we are all somehow caught in an inescapable network of mutuality. Therefore whatever affects one directly affects all indirectly.

As long as there is poverty in the world I can never be rich, even if I have a billion dollars. As

"I Have a Dream"

Martin Luther King, Jr.

Martin Luther King, Jr. (1929–1968) was one of the most influential leaders of the American civil rights movement. He advocated nonviolent resistance during this often turbulent period of American history.

King was born in Atlanta, Georgia. He entered Morehouse College at the age of 15 and was ordained a Baptist minister at the age of 17. During his studies, King became interested in the ideas of the Indian nationalist leader Mohandas K. Gandhi.

In 1959, he travelled to India to gain a better understanding of Ghandi's work. King developed the Indian leader's principles of "satyragraha," or non-violent protest, into the philosophy that would later gain a wide following during the civil rights movement.

In 1955 King led a bus boycott in Montgomery, Alabama, to protest enforced racial segregation in public transportation after the arrest of Rosa Parks, a black woman who had refused to give her seat to a white passenger. The boycott was a victory for nonviolent protest. The Supreme Court banned all forms of segregated public transportation in Montgomery.

In 1963 King led a huge civil rights campaign in Birmingham, Alabama, and organized drives for black voter registration, desegregation, and better education and housing throughout the South. He led the historic March on Washington on August 28 of the same year where he delivered his famous "I Have a Dream" speech. In 1964 King was awarded the Nobel Peace Prize, the youngest recipient of this award.

King became increasingly concerned with the U.S.'s involvement in the war in Vietnam, leading many of his supporters to express concern about King's leadership. On April 3, 1968, King declared that he was confident that these issues would be resolved, as he had "been to the mountain top and seen the Promised Land." People still debate the prophetic nature of these famous words, as the next day King was shot and killed in Memphis, Tennessee, by a white escaped convict, James Earl Ray.

Over 100,000 people attended King's funeral in Atlanta. In 1983, the third Monday in January was designated a national holiday in the U.S. to commemorate Martin Luther King, Jr.'s birthday.

long as diseases are rampant and millions of people in this world cannot expect to live more than twenty-eight or thirty years, I can never be totally healthy even if I just got a good check-up at Mayo Clinic. I can never be what I ought to be until you are what you ought to be. This is the way our world is made. No individual or nation can stand out boasting of being independent. We are interdependent. So John Donne placed it in graphic terms when he affirmed, "No man is an island entire of itself. Every man is a piece of the continent, a part of the main." Then he goes on to say, "Any man's death diminishes me because I am involved in mankind, and therefore never send to know for whom the bell tolls; it tolls for thee." When we discover this, we master the second dimension of life.

Finally, there is a third dimension. Some people never get beyond the first two dimensions of life. They master the first two. They develop their inner powers; they love humanity, but they stop right here. They end up with the feeling that man is the end of all things and that humanity is God. Philosophically or theologically, many of them would call themselves humanists. They seek to live life without a sky. They find themselves bogged down on the horizontal plane without being integrated on the vertical plane. But if we are to live the complete life we must reach up and discover God. H.G. Wells was right: "The man who is not religious begins at nowhere and ends at nothing." Religion is like a mighty wind that breaks down doors and makes that possible and even easy which seems difficult and impossible.

In our modern world it is easy for us to forget this. We so often find ourselves unconsciously neglecting this third dimension of life. Not that we go up and say, "Good-by, God, we are going to leave you now." But we become so involved in the things of this world that we are unconsciously carried away by the rushing tide of materialism which leaves us treading in the confused waters of secularism. We find ourselves living in what Professor Sorokin of Harvard called a sensate civilization, believing that only those things which we can see and touch and to which we can apply our five senses have existence.

Something should remind us once more that the great things in this universe are things that we never see. You walk out at night and look up at the beautiful stars as they bedeck the heavens like swinging lanterns of eternity, and you think you can see all. Oh, no. You can never see the law of gravitation that holds them there. You walk around this vast campus and you probably have a great esthetic experience as I have had walking about and looking at the beautiful buildings, and you think you see all. Oh, no. You can never see the mind of the architect who drew the blueprint. You can never see the love and the faith and the hope of the individuals who made it so. You look at me and you think you see Martin Luther King. You don't see Martin Luther King; you see my body, but, you must understand, my body can't think, my body can't reason. You don't see the me that makes me. You can never see my personality.

In a real sense everything that we see is a shadow cast by that which we do not see. Plato was right: "The visible is a shadow cast by the invisible." And so God is still around. All of our new knowledge, all of our new developments, cannot diminish his being one iota. These new advances have banished God neither from the microcosmic compass of the atom nor from the vast, unfathomable ranges of interstellar space. The more we learn about this universe, the more mysterious and awesome it becomes. God is still here.

So I say to you, seek God and discover him and make him a power in your life. Without him all of our efforts turn to ashes and our sunrises into darkest nights. Without him, life is a meaningless drama with the decisive scenes missing. But with him we are able to rise from the fatigue of despair to the buoyancy of hope. With him we are able to rise from the midnight of desperation to the daybreak of joy. St. Augustine was right—we were made for God and we will be restless until we find rest in him.

Love yourself, if that means rational, healthy, and moral self interest. You are commanded to do that. That is the length of life. Love your neighbor as you love yourself. You are commanded to do that. That is the breadth of life. But never forget that there is a first and even greater commandment, "Love the Lord thy God with all thy heart and all thy soul and all thy mind." This is the height of life. And when you do this you live the complete life.

Thank God for John who, centuries ago, caught a vision of the new Jerusalem. God grant that those of us who still walk the road of life will catch this vision and decide to move forward to that city of complete life in which the length and the breadth and the height are equal.

SOURCE: Martin Luther King, Jr.. *The Measure of a Man.* Christian Education Press. 1959. Reprinted by permission by arrangement with The Heirs to the Estate of Martin Luther King, Jr., c/o Joan Daves Agency as agent for the proprietor.

Questions and Topics for Discussion and Writing

1. What does King mean when he speaks of life's "length, breadth and height?"
2. Why does King assert that "no individual can stand out boasting of being independent?" What is his basis for such an opinion?
3. How does King combine the philosophy of Plato with Christianity? Is this a convincing comparison?

Letter from Birmingham Jail

Martin Luther King, Jr.

Martin Luther King, Jr. (1929-1968) wrote this letter to eight fellow clergymen from his jail cell in Birmingham, Alabama, where he had been detained after being arrested at a nonviolent protest in that city. In it he asks for the assistance of other religious leaders in the civil rights struggle, and answers criticism they had levelled against him for his involvement. This version was edited by King for publication in the book *Why We Can't Wait.*

April 16, 1963

My Dear Fellow Clergymen:

While confined here in the Birmingham city jail, I came across your recent statement calling my present activities "unwise and untimely." Seldom do I pause to answer all the criticism of my work and ideas. If I sought to answer all the criticisms that cross my desk, my secretaries would have little time for anything other than such correspondence in the course of the day, and I would have no time for constructive work. But since I feel that you are men of genuine good will and that your criticisms are sincerely set forth, I want to try to answer your statement in what I hope will be patient and reasonable terms.

I think I should indicate why I am here in Birmingham, since you have been influenced by the view which argues against "outsiders coming in." I have the honor of serving as president of the Southern Christian Leadership Conference, an organization operating in every southern state, with headquarters in Atlanta, Georgia. We have some eighty-five affiliated organizations across the South, and one of them is the Alabama Christian Movement for Human Rights. Frequently we share staff, educational and financial resources with our affiliates. Several months ago the affiliate here in Birmingham asked us to be on call to engage in a nonviolent direct-action program if such were deemed necessary. We readily consented, and when the hour came we lived up to our promise. So I, along with several members of my staff, am here because I was invited here. I am here because I have organizational ties here.

But more basically, I am in Birmingham because injustice is here. Just as the prophets of the eighth century B.C. left their villages and carried their "thus saith the Lord" far beyond the boundaries of their home towns, and just as the Apostle Paul left his village of Tarsus and carried the gospel of Jesus Christ to the far corners of the Greco-roman world, so am I compelled to carry the gospel of freedom beyond my own home town. Like Paul, I must constantly respond to the Macedonian call for aid.

Moreover, I am cognizant of the interrelatedness of all communities and states. I cannot sit idly by in Atlanta and not be concerned about what happens in Birmingham. Injustice anywhere is a threat to justice everywhere. We are caught in an inescapable network of mutuality, tied in a single garment of destiny. Whatever affects one directly, affects all indirectly. Never again can we afford to live with the narrow, provincial "outside agitator" idea. Anyone who lives inside the United States can never be considered an outsider anywhere within its bounds.

You deplore the demonstrations taking place in Birmingham. But your statement, I am sorry to say, fails to express a similar concern for the conditions that brought about the demonstrations. I am sure that none of you would want to rest content with the superficial kind of social analysis that deals merely with effects and does not grapple with underlying causes. It is unfortunate that demonstrations are taking place in Birmingham, but it is even more unfortunate that the city's white power structure left the Negro community with no alternative. In any nonviolent campaign there are four basic steps: collection of the facts to determine whether injustices exist; negotiation; self-purification; and direct action. We have gone through all these steps in Birmingham. There can be no gainsaying the fact that racial injustice engulfs this community. Birmingham is probably the most thoroughly segregated city in the United States. Its ugly record of brutality is widely known. Negroes have experienced grossly unjust treatment in the courts. There have been more unsolved bombings of Negro homes and churches in Birmingham than in any other city in the nation. These are the hard, brutal facts of the case. On the basis of these conditions, Negro leaders sought to negotiate with the city fathers. But the latter consistently refused to engage in good-faith negotiation.

Then, last September, came the opportunity to talk with leaders of Birmingham's economic community. In the course of the negotiations, certain promises were made by the merchants—for example, to remove the stores' humiliating racial signs. On the basis of these promises, the Reverend Fred Shuttlesworth and the leaders of the Alabama Christian Movement for Human Rights agreed to a moratorium on all demonstrations. As the weeks and months went by, we realized that we were the victims of a broken promise. A few signs, briefly removed, returned; the others remained.

As in so many past experiences, our hopes had been blasted, and the shadow of deep disappointment settled upon us. We had no alternative except to prepare for direct action, whereby we would present our very bodies as a means of laying our case before the conscience of the local and the national community. Mindful of the difficulties involved, we decided to undertake a process of self-purification. We began a series of workshops on nonviolence, and we repeatedly asked ourselves: "Are you able to accept blows without retaliating?" "Are you able to endure the ordeal of jail?" We decided to schedule our direct-action program for the Easter season, realizing that except for Christmas, this is the main shopping period of the year. Knowing that a strong economic-withdrawal program would be the by-product of direct action, we felt that this would be the best time to bring pressure to bear on the merchants for the needed change.

Then it occurred to us that Birmingham's mayoral election was coming up in March, and we speedily decided to postpone action until after election day. When we discovered that the Commissioner of Public Safety, Eugene "Bull" Connor, had piled up enough votes to be in the run-off, we decided again to postpone action until the day after run-off so that the demonstrations could not be used to cloud the issues. Like many others, we waited to see Mr. Connor defeated, and to this end we endured postponement after postponement. Having aided in this community need, we felt that our direct-action program could be delayed no longer.

You may well ask: "Why direct action? Why sit-ins, marches and so forth? Isn't negotiation a better path?" You are quite right in calling for negotiation. Indeed, this is the very purpose of direct action. Nonviolent direct action seeks to create such a crisis and foster such a tension that a community which has constantly refused to negotiate is forced to confront the issue. It seeks so to dramatize the issue that it can no longer be ignored. My citing the creation of tension as part of the work the nonviolent-resites may sound rather shocking. But I must confess that I am not afraid of the word "tension." I have earnestly opposed violent tension, but there is a type of constructive, nonviolent tension which is necessary for growth. Just as Socrates felt that it was necessary to create a tension in the mind so that individuals could rise from the bondage of myths and half-truths to the unfettered realm of creative analysis and objective appraisal, so must we see the need for nonviolent gadflies to create the kind of tension in society that will help men rise from the dark depths of prejudice and racism to the majestic heights of understanding and brotherhood.

The purpose of our direct-action program is to create a situation so crisis-packed the it will inevi-

Excerpts

"I Have a Dream..."

"With this faith we will be able to work together, to pray together, to struggle together, to go to jail together, to stand up for freedom together, knowing that we will be free one day. With this faith we will be able to transform the jangling discourse of our nation into a beautiful symphony of brotherhood.

"This will be the day when all of God's children will be able to sing with new meaning 'My country 'tis of thee, sweet land of liberty, of thee I sing. Land where my fathers died, land of the Pilgrim's pride, from every mountainside, let freedom ring!'

"And if America is to be a great nation, this must become true. So, let freedom ring from the prodigious hilltops of New Hampshire. Let freedom ring from the mighty mountains of New York.

"Let freedom ring from the heightening Alleghenies of Pennsylvania.

"Let freedom ring from the snow-capped Rockies of Colorado.

"Let freedom ring from the curvaceous slopes of California.

"But not only that, let freedom ring from Stone Mountain of Georgia.

"Let freedom ring from Lookout Mountain of Tennessee.

"Let freedom ring from every hill and molehill of Mississippi, from every mountainside.

"Let freedom ring and when this happens, when we allow freedom to ring, when we let it ring from every village and every hamlet, from every state and every city, we will be able to speed up that day when all of God's children, black men and white men, Jews and Gentiles, Protestants and Catholics, will be able to join hands and sing in the words of the old Negro spiritual, 'Free at last, free at last. Thank God Almighty, we are free at last.'"

SOURCE: Delivered at the Lincoln Memorial, Wednesday, August 28, 1963.

tably open the door to negotiation. I therefore concur with you in your call to negotiation. Too long has our beloved Southland been bogged down in a tragic effort to live in monologue rather than dialogue.

One of the basic points in your statement is that the action that I and my associates have taken in Birmingham is untimely. Some have asked: "Why didn't you give the new city administration time to act?" The only answer that I can give to this query is that the new Birmingham administration must be prodded about as much as the outgoing one, before it will act. We are sadly mistaken if we feel that the election of Albert Boutwell as mayor will bring the millennium to Birmingham. While Mr. Boutwell is a much more gentle person that Mr. Connor, they are both segregationists, dedicated to maintenance of the status quo. I have hope that Mr. Boutwell will be reasonable enough to see the futility of massive resistance to desegregation. But he will not see this without pressure from devotees of civil rights. My friends, I must say to you that we have not made a single gain in civil rights without determined legal and nonviolent pressure. Lamentable, it is an historical fact that privileged groups seldom give up their privileges voluntarily. Individuals may see the moral light and voluntarily give up their unjust posture; but, as Reinhold Niebuhr has reminded us, groups tend to be more immoral than individuals.

We know through painful experience that freedom is never voluntarily given by the oppressor; it must be demanded by the oppressed. Frankly, I have yet to engage in a direct-action campaign that was "well timed" in the view of those who have not suffered unduly from the disease of segregation. For years now I have heard the word "Wait!" It rings in the ear of every Negro with piercing familiarity. This "Wait" has almost always meant "Never." We must come to see, with one of our distinguished jurists, that "justice too long delayed is justice denied."

We have waited for more than 340 years for our constitutional and God-given rights. The nations Asia and Africa are moving with jet-like speed toward gaining political independence, but we still creep at horse-and-buggy pace toward gaining a cup of coffee at a lunch counter. Perhaps it is easy for those who have never felt the stinging darts of segregation to say, "Wait." But when you have seen vicious mobs lynch your mothers and fathers at will and drown your sisters and brothers at whim; when you have seen hate-filled policemen curse, kick and even kill your black brothers and sisters; when you see the vast majority of your twenty million Negro brothers smothering in an airtight cage of poverty in the midst of an affluent society; when you suddenly find your tongue twisted and you speech stammering as you seek to explain to your six-year-old daughter why she can't go to the public amusement park that has just been advertised on television, and see tears welling up in her eyes when she is told that Funtown is closed to coloured children, and see ominous clouds of inferiority beginning to form in her little mental sky, and see her beginning to distort her personality by developing an unconscious bitterness toward white people; when you have to concoct an answer for a five-year-old son who is asking: "Daddy, why do white people treat coloured people so mean?"; when you take a cross-country drive and find it necessary to sleep night after night in the uncomfortable corners of your automobile because no motel will accept you; when you are humiliated day in day out by nagging signs reading "white" and "coloured;" when your first name becomes "nigger," your middle name becomes "boy" (however old you are) and your last name becomes "John," and your wife and mother are never given the respected title "Mrs.;" when you are harried by day and haunted by night by the fact that you are a Negro, living constantly at tiptoe stance, never quite knowing what to expect next, and are plagued with inner fears and outer resentments; when you are forever fighting a degenerating sense of "nobodiness"—then you will understand why we find it difficult to wait. There comes a time when the cup of endurance runs over, and men are no longer willing to be plunged into the abyss of despair. I hope, sirs, you can understand our legitimate and unavoidable impatience.

You express a great deal of anxiety over our willingness to break laws. This is certainly a legitimate concern. Since we so diligently urge people to obey the Supreme Court's decision of 1954 outlawing segregation in the public schools, at first glance it may seem rather paradoxical for us consciously to break laws. One may well ask: "How can you advocate breaking some laws and obeying others?" The answer lies in the fact that there are two types of laws: just and unjust. I would be the first to advocate obeying just laws. One has not only a legal but a moral responsibility to obey just laws. Conversely, one has a moral responsibility to disobey unjust laws. I would agree with St. Augustine that "an unjust law is no law at all."

Now, what is the difference between the two? How does one determine whether a law is just or unjust? A just law is a man-made code that squares with the moral law or the law of God. An unjust law is a code that is out of harmony with the moral law. To put it in the terms of St. Thomas Aquinas: An unjust law is a human law that is not rooted in eternal law and natural law. Any law that uplifts human personality is just. Any law that degrades human personality is unjust. All segregation statutes are unjust because segregation distorts the soul and damages the personality. It gives the segregator a false sense of superiority and the segregated a false sense of inferiority. Segregation, to use the terminology of the Jewish philosopher Martin Buber, substitutes an "I-it" relationship for an "I-thou" relationship and ends up relegating persons to the status of things. Hence segregation is not only politically, economically and sociologically unsound, it is morally wrong and sinful. Paul Tillich has said that sin is separation. Is not segregation an existential expression of man's tragic separation, his awful estrangement, his terrible sinfulness? Thus it is that I can urge men to obey the 1954 decision of the Supreme Court, for it is morally right; and I can urge them to disobey segregation ordinances, for they morally wrong.

Let us consider a more concrete example of just and unjust laws. An unjust law is a code that a numerical or power majority group compels a minority group to obey but does not make binding on itself. This is *difference* made legal. By the same token, a just law is a code that a majority compels a minority to follow and that it is willing to follow itself. This is *sameness* made legal.

Let me give another explanation. A law is unjust if it is inflicted on a minority that, as a result of being denied the right to vote, had no part in enacting or devising the law. Who can say that the legislature of Alabama which set up that state's segregation laws was democratically elected? Throughout Alabama all sorts of devious methods are used to prevent Negroes from becoming registered voters, and there are some counties in which, even though Negroes constitute a majority of the population, not a single Negro is registered. Can any law enacted under such circumstances be considered democratically structured?

Sometimes a law is just on its face and unjust in its application. For instance, I have been arrested on a charge of parading without a permit. Now, there is nothing wrong in having an ordinance which requires a permit for a parade. But such an ordinance becomes unjust when it is use to maintain segregation and to deny citizens the First-Amendment privilege of peaceful assembly and protest.

I hope you are able to see the distinction I am trying to point out. In no sense do I advocate evading or defying the law, as would the rabid segregationist. That would lead to anarchy. One who breaks an unjust law must do so openly, lovingly, and with a willingness to accept the penalty of imprisonment in order to arouse the conscience of the community over its injustice, is in reality expressing the highest respect for law.

Of course, there is nothing new about this kind of civil disobedience. It was evidenced sublimely in the refusal of Shadrach, Meshach and Abednego to obey the laws of Nebuchadnezzar, on the ground that a higher moral law was at stake. It was practiced superbly by the early Christians, who were willing to face hungry lions and the excruciating pain of chopping clocks rather than submit to certain unjust laws of the Roman Empire. To a degree, academic freedom is a reality today because Socrates practiced civil disobedience. In our own nation, the Boston Tea Party represented a massive act of civil disobedience.

We should never forget that everything Adolf Hitler did was "legal" and everything the Hungarian freedom fighters did in Hungary was "illegal". It was "illegal" to aid and comfort a Jew in Hitler's Germany. Even so, I am sure that, had I lived in Germany at the time, I would have aided and comforted my Jewish brothers. If today I lived in a Communist country where certain principles dear to the Christian faith are suppressed, I would openly advocate disobeying that country's antireligious laws.

I must make two honest confessions to you, my Christian and Jewish brothers. First, I must confess that over the past few years I have been gravely disappointed with the white moderate. I have almost reached the regrettable conclusion that the Negro's great stumbling block in his stride toward freedom is not the White Citizen's Counciler or the Ku Klux Klanner, but the white moderate, who is more devoted to "order" than to justice; who prefers a negative peace which is the absence of tension to a positive peace which is the presence of justice; who constantly says: "I agree with you in the goal you seek, but I cannot agree with the methods of direct action;" who paternalistically believes he can set the timetable for another man's freedom; who lives by a mythical concept of time and who constantly advises the Negro to wait for a "more convenient season." Shallow understanding from people of good will is more frustrating than absolute misunderstanding from people of ill will. Lukewarm acceptance is much more bewildering than outright rejection.

I had hoped that the white moderate would understand that law and order exist for the purpose of establishing justice and that when they fail in this purpose they become dangerously structured dams that back the flow of social progress. I had hoped that the white moderate would understand that the present tension in the South is a necessary phase of the transition from an obnoxious negative peace, in which the negro passively accepted his plight, to a substantive and positive peace, in which all men will respect the dignity and worth of human personality. Actually, we who engage in nonviolent direct action are not the creators of tension. We merely bring to the surface the hidden tension that is already alive. We bring it out in the open, where it can be seen and dealt with. Like a boil that can never be cured so long as it is covered up but must be opened with all its ugliness to the natural medicines of air and light, injustice must be exposed, with all the tension its exposure creates, to the light of human conscience and the air of national opinion before it can be cured.

In your statement you assert our actions, even though peaceful, must be condemned because they precipitate violence. But is this a logical assertion? Isn't this like condemning a robbed man because his possession of money precipitated the evil act of robbery? Isn't this like condemning Socrates because his unswerving commitment to truth and his philosophical inquiries precipitated the act by the misguided populace in which they made him drink hemlock? Isn't this like condemning Jesus because his unique God-consciousness and never-ceasing devotion to God's will precipitated the evil act of crucifixion? We must come to see that, as the federal courts have consistently affirmed, it is wrong to urge an individual to cease his efforts to gain his basic constitutional rights because the quest may precipitate violence. Society must protect the robbed and punish the robber.

I had also hoped that the white moderate would reject the myth concerning time in relation to the struggle for freedom. I have just received a letter form a white brother in Texas. He writes: "All Christians know that the coloured people will receive equal rights eventually, but is it possible that you are in too great a religious hurry. It has taken Christianity almost two thousand years to accomplish what it has. The teachings of Christ take time to come to earth." Such an attitude stems from a tragic misconception of time, from the strangely irrational notion that there is something in the very flow of time that will inevitably cure all ills. Actually, time itself is neutral; it can be use either destructively or constructively. More and more I feel that the people of ill will have used time much more effectively than have the people of good will. We will have to repent in this generation not merely for the hateful words and actions of the bad people but for the appalling silence of the good people. Human progress never rolls in on wheels of inevitability; it comes through the tireless efforts of men willing to be co-workers with God, and without this hard work, time itself becomes an ally of the forces of social stagnation. We must use time creatively, in the knowledge that the times is always ripe to do right. Now is the time to make real the promise of democracy and transform our pending national elegy into a creative psalm of brotherhood. Now is the time to lift our national policy from the quicksand of racial injustice to the solid rock of human dignity.

You speak of our activity in Birmingham as extreme. At first I was rather disappointed that fellow clergymen would see my nonviolent efforts as those of an extremist. I began thinking about the fact that I stand in the middle of two opposing forces in the Negro community. One is a force of complacency, made up in part of Negroes who, as a result of long years of oppression, are so drained of self-respect and a sense of "somebodiness" that they have adjusted to segregation; and in part a few middle-class Negroes who, because of a degree of academic and economic security and because in some way they profit by segregation, have become insensitive to the problems of the masses. The other force is one of bitterness and hatred, and it comes perilously close to advocating violence. It is expressed in the various black nationalist groups that are springing up across the nation, the largest and best-known being Elijah Muhammad's Muslim movement. Nourished by Negro's frustration over the continued existence of racial discrimination, this movement is made up of people who have lost faith in America, who have absolutely repudiated Christianity, and who have concluded that the white man is an incorrigible "devil."

I have tried to stand between these two forces, saying that we need emulate neither the "do-nothingism" of the complacent nor the hatred and despair of the black nationalist. For there is the more excellent way of love and nonviolent protest. I am grateful to God that, through the influence of the Negro church, the way of nonviolence became an integral part of our struggle.

If this philosophy had not emerged, by now many streets of the South would, I am convinced, be flowing with blood. And I am further convinced that if our white brothers dismiss as "rabble-rousers" and "outside agitators" those of us who employ nonviolent direct action, and if they refuse to support our nonviolent efforts, millions of Negroes will, out of frustration and despair, seek solace and security in black-nationalist ideologies—a development that would inevitably lead to a frightening racial nightmare.

Oppressed people cannot remain oppressed forever. The yearning for freedom eventually manifests itself, and that is what has happened to the American Negro. Something within has reminded him of his birthright of freedom, and something without has reminded him that it can be gained. Consciously or unconsciously, he has been caught up by the *Zeitgeist*, and with his black brothers of Africa and his brown and yellow brothers of Asia, South America and the Caribbean, the United States Negro is moving with a sense of great urgency toward the promised land of racial justice. If one recognizes the vital urge that has engulfed the Negro community, one should readily understand why public demonstrations are taking place. The Negro has many pent-up resentments and latent frustrations, and he must release them. So let him march; let him make prayer pilgrimages to the city hall; let him go on freedom rides—and try to understand why he must do so. If his repressed emotions are not released in nonviolent ways, they will seek expression through violence; this is not a threat but a fact of history. So I have not said to my people: "Get rid of your discontent." Rather, I have tried to say that this normal and healthy discontent can be channeled into the creative outlet of nonviolent direct action. And now this approach is being termed extremist.

But though I was initially disappointed at being categorized as an extremist, as I continued to think about the matter I gradually gained a measure of satisfaction from the label. Was not Jesus an extremist for love: "Love your enemies, bless them that curse you, do good to them that hate you, and pray for them which despitefully use you, and persecute you." Was not Amos an extremist for justice: "Let justice roll down like waters and righteousness like an ever-flowing stream." Was not Paul an extremist for the Christian gospel: "I bear in my body the marks of the Lord Jesus." Was not Martin Luther an extremist: "Here I stand; I cannot do otherwise, so help me God." And John Bunyan: "I will stay in jail to the end of my days before I make a butchery of my conscience." And Abraham Lincoln: "This nation cannot survive half slave and half free." And Thomas Jefferson: "We hold these truths to be self-evident, that all men are created equal..." So the question is not whether we will be extremists, but what kind of extremists we will be. Will we be extremists for hate or for love? Will we be extremists for the preservation of injustice or for the extension of justice? In that dramatic scene on Calvary's hill three men were crucified. We must never forget that all three were crucified for the same crime—the crime of extremism. Two were extremists for immorality, and thus fell below their environment. The other, Jesus Christ, was and extremist for love, truth and goodness, and thereby rose above his environment. Perhaps the South, the nation and the world are in dire need of creative extremists.

I had hoped that the white moderate would see this need. Perhaps I was too optimistic; perhaps I expected too much. I suppose I should have realized that few members of the oppressor race can understand the deep groans and passionate yearnings of the oppressed race, and still fewer have the vision to see that injustice must be rooted out by strong, persistent and determined action. I am thankful, however, that some of our white brothers in the South have grasped the meaning of this social revolution and committed themselves to it. They are still all too few in quantity, but they are big in quality. Some—such as Ralph McGill, Lillian Smith, Harry Golden, James McBride Dabbs, Ann Braden and Sarah Patton Boyle—have written about our struggle in eloquent and prophetic terms. Others have marched with us down nameless streets of the South. They have languished in filthy, roach-infested jails, suffering the abuse and brutality of policemen who view them as "dirty nigger-lovers." Unlike so many of their moderate brothers and sisters, they have recognized the urgency of the moment and sensed the need for powerful "action" antidotes to combat the disease of segregation.

Let me take note of my other major disappointment. I have been so greatly disappointed with the white church and its leadership. Of course, there are some notable exceptions. I am not unmindful of the fact that each of you has taken some significant stands on this issue. I commend you, Reverend Stallings, for your Christian stand on this past Sunday, in welcoming Negroes to your worship service on a nonsegregated basis. I commend the Catholic leaders of this state for integrating Spring Hill College several years ago.

But despite these notable exceptions, I must honestly reiterate that I have been disappointed with the church. I do not say this as one of those negative critics who can always find something wrong with the church. I say this as a minister of the gospel, who loves the church; who was nurtured in its bosom; who has been sustained by its spiritual blessings and who will remain true to it as long as the cord of life shall lengthen.

When I was suddenly catapulted into the leadership of the bus protest in Montgomery, Alabama, a few years ago, I felt we would be supported by the white church. I felt that the white ministers, priests and rabbis of the South would be among our strongest allies. Instead, some have been outright opponents, refusing to understand the freedom movement and misrepresenting its leaders; all too many others have been more cautious than courageous and have remained silent behind the anaesthetizing security of stained-glass windows.

In spite of my shattered dreams, I came to Birmingham with the hope that the white religious leadership of this community would see the justice of our cause and, with deep moral concern, would serve as the channel through which our just grievances could reach the power structure. I had hoped that each of you would understand. But again I have been disappointed.

I have heard numerous southern religious leaders admonish their worshippers to comply with a desegregation decision because it is the law, but I have longed to hear white ministers declare: "Follow this decree because integration is morally right and because the Negro is your brother." In the midst of blatant injustices inflicted upon the Negro, I have watched white churchmen stand on the sideline and mouth pious irrelevancies and sanctimonious trivialities. In the midst of a mighty struggle to rid our nation of racial and economic injustice, I have heard many ministers say: "Those are social issues, with which the gospel has no concern." And I have watched many churches commit themselves to a completely otherworldly religion which makes a strange, un-Biblical dis-

Light, at Thirty-Two

Michael Blumenthal

It is the first thing God speaks of
when we meet Him, in the good book
of Genesis. And now, I think
I see it all in terms of light:

How, the other day at dusk
on Ossabaw Island the marsh grass
was the color of the most beautiful hair
I had ever seen, or how—years ago
in the early-dawn light of Montrose Park—
I saw the most ravishing woman
in the world, only to find, hours later
over drinks in a dark bar, that it
wasn't she who was ravishing,
but the light: how it filtered
through the leaves of the magnolia
onto her cheeks, how it turned
her cotton dress to silk, her walk
to a *tour-jeté.*

And I understood, finally,
what my friend John meant,
twenty years ago, when he said: *Love
is keeping the lights on.* And I understood
why Matisse and Bonnard and Gauguin
and Cézanne all followed the light:
Because they knew all lovers are equal
in the dark, that light defines beauty
the way longing defines desire, that
everything depends on how light falls
on a seashell, a mouth... a broken bottle.

And now, I'd like to learn
to follow light wherever it leads me,
never again to say to a woman, *YOU
are beautiful*, but rather to whisper:
*Darling, the way light fell on your hair
this morning when we woke—God,
it was beautiful.* Because, if the light is right,
then the day and the body and the faint
pleasures
waiting at the window... they too are right.
All things lovely there. As that first poet wrote,
in his first book of poems: *Let there be light.*

And there is.

SOURCE: Michael Blumenthal, *Days We Would Rather Know* (NY: Penguin, 1984). Reprinted with permission of the author.

tinction between body and soul, between the sacred and the secular.

I have travelled the length and breadth of Alabama, Mississippi and all the other southern states. On sweltering summer days and crisp autumn mornings I have looked at the South's beautiful churches with their lofty spires pointing heavenward. I have beheld the impressive outlines of her massive religious-education buildings. Over and over I have found myself asking: "What kind of people worship here? Who is their God? Where were their voices when the lips of Governor Barnett dripped with words of interposition and nullification? Where were they when Governor Wallace gave a clarion call for defiance and hatred? Where were their voices of support when bruised and weary Negro men and women decided to rise from the dark dungeons of complacency to the bright hills of creative protest?"

Yes, these questions are still in my mind. In deep disappointment I have wept over the laxity of the church. But be assured that my tears have been tears of love. There can be no deep disappointment where there is not deep love. Yes, I love the church. How could I do otherwise? I am in the rather unique position of being the son, the grandson and the great-grandson of preachers. Yes, I see the church as the body of Christ. But, oh! How we have blemished and scarred that body through social neglect and through fear of being nonconformists.

There was a time when the church was very powerful—in the time when the early Christians rejoiced at being deemed worthy to suffer for what they believed. In those days the church was not merely a thermometer that recorded the ideas and principles of popular opinion; it was a thermostat that transformed the mores of society. Whenever the early Christians entered a town, the people in power became disturbed and immediately sought to convict the Christians for being "disturbers of the peace" and "outside agitators." But the Christians pressed on, in the conviction that they were "a colony of heaven," called to obey God rather than man. Small in number, they were big in commitment. They were too God-intoxicated to be "astronomically intimidated." By their effort and example they brought an end to such ancient evils as infanticide and gladiatorial contests.

Things are different now. So often the contemporary church is a weak, ineffectual voice with an uncertain sound. So often it is an archdefender of the status quo. Far from being disturbed by the presence of the church, the power structure of the average community is consoled by the church's silent—and often even vocal—sanction of things as they are.

But the judgment of God is upon the church as never before. If today's church does not recapture the sacrificial spirit of the early church, it will lose its authenticity, forfeit the loyalty of millions, and be dismissed as an irrelevant social club with no meaning for the twentieth century. Every day I meet young people whose disappointment with the church has turned into outright disgust.

Perhaps I have once again been too optimistic. Is organized religion too inextricably bound to the status quo to save our nation and the world? Perhaps I must turn my faith to the inner spiritual church, the church within the church, as the true *ecclesia* and hope of the world. But again I am thankful to God that some noble souls from the ranks of organized religion have broken loose from the paralysing chains of conformity and joined us as active partners in the struggle for freedom. They have left their secure congregations and walked the streets of Albany, Georgia, with us. They have gone down the highways of the South on tortuous rides for freedom. Yes, they have gone to jail with us. Some have been dismissed from their churches, have lost the support of their bishops and fellow ministers. But they have acted in the faith that right defeated is stronger than the evil triumphant. Their witness has been the spiritual salt that has preserved the true meaning of the gospel in these troubled times. They have carved a tunnel of hope through the dark mountain of disappointment.

I hope the church as a whole will meet the challenge of this decisive hour. But even if the church does not come to the aid of justice, I have no despair about the future. I have no fear about the outcome of our struggle in Birmingham, even if our motives are at present misunderstood. We will reach the goal of freedom in Birmingham and

Prayer for Revolutionary Love

Denise Levertov

That a woman not ask a man to leave meaningful work to follow her.
That a man not ask a woman to leave meaningful work to follow him.

That no one try to put Eros in bondage.
But that no one put a cudgel in the hand of Eros.

That our loyalty to one another and our loyalty to our work
not be set in false conflict.

That our love for each other give us love for each other's work.
That our love for each other's work give us love for one another.

That our love for each other's work give us love for one another.
That our love for each other give us love for each other's work.

That our love for each other, if need be,
give way to absence. And the unknown.

That we endure absence, if need be,
without losing our love for each other.
Without closing doors to the unknown.

all over the nation, because the goal of America is freedom. Abused and scorned though we may be, our destiny is tied up with America's destiny. Before the pilgrims landed at Plymouth, we were here. Before the pen of Jefferson etched the majestic words of the Declaration of Independence across the pages of history, we were here. For more than two centuries our forebears labored in this country without wages; they made cotton king; they built the homes of their masters while suffering gross injustice and shameful humiliation—and yet out of a bottomless vitality they continued to thrive and develop. If the inexpressible cruelties of slavery could not stop us, the opposition we now face will surely fail. We will win our freedom because the sacred heritage of our nation and the eternal will of God are embodied in our echoing demands.

Before closing I feel impelled to mention one other point in your statement that has troubled me profoundly. You warmly commended the Birmingham police force for keeping "order" and "preventing violence." I doubt that you would have so warmly commended the police force if you had seen its dogs sinking their teeth into unarmed, nonviolent Negroes. I doubt that you would have so quickly commended the policemen if you were to observe their ugly and inhumane treatment of Negroes here in the city jail; if you were to watch them push and curse old Negro women and young Negro girls; if you were to see them slap and kick old Negro men and young boys; if you were to observe them, as they did on two occasions, refuse to give us food because we wanted to sing our grace together. I cannot join you in your praise of the Birmingham police department.

It is true that the police have exercised a degree of discipline in handling the demonstrators. In this sense they have conducted themselves rather "nonviolently" in public. But for what purpose? To preserve the evil system of segregation. Over the past few years I have consistently preached that nonviolence demands that the means we use must be as pure as the ends we seek. I have tried to make clear that it is wrong to use immoral means to attain moral ends. But now I must affirm that it is just as wrong, or perhaps even more so, to use moral means to preserve immoral ends. Perhaps Mr. Connor and his policemen have been rather nonviolent in public, as was Chief Pritchett in Albany, Georgia, but they have used the moral means of nonviolence to maintain the immoral end of racial injustice. As T.S. Eliot has said: "The last temptation is the greatest treason: To do the right deed for the wrong reason."

I wish you had commended the Negro sit-inners and demonstrators of Birmingham for their sublime courage, their willingness to suffer and their amazing discipline in the midst of great provocation. One day the South will recognize its real heroes. They will be the James Merediths, with the noble sense of purpose that enables them to face jeering and hostile mobs, and with the agonizing loneliness that characterizes the life of the pioneer. They will be old, oppressed, battered Negro women, symbolized in a seventy-two-year-old woman in Montgomery, Alabama, who rose up with a sense of dignity and with her people decided not to ride segregated buses, and who responded with ungrammatical profundity to one who inquired about her weariness: "My feets is tired, but my soul is at rest." They will be the young high school and college students, the young ministers of the gospel and a host of their elders, courageously and nonviolently sitting in at lunch counters and willingly going to jail for conscience' sake. One day the South will know that when these disinherited children of God sat down at lunch counters, they were in reality standing up for what is best in the American dream and for the most sacred values in our Judaeo-Christian heritage, thereby bringing our nation back to those great wells of democracy which were dug deep by the founding fathers in their formulation of the Constitution and the Declaration of Independence.

Never before have I written so long a letter. I'm afraid it is much too long to take your precious time. I can assure you that it would have been much shorter if I had been writing from a comfortable desk, but what else can one do when he is alone in a narrow jail cell, other than write long letters, think long thoughts and pray long prayers?

If I have said anything in this letter that overstates the truth and indicates unreasonable impatience, I beg you to forgive me. If I have said anything that understates the truth and indicates my having a patience that allows me to settle for anything less than brotherhood, I beg God to forgive me.

I hope this letter finds you strong in the faith. I also hope that circumstances will soon make it possible for me to meet each of you, not as an integrationist or a civil-rights leader but as a fellow clergyman and a Christian brother. Let us all hope that the dark clouds of racial prejudice will soon pass from our fear-drenched communities, and in some not too distant tomorrow the radiant stars of love and brotherhood will shine over our great nation with all their scintillating beauty.

Yours for the cause of Peace and Brotherhood,

Martin Luther King, Jr.

Questions and Topics for Discussion and Writing

1. How does King link the strategy of non-violent direct action and the strategy of negotiation?
2. What justification does King give for breaking laws in the light of the 1954 Supreme Court decision outlawing public school segregation?
3. Why does King claim he has the right to be disappointed by the white religious leaders of Birmingham? What is his view on the "brotherhood" of white and black Americans?

Images of Relationship

Carol Gilligan

In this excerpt from the book *In a Different Voice* (1982) by Harvard psychologist Carol Gilligan, the author explores the way in which the psychological development of women has been trivialized and in many cases ignored by research in the field. She takes particular exception to the work of Lawrence Kohlberg, whose paradigm of child moral development defined the area of child psychology until Gilligan's criticism.

In 1914, with his essay "On Narcissism," Freud swallows his distaste at the thought of "abandoning observation for barren theoretical controversy" and extends his map of the psychological domain. Tracing the development of the capacity to love, which he equates with maturity and psychic health, he locates its origins in the contrast between love for the mother and love for the self. But in thus dividing the world of love into narcissism and "object" relationships, he finds that while men's development becomes clear, women's becomes increasingly opaque. The problem arises because the contrast between mother and self yields two different images of relationships. Relying on the imagery of men's lives in charting the course of human growth, Freud is unable to trace in women the development of relationships, morality, or a clear sense of self. This difficulty in fitting the logic of his theory to women's experience leads him in the end to set women apart, marking their relationships, like their sexual life, as "a 'dark continent' for psychology"...

Thus the problem of interpretation that shadows the understanding of women's development arises from the differences observed in their experience of relationships. To Freud, though living surrounded by women and otherwise seeing so much and so well, women's relationships seemed increasingly mysterious, difficult to discern, and hard to describe. While this mystery indicates how theory can blind observation, it also suggests that development in women is masked by a particular conception of human relationships. Since the imagery of relationships shapes the narrative of human development, the inclusion of women, by changing that imagery, implies a change in the entire account.

The shift in imagery that creates the problem in interpreting women's development is elucidated by the moral judgments of two eleven-year-old children, a boy and a girl, who see, in the same dilemma, two very different moral problems. While current theory brightly illuminates the line and the logic of the boy's thought, it casts scant light on that of the girl. The choice of a girl whose moral judgments elude existing categories of developmental assessment is meant to highlight the issue of interpretation rather than to exemplify sex differences per se. Adding a new line of interpretation, based on the imagery of the girl's thought, makes it possible not only to see development where previously development was not discerned but also to consider differences in the understanding of relationships without scaling these differences from better to worse.

The two children were in the same sixth-grade class at school and were participants in the rights and responsibilities study, designed to explore different conceptions of morality and self. The sample selected for this study was chosen to focus the variables of gender and age while maximising developmental potential by holding constant, at a high level, the factors of intelligence, education, and social class that have been associated which moral development at least as measured by existing scales.

The two children in question, Amy and Jake, were both bright and articulate and, at least in their eleven-year-old aspirations, resisted easy categories of sex-role stereotyping, since Amy aspired to become a scientist while Jake preferred English to math. Yet their moral judgments seem initially to confirm familiar notions about differences between the sexes, suggesting that the edge girls have on moral development during the early school years gives way at puberty with the ascendance of formal logical thought in boys.

The dilemma that these eleven-year-olds were asked to resolve was one in the series devised by Kohlberg to measure moral development in adolescence by presenting a conflict between moral norms and exploring the logic of its resolution. In this particular dilemma, a man named Heinz considers whether or not to steal a drug which he cannot afford to buy in order to save the life of his wife. In the standard format of Kohlberg's interviewing procedure, the description of the dilemma itself—Heinz's predicament, the wife's disease, the druggist's refusal to lower his price—is followed by the question, "Should Heinz steal the drug?" The reasons for and against stealing are then explored through a series of questions that vary and extend the parameters of the dilemma in a way designed to reveal the underlying structure of moral thought.

Jake, at eleven, is clear from the outset that Heinz should steal the drug. Constructing the dilemma, as Kohlberg did, as a conflict between the values of property and life, he discerns the logical priority of life and uses that logic to justify his choice:

> For one thing, a human life is worth more than money, and if the druggist only makes $1,000, he is still going to live, but if Heinz doesn't steal the drug, his wife is going to die. (*Why is life worth more than money?*) Because the druggist can get a thousand dollars later from rich people with cancer, but Heinz can't get his wife again. (*Why not?*) Because people are all different and so you couldn't get Heinz's wife again.

Asked whether Heinz should steal the drug if he does not love his wife, Jake replies that he should, saying that not only is there "a difference between hating and killing," but also, if Heinz were caught, "the judge would probably think it was the right thing to do." Asked about the fact that, in stealing, Heinz would be breaking the law, he says that "the laws have mistakes, and you can't go writing up a law for everything that you can imagine."

Thus, while taking the law into account and recognizing its function in maintaining social order (the judge, Jake says, "should give Heinz the lightest possible sentence"), he also sees the law as man-made and therefore subject to error and change. Yet his judgment that Heinz should steal the drug, like his view of the law as having mistakes, rests on the assumption of agreement, a societal consensus around moral values that allows one to know and expect others to recognize what is "the right thing to do."

Fascinated by the power of logic, this eleven-year-old boy locates truth in math, which, he says, is "the only thing that is totally logical." Considering the moral dilemma to be "sort of like a math problem with humans," he sets it up as an equation and proceeds to work out the solution. Since his solution is rationally derived, he assumes that anyone following reason would arrive at the same conclusion and thus that a judge would also consider stealing to be the right thing for Heinz to do. Yet he is also aware of the limits of logic. Asked whether there is a right answer to moral problems, Jake replies that "there can only be right and wrong in judgment," since the parameters of action are variable and complex. Illustrating how actions undertaken with the best of intentions can eventuate in the most disastrous of consequences, he says, "like if you give an old lady your seat on the trolley, if you are in a trolley crash and that seat goes through the window, it might be that reason that the old lady dies."

Theories of developmental psychology illuminate well the position of this child, standing at the juncture of childhood and adolescence, at what Piaget describes as the pinnacle of childhood intelligence, and beginning through thought to discover a wider universe of possibility. The moment of preadolescence is caught by the conjunction of formal operational thought with a description of self still anchored in the factual parameters of his childhood world—his age, his town, his father's occupation, the substance of his likes, dislikes, and beliefs. Yet as his self-description radiates the self-confidence of a child who has arrived, in Erikson's terms, at a favorable balance of industry over inferiority—competent, sure of himself, and knowing well the rules of the game—so his emergent capacity for formal thought, his ability to think about thinking and to reason things out in a logical way, frees him from dependence on authority and allows him to find solutions to problems by himself.

This emergent autonomy follows the trajectory that Kohlberg's six stages of moral development trace, a three-level progression from an egocentric understanding of fairness based on individual need (stages one and two), to a conception of fairness anchored in the shared conventions of societal agreement (stages three and four), and finally to a principled understanding of fairness that rests on the free-standing logic of equality and reciprocity (stages five and six). While this boy's judgments at eleven are scored as conventional on Kohlberg's scale, a mixture of stages three and four, his ability to bring deductive logic to bear on the solution of moral dilemmas, to differentiate morality from law, and to see how laws can be considered to have mistakes points toward the principled conception of justice that Kohlberg equates with moral maturity.

In contrast, Amy's response to the dilemma conveys a very different impression, an image of development stunted by a failure of logic, an inability to think for herself. Asked if Heinz should steal the drug, she replies in a way that seems evasive and unsure:

> Well, I don't think so. I think there might be other ways besides stealing it, like if he could borrow the money or make a loan or something, but he really shouldn't steal the drug—but his wife shouldn't die either.

Asked why he should not steal the drug, she considers neither property nor law but rather the effect that theft could have on the relationship between Heinz and his wife:

> If he stole the drug, he might save his wife then, but if he did, he might have to go to jail, and then his wife might get sicker again, and he couldn't get more of the drug, and it might not be good. So, they should really just talk it out and find some other way to make the money.

Seeing in the dilemma not a math problem with humans but a narrative of relationships that extends over time, Amy envisions the wife's continuing need for her husband and the husband's continuing concern for his wife and seeks to respond to the druggist's need in a way that would sustain rather than sever connection. Just as she ties the wife's survival to the preservation of relationships, so she considers the value of the wife's life in a context of relationships, saying that it would be wrong to let her die because, "if she died, it hurts a lot of people and it hurts her." Since Amy's moral judgment is grounded in the belief that, "if somebody has something that would keep somebody alive, then it's not right not to give it to them," she considers the problem in the dilemma to arise not from the druggist's assertion of rights but from his failure of response.

As the interviewer proceeds with the series of questions that follow from Kohlberg's construction of the dilemma, Amy's answers remain essentially unchanged, the various probes serving neither to elucidate nor to modify her initial response. Whether or not Heinz loves his wife, he still shouldn't steal or let her die; if it were a stranger dying instead, Amy says that "if the stranger didn't have anybody near or anyone she knew," then Heinz should try to save her life, but he should not steal the drug. But as the interviewer conveys through the repetition of questions that the answers she gave were not heard or nor right, Amy's confidence begins to diminish, and her replies become more constrained and unsure. Asked again why Heinz should not steal the drug, she simply repeats, "Because it's not right." Asked again to explain why, she states again that theft would not be a good solution, adding lamely, "if he took it, he might not know how to give it to his wife, and so his wife might still die." Failing to see the dilemma as a self-contained problem in moral logic, she does not discern the internal structure of its resolution; as she constructs the problem differently herself, Kohlberg's conception completely evades her.

Instead, seeing a world comprised of relation-

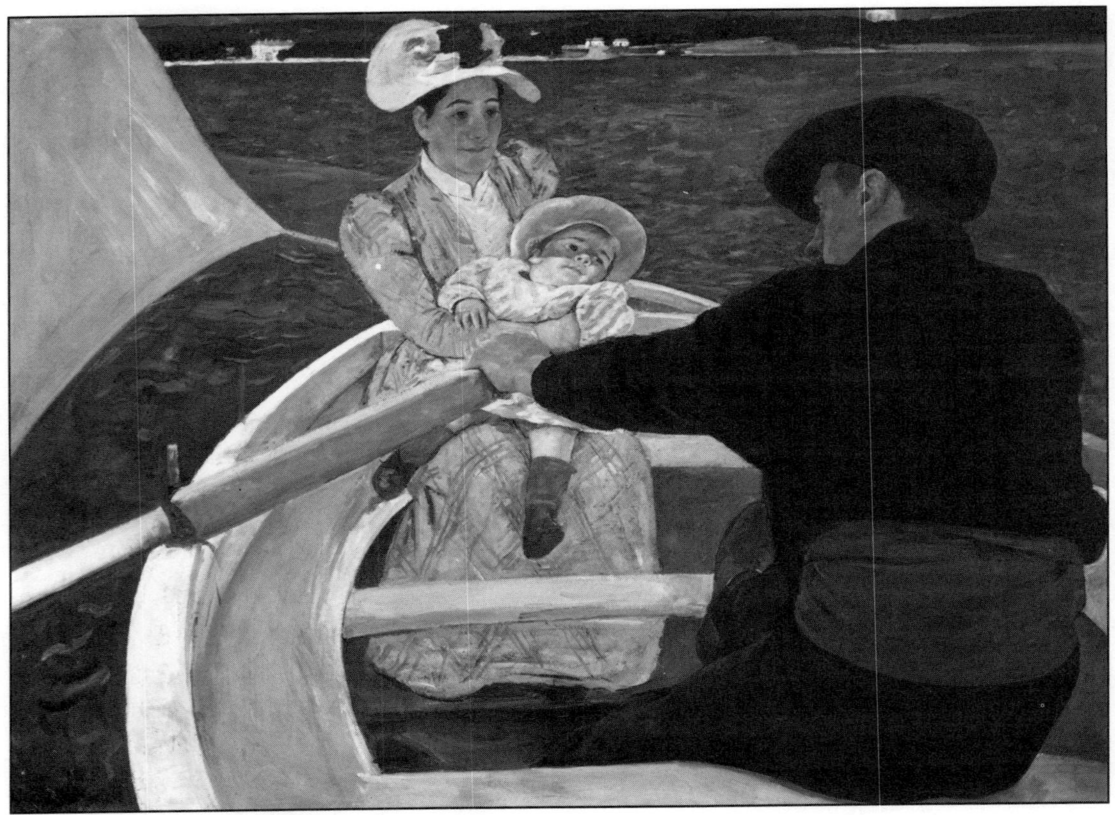

The Boating Party, 1893, by Mary Cassatt (oil on canvas).

Mary Cassatt (1844-1926) was an American painter who lived and worked in France as an important member of the impressionist group.

Courtesy of The National Gallery of Art, Washington, D.C. Chester Dale Collection. © Board of Trustees.

ships rather than of people standing alone, a world that coheres through human connection rather than through systems of rules, she finds the puzzle in the dilemma to lie in the failure of the druggist to respond to the wife. Saying that "it is not right for someone to die when their life could be saved," she assumes that if the druggist were to see the consequences of his refusal to lower his price, he would realize that, "he should just give it to the wife and then have the husband pay back the money later." Thus she considers the solution to the dilemma to lie in making the wife's condition more salient to the druggist or, that failing, in appealing to others who are in a position to help.

Just as Jake is confident the judge would agree that stealing is the right thing for Heinz to do, so Amy is confident that, "if Heinz and the druggist had talked it out long enough, they could reach something besides stealing." As he considers the law to "have mistakes," so she sees this drama as a mistake, believing that "the world should just share things more and then people wouldn't have to steal." Both children thus recognize the need for agreement but see it as mediated in different ways—he impersonally through systems of logic and law, she personally through communication in relationship. Just as he relies on the conventions of logic to deduce the solution to this dilemma, assuming these conventions to be shared, so she relies on a process of communication, assuming connection and believing that her voice will be heard. Yet while his assumptions about agreement are confirmed by the convergence in logic between his answers and the questions posed, her assumptions are belied by the failure of communication, the interviewer's inability to understand her response.

Although the frustration of the interview with Amy is apparent in the repetition of questions and its ultimate circularity, the problem of interpretation is focused by the assessment of her response. When considered in the light of Kohlberg's definition of the stages and sequence of moral development, her moral judgments appear to be a full stage lower in maturity than those of the boy. Scored as a mixture of stages two and three, her responses seem to reveal a feeling of powerlessness in the world, an inability to think systematically about the concepts of morality or law, a reluctance to challenge authority or to examine the logic of received moral truths, a failure even to conceive of acting directly to save a life or to consider that such action, if taken, could possibly have an effect. As her reliance on relationships seems to reveal a continuing dependence and vulnerability, so her belief in communication as the mode through which to resolve moral dilemmas appears naive and cognitively immature.

Yet Amy's description of herself conveys a markedly different impression. Once again, the hallmarks of the preadolescent child depict a child secure in her sense of herself, confident in the substance of her beliefs, and sure of her ability to do something of value in the world. Describing herself at eleven as "growing and changing," she says that she "sees some things differently now, just because I know myself really well now, and I know a lot more about the world." Yet the world she knows is a different world from that refracted by Kohlberg's construction of Heinz's dilemma. Her world is a world of relationships and psychological truths where an awareness of the connection between people gives rise to a recognition of responsibility for one another, a perception of the need for response. Seen in this light, her understanding of morality as arising from the recognition of relationship, her belief in communication as the mode of conflict resolution, and her conviction that the solution to the dilemma will follow from its compelling representation seem far from naive or cognitively immature. Instead, Amy's judgments contain the insights central to an ethic of care, just as Jake's judgments reflect the logic of the justice approach. Her incipient awareness of the "method of truth," the central tenet of nonviolent conflict resolution, and her belief in the restorative activity of care, lead her to see the actors in the dilemma arrayed not as opponents in a contest of rights but as members of a network of relationships on whose continuation they all depend. Consequently her solution to the dilemma lies in activating the network by communication, securing the inclusion of the wife by strengthening rather than severing connections.

But the different logic of Amy's response calls attention to the interpretation of the interview itself. Conceived as an interrogation, it appears instead as a dialogue, which takes on moral dimensions of its own, pertaining to the interviewer's uses of power and to the manifestations of respect. With this shift in the conception of the interview, it immediately becomes clear that the interviewer's problem in understanding Amy's response stems from the fact that Amy is answering a different question from the one the interviewer thought had been posed. Amy is considering not *whether* Heinz should act in this situation ("*should* Heinz steal the drug?") but rather how Heinz should act in response to his awareness of his wife's need ("Should Heinz *steal* the drug?"). The interviewer takes the mode of action for granted, presuming it to be a matter of fact; Amy assumes the necessity for action and considers what form it should take. In the interviewer's failure to imagine a response not dreamt of in Kohlberg's moral philosophy lies the failure to hear Amy's question and to see the logic in her response, to discern that what appears, from one perspective, to be an evasion of the dilemma signifies in other terms a recognition of the problem and a search for a more adequate solution.

Thus in Heinz's dilemma these two children see two very different moral problems—Jake a conflict between life and property that can be resolved by logical deduction, Amy a fracture of human relationship that must be mended with its own thread.

Asking different questions that arise from different conceptions of the moral domain, the children arrive at answers that fundamentally diverge, and the arrangement of these answers as successive stages on a scale of increasing moral maturity calibrated by the logic of the boy's response misses the different truth revealed in the judgment of the girl. To the question, "What does he see that she does not?" Kohlberg's theory provides a ready response, manifest in the scoring of Jake's judgments a full stage higher than Amy's in moral maturity; to the question, "What does she see that he does not?" Kohlberg's theory has nothing to say. Since most of her responses fall through the sieve of Kohlberg's scoring system, her responses appear from his perspective to lie outside the moral domain.

Yet just as Jake reveals a sophisticated understanding of the logic of justification, so Amy is equally sophisticated in her understanding of the nature of choice. Recognizing that "if both the roads went in totally separate ways, if you pick one, you'll never know what would happen if you went the other way," she explains that "that's the chance you have to take, and like I said, it's just really a guess." To illustrate her point "in a simple way," she describes her choice to spend the summer at camp:

> I will never know what would have happened if I had stayed here, and if something goes wrong at camp, I'll never know if I stayed here if it would have been better. There's really no way around it because there's no way you can do both at once, so you've got to decide, but you'll never know.

In this way, these two eleven-year-old children, both highly intelligent and perceptive about life, though in different ways, display different modes of moral understanding, different ways of thinking about conflict and choice. In resolving Heinz's dilemma, Jake relies on theft to avoid confrontation and turns to the law to mediate the dispute. Transposing a hierarchy of power into a hierarchy of values, he defuses a potentially explosive conflict between people by casting it as an impersonal conflict of claims. In this way, he abstracts the moral problem from the interpersonal situation, finding in the logic of fairness an objective way to decide who will win the dispute. But this hierarchical ordering, with its imagery of winning and losing and the potential for violence which it contains, gives way in Amy's construction of the dilemma to a network of connection, a web of relationships that is sustained by a process of communication. With this shift, the moral problem changes from one of unfair domination, the imposition of property over life, to one of unnecessary exclusion, the failure of the druggist to respond to the wife....

SOURCE: From Carol Gilligan *In a Different Voice: Psychological Theory and Women's Development* (Cambridge, Mass.: Harvard University Press).

Questions and Topics for Discussion and Writing

1. Why do psychologists use the "Heinz" dilemma to test ethical judgments in children? What is it about this case that makes it an ideal test?
2. What is the fundamental difference, according to Gilligan's research, in the way in which girls and boys attempt to resolve dilemmas such as the one involving Heinz and his wife?
3. Which psychological approach makes more sense today, Kohlberg's or Gilligan's?

My Confession

Leo Tolstoy

Tolstoy, Leo (1828-1910) was a Russian novelist and social thinker, who is regarded today as one of the all-time great writers of realistic fiction. His best-known works are the classic novels *War and Peace* (1865-69) and *Anna Karenina* (1875-77). In this excerpt, taken from *My Confession* (1882), Tolstoy outlines his increasing confusion about spirituality, and attempts to answer several key questions about human existence.

Although I regarded authorship as a waste of time, I continued to write during those fifteen years. I had tasted of the seduction of authorship, of the seduction of enormous monetary remunerations and applauses for my insignificant labour, and so I submitted to it, as being a means for improving my material condition and for stifling in my soul all questions about the meaning of my life and life in general.

In my writings I advocated, what to me was the only truth, that it was necessary to live in such a way as to derive the greatest comfort for oneself and one's family.

Thus I proceeded to live, but five years ago something very strange began to happen with me: I was overcome by minutes at first of perplexity and then of an arrest of life, as though I did not know how to live or what to do, and I lost myself and was dejected. But that passed, and I continued to live as before. Then those minutes of perplexity were repeated oftener and oftener, and always in one and the same form. These arrests of life found their expression in ever the same questions: "Why? Well, and then?"

At first I thought that those were simply aimless, inappropriate questions. It seemed to me that that was all well known and that if I ever wanted to busy myself with their solution, it would not cost me much labour—that now I had no time to attend to them, but that if I wanted to I should find the proper answers. But the questions began to repeat themselves oftener and oftener, answers were demanded more and more persistently, and, like dots that fall on the same spot, these questions, without any answers, thickened into one black blotch.

There happened what happens with any person who falls ill with a mortal internal disease. At first there appear insignificant symptoms of indisposition, to which the patient pays no attention; then these symptoms are repeated more and more frequently and blend into one temporally indivisible suffering. The suffering keeps growing, and before the patient has had time to look around, he becomes conscious that what he took for an indisposition is the most significant thing in the world to him—is death.

The same happened with me. I understood that it was not a passing indisposition, but something very important, and that if the questions were going to repeat themselves, it would be necessary to find an answer for them. And I tried to answer them. The questions seemed to be so foolish, simple, and childish. But the moment I touched them and tried to solve them, I became convinced, in the first place, that they were not childish and foolish, but very important and profound questions in life, and, in the second, that, no matter how much I might try, I should not be able to answer them. Before attending to my Samara estate, to my son's education, or to the writing of a book, I ought to know why I should do that. So long as I did not know why, I could not do anything. I could not live. Amidst my thoughts of farming, which interested me very much during that time, there would suddenly pass through my head a question like this: "All right, you are going to have six thousand desyatinas of land in the Government of Samara, and three hundred horses—and then?" And I completely lost my senses and did not know what to think farther. Or, when I thought of the education of my children, I said to myself: "Why?" Or, reflecting on the manner in which the masses might obtain their welfare, I suddenly said to myself; "What is that to me?" Or, thinking of fame which my works would get me, I said to myself: "All right, you will be more famous than Gógol, Pushkin, Shakespeare, Molière, and all the writers in the world—what of it?" And I was absolutely unable to make any reply. The question were not waiting, and I had to answer them at once; if I did not answer them, I could not live.

I felt that what I was standing on had given way, that I had no foundation to stand on, that that which I lived by no longer existed, and that I had nothing to live by...

All that happened with me when I was on every side surrounded by what is considered to be complete happiness. I had a good, loving, and beloved wife, good children, and a large estate, which grew and increased without any labour on my part. I was respected by my neighbours and friends, more than ever before, was praised by strangers, and, without any self-deception, could consider my name famous. With all that, I was not deranged or mentally unsound—on the contrary, I was in full command of my mental and physical powers, such as I had rarely met with in people of my age: physically I could work in a field, mowing, without falling behind a peasant; mentally I could work from eight to ten hours in succession, without experiencing any consequences from the strain. And while in such condition I arrived at the conclusion that I could not live, and, fearing death, I had to use cunning against myself, in order that I might not take my life.

This mental condition expressed itself to me in this form: my life is a stupid, mean trick played on me by somebody. Although I did not recognize that "somebody" as having created me, the form of the conception that someone had played a mean, stupid trick on me by bringing me into the world was the most natural one that presented itself to me.

Involuntarily I imagined that there, somewhere, there was somebody who was now having fun as he looked down upon me and saw me, who had lived for thirty or forty years, learning, developing, growing in body and mind, now that I had become strengthened in mind and had reached that summit of life from which it lay all before me, standing as a complete fool on that summit and seeing clearly that there was nothing in life and never would be. And that was fun to him—

But whether there was or was not that somebody who made fun of me, did not make it easier for me. I could not ascribe any sensible meaning to a single act, or to my whole life. I was only surprised that I had not understood that from the start. All that had long ago been known to everybody. Sooner or later there would come diseases and death (they had come already) to my dear ones and to me, and there would be nothing left but stench and worms. All my affairs, no matter what they might be, would sooner or later be forgotten, and I myself should not exist. So why should I worry about all these things? How could a man fail to see that and live—that was surprising! A person could live only so long as he was drunk; but the moment he sobered up, he could not help seeing that all that was only a deception, and a stupid deception at that! Really, there was nothing funny and ingenious about it, but only something cruel and stupid.

Long ago has been told the Eastern story about the traveller who in the steppe is overtaken by an infuriated beast. Trying to save himself from the animal, the traveller jumps into a waterless well, but at its bottom he sees a dragon who opens his jaws in order to swallow him. And the unfortunate man does nor dare climb out lest he perish from the infuriated beast, and does not dare jump down to the bottom of the well, lest he be devoured by the dragon, and so clutches the twig of a wild bush growing in a cleft of the well and holds on to it. His hands grow weak and he feels that soon he shall have to surrender to the peril which awaits him at either side; but he still holds on and sees two mice, one white, the other black, in even measure making a circle around the main trunk of the bush to which he is clinging, and nibbling at it on all sides. Now, at any moment, the bush will break and tear off, and he will fall into the dragon's jaws. The traveller sees that and knows that he will inevitably perish; but while he is still clinging, he sees some drops of honey hanging on the leaves of the bush, and so reaches out for them with his tongue and licks the leaves. Just so I hold on to the branch of life, knowing that the dragon of death is waiting inevitably for me, ready to tear me to pieces, and I cannot understand why I have fallen on such suffering. And I try to lick that honey which used to give me pleasure; but now it no longer gives me joy, and the white and the black mouse day and night nibble at the branch to which I am holding on. I clearly see the dragon, and the honey is no longer sweet to me. I see only the inevitable dragon and the mice, and am unable to turn my glance away from them. That is not a fable, but a veritable, indisputable, comprehensible truth.

The former deception of the pleasures of life, which stifled the terror of the dragon, no longer deceives me. No matter how much one should say to me, "You cannot understand the meaning of life, do not think, live!" I am unable to do so, because I have been doing it too long before. Now I cannot help seeing day and night, which run and lead me up to death. I see that alone, because that alone is the truth. Everything else is a lie.

The two drops of honey that have longest turned my eyes away from the cruel truth, the love of family and of authorship, which I have called an art, are no longer sweet to me.

"My family—" I said to myself, "but my family, my wife and children, they are also human beings. They are in precisely the same condition that I am in: they must either live in the lie or see the terrible truth. Why should I love them, why guard, raise, and watch them? Is it for the same despair which is in me, or for dullness of perception? Since I love them, I cannot conceal the truth from them—every step in cognition leads them up to this truth. And the truth is death."

"Art, poetry?" For a long time, under the influence of the success of human praise, I tried to persuade myself that that was a thing which could be done, even though death should come and destroy everything, my deeds, as well as my memory of them; but soon I came to see that that, too, was a deception. It was clear to me that art was an adornment of life, a decoy of life. But life lost all its attractiveness for me. How, then, could I entrap others? So long as I did not live my own life, and a strange life bore me on its waves; so long as I believed that life had some sense, although I was not able to express it—the reflections of life of every description in poetry and in the arts afforded me pleasure, and I was delighted to look at life through this little mirror or art; but when I began to look for the meaning of life, when I experienced the necessity of living myself, that little mirror became either useless, superfluous, and ridiculous, or painful to me. I could no longer console myself with what I saw in the mirror, namely, that my situation was stupid and desperate. It was all right for me to rejoice so long as I believed in the depth of my soul that life had some sense. At that time the play of lights—of the comical, the tragical, the touching, the beautiful, the terrible in life—afforded me amusement. But when I knew that life was meaningless and terrible, the play in the little mirror could no longer amuse me. No sweetness of honey could be sweet to me, when I saw the dragon and the mice that were nibbling down my support...

In my search after the question of life I experienced the same feeling which a man who has lost his way in the forest may experience.

He comes to a clearing, climbs a tree, and clearly sees an unlimited space before him; at the same time he sees that there are no houses there, and that there can be none; he goes back to the forest, into the darkness, and he sees darkness, and again there are no houses.

Thus I blundered in this forest of human knowledge, between the clearings of the mathematical and experimental sciences, which disclosed to me clear horizons, but such in the direction of which

Author of "War and Peace"

Leo Tolstoy

Tolstoy, Leo (1828–1910) was a Russian novelist and social thinker, who is regarded today as one of the all-time great writers of realistic fiction.

Tolstoy was the son of a noble landowner but was orphaned at the age of nine. He was brought up by relatives and educated by French and German tutors. Tolstoy began university at the age of 16 and dropped out three years later without having completed a degree. After an unsuccessful attempt to improve the condition of the serfs on his family's estate, he immersed himself in the luxuries of Moscow's high society.

In 1851 Tolstoy went to the Caucasus and joined the army. While there, he came into contact with the people who were to be the focus for his 1963 novel, *The Cossacks* (1863). While remaining in the Caucasus, Tolstoy completed an autobiographical novel, *Childhood* (1852), followed by two others, *Boyhood* (1854) and *Youth* (1856). These works, along with the *Sevastopol Stories* (1855–56), based on Tolstoy's participation in the Crimean War, immediately established Tolstoy's reputation as a writer. He returned to Saint Petersburg in 1856 and became interested in the education of peasants, eventually establishing a progressive school. In 1862 he married Sonya (Sofya) Andreyevna Bers, with whom he would have longstanding disputes about his desire to relinquish their material wealth. In the next 15 years he raised a large family, successfully managed his estate, and wrote his two greatest novels, *War and Peace* (1865–69) and *Anna Karenina* (1875–77).

In his *Confession* (1882), Tolstoy outlines his increasing confusion about spirituality and the apparent wastefulness and apathy of Russia's wealthy. Tolstoy developed a profound and radical new faith in religion in *The Kingdom of God is Within You* (1894) and other works. Tolstoy also wrote works about art's relationship to his society, such as *What Is Art?* (1898) in which he argues for art forms that can be understood by everyone, not just the educated members of society.

Tolstoy composed a number of works of imaginative fiction, such as *Stories for the People* (early to mid–1880s), which complied with his assertions about accessible art. He produced pieces intended for a more advanced audience, such as *The Death of Ivan Ilych* (1886) and *Master and Man* (1895), the short story *The Kreutzer Sonata* (1889), the play *The Power of Darkness* (1888); and the novel *Resurrection* (1899). He died at the age of 82.

The caricature (a drawing or sketch of a person in which particular or unusual characteristices are emphasized) above was drawn by Olaf Gulbransson (1873-1958).

there could be no house, and between the darkness of the speculative sciences, where I sunk into a deeper darkness, the farther I proceeded, and I convinced myself at last that there was no way out and could not be.

By abandoning myself to the bright side of knowledge I saw that I only turned my eyes away from the question. No matter how enticing and clear the horizons were that were disclosed to me, no matter how enticing it was to bury myself in the infinitude of this knowledge, I comprehended that these sciences were the more clear, the less I needed them, the less they answered my question.

"Well, I know," I said to myself, "all which science wants so persistently to know, but there is no answer to the question about the meaning of my life." But in the speculative sphere I saw that, in spite of the fact the that the aim of the knowledge was directed straight to the answer of my question, or because of that fact, there could be no other answer than what I was giving to myself: "What is the meaning of my life?"—"None." Or, "What will come of my life?"—"Nothing." Or, "Why does everything which exists exist, and why do I exist?"—"Because it exists."

Putting the question to the one side of human knowledge, I received an endless quantity of exact answers about what I did not ask: about the chemical composition of the stars, about the movement of the sun toward the constellation of Hercules, about the origin of species and of man, about the forms of infinitely small, imponderable particles of ether; but the answer in this sphere of knowledge to my question what the meaning of my life was, was always: "You are what you call your life; you are a temporal, accidental conglomeration of particles. The interrelation, the change of these particles, produces in you that which you call life. This congeries will last for some time; then the interaction of these particles will cease, and that which you call life and all your questions will come to an end. You are an accidentally cohering globule of something. The globule is fermenting. This fermentation the globule calls its life. The globule falls to pieces, and all fermentation and all questions will come to an end." Thus the clear side of knowledge answers, and it cannot say anything else, if only it strictly follows its principles.

With such an answer it appears that the answer is not a reply to the question. I want to know the meaning of my life, but the fact that it is a particle of the infinite not only gives it no meaning, but even destroys every possible meaning.

Those obscure transactions which this side of the experimental, exact science has with speculation, when it says that the meaning of life consists in evolution and the cooperation with this evolution, because of their obscurity and inexactness cannot be regarded as answers.

The other side of knowledge, the speculative, so long as it sticks strictly to its fundamental principles in giving a direct answer to the question, everywhere and at all times has answered one and the same: "The world is something infinite and incomprehensible. Human life is an incomprehensible part of this incomprehensible *all*... "

I lived for a long time in this madness, which, not in words, but in deeds, is particularly characteristic of us, the most liberal and l learned of men. But, thanks either to my strange, physical love for the real working class, which made me understand it and see that it is not so stupid as we suppose, or to the sincerity of my conviction, which was that I could know nothing and that the best that I could do was to hang myself—I felt that if I wanted to live and understand the meaning of life, I ought naturally to look for it, not among those who had lost the meaning of life and wanted to kill themselves, but among those billions departed and living men who had been carrying their own lives and ours upon their shoulders. And I looked around at the enormous masses of deceased and living men—not learned and wealthy, but simple men—and I saw something quite different. I saw that all these billions of men that lived or had lived, all, with rare exceptions did not fit into my subdivisions,[1] and that I could not recognize them as not understanding the question, because they themselves put it and answered it with surprising clearness. Nor could I recognize them as Epicureans, because their lives were composed rather of privations and suffering than of enjoyment. Still less could I recognize them as senselessly living out their meaningless lives, because every act of theirs and death itself was explained by them. They regarded it as the greatest evil to kill themselves. It appeared, then, that all humanity was in possession of a knowledge of the meaning of life, which I did not recognize and which I condemned. It turned out that rational knowledge did not give any meaning to life, excluded life, while the meaning which by billions of people, by all humanity, was ascribed to life was based on some despised, false knowledge.

The rational knowledge in the person of the learned and the wise denied the meaning of life,

Starry Night, 1889, by Vincent van Gogh (oil on canvas; 73.7 x 92.1 cm.).
Vincent van Gogh (1853-1890) was a Dutch post-impressionist painter, whose work represents the archetype of expressionism, the idea of emotional spontaneity in painting.

but the enormous masses of men, all humanity, recognized this meaning in an irrational knowledge. This irrational knowledge was faith, the same that I could not help but reject. That was God as one and three, the creation in six days, devils and angels, and all that which I could not accept so long as I had not lost my senses.

My situation was a terrible one. I knew that I should not find anything on the path of rational knowledge but the negation of life, and there, in faith, nothing but the negation of reason, which was still more impossible than the negation of life. From the rational knowledge it followed that life was an evil and men knew it—it depended on men whether they should cease living and yet they lived and continued to live, all I myself lived, though I had known long ago that life was meaningless and an evil. From faith it followed that in order to understand life, I must renounce reason, for which alone a meaning was needed.

There resulted a contradiction, from which there were two ways out: either what I called rational was not so rational as I had thought, or that which to me appeared irrational was not so irrational as I had thought. And I began to verify the train of thoughts of my rational knowledge.

In verifying the train of thoughts of my rational knowledge, I found that it was quite correct. The deduction that life was nothing was inevitable; but I saw a mistake. The mistake was that I had not reasoned in conformity with the question put by me. The question was, "Why should I live?" that is,

"What real, indestructible essence will come from my phantasmal, destructible life? What meaning has my finite existence in this infinite world?" And in order to answer this question, I studied life.

The solutions of all possible questions of life apparently could not satisfy me, because my question, no matter how simple it appeared in the beginning, included the necessity of explaining the finite through the infinite, and vice versa.

I asked, "What is the extra-temporal, extra-causal, extra-spatial meaning of life?" But I gave an answer to the question, "What is the temporal, causal, spatial meaning of my life?" The result was that after a long labour of mind I answered, "None."

In my reflections I constantly equated, nor could I do otherwise, the finite with the finite, the infinite with the infinite, and so from that resulted precisely what had to result: force was force, matter was matter, will was will, infinity was infinity, nothing was nothing—and nothing else could come from it.

There happened something like what at times takes place in mathematics: you think you are solving an equation, when you have only an identity. The reasoning is correct, but you receive as a result the answer: *a = a, or x = x, or 0 = 0.* The same happened with my reflection in respect to the question about the meaning of my life. The answers given by all science to that question are only identities.

Indeed the strictly scientific knowledge, that knowledge which, as Descartes did, begins with a full doubt in everything, rejects all knowledge which has been taken on trust, and builds everything anew on the laws of reason and experience, cannot give any other answer to the question of life than what I received—an indefinite answer. It only seemed to me at first that science gave me a positive answer—Schopenhaueer's answer: I analyzed the matter, I saw that the answer was not a positive one, but that it was only my feeling which expressed it as such. The answer, strictly expressed, as it is expressed by Brahmins, by Solomon, and by Schopenhauer, is only an indefinite answer, or an identity, *0 = 0*, life is nothing. Thus the philosophical knowledge does not negate anything, but only answers that the question cannot be solved by it, that for philosophy the solution remains insoluble.

When I saw that, I understood that it was not right for me to look for an answer to my question in rational knowledge, and that the answer given

Sweeping The Garden

Olga Broumas

for Debora Hayes

Slowly learning again to love
ourselves working. Paul Eluard

said the body
is that part of the soul
perceptible by the five senses. To love
the body to love its work
to love the hand that praises both to praise
the body to love the soul
that dreams and wakes us back alive
against the slothful odds: fatigue
depression loneliness
the perishable still recognition
what needs

be done. *Sweep the garden, any size*
said the roshi. Sweeping sweeping

alone as the garden grows
large or small. Any song
sung working the garden brings
up from sand gravel soil through
straw bamboo wood and less
tangible elements Power
song for the hands Healing
song for the senses what can
and cannot be perceived
of the soul.

SOURCE: *Soie Sauvage* (Port Townsend, WA: Copper Canyon Press, 1979). Reprinted by permission of the author.

Weeding

Michael Blumenthal

Some say it's woman's work, this bending
and kneeling toward the earth, this task
that separates what feeds from what is fed,
and if it is then I am woman now, pulling
the green from the green, sifting the dirt,
praising the sweet conspiracy that has made
leaf of the seed, and work of my idleness.

Once, I loved a woman who held
the scent of dirt like perfume in her hands,
whose very voice could make the seeds grow
in any weather. Now, I am becoming
that woman, so that the next one I love
need be nothing I have yet a name for.
And someday, I believe, the earth's good works
will belong to anyone, a sweet dream
without gender or contentiousness in which
all who bend with a good heart toward what
survives can be called: *mother.*

Loving a woman now
who makes me man, immune
to any task the mind can simplify,
I bend my body, lovely in its ribs,
toward the earth again, so that the man
and the woman who live inside it may find
peace together, so that all that is separate
inside my life might finally sing: the one song
I have been practicing all these years,
in any place the gods might pause to occupy,
as they do here and now, Amen.

SOURCE: Michael Blumenthal, *Days We Would Rather Know* (New York: Penguin, 1984).

by rational knowledge was only an indication that the answer might be got if the question were differently put, but only when into the discussion of the question should be introduced the question of the relation of the finite to the infinite. I also understood that, no matter how irrational and monstrous the answers might be that faith gave, they had this advantage that they introduced into each answer the relation of the finite to the infinite, without which there could be no answer.

No matter how I may put the question, "How must I live?" the answer is, "According to God's law." "What real result will there be from my life?"—"Eternal torment or eternal bliss." "What is the meaning which is not destroyed by death?"—"The union with infinite God, paradise."

Thus, outside the rational knowledge, which had to me appeared as the only one, I was inevitably led to recognize that all living humanity had a certain other irrational knowledge, faith, which made it possible to live.

All the irrationality of faith remained the same for me, but I could not help recognizing that it alone gave to humanity answers to the questions of life, and, in consequence of them, the possibility of living.

The rational knowledge brought me to the recognition that life was meaningless—my life stopped, and I wanted to destroy myself. When I looked around at people, at all humanity, I saw that people lived and asserted that they knew the meaning of life. I looked back at myself: I lived so long as I knew the meaning of life. As to other people, so even to me, did faith give the meaning of life and the possibility of living.

Looking again at the people of other countries, contemporaries of mine and those passed away, I saw again the same. Where life had been, there faith, ever since humanity had existed, had given the possibility of living, and the chief features of faith were everywhere one and the same.

No matter what answers faith may give, its every answer gives to the finite existence of man the sense of the infinite—a sense which is not destroyed by suffering, privation, and death. Consequently in faith alone could we find the meaning and possibility of life. What, then, was faith? I understood that faith was not merely an evidence of things not seen, and so forth, not revelation (that is only the description of one of the symptoms of faith), not the relation of man to man (faith has to be defined, and then God, and not first God, and faith through him), not merely an agreement with what a man was told, as faith was generally understood—that faith as the knowledge of the meaning of human life, in consequence of which man did not destroy himself, but lived. Faith is the power of life. If a man lives he believes in something. If he did not believe that he ought to live for some purpose, he would not live. If he does not see and understand the phantasm of the finite, he believes in that finite; if he understands the phantasm of the finite, he must believe in the infinite. Without faith one cannot live...

In order that all humanity may be able to live, in order that they may continue living, giving a meaning to life, they, those billions, must have another, a real knowledge of faith, for not the fact that I, with Solomon and Schopenhauer, did not kill myself convinced me of the existence of faith, but that these billions have lived and had borne us, me and Solomon, on the waves of life.

Then I began to cultivate the acquaintance of the believers from among the poor, the simple and unlettered folk, of pilgrims, monks, dissenters, peasants. The doctrine of these people from among the masses was also the Christian doctrine that the quasi-believers of our circle professed. With the Christian truths were also mixed in very many superstitions, but there was this difference: the superstitions of our circle were quite unnecessary to them, had no connection with their lives, were only a kind of an Epicurean amusement, while the superstitions of the believers from among the labouring classes were to such an extent blended with their life that it would have been impossible to imagine it without these superstitions—it was a necessary condition of that life. I began to examine closely the lives and beliefs of these people, and the more I examined them, the more did I become convinced that they had the real faith that their faith was necessary for them, and that it alone gave them a meaning and possibility of life. In contradistinction to what I saw in our circle, where life without faith was possible, and where hardly one in a thousand professed to be a believer, among them there was hardly one in a thousand who was not a believer. In contradistinction to what I saw in our circle, where all life passed in idleness, amusements, and tedium of life, I saw that the whole life of these people was passed in hard work, and that they were satisfied with life. In contradistinction to the people of our circle, who struggled and murmured against fate because of their privations and their suffering, these people accepted diseases and sorrows without any perplexity or opposition, but with the calm and firm conviction that it was all for good. In contradistinction to the fact that the more intelligent we are, the less do we understand the meaning of life and the more do we see a kind of a bad joke in our suffering and death, these people live, suffer, and approach death, and suffer in peace and more often in joy. In contradistinction to the fact that a calm death, a death without terror or despair, is the greatest exception in our circle, a restless, unsubmissive, joyless death is one of the greatest exceptions among the masses. And of such people, who are deprived of everything which for Solomon and from me constitutes the only good of life, and who withal experience the greatest happiness, there is an enormous number. I cast a broader glance about me. I examined the life of past and present vast masses of men, and I saw people who in like manner had understood the meaning of life, who had known how to live and die, not two, not three, not ten, but hundreds, thousands, millions. All of them, infinitely diversified as to habits, intellect, culture, situation, all equally and quite contrary to my ignorance knew the meaning of life and of death, worked calmly, bore privations and suffering, lived and died, seeing in that not vanity, but good.

I began to love those people. The more I penetrated into their life, the life of the men now living, and the life of men departed, of whom I had read and heard, the more did I love them, and the easier it became for me to live. Thus I lived for about two years, and within me took place a transformation, which had long been working within me, and the germ of which had always been in me. What happened with me was that the life of our circle—of the rich and the learned—not only disgusted me, but even lost all its meaning. All our acts, reflections, sciences, arts—all that appeared to me in a new light. I saw that all that was mere pampering of the appetites, and that no meaning could be found in it; but the life of all the working masses, of all humanity, which created life, presented itself to me in its real significance. I saw that that was life itself and that the meaning given to this life was truth, and I accepted it.

Endnote

[1] Tolstoy previously observed that each of his peers assumed one of four attitudes toward life: They lived in ignorance of the problem of life's meaning; ignored the problem and pursued whatever pleasures possible; acknowledged the meaninglessness of life and committed suicide; or acknowledged the meaninglessness but lived on aimlessly, usually lacking the fortitude to take their own lives. [Eds.]

SOURCE: Tolstoy, Leo., translated by Leo Wiener, *My Confession* (London: J.M. Dent & Sons, 1905). Reprinted with permission.

Questions and Topics for Discussion and Writing

1. Why would Tolstoy's position as a member of the landowning class make him so confused about the meaning of human existence?
2. What does Tolstoy say about how his success as a writer has affected his search for meaning?
3. How does Tolstoy ultimately conclude that answers about human life can be found? What other thinkers or writers might disagree with this view?

The Purpose of Philosophy

Isaiah Berlin

In this article, philosopher Isaiah Berlin attempts to discover what exactly it is that he and his colleagues *do* when they "do" philosophy. According to Berlin, while it is easy enough to define the bounds of disciplines like chemistry or history (although there are certainly chemists and historians who would disagree heartily), philosophy suffers from having less well-marked targets.

What is the subject-matter of philosophy? There is no universally accepted answer to this question. Opinions differ, from those who regard it as contemplation of all time and all existence—the queen of the sciences—the keystone of the entire arch of human knowledge—to those who wish to dismiss it as a pseudo-science exploiting verbal confusions, a symptom of intellectual immaturity, due to be consigned together with theology and other speculative disciplines to the museum of curious antiquities, as astrology and alchemy have long ago been relegated by the victorious march of the natural sciences.

Perhaps the best way of approaching this topic is to ask, what constitutes the field of other disciplines? How do we demarcate the province of, say, chemistry or history or anthropology? Here it seems clear that subjects or fields of study are determined by the kind of questions to which they have been invented to provide the answers. The questions themselves are intelligible if, and only if, we know where to look for the answers.

If you ask someone an ordinary question, say "Where is my coat?", "Why was Mr. Kennedy elected President of the United States?", "What is the Soviet system of criminal law?", he would normally know how to set about finding an answer. We may not know the answers ourselves, but we know that in the case of the question about the coat, the proper procedure is to look on the chair, in the cupboard, etc. In the case of Mr. Kennedy's election or the Soviet system of law we consult writings or specialists for the kind of empirical evidence which leads to the relevant conclusions and renders them, if not certain, at any rate probable.

In other words, we know where to look for the answer; we know what makes some answers plausible and others not. What makes this type of question intelligible in the first place is that we think that the answer can be discovered by empirical means, that is, by orderly observation or experiment, or methods compounded of these, namely those of common sense or the natural sciences. There is another class of questions where we are no less clear about the proper route by which the answers are to be sought, namely the formal disciplines: mathematics, for example, or logic, or grammar, or chess or heraldry, defined in terms of certain fixed axioms and certain rules of deduction, etc., where the answer to problems is to be found by applying these rules in the manner prescribed as correct.

We do not know the correct proof of Fermat's Theorem, for example,—no one is known to have found it—but we know along what lines to proceed; we know what kind of methods will, and what kind of methods will not, be relevant to the answer. If anyone thinks that answers to mathematical problems can be obtained by looking at green fields or the behaviour of bees, or that answers to empirical problems can be obtained by pure calculation without any factual content at all,

Interpreting the World

What is Philosophy?

As Isaiah Berlin suggests, the study of philosophy is often made murky by confusion regarding the nature of the discipline itself.

While philosophers debate particular questions about ethics or existence, often disagreeing about the very questions they are supposed to be arguing about, they *do* agree to some extent about the divisions that exist within the formal study of philosophy.

The following are some of the major branches of philosophy:

Metaphysics: Metaphysics is the study of the true nature of objects or events. The famous question about the tree falling in the forest without anyone to see or hear it is an example of a metaphysical problem. Many would suggest that such an event depends on someone being there to witness it before it can be said to have happened, while others would argue that the tree falls no matter who sees or hears it. Metaphysics attempts to address the balance between things as they are and things as we perceive them.

Epistemology: Closely linked to metaphysics, epistemology is the study of knowledge, or of how people know things. It is also concerned with different levels and types of knowledge and questions about how thoroughly we can really know objects or prepositions. Epistemologists often argue over whether or not people can fully comprehend the world around them, or whether it is to some degree an illusion.

Moral philosophy: Moral or ethical philosophers are concerned with questions about life's "shoulds," such as "should everyone do unto others as they would have done unto them?" or "should people always keep their promises, even when doing so can have disastrous consequences?" These questions revolve around people's perceived obligations to each other. Some philosophers, known as "moral relativists" believe that morality is determined by particular situations, while others feel—the "moral absolutists"—that there is a set of moral rules that should be followed at all times, no matter what the situation seems to dictate. Moral or ethical philosophy has important implications for the legal system.

Political philosophy: Political philosophers move from premises about what constitutes "the good life" for individuals and extend them into systems for governing or organizing large groups. Marxism, conservatism and liberalism are examples of political philosophies; all take premises about human nature and expand them into general rules for governing society.

Logic: The study of logic attempts to prove, through both intuition and empirical observation, that certain premises or observations are true or not true. For example, the simplest form of logical argument might be that if A = B, then B = A. Logicians are of course concerned with much more difficult premises, often attaching a whole series of conditions to either A or B, and sometimes conduct their work through a special language of symbolic notation. Smooth scientific experimentation often hinges on the existence of logical premises.

we would today think them mistaken to the point of insanity. Each of these major types of questions—the factual and the formal—possesses its own specialised techniques: discoveries by men of genius in these fields, once they are established, can be used by men of no genius at all in a semi-mechanical manner in order to obtain correct results.

The hallmark of these provinces of human thought is that once the question is put we know in which direction to proceed to try to obtain the answer. The history of systematic human thought is largely a sustained effort to formulate all the questions that occur to mankind in such a way that the answers to them will fall into one or other of two great baskets: the empirical, i.e. questions whose answers depend, in the end, on the data of observation; and the formal, i.e. questions whose answers depend on pure calculation, untrammelled by factual knowledge. This dichotomy is a drastically over-simple formulation: empirical and formal elements are not so easily disentangled; but it contains enough truth not to be seriously misleading. The distinction between these two great sources of human knowledge has been recognised since the first beginning of self-conscious thinking.

Yet there are certain questions that do not easily fit into this simple classification. "What is an okapi?" is answered easily enough by an act of empirical observation. Similarly "What is the cube root of 729?" is settled by a piece of calculation in accordance with accepted rules. But if I ask "What is time?", "What is a number?", "What is the purpose of human life on earth?", "How can I know past facts that are no longer there—no longer where?", "Are all men truly brothers?", how do I set about looking for the answer? If I ask "Where is my coat?" a possible answer (whether correct or not) would be "In the cupboard", and we would all know where to look. But if a child asked me "Where is the image in the mirror?" it would be little use to invite it to look inside the mirror, which it would find to consist of solid glass; or on the surface of the mirror, for the image is certainly not on its surface in the sense in which a postage stamp stuck on it might be; or behind the mirror (which is where the image looks as if it were), for if you look behind the mirror you will find no image there—and so on.

Many who think long enough, and intensely enough, about such questions as "What is time?" or "Can time stand still?", "When I see double, what is there two of?", "How do I know that other human beings (or material objects) are not mere figments of my own mind?", get into a state of hopeless frustration. "What is the meaning of 'the future tense'?" can be answered by grammarians by mechanically applying formal rules; but if I ask "What is the meaning of 'the future'?" where are we to look for the answer?

There seems to be something queer about all these questions—as wide apart as those about double vision, or number, or the brotherhood of men, or purposes of life; they differ from the questions in the other basket in that the question itself does not seem to contain a pointer to the way in which the answer to it is to be found. The other, more ordinary, questions contain precisely such pointers—built-in techniques for finding the answers to them. The questions about time, the existence of others and so on reduce the questioner to perplexity, and annoy practical people precisely because they do not seem to lead to clear answers or useful knowledge of any kind.

This shows that between the two original baskets, the empirical and the formal, there is at least one intermediate basket, in which all those questions live which cannot easily be fitted into the other two. These questions are of the most diverse nature; some appear to be questions of fact, others of value; some are questions about words and a few symbols; others are about methods pursued by those who use them: scientists, artists, critics, common men in the ordinary affairs of life; still others are about the relations between various provinces of knowledge; some deal with the presuppositions of thinking, some with the nature and ends of moral or social or political action.

The only common characteristic which all these questions appear to have is that they cannot be answered either by observation or calculation, either by inductive methods or deductive; and, as a crucial corollary of this, that those who ask them are faced with a perplexity from the very beginning—the do not know where to look for the answers; there are no dictionaries, encyclopedias, compendia of knowledge, no experts, no orthodoxies, which can be referred to with confidence as possessing unquestionable authority or knowledge in these matters. Moreover some of these questions are distinguished by being general and by dealing with matters of principle; and others, while not themselves general, very readily raise or lead to questions of principle.

Such questions tend to be called philosophical.

Lies

Yevgeny Yevtushenko

Telling lies to the young is wrong.
Proving to them that lies are true is wrong.
Telling them that God's in his heaven
and all's well with the world is wrong.
The young know what you mean. The
young are people.
Tell them the difficulties can't be counted,
and let them see not only what will be
but see with clarity these present times.
Say obstacles exist they must encounter
sorrow happens, hardship happens.
The hell with it. Who never knew
the price of happiness will not be happy.
Forgive no error you recognize,
it will repeat itself, increase,
and afterwards our pupils
will not forgive in us what we forgave.

Ordinary men regard them with contempt, or awe, or suspicion, according to their temperaments. For this reason, if for no other, there is a natural tendency to try to reformulate these questions in such a way that all or at any rate parts of them can be answered either by empirical or formal statements; that is to say efforts, sometimes very desperate ones, are made to fit them into either the empirical or the formal basket, where agreed methods, elaborated over the centuries, yield dependable results whose truth can be tested by accepted means.

The history of human knowledge is, to a large degree, a sustained attempt to shuffle all questions into one of the two "viable" categories; for as soon as a puzzling, "queer" question can be translated into one that can be treated by an empirical or a formal discipline, it ceases to be philosophical and becomes part of a recognised science.[1] Thus it was no mistake to regard astronomy in, say, the early Middle Ages as a "philosophical" discipline: so long as answers to questions about stars and planets were not determined by observation or experiment and calculation, but were dominated by such non-empirical notions as those, e.g. of perfect bodies determined to pursue circular paths by their goals or inner essences with which they were endowed by God or Nature, even if this was rendered improbable by empirical observation, it was not clear how astronomical questions could be settled; i.e. what part was to be played by observing actual heavenly bodies, and what part by theological or metaphysical assertions which were not capable of being tested either by empirical or by formal means.

Only when questions in astronomy were formulated in such a manner that clear answers could be discovered by using and depending on the methods of observation and experiment, and these in their turn could be connected in a systematic structure the coherence of which could be tested by purely logical or mathematical means, was the modern science of astronomy created, leaving behind it a cloud of obscure metaphysical notions unconnected with empirical tests and consequently no longer relevant to the new science, and so gradually relegated and forgotten.

So, too, in our own time, such disciplines as economic, psychology, semantics, logic itself, are gradually shaking themselves free from everything that is neither dependent on observation nor formal; if and when they have successfully completed this process they will be finally launched on independent careers of their own as natural or formal sciences, with a rich philosophical past, but an empirical and/or formal present and future. The history of thought is thus a long series of parricides, in which new disciplines seek to achieve their freedom by killing off the parent subjects and eradicating from within themselves whatever traces still linger within them of "philosophical" problems, i.e. the kind of questions that do not carry within their own structure clear indications of the techniques of their own solution.

That, at any rate, is the ideal of such sciences; in so far as some of their problems (e.g. in modern cosmology) are not formulated in purely empirical or mathematical terms, their field necessarily overlaps with that of philosophy. Indeed, it would be rash to say of any developed high-level science that it has finally eradicated its philosophical problems. In physics, for instance, fundamental questions exist at the present time which in many ways seem philosophical—questions that concern the very framework of concepts in terms of which hypotheses are to be formed and observations interpreted. How are wave-models and particle-models related to one another? Is indeterminacy an ultimate feature of sub-atomic theory? Such questions are of a philosophical type; in particular, no deductive or observational programme leads at all directly to their solution. On the other hand, it is of course true that those who try to answer such questions need to be trained and gifted in physics, and that any answers to those questions would constitute advances in the science of physics itself. Although, with the progressive separation of the positive sciences, no philosophers' questions are physical, some physicists' questions are still philosophical.

This is one reason, but only one, why the scope and content of philosophy does not seem greatly diminished by this process of attrition. For no matter how many questions can be so transformed as to be capable of empirical or formal treatment, the number of questions that seem incapable of being so treated does not appear to grow less. This fact would have distressed the philosophers of the Enlightenment, who were convinced that all genuine questions could be solved by the methods that had achieved so magnificent a triumph in the hands of the natural scientists of the seventeenth and early eighteenth centuries.

It is true that even in that clear day men still appeared no nearer to the solution of such central, indubitably philosophical, because apparently unanswerable, questions as whether men and things had been created to fulfil a purpose by God or by nature, and if so what purpose; whether men were free to choose between alternatives, or on the contrary were rigorously determined by the causal laws that governed inanimate nature; whether ethical and aesthetic truths were universal and objective or relative and subjective; whether men were only bundles of flesh and blood and bone and nervous tissue, or the earthly habitations of immortal souls; whether human history had a discernible pattern, or was a repetitive causal sequence or a succession of casual and unintelligible accidents. These ancient questions tormented them as they had their ancestors in Greece and Rome and Palestine and the medieval west.

Physics and chemistry did not tell one why some men were obliged to obey other men and under what circumstances, and what was the nature of such obligations; what was good and what was evil; whether happiness and knowledge, justice and mercy, liberty and equality, efficiency and individual independence, were equally valid goals of human action, and if so, whether they were compatible with one another, and if not, which them were to be chosen, and what were valid criteria for such choices, and how we could be certain about their validity, and what was meant by the notion of validity itself; and many more questions of this type.

Yet—so a good many eighteenth-century philosophers argued—a similar state of chaos and doubt had once prevailed in the realm of the natural sciences too; yet there human genius had finally prevailed and created order.

> Nature and Nature's laws lay hid in night:
> God said "Let Newton be!" and all was light.

If Newton could, with a small number of basic laws, enable us, at least in theory, to determine the position and motion of every physical entity in the universe, and in this way abolish at one blow a vast, shapeless mass of conflicting, obscure, and only half-intelligible rules of thumb which had hitherto passed for natural knowledge, was it not reasonable to expect that by applying similar principles of human conduct and the analysis of the nature of man, we should be able to obtain similar clarification and establish the human sciences upon equally firm foundations?

Philosophy fed on the muddles and obscurities of language; if these were cleared away, it would surely be found that the only questions left would be concerned with testable human beliefs, or expressions of identifiable, everyday human needs or hopes or fears or interests. These were the proper study of psychologists, anthropologists, sociologists, economists; all that was needed was a Newton, or series of Newtons, for the sciences of man; in this way, the perplexities of metaphysics could once and for all be removed, the idle tribe of philosophical speculators eradicated, and on the ground thus cleared, a clear and firm edifice of natural science built.

This was the hope of all the best-known philosophers of the Enlightenment, from Hobbes and Hume to Helvétius, Holbach, Condorcet, Bentham, Saint-Simon, Comte, and their successors. Yet this programme was doomed to failure. The realm of philosophy was not partitioned into a series of scientific successor states. Philosophical questions continued (and continue) to fascinate and torment inquiring minds.

Why is this so? An illuminating answer to this problem was given by Kant, the first thinker to draw a clear distinction between, on the one hand, questions of fact, and, on the other, questions about the patterns in which these facts presented themselves to us—patterns that were not themselves altered however much the facts themselves, or our knowledge of them, might alter. These patterns or categories or forms of experience were themselves not the subject-matter of any possible natural science.

Kant was the first to draw the crucial distinction between facts—the data of experience as it were, the things, persons, events, qualities, relations, that we observed or inferred or thought about—and the categories in terms of which we sensed and imagined and reflected about them. These were, for him, independent of the different cosmic attitudes—the religious or metaphysical frameworks that belonged to various ages and civilisations. Thus, the majority of Greek philosophers, and most of all Aristotle, thought that all things had purposes built into them by nature—ends or goals which they could not but seek to fulfil. The medieval Christians saw the world as a hierarchy in which every object and person was called upon to fulfil a specific function by the Divine Creator; He alone understood the purpose of the entire pattern, and made the happiness and misery of His creatures depend upon the degree to which they followed the commandments that were entailed by the differing purposes for which each entity had been created—the purposes that in fulfilling themselves realised the universal harmony, the supreme pattern, the totality of which was kept from the creatures, and understood by the Creator alone.

The rationalists of the eighteenth and nineteenth centuries saw no purpose in anything but what man himself had created to serve his own needs, and regarded all else as determined by the laws of cause and effect, so that most things pursued no purposes, but were as they were, and moved and changed as they did, as a matter of "brute" fact.

These were profoundly different outlooks. Yet those who held them saw very similar items in the universe, similar colours, tastes, shapes, forms of motion and rest, experienced similar feelings, pursued similar goals, acted in similar fashions.

Kant, in his doctrine of our knowledge of the external world, taught that the categories through which we saw it were identical for all sentient beings, permanent and unalterable; indeed this is what made our world one, and communication possible. But some of those who thought about history, morals, aesthetics, did see change and difference; what differed was not so much the empirical content of what these successive civilisations saw or heard or thought as the basic patterns in which they perceived them, the models in terms of which they conceived them, the category-spectacles through which they viewed them.

The world of a man who believes that God created him for a specific purpose, that he has an immortal soul, that there is an afterlife in which his sins will be visited upon him, is radically different from the world of a man who believes in none of these things; and the reasons for action, the moral codes, the political beliefs, the tastes, the personal relationships of the former will deeply and systematically differ from those of the latter.

Men's views of one another will differ profoundly as a very consequence of their general conception of the world; the notions of cause and purpose, good and evil, freedom and slavery, things and persons, rights, duties, laws, justice, truth, falsehood, to take some central ideas completely at random, depend directly upon the general framework within which they form, as it were, nodal points. Although the facts which are classified and arranged under these notions are not at all identical for all men at all times, yet these differences—which the sciences examine—are not the same as the profounder differences which wearing different sets of spectacles, using different categories, thinking in terms of different models, must make to men of different times and places and cultures and outlooks.

Philosophy, then, is not an empirical study; not the critical examination of what exists or has existed or will exist—this is dealt with by common-sense knowledge and belief, and the methods of the natural sciences. Nor is it a kind of formal deduction as mathematics or logic is. Its subject-matter is to a large degree not the items of experience, but the ways in which they are viewed, the permanent or semi-permanent categories in terms of which experience is conceived and classified. Purpose versus mechanical causality; organism versus mere amalgams; systems versus mere togetherness; spatio-temporal order versus timeless being; duty versus appetite; value versus fact—these are categories, models, spectacles. Some of these are as old as human experience itself; others are more transient. With the more transient, the philosopher's problems take on a more dynamic and historical aspect. Different models and frameworks, with their attendant obscurities and difficulties, arise at different times. The case of contemporary problems in the explanatory framework of physics, already mentioned, is one example of this. But there are other examples, which affect the thought not just of physicists or other specialists, but of reflective men in general.

In politics, for example, men tried to conceive of their social existence by analogy with various models: Plato at one stage, perhaps following Pythagoras, tried to frame his system of human nature, its attributes and goals, following a geometrical pattern, since he thought it would explain all there was. There followed the biological pattern of Aristotle: the many Christian images with which the writings of the Fathers as well as the Old and New Testaments abound; the analogy of the family, which casts light upon human relations not provided by a mechanical model (say that of Hobbes); the notion of an army on the march with its emphasis on such virtues as loyalty, dedication, obedience, needed to overtake and crush the enemy (with which so much play has been made in the Soviet Union); the notion of the state as a traffic policeman and night watchman preventing collisions and looking after property, which is at the back of much individualist and liberal thought; the notion of the state as much more than this—as a great cooperative endeavour of individuals seeking to fulfil a common end, and therefore as entitled to enter into every nook and cranny of human experience, that animates much of the "organic" thought of the nineteenth century; the systems borrowed from psychology, or from theories of games, that are in vogue at present—all these are models in terms of which human beings, groups and societies and cultures, have conceived of their experience.

These models often collide; some are rendered inadequate by failing to account for too many aspects of experience, and are in their turn replaced by other models which emphasize what these last have omitted but in their turn may obscure what the others have rendered clear. The task of philosophy, often a difficult and painful one, is to extricate and bring to light the hidden categories and models in terms of which human beings think (that is, their use of words, images and other symbols), to reveal what is obscure or contradictory in them, to discern the conflicts between them that prevent the construction of more adequate ways of organising and describing and explaining experience (for all description as well as explanation involves some model in terms of

Your Poem, Man...

Edward Lueders

unless there's one thing seen
suddenly against another—a parsnip
sprouting for a President, or
hailstones melting in an ashtray—
nothing really happens. It takes
surprise and wild connections,
doesn't it? A walrus chewing
on a ballpoint pen. Two blue tail-
lights on Tyrannosaurus Rex. Green
cheese teeth. Maybe what we wanted
least. Or most. Some unexpected
pleats. Words that never knew
each other till right now. Plug us
into the wrong socket and see
what blows—or what lights up.
Try
 untried
 circuitry,
new
 fuses.
Tell it like it never really was,
man,
and maybe we can see it
like it is.

SOURCE: From Edward Leuders, *Some Haystacks Don't Even Have Any Needles* (New York: Scott, Foresman & Co., 1969). Reprinted with the permission of the author.

which the describing and explaining is done); and then, at a still "higher" level, to examine the nature of this activity itself (epistemology, philosophical logic, linguistic analysis), and to bring to light the concealed models that operate in the second-order, philosophical, activity itself.

If it is objected that all this seems very abstract and remote from daily experience, something too little concerned with the central interests, the happiness and unhappiness and ultimate fate of ordinary men, the answer is that this charge is false. Men cannot live without seeking to describe and explain the universe to themselves. The models they use in doing this must deeply affect their lives, not least when they are unconscious; much of the misery and frustration of men is due to the mechanical or unconscious, as well as deliberate, application of models where they do not work. Who can say how much suffering has been caused by the exuberant use of the organic model in politics, or the comparison of the state to a work of art, and the representation of the dictator as the inspired moulder of human lives, by totalitarian theorists in our own times? Who shall say how much harm and how much good, in previous ages, came of the exaggerated application to social relations of metaphors and models fashioned after the patterns of paternal authority, especially to the relations of rulers of states to their subjects, or of priests to the laity?

If there is to be any hope of a rational order on earth, or of a just appreciation of the many various interests that divide diverse groups of human beings—knowledge that is indispensable to any attempt to assess their effects, and the patterns of their interplay and its consequences, in order to find viable compromises through which men may continue to live and satisfy their desires without thereby crushing the equally central desires and needs of others—it lies in the bringing to light of these models, social, moral, political, and above all the underlying metaphysical patterns in which they are rooted, with a view to examining whether they are adequate to their task.

The perennial task of philosophers is to examine whatever seems insusceptible to the methods of the sciences or everyday observation, e.g. categories, concepts, models, ways of thinking or acting, and particularly ways in which they clash with one another, with a view to constructing other, less internally contradictory, and (though this can never be fully attained) less pervertible metaphors, images, symbols and systems of categories. It is certainly a reasonable hypothesis that one of the principal causes of confusion, misery and fear is, whatever may be its psychological or social roots, blind adherence to outworn notions, pathological suspicion of any form of critical self-examination, frantic efforts to prevent any degree of rational analysis of what we live by and for.

This socially dangerous, intellectually difficult, often agonizing and thankless, but always important activity is the work of philosophers, whether they deal with the natural sciences or moral or political or purely personal issues. The goal of philosophy is always the same, to assist men to understand themselves and thus operate in the open, and not wildly, in the dark.

The claims of metaphysics or theology to be sciences must rest on the assumption that intuition or revelation are direct sources of knowledge of facts about the world; since they claim to be forms of direct experience, their data, if their existence is allowed, belong, for our purposes, to the "empirical" basket.

Endnote

[1] The claims of metaphysics or theology to be sciences must rest on the assumption that intuition or revelation are direct sources of knowledge of facts about the world: since they claim to be forms of direct experience, their data, if their existence is allowed, belong, for our purposes, to the "empirical" basket.

SOURCE: Isiah Berlin, *Concepts and Categories: Philosophical Essays* (London: Oxford University Press, 1980). Originally published by Hogarth Press.

Questions and Topics for Discussion and Writing

1. According to Berlin, what is the relationship between philosophy and empirical observation?
2. What does Berlin mean when he says that the scope and content of philosophy does not seem greatly diminished by the process of attrition (page 289)?
3. Why, according to Berlin, do people "need" philosophy? Does it do the job better than other sciences or methods of inquiry?

The Universe

May Swenson

What
is it about,
the universe
about
us stretching out? We within our brains within it think
we must unspin the laws that spin it. We think
why because
we think

because.
Because
we think
we think

the universe
about
us.
But does it think,
the universe?
Then what
about?
About
us? If not, must there be cause
in the universe?
Must it have laws? And what
if the universe
is *not about*
us? Then what?
What
is it about
and what
about
us?

SOURCE: Reprinted by permission of the estate of the author.

The Need for a Theology of Experience of God

Denis Edwards

In this piece, author Denis Edwards advocates a "Theology of Experience," or a way of looking at people's relationship with God based on the specifics of their own life. Edwards contends that blanketing, generalized theological systems do not make much sense if they cannot be applied directly to day-to-day life. He argues instead that when people are able to understand their own lives, they will also be better able to understand what has happened to them in relation to God.

Do we have "experience of God?" Is this a legitimate way of speaking about our relationship with God? If we do speak of "experience of God" what kind of experience do we mean?

The answers to these questions are far from obvious. Yet there are few questions that are more important to the men and women of the late twentieth century, whether they be unbelievers, marginal Christians or committed Christians. It takes only a little reflection to see that an adequate theology of experience of God is necessary for effective ministry to each of these groups. Perhaps the best way to show this is by describing four individuals. Each of them, it seems to me, represents a large section of our community.

Julia is a young woman approaching thirty. She finds herself doubting the existence of God. At some times she is inclined to believe in "something" but at other times she thinks of herself as a non-believer, an atheist. Julia was brought up as a Christian and admits to having picked up from her religious background some important values, including a sense of justice. She is generous and compassionate in the way she lives her life, but the word "God" and the language of the Church mean little to her. The Church's idea of God seems far-fetched and alien. It fails to connect with anything which is within the range of her experience. Julia's commitment to social issues is still strong, but she finds within herself an emptiness and an obscure hunger for something more. She knows that she has a need for depth and meaning, but she cannot be satisfied with superficial answers. A properly developed theology of existence of God will have some hope of speaking to those who, like Julia, hold an agnostic position. Instead of rational argument for God's existence (which rarely convinces anyone) this approach would suggest to Julia that she search into her own experience of life, to see if moments of mystery and transcendence can be found there. At this point real dialogue with Julia might begin.

A second set of questions is posed today by the great number of people like Margaret. She finds Christianity irrelevant to her life. Margaret's husband left her six years ago. She has three children, the eldest of them just out of school and unemployed. They live in government housing in one of the poorest parts of the city, where she fears for her children because of the violence of the neighborhood, the gangs that roam the streets and the access to drugs of all kinds. Financial survival is a constant preoccupation and she lives without much hope that life will change for the better. She feels that there is nothing left for her, that she has failed, and she finds herself overwhelmed by bouts of loneliness. Margaret has not abandoned the Church completely but the doctrines and lit-

To Look at Any Thing

John Moffitt

To look at any thing,
If you would know that thing,
You must look at it long:
To look at this green and say
"I have seen spring in these
Woods," will not do—you must
Be the thing you see:
You must be the dark snakes of
Stems and ferny plumes of leaves,
You must enter in
To the small silences between
The leaves,
You must take your time
And touch the very peace
They issue from.

urgy of the Church have little meaning for her. What matters for her is what she experiences each day: the battle to survive, the daily round of work, her hope that her son will find a job, the endurance of loneliness and her hunger for companionship, a hunger that often is met only by the television set. Any kind of pastoral analysis reveals that there are enormous numbers of Christians (many of them in circumstances different from Margaret's) who experience this chasm between what makes up their lives and the faith language of the Church. An adequate understanding of experience of God is, I believe, the only bridge over the chasm. The necessary mediation between personal experience and the language and practice of the Church is the discovery of the depths of what one is experiencing, and the further discovery that these depths open out into the mystery of God. Once this journey of discovery begins the language of the tradition may again have a point of contact with the experience of the person.

Margaret might well be described as a marginal Christian. Like many others she is marginal in terms of her identification with the local church. She is also marginal in terms of society. She is among the poorest and the most hurt. People like Margaret force us to ask ourselves what connection there is between the eucharistic assemblies of Christians and the pain of so many in our world. This question can never receive an adequate answer, except in the cross of Jesus, and this answer remains mysterious. However I want to suggest that one response that ought to be made to this problem is by way of the theology of experience of God, in the link between our experience of those who are pushed to the margins in our world and our experience of God.

Tom, unlike Julia and Margaret, is a Christian committed to his local parish and to Sunday Eucharist. He has worked hard all his life and he and his wife have watched their children leave home to begin their own families. As he begins his retirement from work he finds his life empty. He has high blood pressure and is becoming increasingly conscious that he is in the last stage of life and that his own death must be faced. Tom believes that God exists, that this God has been revealed to us in Jesus Christ, that the Church teaches in the name of Jesus and that we are transformed by God's grace. However he has always believed that grace operates at a level beyond anything he might experience. His faith has always been largely a matter of intellectual assent. Now, as Tom faces the bleak emptiness of his life, his failing health and the possibility of death, his own kind of faith has little to offer him. It makes no connections with his own struggle. He has no access to the richness and joy of a more personal faith that could lead him to wisdom and to peace, and the capacity to love more creatively. A theology of experience of God has some hope of suggesting to Tom, and all those like him, that God does reach out to us in love individually and that there is a way to a more affective and personal faith.

Trevor is also committed to the Church, but his faith has a character entirely different from that of Tom. A family man in his early forties, Trevor recently went through a remarkable conversion experience. In his own language he "found God" and he found Christian community in a charismatic prayer group. All his earlier Church life seems like nothing compared to his new experience. Trevor now speaks easily and often of God and gives the impression of having easy access to him. He believes that God is manifested to those with faith and on different occasions he claims to be directly guided by God in his decisions. Trevor, like many others, has a tendency to identify uncritically his own religious enthusiasm with God, without any awareness that his own psychic state may be contributing to what he experiences. A theological approach to experience of God will offer Trevor a caution against losing sight of the transcendence of God. It will provide a framework for Trevor's experience in the spiritual tradition of the Church. It will show the inner connection between prayerful experience of God and an active engagement in the struggle for justice. Finally, it will offer some guidelines for discernment between genuine experience of God and other human experiences.

There is, then, an urgent need for a theology of experience of God in order that we be able to respond to some of the important questions of our time. I would suggest, as well, that it is only by developing such a theology that we can be faithful to our tradition. Only an adequate theology of experience of God can do justice to the Old and New Testament understanding that God breaks in on our individual lives, that the Spirit moves within us, that God's Word is communicated to us, and that we live in God's presence. Such a theological approach to experience or God can be shown to stand in the tradition of Augustine and Aquinas, and while this tradition may have been obscured in the excessive rationalism of some post-Reformation Scholastic theology, it has always been remembered by the mystics. Without a theology of the experience of God we can make no sense of the works of John of the Cross and the *Spiritual Exercises* of St. Ignatius have no content.

It should be noticed, too, that we cannot develop a theology of revelation which is not built upon an understanding of our experience of God. If one denies all possibility of encounter with God, then the possibility of revelation is either denied or reduced to something entirely extrinsic.

In the project of developing a theology of experience of God careful use of language is extremely important. What do we mean when we use the word "experience" in this context? And what do we mean when we claim that such experience is "of God?" There is a tradition in theology which is hesitant to speak of the human experience of God. There are important reasons for this. One of them is the need to preserve God's transcendence, and any theological language that fails to safeguard this transcendence is automatically and rightly suspect. Where experience is taken to mean the same thing as knowledge or comprehension, then the phrase "experience of God" is rightly called into question. I hope to make clear that experience and conceptual knowledge are not the same thing. It is possible to show that while we do not have access to God's inner being, and while God always transcends our intellectual comprehension, yet we can and do experience the presence and activity of this Holy One in a pre-conceptual way.

If we must speak of experience of God, then it is essential that we clarify what is meant, and is not meant, by the phrase. The first step in this will be an examination of "experience" itself. Then there will be need to show that there are some experiences which are of a pre-conceptual nature. Finally there will be a need to discuss what is meant by the expression "experience of God" as distinct from other common expressions like "religious experience."

The Nature of Experience

It might be helpful to begin an examination of the nature of experience through a reflection about our experience of another person in our lives. What do we mean when we say that we have some experience of this person? Usually we mean (1) that we have had one or more encounters with the person, and (2) that we have formed some kind of interpretation or understanding of this person as a result of these encounters.

First, then, we mean that we have encountered the other person. We would not normally claim to have experience of another person unless we have had some kind of meeting with him or her, even if the meeting occurs only through a telephone call or a letter.

The Red Wheelbarrow

William Carlos Williams

so much depends
upon

a red wheel
barrow

glazed with rain
water

beside the white
chickens.

Second, we mean that we have interpreted these meetings within our own consciousness, and that we now have some understanding of the other person as a result of our encounters with him or her. There is no real experience of another unless we become aware of the encounter. We have to interpret to ourselves the person we encounter by way of images and concepts. Even after speaking with someone on the telephone we form an interpretation of the person encountered through the tone of voice, the warm or cold manner and the accent of the person, as well as by the content of what was said. We have some kind of understanding of the person on the other end of the line. There are many other routine encounters, like sitting next to a person on a bus, which may not deserve to be called experience of another, because we have not really received the other person into our own consciousness in any way.

Experience, then, involves both encounter and the interpretation of the encounter. There is always the reflective, conceptual awareness of what we experience, but this points back to the original experiential encounter.

It is important to stress this double dimension in experience because it is not always noticed. Sometimes people speak of experience as if it involved only encounters with others, and they forget the role their own consciousness has played in selecting and filtering what is received. Others stress only the subjective side and forget that genuine experience depends upon a real meeting with some reality beyond the individual.

Experience is best seen as encounter with some thing or person which has become available to consciousness through reflective awareness. It refers to an encounter that is interpreted within human consciousness. This second element, interpretation, has always already occurred whenever we know that we have experienced something.

However the interpretative element in experience should not be seen as something that occurs only after an encounter, in a moment of reflection. Rather the individual brings to an encounter a receptivity, or lack of it, which has been determined by the person's capabilities, free choices and previous experience. Two people may hear a man describe his difficulties in his relationship with his wife. The first person sees the man as arrogant and self-centered while the second feels empathy and understanding for him. Both have had a similar encounter with him but they have experienced him quite differently. Their own previous experience and their present state of mind have determined how they have received this man. The interpreting self precedes the encounter, enters into the encounter, and reflects upon the encounter.

Even though my original experience of a person can only be present to me through my reflection upon it, it is possible, as I reflect, to distinguish my conceptual understanding from the original encounter. I may become quite aware that my thoughts about a person are inadequate reflections of the original encounter. In fact it is true to say that any real encounter with the humanity of another person has an element of mystery which escapes my comprehension. Not only does my reflection on an encounter with another person enable me to distinguish the encounter from the subsequent interpretation of it, but it also reveals that the original encounter was richer than my reflective conceptual awareness and contained something that escapes rational expression.

The American philosopher John E. Smith speaks of experience as "a product of the intersection of something encountered and a being capable of interpreting the results." This is a good working description of experience. It stresses the two moments or encounter and of interpretation. It makes it clear that both the original encounter and the act of interpretation are essential and necessarily linked together.

The use of the concepts of encounter and interpretation in a description of experience preserves our understanding of experience from distortion. One distortion of experience is to see it as an entirely subjective process, quite unreliable when compared with scientific measurement or logical thought. Those who hold this view of experience dismiss it as unreliable and at the mercy of the whims and prejudices of the individual. The concept of experience as the product of an intersection or an encounter makes it clear that experience has its objective side. The reality encountered, the person who is having the experience, and the actual meeting between the two are clearly objective realities. At the heart of experience is the moment of encounter which is quite objective.

However, experience certainly has its subjective side as well. The concept of experience as an encounter which yet needs interpretation allows that the original encounter has to receive concrete life in a person through the mediation of the person's reflective consciousness. In the interpretative stage of experience there may be distortion because of the biases of an individual, because of dishonesty, because of emotional blockages, because of unconscious motives, or because what has been experienced is too much for a person's ability to conceptualize and express it. However, a human person is capable of checking biases, becoming aware of self-deceptions, admitting limitations and thereby reducing the probability of mistakes or distortion in interpretation of experience.

Awareness of the way the individual enters into the experience (in the interpretation of what is encountered) introduces a critical note into our concept of experience. There is always the need to be critically aware of the way a person's subjectivity shapes his or her reception of experience. At the same time it is important to insist that there is an objective basis to experience in the original encounter, in the person who is experiencing and in what is encountered.

Pre-Conceptual Experiences

There are several different ways in which we experience reality. The most immediate and obvious experiences are those of the five senses. We experience a rose through sight and smell and perhaps through touch. Even much more complex experiences, such as our encounter with another human person, depend upon a basis in the senses. We see a person's facial expressions, or read his or her letters. We listen to a person's voice and so share his or her thoughts.

Needless to say, when we speak of experience of God we are not referring to such sense experience. Of course, experiences of the senses can lead us to a reflective awareness of God, and they can and do act as symbolic mediations of God's presence in our lives. This kind of mediation occurs in a unique way in the Church's sacraments. However, in accurate theological language the phrase "experience of God" means something other than sense experience.

A second way we encounter reality which is external to ourselves is through an intellectual grasp of it. An example of this is the experience we have in reading a book of theology. We are brought into contact with another person's ideas and grapple with them intellectually. We experience reality through concepts and rational judgments. We do this also when we read a newspaper, when we struggle with problems at work and when we engage in the simple interchange of everyday conversation. Such intellectual experience depends, of course, upon sense experience since we depend upon sight and hearing for intellectual encounters. However it is still accurate to speak of such encounters as intellectual experience of reality.

Now it is true that we can form concepts of God and the attributes of God and we can think about the nature of God. We must notice, however, that all of our thinking about God is analogical. We take some reality we know from our everyday world, such as goodness or fatherhood, and we attribute it to God. In doing this there is always

The Elements, 1916, by J.E.H. MacDonald (oil on board; 71.1 x 91.8 cm.).

J.E.H. MacDonald was a founding member of the Group of Seven, a group of Canadian painters formed in 1920 (see page 339).

Courtesy of The Art Gallery of Ontario, Toronto. Gift of Dr. Lorne Pierce, 1958, in memory of Edith Chown Pierce (1890-1954).

the implied reservation that while God is rightly called good he is not good in the way human beings are good, but in a way that totally transcends human goodness. We can think about God, then, but our intellects can approach God only by way of analogy. This "only" is not meant to demean the importance of this kind of knowledge, but simply to point to its proper limits. God is by very definition incomprehensible, and the human intellect must know God as an abiding mystery to it. Our intellects, then, do not grasp God as he is in himself. He always transcends our concepts.

If we do not have sense experience of God and if he escapes the grasp of our intellects, does this mean that we can have no real experience of God at all? Many people would say that this is the case. However this is to ignore another whole area of human experience, the area that I will call preconceptual experience.

The philosopher and scientist Michael Polanyi has shown how much of our knowing occurs at what he calls a "tacit" level. He shows how a great deal of scientific research depends upon unspoken and non-conceptualized assumptions, presuppositions, skills and intuitions. No expert tradesperson can pass on skills to an apprentice simply in concepts or words. Much of what men and women who are gifted in a craft know can never be articulated. They know more then they can tell:

> Although the expert diagnostician, taxonomist and cottonclasser can indicate their clues and formulate their maxims, they know many more things than

they can tell, knowing them only in practice, as instrumental particulars, and nor explicitly, as objects.

Polanyi shows how we operate with "tacit" or pre-conceptual knowledge in many ordinary areas of life. When a woman learns to ride a bicycle it is often impossible for her to explain to another (or herself) the nature of the skill. A man might be able to pick his own raincoat from fifty others at a function and yet be unable to describe it to another person. In these and a thousand other ways we know more than we can tell.

There are other, deeper experiences that occur at a pre-conceptual level. When a man listens to a symphony he depends upon sense experience to hear the individual notes. He uses his intellect to grasp the conceptual order of the music and the interrelationship of part and whole. However he experiences a beauty which transcends the faculties of hearing and thought. The beauty of the symphony is beyond logic, and the man knows that what he experiences cannot adequately be reduced to concepts or words. When he reflects on the experience and tries to speak about it, he has to use concepts, images and words. However he knows that what he has experienced is beyond his ability to verbalize it. Such an experience of beauty is pre-conceptual.

When a woman loves another person, she knows that her love is built upon sense experience of the other and upon an intellectual meeting with him or her. But again the mystery of the other person and the mystery of the love that is shared escapes comprehension. It transcends the senses and the intellect. It can be conceptualized and it can be verbalized (and needs to be verbalized if it is to reach its full human potential) but she knows that her words are inadequate and point to a reality that she despairs of properly expressing. Such love is experienced in a pre-conceptual way.

These two examples, beauty and love, reveal something important to us about our experience. Both experiences depend upon the senses and the intellect but they both transcend the senses and the intellect. They reveal a level of experience which is central to human life and yet one which we cannot intellectually dominate. Such pre-conceptual experiences do become conceptualized and verbalized as we interpret them for ourselves. However, we are quite able to distinguish between our conceptual interpretation, which we know is inadequate, and the original pre-conceptual experience.

There are many other such experiences, some of which will be discussed later. However, even a preliminary reflection on the experiences of beauty and love is enough to show that some of our deepest experiences, and those that we would list as most central to what it is to be human, occur in a pre-conceptual way. This reflection shows how dangerous is the superficial empirical attitude which reduces what is experienced to the senses and what can be measured, and the rationalist view which admits nothing but intellectual comprehension. It must be admitted that some theology has not escaped this kind of empiricism and this kind of rationalism.

When I speak of experience of God I will always mean pre-conceptual experience. God always transcends our senses and our intellects. We do not have access to the inner being of God. However, I will argue, this always transcending God has come close to us in love, and we can experience this presence in our lives in an obscure way. The concept of pre-conceptual experience allows us to speak of a real human awareness of God who yet remains always incomprehensible to our intellects. It is, I will argue, precisely as mystery that we experience God's presence and action.

Why Experience "of God"?

It might be helpful, at this stage, to indicate why I speak directly of experience of God, rather than using other phrases like "religious experience," "experience of grace," "Christian experience," and "mystical experience."

The problem with the expression "religious experience" is that it is not specific enough. It refers to the areas of human life where individuals and groups see themselves as related to the divine, or the sacred. Such religious experience is concerned with the relationship to the sacred which occurs through sacred rites, words, places, things and people. I want to be much more specific than this.

There is a need to pinpoint more precisely within general religious experience the moment of some kind of encounter with God and awareness of him.

The concept of "Christian experience," used by recent Catholic theologians, is also not precise enough. Christian experience refers, according to these theologians, to the personal appropriation of the mystery of Christ within the Church. It includes participation in the Eucharist, Christian community, prayer and everyday life. However the focus of interest in this work is on one experience that may or may not occur in any of these, the sense of some kind of direct union with God. For example, where and how in the celebration of the Eucharist might a person have pre-conceptual experience of God? There is another reason for preferring "experience of God" to "Christian experience:" experience of God occurs outside the Christian tradition, as well as in explicitly Christian experiences.

The phrase "experience of grace" is sometimes used by theologians to mean precisely a pre-conceptual union with God (uncreated Grace) graciously present in our lives. However, the phrase is a little ambiguous, because at times writers use the word grace to mean only a created gift of God. Some who speak of "experience of grace" hold the view that we do not in any real sense have experience of God; rather we experience a created effect (created grace) which he produces in us. I want to go beyond this second position.

"Mystical experience," of course, is experience of God. But mystical experience is usually, and properly, equated with contemplative moments in prayer. Experience of God as I want to speak of it is wider than this, including both contemplative prayer and pre-conceptual experiences of God that occur because grace is poured out in our everyday lives and in our hearts. Some theologians have extended the word "mysticism" to cover our daily experience of God's grace and they speak of the "mysticism of everyday life." It seems preferable, however, to speak of experience of God as a broad term with mystical experience keeping its traditional meaning as one kind of experience of God, that which occurs in contemplative prayer.

In this chapter I have been arguing that not only is it proper to speak of experience of God, but it is essential to do so if we are to be faithful to our tradition and if we are to meet the pressing pastoral needs of our times. The concept of experience has been examined and the original experiential encounter distinguished from the moment of reflective interpretation. It has been shown that experience has objective dimensions, and yet is received by a subject who must interpret it personally. Experience cannot be limited to sense experience or intellectual comprehension, but includes pre-conceptual experiences. These pre-conceptual experiences include some of the most important moments of human life, and our experience of God is always a pre-conceptual experience. Finally it has been argued that it is important to use precisely the phrase "experience of God."

The next step is to look to our human lives and ask how and where such experiences occur. The best procedure is not to describe God and then ask where we experience such a God. Rather, we must first ask where it is in human life that a person experiences moments of mystery and transcendence, and then we can draw upon the traditional, powerful word "God" and use this to speak of the one toward whom such experiences point. Then we can look to the Gospel of Jesus to illuminate our understanding of God. The beginning must be made with human experience.

Questions and Topics for Discussion and Writing

1. How does Edwards recommend applying a theology of experience to someone like "Margaret?" What obstacles would this approach have to overcome before it could be successful?
2. What are the key elements of Edwards' definition of "experience?" What does he mean by the "interpretive element in experience?"

Thirteen Ways of Looking at a Blackbird

Wallace Stevens (1879–1955)

I

Among twenty snowy mountains,
The only moving thing
Was the eye of the blackbird.

II

I was of three minds,
Like a tree
In which there are three blackbirds.

III

The blackbird whirled in the autumn winds.
It was a small part of the pantomime.

IV

A man and a woman
Are one.
A man and a woman and a blackbird
Are one.

V

I do not know which to prefer,
The beauty of inflections,
Or the beauty of innuendoes,
The blackbird whistling
Or just after.

VI

Icicles filled the long window
With barbaric glass.
The shadow of the blackbird
Crossed it, to and fro.
The mood
Traced in the shadow
An indecipherable cause.

VII

O thin men of Haddam,
Why do you imagine golden birds?
Do you not see how the blackbird
Walks around the feet
Of the women about you?

VIII

I know noble accents
And lucid, inescapable rhythms;
But I know, too,
That the blackbird is involved
In what I know.

IX

When the blackbird flew out of sight,
It marked the edge
Of one of many circles.

X

At the sight of blackbirds
Flying in a green light,
Even the bawds of euphony
Would cry out sharply.

XI

He rode over Connecticut
In a glass coach.
Once, a fear pierced him,
In that he mistook
The shadow of his equipage
For blackbirds.

XII

The river is moving.
The blackbird must be flying.

XIII

It was evening all afternoon.
It was snowing
And it was going to snow.
The blackbird sat
In the cedar-limbs.

The Skating Party

Merna Summers

This short story by Canadian author Merna Summers focuses on the universal theme of choice, and the crucial situations in which all of us find ourselves at some point. People must often make choices instantaneously and under considerable stress. Summer's story illustrates that it can be difficult to ascertain the reasons for other people's actions in these situations.

Our house looked down on the lake. From the east windows you could see it: a long sickle of blue, its banks hung with willow. Beyond was a wooded ridge, which, like all such ridges in our part of the country, ran from northeast to south west.

In another part of the world, both lake and ridge would have had names. Here, only people had names. I was Maida; my father was Will, my mother was Winnie. Take us all together and we were the Singletons. The Will Singletons, that is, as opposed to the Dan Singletons, who were my grandparents and dead, or Nathan Singleton, who was my uncle and lived in the city.

In the books I read, lakes and hills had names, and so did ponds and houses. Their names made them more real to me, of greater importance, than the hills and lakes and sloughs that I saw every day. I was eleven years old before I learned that the hill on which our house was built had once had a name. It was called Stone Man Hill. My parents had never thought to tell me that.

It was my uncle, Nathan Singleton, who told me. Uncle Nathan was a bachelor. He had been a teacher before he came to Willow Bunch, but he had wanted to be a farmer. He had farmed for a few years when he was a young man, on a quarter that was now part of our farm. His quarter was just south of what had been my grandfather's home place, and was now ours. But then he had moved to the city and become a teacher again.

In some ways it seemed as if he had never really left Willow Bunch. He spent all his holidays at our place taking walks with me, talking to my mother, helping my father with such chores as he hadn't lost the knack of performing. Our home was his home. I found it hard to imagine him as I knew he must be in his classroom: wearing a suit, chalk dust on his sleeve, putting seat work on the blackboard. He didn't even talk like a teacher.

Uncle Nathan was older than my father, quite a lot older but he didn't seem so to me. In some ways he seemed younger, for he told me things and my father did not. Not that my father was either silent or unloving. He talked as much as anybody, and he was fond of some people—me included—and showed it. What he did not give away was information.

Some children are sensitive: an eye and an ear and a taking-in of subtleties. I wasn't like that. I wanted to be told. I wanted to know how things really were and how people really acted. Sometimes it seemed to me that collecting the facts was uphill work. I persisted because it was important for me to have them. I wanted to know who to praise and who to blame. Until I was in my mid-teens, that didn't seem to me to be too much to ask.

Perhaps my father had a reluctance to look at things too closely himself. He wanted to like people, and he may have found it easier to do if he kept them a little out of focus. Besides that he believed that life was something that children should be protected from knowing about for as long as possible.

I got most of my information from my mother.

She believed that knowledge *was* protection: that children had a right to know and parents had an obligation to teach. She didn't know all there was to know, but what she did know she intended to pass on to me.

I knew this because I heard her say so one night after I had gone to bed. Uncle Nathan, who was at the farm for the weekend, saw things my mother's way. "What you don't know *can* hurt you," he said. "Especially what you don't know about yourself."

So my mother and my uncle talked to me, both as a sort of inoculation against life and because I now believe, both of them liked to talk anyway. I was also willing to listen. My father listened too. He might feel that my mother told me too much, but his conviction wasn't strong enough to stop her.

It was Uncle Nathan, talking for pleasure, not policy, who gave me the pleasure of knowing that I lived in a place with a name. Stone Man Hill was so named, he said, because long ago there had existed on the slopes below our house the shape of a man, outlined in fieldstones.

"He was big," Uncle Nathan said. "Maybe fifteen yards, head to foot."

It was a summer afternoon. I was eleven. My father, in from the fields for coffee was sitting at the kitchen table. His eyelashes were sooty with field dust. My mother was perched on a kitchen stool by the cupboard, picking over berries.

"He must have been quite a sight," my father said.

I walked to the east window of the kitchen and looked out, trying to imagine our hillside field of brome as unbroken prairie sod, trying to picture what a stone man would look like stretched out among the buffalo beans and gopher holes, his face to the sky.

"You get me a writing pad and I'll show you what he looked like," Uncle Nathan said.

I got the pad and Uncle Nathan sat down at the table opposite my father. I sat beside him, watching as he began to trace a series of dots. His hand worked quickly, as if the dots were already visible, but only to his eyes. The outline of a man took shape.

"Who made the stone man?" I asked.

"Indians," Uncle Nathan said. He held the picture up, as if considering additions. "But I don't know when and I don't know why."

"He could have been there a hundred years," my father said. "Maybe more. There was no way of telling"

"I used to wonder why the Indians chose this hill," Uncle Nathan said. "I still do."

He got up and walked to the window looking out at the hill and the lake and the ridge. "It may be that it was some sort of holy place to them," he said.

My mother left the cupboard and came across to the table. She picked up Uncle Nathan's drawing. Looking at it, the corners of her mouth twitched upwards.

"You're sure you haven't forgotten anything?" she asked. "Your mother used to say that the stone man was *very* complete."

Uncle Nathan returned her smile. "The pencil's right here, Winnie," he said. "You're welcome to it."

My father spoke quickly. "It was too bad the folks didn't have a camera," he said. "It would have been nice to have a picture of the stone man."

My mother went back to her berries.

"I've always been sorry I was too young to remember him," my father said. "Before he turned into a rock pile, that is."

I hadn't yet got around to wondering about the stone man's disappearance. Now I did. He should still have been on his hillside for me to look at. My father had been a baby when his people came to Willow Bunch, and he couldn't remember the stone man. My uncle had been a young man and could. But the difference in their ages and experience hadn't kept them from sharing a feeling of excitement at the thought of a stone man on our hillside. Why had my grandfather been insensible to this appeal? Hadn't he liked the stone man?

"Liking wouldn't enter into it," my father said. "Your grandfather had a family to feed. He knew where his duty lay."

"There was 30 acres broke when Pa bought this place," Uncle Nathan said. "He thought he needed more. And this hill was the only land he could break without brushing it first."

Isles of Spruce, 1922, by Arthur Lismer.

Arthur Lismer was a founding member of the Group of Seven, a group of Canadian painters formed in 1920 (see page 339).

Courtesy of Hart House Gallery.

Somebody else had owned our place before my grandfather hadn't they? I asked. He hadn't turned the stone man into a rock pile.

"He was a bachelor," my father said.

"The way your grandfather saw it," Uncle Nathan said, "it was a case of wheat or stones. And he chose wheat."

"Which would you have chosen?" I asked Uncle Nathan. "Which did you want?"

"I wanted both," Uncle Nathan said.

"The choice wasn't yours to make." My mother spoke as if she were defending him.

"That's what I thought then," Uncle Nathan said. "I thought when Pa told me to get those rocks picked, that that was what I had to do. I think now I should have spoken up. I know for years I felt guilty whenever I remembered that I had done just what was expected of me."

He looked up, a half-smile on his face. "I know it sounds crazy," he said, "but I felt as if the stone man had more claim on me than my own father did."

"We all of us think some crazy things sometimes," my father said.

From my point of view, Uncle Nathan had only one peculiarity. He had never married. And though I sometimes asked him why, I never found any satisfaction in his answers.

"Maybe it wasn't every girl who took my eye," he told me once. "I'd pity the girl who had to count on me to take care of her," he said another time.

Then my mother told me about the skating party. It had been a dark night in November, and my mother, five years old, had come to our lake with her parents, and spent the night pushing a kitchen chair in front of her across the ice, trying to learn to skate. The party was being held in honour of Uncle Nathan and a girl called Eunice Lathem. The were to be married soon, and their friends planned after the skating, to go up to the house and present a gift to them. The gift and the fact that the party was in her honour were to be a surprise to Eunice. Nathan, for some reason, had been told about it.

There had been cold that year but no snow, so you could skate all over the lake. My mother remembered them skimming by, the golden lads and girls who made up the world when she was small, and Nathan and Eunice the most romantic of all. Nathan was handsome and Eunice was beautiful and they were very much in love, she said.

She remembered the skaters by moonlight, slim black shapes mysterious against the silver fields. There were a lot of clouds in the sky that night and when the moon went behind one of them friends, neighbours, and parents' friends became alike: all equally unknown, unidentifiable.

My grandfather and Uncle Nathan had built a big wood fire at the near end of the lake. My mother said that it was a grand experience to skate off into the darkness and the perils and dangers of the night, and then turn and come back toward the light, following the fire's reflection on the ice.

Late on, when some people were already making their way up the hill to the house, Eunice Lathem went skating off into the darkness with her sister. They didn't skate up the middle of the lake as most of the skaters had been doing. Instead they went off toward the east bank. There is a place there where a spring rises and the water is deep but they didn't know that. The ice was thinner there. They broke through.

Near the fire, people heard their cries for help. A group of men skated out to rescue them. When the men got close to the place where the girls were in the water, the ice began to crack under their feet.

All the men lay down then and formed a chain, each holding the ankles of the man in front of him. Uncle Nathan was at the front. He inched forward, feeling the ice tremble beneath his body until he came to the point where he could reach either of two pairs of hands clinging to the fractured edge.

It was dark. He couldn't see the girls' faces. All he could do was grasp the nearest pair of wrists and pull. The men behind him pulled on his feet. Together they dragged one girl back to safety. But as they were doing it, the ice broke away beneath them and the second girl went under. The moon came out and they saw it was Eunice Lathem's sister they had saved. They went back to the hole, but Eunice had vanished. There wasn't any way they could even get her body.

"It was an awful thing to have happen on our place," my father said.

"Your Uncle Nathan risked his life," my mother said. Her voice was earnest, for she too believed in identifying heroes and villains.

"There was no way on earth he could save both girls," she said. "The ice was already breaking, and the extra weight of the first one was bound to be too much for it."

Why hadn't he saved Eunice first?

"I told you," my mother said. "He couldn't see their faces."

It troubled me that he hadn't had some way of knowing. I would have expected love to be able to call out to love. If it couldn't do that, what was it good for? And why had the moon been behind a cloud anyway?

"Your grandmother used to say that the Lord moves in a mysterious way," my father said.

"What does that mean?" I asked.

"It means that nobody knows," my mother said.

I'd seen Eunice Lathem's name on a grave in the yard of St. Chad's, where we attended services every second Sunday. If I'd thought of her at all, it was as a person who had always been dead. Now she seemed real to me, almost like a relative. She was a girl who had loved and been loved. I began to make up stories about her. But I no longer skated on the lake alone. Eunice Lathem's sister, whose name was Delia Sykes, moved away from Willow Bunch right after the accident. She didn't wait until her husband sold out; she went straight to Edmonton and waited for him there. Even when they buried Eunice in the spring, she didn't come back.

Years later, someone from Willow Bunch had seen her in Edmonton. She didn't mention Eunice or the accident or even Willow Bunch.

"It must have been a short conversation," my mother said practically.

Is it surprising that I continued to wonder why Uncle Nathan didn't marry? Some people remember their childhoods as a time when they thought of anybody over the age of 25 as being so decrepit as to be beyond all thought of romance or adventure. I remember feeling that way about *women*, but I never thought of men that way, whatever their ages. It seemed to me that Uncle Nathan could still pick out a girl and marry her if he set his mind to it.

"No," he said when I asked him. "Not 'still' and not 'pick out a girl.' A person doesn't have that much say in the matter. You can't love where you choose."

And then, making joke of it, "See that you remember that when your time comes," he said.

One day my mother showed me a picture of Eunice Lathem and her sister. Two girls and a pony stood looking at the camera. Both girls were pretty. The one who wasn't Eunice was laughing; she looked like a girl who loved to laugh. Eunice was pretty too but there was a stillness about her, almost a sternness. If she hadn't been Eunice Lathem, I would have said she was sulking.

I felt cheated. Was the laughing one also prettier?

"She may have been," my mother said. "I remember Eunice Lathem as being beautiful. But since Delia Sykes was married I don't suppose I gave her looks a thought one way or the other."

As I grew older I spent less time wondering about the girl who'd been Eunice Lathem. I'd never wondered about her sister, and perhaps never would have if I hadn't happened to be with Uncle Nathan the day he heard that Delia Sykes had died.

It was the spring I was fifteen. My parents were away for the weekend, attending a silver wedding in Rochfort Bridge. Uncle Nathan and I were alone on the farm and so, if he wanted to talk about Delia Sykes, he hadn't much choice about who to talk to.

It was a morning for bad news. The frost was coming out of the ground, setting the very ditches and wheel-ruts to weeping. Out in the barn, a ewe was mourning her lost lamb. We had put her in a pen by herself and we were saving the dead lamb, so we could use its skin to dress another lamb in case one of the ewes died in lambing or had no milk.

Uncle Nathan and I left the barn and walked out to the road to pick up the mail. The news of Delia's death was in the local paper. "Old-timers will be saddened to learn of the death in Duncan, B.C. of Mrs. Delia Sykes, a former resident of this district," the paper said.

Uncle Nathan shook his head slowly, as if he found the news hard to believe. "So Delia's gone," he said. "She was a grand girl, Delia Sykes. No matter what anybody said she was a grand girl."

There was a picture of Mrs. Sykes with the death notice. I saw a middle-aged woman who had gone from the hairdresser's to the photographer's. Her cheeks were as firm and round as two peach halves, and she had snappy eyes. She was wearing a white dress. She looked as if she might have belonged to the Eastern Star or the Rebekahs.

Uncle Nathan looked at the picture too. "Delia always was a beauty," he said.

He sat in silence for a while and then bit by bit, he began to tell me the story of how he had met Delia Sykes and before her, her husband.

"Only I didn't realize that he was her husband," Uncle Nathan said. "I thought when I met her that she was single, that was the joke of it."

It was late July and late afternoon. Uncle Nathan was teaching school, to make enough money to live on until his farm got going. But he was hoping to get out of it.

"The land was new then and we thought there was no limit to how rich we were all going to be some day. Besides that," he added, "what I wanted to do was farm. School-teaching seemed to me to be no proper job for a man."

There were two things Uncle Nathan wanted. One was to stop teaching. The other was to find a wife.

There were more men than girls around then, he told me, so the man who wanted a good selection had to be prepared to cover a lot of territory.

"Harold Knight and I took in dances and ball games as far away as Hasty Hills," he said.

They'd already seen a fair sampling, but there were still girls they hadn't seen.

"I had a pretty fair idea of what I was looking for," Uncle Nathan said. "I imagine it was the same sort of thing every young fellow thinks he's looking for, but I thought I had standards. I wasn't willing to settle for just anyone."

It was with the idea of looking over another couple of girls that he went to see Harold Knight that late July afternoon. A family with two daughters was rumoured to have moved in somewhere near Morningside School. He'd come to suggest to Harold that they take in the church service at the school the next Sunday.

The Knights, Uncle Nathan said, had hay and seed wheat to sell to people with the money to buy it. When Uncle Nathan walked into their yard that day, he saw that Mr. Knight was talking to a buyer. It was a man he'd never seen before, but he guessed by the cut of the man's rig that he must be well fixed.

"Nathan," Mr. Knight said, "meet Dobson Sykes."

Mr. Sykes was a straight-standing man with greying hair. He put out his hand and Uncle Nathan shook it.

"His driving horses," Uncle Nathan said "were as showy a team as I'd ever seen—big bays with coats the colour of red willow."

"You'd go a long way before you'd find a better-matched team than that," Mr. Knight said.

"Oh, they match well enough." Dobson Sykes spoke as if that was a matter of little importance to him, as if no effort was made in the acquiring of such a team. "I'd trade them in a minute if something better came along," he said carelessly. "I have a job to keep Spark, here, up to his collar."

"I had a fair amount of respect then for men who'd done well in life," Uncle Nathan told me. "This man was about my father's age, old enough to have made it on his own. When a man like that came my way, I studied him. I thought if I was going to be a farmer instead of a teacher, I'd have to start figuring out how people went about getting things in life."

"I wasn't really surprised when Mr. Knight said that Sykes had a crew of men—men he was paying—putting up a set of buildings for him on a place he'd bough t near Bannock Hill. He looked like a man with that kind of money."

"We're not building anything fancy," Dobson Sykes said. "If I'd wanted to stay farming on a big scale, I wouldn't have moved from Manitoba."

After a while Uncle Nathan left the two older men talking and walked out toward the meadow, where Harold was fetching a load of hay for Mr. Sykes.

It was on the trail between buildings and meadow that he met Delia Sykes.

He didn't see her at first because she wasn't sitting up front with Harold. She must have been lying back in the hay, Uncle Nathan said, just watching the clouds drift by overhead. She sat up.

Uncle Nathan saw at once that she was not very old; he had girls almost as old as she was in his classroom. But there was nothing of the schoolgirl about Delia. She was young but womanly. Everything about her curved, from the line of her cheek to the way she carried her arms.

Uncle Nathan saw all this in the instant that she appeared looking down over the edge of the load. He saw too that she had a kind of class he'd never seen around Willow Bunch. She looked like a girl perfectly suited to riding around the country behind a team of perfectly matched bays.

She reached behind her into the hay and came up with a crown of french-braided dandelions. She set it on top of her hair and smiled.

He knew right then, Uncle Nathan said, that his voice wouldn't be among those swelling the hymns at Morningside School next Sunday. And he felt as if he understood for the first time how men must feel when they are called to the ministry. Choosing and decision and standards have nothing to do with it. You're called or you're not called, and when you're called you know it.

The girl smiled and opened her arms as if to take in the clouds in the sky and the bees buzzing in the air and the red-topped grasses stirring in the wind. Then she spoke.

"You've got no worries on a load of hay," she said. Those were the first words Uncle Nathan heard Delia Sykes say. "You've got no worries on a load of hay."

There was a patch of milkweed blooming near the path where Uncle Nathan was standing. In late July, small pink blossoms appear and the milk, rich and white, is ready to run as soon as you break the stalk. Uncle Nathan picked a branch, climbed the load of hay, and presented it to the girl.

"It's not roses," he said "but the sap is supposed to cure warts."

She laughed. "My name is Delia Sykes," she said.

"I thought she was Dobson's daughter," Uncle Nathan said, "and it crossed my mind to wonder if he'd have traded her off if she hadn't moved along smart in her harness."

"There didn't seem to be much fear of that. You could see right away she had spirit. If she had too much, it was nothing that marriage to a good man wouldn't cure, I thought."

Uncle Nathan gave a rueful smile. "Of course when we got back to the yard I found out that she wasn't Dobson's daughter but his wife. Later I wonder why she hadn't introduced herself as *Mrs.* Sykes. And she'd called me *Nathan* too, and girls didn't do that then.

"The truth is," Uncle Nathan said, "I had kind of fallen for her."

Did she feel the same way about him?

If she did, Uncle Nathan wasn't willing to say so. "Delia was only nineteen," he said. "I don't think she knew what she wanted."

He was silent for a while. Then he went on with his story. "Once I knew she was married," he said "I knew right away what I had to do. I remember I gave myself a good talking to. I said, 'If you can fall in love in twenty minutes, you can fall out of love just as fast.'"

"And could you?"

"Some people could, I guess," Uncle Nathan said. "It seemed to take me a bit longer than that."

The story stopped then because we had to go out to the barn to check the sheep. While we'd been in the house, another ewe had dropped her lamb. We heard it bleat as we came in the barn, and the ewe whose lamb had died heard it too. It was at the far end of the barn, out of sight, but at the sound of it, milk began to run from her udder. She couldn't help herself.

We checked the rest of the sheep and then we went back into the house. I made us a pot of tea.

"I was afraid to go to see Dobson and Delia after they got moved in," Uncle Nathan said. "I think I was afraid somebody would read my mind."

He went, he said, because Delia soon made her house a gathering place for all the young people of the district, and he didn't see how he could be the only one to stay away. Delia didn't make things any easier for him.

"She used to keep saying she'd only been married three months...as if that made it any less final. And when she spoke of anything they had—whether it was a buggy or a kitchen safe or the pet dog—she would say 'my buggy' or 'my kitchen safe' or 'my dog.' 'We' and 'us' were words she didn't use at all."

I poured our tea then, trying to imagine the house that Delia Sykes had lived in.

"It was something of a showplace for its time," Uncle Nathan told me. Everything in it was the best of its kind, he said, from the Home Comfort stove in the kitchen to the pump organ in the parlour. What puzzled Uncle Nathan was Delia's attitude to her things. She'd picked them out herself in Winnipeg and ordered them sent, but when they got here, she seemed to feel they weren't important.

"The more things you've got, the more things you've got to take care of," she said. She didn't even unpack most of her trunks.

Dobson was worried. He thought that moving

Race, 1984, by Michael Snow (photograph and paint on board; 176 x 79 cm.).

Courtesy of Agnes Etherington Art Centre, Queens University. Reprinted with the permission of Michael Snow.

away from her family had unsettled her. "Delia wasn't like this in Manitoba," he said.

"I kept wondering," Uncle Nathan said, "where we would go from here. It never occurred to me that there could be another girl for me. And then Eunice came along."

It was on an October afternoon, Uncle Nathan said, that he met Eunice Lathem.

The sun was low in the southwest when he drove into the Sykes yard, and Dobson, as usual, was out around the buildings showing the younger men his grinding mill, his blacksmith shop, his threshing machine.

Uncle Nathan remembered that the trees were leafless except for the plumes of new growth at the top. He tied up his horse and, as he headed for the house, saw that the afternoon sun was turning the west-facing walls all gold and blue. It looked like a day for endings, not beginnings. But he went into the house, and there stood Eunice Lathem.

Eunice was a year or two older than Delia but she looked just like her. Uncle Nathan noticed that she was quieter.

Supper was already on the table when Uncle Nathan got there. The news of Eunice's arrival had attracted such a company of bachelors that there weren't enough plates or chairs for everybody to eat at once.

"I don't know about anybody else, but I'm starving," Delia announced, taking her place at the head of the table. Eunice, though she was the guest of honour, insisted on waiting until the second sitting.

As the first eaters prepared to deal with their pie, Eunice began to ladle water out of a stonewear crock into a dishpan. Uncle Nathan went to help her. He said something funny and she laughed.

Delia's voice startled them both. "I invited Eunice out here to find a husband," she said with a high-pitched laugh. "I said to myself, 'With all the bachelors we've got around, if she can't find a husband here there's no hope for her.'"

Delia spoke as if she was making a joke and there was a nervous round of laughter. Blood rose in Eunice's face.

"If I'd known that was why you were asking me," Eunice said, "I would never have come."

And indeed, Uncle Nathan said, Eunice wasn't the sort of girl to need anyone's help in finding a husband. She was, if anything, prettier than Delia. Not as showy, perhaps, perhaps not as rounded. But if you went over them point by point comparing noses, chins, teeth and all the rest of it, Eunice's might well have come out on top.

Later, when the others had gone, Delia apologized. "I shouldn't have said that," she said. "It sounded awful." She didn't even claim to have been making joke.

"I want you two to be friends," she said.

In the weeks that followed, Uncle Nathan saw that Delia was pushing her sister his way. He didn't know why, but he didn't find the idea unpleasant.

"I suppose I liked Eunice at first because she looked so much like Delia," he said, "but as I got to know her better it seemed to me that she might be easier to get along with in the long run. I wouldn't be the first man to marry the sister of the girl who first took his fancy, nor the last one either.

"It seemed to me that a man could love one girl as easily as another if he put his mind to it. I reasoned it out. How much did the person matter anyway? That was what I asked myself. It seemed to me that when all was said and done, it would be the life that two people made together that would count, not who the people were.

"I remember thinking that getting married would be like learning to dance. Some people are born knowing how; they have a natural beat. Other people have to make an effort to learn. But all of them, finally, are moving along to the music one way or the other.

"Anyway," Uncle Nathan said "I spoke to Eunice and she agreed, and we decided to be married at Christmas.

"It was September, I think, when we got engaged," Uncle Nathan said. "I remember thinking about telling Dobson and Delia. I could imagine the four of us—Dobson and Delia, Eunice and me—living side by side, spending our Sundays together, raising children who would be cousins and might even look like each other.

"I came over early on the Sunday and we told them. Delia didn't have very much to say then. But in the afternoon when quite a crowd had gathered and Eunice and I were waiting for the rest of them to get there before we made our announcement, a strange thing happened.

"The day before, Dobson had brought home a new saddle pony and Delia had wanted to ride it. Dobson didn't know how well broke it was, or if it could be trusted, and he refused. I guess that refusal rankled. Delia didn't like to be told she couldn't do a thing or have a thing she had set her heart on.

"Anyway, on Sunday afternoon Eunice was sitting at the pump organ playing for us, and she looked beautiful. We were all sitting around looking at her.

"And then somebody happened to glance out of the window," Uncle Nathan said. "And there was Delia on the pony and the pair of them putting on a regular rodeo.

"She didn't break her neck which was a wonder. By the time she finally got off the pony, we were all out in the yard, and somebody had the idea of taking a picture of Delia and Eunice and the pony."

After that, Uncle Nathan said, Delia seemed to want to get the wedding over with as soon as possible. She hemmed sheets and ordered linen and initialled pillow-cases. When November finally came and the neighbours decided on a skating party for Eunice and Uncle Nathan, it was Delia who sewed white rabbit fur around the sleeves and bottom of Eunice's coat, so that it would look like a skating dress.

The night of the party was dark. There was a moon, but the sky was cloudy. They walked down the hill together, all those young people laughing and talking.

"One minute you could see their faces and the next they would all disappear," Uncle Nathan said. "I touched a match to a bonfire we had laid in the afternoon, and we all sat down to screw on our skates.

"I skated first with Eunice. She wanted to stay

near the fire so we could see where we were going. I skated with several other girls, putting off, for some reason, the time when I would skate with Delia. But then she came gliding up to me and held out her hands and I took them and we headed out together into the darkness.

"As soon as we turned our backs on the fire it was as if something came over us. We wanted to skate out farther and farther. It seemed to me that we could keep on like this all our lives, just skating outward farther and farther, and the lake would keep getting longer and longer so that we would never come to the end of it."

Uncle Nathan sighed. "I didn't know then that in three days Delia would have left Willow Bunch for good, and in six months I would have followed her," he said.

Why had he given up farming?

"Farming's no life for a man alone," he said. "And I couldn't imagine ever wanting to marry again."

He resumed his story. "Once the moon came out and I could see Delia's face, determined in the moonlight.

"'Do you want to turn back?' I asked her.

"'I'm game as long as you are,' she said.

"Another time, 'I don't ever want to turn back,' she said.

"I gave in before Delia did," Uncle Nathan said. "'If we don't turn around pretty soon,' I told her 'we're going to be skating straight up Pa's stubble fields.'

"We turned around then, and there was the light from the fire and our feet already set on its path. And I found I wanted to be back there with all the people around me. Eunice deserved better, and I knew it."

As they came toward the fire, Eunice skated out to meet them. "I might as well have been someplace else for all the attention she paid me," Uncle Nathan said. Her words were all for Delia.

"If this is what you got me out here for," Eunice said, "you can just forget about it. I'm not going to be your window blind."

"I don't know what you're talking about," Delia said.

She looked unhappy. "She knew as well as I did," Uncle Nathan said "that whatever we were doing out there it was more than just skating."

"We were only skating," Delia said. And then her temper rose. "You always were jealous of me," she said.

"Who would you say was jealous now?" Eunice asked.

"We were far enough away from the fire for the girls not to be heard," Uncle Nathan said. "At least I hoped we were.

"What was worrying me was the thought of Eunice having to meet all the people up at the house, and finding out she was the guest of honour, and having to try to rise to the occasion.

"That was why I suggested that the two of them go for a skate. I thought it would give them a chance to cool down. Besides," he added, "I couldn't think of anything else to do."

The girls let themselves be persuaded. They skated off together and Uncle Nathan watched them go. First he could see their two silhouettes, slim and graceful against the silver lake. Then all he could see was the white fur on Eunice's coat. And then they were swallowed up by the darkness.

"It was several minutes before we heard them calling for help," Uncle Nathan said.

Uncle Nathan and I sat silent for some time then: he remembering, I pondering. "If only you could have seen how beautiful she was" he said at last, and I didn't know whether it was Eunice he was speaking of, or Delia.

"I wonder if I would have felt any better about it if I'd got Eunice instead of Delia," he said. I realized that he'd been trying to make the judgment for 30 years.

"You didn't have any choice," I reminded him. "It was dark. You couldn't see their faces."

"No," Uncle Nathan said. "I couldn't see their faces." The sound of old winters was in his voice, a sound of infinite sadness.

"But I could see their hands on the edge of the ice," he said. "The one pair of arms had white fur around them.

"And I reached for the other pair."

Rowing

Anne Sexton

A story, a story!
(Let it go. Let it come.)
I was stamped out like a Plymouth fender
into this world.
First came the crib
with its glacial bars.
Then dolls
and the devotion to their plastic mouths.
Then there was school,
the little straight rows of chairs,
blotting my name over and over,
but undersea all the time,
a stranger whose elbows wouldn't work.
Then there was life
with its cruel houses
and people who seldom touched—
though touch is all—
but I grew,
like a pig in a trenchcoat I grew,
and then there were many strange apparitions,
the nagging rain, the sun turning into poison
and all of that, saws working through my heart,
but I grew, I grew,
and God was there like an island I had not rowed to,
still ignorant of Him, my arms and my legs worked,
and I grew, I grew,
I wore rubies and bought tomatoes
and now, in my middle age,
about nineteen in the head I'd say,
I am rowing, I am rowing,
though the oarlocks stick and are rusty
and the sea blinks and rolls
like a worried eyeball,
but I am rowing, I am rowing,
though the wind pushes me back
and I know that that island will not be perfect,
it will have the flaws of life,
the absurdities of the dinner table,
but there will be a door
and I will open it
and I will get rid of the rat inside of me,
the gnawing pestilential rat.
God will take it with his two hands
and embrace it.

As the African says:
This is my tale which I have told,
if it be sweet, if it be not sweet,
take somewhere else and let some return to me.
This stoy ends with me still rowing.

The Rowing Endeth

Anne Sexton

I'm mooring my rowboat
at the dock of the island called God.
This dock is made in the shape of a fish
and there are many boats moored
at many different docks.
"It's okay," I say to myself,
with blisters that broke and healed
and broke and healed—
saving themselves over and over.
And salt sticking to my face and arms like
a glue-skin pocked with grains of tapioca.
I empty myself from my wooden boat
and onto the flesh of The Island.

"On with it!" He says and thus
we squat on the rocks by the sea
and play—can it be true—
a game of poker.
He calls me.
I win because I hold a royal straight flush.
He wins because He holds five aces.
A wild card had been announced
but I had not heard it
being in such a state of awe
when He took out the cards and dealt.
As he plunks down His five aces
and I sit grinning at my royal flush,
He starts to laugh,
the laughter rolling like a hoop out of His mouth
and into mine,
and such laughter that He doubles right over me
laughing a Rejoice-Chorus at our two triumphs.
Then I laugh, the fishy dock laughs
the sea laughs. The Island laughs.
The Absurd laughs.

Dearest dealer,
I with my royal straight flush,
love you so for your wild card,
that untamable, eternal, gut-driven *ha-ha*
and lucky love.

What We Talk about When We Talk about Love

Raymond Carver

American writer Raymond Carver's work probes relationships between people in an increasingly complex modern world, where confusion about love, or lack of it, is often the norm. In this piece from the 1981 short story collection of the same name, Carver looks at the relationship between two men and two women as they discuss relationships and their pasts. Carver's stories were combined in a 1993 film entitled *Short Cuts*.

My friend Mel McGinnis was talking. Mel McGinnis is a cardiologist, and sometimes that gives him the right. The four of us were sitting around his kitchen table drinking gin. Sunlight filled the kitchen from the big window behind the sink. There were Mel and me and his second wife, Teresa—Terri, we called her—and my wife, Laura. We lived in Albuquerque then. But we were all from somewhere else.

There was an ice bucket on the table. The gin and the tonic water kept going around, and we somehow got on the subject of love. Mel thought real love was nothing less than spiritual love. He said he'd spent five years in a seminary before quitting to go to medical school. He said he still looked back on those years in the seminary as the most important years in his life.

Terri said the man she lived with before she lived with Mel loved her so much to tried to kill her. Then Terri said, "He beat me up one night. He dragged me around the living room by my ankles. He kept saying 'I love you, I love you, you bitch.' He went on dragging me around the living room. My head kept knocking on things." Terri looked around the table. "What do you do with love like that?"

She was a bone-thin woman with a pretty face, dark eyes, and brown hair that hung down her back. She liked necklaces made of turquoise, and long pendant earrings.

"My God, don't be silly. That's not love, and you know it," Mel said. "I don't know what you'd call it, but I sure know you wouldn't call it love."

"Say what you want to, but I know it was," Terry said. "It may sound crazy to you, but it's true just the same. People are different, Mel. Sure, sometimes he may have acted crazy. Okay. But he loved me. In his own way maybe, but he loved me. There was love there, Mel. Don't say there wasn't."

Mel let out his breath. He held his glass and turned to Laura and me. "The man threatened to kill me," Mel said. He finished his drink and reached for the gin bottle. "Terri's a romantic. Terri's of the kick-me-so-I'll-know-you-love-me school. Terri, hon, don't look that way." Mel reached across the table and touched Terri's cheek with his fingers. He grinned at her.

"Now he wants to make up," Terri said.

"Make up what?" Mel said. "What is there to make up? I know what I know. That's all."

"How'd we get started on this subject, anyway?" Terri said. She raised her glass and drank from it. "Mel always has love on his mind," she said. "Don't you, honey?" she smiled. and I thought that was the last of it.

"I just wouldn't call Ed's behavior love. That's all I'm saying, honey," Mel said. "What about you guys?" Mel said to Laura and me. "Does that sound like love to you?"

"I'm the wrong person to ask," I said "I didn't even know the man. I've only heard his name mentioned in passing. I wouldn't know. You'd have to know the particulars. But I think what you're saying is that love is an absolute."

Mel said, "The kind of love I'm talking about is. The kind of love I'm talking about, you don't try to kill people."

Laura said, "I don't know anything about Ed, or anything about the situation. But who can judge anyone else's situation?"

I touched the back of Laura's hand. She gave me a quick smile. I picked up Laura's hand. It was warm, the nails polished, perfectly manicured. I encircled the broad wrist with my fingers, and I held her.

"When I left, he drank rat poison," Terri said. She clasped her arms with her hands. "They took him to the hospital in Santa Fe. That's where we lived then, about ten miles out. They saved his life. But his gums went crazy from it. I mean they pulled away from his teeth. After that, his teeth stood out like fangs. My God," Terri said. She waited a minute, then let go of her arms and picked up her glass.

"What people won't do!" Laura said.

"He's out of the action now," Mel said. "He's dead."

Mel handed me the saucer of limes. I took a section, squeezed it over my drink, and stirred the ice cubes with my finger.

"It gets worse," Terri said. "He shot himself in the mouth. But he bungled that too. Poor Ed," She said. Terri shook her head.

"Poor Ed nothing," Mel said. "He was dangerous."

Mel was forty-five years old. He was tall and rangy with curly soft hair. His face and arms were brown from the tennis he played. When he was sober, his gestures, all his movements, were precise, very careful.

"He did love me though, Mel. Grant me that," Terri said. "That's all I'm asking. He didn't love me that way you love me. I'm not saying that. But he loved me. You can grant me that, can't you?"

"What do you mean, he bungled it?" I said.

Laura leaned forward with her glass. She put her elbows on the table and held her glass in both hands. She glanced from Mel to Terri and waited with a look of bewilderment on her open face, as if amazed that such things happened to people you were friendly with.

"How'd he bungle it when he killed himself?" I said.

"I'll tell you what happened," Mel said. "He took this twenty-two pistol he'd bought to threaten Terri and me with. Oh, I'm serious, the man was always threatening. You should have seen the way we lived in those days. Like fugitives. I even bought a gun myself. Can you believe it? A guy like me? But I did. I bought one for self-defense and carried it in the glove compartment. Sometimes I'd have to leave the apartment in the middle of the night. To go to the hospital, you know? Terri and I weren't married then, and my first wife had the house and kids, the dog, everything, and Terri and I were living in this apartment here. Sometimes, as I say, I'd get a call in the middle of the night and have to go in to the hospital at two or three in the morning. It'd be dark out there in the parking lot, and I'd break into a sweat before I could even get to my car. I never knew if he was going to come up out of the shrubbery or from behind a car and start shooting. I mean, the man was crazy. He was capable of wiring a bomb, anything. He used to call my service at all hours and when I'd return the call, he'd say, 'Son of a bitch, your days are numbered.' Little things like that. It was scary, I'm telling you."

"I still feel sorry for him," Terri said.

"It sounds like a nightmare," Laura said. "But what exactly happened after he shot himself?"

Laura is a legal secretary. We'd met in a professional capacity. Before we knew it, it was a courtship. She's thirty five, three years younger than I am. In addition to being in love, we like each other and enjoy one another's company. She's easy to be with.

"What happened?" Laura said.

Mel said, "He shot himself in the mouth in his room. Someone heard the shot and told the manager. They came in with a passkey, saw what had happened, and called an ambulance. I happened to be there when they brought him in, alive but past recall. The man lived for three days. His head swelled up to twice the size of a normal head. I'd never seen anything like it, and I hope I never do again. Terri wanted to go in and sit with him when she found out about it. We had a fight over it. I didn't think she should see him like that. I didn't think she should see him, and I still don't."

"Who won the fight?" Laura said.

"I was in the room with him when he died," Terri said. "He never came up out of it. But I sat with him. He didn't have anyone else."

"He was dangerous," Mel said. "If you call that love, you can have it."

"It was love," Terri said. "Sure, it's abnormal in most people's eyes. But he was willing to die for it. He did die for it."

"I sure as hell wouldn't call it love," Mel said. "I mean, no one knows what he did it for. I've seen a lot of suicides, and I couldn't say anyone ever knew what they did it for."

Mel put his hands behind his neck and tilted his chair back. "I'm not interested in that kind of love," he said. "If that's love, you can have it."

Terri said, "We were afraid. Mel even made a will out and wrote to his brother in California who used to be a Green Beret. Mel told him who to look for if something happened to him."

Terri drank form her glass. She said, "But Mel's right—we lived like fugitives. We were afraid. Mel was, weren't you, honey? I even called the police at one point, but they were no help. They said they couldn't do anything until Ed actually did something. Isn't that a laugh?" Terri said. She poured the last of the gin into her glass and waggled the bottle. Mel got up form the table and went to the cupboard. He took down another bottle.

"Well, Nick and I know what love is," Laura said. "For us, I mean," Laura said. She bumped my knee with her knee. "You're supposed to say something now," Laura said, and turned her smile on me.

For an answer, I took Laura's hand and raised it to my lips. I made a big production out of kissing her hand. Everyone was amused.

"We're lucky," I said.

"You guys, Terri said. "Stop that now. You're making me sick. You're still on the honeymoon, for God's sake. You're still gaga, for crying out loud. Just wait. How long have you been together now? How long has it been? A year? Longer than a year?"

"Going on a year and a half," Laura said, flushed and smiling.

"Oh, now," Terri said. "Wait awhile."

She held her drink and gazed at Laura.

"I'm only kidding," Terri said.

Mel opened the gin and went around the table with the bottle.

"Here, you guys," he said. "Let's have a toast. I want to propose a toast. a toast to love. To true love," Mel said.

We touched glasses.

"To love," we said.

Outside in the backyard, one of the dogs began to bark. The leaves of the aspen that leaned past the window ticked against the glass. The afternoon sun was like a presence in this room the spacious light of ease and generosity. We could have been anywhere, somewhere enchanted. We raised our glasses again and grinned at each other like children who had agreed on something forbidden.

"I'll tell you what real love is," Mel said. "I mean, I'll give you a good example. And then you can draw you own conclusion." He poured more gin into his glass. He added an ice cube and a sliver of lime. We waited and sipped our drinks. Laura and I touched knees again. I put a hand on her warm thigh and left it there.

"What do any of us know about love?" Mel said. "It seems to me we're just beginners at love. We say we love each other and we do, I don't doubt it. I love Terri and Terri loves me, and you guys love each other too. You know the kind of love I'm talking about now. Physical love, that impulse that drives you to someone special, as well as love of the other person's being, his or her essence, as it were. Carnal love and, well call it sentimental love, the day-to-day caring about the other person. But sometimes I have a hard time accounting for the fact that I must have loved my first wife too. But I did, I know I did. So I suppose I am like Terri in that regard. Terri and Ed." He thought about it and then he went on. "There was a time when I thought I loved my first wife more than life itself. But now I hate her guts. I do. How do you explain that? What happened to that love? What happened to it, is what I'd like to know. I wish someone could tell me. Then there's Ed. Okay, we're back to Ed. He loves Terri so much he tries to kill her and he winds up killing himself." Mel stopped talking and swallowed from his glass. "You guys have been together eighteen months and you love each other. It shows all over you. You glow with it. But you both loved other people before you met each other. You've both been married before, just like us. And you probably loved other people before that too, even. Terri and I have been together five years, been married for four. And the terrible thing, the terrible thing is, but the good thing too, the saving grace, you might say, is that if something happened to one of us—excuse me for saying this—but if something happened to one of us tomorrow, I think the other one, the other person, would grieve for a while, you know, but then the surviving party would go out and love again, have someone else soon enough. All this, all of this love we're talking about, it would just be a memory. Maybe not even a memory. Am I wrong? Am I way off base? Because I want you to set me straight if you think I'm wrong. I want to know. I mean, I don't know anything, and I'm the first one to admit it."

"Mel, for God's sake," Terri said. She reached out and took hold of his wrist. "Are you getting drunk? Honey? Are you drunk?"

"Honey, I'm just talking," Mel said. "All right? I don't have to be drunk to say what I think. I mean, we're all just talking, right?" Mel said. He fixed his eyes on her.

"Sweetie, I'm not criticizing," Terri said.

She picked up her glass.

"I'm not on call today," Mel said. "Let me remind you of that. I am not on call," he said.

"Mel, we love you," Laura said.

Mel looked at Laura. He looked at her as if he could not place her, as if she was not the woman she was.

"Love you too, Laura," Mel said. "And you, Nick, love you too. You know something?" Mel said. "You guys are our pals," Mel said.

He picked up his glass.

Mel said, "I was going to tell you about something. I mean, I was going to prove a point. You see, this happened a few months ago, but it's still going on right now, and it ought to make us feel ashamed when we talk like we know what we're talking about when we talk about love."

"Come on now," Terri said. "Don't talk like you're drunk if you're not drunk."

"Just shut up for once in your life," Mel said very quietly. "Will you do me a favor and do that for a minute? So as I was saying, there's this old couple who had this car wreck out on the interstate. A kid hit them and they were all torn to shit and nobody was giving them much chance to pull through."

Terri looked at us and then back at Mel. She seemed anxious, or maybe that's too strong a word.

Mel was handing the bottle around the table.

"I was on call that night," Mel said. "It was May or maybe it was June. Terri and I had just sat down to dinner when the hospital called. There'd been this thing out on the interstate. Drunk kid, teenager, plowed his dad's pickup into this camper with this old couple in it. They were up in their mid-seventies, that couple. The kid—eighteen, nineteen, something—he was DOA. Taken the steering wheel through his sternum. The old couple, they were alive, you understand. I mean, just barely. But they had everything. Multiple fractures, internal injuries, hemorrhaging, contusions, lacerations, the works, and they each of them had themselves concussions. They were in a bad way, believe me. And, of course, their age was two strikes against them. I'd say she was worse off than he was. Ruptured spleen along with everything else. Both kneecaps broken. But they'd been wearing seatbelts and, God knows, that's what saved them for the time being."

"Folks, this is an advertisement for the National Safety Council," Terri said. "This is your spokesman, Dr. Melvin R. McGinnis, talking." Terri laughed. "Mel," she said, "sometimes you're just too much. But I love you, hon," she said.

"Honey, I love you," Mel said.

He leaned across the table. Terri met him halfway. They kissed.

"Terri's right," Mel said as he settled himself

again. "Get those seatbelts on. But seriously, they were in some shape, those oldsters. By the time I got down there, the kid was dead, as I said. He was off in a corner, laid out on a gurney. I took one look at the old couple and told the ER nurse to get me a neurologist and an orthopedic man and a couple of surgeons down there right away."

He drank from his glass. "I'll try to keep this short," he said. "So we took the two of them up to the OR and worked like fuck on them most of the night. They had these incredible reserves, those two. You see that once in a while. So we did everything that could be done, and toward morning we're giving them a fifty-fifty chance, maybe less than that for her. So here they are, still alive the next morning. So, okay, we move them into the ICU, which is where they both kept plugging away at it for two weeks, hitting it and better on all the scopes. So we transfer them out to their own room."

Mel stopped talking. "Here," he said, "let's drink this cheapo gin the hell up. Then we're going to dinner, right? Terri and I know a new place. That's where we'll go, to this new place we know about. But we're not going until we finish up this cut-rate, lousy gin."

Terri said, "We haven't actually eaten there yet. But it looks good. From the outside, you know."

"I like food," Mel said. "If I had it to do all over again, I'd be a chef, you know? Right, Terri?" Mel said.

He laughed. He fingered the ice in his glass.

"Terri knows," he said. "Terri can tell you. But let me say this. If I could come back again in a different life, a different time and all, you know what? I'd like to come back as a knight. You were pretty safe wearing all that armour. It was all right being a knight until gunpowder and muskets and pistols came along."

"Mel would like to ride a horse and carry a lance," Terri said.

"Carry a woman's scarf with you everywhere," Laura said.

"Or just a woman," Mel said.

"Shame on you," Laura said.

Terri said, "Suppose you came back as a serf. The serfs didn't have it so good in those days," Terri said.

"The serfs never had it good," Mel said. "But I guess even the knights were vessels to someone. Isn't that the way it worked? But then everyone is always a vessel to someone. Isn't that right? Terri? But what I liked about knights, besides their ladies, was that they had that suit of armour, you know, and they couldn't get hurt very easy. No cars in those days, you know? No drunk teenagers to tear into your ass."

"Vassals," Terri said.

"What?" Mel said.

"Vassals, vessels," Mel said, "what the fuck's the difference? You knew what I meant anyway. All right," Mel said. "So I'm not educated. I learned my stuff. I'm a heart surgeon, sure, but I'm just a mechanic. I go in and I fuck around and I fix things. Shit," Mel said.

"Modesty doesn't become you," Terri said.

"He's just a humble sawbones," I said. "But sometimes they suffocated in all that armour, Mel. They'd even have heart attacks if it got too hot and they were too tired and worn out. I read somewhere that they'd fall off their horses and not be able to get up because they were too tired to stand with all that armour on them. They got trampled by their own horses sometimes."

"That's terrible," Mel said. "That's a terrible thing, Nicky. I guess they'd just lay there and wait until somebody came along and made a shish kebab out of them."

"Some other vessel," Terri said.

"That's right," Mel said. "Some vassal would come along and spear the bastard in the name of love. Or whatever the fuck it was they fought over in those days."

"Same things we fight over these days," Terri said.

Laura said, "Nothing's changed."

The color was still high in Laura's cheeks. Her eyes were bright. She brought her glass to her lips.

Mel poured himself another drink. He looked at the label closely as if studying a long row of numbers. Then he slowly put the bottle down on the table and slowly reached for the tonic water.

"What about the old couple?" Laura said. "You didn't finish that story you started."

Laura was having a hard time lighting her cigarette. Her matches kept going out.

The sunshine inside the room was different now, changing, getting thinner. But the leaves outside the window were still shimmering, and I stared at the pattern they made on the panes and on the Formica counter. They weren't the same patterns, of course.

"What about the old couple?" I said.

"Older but wiser," Terri said.

Mel stared at her.

Terri said, "Go on with your story, hon. I was only kidding. Then what happened?"

"Terri, sometimes," Mel said.

"Please, Mel," Terri said. "Don't always be so serious, sweetie. Can't you take a joke?"

"Where's the joke?" Mel said.

He held his glass and gazed steadily at his wife.

"What happened?" Laura said.

Mel fastened his eyes on Laura. He said, "Laura, if I didn't have Terri and if I didn't love her so much, and if Nick wasn't my best friend, I'd fall in love with you. I'd carry you off, honey," he said.

"Tell you story," Terri said. "Then we'll go to that new place, okay?"

"Okay," Mel said. "Where was I?" he said. He stared at the table and then he began again.

"I dropped in to see each of them every day, sometimes twice a day if I was up doing other calls anyway. Casts and bandages, head to foot, the both of them. You know, you've seen it in the movies. That's just the way they looked, just like in the movies. Little eye-holes and nose-holes and mouth-holes. And she had to have her legs slung up on top of it. Well, the husband was very depressed for the longest while. Even after he found out that his wife was going to pull through, he was still very depressed. Not about the accident, though. I mean, the accident was one thing, but it wasn't everything. I'd get up to his mouth-hole, you know, and he'd say no, it wasn't the accident exactly but it was because he couldn't see her through his eye-holes. He said that was what was making him feel so bad. Can you imagine? I'm telling you, the man's heart was breaking because he couldn't turn his goddamn head and *see* his goddamn wife."

Mel looked around the table and shook his head at what he was going to say.

"I mean, it was killing the old fart just because he couldn't *look* at the fucking woman."

We all looked at Mel.

"Do you see what I'm saying?" he said.

Maybe we were a little drunk by then. I know it was hard keeping things in focus. The light was draining out of the room, going back through the window where it had come from. Yet nobody made a move to get up form the table to turn on the overhead light.

"Listen," Mel said. "Let's finish this fucking gin. There's about enough left here for one shooter all around. Then let's go eat. Let's go to the new place."

"He's depressed," Terri said. "Mel, why don't you take a pill?"

Mel shook his head. "I've taken everything there is."

"We all need a pill now and then," I said.

"Some people are born needing them," Terri said. She was using her finger to rub at something on the table. Then she stopped rubbing.

"I think I want to call my kids," Mel said. "Is that all right with everybody? I'll call my kids," he said.

Terri said, "What if Marjorie answers the phone? You guys, you've heard us on the subject of Marjorie. It'll make you feel even worse."

"I don't want to talk to Marjorie." Mel said. "But I want to talk to my kids."

"There isn't a day goes by that Mel doesn't say he wishes she'd get married again. Or else die," Terri said. "For one thing," Terri said, "she's bankrupting us. Mel says it's just to spite him that she won't get married again. She has a boyfriend who lives with her and the kids, so Mel is supporting the boyfriend too."

"She's allergic to bees," Mel said. "If I'm not praying she'll get married again, I'm praying she'll get herself stung to death by a swarm of fucking bees."

"Shame on you," Laura said.

"Bzzzzzzz," Mel said, turning his fingers into bees and buzzing them at Terri's throat. Then he let his hands drop all the way to his sides.

"She's vicious," Mel said. "Sometimes I think I'll go up there dressed like a beekeeper. You know, that hat that's like a helmet with the plate that comes down over you face, the big gloves, and the padded coat? I'll knock on the door let loose a hive of bees in the house. But first I'd make sure the kids were out, of course."

He crossed one leg over the other. It seemed to take him a lot of time to do it. Then he put both feet on the floor and leaned forward, elbows on the table, his chin cupped in his hands.

"Maybe I won't call the kids, after all. Maybe it isn't such a hot idea. Maybe we'll just go eat. How does that sound?"

Sounds fine to me," I said. "Eat or not eat. Or keep drinking. I could head right on out into the sunset."

"What does that mean, honey?" Laura said.

"It just means what I said," I said. "It means I could just keep going. That's all it means."

"I could eat something myself," Laura said. "I don't think I've ever been so hungry in my life. Is there something to nibble on?"

"I'll put out some cheese and crackers," Terri said.

But Terri just sat there. She did not get up to get anything.

Mel turned his glass over. He spilled it out on the table.

"Gin's gone," Mel said.

Terri said, "Now what?"

I could hear my heart beating. I could hear everyone's heart. I could hear the human noise we sat there making, not one of us moving, not even when the room went dark.

Ecclesiastes

The New Jerusalem Bible

There is a season for everything, a time
for every occupation under heaven:
A time for giving birth,
a time for dying;
a time for planting,
a time for uprooting what has been
planted.
A time for killing,
a time for healing;
a time for knocking down,
a time for building.
A time for tears,
a time for laughter;
a time for mourning,
a time for dancing.
A time for throwing stones away,
a time for gathering them;
a time for embracing,
a time to refrain from embracing.
A time for searching,
a time for losing;
a time for keeping,
a time for discarding.
A time for tearing,
a time for sewing;
a time for keeping silent,
a time for speaking.
A time for loving,
a time for hating;
a time for war,
a time for peace.

SOURCE: Ecclesiastes, 3:1. *The New Jerusalem Bible.* Garden City, N.Y.: Doubleday & Company, Inc., 1966.

Turn, Turn, Turn

The Byrds (lyrics by Pete Seeger, adapted from Ecclesiastes 3:1)

Chorus:
To everything (turn, turn, turn)
There is a season (turn, turn, turn)
And a time for ev'ry purpose under heaven.

A time to build up, a time to break down;
A time to dance, a time to mourn;
A time to cast away stones, a time to
gather stones together.
Chorus

A time of love, a time of hate;
A time of war, a time of peace;
A time you may embrace, a time to refrain
from embracing.
Chorus

A time to gain, a time to lose;
A time to rend, a time to sew;
A time to love, a time to hate; a time of
peace, I swear it's not too late.
Chorus—repeat last line

Three Poems

Weary, I Lie Alone

Anonymous

By day my eyes, by night my soul desires you,
Weary, I lie alone.
Once in a dream it seemed you were beside me
O far beyond all dreams, if you would come!

Medieval Latin Lyrics:

Te vigilans oculis, animo te nocte requiro,
victa iacent solo cum mea membra toro.
vidi ego me tecum falsa sub imagine somni.
somnia tu vinces, si mihi vera venis.

SOURCE: Helen Waddell, *Mediaeval Latin Lyrics* (London, UK: Constable & Company Ltd.).

Bhartrhari

Translated from Sanskrit

In former days we'd both agree
That you were me, and I was you.
What has now happened to us two,
That you are you, and I am me?

SOURCE: From *Poems from the Sanskrit*, translated by John Brough, (London: Penguin Classics, 1968) copyright © John Brough, 1968.

Absence

Abu Bakr al-Turtushi

Every night I scan
the heavens with my eyes
seeking the star
that you are contemplating.

I question travellers
from the four corners of the earth
hoping to meet one
who has breathed your fragrance.

When the wind blows
I make sure it blows in my face:
the breeze might bring me
news of you.

I wander over roads
without aim, without purpose.
Perhaps a song
will sound your name.

Secretly I study
every face I see
hoping against hope
to glimpse a trace of your beauty.

SOURCES: *Poems of Arab Andalusia*, translated by Carla Franzen (San Francisco: City Lights Books).

The Color Purple

Alice Walker

The American writer Alice Walker (1944-) was born into a sharecropping family in Eatonton, Georgia. Her poems, novels and short stories depict black life in the southern U.S. Her best-known work, *The Color Purple* (1982), from which this excerpt was taken was made into a popular movie in 1985. This novel won the Pulitzer Prize and the American Book Award in the year it was published.

Dear Nettie,

I don't write to God no more, I write to you.

What happen to God? ast Shug.

Who that? I say.

She look at me serious.

Big a devil as you is, I say, you not worried bout no God, surely.

She say, Wait a minute. Hold on just a minute here. Just because I don't harass it like some peoples us know don't mean I ain't got religion.

What God do for me? I ast.

She say, Celie! Like she shock. He gave you life, good health, and a good woman that love you to death.

Yeah, I say, and he give me a lynched daddy, a crazy mama, a lowdown dog of a step pa and a sister I probably won't ever see again. Anyhow, I say, the God I been praying and writing to is a man. And act just like all the other mens I know. Trifling, forgitful and lowdown.

She say, Miss Celie. You better hush. God might hear you.

Let 'im hear me, I say. If he ever listened to poor colored women the world would be a different place, I can tell you.

She talk and she talk, trying to budge me way from blasphemy. But I blaspheme much as I want to.

All my life I never care what people thought bout nothing I did, I say. But deep in my heart I care about God. What he going to think. And come to find out, he don't think. Just sit up there glorying in being deef, I reckon. But it ain't easy, trying to do without God. Even if you know he ain't there, trying to do without him is a strain.

I is a sinner, say Shug. Cause I was born. I don't deny it. But once you find out what's out there waiting for us, what else can you be?

Sinners have more good times, I say.

You know why? she ast.

Cause you ain't all the time worrying bout God, I say.

Naw, that ain't it, she say. Us worry bout God a lot. But once us feel loved by God, us do the best us can to please him with what us like.

You telling me God love you, and you ain't never done nothing for him? I mean, not go to church, sing in the choir, feed the preacher and all like that?

But if God love me, Celie, I don't have to do all that. Unless I want to. There's a lot of other things I can do that I speck God likes.

Like what? I ast.

Oh, she say. I can lay back and just admire stuff. Be happy.

Have a good time.

Well, this sound like blasphemy sure nuff.

She say, Celie, tell the truth, have you ever found God in church? I never did. I just found a bunch of folks hoping for him to show. Any God I ever felt in church I brought in with me. And I think all the other folks did too. They come to church to *share* God, not find God.

Some folks didn't have him to share, I said. They the ones didn't speak to me while I was there struggling with my big belly and Mr. _______ children.

Right, she say.

Then she say: Tell me what your God look like, Celie.

Aw naw, I say. I'm too shame. Nobody ever ast me this before, so I'm sort of took by surprise. Besides, when I think about it, it don't seem quite right. But it all I got. I decide to stick up for him, just to see what Shug say.

Okay, I say. He big and old and tall and gray-bearded and white. He wear white robes and go barefooted.

Blue eyes? she ast.

Sort of bluish-gray. Cool. Big though. White lashes, I say.

She laugh.

Why you laugh? I ast. I don't think it so funny. What you expect him to look like, Mr. _______ ?

That wouldn't be no improvement, she say. Then she tell me this old white man is the same God she used to see when she prayed. If you wait to find God in church, Celie, she say, that's who is bound to show up, cause that's where he live.

How come? I ast.

Cause that's the one that's in the white folks' white bible.

Shug! I say. God wrote the bible, white folks had nothing to do with it.

How come he look just like them, then? she say. Only bigger? And a heap more hair. How come the bible just like everything else they make, all about them doing one thing and another, and all the coloured folks doing is gitting cursed?

I never thought bout that.

Nettie say somewhere in the bible it say Jesus' hair was like lamb's wool, I say.

Well, say Shug, if he came to any of these churches we talking bout he'd have to have it conked before anybody paid him any attention. The last thing niggers want to think about they God is that his hair kinky.

That's the truth, I say.

Ain't no way to read the bible and not think God white, she say. Then she sigh. When I found out I thought God was white, and a man, I lost interest. You mad cause he don't seem to listen to your prayers. Humph! Do the mayor listen to anything coloured say? Ask Sofia, she say.

But I don't have to ast Sofia. I know white people never listen to coloured, period. If they do, they only listen long enough to be able to tell you what to do.

Here's the thing, say Shug. The thing I believe. God is inside you and inside everybody else. You come into the world with God. But only them that search for it inside find it. And sometimes it just manifest itself even if you not looking, or don't know what you looking for. Trouble do it for most folks, I think. Sorrow, lord. Feeling like shit.

It? I ast.

Yeah, It. God ain't a he or a she, but a It.

But what do it look like? I ast.

Don't look like nothing, she say. It ain't a picture show. It ain't something you can look at apart from anything else, including yourself. I believe God is everything, say Shug. Everything that is or ever was or ever will be. And when you can feel that, and be happy to feel that, you've found It.

Shug a beautiful something, let me tell you. She frown a little, look out cross the yard, lean back in her chair, look like a big rose.

She say, My first step from the old white man was trees. Then air. Then birds. Then other people. But one day when I was sitting quiet and feeling like a motherless child, which I was, it come to me: that feeling of being part of everything, not separate at all. I knew that if I cut a tree, my arm would bleed. And I laughed and I cried and I run all round the house. I knew just what it was. In fact, when it happen, you can't miss it. It sort of like you know what, she say, grinning and rubbing high up on my thigh.

Shug! I say.

Oh, she say. God love all them feelings. That's some of the best stuff God did. And when you know God loves 'em you enjoys 'em a lot more. You can just relax, go with everything that's going, and praise God by liking what you like.

God don't think it dirty? I ast.

Naw, she say. God made it. Listen, God love everything you love—and a mess of stuff you don't. But more than anything else, God love admiration.

You saying God vain? I ast.

Naw, she say. Not vain, just wanting to share a good thing. I think it pisses God off if you walk by the color purple in a field somewhere and don't notice it.

What it do when it pissed off? I ast.

Oh, it make something else. People think pleasing God is all God care about. But any fool living in the world can see it always trying to please us back.

Yeah? I say.

Yeah, she say. It always making little surprises and springing them on us when us least expect.

You mean it want to be loved, just like the bible say.

Yes, Celie, she say. Everything want to be loved. Us sing and dance, make faces and give flower bouquets, trying to be loved. You ever notice that trees do everything to git attention we do, except walk?

Well, us talk and talk bout God, but I'm still adrift. Trying to chase that old white man out of my head. I been so busy thinking bout him I never truly notice nothing God make. Not a blade of corn (how it do that?) not the color purple (where it come from?). Not the little wildflowers. Nothing.

Now that my eyes opening, I feels like a fool. Next to any little scrub of a bush in my yard, Mr. _______ 's evil sort of shrink. But not altogether. Still, it is like Shug say, You have to git man off your eyeball, before you can see anything a'tall.

Man corrupt everything, say Shug. He on your box of grits, in your head, and all over the radio. He try to make you think he everywhere. Soon as you think he everywhere, you think he God. But he ain't. Whenever you trying to pray, and man plop himself on the other end of it, tell him to git lost, say Shug. Conjure up flowers, wind, water, a big rock.

But this hard work, let me tell you. He been there so long, he don't want to budge. He threaten lightening, floods and earthquakes. Us fight. I hardly pray at all. Every time I conjure up a rock, I throw it.

Amen

SOURCE: Alice Walker, *The Color Purple* (New York: Harcourt Brace Jovanovich, Publishers, 1982) pp.164–168.

Tenderness

Stephen Dunn

Back then when so much was clear
    and I hadn't learned
young men learn from women

what it feels like to feel just right,
    I was twenty-three,
she thirty-four, two children, a husband

in prison for breaking someone's head.
    Yelled at, slapped
around, all she knew of tenderness

was how much she wanted it, and all
    I knew
were back seats and a night or two

in a sleeping bag in the furtive dark.
    We worked
in the same office, banter and loneliness

leading to the shared secret
    that to help
National Biscuit sell biscuits

was wildly comic, which led to my body
    existing with hers
like rain that's found its way underground

to water it naturally joins.
    I can't remember
ever saying the exact word, tenderness,

though she did. It's a word I see now
    you must be older to use,
you must have experienced the absence of it

often enough to know what silk and deep
    balm it is
when at last it comes. I think it was terror

at first that drove me to touch her
    so softly,
then selfishness, the clear benefit

of doing something that would come back
    to me twofold,
and finally, sometime later, it became

reflexive and motiveless in the high
    ignorance of love.
Oh abstractions are just abstract

until they have an ache in them. I met
    a woman never touched
gently, and when it ended between us

I had new hands and new sorrow,
    everything it meant
to be a man changed, unheroic, floating.

SOURCE: Stephen Dunn, *Between Angles*, (New York: W.W. Norton & Co., 1989). Reprinted with the permission of the publishers.

The One Sitting There

Joanna H. Woś

The difficult emotions surrounding the loss of a loved one is the focus of Joanna Woś's *The One Sitting There*. Through the author's descriptions it is easy to imagine the story's setting; through Woś's moving narrative it is equally easy to know what the story's character is feeling. The final result of the combination of these devices is an emotionally gripping short story.

I threw away the meat. The dollar ninety-eight a pound ground beef, the boneless chicken, the spareribs, the hamsteak. I threw the soggy vegetables into the trashcan: the carrots, broccoli, peas, the Brussels sprouts. I poured the milk down the drain of the stainless steel sink. The cheddar cheese I ground up in the disposal. The ice cream, now liquid, followed. All the groceries in the refrigerator had to be thrown away. The voice on the radio hinted of germs thriving on the food after the hours without power. Throwing the food away was rational and reasonable.

In our house, growing up, you were never allowed to throw food away. There was a reason. My mother saved peelings and spoiled things to put on the compost heap. That would go back into the garden to grow more vegetables. You could leave meat or potatoes to be used again in soup. But you were never allowed to throw food away.

I threw the bread away. The bread had gotten wet. I once saw my father pick up a piece of Wonder Bread he had dropped on the ground. He brushed his hand over the slice to remove the dirt and then kissed the bread. Even at six I knew why he did that. My sister was the reason. I was born after the war. She lived in a time before. I do not know much about her. My mother never talked about her. There are no pictures. The only time my father talked about her was when he described how she clutched the bread so tightly in her baby fist that the bread squeezed out between her fingers. She sucked at the bread that way.

So I threw the bread away last. I threw the bread away for all the times I sat crying over a bowl of cabbage soup my father said I had to eat. Because eating would not bring her back. Because I would still be the one sitting there. Now I had the bread. I had gotten it. I had bought it. I had put it in the refrigerator. I had earned it. It was mine to throw away.

So I threw the bread away for my sister. I threw the bread away and brought her back. She was twenty-one and had just come home from Christmas shopping. She had bought me a doll. She put the package on my dining room table and hung her coat smelling of perfume and the late fall air on the back of one of the chairs. I welcomed her as an honored guest. As if she were a Polish bride returning to her home, I greeted her with a plate of bread and salt. The bread, for prosperity, was wrapped in a white linen cloth. The salt, for tears, was in a small blue bowl. We sat down together and shared a piece of bread.

In a kitchen, where such an act was an ordinary thing, I threw away the bread. Because I could.

SOURCE: Joanna H. Woś, *"The One Sitting There."* From *Flash Fiction*, edited by James Thomas, Denise Thomas and Tom Hazaka (New York: W.W. Norton, 1992).

"Guernica"

Stephen Spender

Stephen Spender's 1938 critique of Pablo Picasso's *Guernica* is a chronicling of one man's emotions and opinions upon seeing this well-known painting. Spender's piece serves as a combination of formal art criticism and analysis, and personal reflection. It reads as an intelligent and well-considered reaction to Picasso's famous work.

André Gide writes in *Verve* that *Guernica* fails because it is *eccentric*, it breaks away from its centre, or has no centre. Other critics complain that it is neither expressionist nor abstract, but falls between two stools; that it is terrifying without producing any sensation of pity; and so on. All these criticism are attempts to answer the question whether or not this picture is a great masterpiece. Otherwise, they could not be criticisms at all, but just descriptions, which so far from being *against* it, might well be an account of its merits.

Guernica affects one as an explosion, partly no doubt because it is a picture of an explosion. If one attempts to criticize it, one attempts to relate it to the past. So long as a work of art has this explosive quality of newness it is impossible to relate it to the past. People who say that it is *eccentric*, or that it falls between two stools, or that it is too horrible, and so on, are only making the gasping noises they might make if they were blown off their feet by a high-explosive bomb. All I can try to do is to report as faithfully as possible the effect that this very large and very dynamic picture makes on me.

In the first place, it is certainly not realistic in the sense that Goya's etchings of another tragedy in Spain are realistic. *Guernica* is in no sense reportage; it is not a picture of some horror which Picasso has seen and been through himself. It is the picture of a horror reported in the newspapers, of which he has read accounts and perhaps seen photographs.

This kind of second-hand experience, from the newspapers, the news-reel, the wireless, is one of the dominating realities of our time.

The many people who are not in direct contact with the disasters falling on civilization live in a waking nightmare of second-hand experiences which in a way are more terrible than real experiences because the person overtaken by a disaster has at least a more limited vision than the camera's wide, cold, recording eye, and at least has no opportunity to imagine horrors worse than what he is seeing and experiencing. The flickering black, white and grey lights of Picasso's picture suggest a moving picture stretched across an elongated screen; the flatness of the shapes again suggests the photographic image, even the reported paper words. The centre of this picture is like a painting of a *collage* in which strips of newspaper have been pasted across the canvas.

The actual figures on the canvas, the balloon-like floating head of a screaming woman; the figure throwing arms up in despair, the woman running forwards, and leaving behind one reluctant, painful, enormous, clumsy leg, the terror of a horse with open mouth and skin drawn back over the teeth; the hand clutching a lamp and the electric lamp glowing so that it shows the wires, as though at any moment the precious light may go out; the groaning bull, the woman clutching her child, a complex of clustered fingers like over-ripe fruit; all this builds up a picture of horror, but to me there is grandeur in the severed arm of a hero

Guernica, 1937, by Pablo Picasso.

Picasso's monumental anti-war painting was first exhibited at the Spanish Pavillion of the 1937 World Exposition in Paris. It expresses the artist's outrage at the distruction of the Basque town of Guernica by the air force of Nazi Germany, then allied with General Franco during the Spanish Civil war.

Courtesy of Museo Nacional Centro de Arte Reina Sofia, Madrid.

lying in the foreground, clutching the noble, broken, ineffective sword with which he has tried to ward off the horrors of mechanical destruction; and there is pity in the leaves of the little plant growing just above this hand.

Picasso uses every device of expressionism, abstractionism and effects learnt from *collage*, to build up the horror of *Guernica*. Diagonal lines of light and shade in the background, suggest searchlights and confusion, and the violent contrasts of the faces revealed in a very white light suggest the despair of light and darkness in air raids; despair of the darkness because it is too complete and you are lost; despair of the light because it is too complete and you are revealed to the enemy raiders.

The impression made on me by this picture is one that I might equally get from a great masterpiece, or some very vivid experience. That, of course, does not mean that it *is* a masterpiece. I shall be content to wait some years before knowing that. But it is certainly worth seeing. And if you don't like, or resist, or are overwhelmed by explosions, there are the sixty-seven studies for *Guernica*, some of them quite unlike anything in the picture itself, which are certainly amongst the most beautiful and profound drawings Picasso has ever made.

SOURCE: From *New Statesman & Nation*, 15 October 1938.

Last Night Train

Robert Penn Warren

In that slick and newfangled coach we go slam-banging
On rackety ruin of a roadbed, past caterpillar-
Green flash of last light on deserted platforms,
And I watch the other passenger at this
Late hour—a hundred and eighty pounds of
Flesh, black, female, middle-aged,
Unconsciously flung by roadbed jerks to wallow,
Unshaped, unhinged, in
A purple dress. Straps of white sandals
Are loosened to ease the bulge of contrasting bare instep.
Knees wide, the feet lie sidewise, sole toward sole. They have walked
So far. Head back, flesh snores.
I wonder what she has been doing all day in N.Y.

My station at last. I look back once.
Is she missing hers? I hesitate to ask, and the snore
Is suddenly snatched into eternity.

The last red light fades in distance and darkness like
A wandering star. Where the brief roar just now was,
A last cricket only is audible. That lost
Sound makes me think, with quickly suppressed
Nostalgia, of
A country lane, late night, late autumn—and there
Alone I stood, part of all.
Alone, I now stand under the green station light,
Part of nothing but years.

I stare skyward at uncountable years beyond
My own little aura of pale-green light—
The complex of stars is steady in its operation.
Smell of salt sedge drifts in from seaward,
And I think of the joy of swimming, naked and seaward,
In starlight forever.

By habit, I put hand in pocket, find keys there.
Bemused, I stare at them, and gradually
Grow aware of their preciousness. I discover
The blessedness of the world. Ah, Time! Why so short?

I look up the track toward Bridgeport. I feel
Like blessing the unconscious wallow of flesh-heap
And white sandals unstrapped at bulging of instep.

I hear my heels crunch on the gravel, making
My way to the parked car.

SOURCE: Robert Penn Warren, *Last Night Train* (New York: Random House, 1985).

Canadian and Colonial Painting

Northrop Frye

Herman Northrop Frye (1912-1991) was one of the most innovative and well-respected literary critics of his time. Frye developed a complex and fascinating theory which connected literature, myth and society and explained their role in Western civilization. The following piece is an example of Frye applying his critical ideas to the field of Canadian art.

The countries men live in feed their minds as much as their bodies: the bodily food they provide is absorbed in farms and cities: the mental, in religion and arts. In all communities this process of material and imaginative *digestion* goes on. Thus a large tract of vacant land may well affect the people living near it as too much cake does a small boy: an unknown but quite possibly horrible Something stares at them in the dark: hide under the bedclothes as long as they will, sooner or later they must stare back. Explorers, tormented by a sense of the unreality of the unseen, are first: pioneers and traders follow. But the land is still not imaginatively absorbed, and the incubus moves on to haunt the artists. It is a very real incubus. It glares through the sirens, gorgons, centaurs, griffins, cyclops, pygmies and chimeras of the poems which followed the Greek colonies: there the historical defeat which left a world of mastery outside the Greek clearing increased the imaginative triumph. In our own day the exploration and settlement has been far more thorough and the artistic achievement proportionately less: the latter is typified in the novels of Conrad which are so often concerned with finding a dreary commonplace at the centre of the unknown. All of which is an elaborate prologue to the fact that I propose to compare Tom Thomson with Horatio Walker, as suggested by a recent showing of them at the Art Gallery of Toronto; still, when in Canadian history the sphinx of the unknown land takes its riddle from Frazer and Mackenzie to Tom Thomson, no one can say that there has been an anti-climax.

Griffins and gorgons have no place in Thomson certainly, but the incubus is there, in the twisted stumps and sprawling rocks, the strident colouring, the scarecrow evergreens. In several pictures one has the feeling of something not quite emerging which is all the more sinister for its concealment. The metamorphic stratum is too old: the mind cannot contemplate the azoic without turning it into the monstrous. But that is of minor importance. What is essential in Thomson is the imaginative instability, the emotional unrest and dissatisfaction one feels about a country which has not been lived in: the tension between the mind and a surrounding not integrated with it. This is the key to both his colour and his design. His underlying "colour harmony" is not a concord but a minor ninth. Sumachs and red maples are conceived, quite correctly, as a *surcharge* of colour: flaming reds and yellows are squeezed straight out of the tube on to an already brilliant background: in softer light ambers and pinks and blue-greens carry on a subdued cats' chorus. This in itself is mere fidelity to the subject, but it is not all. Thomson has a marked preference for the transitional over the full season: he likes the delicate pink and green tints on the birches in early spring and the irresolute sifting of the first snow through the spruces; and his autumnal studies are sometimes a Shelleyan hectic decay in high winds and spinning leaves, sometimes a Keatsian opulence and glut. His sense of design, which, of course, is derived from the trail and the canoe, is the exact opposite of the academic "establishing of foreground." He

West Wind, 1917, by Tom Thomson (oil on canvas; 120.7 x 137.2 cm.).
The work of the Group of Seven (see page 339) was profoundly affected by the Canadian landscape painter Tom Thomson. Thomson died in 1917, three years before the Group of Seven was founded.

Courtesy of The Art Gallery of Ontario, Toronto. Gift of the Canadian Club of Toronto, 1926.

is primarily a painter of linear distance. Snowed-over paths wind endlessly through trees, rivers reach nearly to the horizon before they bend and disappear, rocks inch by inch under water, and the longest stretch of mountains dips somewhere and reveals the sky beyond. What is furthest in distance is often nearest in intensity. Or else we peer through a curtain of trees to a pool and an opposite shore. Even when there is no vista a long tree-trunk will lean away from us and the whole picture will be shattered by a straining and pointing diagonal.

This focusing on the farthest distance makes the foreground, of course, a shadowy blur: a foreground tree—even the tree in "West Wind"—may be only a green blob to be looked past, not at. Foreground leaves and flowers, even when carefully painted, are usually thought of as obstructing the vision and the eye comes back to them with a start. Thomson looks on a flat area with a naive Rousseauish stare (see the "decorative panels"). In fact, of all important Canadian painters, only David Milne seems to have a consistent foreground focus, and even he is fond of the obstructive blur.

When the Canadian sphinx brought her riddle of unvisualized land to Thomson it did not occur to him to hide under the bedclothes, though she

Elevator Court, Halifax, 1921, by Lawren Harris (oil on canvas; 96.5 x 112.1 cm.).

Lawren Harris was a founder and leader of the Canadian Group of Painters, which succeeded the Group of Seven (which he also helped to form in 1920—see page 339).

did not promise him money, fame, happiness or even self-confidence, and when she was through with him she scattered his bones in the wilderness. Horatio Walker, one of those wise and prudent men from whom the greater knowledges are concealed, felt differently. It was safety and bedclothes for him. He looked round wildly for some spot in Canada that had been thoroughly lived in, that had no ugly riddles and plenty of picturesque clichés. He found it in the Ile d'Orléans. That was a Fortunate Isle with rainbows and full moons instead of stumps and rocks: it had been cosily inhabited for centuries, and suggested relaxed easy-going narratives rather than inhuman landscapes. Pictures here were ready-made. There was Honest Toil with the plough and the quaint Patient Oxen: there were pastoral epigrams of sheep-shearing and farmers trying to gather in hay before the storm broke; there was the note of Tender Humour supplied by small pigs and heraldic turkeys; there was the Simple Piety which bowed in Childlike Reverence before a roadside *calvaire*. Why, it was as good as Europe, and had novelty besides. And for all Canadians and Americans under the bedclothes who wanted, not new problems of form and outlines, but the predigested picturesque, who preferred dreamy association-responses to detached efforts of organized vision, and who found in a queasy and maudlin nostalgia the deepest appeal of art, Horatio Walker was just the thing. He sold and sold and sold.

SOURCE: Northrop Frye, *The Bush Garden, Essays on the Canadian Imagination* (Toronto: House of Anansi Press Ltd., 1971). Reprinted by permission of the publishers.

Figures and Portraits: The Canadian Identity

Judi Schwartz

In these notes to an exhibition of Canadian Art at the University of Toronto's Hart House Gallery, curator and director Judi Schwartz explains how Canadian art has evolved from the nineteenth century to the present. This evolution was helped along most notably by the Group of Seven, who Schwartz credits with artistically rediscovering the "True North."

Hart House is the cultural, social and recreational centre of the University of Toronto. Built between 1911 and 1919, this neo-Gothic building was the gift of the Massey Foundation.

The University of Toronto Sketch Club (organized in 1917) found a home in Hart House when it opened in 1919. The club evolved into the Art Committee of Hart House, composed of a majority of students plus alumni and faculty representatives. The Committee was soon organizing exhibitions, art classes, and lectures. It also began in 1924 to purchase works of Canadian art to be hung throughout the building. The Committee's activities became an important focus and stimulus for the visual arts on campus and beyond.

By 1925, the Committee had already set its goal: to "form a collection of pictures representative of the best of Canadian art." The Hart House Permanent collection is now one of the largest and most significant private collections of Canadian art.

Although the Collection was never intended to be a comprehensive collection of Canadian Art History, certain periods and art forms are, nonetheless, well represented. Portrait and figure paintings, particularly from the interwar period, form an important part of the Collection.

The popularity of portraiture has fluctuated through the centuries. The rise of portraiture as an art form in the fifteenth century echoed the belief in Renaissance thought that the significance of the individual is central. In the ensuing periods prevailing philosophies and cultural outlooks can be witnessed through portraiture. Historically portraiture was a study of significant events and important people. It was an elitist tradition catering to the upper classes.

The growth of humanistic thought and philosophy in the nineteenth century challenged the doctrines of previous practices establishing the men and women of the street as subject matter.

By the middle of the nineteenth century, portrait painting met its rival in the form of photography. Economically, photography presented itself as a viable alternative to the painted image. As an art form, artists looked upon photography with defiance. Nonetheless, they were forced to explore new directions in their painting. It is at this time a shift in emphasis took place. Exact representation was replaced with subjective interpretation with exploration into the region of colour. The rage for colour was to carry on into the twentieth century. By this time subjectivity had broken away from all restrictions placed upon the artists by society. The artists embarked on the search for essence within each of their sitters. The individual gave way to an interest in "type." Although commissioned portraits were a "necessity" for their livelihood, the artists also, in the interest of their art form, worked from unknown sitters or family and

Isolation Peak, 1930, by Lawren Harris.

Courtesy of Hart House Gallery.

friends. The painting became timeless as details evaporated and the humanity of the sitter came to light. The artists had become committed to the conceptual investigation of the art form of portraiture.

In Canada, by the 1920s, portrait and figure painters encountered a rival of their own, the Canadian landscape. The Group of Seven set out to rediscover the "True North." The growing impact of the Group's interpretation of the landscape can be felt even today, sometimes to the exclusion of the important movement of portrait and figure painters of the time. Upon closer examination, an interesting phenomenon can be found within The Group itself. Frederick Varley, one of the Group members, created some of his best paintings in the form of portraits or figures. Group members tried to convince Varley that the truly Canadian subject to paint was the northern landscape. The art of portrait painting to Varley presented much more than the representation of his subject matter. He reflected on the importance of colour and the "psychology" of the art form: "Green is a 'spiritual' colour, the colours of the earth are 'lusty', pale violet is 'aesthetic'. Colour vibrations, emanating from the object portrayed, enter into the maze of light and colour already present about the object portrayed, and this relationship has to be carefully analyzed and mastered before one can complete a satisfactory portrait. This analysis becomes all the more essential if one wishes to link the personality of the sitter to the mood of time and place."

A later addition to the Group, Edwin Holgate, found inspiration on many trips he took north of Montreal into the Laurentians. Perhaps his most striking image done in 1925 is not that of a landscape, but that of a forest ranger, *Garde Forestier*, personifying the spirit of the north. Holgate writes of this subject: "...at the age when I painted him (he) could still run the young lads ragged in the bush...(he) was a game warden, fire ranger, cook, guide, north of Lac Trembland in the Laurentians."

A contemporary of Holgate's, Prudence Heward, showed a preference for figurative subject matter in her paintings, setting her apart from the Group of Seven in the early 1920s. She was one of a group of talented Montreal-born women artists who dominated the Beaver Hall Group, a short-lived association of artists with studio space in Montreal's Beaver Hall Square. Heward created many striking portrait studies which places her in the forefront of Canadian figurative artists. She employed an interesting technique in her paintings. She would use her landscape sketches as the background for her figurative paintings.

Another member of the Beaver Hall Group, Lilias Torrance Newton, joins the ranks of portrait painters who were consistently well-received for their portraits. Her style, somewhat informal, has sometimes been referred to as a "psychological statement in visual terms."

By the late 1920s The Group of Seven was coming under fire of criticism for its "exclusive" nature. Artists of different political, intellectual and painterly concerns had emerged across the country. Early in 1933, the Canadian Group of Painters was formed. Along with some of the Group of Seven members, the Canadian Group of Painters consisted of artists from across Canada, including Prudence Heward and Lilias Torrance Newton. Although the emphasis in the new group was still in landscape painting, there was also an emergence of new themes, including figure studies, still-lifes and industrial scenes. The activities of The Canadian Group of Painters was primarily concentrated in three cities, Toronto, Montreal and Vancouver.

It is in the city of Montreal that the portrait and figure artists flourished. This is owing partly to the efforts of John Lyman. In 1931, he returned to Montreal after spending 24 years in Europe. He believed that "...the essential qualities of a work lie in the relationship of form to form and colour to colour." He shared his beliefs in teaching and through exhibitions which included Edwin Holgate and Goodridge Roberts. In December 1938 Lyman, Roberts, Jack Humphrey and others who were like-minded exhibited as The Eastern Group. By 1939 this group had expanded into The Contemporary Arts Society with twenty-six members including Lyman, Roberts, Humphrey, Heward and Jacques de Tonnancour. Out of this group came some of the finest work produced by Canadian artists—a distinct contrast to the landscape art made so popular in the 1920s.

The 1930s and the Depression era presented the young artists with new challenges and provoked

Famous Canadian Artists

The Group of Seven

The image of Canada as a northern country is a recurring theme in Canadian literature and art, no more so perhaps than in the paintings of the Canadian artists known as the Group of Seven.

In May 1920, seven Canadian artists met in Toronto and decided to bring attention to their common creative aims by holding a show at the Art Gallery of Toronto. The exhibit focused on getting public attention for the Group of Seven, a name that became a familiar cultural symbol.

Although the group's membership changed occasionally, the core remained. The founding members were Franklin Carmichael, Lawren Harris, A.Y. Jackson, Frank Johnson, Arthur Listmer, J.E.H. MacDonald and Frederick H. Varley. Tom Thomson, whose life and work profoundly affected these founders of the Group, was not a member—he died in a canoeing accident in 1917.

In 1933, the disbanded Group of Seven spearheaded the creation of a more broadly based society to be called The Canadian Group of Painters. Until it disbanded in 1969, the new group offered an exhibition base for the country's most creative artists.

new directions in thought that manifested themselves in their work. The social and economic realities of the troubled Depression decade helped develop a critical change in subject matter. The people chosen for these figure studies were a vehicle to express the feelings of the times. Perhaps the painting most often used to illustrate this period of art, is *Young Canadian* by Charles Comfort. Charles Comfort painted large portraits in watercolour. *Young Canadian* gives the impression of an oil painting and yet has the subtleness of a watercolour. A portrait of fellow artist, Carl Schaeffer, it has come to symbolize the state of mind of Canadian youth during the difficult Depression era.

Another strong example of the effect of the Depression on artists is that of *Dark Girl* by Prudence Heward. This painting was a first in a series of black nudes. It depicts a black woman as a vincible human being. A melancholy mood permeates the painting. This is sharply contrasted by the lush background of Canadian sumach.

Jack Humphrey, a maritime artist, aptly describes his feelings as expressed in the painting *Draped Head*. "*Draped Head* is not a portrait. Instead it is a symbol and a generality, but specific in its language of volume and point. It may seem surprising that I painted a self-portrait to express this aspiration. Two other heads, more portrait-like, had preceded it and were discarded. It does not express the sense of person or place...but the environment and ideas I had lately been experiencing."

Montreal was established as a centre with artist groups of both French and English origins working at developing a reputation for figurative art. Jacques de Tonnancour, Stanley Cosgrove and Goodridge Roberts come out of this grouping.

Another Montreal grouping of note was that of the Jewish artists such as Louis Muhlstock and Herman Heimlich. Louis Muhlstock's sensitive drawings and paintings of people caught by the Depression are haunting. His subjects were drawn from the ranks of the unemployed or homeless. He paid them to sit for him giving him the freedom of self-expression. Herman Heimlich favoured the portrait style, inviting people of the streets or students from his classes to pose for him. In *Portrait of a Young Man*, with his handling of pastel using few lines and just a hint of colouring, he manages to convey the earnestness and sensitivity of the young student.

The advent of World War II offered a new vehicle of expression for portrait/figurative artists. They were recruited as official war artists to capture and record in their art the wartime activities in Canada and abroad. Later in the 1940s, figurative art no longer was popular. "Experimental Art" had arrived. Cubist, surrealist or abstract styles were now being embraced by the Canadian art scene. At this time, when some figurative artists were trying these new art forms, Canadian women artists continued to work in the painting style that had established them as artists and would make new gains for them. Prudence Heward exhibited her own sensitivity to people with her richly coloured canvasses. Pegi Nicol McLeod's masses of restless figures revealed a fascination with the activities of daily life. People she knew, such as her daughter Jane and her friends, as well as views from her window were all captured in her paintings.

Jacques de Tonnancour was one artist to bridge the gap between figurative and abstract art. He studied the works of Picasso and Matisse and incorporated some of their ideas and techniques into his work. He acknowledges this influence when he wrote about *La Robe Bleue*: "The painting was done at a moment when I was still very much under the influence of Matisse. I was conscious of the fact and made no efforts to by-pass it (or any other influence). On the contrary, I felt that the only way was through it and not around it."

The development of portraiture as an art form in Canada has experienced its ups and downs and yet has survived to be recognized as a significant factor in our art history. The two strong traditions in Canadian art are that of the landscape artist and that of the portrait artist. At times it may have seemed that the two styles of art were in conflict. In retrospect, both have proven important to the establishment of a Canadian identity through art.

Presented here is an exhibition of fellow Canadians as seen through artists' eyes.

SOURCE: Courtesy of the author.

APPENDICES

Appendix 1

Terms Used in Essays

Compiled by Kathryn Kearney and Marilyn White

ANALYZE
Analyze has two meanings: (1) you look for main ideas or themes and say why they are important; also, you point out underlying assumptions and their implications; (2) you break something down into its parts, and then examine the relationships between those parts.

COMPARE
When you *compare*, you try to find ways in which one thing is similar to another.

COMMENT ON
This requires that you discuss, criticize, or explain the meaning of a topic as completely as possible, and give your personal opinion.

CONTRAST
When you *contrast*, you look for ways in which things are different from each other.

CRITICIZE
In *criticizing*, you both compare and contrast. Begin by briefly describing the position or issue. In the body of your argument, discuss both the strengths and the limitations of the plan, work, or material in question. In your conclusion, summarize the points you have made and give your own opinion. Be sure to give reasons to support your position.

DEFINE
State an accurate meaning for the term. Be brief. Give a specific example of the term or concept.

DESCRIBE
Try to portray in words the person, place, or thing being described. State details, facts, characteristics, or anything that will give the reader an accurate mental picture.

DIAGRAM
Make a drawing, chart, plan or graphic representation. Label the diagram, and add a brief explanation if necessary.

DISCUSS
Analyze the subject or items involved. Present arguments or ideas both for and against. Make your answer complete and detailed in order to show that you understand the topic.

EVALUATE
Evaluation requires you to make a judgment on the material in question and give reasons to support your position. You should discuss what authorities have to say and then give your own personal assessment.

EXPLAIN
When you *explain*, you try to make clear what is meant by giving details; by interpreting; by giving reasons or causes; or by answering questions such as "How? or Why?"

ILLUSTRATE
A question which asks you to *illustrate* usually requires you to explain or clarify by presenting a figure, picture, or concrete example.

INTERPRET

Interpretation is similar to explanation. When you are asked to *interpret*, you should comment on the subject, giving your own understanding of or reaction to the problem.

JUSTIFY

In *justifying*, you should give evidence or reasoned arguments to support your answer or position

LIST

This simply means to present your answer in an itemized series of concise, numbered points.

OUTLINE

When you *outline*, you give the main points in an organized sequence, including whatever supporting information is necessary, omitting minor details.

PROVE

When you are asked to *prove* a point, you must give details that would lead to an inescapable conclusion.

RELATE

When you are asked to *relate* or show a *relationship* between two things, you show how they are connected or associated.

REVIEW

A *review* is a critical examination of a topic, text, or idea. You summarize the major points, say what you liked and disliked, and give a general critical evaluation.

STATE

Express the main points briefly and clearly. Details, illustrations, and examples may be omitted.

SUMMARIZE

When you summarize, just give the main points in a condensed form, omitting details, illustrations, and elaborations.

Improve Your Writing

The point of writing is to convey what you want to say and nothing more. The first key to good writing, therefore, is clear thinking. Be sure you know what you are writing about, more or less. *That is Cardinal Rule Number 1.*

Like anything else done well, good writing does not come easily. To write well, one needs to write often and to read good writing often. So, as in other areas of life, **practice is essential**. *That is Cardinal Rule Number 2.*

Meanwhile, here are some quick writing tips that may be helpful to you:

- **Shorter sentences:** A good first tip to improve your writing is: *write shorter sentences.* Probably the most common fault in writing is trying to pack too many thoughts into one (unending) sentence. Writing short sentences also helps you to think through your logic (and thus helps the reader understand your point). So, shorten up the sentences: count the words, if necessary. If the sentence is more than 15-20 words, unless you are an experienced writer, you've likely gone on too long...and lost the reader to boot!
- **Shorter words:** A second tip is to *use short words,* where possible. In writing you are trying to convey a message, not show off your vocabulary. The message (always the most important thing) can be lost simply because the words are over-blown. Never use a long word where a short word will do. Look through what you have written and find shorter words where possible.
- **Shorter paragraphs:** It is important to contain your thoughts on one issue at a time in a separate paragraph. Quite often paragraphs are not frequent enough, nor clearly distinguished. Keep the number of sentences in each paragraph down to a minimum, at first anyway. Try for a half dozen or so sentences at the outset. Again, this way you will be able to work through the logic of your argument and the reader will be able to follow you.
- **Shorter essays:** Generally, you can pare down your words and paragraphs considerably and get across the same message. *Edit your work.* Remember it is the message that counts, not the number of words or the length of paragraphs. Editing also helps clarity of thought. If you have not been through your work many times over, trying always to improve it, then probably it is not the best you can do.

Remember, your essay as a whole is, or should be, greater than the sum of its parts. Somehow the words, paragraphs and sections all must work together to convey your message. It is the content of the message that is paramount. The final essay must appear, like a symphony, *as if* it were cleverly crafted from the beginning. This is not easy to achieve but the effort can be fun: if done well, it will also be enjoyable to your audience.

Finally, the above rules (like most rules) are not iron-clad. If you get good marks without following them, good for you—you are obviously conveying your message, which is what is important. Carry on. On the other hand, if you think you are having trouble, try to apply these writing tips. They won't make you a great writer, but they will help.

Always keep in mind the two **Cardinal Rules**: (1) clear thinking always underlies clear writing and (2) practice (reading good writing and writing more often), as always, leads to perfection.

Happy writing!

Read and Study with Better Results

Reading is key to being a successful student. Fortunately, good reading habits (like a good tennis serve) can be developed and improved, *but it takes practice.*

A common method for improving your reading skills is SQ3R. The technique is simple:

- **S**urvey the material first; then
- **Q**uestions should be put down on paper; then
- **R**ead the material and underline important passages; then
- **R**ecite the material from memory and write; and finally,
- **R**eview as often, if possible setting yourself a schedule.

Let's review each in turn.

- **Survey.** When you *Survey*, you are simply making a quick pass over the material you are reading. Take notice of subheadings, diagrams or other graphics, notes or questions at the end of the each chapter. This preview should take no more than 10 minutes per chapter. Since people are not generally in the habit of doing this, you might have to force yourself to do it at first.
- **Question.** When you *Question*, you are reading with the intention of asking certain questions about what you read. Use each subheading in the chapter to assist you. For example, when you see the subheading "The Worst Relief Pitchers of All Time" in a chapter about baseball, mentally or on paper ask yourself "just *who* were these hapless relief pitchers?" and "why do they deserve to be on an all-time worst list?"
- **Read.** Having developed the questions you want answered, you are now ready to actually *Read and underline* (or highlight) the material carefully, keeping the questions in mind. Re-read difficult sentences and paragraphs if you have to. There's nothing wrong with having to read something two or three times, but there *is a lot* wrong with glossing over something you don't understand! Use a dictionary if you have to. There are all kinds of techniques for underlining or circling key words, but as long as you develop a system that is easy to understand and helps you ascertain the key ideas, you will be well on the way.
- **Recite.** The next step is to *Recite* aloud the questions you formulated, followed by their answers, which you discovered in the reading/underlining process. While you are reciting (which is maybe best done in private, unless you are the type of person who doesn't mind being seen talking to yourself on the subway!), jot down some study notes. This will help you remember and will come in handy later.
- **Review.** Finally, *Review* the material again (and, if possible, again). You can do this by going over headings, looking over your underlining and annotations, answering the questions you devised for each section, and reflecting on the study notes you've written.

A note of caution, however. No matter how thorough the system used, or how experienced the reader, *nobody understands everything they read, all the time.* Due to unclear writing, complex language or just your own flagging interest, there are times when reading just does not come easily. Moreover, time pressure may force you to read to a deadline, and there is nothing more frustrating than ploughing through the same paragraph over and over and getting nowhere. Taking a break usually helps. Then get back to SQ3R system, or your variant of it. Applied consistently, SQ3R will not fail.

Now you're on your way to effective reading!

Appendix 4

Present Your Essays in Style ... Please

Imagine having to read 400 essays six times a year or so. You will now realize how important presentation is to the person having to mark all these essays. Clean essays also help develop clear ideas. So, take the time to type up your essays, ensure that proper formatting is done, and ensure the bibliography is complete.

Here are some tips to help you do this:

- **Type your essays.** Whenever possible, always type your essays. Nowadays typing is usually done using a word processor on a computer and sending the final version to a printer. Make sure the ribbon (or laser toner) is good and the final output is crisp. Also use white paper.
- **Use double spacing.** Double space the lines on your page. Also include an extra line space above subheadings. This spacing will allow you to edit your work on paper before printing the final version. It also will allow the person marking it to write in comments and corrections.
- **Ensure good margins all around.** Allow good margins on the top, bottom and sides of each page. Again, this will allow room for comments. The margins should be about 1 inch. Make sure they are consistent for each page; otherwise your paper as a whole will appear messy.
- **Number your pages and staple them.** Be sure that each page is numbered in sequence (and that the number appears at the same spot on each page). It is also a good idea to staple the pages together (or put them in a bound folder). The pages might get out of sequence otherwise.
- **Use subheadings.** Pages and pages of text can be more lively and interesting if there are subheadings. Subheadings give clues to the reader and pique his or her interest in what you have to say. They also show that you have taken your assignment seriously.
- **Include a cover page.** Make sure you include a cover page if you want to get a mark! This page should come first and it should contain, at a minimum, the following: (1) the title of your essay (and subtitle if you have one), (2) your own name in full, (4) the course name (and your class number if there is one), (4) your professor's name, and (5) the date (including the year).
- **Include a complete bibliography.** A bibliography directs the reader, should he or she be so inclined, to the sources you consulted while writing your essay. These bibliographical references should be included at the end of your essay under the heading "Bibliography." The entries should be in alphabetical order according to the author's surname. It is important that the references are complete and in a consistent style. Each bibliographical reference should include: (1) the author's surname and first name or initials, (2) the title of the book (underlined or in italics) or article (within quotation marks), (3) the magazine or journal (underlined or in italics) in which the piece appeared if it is an article, (4) the publisher and place of publication, (4) the publication date, and (6) the pages on which the material you used is to be found (if you are not referring to the whole piece). You can consult a style manual for the exact format of the bibliographical entry or you can simply look at a few good books to see how they have done it, but make sure all the above items are included in each reference.

Now you have the basis of a good-looking term paper. You will find that this gets easier each time you do it. You will also find that giving more attention to presentation will help you to improve the content of your paper too.

So, do it up in style.

Glossary

When reading and studying (not to mention writing), it is essential to have a dictionary nearby. Even the most experienced reader will come across words that are difficult or unclear. Your bookstore will be able to recommend a good one that is not expensive.

Below are some words and terms that you may have come across in the course of reading this book. This list includes only some of the more common ones. It will get you started. For the rest, you will have to use your own dictionary.

Abstraction: The act or process of removing or separating out the essentials; eg., an abstract idea or abstract work of art.

Ambiguous: Capable of being interpreted in more than one way; doubtful or uncertain.

Ambivalent: The simultaneous existence of two conflicting feelings about a person, object, or idea.

Analogy: Correspondence in some respects between things otherwise dissimilar; an inference that if two things are alike in some respects they must be alike in others.

Anthropology: The science of the origin, culture, and development of human beings.

Antisocial: Not sociable; interfering with society; eg., antisocial behaviour.

Antithesis: The direct opposite.

Behaviourism: The psychological school that believes that objectively observable behavior rather than mental conditions constitutes the essential scientific basis of psychological data and investigation.

Biodiversity: Pertaining to the vast array of life forms that exist and are continually being created in nature.

Biomes: An extensive ecological community, especially one having one dominant type of vegetation; eg., the tundra biome.

Biotechnology: The marriage of the biological science on the one hand and technology on the other so as to enable the scientific discoveries of biology to be applied to everyday life.

Boreal: Pertaining to or located in the north; northern.

Bureaucracy: Government administered through bureaus and departments; the departments and their officials as a group; an unwieldy administrative system.

Cognizant: Conscious knowledge or recognition; awareness.

Contradiction: To assert the opposite; to deny; to be contrary to or inconsistent with.

Counterintuitive: Running contrary to what one might assume without conscious reasoning.

Coup de grâce: A finishing stroke; eg., a sudden and decisive blow that gives a merciful death to a suffering animal or person.

Creationism: The belief that all things, including humans, were especially created by God and are not the act of accident or evolution.

Criticism: The act of making judgments and evaluations.

Cyberspace: This term is used to describe the intertwining of more than 15,000 computer networks around the world whereby people can communicate through the use of computers and the internet system.

Deduction: The act or process of reasoning, especially a logical method in which a conclusion necessarily follows from the propositions stated. (*See also* induction.)

Determinism: The philosophical doctrine asserting

a correspondence between determining causes and effects.

Dialogue: A conversation between two or more people; a conversational passage in a play or narrative; an exchange of ideas or opinions.

Digitally optimized: When the quality (or colour balance) of an digital image (or other digitized object) is improved electronically using computer calculations and adjustments.

Dilation: To make or become wider or larger; to expand.

Dilemma: A situation that requires a choice between two equal, usually unpleasant alternatives.

Dysfunctional: Not working as it should or was supposed to work.

Ellipse: An oval. The path a point moves so that the sum of its distances from two fixed points remains the same.

Empirical: Based on observation or experiment; relying on practical experience rather than theory.

Episodic: One isolated incident in the course of an experience.

Equilibrium: A condition of balance between opposed forces, influences, or actions.

Ethical: In accordance with accepted principles governing the conduct of a group.

Ethos: The character or attitude peculiar to a specific culture or group.

Figments: Something imagined; eg., a figment of one's imagination.

Figuratist: One who knows what is appropriate to think and say about a given phenomenon; who engages in mind play rather than passively existing. (*See also* literalist.)

Finite: Having bounds; limited; neither infinite nor infinitesimal.

Focal point: A point to which something converges or from which it diverges.

Fundamentalism: A religious-type movement insisting on adherence to the original texts as the sole historical and prophetic authority.

Geo-political: The study of how geography influences international relations.

Helix: A three-dimensional curve that lies on a cylinder or cone and cuts the elements at a constant angle.

Heterodoxies: Not in agreement with accepted beliefs, especially departing from religious doctrine; holding unorthodox opinions.

Humanism: A doctrine or attitude concerned primarily with human beings and their values, capacities, and achievements.

Ideology (ideologues): Bodies of ideas reflecting the social needs and aspirations of an individual, group, class, or culture.; eg., fascism, nationalism. Ideologues are those who advocate such views.

Idiosyncratic: A structural or behavioral peculiarity; eccentricity.

Induction: Reasoning in which general principles are derived from particular facts or instances. (*See also* deduction.)

Infrastructure: The underlying basis of something; eg., the economy might be considered part of the infrastructure of society.

Intuition: The faculty of knowing as if by instinct, without conscious reasoning.

Languor: A deficiency in mental and physical alertness and activity; lethargy, stupor, dullness, sluggishness.

Laudatory: Expressing praise; eulogistic.

Literalist: One who sees specific instances rather than general principles; who moves from point A to point B in a thought sequence without grasping the essential point of a discussion. (*See also* figuratist.)

Metaphor: A figure of speech in which a term that ordinarily designates an object or idea is used to designate a dissimilar object or idea in order to suggest comparison or analogy, as in the phrase evening of life.

Metaphysical: Based on speculative or abstract reasoning.

Methodology: The system of principles and procedures applied to a science or discipline.

Microelectronics: The branch of electronics dealing with miniature components.

Monologue: A long speech.

Moratorium: A deferment or delay of any action.

Multiculturalism: Of, relating to, or intended for several cultures; with much of its population coming from many different parts of the world, Canada is a very multicultural country and has instituted policies to help these various cultures develop and coexist.

Norm (i.e., social norm): A standard or accepted belief or practice of a particular social group.

Omnipotent: Having unlimited power, authority, or force.

Orthodoxy: Adhering to traditional or established beliefs, especially in religion.

Paradox: A statement that appears to contradict itself or be contrary to common sense but that may be true.

Pastoral: Of or having to do with shepherds or country life; simple or naturally beautiful like the country; or pertaining to a pastor and his duties.

Peripheral: Relatively unimportant.

Phantasm: A phantom; something apparently seen, heard, or sensed, but having no physical reality; ghost; specter; an illusory mental image.

Phenomenon: An occurrence or fact that can be perceived by the senses.

Philanthropic: The effort to increase the well-being of humankind, as by charitable donations; love of humankind in general; a charitable action or institution.

Pluralistic: Of or relating to a form that designates more than one of the things specified; eg., a country is usually seen as politically pluralistic if there is more than one political party running for office.

Proselytize: To convert from one belief or faith to another.

Protagonist: The leading character in a story or drama.

Québecois: Some one who lives in the province of Québec, Canada.

Prescribed: To set down as a rule or guide.

Quantified: To describe something using numbers, thus permitting mathematical calculations to analyze that thing.

Quantum mechanics: A branch of physics dealing with the interpretation of the behaviour of atoms and elementary particles, such as electrons.

Relativity, theory of: The physical theory of time and space developed by Albert Einstein.

Remuneration: Payment for goods provided, services rendered, or losses incurred.

Replication: To make a replica of; duplicate.

Reptilian: Any of various cold-blooded vertebrates, as a snake or crocodile, that are covered with scales or horny plates.

Segregation: To separate or isolate from others or from a main body or group; to impose the separation of (a race or class) from the rest of society.

Opaque: Impenetrable by light; not clear; dull; obtuse.

Pinnacle: the highest point; acme.

Senescence: Aging; elderly.

Simultaneity: Happening, existing, or done at the same time.

Skepticism: The philosophical doctrine that absolute knowledge is impossible.

Stewardship: One who manages another's property, finances, or other affairs.

Stigma: A mark or token of shame or disgrace.

Synergistic: The action of two or more substances, organs, or organisms to achieve an effect of which each is individually incapable.

Systematic: A group of interacting elements functioning as a complex whole; regular method; orderliness.

Tacit: Not spoken: tacit consent; implied by or inferred from actions or statements.

Technocratic: Government by technical scientists and engineers.

Trailblazers: A leader in a field; pioneer.

Transmutation: To change from one form, nature, condition, and so forth, into another; transform.

Ubiquity: Being or seeming to be everywhere at the same time; omnipresent.

Vestal maiden: Having to do with the Roman goddess Vesta; chaste; pure.

Wampum: Beads made of polished shells strung together into strands or belts formerly used by North American Indians as money or jewelry.

Worst-case scenario: The worst thing that could possibly happen.